# COMPUTER PACKAGES AND RESEARCH DESIGN

With Annotations of Input and Output from the BMDP, SAS, SPSS and SPSSX Statistical Packages

## Volume 3: SPSS and SPSSX

Edited by

## Robert S. Barcikowski

Contributions by

Robert S. Barcikowski
James D. Brodzinski
Tom D. Daniels
Charles Kufs
Charles E. Rich
Barry K. Spiker

DISCARD

UNIVERSITY
PRESS OF
AMERICA

LANHAM • NEW YORK • LONDON

**Library of Congress Cataloging in Publication Data**
Main entry under title:

Computer packages and research design.

    Includes bibliographies and indexes.
    Contents: v. 1. BMDP–v. 2. SAS–v. 3. SPSS and
SPSSX.
    1. Mathematical statistics–Computer programs. 2.
Statistics–Computer programs. 3. Biometry–Computer
programs. I. Barcikowski, Robert S.
QA276.4.C576  1983   519.5'028'5425   83–1469.
ISBN 0–8191–3494–5 (pbk. : v. 1 : alk. paper)
ISBN 0–8191–3495–3 (pbk. : v. 2 : alk. paper)
ISBN 0–8191–3496–1 (pbk. : v. 3 : alk. paper)

To our parents,


Leo and Lillian Barcikowski


Alfons and Theresa Brodzinski


Harlin and Doris Daniels


Charles, Sr. and Edith Kufs


Ruth and Elmer Rich


William and Imogene Spiker

# ACKNOWLEDGEMENTS

I would like to express my appreciation to Chuck Rich and James Brodzinski who performed yeoman's service in helping to create the final version of this manuscript. Special thanks are also due to Barbara Lapp Rush and Michael Held whose initial assistance and support are reflected in this manuscript. I am also indebted to Pamela Boger for her tremendous effort in preparing the text of this book for our word processor, and to Randy Robey and Gretchen Rauschenberg for their insightful comments. Very special thanks are given to my wife, Beth Barcikowski, without whose help much of this manuscript would still be in a heap on my office floor.

I am indebted to Larry Buell, George Hinkle, Jr. and their staff at Ohio University's Computing and Learning Services for their assistance in providing me access to the most recent versions of the statistical packages. I am also indebted to Allen Meyers, Dean of Ohio University's College of Education, for assistance in obtaining the hardware that greatly facilitated my work on this book.

The authors of this book would like to thank the people associated with each of the statistical packages for allowing us to use the input and output from their programs. It is important to note, however, that we bear sole responsibility for our interpretations and that they are not necessarily those that would be given by BMDP, SAS, or SPSS. The BMDP programs were developed at the Health Sciences Computing Facility at UCLA and are now distributed by BMDP Statistical Software Incorporated. SAS was copyrighted in 1982 by SAS INSTITUTE INC. SPSS was copyrighted in 1981 by C. Hadlai Hull and Norman H. Nie. SPSS and SPSSX are registered trademarks for SPSS, Inc.

Robert S. Barcikowski

May 1983

## CONTENTS: Volume III

# PREFACE

Many commercial computer programs are available to help researchers do statistical analyses of their data. Unfortunately, the output provided by most of these 'canned' packages is frequently misunderstood or is misinterpreted by many researchers. For instance, how many researchers realize that it is possible to arrive at entirely different results and conclusions depending on the computer program used to analyze a two factor, unequal $n$, analysis of variance? Or, how many researchers can write the control cards for, and interpret the output from, designs utilizing analysis of covariance, nested factors, or repeated measures (univariate or multivariate)? This book was written primarily to help researchers understand the meaning, interpretation, and use of the output they obtain from computer programs which analyze data from standard research designs.

As a teacher, graduate advisor, and consultant, I have met many researchers who have difficulty with the processes of: (a) melding their research problem(s) and hypotheses into a research design, (b) finding an appropriate computer package to analyze their data, (c) understanding the input and output from a computer package, and (d) reporting what they have found. This book will aid these researchers by providing information on each of these processes. Therefore, this book should also be of value to students in their courses on research design and univariate and multivariate statistics. People who have little difficulty with the latter processes will find it useful as a reference for the output available on standard research designs from three widely used statistical packages. The statistical packages employed in this book are: Biomedical Computer Programs, BMDP (Dixon, 1981), Statistical Analysis System, SAS (SAS Institute, 1982a, 1982b), the Statistical Package for the Social Sciences, SPSS (Nie, Hull, Jenkins, Steinbrenner, and Brent, 1975; Nie and Hull, 1979, 1981), and SPSSX (SPSS Inc, 1983).

This book consists of three volumes, one for each statistical package. In each volume we have repeated our discussions of different research designs, but the associated input and output is from a given statistical package. The first volume contains input and output from BMDP; the second from SAS; and the third from SPSS and SPSSX. Each volume is self-contained so that the reader may decide to purchase only one or two volumes of interest. The entire book is useful as a means of comparing input and output from the packages and as a reference for those who use all of the packages. The first chapter is also repeated in each volume and is recommended reading for all users of the book. It provides the reader with an orientation to the contents of the book, and presents a concise discussion of the statistical packages employed. Chapters 2 through 7 of each volume each contain a discussion of one research design with annotated input/output from a given package. The research designs discussed are: one factor (one-way classification), two factor (two-way classification), three factor (three-way classification), analysis of covariance, nested, and repeated measures.

The mode of presentation in Chapters 2-7 of each volume is primarily through example. The authors of each chapter selected a research problem and then found data, in a well known statistics text, e.g., Winer, 1971, that would fit the problem and research hypotheses. This method allows the reader to easily consult other texts for further discussion of the design and description of the analysis. We recognize that reading more than one source is invaluable in understanding a research design.

The discussion of the statistical design in each chapter consists of: a listing of the programs run, a rationale for using the design, a univariate example problem, and a multivariate example problem. In each volume this discussion is followed by annotated input/output from a given statistical package that can be used to analyze the data. The univariate (one dependent variable) and multivariate (more than one dependent variable) discussions, and input/output, were kept separate in each chapter. This enables the reader who is unfamiliar with multivariate analysis of variance to concentrate solely on the univariate problems. Each univariate and multivariate section includes: a statement of the problem, the research hypotheses, the statistical hypotheses, a statistical table derived from the program output, and planned and/or post hoc comparisons. These sections were written to aid researchers in writing a dissertation, thesis, or research report.

The input control options for each package were selected so that the user could check on the accuracy of his data and would be supplied with information for planned or post hoc comparisons (i.e., information to answer his research hypotheses). The purpose of each input control specification is explained by comments on the program control card listings. In the annotated output, important statistics are identified, and a brief discussion is given, illustrating how these statistics are used and how they may be interpreted for the example problem.

Five appendices were written to help the reader interpret the significance test output from the packaged programs. For the convenience of the reader these appendices have been repeated in each volume. The topics covered are: Two-Way Nonorthogonal (Unequal n) Analyses (Appendix A), Multivariate Statistical Tests (Appendix B), Step-Down Analysis (Appendix C), Statistical Tests When the Factors Have Fixed, Random, and Mixed Levels (Appendix D), and Skewness and Kurtosis Measures in SAS (Appendix E). These appendices were included because the topics are either not available in most statistics texts or are controversial (e.g., the methods of analysis with unequal n).

## The Book And Its Authors

The idea for this book came from a computer project I assigned to the students in my Advanced Computer Applications in Education II course at Ohio University during the summer of 1977. The assignment was for each student to execute several packaged programs for a specific research design and then annotate the input/output. It soon became apparent to many of us, although Barry Spiker claims initial credit, that what we were doing could be of great value both as a mode of learning statistics and research design and as a reference for researchers who use statistical packages. The "I want a copy" responses from students and staff, both on and off campus, provided us with the needed motivation to write this book. And so, the next few years were spent running and rerunning programs, and writing.

For the designs we wanted to consider we were initially faced with three major problems: 1. Which statistical packages do we choose? 2. How should we display all of the input/output from the packaged programs? and, 3. Which options from these packages should be selected? The first problem was settled when we decided to work with packaged programs, one or more of which should be available at every academic computer center. The second problem was settled when we decided to include complete program input (without the systems cards) for all programs; to provide a full program output listing of each program the first time the program is used, and to provide only important output, particularly that needed for statistical tables, for all other programs. This meant that complete program listings of most programs may be found in Chapter 2. The third problem was not so easy. At first, we thought we would provide examples illustrating every program option. This resulted in a mountain of output, and this approach was quickly discarded. Then, we decided not to use any options. This resulted in output which primarily yielded overall statistical tests and that would require a second run with options to answer most research questions. We finally decided to use those options which would provide us with:

(1) a check on the input accuracy of our data,

(2) information that would enable us to complete the kind of ANOVA and MANOVA statistical tables found in most research reports, theses, and dissertations, and

(3) information that would enable us to perform either "planned" or post hoc comparison tests. To emphasize this last requirement, a different post hoc comparison test was discussed and used in each chapter.

The coauthors of this book are five of my former students in statistics and computer science. Each student had at least four, and most had all seven, statistics-computer applications courses offered by the Research and Evaluation Program Area in the College of Education at Ohio University. The students representing a broad range of backgrounds are: Barry Spiker, B.A. General Studies, M.A. Political Science, Ph.D. in Interpersonal Communication; James Brodzinski, B.F.A. Photography, M.A. Interpersonal Communication, Ph.D. in Interpersonal Communication; Charlie Kufs, A.B. Geology, M.A. Geology; Tom Daniels, B.A. Communication, M.A. Rhetoric and Public Address, Ph.D. in Interpersonal Communication; Chuck Rich, B.A. Psychology, M.S. Experimental Psychology, Ph.D. in Guidance and Counseling. The editor has a B.A. in Mathematics and Ph.D. in Educational Psychology (1970, State University of New York at Buffalo).

I believe that this book will be of great value to students because it was written by students with varied backgrounds who were not too far removed from the problems encountered by newcomers to the use of statistics and computer statistical packages. This will be particularly true if I was able to live up to my part of our bargain, by providing proper guidance and explanations on applied statistical methodology.

Robert S. Barcikowski

May 1983

# CHAPTER 1

## INTRODUCTION
### by Robert S. Barcikowski

Packaged statistical computer programs are available to perform all of the data manipulations commonly desired by researchers. This book is divided into three volumes which are designed to assist you in understanding the input and output from BMDP, SAS, SPSS, and SPSSX programs used to analyze standard research designs. (From this point on we generally refer to SPSS and SPSSX using the acronym SPSS; we discuss the difference between them in the section of this chapter entitled "Selection of Programs and Program Options.") The standard designs discussed are: one factor (one-way classification), two factor (two-way classification), three factor (three-way classification), analysis of covariance, nested, and repeated measures. The purpose of this chapter is to introduce you to the following chapters and their program input/output through a brief discussion of:

1. design terminology,

2. chapter contents,

3. selection of programs and program options,

4. appendices,

5. systems cards.

## Design Terminology

### An Example

Research design and analysis is an area of study with its own special language. This language is fairly standard but may vary slightly among textbooks. So that the readers of this book are sure of what is meant by the design terminology employed, the design terms to be used here are presented through the example design illustrated in Figure 1.1.

The design in Figure 1.1 is called a two-way analysis of variance because there are two factors under study. The researcher who used this design was interested in answering three main questions:

1. Does the method of studying for an exam affect the score that one achieves on the exam?

2. Does the method of presentation of the material on

1

which the exam is based affect the score that one achieves on the exam?

3. Is there an interaction between the method of studying for an exam and the presentation of the material on which the exam is based which affects the score that one achieves on the exam?

Method of Presentation[2]

|   |   | (LEVEL 1)<br>Lecture | (LEVEL 2)<br>TV Lecture | (LEVEL 3)<br>Small Group |
|---|---|---|---|---|
| M<br>e<br>t S[1]<br>h t<br>o u<br>d d<br>y<br>o<br>f | (LEVEL 1)<br>Picture<br>Outline | English[3]<br>Science[4]<br>30 Students[5]<br>Cell 11[6] | English<br>Science<br>28 Students<br>Cell 12 | English<br>Science<br>25 Students<br>Cell 13 |
|   | (LEVEL 2)<br>Written<br>Outline | English<br>Science<br>34 Students<br>Cell 21 | English<br>Science<br>19 Students<br>Cell 22 | English<br>Science<br>28 Students<br>Cell 23 |

[1]First factor (independent variable).
[2]Second factor (independent variable).
[3]First dependent variable.
[4]Second dependent variable.
[5]Units of analysis (observations of $\underline{n}$ per cell).
[6]Cell indentification.

Figure 1.1 The terminology used in a two-way (two factor) analysis of variance design

In this design, the two independent variables (factors) were Method of Study and Method of Presentation. The types (levels) of Method of Study investigated were Picture Outline and Written Outline. The levels of the second factor, Method of Presentation, were Lecture, TV Lecture and Small Group class presentations.

Each level of the first factor and each level of the second factor combined to form the six treatment combinations, called cells, shown in Figure 1.1. The cells of the design are numbered 11 (one-one), 12 (one-two), etc., where the first digit indicates the level of the first factor, Method of Study, and the second digit indicates the level of the second factor, Method of Presentation. For instance, cell 21 indicates the treatment combination Written Outline, level 2, and Lecture, Level 1. The students, called units of analysis or observations, were randomly assigned to each cell. The letter n refers to the number of students in each cell, i.e., the cell frequency. The 30 students in cell 11 were given lectures in English and Science and they studied for their examinations in these subjects using a picture outline method. The examination scores in English and Science are measures of the dependent variables, achievement in English and Science. Given two dependent variables, this design would call for a multivariate analysis of variance; if there were only one dependent variable, this design would require a univariate analysis of variance. Finally, since there are an unequal number of observations across the cells of the design, (viz., 30, 28, 25, etc.) this design is referred to as an unequal n or nonorthogonal design. Unequal n designs are discussed further in Appendix A, because they require special attention.

In the designs that we present, each design may at first be generally conceptualized with an equal number of observations in its cells and with multiple dependent variables. A univariate design is arrived at by deleting all but one dependent variable. Univariate and multivariate unequal n designs are arrived at by deleting observations from one or more cells of the design.

## Analysis Backbone

In this section we focus on three of the elements of a good research design: 1) the statement of a problem, 2) the research hypothesis, and 3) the statistical hypotheses. We believe that the line of reasoning established from the problem, to the research hypotheses, to the statistical hypotheses, forms the backbone of most good data analysis. This line of reasoning allows the researcher to effectively ask questions, and have them answered using the designs discussed in the following chapters. We leave to others, e.g., Kerlinger (1973), Cook and Campbell (1979), the discussion of the other elements of research design, e.g., how one arrives at a problem and the difficulties of interpreting results.

Problem. The first and most important element that we focus on is the statement of the problem. Here we followed the recommendation of Kerlinger (1973) and placed all of our problems in question form. Throughout the book we tried to keep the problems at a fairly simple level, but in Chapter 3 with our 3 X 2 data, you can begin to see how complex a problem can become.

Research Hypothesis. The second key element is the research hypothesis which is basically an answer to the problem and is based on past research and/or theory.

3

Again, we followed Kerlinger's recommendation and stated all of our research hypotheses as declarative sentences. For example, in the design we just discussed, a response to the first problem might be: "The Written Outline method of study will yield higher mean achievement than will the Picture Outline method."

Statistical Hypotheses. The third key element is the statement of the statistical hypotheses ,i.e., the null (HO) and alternative (HA) hypotheses. Statistical hypotheses are written in symbolic form using the symbol of the population parameter under consideration. In this book we present examples of hypotheses that are tested using planned and overall (omnibus) F-tests. Our planned questions are always about treatment means and so our statistical hypotheses are always made up of mean comparisons with the symbol "u" used to represent a population mean. The statement of the null hypothesis is that a comparison among the treatment means is equal to a constant, usually zero. For example, in the latter design, the univariate null hypothesis for the first problem is: $HO: u(1) - u(2) = 0$. Here $u(1)$ and $u(2)$ are the population means on English achievement for treatments 1 and 2, respectively. In other words this null hypothesis indicates that there are no differences in English achievement between the Picture Outline and Written Outline methods of studying for an examination. The alternative hypothesis is dependent on what is said in the research hypothesis. If on the basis of past research and/or theory the researcher is able to make a directional prediction concerning the treatment means (i.e., make a planned comparison among the treatment means), then the alternate hypothesis reflects this prediction, i.e., $HA: u(1) > u(2)$ or $HA: u(1) < u(2)$. However, if the researcher is unable to predict a directional difference or if he or she agrees with the null hypothesis (i.e., will use an overall F-test), then the alternate hypothesis is nondirectional, i.e., $u(1) - u(2) \neq 0$.

## Chapter Contents

In each of the chapters is a discussion of one design and annotated computer input/output based on this design. The designs discussed include: one factor (one-way classification), two factor (two-way classification), three factor (three-way classification), analysis of covariance, nested, and repeated measures. Each design is considered in two forms: univariate analysis of variance, ANOVA, and multivariate analysis of variance, MANOVA, and with equal and unequal n's.

The main focus in each chapter is the annotated computer input/output from one of the three major statistical packages, BMDP, SAS and SPSS. For all programs a complete listing of the program input, without systems cards, is provided. (Systems cards are described in the last section of this chapter.) For program output, most programs are fully listed using the one-way output in Chapter 2 of each volume. Specialized programs are fully listed in the chapters where they apply, i.e., BMDP8V and SAS(NESTED) in Chapter 6 of Volumes 1 and 2, respectively, and SPSS(RELIABILITY) in Chapter 7 of Volume 3. For the output in Chapters 3 through 6 of each volume we primarily present that part of the output that is useful in constructing source tables and/or testing assumptions.

The discussion of the statistical design in each chapter consists of: a table listing the programs run and some of their features; a rationale for using the statistical design; a univariate example problem; and a multivariate example problem. The univariate and multivariate example problems contain: a statement of the problem, the research hypotheses, the statistical hypotheses, a statistical table derived from the program output, and planned and/or post hoc comparisons. The latter information was included as an aid to researchers writing a dissertation, thesis or research report. The statistical design presentation in each chapter is meant to serve as a review and should serve to support, not replace, the discussion of that design in one of the statistical texts mentioned in the chapter.

The chapters were written so that readers who are unfamiliar with multivariate analysis of variance (i.e., statistical designs with more than one dependent variable) would be able to skip over this material and concentrate solely on the univariate (i.e., one dependent variable) input/output. The volumes and chapters were also written to be as self-contained as possible. That is, each chapter in a volume has information which enables the reader to review what a particular design is supposed to accomplish and the meaning of the computer output for that design. For example, if you wanted to run a univariate one-way analysis of variance you could turn to Chapter 2 in any volume and find a short review of why one uses one-way designs. Then, you could turn to the annotated input and output in each volume. You could then make a decision on which program or combination of programs you would want to run, and use the annotated input as an aid to compiling the control cards necessary to run the program, and the annotated output with the example problem discussion as an aid in interpreting your own output. Appendices, which are discussed in a following section, are also available to aid you in interpreting some components of the program output.

## Table 1.1
## Statistical Package Programs and
## Designs Discussed
## in this Book

---

### Statistical Packages

| Design | BMDP | SAS | SPSS & SPSSX |
|--------|------|-----|--------------|
| One-way | 3D | ANOVA | ANOVA |
|  | 7D | CANDISC | DISCRIMINANT |
|  | 7M | DISCRIM | MANOVA |
|  | 1V | GLM | ONEWAY |
|  | 2V | REG |  |
|  | 4V | STEPDISC |  |
| Two-way | 7D | GLM | ANOVA |
|  | 2V |  | MANOVA |
|  | 4V |  |  |
| Three-way | 2V | ANOVA | ANOVA |
|  | 4V | GLM | MANOVA |
| Analysis of | 1V | GLM | ANOVA |
| Covariance | 2V |  | MANOVA |
|  | 4V |  |  |
| Nested | 4V | GLM | MANOVA |
|  | 8V | NESTED |  |
| Repeated | 2V | GLM | MANOVA |
| Measures | 4V | REG | RELIABILITY |

---

### Selection of Programs and Program Options

### Selection of Programs and A Word of Caution

All of the statistical packages contain a variety of programs which will allow you to perform both simple and complex data analyses relatively easily. These programs are called "programs" in BMDP, "procedures" in SAS, and "subprograms" in SPSS. They are all generally referred to as programs in this book. The programs used to analyze data from the various designs considered in this book are listed above in Table 1.1. In each package we tried to run all of the programs that could generally be used to analyze data for a given design. However, we did not include some programs which we decided were not as pertinent as others, e.g., some single factor designs could be analyzed using BMDP9D, SAS(TTEST), SPSS(BREAKDOWN), or SPSS(T-TEST).

6

We want to emphasize that the reader should exercise care in using the input, output, and annotations provided in the following chapters. The reason for this is that the statistical packages are continually being revised with program features, and programs, added and/or deleted. Also, many computer centers contain old and/or experimental versions. For example, BMDP4V and SPSS (MANOVA) were introduced in 1981, and SPSSX (MANOVA) in 1983; your center may not have these versions. On the other hand, we have found that most of the input/output for the programs described in this book has remained unchanged over the past several years. Our advice is that you check with your computer center as to which version they have and then compare the I/O with ours. Our experience indicates that over 90% of our annotations are appropriate for old versions.

SPSS and SPSSX

In 1983 SPSS was modified to become the SPSSX Batch System. This new system greatly improved SPSS's ability to manage, analyze and display data. To illustrate the use of SPSSX, and to show changes from the old system, we have presented annotated examples of both SPSS and SPSSX control card listings in the last section of this chapter. We have likewise annotated the SPSS output in Volume III of this book so as to point out the small number of changes in output from equivalent SPSSX programs. Therefore, this book should aid the users of either system and be of special value to SPSS users who wish to change to the new SPSSX system.

Program Options

For the programs run in this book we tried to select program options which would allow the user to complete the following processes:

1. Check the data to be sure it was accurately recorded.

2. Check the data for scores that are impossible or markedly deviant. Scores of this type are called outliers, e.g., an IQ score of -50 or 160 on the Wechsler Adult Intelligence test.

3. Check the program control cards for accuracy. These cards determine what statistical program will be used and how the program will function.

4. Check some of the output by hand (e.g., means, variances) to be sure of its accuracy.

7

5. Check for violations of the assumptions of the statistical model used.

6. Consider the question(s) to be answered with the aid of statistical tests. This entails one or more of the following types of statistical tests:

    a. Overall (omnibus) statistical tests (e.g., the overall F test in a one-way ANOVA).

    b. A priori statistical tests (e.g., planned-comparisons).

    c. Post-hoc statistical tests (e.g., Scheffe or Tukey).

Process 6 requires further discussion. In research studies we have all too frequently found an overall analysis of variance (e.g. a one-way analysis with a single omnibus F test) followed by a post hoc test such as Scheffe's or Tukey's. For some studies this approach is correct, but for many others it is not. We find that in many of these research studies--indeed, perhaps most of them--the researchers could have asked questions of their data and predicted outcomes. Had this been done on an a priori basis, the researcher would have been in a position to use statistical techniques that are far more sensitive to treatment effects than is an omnibus F test followed by an extremely conservative post hoc technique. Therefore, in order to place more emphasis on asking planned questions in research studies, we have discussed their use for all problems prior to considering an overall analysis. Chronologically, of course, an overall analysis would precede a planned analysis, but we feel that the latter analysis needs more attention. In the following subsection we discuss input accuracy which is closely related to the first five processes.

Input Accuracy

Outliers. A frequent cause of difficulty in data analysis are scores that are called 'outliers.' Outliers are scores that do not appear to belong with the other scores. They are "mavericks" or as Daniel and Wood (1971) call them "wild points." Such scores may lie three, four or more standard deviations from the other scores, and hence, merit close scrutiny. Outliers may be caused by an error in scoring or recording, or by an anomalous observation such as one caused by a subject who scored all 3's on a five option fifty-item multiple choice test. Frequently outliers should simply be removed from the data set or corrected. Draper and Smith (1981), however, caution researchers about the automatic removal of outliers

8

from a data set when they state: "Sometimes the outlier is
providing information which other data points cannot due to
the fact that it arises from an unusual combination of
circumstances which may be of vital interest and requires
further investigation rather than rejection" (p. 152). An
informative paper entitled "The Rejection of Outliers" was
written by Anscombe (1960); an entire text on this subject
was written by Barnett and Lewis (1978).

"Garbage in Garbage out." Most users of statistical
computer packages have heard the saying "garbage in,
garbage out." This phrase means that if you have provided
a program with either inaccurate data or incorrect
directions (control cards), i.e., "garbage in," the program
will often run with no indication that an error has been
made, yielding incorrect output, i.e., "garbage out". The
author is reminded of an early painful experience when as a
graduate student, he failed to check the input accuracy of
his data. As a consultant to a school system the author
was in the process of explaining the output from an
evaluation. The school people were happy since their
experimental group had done significantly better than the
control group. The dependent variable was a measure of
verbal ability where the highest possible score was 200.
Needless to say, it was very embarrassing when it was
noticed that the mean for the experimental group was over
300. This blatant error was caused when one score was
mispunched as 6000 instead of 60. From that time on the
author has been a strong advocate of diligently checking
all data for outliers before looking at the rest of the
program results. This can usually be done by having the
computer package list the data that is to be analyzed.
This data list should then be proofread like a manuscript.

Large Data Sets. Students frequently complain that if
they listed all their data they would have twenty to thirty
pages of extra output. Because this would involve numerous
additional pages, and might delay the execution of the
program, a data list is all too commonly omitted. The
desire to get to the results of statistical tests as soon
as possible probably reflects the emphasis placed on these
tests in most statistics courses. Too little attention is
given to checking for input accuracy in many of these
courses. Certainly, with a large amount of data, it is all
the more important that the student check his or her data
carefully, because it is all the more likely that errors
have occurred.

Program Control Cards. It is also very important to
check the program control cards to be sure that the program
was given the correct directions. A common error
encountered with control cards is that the user has read
the wrong variable from a set of cards containing many

variables, or that he or she has mislabeled a variable. These types of errors will usually <u>not</u> cause a program to give you an error message or to terminate its execution. They can be detected either through a careful review of the program control cards and the output from these cards found in the program, or through manual computation of some of the program output.

Unfortunately, research and statistics texts and courses often fail to place much emphasis on checking data for input accuracy. The author's hope is that this small section, and his embarrassing experience, will encourage researchers to expend more effort on data and control card input checking. Although tedious, it is certainly less painful than discovering data or control card errors after a manuscript has been written or, worse yet, put into print.

## Appendices

The appendices in this book contain information which should enable you to further understand some of the statistical tests performed by the computer package programs. The appendices are repeated in each volume. The topics covered in the appendices include:

Two-Way Nonorthogonal (Unequal $n$) Analyses (Appendix A),

Multivariate Statistical Tests (Appendix B),

Step-Down Analysis (Appendix C)

Statistical Tests When the Factors have Fixed, Random and Mixed Levels (Appendix D),

Skewness and Kurtosis Measures in SAS (Appendix E).

Appendix A was included because there is disagreement among statisticians on how one should analyze designs with unequal cell sizes, i.e., unequal $n$'s. In Appendix A we discuss some of the methods that are available to analyze unequal $n$ designs, and present reasons as to why we selected a method called "weighted squares of means" for use throughout this book. We also give reasons why we did not use the other methods. Appendix B was written in order to assist researchers in choosing an appropriate multivariate test statistic. Appendices C through E were written as a convenience for the reader. In these appendices we discuss tests that are available from some of the packages.

## Systems Cards

Throughout this book we provide you with a complete listing of the control cards used to derive every program output. Control cards are the cards which control the operation of the statistical package. (Here the word "card" is synonymous with a "line" on a computer terminal.) However, we do not include the systems cards in these listings because systems cards are dependent upon the operating system available at a given computer center. Systems cards are the cards you need to gain access to a computer and to its statistical packages. In input listings 1-1 through 1-6 we present five complete card listings in order to illustrate how systems cards may be used for different purposes.

Input listings 1-1, 1-2, 1-3, and 1-4 contain a complete listing of the programs used to execute BMDP1V, SAS(GLM), SPSS(MANOVA) and SPSSX(MANOVA), respectively, for the one-way analysis of variance data found in Chapter 2. These listings contain the systems cards which are needed to execute these programs at Ohio University. Remember, the systems cards shown in these input listings probably will not execute this program on your computer system because systems cards are specific to a given system. Therefore, before running one of the programs listed in this book you should insert the systems cards necessary for your computer system.

In input listing 1-5 we present the systems and control cards that were used to execute two programs (BMDP1D and BMDP1V) in a single run from the BMDP package. In Volume 1 we do not execute other BMDP programs in this fashion and so we took this opportunity to show you that it can be done. This linkage of BMDP programs is especially valuable for obtaining data lists or in transferring factor scores or correlation matrices between programs for further analysis.

In input listing 1-6 we present the systems and control cards which enabled us to send data from SAS to BMDP and then to SPSS. We did this to show you that it is possible to send data from one package to the next. However, this may not be true at your computer center, so check. In SAS it is also possible to interface other packages without using special system cards as just described. For example, SAS's PROC BMDP allows you to utilize BMDP programs from within a SAS job. SAS also has PROC CONVERT which converts system files from other packages (including BMDP and SPSS) to SAS data sets, then useable by other SAS procedures.

Finally, BMDP, SAS, and SPSS have "interactive"

versions of their packages, which means that in those versions the system cards as discussed here are not used. Also, some of the interactive control cards may differ somewhat from those shown in this book. However, the necessary adjustments which result from computing interactively should be easily discerned by the reader.

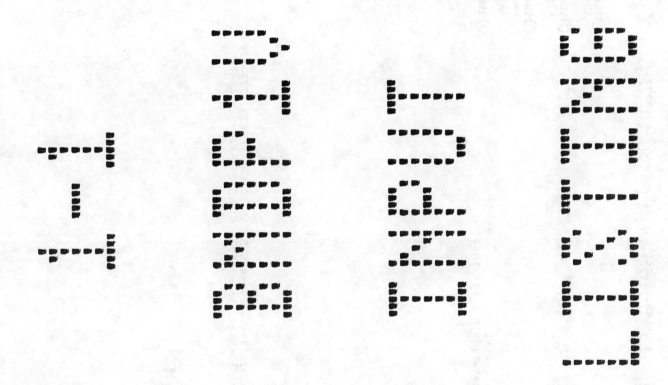

① These are column identifiers and are not part of the program content.

② These are the systems cards used at Ohio University to execute BMDP1V.

③ The control cards for BMDP1V follow the systems cards (they may also follow the data but do not in this example).

④ These are the data cards.

```
① 0000000001111111111222222222233333333334444444444555555555566666666667777777778
   1234567890123456789012345678901234567890123456789012345678901234567890

② //H1001BMD JOB (,
② //   N3366KGB),ROBERT.BARCIKOWSKI
② //   EXEC BIMED,PROG=BMDP1V
③ /PROB TITLE IS 'SPIKER: ONE-WAY ANCVA, UNEQUAL N
                 DATA FROM WINER, P. 237, 1971'.
   /INPUT  VARIABLE = 2.
           FORMAT = '(2F3.0)'.
   /VARIABLE NAME = TREAT,CREDBY.
              GROUP = TREAT.
   /GROUP CODES(1) = 1 TO 3.
          NAME(1) = 'ORAL-VIS','VISUAL,ORAL.
   /DESIGN TITLE IS 'METHOD OF PRESENTATION ONE-WAY ANCVA'.
           DEPEND = CREDBY.
           CONTR = 1,-.5,-.5.
           CCNTR = 0,1,-1.
   /PRINT MIN. MAX. NEWS.
   /END
④  1 10
   1  4
   1 10
   2  8
   2  4
   2  4
   2  2
   2  9
   3  3
   3  5
   3  4
   3  1
```

14

```
① 0000000001111111111222222222233333333334444444444555555555566666666667777777778
   1234567890123456789012345678901234567890123456789012345678901234567890
```

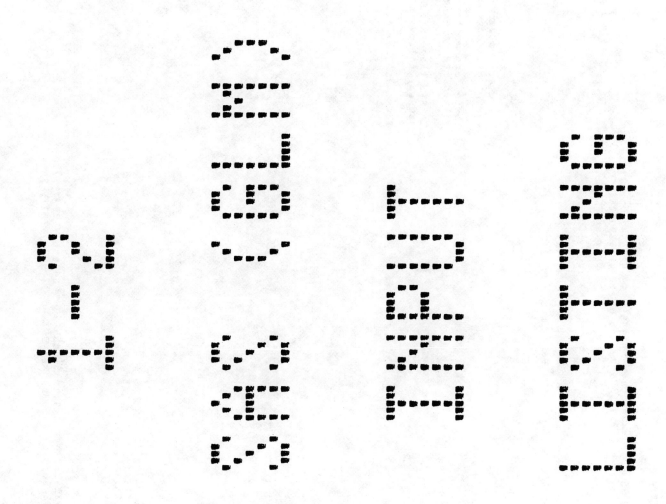

```
①0000000000111111111122222222223333333333444444444455555555556666666666777777777 8
  1234567890123456789012345678901234567890123456789012345678901234567890123456789 0

②//H1002SAS JOB (,
②// N3366QED),ROBERT.BARCIKOWSKI
②// EXEC SAS
③COMMENT SPIKER: ONE-WAY ANOVA, UNEQUAL N -- DATA FROM WINER, P. 237, 1971;
DATA SPIKER:
INPUT TREAT CREDBY;
LABEL TREAT = METHOD OF PRESENTATION;
CARDS;
④ 1 10
  1  4
  1 10
  2  8
  2  4
  2  4
  2  2
  2  9
  2  3
  3  5
  3  4
  3  1

PROC FORMAT PRINT;
VALUE LEVEL 1 = A:  ORAL/VISUAL
            2 = B:  VISUAL
            3 = C:  ORAL;

TITLE METHOD OF PRESENTATION ONE-WAY ANOVA;
PROC SORT;
BY TREAT;
PROC PRINT;
BY TREAT;
FORMAT TREAT LEVEL.;
PROC UNIVARIATE PLOT FREQ NORMAL;
VAR CREDBY;
BY TREAT;
FORMAT TREAT LEVEL.;
PROC GLM;
CLASS TREAT;
MODEL CREDBY = TREAT;
CONTRAST 'O-V VS AVE OF O & V' TREAT 1 -.5 -.5;
CONTRAST 'ORAL VS VISUAL' TREAT 0 1 -1;
ESTIMATE 'O-V VS AVE OF O & V' TREAT 1 -.5 -.5/E;
ESTIMATE 'ORAL VS VISUAL' TREAT 0 1 -1/E;
LSMEANS TREAT/ STDERR PDIFF;
FORMAT TREAT LEVEL.;

①0000000000111111111122222222223333333333444444444455555555556666666666777777777 8
  1234567890123456789012345678901234567890123456789012345678901234567890123456789 0
```

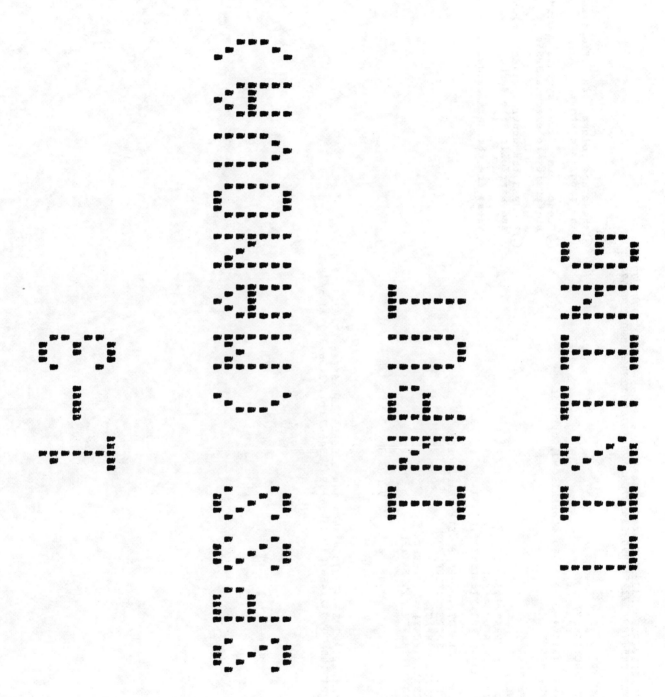

```
①00000000011111111112222222222333333333344444444445555555555666666666677777777778
   12345678901234567890123456789012345678901234567890123456789012345678901234567890

②//H1OO3RSB JOB (,
②// N366CIA),ROBERT.BARCIKCWSKI
②// EXEC SPSS
③RUN NAME       ONE-WAY (ANOVA):    PLANNED COMPARISONS, UNEQUAL N
 VARIABLE LIST  TREAT,CREDBY
 INPUT MEDIUM   CARD
 INPUT FORMAT   FREEFIELD
 N OF CASES     UNKNOWN
 MANOVA         CREDBY BY TREAT(1,3)/
                PRINT=CELLINFO(MEANS)
                  HOMOGENEITY(EARTLETT,CCCHRAN)
                  POBS/
                PLOT = CELLPLOTS,BOXPLOTS,STEMLEAF,POBS/
                METHOD = SSTYPE(UNIQUE)/
                PARTITICN(TREAT)/
                CONTRAST(TREAT) = HELMERT/
                DESIGN = TREAT(1),TREAT(2)/
 READ INPUT DATA
④1 1 10   1 4 1 10   2 8   2 4   2 2   2 9   3 3   3 5   3 4   3 1
 END INPUT DATA

①00000000011111111112222222222333333333344444444445555555555666666666677777777778
   12345678901234567890123456789012345678901234567890123456789012345678901234567890
```

18

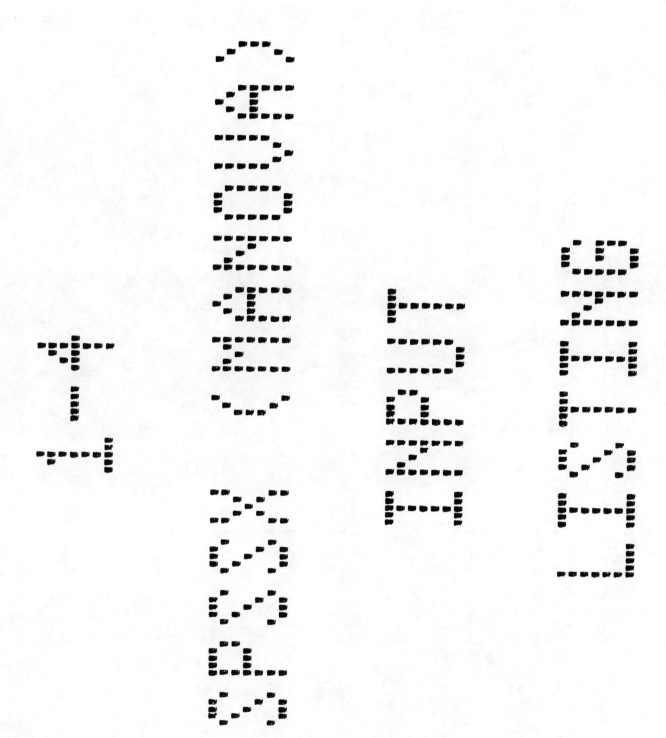

```
② //H1004SPS JOB (,
② // N6633AIC),ROBERT.BARCIKOWSKI
② //EXEC SPSSX
③ TITLE     ONE-WAY (ANOVA):    PLANNED COMPARISONS, UNEQUAL N
  DATA LIST FREE/ TREAT,CREDBY
  MANOVA       CREDBY BY TREAT(1,3)/
               PRINT=CELLINFO(MEANS)
                     HOMOGENEITY(BARTLETT,COCHRAN)
                     POBS/
               PLOT = CELLPLOTS,BOXPLOTS,STEMLEAF,POBS/
               METHOD = SSTYPE(UNIQUE)/
               PARTITION(TREAT)/
               CONTRAST(TREAT) = HELMERT/
               DESIGN = TREAT(1),TREAT(2)/
④ BEGIN DATA
  1 10    1 4    1 10    2 8    2 4    2 4    2 2    2 9    3 3    3 5    3 4    3 1
  END DATA
```

① These are column identifiers and are not part of the program content.

② These are the systems cards used at Ohio University to execute SPSSX.

③ In SPSSX the control cards follow the systems cards and may follow the data.

④ These are the data cards.

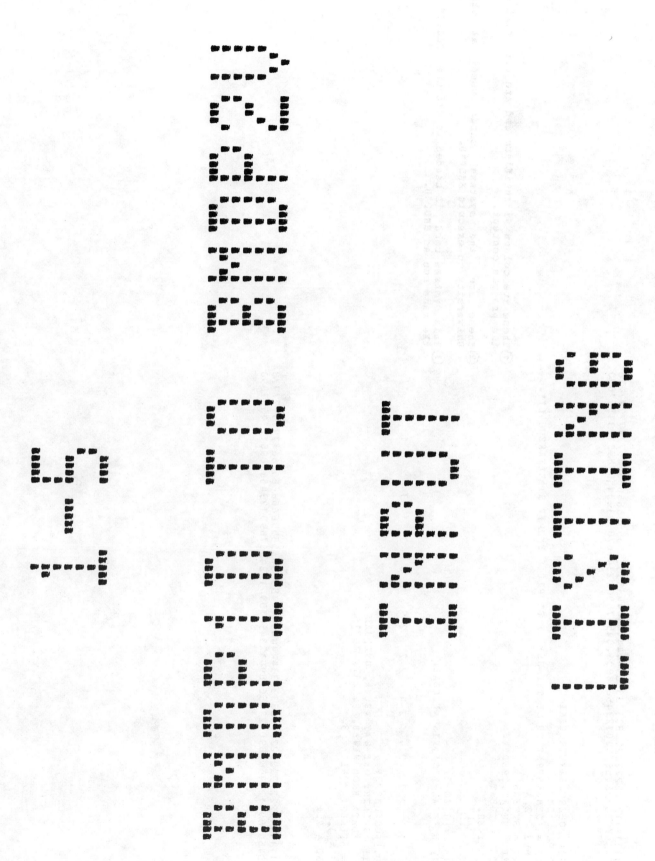

```
①0000000000111111111122222222223333333333444444444455555555556666666666777777778
   1234567890123456789012345678901234567890123456789012345678901234567890123456789 0

② //H1004BMD JOB (,
② // N366CIA,30),ROBERT.BARCIKCWSKI
② // EXEC BIMED,PROG=BMDP1D
/PROBLEM TITLE = 'DEMONSTRATICN OF THE USE CF BMDP1D & BMDP2V SIMULTANEOUSLY'.
/INPUT VARIABLE = 2.
       FORMAT = STREAM.
/VARIABLE NAME = TREAT,CREDBY.
          GROUP = TREAT.
/SAVE CODE = SPIKER.
     UNIT = 3.
     NEW.
/GROUP CODES(1) = 1 TO 3.
       NAME(1) = 'ORAL-VIS',VISUAL,CRAL.
/PRINT DATA.
/END
1 10   1 4   1 10   2 8   2 4   2 4   2 2   2 9   3 3   3 5   3 4   3 1
/END
③ // EXEC BIMED,PROG=BMDP2V
/PROB TITLE IS 'SPIKER: ONE-WAY ANCVA, UNEQUAL N
               DATA FROM WINER, P. 237, 1971'.
/INPUT CCDE = SPIKER. UNIT = 3.
/DESIGN GRCUP = 1.
        DEPEND = 2.
/END

①0000000000111111111122222222223333333333444444444455555555556666666666777777778
   1234567890123456789012345678901234567890123456789012345678901234567890123456789 0
```

① These are column identifiers and are not part of the program content.

② These are the systems cards used at Ohio University to execute BMDP1D.

③ This systems card is needed to execute BMDP2V in the same run as BMDP1D.

22

COLLECTION IDS: 1,0

am  83-14693     db   10/11/83  07/30/85  10/31/83  LC        LC

LON    :a
TILNO  :abc

:(WaOLN)2827900
:Computer packages and research design :;with annotations of input and output from the BMDP, SAS, SPSS, and SPSSX statistical packages /;edited by Robert S. Barcikowski ; contributions by Robert S. Barcikowski ... [et al.].
:Lanham, MD :;University Press of America,;c1983.
:3 v. ;;28 cm.
:Includes bibliographies and indexes.
:v. 1- BMDP -- v. 2. SAS -- v. 3. SPSS and SPSSX.
:Mathematical statistics;Computer programs.
:Statistics;Computer programs.
:Biometry;Computer programs.
:Barcikowski, Robert S.
:0819134945 (pbk. :;v. 1 : alk. paper) :;$26.50 (varies for each vol.)

IMP    :abc
COL    :ac
NOB    :a
NOCC   :a
SUT-L  :ax
SUT-L  :ax
SUT-L  :ax
AEPSA  :a
SBN    :ac

CALL   :ab      :QA276.4:.C576 1983
DDCF   :a2      :519.5/028/5425;19
LCDN   :abcde   :2;3;3;3;3
FFD    CONF==       FEST==        INDEX= x    ME IN B==    LAN= eng
INTEL LV==       FIC==         BIOG==       DAT KY= s     REPRO==
DATE1= 1983  DATE2=        CNTRY= mdu   ILLUS==      CAT FORM= a
CONTENTS= b  MODRC==       CAT S==      GOV PUB==

wait a few days

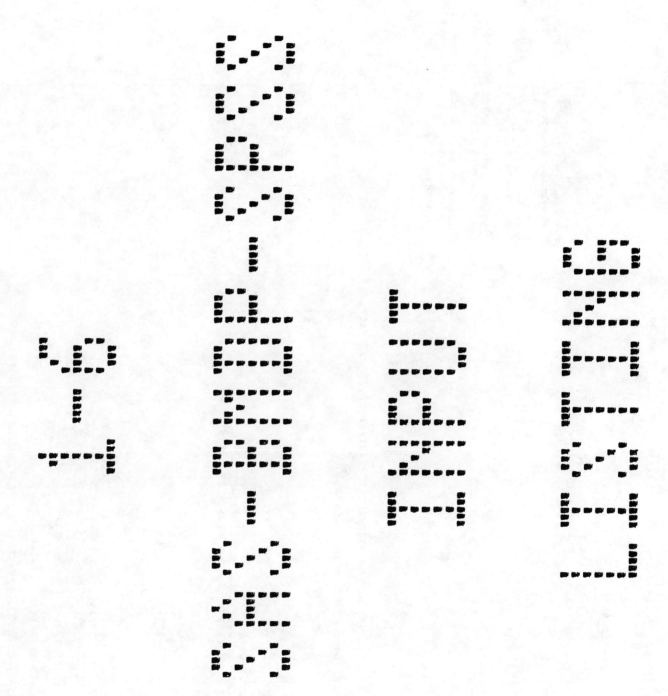

```
00000000011111111112222222222333333333344444444445555555555666666666677777777778
12345678901234567890123456789012345678901234567890123456789012345678901234567890

//H1005RSB JOB (,
//  N3366KGB,30),ROBERT.BARCIKCWSKI
//STEP0010 EXEC SAS
//EXAMPLE DD DSN=&EXAMPLE,DISP=(NEW,PASS,DELETE),SPACE=(CYL,(1,1)),
//  UNIT=DISK,DCB=(LRECI=80,ELKSIZE=800,RECFM=FB)
DATA SPIKER:
INPUT TREAT CREDBY EFFECT:
LIST:
CARDS:
 1 10 16
 1  4 10
 1 10 18
 2  8 12
 2  4  8
 2  4  6
 2  2  6
 2  9 14
 3  3 10
 3  5 16
 3  4 14
 3  1  9
PRCC PRINT:
PROC FACTOR NPACT=2 MINEIGEN=-1 METHOD=PRIN ROTATE=VARIMAX SCORE OUT=FACT:
VAR CREDBY EFFECT:
PROC SCORE DATA=SPIKER SCORE = FACT OUT = SCORE1;
VAR CREDBY EFFECT:
PROC PRINT:
DATA GRAPE:
SET SCORE1:
FILE EXAMPLE:
PUT @1 TREAT 1. @2 FACTOR1 7.4 @9 FACTOR2 7.4:
/*
//STEP0020 EXEC BIMED,PROG=BMDP7M
//FT09F001 DD DSN=&EXAMPLE,DISP=(OLD,PASS),UNIT=DISK
/PROB TITLE IS 'LINK EXAMPLE WITH FACTOR SCORES FROM SAS'.
/VARIABLE NAME IS TREAT,FS1,FS2.
   GROUP IS TREAT.
/INPUT UNIT IS 9.
   VARIABLES ARE 3.
   FORMAT = '(F1.0,2F7.4)'.
/GROUP CODES(1) = 1 TO 3.
/DISC CONTR = 2,-1,-1.
/END
/*
//STEP0030 EXEC SPSS
//FT08F001 DD DSN=&EXAMPLE,DISP=(OLD,DELETE),UNIT=DISK
RUN NAME       EXAMPLE LINK WITH BMDP
VARIABLE LIST  TREAT,FS1,FS2
INPUT FORMAT   FIXED(F1-0,2F7-4)
PRINT FORMATS  TREAT TO FS2 (4)
LIST CASES     CASES=15/VARIABLES=TREAT,FS1,FS2
INPUT MEDIUM   DISK
DISCRIMINANT   GROUPS = TREAT (1,3)/VARIABLES = FS1,FS2/ANALYSIS=FS1,FS2
STATISTICS     ALL,
OPTIONS        6,7,11
READ INPUT DATA

00000000011111111112222222222333333333344444444445555555555666666666677777777778
12345678901234567890123456789012345678901234567890123456789012345678901234567890
```

① These are column identifiers and are not part of the program content.

② These systems cards allowed us to store data generated by SAS.

③ These systems cards allowed us to access the data generated by SAS and to analyze it with BMDP7M.

④ These systems cards allowed us to access the data generated by SAS and to analyze it with an SPSS program.

CHAPTER 2

ONE-WAY ANALYSIS OF VARIANCE
by Robert S. Barcikowski and Barry K. Spiker

## Introduction

One-way analysis of variance is an analytical tool used in experiments where groups are exposed to different treatment levels of one independent variable. The problem in such designs is to determine if the groups differ on one or more dependent variables. In univariate analysis of variance, ANOVA, there is one dependent variable, while in multivariate analysis of variance, MANOVA, there is more than one dependent variable. In this chapter, researchers can gain a basic understanding of one-way analysis of variance and its use through example output from various "canned" computer programs.

In planning an experiment, there is a temptation to include many experimental treatments and variables, especially if the data are inexpensive or are available. However, this is not a good approach to research design, especially if the researcher is interested in making meaningful inferences from his data. Interpretation of data should be made according to the nature and history of the problem under investigation and not left entirely to the statistical results. Other things being equal, the simpler the experiment the more interpretable and meaningful the results will be. One-way analysis of variance designs represent one of the simplest and most powerful analytical tools available to researchers.

## Organization of the Programs

To illustrate several ways data from a one-way analysis of variance design may be analyzed, 27 computer runs were made with the data from this chapter. Because this book is to be used both as a reference and a teaching guide, some input/output (I/O) is labeled "Standard" and some input/output is labeled "Instruction." "Standard" I/O supplies the reader with data checks and material required for most research reports. It contains I/O that a researcher would desire from a single program execution. "Instruction" I/O demonstrates a special feature of a program or highlights a point made in one of the Appendices. Table 2.1 contains a list of the programs run for this chapter and indicates whether they are univariate or multivariate and standard or instruction runs. The output from the standard runs is discussed in the

Table 2.1
Descriptions of the Programs Run on the
Single Factor (One-Way) Data From Chapter 2

| Program | Program Number | Model[1] | Type[2] | Page | I/C Features |
|---------|---------|--------|-------|------|--------------|
| | | | | | |
| Volume 1: BMDP | | | | | |
| BMDP1V | 2-1 | U | S | 55 | unequal n, fixed format, overall and planned analyses, t-test matrix |
| BMDP4V | 2-2 | U | S | 62 | unequal n, free format, planned analysis |
| BMDP2V | 2-3 | U | S | 70 | unequal n, stream format, overall analysis |
| BMDP7D | 2-4 | U | S | 76 | unequal n, fixed format with cases= specification, data list, overall analyses, with assumed equal and unequal (Welch, Brown-Forsythe) variances side-by-side histograms of treatment levels, Levene's test for equal variances |
| BMDP4V | 2-5 | U | S | 85 | unequal n, slash format, overall analysis |
| BMDP4V | 2-6 | M | S | 91 | unequal n, planned analysis |
| BMDP4V | 2-7 | M | S | 100 | unequal n, overall analysis |
| BMDP7M | 2-8 | M | S | 108 | unequal n, overall analysis through stepwise discriminant analysis |
| BMDP3D | 2-9 | M | I | 121 | unequal n, Hotelling's T**2 with separate and pooled univariate t's, Levene's test for equal (pair-wise) variances |
| BMDP7M | 2-10 | M | I | 129 | unequal n, planned contrast through stepwise discriminant analysis |

| Program | Program Number | Mode[1] | Type[2] | Page | I/O Features |
|---------|---------|---------|---------|------|--------------|
| | | | | Volume 2: SAS | |
| SAS (GLM) | 2-1 | U | S | 55 | unequal $\underline{n}$, list input, PROC UNIVARIATE, overall and planned analyses |
| SAS (ANOVA) | 2-2 | U | S | 69 | equal $\underline{n}$, PROC MEANS, overall analysis |
| SAS (GLM) | 2-3 | M | S | 77 | unequal $\underline{n}$, column input, overall multivariate analysis with overall and planned univariate analyses |
| SAS (REG) | 2-4 | M | I | 91 | unequal $\underline{n}$, overall and planned multivariate analysis |
| SAS (STEPDISC) | 2-5 | M | S | 100 | unequal $\underline{n}$, formatted input, overall analysis through stepwise discriminant analysis |
| SAS (DISCRM) | 2-6 | M | I | 109 | unequal $\underline{n}$, mixed (i.e. column, formatted, and list) input, PROC SUMMARY, classification analysis, Kendall and Stuart test of homogeneity of within covariance matrices |
| SAS (CANDISC) | 2-7 | M | S | 122 | unequal $\underline{n}$, overall analysis through discriminant analysis |

Table 2.1, continued

| Program | Program Number | Mode[1] | Type[2] | Page | I/O Features |
|---|---|---|---|---|---|

Volume 3: SPSS and SPSSX

| Program | Program Number | Mode[1] | Type[2] | Page | I/O Features |
|---|---|---|---|---|---|
| SPSS-SPSSX (MANOVA) | 2-1 | U | S | 55 | unequal n, freefield input format, UNKNOWN number of cases, Helmert contrasts, planned analysis, Cochran and Bartlett-Box tests for equal variances, plots of means versus standard deviations, and cell means, box-plots, stem-and-leaf display, listing of observed, predicted, raw residual, and standardized residuals, plots of predicted and residual case values |
| SPSS-SPSSX (ONEWAY) | 2-2 | U | S | 71 | unequal n, DATA LIST Input, overall and planned analyses, Cochran and Bartlett-Box tests for equal variances, second run with Tukey's test run on harmonic means |
| SPSS-SPSSX (ONEWAY) | 2-3 | U | S | 84 | equal n, fixed format input run with Tukey's test for equal n's |
| SPSS-SPSSX (ANOVA) | 2-4 | U | S | 93 | unequal n, overall analysis |

| Program | Program Number | Mode[1] | Type[2] | Page | I/O Features |
|---------|----------------|---------|---------|------|--------------|
| SPSS-SPSSX (MANOVA) | 2-5 | U | S | 103 | unequal n, overall analysis |
| SPSS-SPSSX (MANOVA) | 2-6 | U | I | 112 | equal n, simple contrasts |
| SPSS-SPSSX (MANOVA) | 2-7 | U | I | 115 | equal n, repeated contrasts |
| SPSS-SPSSX (MANOVA) | 2-8 | U | I | 120 | equal n, special contrasts |
| SPSS-SPSSX (MANOVA) | 2-9 | U | I | 125 | equal n, polynomial contrasts |
| SPSS-SPSSX (MANOVA) | 2-10 | M | S | 130 | unequal n, TASK NAME, first run planned analysis; second run overall analysis, each with stepdown analysis |
| SPSS-SPSSX (DISCRIMINANT) | 2-11 | M | S | 160 | unequal n, overall analysis through stepwise discriminant analysis |

[1] Mode is coded U for univariate or M for multivariate.
[2] Type is coded S for standard or I for instruction.

succeeding analysis of variance sections. A discussion of the special runs follows the analysis of variance presentations. In Table 2.1 we also number the programs, indicate the pages on which a given program's I/O is described, and present some I/O features that you might be interested in. For example, in the programs we made an attempt to illustrate a variety of methods available in each package to input data. Therefore, in the I/O Features section of Table 2.1, we indicate which programs illustrate different input methods. Here, the first three BMDP programs illustrate this package's fixed, free, and stream formats; SAS programs number 2-1, 2-3, and 2-5 illustrate this package's list, column, and formatted input; and, SPSS (SPSSX) programs numbered 2-1, 2-2, and 2-3 illustrate this package's freefield (free), data list (data list), and fixed (formatted) format methods of inputing data.

## Analysis of Variance Presentations

For the univariate and multivariate presentations that follow, data were taken from a problem discussed in Winer (1971, p. 237). To give this data meaning, a fictitious problem was created concerning the study of effects of modes of message presentation. The problem and research hypotheses are stated in the question and answer format suggested by Kerlinger (1973, pp. 16-20).

Both the univariate and multivariate analyses are approached in two ways. First the researcher is assumed to have knowledge based on theory and /or past research which supports an analysis with planned questions. This approach is discussed in sections concerned with what are known as "planned comparisons." Second, the researcher is assumed to be in an exploratory phase of analysis with little supporting research and/or theory. This type of analysis is discussed in sections concerned with overall tests and post hoc comparisons. A brief discussion of the nature of the problem follows.

## Problem

A New York publishing house wishes to promote what they consider to be a revolutionary textbook. The marketing department was called upon to perform a feasibility study as to the best way of selling such a book. To determine the best method of presentation, a persuasive sales pitch was produced in three forms. The three forms or levels of presentation were given to a randomly selected group of subjects as: oral-visual (live, face-to-face presentation), visual (written presentation), and oral (audio cassette tape presentation). A review of the following pertinent literature provided the warrant for such a study.

The manner in which a message is delivered has great influence over the effectiveness of that presentation. Early research (Knower, 1935, 1936) on the credibility of live versus non-live presentations showed that the live or face-to-face presentation was significantly better than the taped presentation. Bettinghaus (1980) demonstrated that oral communication will be more effective than written communication. Croft, Stimpson, Ross, Bray and Breglio (1969) suggest that source credibility will differ depending on the mode of presentation even though Meyer and Gute (1972) found no differences in the rating of the credibility of messages presented as live, audio, or video. The problem area and its supporting research suggests the following question: is a message's credibility dependent on the mode of presentation? Basically, the publishing house would like to use the information provided through the following analyses to determine if they can best promote their book using salesmen (live, face-to-face presentation), through mailed brochures (visual presentation), or by mailing a tape to prospective buyers (audio-tape presentation).

## Univariate Analysis: Planned Comparisons

We recommend that the reader consult other texts for further discussion of univariate one-way ANOVA designs. Good books on this topic are: Cohen & Cohen, 1975; Dayton, 1970; Glass & Stanley, 1970; Hays, 1973; Kennedy, 1978; Keppel, 1973; Kerlinger & Pedhazur, 1973; Kirk, 1968; Snedecor & Cochran, 1967; Winer, 1971. Hays (1973, Chapter 14) and Kirk (1968, Chapter 3) provide excellent discussions and examples of planned comparisons.

Problem. Is a message's credibility dependent on the mode of message presentation?

Research Hypotheses. The research hypotheses were formulated based on theory and previous research before the data were collected.

Research Hypothesis (1): of three modes of message presentation, oral-visual, visual, and oral, the combined oral-visual message presentation will not differ from the average effect of the visual and oral message presentations in enhancing message credibility.

Research Hypothesis (2): the visual mode of message presentation will be more effective than the oral mode.

31

Statistical Hypotheses. The statistical hypotheses
are written in symbolic form to match the research
hypotheses. Here the symbol u(i) represents the population
mean for group $i$ ( $i$ = 1, 2, 3); H(0h) represents the null
and H(Ah) the alternate hypotheses for research hypothesis
$h$ ( $h$ = 1, 2). Here oral-visual is treatment 1, visual is
treatment 2, and oral is treatment 3.

Null Hypothesis (1) H(01): $u(1) = \frac{(u(2) + u(3))}{2}$

Alternate Hypothesis (1) H(A1): $u(1) \neq \frac{(u(2) + u(3))}{2}$

Null Hypothesis (2) H(02): $u(2) = u(3)$

Alternate Hypothesis (2) H(A2): $u(2) > u(3)$

Each null hypothesis will be tested at the .05 level
of significance, making the experimentwise level of
significance .10.

Data. The data are presented in Table 2.2 as a
univariate, equal $n$ problem. The design has one factor
with three levels, and the dependent variable is message
credibility. A measure of the dependent variable was
arrived at by taking ratings of each message's credibility
using Spiker's credibility form. The subjects (prospective
buyers) were randomly sampled from the population of
subjects and were then randomly assigned to the treatment
levels. Three subjects were dropped (represented by *) for
most computer runs in order to demonstrate the effects of
unequal $n$s. If this were an actual experiment the
researcher would have to check to be sure that these
subjects were not absent because of the treatment effects.[1]
(Footnotes are at the end of the text for each chapter,
i.e., preceding the program I/O.) The analysis that
follows is based on the unequal $n$ data.

Table 2.2
Data[1] for a
One-Way Univariate ANOVA Design

| Oral/Visual Live Presentation | Visual Presentation | Oral Presentation |
|---|---|---|
| 10 | 8 | 3 |
| 4 | 4 | 5* |
| 10 | 4 | 5 |
| 4* | 2 | 4 |
| 10* | 9 | 1 |

$\bar{X}(1)=7.60$   $\bar{X}(2)=5.40$   $\bar{X}(3)=3.60$
$*\bar{X}(1)=8.00$   $*\bar{X}(2)=5.40$   $*\bar{X}(3)=3.25$

[1]The data is from Winer (1971, p. 237); "*"
scores were removed to create an unequal n
problem. For this presentation, the data
in Winer's cells 1 & 3 were reversed.


One-Way ANOVA Table. Table 2.3 is the planned
comparison one-way ANOVA table (for unequal n's) which
would appear in a research report on this experiment. The
contents of this table could be drawn from runs of the
programs: BMDP1V (2-1), BMDP4V (2-2), SAS(GLM) (2-1),
SPSS(MANOVA) (2-1), and SPSS(ONEWAY) (2-2).

For an equal n design a similar table could be
constructed with output from all of the above programs. In
the program output SPSS(MANOVA) (2-6), (2-7), (2-8) and (2-
9) was run with equal n's to illustrate different types of
contrasts. (SAS(ANOVA) (2-2) was run on equal n's, but it
only yields an overall analysis).

The results in Table 2.3 indicate that the data from
this experiment do support both null hypotheses (p<.0762;
p<.1367). Support was found for the first research
hypothesis[2], but no support was found for the second
research hypothesis. Therefore, the publishers decided to
mail brochures to prospective buyers because this was the
cheapest method of presentation and it did not vary
significantly from the other methods[3].

## Table 2.3
## Univariate Planned Comparisons Analysis
## of Variance for the Type of Presentation Experiment

| Source of Variation | Degrees of Freedom | Sum of Squares | Mean Square | t Statistic | Prob |
|---|---|---|---|---|---|
| Treatments (between groups) Comparisons | 2 | 38.72 | | | |
| 1 | 1 | 30.29 | 30.29 | 2.00 | .0762 |
| 2 | 1 | 10.27 | 10.27 | 1.17 | .1367[1] |
| Error (within groups) | 9 | 67.95 | 7.55 | | |
| Total (adjusted for grand mean) | 11 | 106.67 (treatments plus error) | | | |

[1]This value is for a one-tailed t-test and is half of the two-tailed probability (.2734) reported in BMDP1V and SAS(GLM).

## Univariate Analysis: Overall Test and Post Hoc Comparisons

If a researcher has no planned questions that he feels are appropriate (i.e., on the basis of theory or past research) to ask about his treatments, then he might conduct an overall test of significance. If the overall test is significant, then he would test differences among the treatment means using a post hoc test. In this case the problem statement would probably be the same as in a planned comparison example, but the research hypotheses would change.

Problem. Is a message's credibility dependent on the mode of message presentation?

Research Hypothesis. In this case the researcher believes that differences will appear among his group means, but past research was inconclusive, and his theory is not formulated well enough for him to make predictions.

Research Hypothesis: one of the modes of message presentation, oral-visual, visual, oral, will be more effective than the others in enhancing message credibility.

Statistical Hypotheses.

Null Hypothesis $H(0)$: $u(1) = u(2) = u(3)$

Alternate Hypothesis $H(A)$: $u(i) \neq u(j)$ $(i \neq j;$ $i, j = 1, 2, 3)$

The alternate hypothesis indicates that some of the population means are different from others.

This null hypothesis will be tested at the .05 level of significance.

Data. The data are the unequal n data presented in Table 2.2 .

One-Way ANOVA Table. Table 2.4 is the one-way ANOVA source table that would appear in a research report on this experiment. The contents of this table could be derived from all of the overall analysis univariate unequal n program runs for this chapter. A similar table for the equal n design could be constructed from all of the programs where equal n data was used. The results in Table 2.4 indicate that the data from this experiment support the null hypothesis (p<.1314). Therefore, the research hypothesis is not supported. Based on this result the publishers would probably mail brochures to prospective buyers because this is the cheapest method of presentation and it did not differ significantly from the other methods.

Table 2.4
Univariate Analysis of Variance
for the Type of Presentation Experiment

| Source of Variation | Degrees of Freedom | Sum of Squares | Mean Square | F-Ratio | Prob > F |
|---|---|---|---|---|---|
| Treatments (between groups) | 2 | 38.72 | 19.36 | 2.56 | .1314 |
| Error (within groups) | 9 | 67.95 | 7.55 | | |
| Total (adjusted for the grand mean) | 11 | 106.67 | | | |

Tukey's (HSD) Post Hoc Contrasts. Because there are no significant differences among the means of the groups in this study, no post hoc tests would be done. However, in order to demonstrate how Tukey's test works, the following material is presented. The reader is reminded that this post hoc test would be done only if a significant overall F test were found.

This presentation is based on Kirk (1968, pp. 88-90) for the case when the cells have equal ns, and on Games and Howell (1976) for the case when the cells have unequal ns. (The Games and Howell modification of Tukey's test was further corroborated in Keselman and Rogen (1978).) Tukey's HSD (honestly significant difference) test was designed for making all pairwise comparisons among cell means while holding the experimentwise error rate at alpha. The following steps indicate how Tukey's test is calculated in general and for the presentation experiment.

Step 1.

Equal n. If you have equal ns in your treatment levels, go to step 2, and use the number of subjects in one treatment as your n in step 3. (The results for equal n can be found in the SPSS (program 2-3) standard, univariate, one-way, equal n output from the subprogram ONEWAY.)

Unequal n. Calculate the estimated variance error of the mean $(S^2(\bar{X}i))$ for each treatment using:

$$S^2(\bar{X}i) = S^2(i) / n(i).$$

Here, $S^2(i)$ = estimated variance in treatment $i$, and $n(i)$ is the number of subjects in treatment $i$:

$$S^2(i) = [n(i) \sum X(ik)^2 - (\sum X(ik))^2] / [n(i) * (n(i)-1)],$$

where $X(ik)$ = observation k in treatment i.

> Example:
>
> $S^2(\bar{X}1) = 12.00/3.00 = 4.00$
> $S^2(\bar{X}2) = 8.80/5.00 = 1.76$
> $S^2(X3) = 2.92/4.00 = .73$

Step 2.

Equal n. Find the statistic q from tables of the studentized range distribution. To enter the table for q, one needs three values: the error degrees of freedom, V, the number of treatment levels, I, and the level of significance, . Tables for q can be found in Glass and Stanley (1970, pp. 529-533), Kirk (1968, pp. 531-532), and Winer (1971, pp. 870-871).

Unequal n. For unequal n the q statistic is found as described above for equal n, but the degrees of freedom for error are found separately for each possible comparison using:

$$V(ii') = \frac{(S^2(\overline{X}i) + S^2(\overline{X}i'))^2 (n(i)-1)(n(i')-1)}{(n(i')-1)(S^2(\overline{X}i))^2 + (n(i)-1)(S^2(\overline{X}i'))^2}$$

Here $V(ii')$ is the degrees of freedom for a comparison between treatment levels (i) and (i'). This may not result in a whole number for $V(ii')$, in which case the nearest whole number will be accurate enough for most cases. Therefore, a different q, written q(ii') is found for each comparison.

Example:

```
I = 3
Alpha = .01
V(12) = 3.78    4.00
V(13) = 2.74    3.00
V(23) = 6.51    7.00
```

Therefore,

```
q(12) =  8.12
q(13) = 10.60
q(23) =  5.92
```

Step 3.

Equal n. Find the HSD statistic as:

$$HSD = q\sqrt{\text{Mean Square Error} / n}$$

Unequal n. Find the HSD(ii') statistic for each comparison as:

$$HSD(ii') = (q(ii')/\sqrt{2})\sqrt{S^2(\overline{X}i) + S^2(\overline{X}i')}$$

Example:

```
HSD(12) = 13.78
HSD(13) = 16.30
HSD(23) =  6.61
```

Step 4.

Equal and Unequal n. Arrange the treatment means in order, and then prepare a table of absolute differences between all pairs of means.

Example:

|  | | $\bar{X}(1)$ | $\bar{X}(2)$ | $\bar{X}(3)$ |
|---|---|---|---|---|
|  | | 8.00 | 5.40 | 3.25 |
| $\bar{X}(1)$ | 8.00 | | 2.60 | 4.75 |
| $\bar{X}(2)$ | 5.40 | | | 2.15 |

Step 5.

Equal n. Any absolute difference between the means that exceeds HSD is significant.

Unequal n. A difference, (D(ii')), between treatment level means that is larger than HSD(ii') indicates a significant difference.

Example:

| $D(ii')$ | | $HSD(ii')$ |
|---|---|---|
| 2.60 | < | 13.78 |
| 4.75 | < | 16.30 |
| 2.15 | < | 6.61 |

Here no significant differences were found. This was to be expected because the overall test was not significant.


## Multivariate Analysis of Variance

We recommend that the reader consult other texts for further discussion of one-way MANOVA designs. Books available on this topic are: Amick & Walberg (1975), Bock (1975), Cooley & Lohnes (1971), Finn (1974), Harris (1975), Lindeman, Merenda, and Gold (1980), Morrison (1967), Overall & Klett (1972), Press (1972), Stevens & Barcikowski (1984), Tatsuoka (1971), Timm (1975), Winer (1971).


## Multivariate Analysis: Planned Comparisons

The multivariate analysis presented here is an extension of the univariate planned comparisons analysis discussed earlier in this chapter. These contiguous presentations should allow readers who are unfamiliar with the multivariate model to compare it with the univariate model. In our MANOVA example, the design remains the same, but an additional dependent variable, message effectiveness, is added. Finn (1974, p. 4) makes the important point that, "it is critical that the variables of any set share a common conceptual meaning, in order for the multivariate results to be valid. It is an easy matter to abuse, say, an extensive computer program to perform analyses on sets of variables which bear no 'real-life' counterpart as a group." In our MANOVA example, the two dependent variables, credibility and effectiveness, are dimensions of message presentation; the researcher is interested in testing the effects of the different levels of the independent variable on the two dependent variables considered together.

Problem. Is a message's credibility and effectiveness dependent on the mode of message presentation?

Research Hypothesis. The research hypotheses were formulated based on theory and previous research before the data were collected.

Research Hypothesis (1): of three modes of message presentation, oral-visual, visual, and oral the combined oral-visual speaker presentation does not differ from the average effect of the visual and oral presentations in enhancing message credibility and effectiveness.

Research Hypothesis (2): there will be a difference in message credibility and effectiveness between the visual and oral modes of presentation.

Statistical Hypotheses. The statistical hypotheses are written in symbolic form to match the research hypotheses. Here the symbol $u(pi)$ represents the population mean for variable $p$ ( $p = 1, 2$) in group $i$ ( $i = 1, 2, 3$), and the symbol $u(i)$ represents the vector of means containing both dependent variable means from group $i$. Here oral-visual is treatment 1, visual is treatment 2, and oral is treatment 3.

$$
\text{Null Hypothesis (1) } H(01): \begin{bmatrix} u(11) \\ u(21) \end{bmatrix} = .5 \begin{bmatrix} u(12) \\ u(22) \end{bmatrix} + .5 \begin{bmatrix} u(13) \\ u(23) \end{bmatrix}
$$

$$
\text{i.e., } H(01): \underline{u}(1) = .5 \, \underline{u}(2) + .5 \, \underline{u}(3)
$$

$$
\text{Alternate Hypothesis (1) } H(A1): \begin{bmatrix} u(11) \\ u(21) \end{bmatrix} \neq .5 \begin{bmatrix} u(12) \\ u(22) \end{bmatrix} + .5 \begin{bmatrix} u(13) \\ u(23) \end{bmatrix}
$$

$$
\text{i.e., } H(A1): \underline{u}(1) \neq .5 \, \underline{u}(2) + .5 \, \underline{u}(3)
$$

Null
Hypothesis (2) H(O2):  $\begin{bmatrix} u(12) \\ u(22) \end{bmatrix} = \begin{bmatrix} u(13) \\ u(23) \end{bmatrix}$

i.e., H(O2):  $\underline{u}(2) = \underline{u}(3)$


Alternate
Hypothesis (2) H(A2):  $\begin{bmatrix} u(12) \\ u(22) \end{bmatrix} \neq \begin{bmatrix} u(13) \\ u(23) \end{bmatrix}$

i.e., H(A2):  $\underline{u}(2) \neq \underline{u}(3)$


Each null hypothesis will be tested at the .05 level of significance.

Data. The data is presented in Table 2.5 as a multivariate, equal n problem. The design has one factor with three levels, and the dependent variables are message credibility and effectiveness.

Table 2.5
Data[1] for a One-Way Multivariate Design

| Oral/Visual Presentation | | Visual Presentation | | Oral Presentation | |
|---|---|---|---|---|---|
| Credblty | Effectness | Credblty | Effectness | Credblty | Effectness |
| 10 | 16 | 8 | 12 | 3 | 10 |
| 4 | 10 | 4 | 8 | 5* | 16* |
| 10 | 18 | 4 | 6 | 5 | 16 |
| 4* | 14* | 2 | 6 | 4 | 14 |
| 10* | 16* | 9 | 14 | 1 | 9 |
| $\overline{X}1=7.60$ | 14.80 | $\overline{X}2=5.40$ | 9.20 | $\overline{X}3=3.60$ | 13.00 |
| *$\overline{X}1=8.00$ | 14.67 | *$\overline{X}2=5.40$ | 9.20 | *$\overline{X}3=3.25$ | 12.25 |

[1]The data is from Winer (1971, p. 237), "*" scores were removed to create an unequal n problem.

Measures of each dependent variable were arrived at by taking subjects' ratings of message credibility using Spiker's credibility form, and subjects' ratings of message effectiveness using the Waters' speaker effectiveness scale. The subjects (prospective buyers) were randomly selected from the population and then were randomly assigned to three treatment levels. Three subjects were dropped (represented by *) for all computer runs in order to demonstrate the effects of unequal ns. If this were an actual experiment the researcher would have to check to be sure that these subjects were not absent because of the treatment effects (e.g., they may have been intimidated by the mode of presentation).

One-Way MANOVA Table. Table 2.6 is the planned comparison one-way MANOVA table that would appear in a research report on this experiment. The complete contents of this table can be drawn from BMDP4V (2-6), SAS(REG) (2-4), and SPSS(MANOVA) multivariate output, and the statistical test results can be drawn from BMDP7M (2-8). The same type of table would be constructed for an equal $\underline{n}$ design .

The results in Table 2.6 indicate that the first null hypothesis was supported (p<.1853), and that the second null hypothesis was rejected (p<.0005). After a multivariate test is found to be significant, researchers frequently calculate univariate tests on each dependent variable (see, Hummel & Sligo, 1971). Because[4] the multivariate test of the second comparison was significant, the corresponding univariate results were of interest and are shown in Table 2.6. These tests indicate that neither dependent variable, by itself, was able to differentiate between groups. Therefore, only the combined effects of both message credibility and effectiveness were responsible for the group differences found in the second comparison.

The mean vector difference, shown below, for the second planned comparison is informative.

$$
\begin{array}{lccc}
 & \text{Visual} & \text{Oral} & \text{Difference} \\
\text{Credibility} & \begin{bmatrix} 5.40 \\ 9.20 \end{bmatrix} & - \begin{bmatrix} 3.25 \\ 12.25 \end{bmatrix} & = \begin{bmatrix} 2.15 \\ -3.05 \end{bmatrix} \\
\text{Effectiveness} & & &
\end{array}
$$

The significant difference between the groups found by the multivariate test appears to be due to an interaction between the treatments and the type of message mode being rated. That is, in the visual mode of message presentation the messages were rated higher on credibility and lower on effectiveness than in the oral mode of presentation. This result might indicate that the oral/visual mode of presentation should be further refined and studied as a means of influencing both message credibility and effectiveness.

41

Table 2.6
Multivariate Planned Comparisons Analysis
of Variance for the Type of Presentation Experiment

| Source of Variation | Sums of Squares and Products[1] Credibility Effectness | | Multivariate Wilks' Lambda | Df | F(Probability) | Df | Univariate F(Probability) Credibility | F(Probability) Effectiveness |
|---|---|---|---|---|---|---|---|---|
| Treatments (between groups) | 38.72 18.32 | 18.32 58.70 | | | | | | |
| Comparisons 1 | 30.29 32.49 | 32.49 34.85 | .66 | 2,8 | 2.10 (.1853) | 1 | 4.01(.0762) | 2.61(.1407) |
| 2 | 10.27 -14.57 | -14.57 20.67 | .15 | 2,8 | 23.20*(.0005) | 1 | 1.36(.2734) | 1.55(.2449) |
| Error (within groups) | 67.95 85.35 | 85.35 120.22 | | | | 9 | | |
| Total (adjusted for grand mean) | 106.67 103.67 | 103.67 178.92 | | | | | | |

[1]With more than two variables we suggest that these matrices be placed in an appendix.
*Significant at p<.05

42

Kerlinger and Pedhazur (1973, pp. 352-360) present an excellent discussion of a similar multivariate analysis where there was a significant multivariate test; none of the univariate tests were significant, and there was an interaction between the treatment and the dependent variables. These authors finish their presentation by indicating that results like those found in our example are very possible, especially in education.

> Methods of teaching, for example, may work well for certain kinds of students in some subjects, while they may not work too well for other kinds of students in other subjects. Clearly, the search for a "best" universal teaching method is probably doomed. The real world of education, like the real world of changing attitudes and prejudice, is much too complex - too multivariate, if we can be forgiven for repeating the point a bit too much (p. 360).

## Multivariate Analysis: Overall Test and Post Hoc Comparisons

A researcher who has no planned questions that he feels are appropriate (i.e., on the basis of theory or past research) to ask about his treatments, might conduct an overall test of significance. If the overall multivariate test is not significant, further testing is considered inappropriate. This last statement is frequently difficult for some researchers to practice because in their computer output univariate tests are automatically provided, and one of them may be significant. The temptation is to interpret this significant univariate test. However, if the study has been properly composed, there is a good chance that one or more significant univariate tests, following a nonsignificant overall multivariate test, represent spurious results. The best approach to this problem is for the researcher to conduct another study.

Given a significant overall multivariate test, there are several tests that one could perform next (e.g., see Stevens, 1972; 1973). One approach that is used (Bock, 1975; Finn, 1974) is to perform univariate tests on each dependent variable. Given the protection against Type I error provided by the previous two tests (overall multivariate and univariate), one might then conduct univariate post hoc comparisons. We know of no empirical or mathematical support for this last course of action, but it seems reasonable in light of results presented by Hummel and Sligo (1971) which indicate that a hierarchical testing pattern (overall multivariate followed by univariate tests) controls the Type I experimentwise error rate.

Another approach to doing multivariate research where an overall significance test is used, would be the following three stage testing process. Step 1, conduct the overall multivariate significance test. If it is not significant, stop; if it is significant go to step 2. Step 2, conduct all possible multivariate (Hotellings) $T^2$ between the treatment groups. If none are significant, stop; if some are significant, go to step 3. Step 3, conduct univariate t-tests, or Tukey's HSD test between the groups found to have significant differences in step 3. Again, we know of no empirical or mathematical support for these steps but they seem logical in light of Hummel and Sligo's (1971) results.

Problem. Is a message's credibility and effectiveness dependent on the mode of message presentation?

Research Hypothesis. In this case the researcher believes that differences will appear among his group means, but past research was inconclusive, and his theory is not formulated well enough for him to make predictions.

Research Hypothesis: one of the modes of message presentation, oral-visual, visual, oral will be more effective than the others in enhancing message credibility and effectiveness.

Statistical Hypotheses

$$\text{Null Hypothesis } H(0): \begin{bmatrix} u(11) \\ u(21) \end{bmatrix} = \begin{bmatrix} u(12) \\ u(22) \end{bmatrix} = \begin{bmatrix} u(13) \\ u(23) \end{bmatrix}$$

$$\text{i.e., } H(0): \underline{u}(1) = \underline{u}(2) = \underline{u}(3)$$

$$\text{Alternate Hypothesis } H(A): \begin{bmatrix} u(1i) \\ u(2i) \end{bmatrix} \neq \begin{bmatrix} u(1j) \\ u(2j) \end{bmatrix} \quad (i \neq j; i,j = 1,2,3)$$

$$\text{i.e., } H(A): \underline{u}(i) \neq \underline{u}(j)$$

This null hypothesis will be tested at the .05 level of significance.

Data. The data are the unequal $\underline{n}$ data presented in Table 2.5.

One-Way MANOVA Table. Table 2.7 is the one-way MANOVA source table that would appear in a research report on this experiment. The contents of this table could be derived from all of the standard overall analysis unequal n multivariate program runs for this chapter. A table with the same information would be constructed for an equal n design.

The results in Table 2.7 indicate that the null hypothesis was rejected (p<.0008). Therefore, the research hypothesis is supported.

Post Hoc Tests. All possible multivariate $T^2$ tests were conducted among the treatment level mean vectors using BMDP3D (2-9). The level of significance was set at .01. The results indicate that: 1. There is no significant difference between the oral-visual and visual modes of presentation ($T^2$ = 12.87, p<.057). 2. There is no significant difference between the oral-visual and oral modes of presentation ($T^2$ = 20.65, p<.038). 3. There is a significant difference between the visual and oral modes of speaker presentation ($T^2$ = 51.41, p<.002). A brief discussion of the meaning of the significant difference between the visual and oral modes of presentation mean vectors was provided when this same comparison was tested as a planned comparison (see page 41). The latter discussion indicated that further research should be devoted to testing and improving the integrated oral/visual presentation, since the message's credibility appears to be most affected by the visual presentation and the message's effectiveness appears to be most affected by the oral presentation--note, however, that the univariate tests of this were not significant. The results here seem to indicate the same course of action. Again, although all of the tests were not significant, it appears that, based on the direction of the statistical tests, the oral/visual method, when improved, would yield the best method of presentation.

The BMDP program BMDP3D (2-9) was used to calculate all possible $T^2$ tests between the treatment groups. The same results could have been obtained by running any one of the multivariate programs on each pair of treatments. The latter approach requires several runs however. In these multivariate programs the error sums of squares and cross-products, E-SSCP, matrix is found using the data from the two treatments being compared. This E-SSCP matrix is recommended (see the BMDP3D program notes), especially with unequal ns, because the use of the overall E-SSCP when the assumption of homogeneity of variance-covariance matrices is violated, can seriously affect the probability of making a Type I error. If the use of the overall E-SSCP matrix is warranted, BMDP7M, BMDP4V or several runs of SPSS(MANOVA) with different combinations of simple contrasts will yield the desired results.

Table 2.7

Multivariate Analysis of Variance for
the Type of Presentation Experiment

| Source of Variation | Sums of Squares and Products[1] | | Multivariate | | | Univariate | | |
|---|---|---|---|---|---|---|---|---|
| | Credbility | Effectness | Wilks' Lambda | Df | F(Probability) | Df | F(Probability) Credibility | Credibility Effectiveness |
| Treatments (between groups) | 38.72  18.32 | 18.32  58.70 | .11 | 4,16 | 8.28*(.0008) | 2 | 2.56(.1314) | 2.20(.1671) |
| Error (within groups) | 67.95  85.35 | 85.35  120.22 | | | | 9 | | |
| Total (adjusted for grand mean) | 106.67  103.67 | 103.67  178.92 | | | | | | |

[1] With more than two variables we suggest that these matrices be placed in an appendix.
*significant at p<.05

Tukey's HSD test (alpha = .01) was used to determine if significant differences exist between the dependent variables of the visual and oral groups. The HSD test for mean differences between these groups on message credibility was found to be nonsignificant when this comparison was considered as a univariate problem (see pp. 36-38). The HSD test (not shown here) for mean differences on message effectiveness was also found to be nonsignificant. That is, the group differences were due to the effects of both dependent variables considered together.

## Canonical Discriminant Analysis

The one-way overall multivariate test of significance can be found in the discriminant analysis output. However, in this section we primarily focus on discriminant analysis in its functions as a follow-up to MANOVA (Borgen & Seling, 1978; Stevens, 1972). Therefore, we are interested in investigating what Huberty (1975) called:

(1) separation - determining inter-group significant differences of group centroids (i.e., mean vectors), and
(2) discriminations - studying group separation with respect to dimensions and to (discriminator) variable contribution to separation. (p. 545)

## Packaged Program Confusion

Huberty also discussed two other functions of discriminant analysis: estimation and classification, but we have found that these two functions have caused some confusion among the users of computer packages. Green (1979) indicates that the confusion is caused by the use of the same term "discriminant analysis" to describe two different processes: that which we will briefly describe in the next section, and which Green calls "canonical discriminant analysis," and that used to classify subjects into groups which he calls "classification analysis". The confusion encountered by many researchers is that BMDP7M reports coefficients for both types of analyses; BMDP4V only reports cannonical discriminant function coefficients; SAS(DISCRIM) only reports classification function coefficients, but canonical discriminant information is available from SAS(CANDISC), SAS(GLM) and SAS(STEPDISC); SPSS (DISCRIMINANT) reports canonical discriminant function coefficients for standard runs, but classification output is available through options, and SPSS(MANOVA) only reports canonical discriminant function coefficients. Researchers, who usually have only studied canonical discriminant analysis (described in the next section), are frequently confused by the classification function output. Here, we will only discuss canonical discriminant functions; the reader interested in classification analysis will find an excellent elementary discussion in Tatsuoka (1974) with further discussions in Cooley and Lohnes (1971), Overall and Klett (1972) and Tatsuoka (1971).

## Canonical Discriminant Functions

Basically canonical discriminant analysis provides the researcher with one or more linear combinations, called canonical discriminant functions, of the dependent variables which are used to discriminate between the treatment levels in a MANOVA. The number of such linear combinations that can be found is either equal to the number of dependent variables or the number of treatment levels minus one, whichever is smaller. The first canonical discriminant function is a linear combination that is similar to a regression equation, but the score that it produces (in a regression context the score that it predicts) yields the largest possible F statistic which can be found in performing a univariate ANOVA using these scores with the given treatment levels. The second canonical discriminant function yields scores that are independent of the first set and that yield the largest possible F statistic for such scores which can be found in performing an ANOVA. In like manner further canonical discriminant functions yield scores that are independent of those produced by previous functions and that yield the largest possible F statistic for such scores in an ANOVA on the given treatment levels.

Like the coefficients in regression analysis, the canonical discriminant function coefficients are affected by the intercorrelations among the dependent variables, and therefore, like regression coefficients, the magnitude of a discriminant function coefficient does not necessarily indicate its importance in explaining the underlying construct which is measured by the function. (Note that the latter sentence implies that you are working with dependent variables that make some conceptual sense when considered together.) The correlations between the dependent variables and the canonical discriminant function scores aid in helping to name the construct which underlies the canonical discriminant function (i.e., the construct which characterizes the group differences). These correlations are often called "discriminant structure coefficients," where the nomenclature was borrowed from factor analysis. There are two ways that these correlations can be found: 1. by correlating the canonical discriminant function scores with the scores in the design, and 2. by considering group membership and correlating the canonical discriminant function scores with the design deviation scores (a deviation score is a score that has had its cell mean subtracted from it). The first method yields correlations based on total-group information and the second yields correlations based on within group information.

This short subsection was meant to briefly aid the reader in understanding the output found in the packages and the discussion that follows. Good discussions of canonical discriminant analysis (usually simply called discriminant analysis) can be found in the multivariate books referenced at the beginning of the multivariate section.

## Results for the Type of Presentation Experiment

Before presenting the results for the type of presentation experiment two points should be made about this data: first, the sample size is small so that the function coefficients and the function-variable correlations may be unstable (i.e., have large error variances -- see Barcikowski and Stevens, 1975); second, canonical discriminant analysis would be exhibited in a better light if there were more dependent variables and treatment levels so that its variable reduction properties could be illustrated.

The data from the canonical discriminant analysis for the multivariate type of presentation scores (Table 2.5) is shown in Table 2.8. The information in Table 2.8 can be gathered entirely from the SAS (CANDISC) (2-7), SPSS (DISCRIMINANT) (2-11) and (MANOVA) (2-10) programs; can be partially gathered from BMDP7M (2-8); cannot be gathered from SAS(DISCRIM) (2-6); and can be partially gathered (no statistical test of the second root is provided) from SAS(GLM) (2-3) and (STEPDISC) (2-5).

In Table 2.8 the value of Wilks' lambda is .11 (the same value that we obtained for overall multivariate significance in Table 2.7), and its associated F-Statistic is 8.28 which is significant at $p < .05$. These results indicate two things:

Table 2.8

Canonical Discriminant Analysis for the Type of Presentation Experiment

| Variable | Coefficients | | Function-Variable Correlations[1] | Variance[2] (% Variance) | Canonical Correlation[3] | Df | Wilks' Lambda | F-Statistic[4] (Probability) |
|---|---|---|---|---|---|---|---|---|
| | Raw | Standard | | | | | | |

First Canonical Discriminant Function

| Variable | Raw | Standard | Function-Variable Correlations[1] | Variance[2] (% Variance) | Canonical Correlation[3] | Df | Wilks' Lambda | F-Statistic[4] (Probability) |
|---|---|---|---|---|---|---|---|---|
| Credibility | 1.09 | 3.01 | .19 | 5.87 (94.01) | .92 | 4,16 | .11 | 8.28* (.0008) |
| Effectiveness | -.82 | -2.98 | -.14 | | | | | |

Second Canonical Discriminant Function

| Variable | Raw | Standard | Function-Variable Correlations[1] | Variance[2] (% Variance) | Canonical Correlation[3] | Df | Wilks' Lambda | F-Statistic[4] (Probability) |
|---|---|---|---|---|---|---|---|---|
| Credibility | .16 | .44 | -.98 | .37 (5.99) | .52 | 1,9 | .73 | 3.36 (.0999) |
| Effectiveness | .16 | .57 | -.99 | | | | | |

Note. A test of the assumption of homogeneity of within group variance-covariance matrices was not significant.

[1]Based on the pooled within-groups correlation matrix.

[2]In the program output this number is referred to as 'eigenvalue,' 'characteristic root,' and 'canonical variance.'

[3]Canonical correlation between the grouping variable (independent variable) and the discriminant function.

[4]SPSS(DISCRIMINANT) provides Chi-Square approximations.

*Significant at $p < .05$.

1. That there is a significant multivariate difference between the three treatment levels, and 2. That the first canonical discriminant function plays a significant role in differentiating between treatment levels. Wilks' lambda for the second canonical discriminant function is large, .73, and its corresponding F-Statistic of 3.36 is not significant at the .05 level of significance. Therefore, the second canonical discriminant function does not play a significant role in differentiating among the treatments. The difference between the first and second canonical discriminant functions is further high-lighted by the fact that the proportion of discriminatory power attributed to the first function is 94.01% with only 5.99% attributable to the second function. A plot of the treatment means and the individual scores when converted to canonical discriminant function scores is found as part of the output for BMDP7M, SAS (CANDISC & PLOT) and SPSS (DISCRIMINANT); we feel that this plot should be a part of any report using canonical discriminant analysis. This plot also clearly shows that the treatment groups are differentiated on the first discriminant function and not differentiated as well on the second function.

Interestingly, both credibility and effectiveness have standarized function coefficients and function-variable correlations of about the same magnitude, but differing in sign. This indicates that the construct that yields group differences is bipolar; however, the low function-variable correlations indicate that it is not strongly related to either variable. This result is a reflection of the interaction between the treatments and the type of message mode being rated. This interaction led to the weight and correlation differences in sign. In light of this, the same advice as was given earlier seems appropriate. That is, the oral-visual mode might be further refined and studied because if the credibility scores in this mode could be sufficiently increased (i.e. especially those scores of 4), then the oral-visual mode of presentation would clearly be superior to the other methods. Also, because the two dependent variables are so highly intercorrelated, with further refinement we might expect to find a discriminant function like the second function that would discriminate effectively between the groups. Note that in Table 2.8 both variables are highly correlated with the second discriminant function. (It should also be noted that varimax rotation of the structure matrix, available as option 13 in SPSS (DISCRIMINANT) and as an option in SPSS(MANOVA), does not appear to add to this interpretation.)

## Conclusion

In conclusion we would recommend that future work be done to improve the credibility scores in the oral-visual mode of presentation. Work in this direction might begin by interviewing the people in that treatment in order to try and identify why two of them scored this presentation so low on the credibility scale. Then, another study with suitable modifications and more subjects might be planned where the prediction is made that the oral-visual mode of presentation will yield higher scores on presentation credibility and effectiveness than either the visual or oral modes of presentation. Also, using canonical discriminant analysis, one discriminant function might be predicted to differentiate between the treatments and to have high correlations with both credibility and effectiveness, and a second function might be predicted that would look like the first function found with this data and which reflects the interaction of the dependent variables with the mode of presentation, primarily in the visual and oral treatments. We believe that it is important for the reader to note that our recommendations for future work were not the result of a single analysis, but were formed by considering discriptive information (e.g. individual scores, means, intercorrelations) and multivariate information (e.g. Wilks' lambda, Hotelling's $T^2$, and canonical discriminant functions) along with knowledge of the variables, both dependent and independent, that we were working with. In this regard we agree with Borgen and Seling (1978) who agreed with Wiley's (1978) comments on Tukey's (1977) text. Wiley indicated that Tukey "is a part of a revolution currently shaking the field of statistics," based on a completely new set of principles, including the following: (a) For a single category of problem, there is no single best technique and there never will be, (b) There is much to be found in any data set which cannot be anticipated, and (c) A summary picture is worth a thousand summary numbers (p. 153).

## Instruction Programs

The BMDP3D program (2-9) was executed as an instructional program to illustrate the calculation of Hotelling's $T^2$ for all pairs of treatment levels, and the BMDP7M (2-10) program was executed to illustrate how the univariate and multivariate test statistics for planned comparisons (see Table 2.6) could be found using this program.

SAS(REG) (2-4) was included to illustrate how planned comparisons could be made in SAS, and to illustrate some of this package's programming language. The SAS(DISCRIM) (2-6) program was included to indicate that it is primarily a classification program (see the previous discussion on discriminant analysis).

The SPSS instruction runs focus on the optional contrasts that are possible through the subprogram MANOVA. The contrasts illustrated are simple (2-6), repeated (2-7), special (2-8), and polynomial (2-9). The Helmert (2-1) and deviation (2-5) contrasts are illustrated as part of the standard output, and the difference contrasts (the reverse of the Helmert contrasts) were not run to save space.

# Notes

[1] For example, subjects might appear for the oral or visual presentations but be too intimidated to appear for the oral-visual presentation.

[2] Cook and Campbell (pp. 44-50, 1979) present an excellent discussion of the problems involved in "accepting" the null hypothesis.

[3] It is interesting to note that if the researcher had predicted that the oral/visual method would yield more credibility than the visual method, then this planned comparison would have been significant ($p < .025$). Furthermore, further testing using post hoc methods will not yield this significant result (see the results of Tukey's HSD test in the "Univariate Analysis: Overall Test and Post Hoc Comparison" section). The planned comparison test of the oral/visual and visual methods would require another experiment.

[4] All univariate tests are generally included in this table because other researchers may have chosen different significance levels for the multivariate tests.

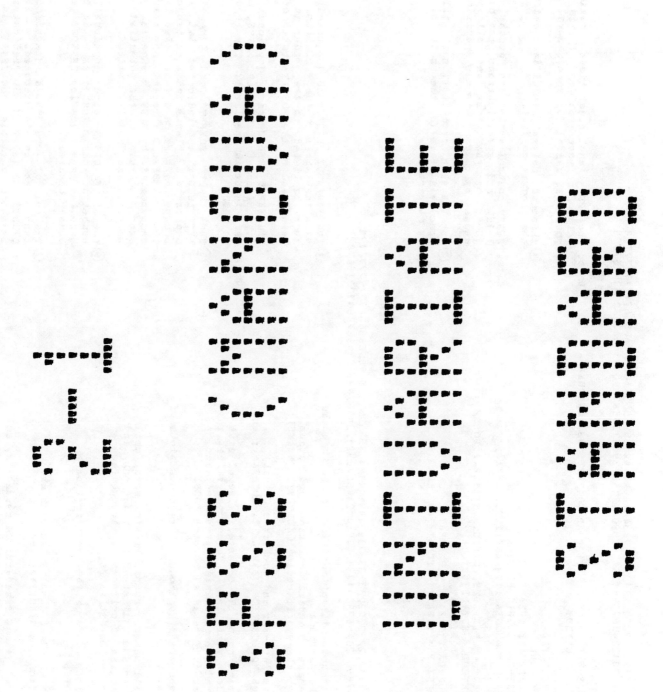

(1) 

(2) RUN NAME       ONE-WAY (ANOVA): PLANNED COMPARISONS, UNEQUAL N
(3) VARIABLE LIST  TREAT,CREDBY
(4) INPUT MEDIUM   CARD
(5) INPUT FORMAT   FREEFIELD
(6) N OF CASES     UNKNOWN
(7) MANOVA         CREDBY BY TREAT(1,3)/
(8)                PRINT=CELLINFO(MEANS)
                   HOMOGENEITY(BARTLETT,COCHRAN)
                   POBS/
(9)                PLOT = CELLPLOTS,BOXPLOTS,STEMLEAF,POBS/
(10)               METHOD = SSTYPE(UNIQUE)/
(11)               PARTITION(TREAT)/
(12)               CONTRAST(TREAT) = HELMERT/
(13)               DESIGN = TREAT(1),TREAT(2)/
(14) READ INPUT DATA
     1 10   1 10   2 8   2 4   2 4   2 2   2 9   3 3   3 5   3 4   3 1
(15) END INPUT DATA

**Note:** The SPSS input annotations provided here are of value for most problems of this type. Consult your SPSS manual for more general information.

(1) These are column identifiers and are not part of the program content.

**Note:** SPSS control words are punched between columns 1-15, and specifications are placed in columns 16-80 on the first and all succeeding cards necessary to complete the specifications.

(2) The RUN NAME card (optional) allows the user to specify a title for the analysis; it is limited to 64 characters.

(3) The VARIABLE LIST card (required) provides SPSS with the names of the variables. The variables must be listed in the order in which they are being read by the FORMAT statement.

(4) The INPUT MEDIUM card (optional) specifies the type of input (CARD, TAPE, DISK, or OTHER). Here card input is specified. The input medium default is CARD.

(5) The INPUT FORMAT card (required) specifies that the data must be FREEFIELD which indicates that the data must be separated by blanks and that two or more cases may occupy the same card (see also input number 2-5). The FREEFIELD format specification is not recommended by SPSS, especially in large data sets, because of the potential for errors if a value is accidentally omitted.

(6) The N OF CASES card (optional) specifies the number of cases (subjects) in the problem run. Here the specification UNKNOWN requests SPSS to count the cases.

(7) The control word MANOVA (required) indicates the subprogram to be executed. The specification CREDBY BY TREAT (1,3) indicates CREDBY is the dependent variable and TREAT is the factor name with levels 1 through 3. The slash informs SPSS that the specification is ended and that another one may follow.

(8) The PRINT subcommand (optional) requests that the following be printed:

the cell means, standard deviations and counts, through the specification CELL INFO (MEANS):

the Bartlett-Box and Cochran's C test, through HOMOGENEITY (BARTLETT, COCHRAN); and,

the printing of the observed value of each dependent variable, its predicted value, raw residual (observed minus predicted) and standardized residual through POBS.

(9) The PLOT subcommand (optional) requests plots of the following:

the cell means versus cell variances, cell means versus cell standard deviations, and a histogram of cell means, through the specification CELLPLOTS:

box plots, through the specification BOXPLOTS:

a stem-and-leaf display, through the specification STEMLEAF; and,

observed versus standardized residuals, cell means versus standardized residuals, case number versus standardized residuals, a normal probability plot, and a detrended normal probability for the standardized residuals, through the specification POBS.

(10) The METHOD subcommand requests the method of weighted squares of means analysis (see Appendix A) through the specification SSTYPE (UNIQUE).

(11) The PARTITION subcommand allows for single degree of freedom partitioning of the between-groups sums of squares on the independent variable TREAT.

(12) The CONTRAST subcommand requests HELMERT contrasts for the independent variable TREAT. This subcommand interacts with the PARTITION subcommand to yield the planned comparisons desired in Chapter 2.

(13) The DESIGN subcommand specifies the between-subjects model to be analyzed. Here TREAT(1) and TREAT(2) refer to the first and second partitions of TREAT as previously specified in the PARTITION subcommand.

(14) The READ INPUT DATA card (required) signals that the data begins with the next card.

(15) The END INPUT DATA card (required) signals the end of the data. This card is required here because the number of cases was not specified.

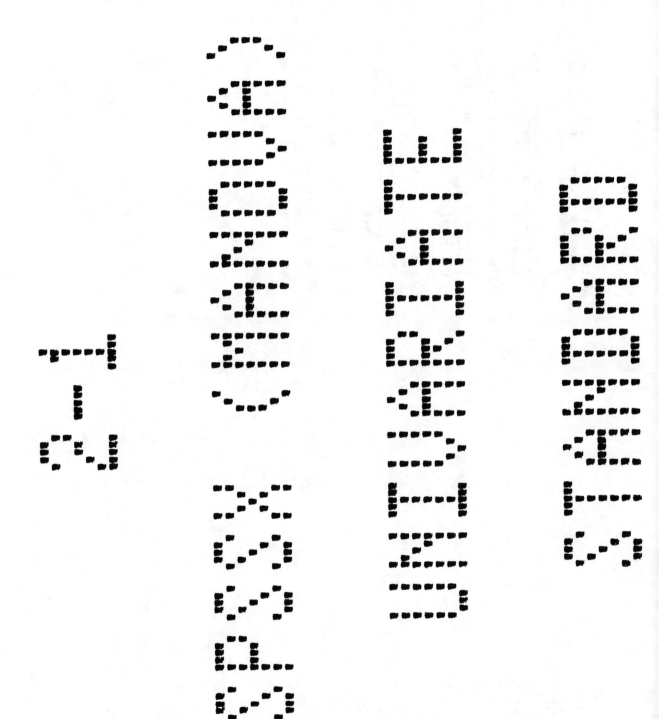

```
00000000011111111112222222222333333333344444444445555555555666666666677777777778
12345678901234567890123456789012345678901234567890123456789012345678901234567890
```

① 

② TITLE    ONE-WAY (ANOVA):    PLANNED COMPARISONS, UNEQUAL N

③ DATA LIST FREE/ TREAT,CREDBY
MANOVA    CREDBY BY TREAT(1,3)/
          PRINT=CELLINFO(MEANS)
               HOMOGENEITY(BARTLETT,COCHRAN)
               POBS/
          PLOT = CELLPLOTS,BOXPLOTS,STEMLEAF,POBS/
          METHOD = SSTYPE(UNIQUE)/
          PARTITION(TREAT)/
          CONTRAST(TREAT) = HELMERT/
          DESIGN = TREAT(1),TREAT(2)/

④ BEGIN DATA
  1 10   1 14   1 10   2 8   2 4   2 4   2 2   2 9   3 3   3 5   3 4   3 1
⑤ END DATA

```
00000000011111111112222222222333333333344444444445555555555666666666677777777778
12345678901234567890123456789012345678901234567890123456789012345678901234567890
```

① 

**Note:** The SPSSX input annotations provided here are of value for most problems of this type. Consult your SPSSX manual for more general information.

① These are column identifiers and are not part of the program content.

**Note:** SPSSX command keywords begin in column 1; specifications, separated by at least one blank, follow the command keywords. Specifications which continue beyond the first card must be indented by at least one column, and may continue for as many cards as is necessary.

② The TITLE card (optional) allows the user to specify a title for the analysis; it is limited to 60 characters.

③ The DATA LIST card (required) provides SPSSX with the names of the variables. The variables must be listed in the order in which they are being read by the format specification. Here the FREE format specification was used. This input specification indicates that the scores for more than one case may be found on one card. The FREE input specification requires that the scores be separated by at least one blank or comma. (See other programs for examples of different ways SPSSX allows data to be read.)

④ The BEGIN DATA card (required) signals that the data begins with the next card.

⑤ The END DATA card (required) signals the end of the data.

59

SPSS FOR OS/360, VERSION H, RELEASE 9.1, FEBRUARY 1, 1982

                              CURRENT DOCUMENTATION FOR THE SPSS BATCH SYSTEM
ORDER FROM MCGRAW-HILL:    SPSS, 2ND ED. (PRINCIPAL TEXT)        SPSS STATISTICAL ALGORITHMS
                          SPSS UPDATE 7-9 (USE W/SPSS,2ND FOR REL. 7, 8, 9)    ORDER FROM SPSS INC.:
                          SPSS POCKET GUIDE, RELEASE 9                  KEYWORDS: THE SPSS INC. NEWSLETTER
                          SPSS INTRODUCTORY GUIDE:  BASIC STATISTICS AND OPERATIONS
                          SPSS PRIMER (BRIEF INTRO TO SPSS)
                                                      ①SPSS provides a listing of program control cards.
                                                          This listing should be checked for input accuracy.

DEFAULT SPACE ALLOCATION..       ALLOWS FOR..    102 TRANSFORMATIONS
WORKSPACE    71680 BYTES                         409 RECODE VALUES + LAG VARIABLES
TRANSPACE    10240 BYTES                        1641 IF/COMPUTE OPERATIONS

    ①   1  RUN NAME          ONE-WAY (ANOVA):   PLANNED COMPARISONS, UNEQUAL N
         2  VARIABLE LIST     TREAT,CREDBY
         3  INPUT MEDIUM      CARD
         4  INPUT FORMAT      FREEFIELD
         5  N OF CASES        UNKNOWN
         6  MANOVA            CREDBY BY TREAT(1,3)/
         7                    PRINT=CELLINFO(MEANS)
         8                         HOMOGENEITY(BARTLETT,COCHRAN)
         9                         POBS/
        10                    PLOT = CELLPLOTS,BOXPLOTS,STEMLEAF,POBS/
        11                    METHOD = SSTYPE(UNIQUE)/
        12                    PARTITION(TREAT)/
        13                    CONTRAST(TREAT) = HELMERT/
        14                    DESIGN = TREAT(1),TREAT(2)/
        15  READ INPUT DATA

AFTER READING    12 CASES FROM SUBFILE NONAME  ,   END OF DATA WAS ENCOUNTERED ON LOGICAL UNIT # 5

* * * * * * * * * * * * * * * * * A N A L Y S I S   O F   V A R I A N C E * * * * * * * * * * * * * * * *

CELL MEANS AND STANDARD DEVIATIONS

VARIABLE .. CREDBY

② The input data check should include: identification of the factor levels, number of subjects per cell, and the total number of subjects.

| FACTOR ② | CODE | MEAN | STD. DEV. ④ | N ② | 95 PERCENT CONF. INTERVAL ⑤ | |
|---|---|---|---|---|---|---|
| TREAT | 1 | ③ 8.00000 | ④ 3.46410 | 3 | -.60540 | 16.60540 |
| TREAT | 2 | 5.40000 | 2.96648 | 5 | 1.71669 | 9.08331 |
| TREAT | 3 | 3.25000 | 1.70783 | 4 | .53251 | 5.96749 |
| FOR ENTIRE SAMPLE | | ⑥ 5.33333 | 3.11400 | 12 | 3.35480 | 7.31187 |

③ Cell means may be used in a priori or post hoc analyses. The user may calculate these means by hand to further check on input accuracy and program execution.

UNIVARIATE HOMOGENEITY OF VARIANCE TESTS

VARIABLE .. CREDBY

⑧ COCHRANS $C(3,3)$ =           .50597, P = .417 (APPROX.)
⑨ BARTLETT-BOX $F(2,152)$ =     .56321, P = .571

⑩ 12 CASES ACCEPTED.
0 CASES REJECTED BECAUSE OF OUT-OF-RANGE FACTOR VALUES.
0 CASES REJECTED BECAUSE OF MISSING DATA.
3 NON-EMPTY CELLS.

④ cell standard deviations should be approximately equal (a check on the assumption of homogeneity of variance). This check is particularly important when the cells have unequal n's.

⑤ The 95% confidence interval provides the researcher with an idea of the possible mean (cell and overall) values.

⑥ This is the weighted (by cell sizes) grand mean.

⑦ The tests for homogeneity of variance are not significant which indicates the homogeneity of variance assumption has been met. However, with small n, these tests are unreliable.

⑧ Cochran's C test is found as the largest variance divided by the sum of all of the variances. Here the sum of the variances is: 12.0000 + 8.8000 + 2.9167 = 23.7167. Therefore, Cochran's C = 12.0000/23.7167 = .50597. Critical values for Cochran's C are available in Dixon and Massey (1969, pp. 536-537) and Winer (1971, p. 876).

⑨ The Bartlett-Box test was developed by Bartlett (1937) for the univariate case and was extended by Box (1949) for the multivariate case. The test used here is based on Box's extension, but the calculations are done for one dependent variable. The formulas for this test are complex, but are well illustrated in Cooley and Lohnes (1971, pp. 228-230).

⑩ The number of cases accepted/rejected, and the number of cells with data should be reviewed as part of the data check.

\* \* \* \* \* \* \* \* \* \* \* \* \* \* \* \* A N A L Y S I S   O F   V A R I A N C E \* \* \* \* \* \* \* \* \* \* \* \* \* \* \* \* \* \*

MEANS VS. VARIANCES FOR CREDBY

MEANS VS. STD. DEVS. FOR CREDBY

⑪ If the assumption of homogeneity of variance was met, all of the points in the 'means vs. variances' and the 'means vs. std. devs.' plots would fall on a horizontal line. Here we have the heterogeneity of the scores in treatments 1 and 2 contrasted with the homogeneity of the scores in treatment 3. (For further discussion of this plot see BMD2V (2-3) ).

DISTRIBUTION OF CELL MEANS FOR CREDBY

⑫

| FREQUENCY | 1 | 0 | 0 | 1 | 0 | 0 | 1 | 0 | 1 | 0 |
|-----------|---|---|---|---|---|---|---|---|---|---|
| 1 | * | | | * | | | * | | * | |
| INTERVAL : | 3.300 | 3.900 | 4.500 | 5.100 | 5.700 | 6.300 | 6.900 | 7.500 | 8.100 | 8.700 |
| MID-POINTS: | | | | | | | | | | |

⑫ The cell means appear to be spread out, but the differences are not significant at the .05 level of significance (shown later in this output).

(13) BOX-PLOTS FOR VARIABLE -- CREDEY

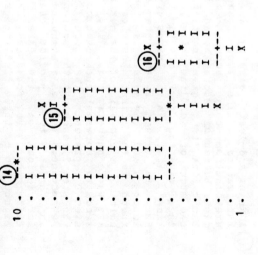

(13) The box-plots, more descriptively called by Tukey(1977, p.39) the 'box-and-whisker plots', picture the range, median, and hinges (similar to quartiles) of the scores in each cell. They provide the user with further information with which to check statistical assumptions, and a visual comparison of the differences among the cells and their scores.

(14) The first box-plot pictures the scores, i.e., 10,10,4, from the Oral/visual treatment. In this plot the vertical I's represent the distance from the highest score of 10 to the lowest score of 4. (The double column of I's usually represent the distance between the 'hinges,' but in this data set the hinges and the extremes are the same.) The * at the top of this plot indicates that 10 is the median, middle score, of this set of scores. At this point one would observe that this treatment contains a score, 4, that might require further study (see the discussion in Chapter 2).

(15) The second box-plot pictures the scores from the visual treatment, i.e., 9,8,4,4,2. The extremes, denoted by X's, are at 9 and 2; these scores are found at the end of Tukey's 'whiskers,' i.e., the single column of I's. The vertical lines, dashes with a + sign between them, represent 'hinges.' A hinge is a score that falls half-way between an extreme and the median. In this treatment the hinges are at 8 and 4. The median, represented by an *, is the middle score of 4.

(16) In the third set of data, the Oral treatment, the scores are: 5,4,3,1. Here the extremes are at 5 and 1; the hinges are at 4 and 3; and, the median is at 3.5.

63

* * * * * * * * * * * * * * * * A N A L Y S I S   O F   V A R I A N C E * * * * * * * * * * * * * * * * * * * * * * * * * * * * *

STEM-AND-LEAF DISPLAY FOR VARIABLE -- CREDBY

⑰  0 . 0
    2 . 00
    4 . 00000
    6 . 00
    8 . 00
   10 . 00

- - - - - - - - - - - - - - - - - - - - - - - - - - - - - - - - - - - - - - - - - - - - - - - - - - - - - - - - - - - - - -

CORRESPONDENCE BETWEEN EFFECTS AND COLUMNS OF BETWEEN-SUBJECTS DESIGN

    STARTING  ENDING
⑱   COLUMN    COLUMN     EFFECT NAME
      1         1        CONSTANT
      2         2        TREAT(1)
      3         3        TREAT(2)

- - - - - - - - - - - - - - - - - - - - - - - - - - - - - - - - - - - - - - - - - - - - - - - - - - - - - - - - - - - - - -

⑰ A stem-and-leaf display is used to provide information, like that found in a frequency distribution--only more-- of the type and distribution of scores found in a design. The basic idea 'is to give part of the information at the start of each line', i.e., at the stem, 'and then give the rest of the information in the line', i.e., in the leaves (Tukey, 1977, p.8). Here the values in the stem are given at even integers and the values in the leaves are those found in the first position after the decimal point. Since all of the numbers in this design are whole numbers, e.g., 1.0, the computer listed zeros to represent each number. The leaf for the stem 0 represents the score 1.0, the leaves for the stem 2 represent the scores 2.0 and 3.0, etc. We recommend this as a standard part of the output in order to provide further discriptive information on the data. If significant differences were found among the groups we might expect two or three distinct groups of scores.

⑱ The between-subjects design matrix is made up of three columns: one for the constant, grand mean, one for the first contrast on TREAT, and one for the second contrast on TREAT. This output should be checked to see that you have correctly specified your design.

64

\* \* \* \* \* \* \* \* \* \* \* \* \* \* \* \* \* A N A L Y S I S   O F   V A R I A N C E \* \* \* \* \* \* \* \* \* \* \* \* \* \* \* \* \*

(19)(20) TESTS OF SIGNIFICANCE FOR CREDBY USING UNIQUE SUMS OF SQUARES

| SOURCE OF VARIATION | SUM OF SQUARES | DF | MEAN SQUARE | F | SIG. OF F |
|---|---|---|---|---|---|
| WITHIN CELLS | 67.95000 | 9 | 7.55000 | | |
| (21) CONSTANT | 353.90106 | 1 | 353.90106 | 46.87431 | .000 |
| TREAT(1) | 30.29299 | 1 | 30.29299 | 4.01232 | .076 |
| TREAT(2) | 10.27222 | 1 | 10.27222 | 1.36056 | .273 (22) |

(19) This information would be found in an ANOVA source table (see Table 2.4, Chapter 2).

ESTIMATES FOR CREDBY

CONSTANT

| PARAMETER | COEFF. | STD. ERR. | T-VALUE | LOWER .95 CL | UPPER .95 CL | SIG. OF T |
|---|---|---|---|---|---|---|
| 1 | 5.5500000000 | .81064 | 6.84648 | 3.71622 | 7.38378 | .000 |

TREAT(1)

| PARAMETER | COEFF. | STD. ERR. | T-VALUE | LOWER .95 CL | UPPER .95 CL | SIG. OF T |
|---|---|---|---|---|---|---|
| (24) 2 | 3.6750000000 | 1.83468 | (25) 2.00308 | -.47533 | (23) 7.82533 | (26) .076 (27) |

TREAT(2)

| PARAMETER | COEFF. | STD. ERR. | T-VALUE | LOWER .95 CL | UPPER .95 CL | SIG. OF T |
|---|---|---|---|---|---|---|
| (24) 3 | 2.1500000000 | 1.84323 | 1.16643 | -2.01968 | (23) 6.31968 | (26) .273 (27) |

(20) This is the overall analysis of variance for the Mode of Message Presentation (TREAT) effects (see discussion, Chapter 2).

(21) This is the test of the null hypothesis that the grand mean is equal to zero. This test is usually significant and not of much interest, because the grand mean is generally larger than zero.

(22) These are the probabilities of obtaining F ratios larger than the calculated F ratios of 4.01232 and 1.36056. Since they are both greater than .05, we fail to reject both null hypotheses (see the discussion in Chapter 2).

(23) The 95 percent confidence intervals for the contrasts of interest both contain zero. This further reflects the fact that the contrasts do not differ significantly from zero.

(24) The COEFF. are the linear contrasts (here Helmert) on the cell means. The first parameter estimated is the unweighted grand mean (5.55); the second parameter estimated is $1(8.0) -.5(5.4) -.5(3.25) = 3.675$, the first planned comparison; the third parameter estimated is the second planned contrast $0(8.0) + 1(5.4) - (3.25) = 2.15$.

(25) The contrast COEFF. when divided by its STD. ERR. (standard error) yields the T-VALUE (t-statistic).

(26) Also reported for each contrast is the SIG. OF T (significance of t) and the upper and lower .95 confidence limits on the contrast.

(27) Here the probability results reported for each contrast agree with those found above. This is true because with one degree of freedom $F = t^2$.

ONE-WAY (ANOVA): PLANNED COMPARISONS, UNEQUAL N

***** * * * * * * * * * * A N A L Y S I S  O F  V A R I A N C E * * * * * * * * * * * * * * * * * * * * * *  02/03/83     PAGE   8

OBSERVED AND PREDICTED VALUES FOR EACH CASE

DEPENDENT VARIABLE.. CREDBY

| CASE NO. | OBSERVED ②⑧ | PREDICTED ②⑨ | RAW RESID. ③⓪ | STD RESID. ③① ③② |
|---|---|---|---|---|
| 1 | 10.00000 | 8.00000 | 2.00000 | .72787 |
| 2 | 4.00000 | 8.00000 | -4.00000 | -1.45575 |
| 3 | 10.00000 | 8.00000 | 2.00000 | .72787 |
| 4 | 8.00000 | 5.40000 | 2.60000 | .94624 |
| 5 | 4.00000 | 5.40000 | -1.40000 | -.50951 |
| 6 | 4.00000 | 5.40000 | -1.40000 | -.50951 |
| 7 | 2.00000 | 5.40000 | -3.40000 | -1.23739 |
| 8 | 9.00000 | 5.40000 | 3.60000 | 1.31017 |
| 9 | 3.00000 | 3.25000 | -.25000 | -.09098 |
| 10 | 5.00000 | 3.25000 | 1.75000 | .63689 |
| 11 | 4.00000 | 3.25000 | .75000 | .27295 |
| 12 | 1.00000 | 3.25000 | -2.25000 | -.81886 |

②⑧ The observed scores for each cell should be proofread to ensure that the correct observations have entered the analysis.

②⑨ The predicted score for each observation in a cell will be the cell mean.

③⓪ The raw residual for each observation is the difference between it and its cell mean (i.e., for case no. 1, 10.0 - 8.0 = 2.0).

③① The standardized residual is the raw residual divided by the standard error of the mean (i.e., the square root of the mean square within cell). In the first case the standardized residual is 2/2.7477 = .72787, where the square root of 7.55 = 2.7477.

③② Standardized residuals that are larger than 3.0 or smaller than -3.0 should be considered as potential outliers; no such values appear in this data set.

66

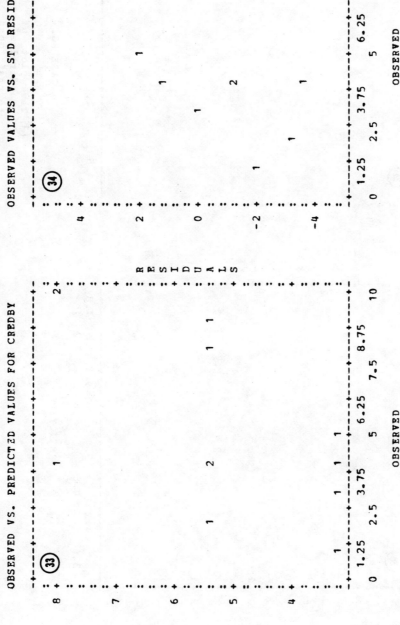

* * * * * * * * * * * * * * * * * A N A L Y S I S   O F   V A R I A N C E * * * * * * * * * * * * * * * * * * * * * * * * * * * *

PLOTS OF OBSERVED, PREDICTED, AND RESIDUAL CASE VALUES

OBSERVED VS. PREDICTED VALUES FOR CREDBY

OBSERVED VALUES VS. STD RESID. FOR CREDBY

(33) Because the predicted value for each cell is the cell mean, the plot of the observed versus the predicted values for CREDBY displays the spread of the scores from each cell horizontally. This plot permits us to check for outliers and to check on the homogeneity of the cell variances. By viewing the scores vertically, we can see that the scores overlapped across the cells—an indication of no significant treatment differences.

(34) In observing the plot of the observed values versus the standardized residuals for CREDBY, we see that the low values were predicted to be higher and that the high values were predicted to be lower. Since we expected a horizontal band of points around a residual of zero, this linear trend may indicate that another independent variable (e.g. personality type of the subjects) may help to explain the results. (Of course, this plot may simply reflect the small sample size.)

67

\*\*\*\*\*\*\*\*\*\*\*\*\*\*\*\*\*\*\*\*\*\* A N A L Y S I S   O F   V A R I A N C E \*\*\*\*\*\*\*\*\*\*\*\*\*\*\*\*\*\*\*\*\*\*\*\*\*\*\*

PLOTS OF OBSERVED, PREDICTED, AND RESIDUAL CASE VALUES (CONT.)

PREDICTED VALUES VS. STD RESID. FOR CREDBY          CASE NUMBER VS. STD. RESIDUALS FOR CREDBY

③⑤ The plot of the predicted values versus the standardized residuals yields information similar to that found in the plot of the observed versus the predicted value, only with the axes changed.

③⑥ The plot of the case numbers versus the standardized residuals indicates, through the more-or-less horizontal band of points, that there is no relationship between the standardized residuals and the case numbers.

PLOTS OF OBSERVED, PREDICTED, AND RESIDUAL CASE VALUES (CONT.)

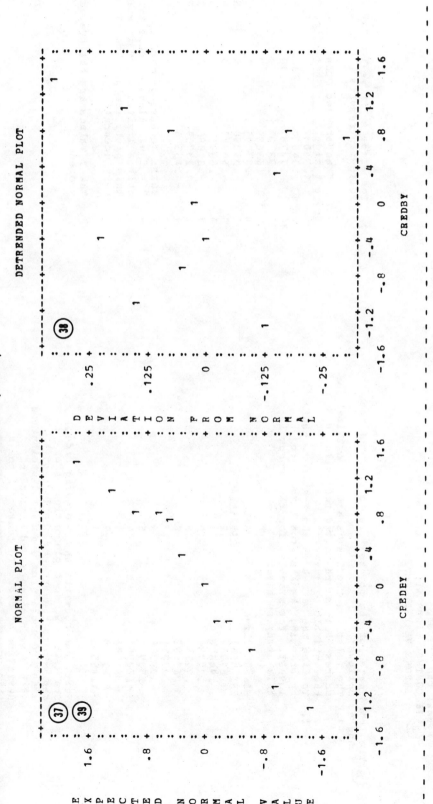

NORMAL PLOT

DETRENDED NORMAL PLOT

③⑦ One uses a NORMAL PLOT to visually check on the assumption that the scores on a variable have a normal distribution (although it may also be used to estimate the mean and standard deviation of the scores). If the normality assumption is viable, the points will fall on a straight line (the mean is estimated as the X coordinate at Y=0, and the standard deviation is the slope of this straight line). The process is described by Draper and Smith (pp.177-179, 1981) and by Barnett (1975).

③⑧ The detrended normal plot is another method of checking on normality. Here the X scores are the standardized residuals and the Y scores are the differences between the Y scores found for a normal plot and the X scores converted to standard scores from a normal distribution (mean 0, variance 1). Therefore, if the X scores follow a normal distribution, the scatter of points in a detrended normal plot should be close to zero, with roughly an equal number above and below zero. The standardized residuals plotted here appear to have come from a normal distribution.

ONE-WAY (ANOVA):  PLANNED COMPARISONS, UNEQUAL N

CPU TIME REQUIRED..  2.32 SECONDS

7960 BYTES OF WORKSPACE NEEDED FOR MANOVA EXECUTION.

(40) 16 FINISH    (SPSS GENERATED)

NORMAL END OF JOB.
(41) 16 CONTROL CARDS WERE PROCESSED.
  0 ERRORS WERE DETECTED.

(39) The coordinates of the points in a normal plot are found as follows:

1. The values on the X-axis are the original scores, here standardized residuals, on the variable of interest.

2. To find the values on the Y-axis we begin by ordering the X's from highest to lowest. For example, for the scores in this study we have:

| Standardized Residual | Order Statistic(i) |
| --- | --- |
| 1.31017 | 12 |
| .94624 | 11 |
| .72787 | 10 |
| .72787 | 9 |
| .63689 | 8 |
| .27295 | 7 |
| -.09098 | 6 |
| -.50951 | 5 |
| -.50951 | 4 |
| -.81886 | 3 |
| -1.23739 | 2 |
| -1.45575 | 1 |

3. Next, one converts the preceding order statistic, i, to a proportion which represents the area to the left of a standard score from a normal distribution with a mean of zero and a standard deviation of one. To convert i to this proportion, p, several approaches are described by Barnett (1975), namely:

$p = i/(n+1)$, referred to as the Weibull distribution,

$p = (i-1/2)/n$,

$p = (i-3/8)/(n+1/4)$,

$p = (i-.3)/(n+.4)$,

$p = i/n$,

$p = (3i-1)/(3n+1)$ (recommended and used by BMDP).

For example, if we let p = i/n, then the following results are found.

| Raw Score | Standardized Residual | Order Statistic | P | Standard score |
| --- | --- | --- | --- | --- |
| 9 | 1.31017 | 12 | 1.0 | 2.00 |
| 8 | .94624 | 11 | .92 | 1.38 |
| 10 | .72787 | 10 | .83 | .96 |
| 10 | .72787 | 9 | .75 | .67 |
| 5 | .63689 | 8 | .67 | .43 |
| 4 | .27295 | 7 | .58 | .21 |
| 3 | -.09098 | 6 | .50 | 0.00 |
| 4 | -.50951 | 5 | .42 | -.20 |
| 4 | -.50951 | 4 | .33 | -.43 |
| 1 | -.81886 | 3 | .25 | -.67 |
| 2 | -1.23739 | 2 | .17 | -.96 |
| 4 | -1.45575 | 1 | .08 | -1.38 |

NOTE: We have guessed that SPSS is using p = i/n. Also, because the computer has only a limited space in which to make this plot, the plotted values are not very accurate.

4. The Y values are the preceding standard scores.

(40) A FINISH card may follow the last card in an SPSS run; if one is not present (as is the case here) SPSS generates this card internally.

(41) This is the first place you might check after receiving your output. It tells you if you've had any errors and how many SPSS control cards were processed. The control card count includes the FINISH card, but does not include the data cards.

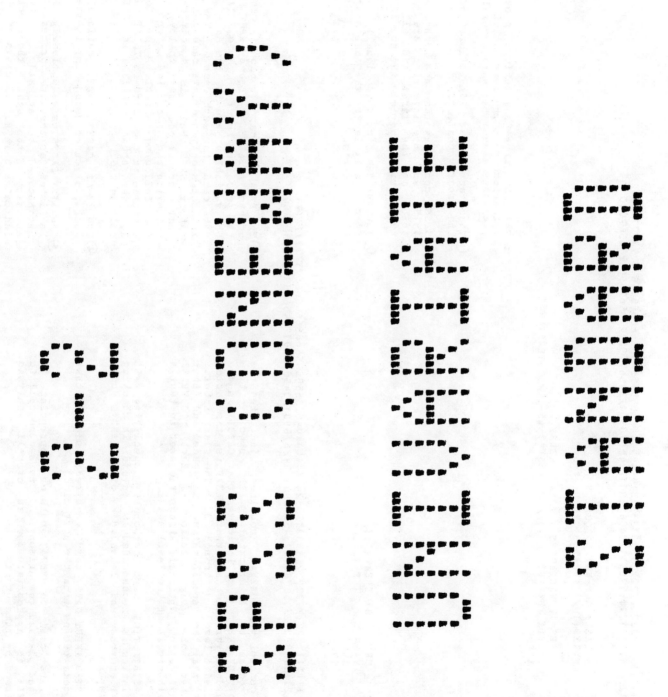

```
0000000001111111111222222222233333333334444444444555555555566666666667777777778
1234567890123456789012345678901234567890123456789012345678901234567890
```

① RUN    ME       SPIKER: ONE-WAY UNEQUAL N
② DATA LIST       FIXED(1)/1 TREAT 3 CREDBY 4-6
③ N OF CASES      12
④ LIST CASES      CASES=12/VARIABLES = TREAT,CREDBY
⑤ ONEWAY          CREDBY BY TREAT(1,3)/CONTRAST=1 -.5 -.5/CONTRAST=0 1 -1/
⑥ STATISTICS      ALL
⑧ READ INPUT DATA
```
        1 10
        1  4
        1 10
        2  8
        2  4
        2  4
        2  9
        3  3
        3  5
        3  4
        3  1
```
⑨ ONEWAY  ⑩      CREDBY BY TREAT(1,3)/
         ⑪      RANGES = TUKEY(.05)/
⑦ STATISTICS      ALL
⑫ OPTIONS         10

**Note:** The SPSS input annotations provided here are of value for most problems of this type. Consult your SPSS manual for more general information.

① These are column identifiers and are not part of the program content.

**Note:** SPSS control words are punched between columns 1-15, and specifications are placed in columns 16-80 on the first and all succeeding cards necessary to complete the specifications.

② The RUN NAME card (optional) allows the user to specify a title for the analysis; it is limited to 64 characters.

③ The DATA LIST card (optional) can be used in place of the VARIABLE LIST and INPUT FORMAT CARDS (see the preceding input). Here, FIXED indicates that the variables are in the same position on each data card for each case. The '1' in the '(1)' indicates only one data card per case. The slash informs SPSS that this specification is ended and that another one may follow. The number '1' following the slash indicates the card on which the following variables are found. The first variable on the card is TREAT which is in column 3, the second variable is CREDBY which is in columns 4-6.

④ The N OF CASES card (optional) specifies the number of cases (subjects) in the problem run.

⑤ The LIST CASES card (optional) will cause cases to be listed as they are processed. This card is recommended as an aid in checking the input accuracy of the data. The specification CASES=12 indicates that all 12 cases are to be listed. The slash indicates that the specification is ended and that another one may follow. The variables to be listed are specified next.

```
0000000001111111111222222222233333333334444444444555555555566666666667777777778
1234567890123456789012345678901234567890123456789012345678901234567890
```

⑥ The control word ONEWAY (required) indicates the subprogram to be executed. The specification CREDBY BY TREAT(1,3) indicates that CREDBY is the dependent variable and that TREAT is the factor name with levels 1 through 3. The slash informs SPSS that the specification is ended and that another one may follow. Each CONTRAST specification (optional) allows the user to test a hypothesis about the level means.

⑦ The STATISTICS card (optional) specifying ALL statistics is recommended as an aid in checking input accuracy and the validity of the ANOVA model assumptions.

⑧ The READ INPUT DATA card (required) signals that the data begins with the next card.

⑨ The first call to ONEWAY would be appropriate if one had planned comparisons. The second call to ONEWAY is appropriate for an overall analysis followed by Tukey tests.

⑩ In SPSS a data set may be re-analysed by the same or other subprograms by listing the subprogram specifications following the data.

```
0000000001111111111222222222233333333334444444444555555555566666666667777777778
1234567890123456789012345678901234567890123456789012345678901234567890
```

⑪ The specification RANGES calls for TUKEY tests between all pairs of treatment level means, at the .05 level of significance.

⑫ The CPTIONS statement requests a specific type of analysis. Here option 10 is recommended by SPSS when the cells have unequal $n$'s. It requests that the harmonic mean of the cell sizes be used to represent the cell size for the Tukey tests.

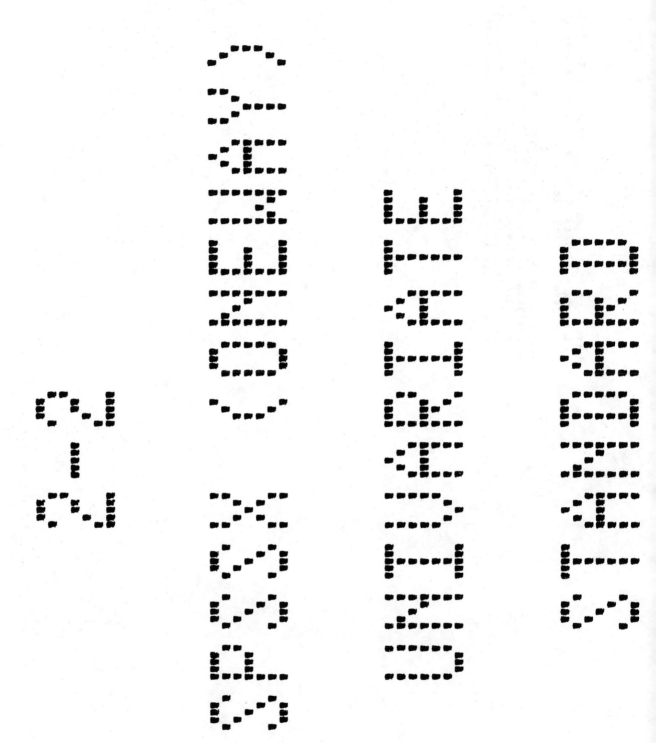

```
①0000000001111111111222222222233333333334444444444555555555566666666667777777777 8
 123456789012345678901234567890123456789012345678901234567890123456789012345678 90
② TITLE      SPIKER: ONE-WAY UNEQUAL N
③ DATA LIST  RECORD=1/1 TREAT 3 CREDBY 4-6
   ONEWAY     CREDBY BY TREAT(1,3)/CONTRAST=1-.5-.5/CONTRAST=0 1 -1/
   STATISTICS ALL
④ BEGIN DATA
    1 10
    1  4
    1 10
    2  8
    2  4
    2  4
    2  2
    2  9
    2  3
    3  3
    3  5
    3  4
    3  3
    3  1
⑤ END DATA
⑥ LIST VARIABLES = TREAT,CREDBY
   ONEWAY     CREDBY BY TREAT(1,3)/
              RANGES = TUKEY(.05)/
   STATISTICS ALL
   OPTIONS    10
①0000000001111111111222222222233333333334444444444555555555566666666667777777777 8
 123456789012345678901234567890123456789012345678901234567890123456789012345678 90
```

Note: The SPSSX input annotations provided here are of value for most problems of this type. Consult your SPSSX manual for more general information.

① These are column identifiers and are not part of the program content.

Note: SPSSX command keywords begin in column 1; specifications, separated by at least one blank, follow the command keywords. Specifications which continue beyond the first card must be indented by at least one column, and may continue for as many cards as is necessary.

② The TITLE card (optional) allows the user to specify a title for the analysis; it is limited to 60 characters.

③ The DATA LIST card provides SPSSX with the names of the variables. When no input format specification is specified, the specification FIXED is implied. Here, FIXED indicates that the variables are in the same position on each data card for each case. The '1' in 'RECORD=1' indicates only one data card per case. The slash informs SPSSX that this specification is ended and that another one may follow. The number '1' following the slash indicates the card on which the following variables are found. The first variable on the card is TREAT which is in column 3, the second variable is CREDBY which is in columns 4-6.

④ The BEGIN DATA card (required) signals that the data begins with the next card.

⑤ The END DATA card (required) signals the end of the data.

⑥ The LIST card (optional) will cause cases to be listed. This card is recommended as an aid in checking the input accuracy of the data. Here the scores for the variables listed will be printed for all of the cases.

                    CURRENT DOCUMENTATION FOR THE SPSS BATCH SYSTEM
ORDER FROM MCGRAW-HILL:   SPSS, 2ND ED. (PRINCIPAL TEXT)      SPSS STATISTICAL ALGORITHMS
                          SPSS UPDATE 7-9 (USE W/SPSS,2ND FOR REL. 7, 8, 9)
                          SPSS POCKET GUIDE, RELEASE 9         KEYWORDS: THE SPSS INC. NEWSLETTER
                          SPSS INTRODUCTORY GUIDE:  BASIC STATISTICS AND OPERATIONS
                          SPSS PRIMER (BRIEF INTRO TO SPSS)

DEFAULT SPACE ALLOCATION..       ALLOWS FOR..      102  TRANSFORMATIONS
WORKSPACE    71680 BYTES                           409  RECODE VALUES + LAG VARIABLES
TRANSPACE    10240 BYTES                          1641  IF/COMPUTE OPERATIONS

       (1)  1 RUN NAME        SPIKER: ONE-WAY UNEQUAL N
            2 DATA LIST       FIXED(1)/1 TREAT 3 CREDBY 4-6

THE DATA LIST PROVIDES FOR   2 VARIABLES AND  1 RECORDS ('CARDS') PER CASE. A MAXIMUM OF   6 COLUMNS ARE USED ON A RECORD.

LIST OF THE CONSTRUCTED FORMAT STATEMENT..
     (2X,F1.0,F3.0)

            3 N OF CASES      12
            4 LIST CASES      CASES=12/VARIABLES = TREAT,CREDBY
            5 ONEWAY          CREDBY  BY TREAT(1,3)/CONTRAST=1-.5-.5/CONTRAST=0  1 -1/
            6 STATISTICS      ALL

***** ONEWAY PROBLEM REQUIRES      136 BYTES WORKSPACE *****

            7 READ INPUT DATA

(1) SPSS provides a listing  of program control cards.
    This listing should be checked for input accuracy.

SPIKER: ONE-WAY UNEQUAL N

FILE  NONAME  (CREATION DATE = 02/02/83)

| CASE-N | TREAT | CREDBY |
|--------|-------|--------|
| ② 1 | 1. | 10. |
| 2 | 1. | 4. |
| 3 | 1. | 10. |
| 4 | 2. | 8. |
| 5 | 2. | 4. |
| 6 | 2. | 4. |
| 7 | 2. | 2. |
| 8 | 3. | 9. |
| 9 | 3. | 3. |
| 10 | 3. | 5. |
| 11 | 3. | 4. |
| 12 | 3. | 1. |

② The LIST CASES card produced this data list which should be proofread.

77

SPIKER: ONE-WAY UNEQUAL N

FILE   NONAME   (CREATION DATE = 02/02/83)

02/02/83      PAGE   3

- - - - - - - - - - - - - - - - - O N E W A Y - - - - - - - - - - - - - - - - -

VARIABLE  CREDBY
BY VARIABLE  TREAT

③④

ANALYSIS OF VARIANCE

| SOURCE | D.F. | SUM OF SQUARES | MEAN SQUARES | F RATIO ⑤ | F PROB. |
|---|---|---|---|---|---|
| BETWEEN GROUPS | 2 | 38.7167 | 19.3583 | 2.564 | 0.1314 |
| WITHIN GROUPS | 9 | 67.9500 | 7.5500 | | |
| TOTAL | 11 | 106.6667 | | | |

| GROUP | COUNT | MEAN ⑥ | STANDARD DEVIATION ⑦ | STANDARD ERROR | MINIMUM ⑧ | MAXIMUM | 95 PCT CONF INT FOR MEAN ⑨ |
|---|---|---|---|---|---|---|---|
| GRP01 | 3 | 8.0000 | 3.4641 | 2.0000 | 4.0000 | 10.0000 | -0.6054 TO 16.6054 |
| GRP02 | 5 | 5.4000 | 2.9665 | 1.3266 | 2.0000 | 9.0000 | 1.7167 TO 9.0833 |
| GRP03 | 4 | 3.2500 | 1.7078 | 0.8539 | 1.0000 | 5.0000 | 0.5325 TO 5.9675 |
| TOTAL ⑪ | 12 | 5.3333 | 3.1140 | 0.8989 | 1.0000 | 10.0000 | 3.3548 TO 7.3119 |
| FIXED EFFECTS MODEL | | | 2.7477 | 0.7932 | | | 3.5390 TO 7.1277 |
| RANDOM EFFECTS MODEL | | | | ⑩ 1.2946 | | | -0.2370 TO 10.9036 |

RANDOM EFFECTS MODEL - ESTIMATE OF BETWEEN COMPONENT VARIANCE          3.0149

③ This information would be found in an ANOVA source table (see Table 2.4, Chapter 2).

④ This is the overall analysis of variance for the Mode of Message Presentation (TREAT) effects (see discussion, Chapter 2).

⑤ This is the probability of obtaining an F ratio larger than the calculated F ratio of 2.56. Therefore, if the level of significance, alpha, was .05, one would fail to reject the overall null hypothesis that the treatment means are all equal to each other. That is, for the F statistic to indicate that significant differences are present, the obtained 'F PROB.' must be less than the predetermined level of significance.

⑥ cell means may be used in a priori or post hoc analyses. The user may calculate these means by hand to further check on input accuracy and program execution.

⑦ cell standard deviations should be approximately equal (a check on the assumption of homogeneity of variance). This check is particularly important when the cells have unequal n's.

⑧ A further data check is provided by printing the minimum and maximum values per cell of the dependent (CREDBY) variable.

⑨ The 95% confidence interval provides the researcher with an idea of the possible mean (cell and overall) values.

⑩ The computation of the standard deviation for the 'RANDOM EFFECTS MODEL' (see Appendix D) is not explained in SPSS and is complicated with unequal n's (see Scheffe', 1959, p. 224).

⑪ The input data check should include: identification of the factor levels, number of subjects per cell, and the total number of subjects.

- - - - - - - - - - - - O N E W A Y - - - - - - - - - - - -

VARIABLE   CREDBY
BY VARIABLE   TREAT

CONTRAST COEFFICIENT MATRIX

|  | GRP01 | GRP02 | GRP03 |
|---|---|---|---|
| (12) CONTRAST 1 | 1.0 | -0.5 | -0.5 |
| CONTRAST 2 | 0.0 | 1.0 | -1.0 |

POOLED VARIANCE ESTIMATE

|  | VALUE | S. ERROR | T VALUE | D.F. | T PROB. |
|---|---|---|---|---|---|
| CONTRAST 1 | 3.6750 | 1.8347 | (15) 2.003 | 9.0 | (13) 0.076 |
| CONTRAST 2 | 2.1500 | 1.8432 | 1.166 | 9.0 | 0.273 |

SEPARATE VARIANCE ESTIMATE

|  | S. ERROR | T VALUE | D.F. | T PROB. |
|---|---|---|---|---|
| | 2.1500 | (14) 1.709 | 2.7 | (13) 0.186 |
| | 1.5777 | 1.363 | 6.5 | 0.215 |

TESTS FOR HOMOGENEITY OF VARIANCES

(18) COCHRANS C = MAX. VARIANCE/SUM(VARIANCES) = 0.5060, P = 0.626   (16) (APPROX.)
(17) BARTLETT-BOX F =                                0.563, P = 0.571
(19) MAXIMUM VARIANCE / MINIMUM VARIANCE = 4.114

---

(12) These are the user-constructed contrasts comparing the mean of cell 1 with the average of the means of cells 2 and 3 (1.,-.5,-.5), and comparing the mean of cell 2 to the mean of cell 3 (0,1,-1).

(13) These contrasts are tested with a t-test, and neither contrast is significant at the .05 level of confidence (see discussion in Chapter 2).

Note: Because the sample size in this study was relatively small, further investigation in this area would be dependent on the insight gained by the investigator. For a discussion on sample size see Cohen (1977).

(14) The individual contrast sums of squares (i.e., planned comparison ANOVA source table, Table 2.3) are needed for the comparison ANOVA source table, Table 2.3. We can find these sums of square from the information given in this program using the following formula:

$$t^2 = SS(Contrast)/Mean Square Error$$

(see Hays,1973, Chapter 14). Here, SS(Contrast) is the sum of squares associated with contrast i (i = 1,2), and the MEAN SQUARE ERROR for each contrast is found in the above ANOVA source table. Then, using the above formula, we have
SS(1st. Contrast) = $7.55(2.0031)^2$ = 30.29,
and
SS(2nd. Contrast) = $7.55(1.164)^2$ = 10.27.

(15) An excellent discussion of the pooled and separate variance estimate t test may be found in (Hays, 1973, p.410). Hays indicates that the separate variance estimate t test should be interpreted when the groups have unequal n's.

(16) The tests for homogeneity of variance are not significant, which indicates the homogeneity of variance assumption has been met. However, with small n, these tests are unreliable.

(17) Cochran's C test is found as the largest variance divided by the sum of all of the variances. Here the sum of the variances is: 12.0000 + 8.8000 + 2.9167 = 23.7167. Therefore, Cochran's C = 12.0000/23.7167 = .50597. Critical values for Cochran's C are available in Dixon and Massey (1969, pp. 536-537) and Winer (1971, p. 876).

(18) The Bartlett-Box test was developed by Bartlett (1937) for the univariate case and was extended by Box (1949) for the multivariate case. The test used here is based on Box's extension, but the calculations are done for one dependent variable. The formulas for this test are complex, but are well illustrated in Cooley and Lohnes (1971, pp. 228-230).

(19) The ratio of the largest variance (12.0000) to the smallest variance (2.9165) is 4.114. This is a descriptive measure of variance heteroscedasticity, which does not appear to be serious here (see Hopkins and Glass (1978, pp. 257-259)) for an elementary discussion of these points.

CPU TIME REQUIRED..     0.34 SECONDS

(20)  8 ONEWAY          CREDEY BY TREAT(1,3)/
      9                 RANGES = TUKEY(.05)/
     10 STATISTICS      ALL
     11 OPTIONS         10

***** ONEWAY PROBLEM REQUIRES    128 BYTES WORKSPACE *****

(20) Control cards which follow the data are listed prior to the analyses which they generate. They should be checked for input accuracy.

FILE   NONAME   (CREATION DATE = 02/02/83)

- - - - - - - - - - - - - - O N E W A Y - - - - - - - - - - - - - -

VARIABLE   CREDBY
BY VARIABLE   TREAT

㉑ The analysis on this page was explained on the preceding pages.

ANALYSIS OF VARIANCE

| SOURCE | D.F. | SUM OF SQUARES | MEAN SQUARES | F RATIO | F PROB. |
|---|---|---|---|---|---|
| BETWEEN GROUPS | 2 | 38.7167 | 19.3583 | 2.564 | 0.1314 |
| WITHIN GROUPS | 9 | 67.9500 | 7.5500 | | |
| TOTAL | 11 | 106.6667 | | | |

| GROUP | COUNT | MEAN | STANDARD DEVIATION | STANDARD ERROR | MINIMUM | MAXIMUM | 95 PCT CONF INT FOR MEAN | | |
|---|---|---|---|---|---|---|---|---|---|
| GRP01 | 3 | 8.0000 | 3.4641 | 2.0000 | 4.0000 | 10.0000 | -0.6054 | TO | 16.6054 |
| GRP02 | 5 | 5.4000 | 2.9665 | 1.3266 | 2.0000 | 9.0000 | 1.7167 | TO | 9.0833 |
| GRP03 | 4 | 3.2500 | 1.7078 | 0.8539 | 1.0000 | 5.0000 | 0.5325 | TO | 5.9675 |
| TOTAL | 12 | 5.3333 | 3.1140 | 0.8989 | 1.0000 | 10.0000 | 3.3548 | TO | 7.3119 |
| FIXED EFFECTS MODEL | | | 2.7477 | 0.7932 | | | 3.5390 | TO | 7.1277 |
| RANDOM EFFECTS MODEL | | | | 1.2946 | | | -0.2370 | TO | 10.9036 |

RANDOM EFFECTS MODEL - ESTIMATE OF BETWEEN COMPONENT VARIANCE     3.0149

TESTS FOR HOMOGENEITY OF VARIANCES

COCHRANS C = MAX. VARIANCE/SUM(VARIANCES) = 0.5060, P = 0.626 (APPROX.)
BARTLETT-BOX F = 0.563, P = 0.571
MAXIMUM VARIANCE / MINIMUM VARIANCE = 4.114

- - - - - - - - - - - - - - - - - - - - - - O N E W A Y - - - - - - - - - - - - - - - - - - - - - -

    VARIABLE  CREDBY
  BY VARIABLE  TREAT

MULTIPLE RANGE TEST

(22)
(23) TUKEY-HSD PROCEDURE
     RANGES FOR THE 0.050 LEVEL -

        3.94  3.94

HARMONIC MEAN CELL SIZE =    3.8298
THE ACTUAL RANGE USED IS THE LISTED RANGE *       1.4041

     HOMOGENEOUS SUBSETS    (SUBSETS OF GROUPS, WHOSE HIGHEST AND LOWEST MEANS DO NOT DIFFER BY MORE THAN THE SHORTEST
                             SIGNIFICANT RANGE FOR A SUBSET OF THAT SIZE)

SUBSET   1
(24)
GROUP    GRP03      GRP02      GRP01
MEAN     3.2500     5.4000     8.0000

82

- - - - - - - - - - - - - - - - - - - - - - - - - - - - - - - - - - - - - - - - - - - - - - - - -

(22) Note that the Tukey test completed by SPSS for the
     case with unequal n's is not the same test as
     that described for unequal n's in Chapter 2.
     (The test in Chapter 2 controls Type I error
     better).

(23) To calculate the Tukey test,   SPSS   uses   the
     formula:

$$HSD = R\sqrt{MSW/n},$$

     where,
           R=is the statistic from the studentized range
             distribution (our q in step 2 of the Tukey
             presentation in Chapter 2),
           MSW=mean square within, and
           n=the harmonic mean of the sample sizes across
             all treatment levels.
     The harmonic mean is found using the formula

$$n = P/\Sigma[1/n(i)]$$

     where
           P=the number of treatment levels, and
           n(i)=the number of subjects per treatment.

     For option 10 this number is $\sqrt{MSW/n}$.

(24) Because all of our treatment level means have been
     printed here (i.e. as a homogeneous set), this
     indicates  that  there  are  no  significant
     differences among our treatments at the .05 level
     of significance.

CPU TIME REQUIRED.-- 0.25 SECONDS

(25) 12 FINISH (SPSS GENERATED)

(26) NORMAL END OF JOB.
12 CONTROL CARDS WERE PROCESSED.
0 ERRORS WERE DETECTED.

(25) A FINISH card may follow the last card in an SPSS run; if one is not present (as is the case here) SPSS generates this card internally.

(26) This is the first place you might check after receiving your output. It tells you if you've had any errors and how many SPSS control cards were processed. The control card count includes the FINISH card, but does not include the data cards.

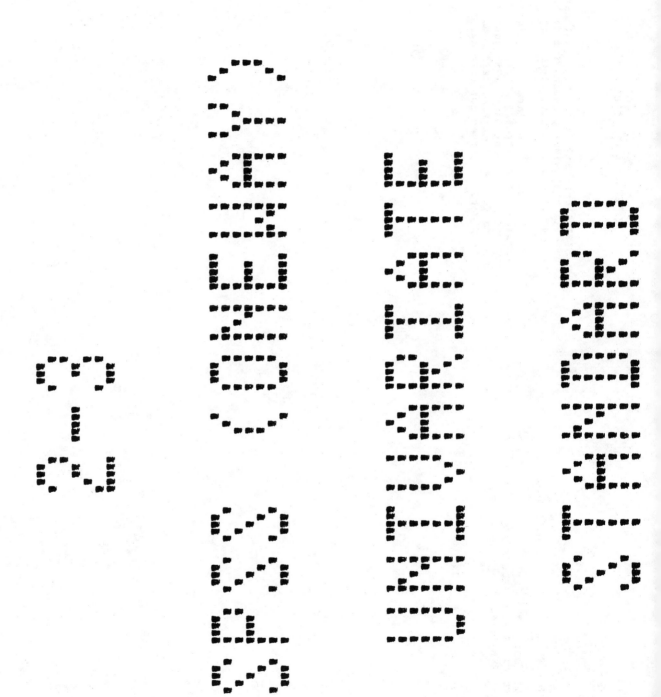

```
① 0000000000111111111122222222223333333333444444444455555555556666666666777777777 7778
  1234567890123456789012345678901234567890123456789012345678901234567890123456789 0

② RUN NAME        ONE-WAY (ANOVA):    EQUAL N
③ VARIABLE LIST   TREAT,CREDBY
④ INPUT FORMAT    FIXED(2F3.0)
⑤ LIST CASES      CASES = 1000/VARIABLES = TREAT,CREDBY
⑥ ONEWAY          CREDBY BY TREAT(1,3)/
⑦                 RANGES = TUKEY(.05)/
⑧ STATISTICS      ALL
⑨ READ INPUT DATA

         1  10
         1   4
         1  10
         1   4
         1  10
         2   8
         2   4
         2   4
         2   2
         2   9
         3   3
         3   5
         3   5
         3   4
         3   1

⑩ END INPUT DATA

  0000000000111111111122222222223333333333444444444455555555556666666666777777777 7778
① 1234567890123456789012345678901234567890123456789012345678901234567890123456789 0
```

85

**Note:** The SPSS input annotations provided here are of value for most problems of this type. Consult your SPSS manual for more general information.

① These are column identifiers and are not part of the program content.

**Note:** SPSS control words are punched between columns 1-15, and specifications are placed in columns 16-80 on the first and all succeeding cards necessary to complete the specifications.

② The RUN NAME card (optional) allows the user to specify a title for the analysis; it is limited to 64 characters.

③ The VARIABLE LIST card (required) provides SPSS with the names of the variables. The variables must be listed in the order in which they are being read by the FORMAT statement.

④ The control words INPUT FORMAT indicate that a format for the data will be specified. Here the subcommand FIXED indicates that the data is in the same columns on all cards, and the Fortran specification (2F3.0) indicates that the variables being read are in the first three (1-3) and the next three (4-6) columns.

⑤ The LIST CASES card (optional) requests the cases to be listed. The subcommand CASES=1000 was made so that all cases would be listed (specify more cases than you know you have when you are unsure of the number of cases); the subcommand VARIABLES=TREAT, CREDBY indicates which variables are to be listed. This card is recommended as an aid in checking the input accuracy of the data.

⑥ The control word ONEWAY (required) indicates the subprogram to be executed. The specification CREDBY BY TREAT (1,3) indicates that CREDBY is the dependent variable and that TREAT is the factor name with levels 1 through 3. The slash informs SPSS that the specification is ended and that another one may follow.

⑦ The RANGES specification calls for TUKEY tests between all pairs of treatment level means, at the .05 level of significance.

⑧ The STATISTICS card (optional) specifying ALL statistics is recommended as an aid in checking input accuracy and the validity of the ANOVA model assumptions.

⑨ The READ INPUT DATA card (required) signals that the data begins with the next card.

⑩ The END INPUT DATA card (required) signals the end of the data. This card is required here because the number of cases was not specified.

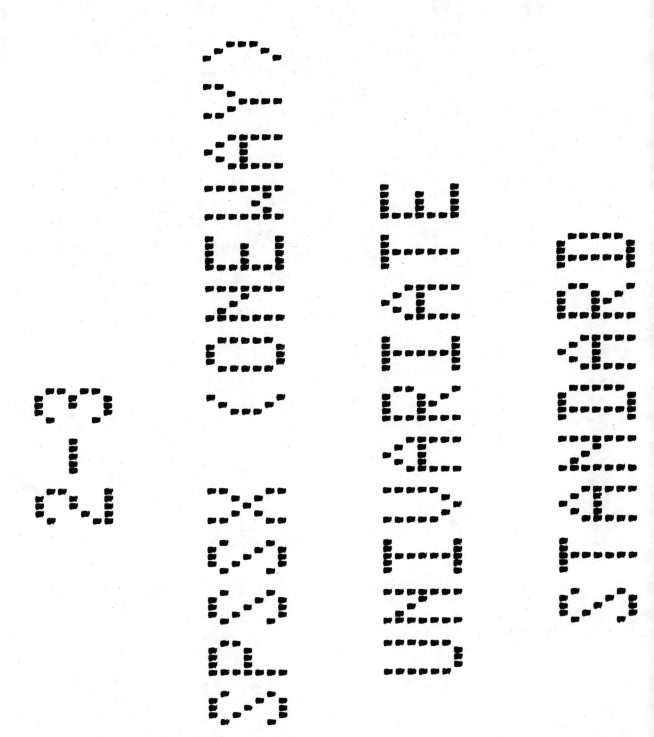

① These are column identifiers and are not part of the program content.

Note: SPSSX command keywords begin in column 1; specifications, separated by at least one blank, follow the command keywords. Specifications which continue beyond the first card must be indented by at least one column, and may continue for as many cards as is necessary.

② The TITLE card (optional) allows the user to specify a title for the analysis; it is limited to 60 characters.

③ The DATA LIST card provides SPSSX with the names of the variables. When no input format specification is specified, the specification FIXED is implied. Here, FIXED indicates that the variables are in the same position on each data card for each case. Following the variable names is a Fortran specification, i.e., (2F3.0), which indicates that the variables being read are in the first three (1-3) and the next three (4-6) columns.

④ The BEGIN DATA card (required) signals that the data begins with the next card.

⑤ The END DATA card (required) signals the end of the data.

⑥ The LIST card (optional) will cause cases to be listed. This card is recommended as an aid in checking the input accuracy of the data. Here the scores for the variables listed will be printed for all of the cases.

```
① 0000000001111111111222222222233333333334444444444555555555566666666667777777778
   1234567890123456789012345678901234567890123456789012345678901234567890

② TITLE      ONE-WAY (ANOVA): EQUAL N
③ DATA LIST/ TREAT,CREDBY (2F3.0)
④ BEGIN DATA
   1  10
   1  10
   1   4
   1  10
   2   8
   2   4
   2   2
   2   9
   3   3
   3   5
   3   5
   3   4
   3   1
⑤ END DATA
⑥ LIST       VARIABLES = TREAT,CREDBY
   ONEWAY        CREDBY BY TREAT(1,3)/
                 RANGES = TUKEY(.05)/
   STATISTICS    \LL

① 0000000001111111111222222222233333333334444444444555555555566666666667777777778
   1234567890123456789012345678901234567890123456789012345678901234567890
```

SPSS FOR OS/360, VERSION H, RELEASE 9.1, FEBRUARY 1, 1982

ORDER FROM MCGRAW-HILL:    CURRENT DOCUMENTATION FOR THE SPSS BATCH SYSTEM
                           SPSS, 2ND ED. (PRINCIPAL TEXT)    ORDER FROM SPSS INC.:    SPSS STATISTICAL ALGORITHMS
                           SPSS UPDATE 7-9 (USE W/SPSS,2ND FOR REL. 7, 8, 9)         KEYWORDS: THE SPSS INC. NEWSLETTER
                           SPSS POCKET GUIDE, RELEASE 9
                           SPSS INTRODUCTORY GUIDE:  BASIC STATISTICS AND OPERATIONS
                           SPSS PRIMER (BRIEF INTRO TO SPSS)

DEFAULT SPACE ALLOCATION-    ALLOWS FOR--    102 TRANSFORMATIONS
WORKSPACE    71680 BYTES                     409 RECODE VALUES + LAG VARIABLES
TRANSPACE    10240 BYTES                    1641 IF/COMPUTE OPERATIONS

① 1 RUN NAME       ONE-WAY (ANOVA):  EQUAL N              ① SPSS provides a listing of program control cards.
  2 VARIABLE LIST  TREAT,CREDBY                              This listing should be checked for input accuracy.
  3 INPUT FORMAT   FIXED(2F3.0)

   ACCORDING TO YOUR INPUT FORMAT, VARIABLES ARE TO BE READ AS FOLLOWS

   VARIABLE    FORMAT    RECORD    COLUMNS

   TREAT       F 3. 0      1        1-  3
   CREDBY      F 3. 0      1        4-  6

THE INPUT FORMAT PROVIDES FOR    2 VARIABLES.    2 WILL BE READ
IT PROVIDES FOR   1 RECORDS ('CARDS') PER CASE.  A MAXIMUM OF     6 'COLUMNS' ARE USED ON A RECORD.

② 4 LIST CASES     CASES = 1000/VARIABLES = TREAT,CREDBY
  5 ONEWAY         CREDBY BY TREAT(1,3)/
  6               RANGES = TUKEY(-.05)/
  7 STATISTICS     ALL

***** ONEWAY PROBLEM REQUIRES    128 BYTES WORKSPACE *****

  8 READ INPUT DATA

88

FILE NONAME (CREATION DATE = 02/27/83)

(2) The LIST CASES card produced this data list which should be proofread.

| CASE-N | TREAT | CREDBY |
|--------|-------|--------|
| (2) 1  | 1.    | 10.    |
| 2      | 1.    | 4.     |
| 3      | 1.    | 10.    |
| 4      | 1.    | 4.     |
| 5      | 1.    | 10.    |
| 6      | 2.    | 8.     |
| 7      | 2.    | 4.     |
| 8      | 2.    | 4.     |
| 9      | 2.    | 2.     |
| 10     | 3.    | 9.     |
| 11     | 3.    | 3.     |
| 12     | 3.    | 5.     |
| 13     | 3.    | 5.     |
| 14     | 3.    | 4.     |
| 15     | 3.    | 1.     |

AFTER READING   15 CASES FROM SUBFILE NONAME ,   END OF DATA WAS ENCOUNTERED ON LOGICAL UNIT # 5

VARIABLE CREDBI
BY VARIABLE TREAT ④

- - - - - - - - - - - O N E W A Y - - - - - - - - - - -

③ This information would be found in an ANOVA source table.

③ ANALYSIS OF VARIANCE

| SOURCE | D.F. | SUM OF SQUARES | MEAN SQUARES | F RATIO | F PROB. |
|---|---|---|---|---|---|
| BETWEEN GROUPS | 2 | 40.1333 | 20.0667 | 2.688 | 0.1085 ⑤ |
| WITHIN GROUPS | 12 | 89.6000 | 7.4667 | | |
| TOTAL | 14 | 129.7333 | | | |

④ This is the overall analysis of variance for the Mode of Message Presentation (TREAT) effects (see discussion, Chapter 2).

⑧

| GROUP ⑥ | COUNT | MEAN ⑦ | STANDARD DEVIATION | STANDARD ERROR | MINIMUM ⑪ | MAXIMUM | 95 PCT CONF INT FOR MEAN ⑫ |
|---|---|---|---|---|---|---|---|
| GRP01 | 5 | 7.6000 | 3.2863 | 1.4697 | 4.0000 | 10.0000 | 3.5195 TO 11.6805 |
| GRP02 | 5 | 5.4000 | 2.9665 | 1.3266 | 2.0000 | 9.0000 | 1.7167 TO 9.0833 |
| GRP03 | 5 | 3.6000 | 1.6733 | 0.7483 | 1.0000 | 5.0000 | 1.5223 TO 5.6777 |
| TOTAL | 15 | 5.5333 | 3.0441 | 0.7860 | 1.0000 | 10.0000 | 3.8476 TO 7.2191 |
| FIXED EFFECTS MODEL | | | 2.7325 | 0.7055 | | | 3.9961 TO 7.0706 |
| RANDOM EFFECTS MODEL | | | | 1.1566 | | | 0.5567 TO 10.5099 |

⑬ RANDOM EFFECTS MODEL - ESTIMATE OF BETWEEN COMPONENT VARIANCE    2.5200

⑭ TESTS FOR HOMOGENEITY OF VARIANCES

⑨ COCHRANS C = MAX. VARIANCE/SUM(VARIANCES) = 0.4821, P = 0.632 (APPROX.)
⑩ BARTLETT-BOX F = 0.805, P = 0.448
MAXIMUM VARIANCE / MINIMUM VARIANCE = 3.857

⑨ Cochran's C test is found as the largest variance divided by the sum of all of the variances. Here the sum of the variances is: 12.0000 + 8.8000 + 2.9167 = 23.7167. Therefore, Cochran's C = 12.0000/23.7167 = .50597. Critical values for Cochran's C are available in Dixon and Massey (1969, pp. 536-537) and Winer (1971, P. 876).

⑩ The Bartlett-Box test was developed by Bartlett (1937) for the univariate case and was extended by Box (1949) for the multivariate case. The test used here is based on Box's extension, but the calculations are done for one dependent variable. The formulas for this test are complex, but are

⑤ This is the probability of obtaining an F ratio larger than the calculated F ratio of 2.688. Therefore, if the level of significance, alpha, was .05, one would fail to reject the overall null hypothesis that the treatment means are all equal to each other. That is, for the F statistic to indicate that significant differences are present, the obtained 'F PROB.' must be less than the predetermined level of significance.

⑥ The input data check should include: identification of the factor levels, number of subjects per cell, and the total number of subjects.

⑦ Cell means may be used in a priori or post hoc analyses. The user may calculate these means by hand to further check on input accuracy and program execution.

⑧ Cell standard deviations should be approximately equal (a check on the assumption of homogeneity of variance). This check is particularly important

90

------- O N E W A Y -------

VARIABLE    CREDBY
BY VARIABLE  TREAT

MULTIPLE RANGE TEST

TUKEY-HSD PROCEDURE  (15)
RANGES FOR THE 0.050 LEVEL -
3.77  3.77

THE RANGES ABOVE ARE TABLE RANGES. THE VALUE ACTUALLY COMPARED WITH MEAN(J)-MEAN(I) IS--
(16)  $1.9322 * \text{RANGE} * \text{SQRT}(1/N(I) + 1/N(J))$

HOMOGENEOUS SUBSETS    (SUBSETS OF GROUPS, WHOSE HIGHEST AND LOWEST MEANS DO NOT DIFFER BY MORE THAN THE SHORTEST
                        SIGNIFICANT RANGE FOR A SUBSET OF THAT SIZE)

SUBSET  1  (17)(18)

| GROUP | GRP03 | GRP02 | GRP01 |
|-------|-------|-------|-------|
| MEAN  | 3.6000 | 5.4000 | 7.6000 |

91

(11) A further data check is provided by printing the minimum and maximum values per cell of the dependent (CREDBY) variable.

(12) The 95% confidence interval provides the researcher with an idea of the possible mean (cell and overall) values.

(13) The computation of the standard deviation for the 'RANDOM EFFECT MODEL' (see Appendix D) is not explained in SPSS and is complicated with unequal n's (see Scheffe', 1959, p. 224).

(14) The tests for homogeneity of variance are not significant, which indicates the homogeneity of variance assumption has been met. However, with small n, these tests are unreliable.

(15) Note that the Tukey test completed by SPSS for the case with equal n's is the same test as that described for equal n's in Chapter 2. (The test in Chapter 2 controls Type I error better).

(16) To calculate the Tukey test SPSS uses the formula:

$$\text{HSD} = R\sqrt{\text{MSW}/n},$$

where,

R=is the statistic from the studentized range distribution (our q in step 2 of the Tukey presentation in Chapter 2).

MSW=mean square within, and

n=the number of subjects in a cell.

(17) For equal n's this number is $\sqrt{\text{MSW}/2}$.

(18) Because all of our treatment level means have been printed here (i.e. as a homogenous set), this indicates that there are no significant differences among our treatments at the .05 level of significance.

ONE-WAY (ANOVA): EQUAL N

CPU TIME REQUIRED..    0.36 SECONDS

(19) 9 FINISH          (SPSS GENERATED)

NORMAL END OF JOB.
    9 CONTROL CARDS WERE PROCESSED.
    0 ERRORS WERE DETECTED.
(20)

(19) A FINISH card may follow the last card in an SPSS run; if one is not present (as is the case here) SPSS generates this card internally.

(20) This is the first place you might check after receiving your output. It tells you if you've had any errors and how many SPSS control cards were processed. The control card count includes the FINISH card, but does not include the data cards.

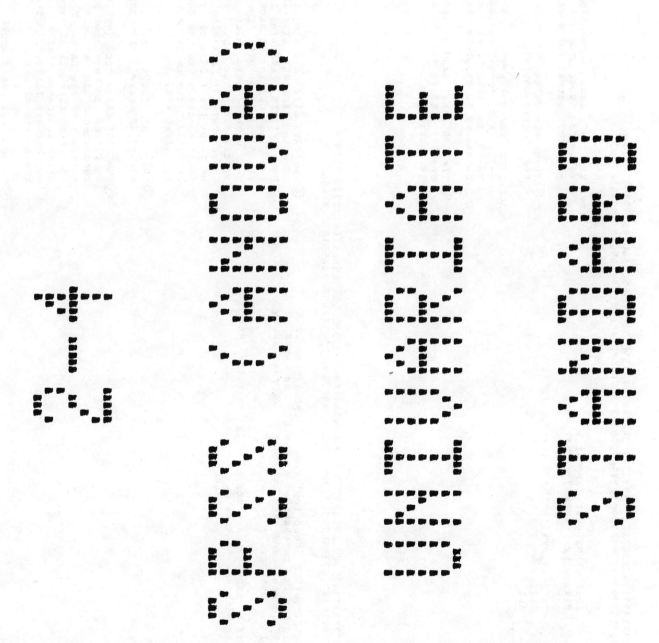

```
② RUN NAME         SPIKER: ONE-WAY UNEQUAL N
③ DATA LIST        FIXED(1)/1 TREAT 3 CREDBY 4-6
④ N OF CASES       12
⑤ LIST CASES       CASES=12/VARIABLES = TREAT,CREDBY
⑥ ANOVA            CREDBY BY TREAT(1,3)/
⑦ STATISTICS       ALL
⑧ READ INPUT DATA
   1 10
   1  4
   1 10
   2  8
   2  4
   2  2
   2  9
   3  3
   3  5
   3  4
   3  1
```

Note: The SPSS input annotations provided here are of value for most problems of this type. Consult your SPSS manual for more general information.

① These are column identifiers and are not part of the program content.

Note: SPSS control words are punched between columns 1-15, and specifications are placed in columns 16-80 on the first and all succeeding cards necessary to complete the specifications.

② The RUN NAME card (optional) allows the user to specify a title for the analysis; it is limited to 64 characters.

⑦ The STATISTICS card (optional) specifying ALL statistics is recommended as an aid in checking input accuracy and the validity of the ANOVA model assumptions.

⑧ The READ INPUT DATA card signals that the data begins with the next card.

③ The DATA LIST card (required) can be used in place of the VARIABLE LIST and INPUT FORMAT CARDS. Here, FIXED indicates that the variables are in the same position on each data card for each case. The '1' in the '(1)' indicates only one data card per case. The slash informs SPSS that this specification is ended and another one follows. The number '1' following slash indicates the card on which the following variables are found. The first variable on the card is TREAT which is in column 3, the second variable is CREDBY which is in column 4-6.

④ The N OF CASES card (optional) specifies the number of cases (subjects) in the problem run.

⑤ The LIST CASES card (optional) will cause cases to be listed as they are processed. This card is recommended as an aid in checking the input accuracy of the data. The specification CASES: 12 indicates that all 12 cases are to be listed. The slash indicates that a specification is ended and another one follows. The variables to be listed are specified next.

⑥ The control word ANOVA (required) indicates the subprogram to be executed. The specification CREDBY BY TREAT (1,3) indicates that CREDBY is the dependent variable and that TREAT is the factor name with levels 1 through 3.

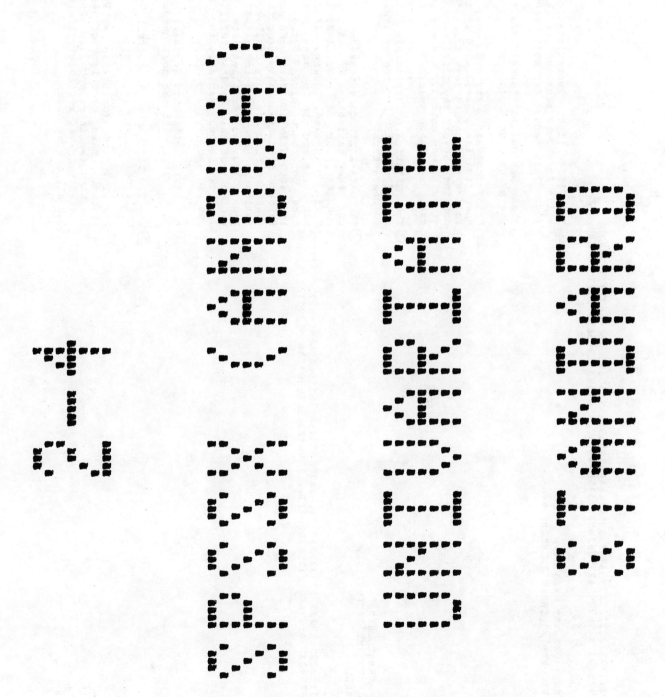

```
①00000000011111111112222222222333333333344444444445555555555666666666677777777778
  12345678901234567890123456789012345678901234567890123456789012345678901234567890

②TITLE       SPIKER: ONE-WAY UNEQUAL N
③DATA LIST   RECORD=1/1 TREAT 3 CREDBY 4-6
④BEGIN DATA
            1 10
            1  4
            1 10
            2  8
            2  4
            2  4
            2  2
            2  9
            3  3
            3  5
            3  4
            3  1
⑤END DATA
⑥LIST VARIABLES = TREAT,CREDBY
 ANOVA          CREDBY BY TREAT (1,3)/
 STATISTICS     ALL

①00000000011111111112222222222333333333344444444445555555555666666666677777777778
  12345678901234567890123456789012345678901234567890123456789012345678901234567890
```

Note: The SPSSX input annotations provided here are of value for most problems of this type. Consult your SPSSX manual for more general information.

① These are column identifiers and are not part of the program content.

Note: SPSSX command keywords begin in column 1; specifications, separated by at least one blank, follow the command keywords. Specifications which continue beyond the first card must be indented by at least one column, and may continue for as many cards as is necessary.

② The TITLE card (optional) allows the user to specify a title for the analysis; it is limited to 60 characters.

③ The DATA LIST card provides SPSSX with the names of the variables. When no input format specification is specified, the specification FIXED is implied. Here, FIXED indicates that the variables are in the same position on each data card for each case. The '1' in 'RECORD=1' indicates only one data card per case. The slash informs SPSSX that this specification is ended and that another one may follow. The number '1' following the slash indicates the card on which the following variables are found. The first variable on the card is TREAT which is in column 3, the second variable is CREDBY which is in columns 4-6.

④ The BEGIN DATA card (required) signals that the data begins with the next card.

⑤ The END DATA card (required) signals the end of the data.

⑥ The LIST card (optional) will cause cases to be listed. This card is recommended as an aid in checking the input accuracy of the data. Here the scores for the variables listed will be printed for all of the cases.

96

SPSS BATCH SYSTEM

SPSS FOR OS/360, VERSION H, RELEASE 9.1, FEBRUARY 1, 1982

ORDER FROM MCGRAW-HILL:    CURRENT DOCUMENTATION FOR THE SPSS BATCH SYSTEM
                           SPSS, 2ND ED. (PRINCIPAL TEXT)        SPSS STATISTICAL ALGORITHMS
                           SPSS UPDATE 7-9 (USE W/SPSS,2ND FOR REL. 7, 8, 9)    ORDER FROM SPSS INC.:
                           SPSS POCKET GUIDE, RELEASE 9          KEYWORDS: THE SPSS INC. NEWSLETTER
                           SPSS INTRODUCTORY GUIDE: BASIC STATISTICS AND OPERATIONS
                           SPSS PRIMER (BRIEF INTRO TO SPSS)

                                                                ① SPSS provides a listing of program control cards.
                                                                   This listing should be checked for input accuracy.

DEFAULT SPACE ALLOCATION.-      ALLOWS FOR..      102 TRANSFORMATIONS
WORKSPACE    71680 BYTES                          409 RECODE VALUES + LAG VARIABLES
TRANSPACE    10240 BYTES                         1641 IF/COMPUTE OPERATIONS

          ① 1 RUN NAME        SPIKER: ONE-WAY UNEQUAL N
             2 DATA LIST       FIXED(1)/1 TREAT 3 CREDBY 4-6

THE DATA LIST PROVIDES FOR  2 VARIABLES AND  1 RECORDS ('CARDS') PER CASE. A MAXIMUM OF   6 COLUMNS ARE USED ON A RECORD.

LIST OF THE CONSTRUCTED FORMAT STATEMENT.-
   (2X,F1.0,F3.0)

          ② 3 N OF CASES     12
             4 LIST CASES     CASES=12/VARIABLES = TREAT,CREDBY
             5 ANOVA          CREDBY BY TREAT(1,3)/
             6 STATISTICS     ALL

'ANOVA' PROBLEM REQUIRES    183 BYTES OF SPACE.

             7 READ INPUT DATA

97

② The LIST CASES card produced this data list, which should be proofread.

Note: The input data check should include: identification of the factor levels, number of subjects per cell, and the total number of subjects.

SPIKER: ONE-WAY UNEQUAL N

FILE   NONAME   (CREATION DATE = 02/02/83)

| CASE-N | TREAT | CREDBY |
|--------|-------|--------|
| ② 1 | 1. | 10. |
| 2 | 1. | 4. |
| 3 | 1. | 10. |
| 4 | 2. | 8. |
| 5 | 2. | 4. |
| 6 | 2. | 4. |
| 7 | 2. | 2. |
| 8 | 2. | 9. |
| 9 | 3. | 3. |
| 10 | 3. | 5. |
| 11 | 3. | 4. |
| 12 | 3. | 1. |

FILE   NONAME   (CREATION DATE = 02/02/83)

* * * * * * * * * * * * * *    C E L L   M E A N S    * * * * * * * * * * * * * * * * * * * * * * * *

              CREDBY
           BY TREAT

* * * * * * * * * * * * * *    * * * * * * * * * * * * * * * * * * * * * * * * * * * * * * * * * * *

TOTAL POPULATION

    5.33
  (   12)

TREAT      1          2          3

         8.00       5.40       3.25
       (   3)     (   5)     (   4)

③ Cell means may be used in a priori or post hoc analyses. The user may calculate these means by hand to further check on input accuracy and program execution.

FILE   NCNAME   (CREATION DATE = 02/02/83)

* * * * * * * * * A N A L Y S I S   O F   V A R I A N C E * * * * * * * * * * * * * * * *
* * * * * * * * *           CREDBY                    * * * * * * * * * * * * * * * * * *
* * * * * * * * *        BY TREAT  (4)                * * * * * * * * * * * * * * * * * *
* * * * * * * * * * * * * * * * * * * * * * * * * * * * * * * * * * * * * * * * * * * * *

| SOURCE OF VARIATION | SUM OF SQUARES | DF | MEAN SQUARE | F | SIGNIF OF F (6) |
|---|---|---|---|---|---|
| MAIN EFFECTS | 38.717 | 2 | 19.358 | 2.564 | 0.131 |
| TREAT (5) | 38.717 | 2 | 19.358 | 2.564 | 0.131 |
| EXPLAINED | 38.717 | 2 | 19.358 | 2.564 | 0.131 |
| RESIDUAL | 67.950 | 9 | 7.550 | | |
| TOTAL | 106.667 | 11 | 9.697 | | |

12 CASES WERE PROCESSED.
 0 CASES ( 0.0 PCT) WERE MISSING.

(4) This information would be found in an ANOVA source table (see Table 2.4, Chapter 2).

(5) This is the overall analysis of variance for the Mode of Message Presentation (TREAT) effects (see discussion, Chapter 2).

(6) This is the probability of obtaining an F ratio larger than the calculated F ratio of 2.564. Therefore, if the level of significance, alpha, was .05, one would fail to reject the overall null hypothesis that the treatment means are all equal. That is, for the F statistic to indicate that significant differences are present, this obtained 'SIGNIF. OF F' must be less than the predetermined level of significance.

SPIKER: ONE-WAY UNEQUAL N

FILE    NONAME    (CREATION DATE = 02/02/83)

\* \* \*   M U L T I P L E   C L A S S I F I C A T I O N   A N A L Y S I S   \* \* \*
        CREDBY
   EY   TREAT
\* \* \* \* \* \* \* \* \* \* \* \* \* \* \* \* \* \* \* \* \* \* \* \* \* \* \* \* \* \* \* \*

GRAND MEAN =    5.33

| VARIABLE + CATEGORY | N | UNADJUSTED DEV'N ETA (7) (9) | ADJUSTED FOR INDEPENDENTS DEV'N ETA (8) | ADJUSTED FOR INDEPENDENTS + COVARIATES DEV'N BETA (7) |
|---|---|---|---|---|
| TREAT | | | | |
| 1 | 3 | 2.67 | | 2.67 |
| 2 | 5 | 0.07 | | 0.07 |
| 3 | 4 | -2.08 | | -2.08 |
| | | 0.60 | | 0.60 |

MULTIPLE R SQUARED (10)                 0.363
MULTIPLE R                              0.602

(7) These are estimates of the treatment effects, i.e., the difference between each treatment level mean and the grand mean.

(8) These values are the same as the UNADJUSTED DEV'N because there is only one dependent variable in the study (i.e., an adjustment cannot be made for another independent variable.)

(9) 'ETA' and 'MULTIPLE R' represent the correlation between the cell means and the treatment effect vectors (see Kerlinger and Pedhazur, 1973).

(10) 'MULTIPLE R SQUARED' is the multiple correlation coefficient squared (the coefficient of determination). It represents the proportion of variation in the dependent variable accounted for by the independent variable. Here 36% of the variation in speaker credibility was accounted for by mode of presentation.

Note: Because the sample size in this study was relatively small, further investigation in this area would be dependent on the insights gained by the investigator. For a discussion of sample size see Cohen (1977).

101

CPU TIME REQUIRED..    0.35 SECONDS

(11) 8 FINISH          (SPSS GENERATED)

NORMAL END OF JOB.
(12) 8 CONTROL CARDS WERE PROCESSED.
   0 ERRORS WERE DETECTED.

(11) A FINISH card may follow the last card in an SPSS run; if one is not present (as is the case here) SPSS generates this card internally.

(12) This is the first place you might check after receiving your output. It tells you if you've had any errors and how many SPSS control cards were processed. The control card count includes the FINISH card, but does not include the data cards.

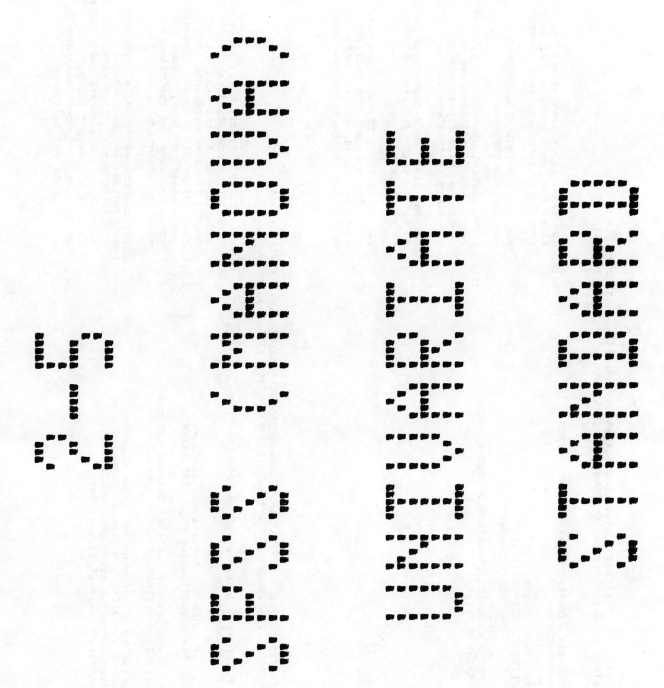

```
① 0000000000111111111122222222223333333333444444444455555555556666666666777777778
   1234567890123456789012345678901234567890123456789012345678901234567890

② RUN NAME      ONE-WAY (ANOVA) :  OVERALL TEST, UNEQUAL N
③ VARIABLE LIST TREAT,CREDBY
④ INPUT FORMAT  FREEFIELD
⑤ MANOVA        CREDBY BY TREAT(1,3)/
⑥              PRINT=CELLINFO(MEANS)
                   HOMOGENEITY(BARTLETT,COCHRAN)
                   POBS/
⑦              PLOT = CELLPLOTS,BOXPLOTS,STEMLEAF,POBS/
⑧              DESIGN = TREAT/
⑨ READ INPUT DATA
   1  10
   1   4
   1  10
   2   8
   2   4
   2   4
   2   9
   2   3
   3   3
   3   5
   3   4
   3   1
⑩ END INPUT DATA

① 0000000000111111111122222222223333333333444444444455555555556666666666777777778
   1234567890123456789012345678901234567890123456789012345678901234567890
```

Note: The SPSS input annotations provided here are of value for most problems of this type. Consult your SPSS manual for more general information.

① These are column identifiers and are not part of the program content.

Note: SPSS control words are punched between columns 1-15, and specifications are placed in columns 16-80 on the first and all succeeding cards necessary to complete the specifications.

② The RUN NAME card (optional) allows the user to specify a title for the analysis; it is limited to 64 characters.

③ The VARIABLE LIST card (required) provide SPSS with the name of the variables. The variables must be listed in the order in which they are being read by the FORMAT statement.

④ The INPUT FORMAT card (required) specifies FREEFIELD which indicates that the data must be separated by blanks and that two or more cases may occupy the same card (see also input number 2-21). The FREEFIELD format specification is not recommended by SPSS, especially in large data sets, because of the potential for errors if a value is accidentally omitted.

⑤ The control word MANOVA (required) indicates the specification subprogram to be executed. The CREDBY BY TREAT (1,3) indicates that CREDBY is the dependent variable and that TREAT is the factor name with levels 1 through 3. The slash informs SPSS that the specification is ended and that another one may follow.

⑥ The PRINT subcommand (optional) requests that the following be printed:

cell means, standard deviations, and counts, through the specification CELL INFO (MEANS);

the Bartlett-Box and Cochran' C test, through HOMOGENEITY (Bartlett, Cochran); and,

the printing of the observed value of each dependent variable, its predicted value, raw residual (observe1 minus predicted) and standardized residual through POBS.

⑦ The PLOT subcommand (optional) requests plots of the following:

the cell means versus cell variances, cell means versus cell standard deviations, and a histogram of cell means, through the specification CELLPLOTS;

boxplots, through the specification BOXPLOTS;

a stem-and-leaf display, through the specification STEMLEAF; and,

observed versus standardized residuals, cell means versus standardized residuals, case number versus standardized residuals, a normal probability plot, and a detrended normal probability for the standardized residuals, through the specification POBS. (Note: the plots requested by POBS will not be produced unless POBS also appears in the PRINT subcommand).

⑧ The DESIGN subcommand (which is optional here) specifies the between-subjects model to be analyzed.

⑨ The READ INPUT DATA card (required) signals that the data begins with the next card.

⑩ The END INPUT DATA card (required) signals the end of the data. This card is required here because the number of cases was not specified.

Note: SPSS output pages 2-6 and 8-12 are exactly the same as those found in SPSS (MANOVA) (2-17). Therefore, these pages were not included as part of this output.

105

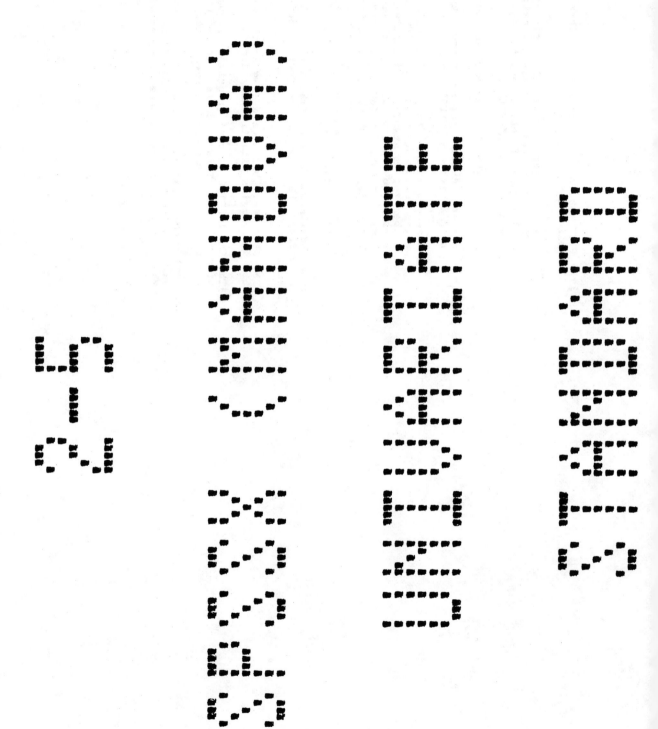

```
① 0000000000111111111122222222223333333333444444444455555555556666666666777777777 8
   1234567890123456789012345678901234567890123456789012345678901234567890123456789 0

② TITLE     ONE-WAY (ANOVA):  OVERALL TEST, UNEQUAL N
③ DATA LIST LIST/ TREAT,CREDBY
   MANOVA    CREDBY BY TREAT(1,3)/
             PRINT=CELLINFO(MEANS)
                   HOMOGENEITY(BARTLETT,COCHRAN)
                   POBS/
             PLOT = CELLPLOTS,BOXPLOTS,STEMLEAF,POBS/
             DESIGN = TREAT/
④ BEGIN DATA
   1 10
   1 4
   1 10
   2 8
   2 4
   2 4
   2 2
   2 9
   3 3
   3 5
   3 4
   3 1
⑤ END DATA
① 0000000000111111111122222222223333333333444444444455555555556666666666777777777 8
   1234567890123456789012345678901234567890123456789012345678901234567890123456789 0
```

Note: The SPSSX input annotations provided here are of value for most problems of this type. Consult your SPSSX manual for more general information.

① These are column identifiers and are not part of the program content.

Note: SPSSX command keywords begin in column 1: specifications, separated by at least one blank, follow the command keywords. Specifications which continue beyond the first card must be indented by at least one column, and may continue for as many cards as is necessary.

② The TITLE card (optional) allows the user to specify a title for the analysis; it is limited to 60 characters.

③ The DATA LIST card (required) provides SPSSX with the names of the variables. The variables must be listed in the order in which they are being read by the format specification. Here the LIST format specification was used. This input specification indicates that the scores for each case will be found on one card (record). The LIST input specification requires that the scores be separated by at least one blank or comma.

④ The BEGIN DATA card (required) signals that the data begins with the next card.

⑤ The END DATA card (required) signals the end of the data.

ORDER FROM MCGRAW-HILL:    SPSS, 2ND ED. (PRINCIPAL TEXT)         SPSS STATISTICAL ALGORITHMS
                           SPSS UPDATE 7-9 (USE W/SPSS,2ND FOR REL. 7, 8, 9)    KEYWORDS: THE SPSS INC. NEWSLETTER
                           SPSS POCKET GUIDE, RELEASE 9
                           SPSS INTRODUCTORY GUIDE:  BASIC STATISTICS AND OPERATIONS
                           SPSS PRIMER (BRIEF INTRO TO SPSS)

                           CURRENT DOCUMENTATION FOR THE SPSS BATCH SYSTEM
                                                    ORDER FROM SPSS INC.:

DEFAULT SPACE ALLOCATION.-     ALLOWS FOR.-    102 TRANSFORMATIONS
WORKSPACE      71680 BYTES                     409 RECODE VALUES + LAG VARIABLES
TRANSPACE      10240 BYTES                    1641 IF/COMPUTE OPERATIONS

    1 RUN NAME          ONE-WAY (ANOVA):  OVERALL TEST, UNEQUAL N
    2 VARIABLE LIST     TREAT,CREDBY
    3 INPUT FORMAT      FREEFIELD
    4 MANOVA            CREDBY BY TREAT(1,3)/
    5                   PRINT=CELLINFO(MEANS)
    6                         HOMOGENEITY(BARTLETT,COCHRAN)
    7                         POBS/
    8                   PLOT = CELLPLOTS,BOXPLOTS,STEMLEAF,POBS/
    9                   DESIGN = TREAT/
   10 READ INPUT DATA

AFTER READING    12 CASES FROM SUBFILE NONAME  ,   END OF DATA WAS ENCOUNTERED ON LOGICAL UNIT # 5

108

* * * * * * * * * * * * * * * * * *A N A L Y S I S   O F   V A R I A N C E* * * * * * * * * * * * * * * * * * *

TESTS OF SIGNIFICANCE FOR CREDBY USING SEQUENTIAL SUMS OF SQUARES  (1)(2)

| SOURCE OF VARIATION | SUM OF SQUARES | DF | MEAN SQUARE | F | SIG. OF F |
|---|---|---|---|---|---|
| (4) WITHIN CELLS | 67.95000 | 9 | 7.55000 | | |
| CONSTANT | 341.33333 | 1 | 341.33333 | 45.20971 | .000 |
| TREAT | 38.71667 | 2 | 19.35833 | 2.56402 | .131 (3) |

ESTIMATES FOR CREDBY

CONSTANT

| PARAMETER | COEFF. (5) | STD. ERR. | T-VALUE (6) | SIG. OF T (7) | LOWER .95 CL | UPPER .95 CL (8) |
|---|---|---|---|---|---|---|
| 1 | 5.5500000000 | .81064 | 6.84648 | .000 | 3.71622 | 7.38378 |

TREAT

| PARAMETER | COEFF. | STD. ERR. | T-VALUE | SIG. OF T | LOWER .95 CL | UPPER .95 CL |
|---|---|---|---|---|---|---|
| 2 | 2.4500000000 | 1.22312 | 2.00308 | .076 | -.31688 | 5.21688 |
| 3 | -.1500000000 | 1.07725 | -.13924 | .892 | -2.58690 | 2.28690 |

(1) This information would be found in an ANOVA source table (see Table 2.4, Chapter 2).

(2) This is the overall analysis of variance for the Mode of Message Presentation (TREAT) effects (see discussion, Chapter 2).

(3) This is the probability of obtaining an F ratio larger than the calculated F ratio of 2.56. Therefore, if the level of significance, alpha, was .05, one would fail to reject the overall null hypothesis that the treatment means are all equal to each other. That is, for the F statistic to indicate that significant differences are present, the obtained 'SIG. OF F' must be less than the predetermined level of significance.

(4) This is the test of the null hypothesis that the grand mean is equal to zero. This test is usually significant and not of much interest, because the grand mean is generally larger than zero.

(5) The COEFF. are linear contrasts (here the default is deviation, see SPSS Update 7-9, 1981, p. 72). The first parameter estimated is the unweighted grand mean (5.55); the second parameter estimated is the contrast 2/3(8.0) - 1/3(5.4) - 1/3(3.25) = 2.45; the third parameter estimated is the contrast -1/3(8.0) + 2/3(5.4) - 1/3(3.25) = -.15. Note that deviation contrasts yield the same results as subtracting the unweighted grand mean from each cell mean, e.g., for the second contrast we have that 8.0 - 5.55 = 2.45.

(6) The contrast COEFF when divided by its STD. ERR. (standard error) yields the T-VALUE (t-statistic).

(7) Also reported for each contrast is the SIG. OF T (significance of t) and the upper and lower .95 confidence limits on the contrast.

(8) The 95 percent confidence intervals for the contrasts of interest both contain zero. This further reflects the fact that the contrasts do not differ significantly from zero.

109

```
0000000001111111111222222222233333333334444444444555555555566666666667777777778
1234567890123456789012345678901234567890123456789012345678901234567890123456789 0

RUN NAME      ONE-WAY (ANOVA):  SIMPLE CONTRASTS, EQUAL N
VARIABLE LIST TREAT,CREDBY
INPUT FORMAT  FREEFIELD
MANOVA        CREDBY BY TREAT(1,3)/
              PRINT=CELLINFO(MEANS)
                    HOMOGENEITY(BARTLETT,COCHRAN)
                    POBS/
              PLOT = CELLPLOTS,BOXPLOTS,STEMLEAF,POBS/
①             DESIGN = TREAT/
              METHOD = SSTYPE(UNIQUE)/
              PARTITION(TREAT)/
②             CONTRAST (TREAT) = SIMPLE/
              DESIGN = TREAT(1),TREAT(2)/

READ INPUT DATA
  1  10
  1  10
  1  10
  1   4
  1  10
  2   8
  2   4
  2   4
  2   2
  2   9
  3   3
  3  10
  3   5
  3   4
  3   1
END INPUT DATA

0000000001111111111222222222233333333334444444444555555555566666666667777777778
1234567890123456789012345678901234567890123456789012345678901234567890123456789 0
```

Note: This is an 'instruction' program.  It illustrates ANOVA results with simple contrasts and equal n's.

Note: Most of these input cards have been annotated in SPSS(MANOVA) (2-1), but with unequal n's.

① The DESIGN subcommand set at TREAT requests SPSS to print an overall ANOVA.

② The CONTRAST (TREAT) subcommand specifies the use of SIMPLE contrasts.

Note: The output for this program is similar to that found for the previous runs of the SPSS subprogram MANOVA, and was eliminated here to save space. The only page of output presented focuses on the simple contrasts.

Note: The annotations for this page can be found in SPSS(MANOVA) (2-1).

111

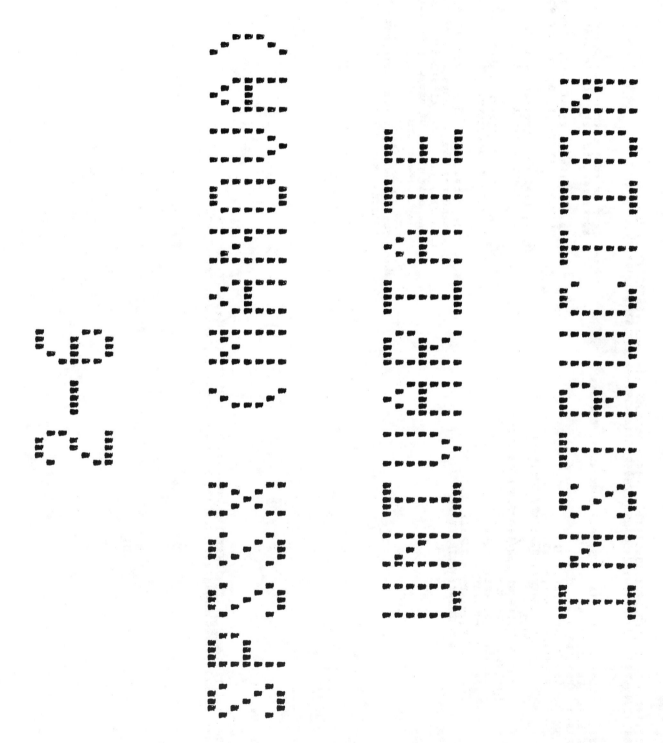

```
① 00000000011111111112222222222333333333344444444445555555555666666666677777777778
   12345678901234567890123456789012345678901234567890123456789012345678901234567890

② TITLE     ONE-WAY (ANOVA):  SIMPLE CONTRASTS, EQUAL N
③ DATA LIST LIST/ TREAT,CREDBY
   MANOVA    CREDBY BY TREAT(1,3)/
             PRINT=CELLINFO(MEANS)
                   POBS/
             PLOT = CELLPLOTS,BOXPLOTS,STEMLEAF,POBS/
             DESIGN = TREAT/
             METHOD = SSTYPE(UNIQUE)/
             PARTITION(TREAT)/
             CONTRAST(TREAT) = SIMPLE/
             DESIGN = TREAT(1),TREAT(2)/
④ BEGIN DATA
   1 10
   1  4
   1 10
   1  4
   1 10
   2  8
   2  4
   2  4
   2  2
   2  9
   3  3
   3  5
   3  5
   3  4
   3  1
⑤ END DATA

① 00000000011111111112222222222333333333344444444445555555555666666666677777777778
   12345678901234567890123456789012345678901234567890123456789012345678901234567890
```

Note: The SPSSX input annotations provided here are of value for most problems of this type. Consult your SPSSX manual for more general information.

① These are column identifiers and are not part of the program content.

Note: SPSSX command keywords begin in column 1; specifications, separated by at least one blank, follow the command keywords. Specifications which continue beyond the first card must be indented by at least one column, and may continue for as many cards as is necessary.

② The TITLE card (optional) allows the user to specify a title for the analysis; it is limited to 60 characters.

③ The DATA LIST card (required) provides SPSSX with the names of the variables. The variables must be listed in the order in which they are being read by the format specification. Here the LIST format specification was used. This input specification indicates that the scores for each case will be found on one card (record). The LIST input specification requires that the scores be separated by at least one blank or comma.

④ The BEGIN DATA card (required) signals that the data begins with the next card.

⑤ The END DATA card (required) signals the end of the data.

113

\* \* \* \* \* \* \* \* \* \* \* \* \* \* \* \* \* \* A N A L Y S I S   O F   V A R I A N C E \* \* \* \* \* \* \* \* \* \* \* \* \* \* \* \* \* \* \* \*

TESTS OF SIGNIFICANCE FOR CREDBY USING UNIQUE SUMS OF SQUARES

| SOURCE OF VARIATION | SUM OF SQUARES | DF | MEAN SQUARE | F | SIG. OF F |
|---|---|---|---|---|---|
| WITHIN CELLS | 89.60000 | 12 | 7.46667 | | |
| CONSTANT | 459.26667 | 1 | 459.26667 | 61.50893 | .000 |
| TREAT(1) | 40.00000 | 1 | 40.00000 | 5.35714 | .039 |
| TREAT(2) | 8.10000 | 1 | 8.10000 | 1.08482 | .318 |

ESTIMATES FOR CREDBY

CONSTANT

| PARAMETER | COEFF. | STD. ERR. | T-VALUE | | SIG. OF T | LOWER 95% CL | UPPER 95% CL |
|---|---|---|---|---|---|---|---|
| 1 | 5.5333333333 | .70553 | 7.84276 | (1) | .000 | 3.99611 | 7.07056 |

TREAT(1)

| PARAMETER | COEFF. | STD. ERR. | T-VALUE | | SIG. OF T | LOWER 95% CL | UPPER 95% CL |
|---|---|---|---|---|---|---|---|
| 2 | 4.0000000000 | 1.72820 | 2.31455 | (2) | .039 | .23458 | 7.76542 |

TREAT(2)

| PARAMETER | COEFF. | STD. ERR. | T-VALUE | | SIG. OF T | LOWER 95% CL | UPPER 95% CL |
|---|---|---|---|---|---|---|---|
| 3 | 1.8000000000 | 1.72820 | 1.04155 | (3) | .318 | -1.96542 | 5.56542 |

(1) Simple contrasts may be used to perform Dunnett's t test, but the probability values reported by the program for each contrast are not correct for this test. Instead, one can compare the t value given here with tabled values (e.g. Winer, 1971, pp. 373-374).

(2) The tabled Dunnett's t's at alpha = .05 are 2.18 (nondirectional H(A)) and 1.78 (directional H(A)). For either of the preceding H(A)'s we have a significant result, i.e., the oral/visual presentation is more credible than the oral presentation alone.

(3) The tabled Dunnett's t's at alpha= .05 are 2.18 (non directional H(A)) and 1.78 (directional H(A)) for either of these H(A)'s we have no significant result, i.e., there is no difference in

114

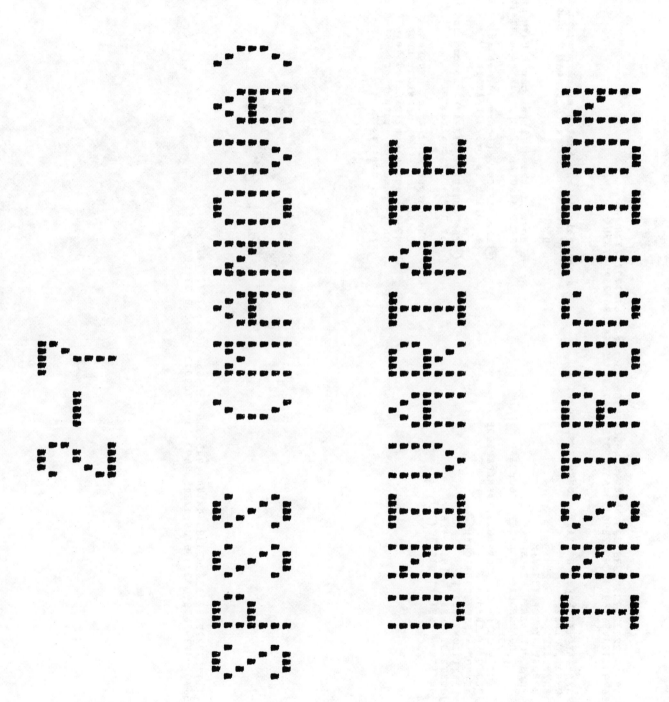

```
00000000011111111112222222222333333333344444444445555555555666666666677777777778
12345678901234567890123456789012345678901234567890123456789012345678901234567890

RUN NAME         ONE-WAY (ANOVA):    REPEATED CONTRASTS, EQUAL N
VARIABLE LIST    TREAT,CREDBY
INPUT FORMAT     FREEFIELD
MANOVA           CREDBY BY TREAT(1,3)/
                 PRINT=CELLINFO(MEANS)
                     HOMOGENEITY(BARTLETT,COCHRAN)
                     POBS/
                 PLOT = CELLPLOTS,BOXPLOTS,STEMLEAF,POBS/
①                DESIGN = TREAT/
                 METHOD = SSTYPE(UNIQUE)/
                 PARTITION(TREAT)/
②                CONTRAST(TREAT) = REPEATED/
                 DESIGN = TREAT(1),TREAT(2)/

READ INPUT DATA
1 10
1 4
1 10
1 4
1 10
2 8
2 4
2 2
2 9
2 3
3 5
3 5
3 4
3 1

END INPUT DATA

00000000011111111112222222222333333333344444444445555555555666666666677777777778
12345678901234567890123456789012345678901234567890123456789012345678901234567890
```

Note: This is an 'instruction' program. It illustrates ANOVA results with repeated contrasts and equal n's.

Note: Most of these input cards have been annotated in SPSS (MANOVA) (2-1), but with unequal n's.

① The DESIGN subcommand set at TREAT requests SPSS to print an overall ANOVA.

② The CONTRAST (TREAT) subcommand specifies the use of REPEATED contrasts.

Note: The output for this program is similar to that found for the previous runs of SPSS (MANOVA) (2-1), and was eliminated here to save space. The only page of output presented focuses on the repeated contrasts.

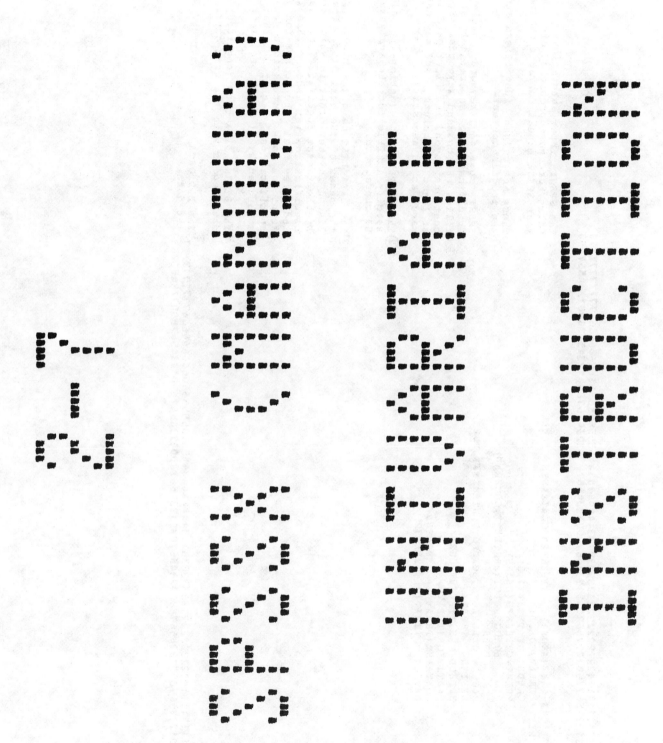

```
0000000001111111111222222222233333333334444444444555555555566666666667777777777 8
1234567890123456789012345678901234567890123456789012345678901234567890123456789 0
```

① ② TITLE    ONE-WAY (ANOVA):    REPEATED CONTRASTS, EQUAL N
③ DATA LIST LIST/ TREAT,CREDBY
MANOVA       CREDBY BY TREAT(1,3)/
             PRINT=CELLINFO(MEANS)
                   HOMOGENEITY(BARTLETT,COCHRAN)
                   POBS/
             PLOT = CELLPLOTS,BOXPLOTS,STEMLEAF,POBS/
             DESIGN = TREAT/
             METHOD = SSTYPE(UNIQUE)/
             PARTITION(TREAT)/
             CONTRAST(TREAT) = REPEATED/
             DESIGN = TREAT(1),TREAT(2)/
④ BEGIN DATA
   1 10
   1  4
   1 10
   1  4
   1 10
   2  8
   2  4
   2  4
   2  2
   2  9
   3  3
   3  5
   3  5
   3  5
   3  4
   3  1
⑤ END DATA

```
0000000001111111111222222222233333333334444444444555555555566666666667777777777 8
1234567890123456789012345678901234567890123456789012345678901234567890123456789 0
```

Note:  The SPSSX   input annotations provided here  are of
       value for  most problems of this type.  Consult
       your SPSSX manual for more general information.

① These are column  identifiers and are not  part of
   the program content.

Note:  SPSSX command   keywords begin  in  column  1;
       specifications,  separated by at  least one blank,
       follow the command keywords.  Specifications which
       continue beyond the first card must be indented by
       at least one column,  and may continue for as many
       cards as is necessary.

② The  TITLE card   (optional)   allows  the user  to
   specify a title for the analysis; it is limited to
   60 characters.

③ The DATA LIST card (required)   provides SPSSX with
   the names of the variables.  The variables must be
   listed in the  order in which they are being read
   by the format specification.  Here the LIST format
   specification was used.  This input specification
   indicates that  the scores for  each case will be
   found  on one  card (record).    The LIST input
   specification   requires that   the  scores  be
   separated by at least one blank or comma.

④ The BEGIN DATA card (required)  signals  that the
   data begins with the next card.

⑤ The END DATA  card (required)  signals the  end of
   the data.

118

* * * * * * * * * * * * * * * * * * * * * * A N A L Y S I S   O F   V A R I A N C E * * * * * * * * * * * * * * * * * * * * * *

TESTS OF SIGNIFICANCE FOR CREDBY USING UNIQUE SUMS OF SQUARES

| SOURCE OF VARIATION | SUM OF SQUARES | DF | MEAN SQUARE | F | SIG. OF F |
|---|---|---|---|---|---|
| WITHIN CELLS | 89.60000 | 12 | 7.46667 | | |
| CONSTANT | 459.26667 | 1 | 459.26667 | 61.50893 | 0.0 |
| TREAT(1) ① | 12.10000 | 1 | 12.10000 | 1.62054 | .227 |
| TREAT(2) | 8.10000 | 1 | 8.10000 | 1.08482 | .318 |

ESTIMATES FOR CREDBY

CONSTANT

| PARAMETER | COEFF. | STD. ERR. | T-VALUE | SIG. OF T | LOWER .95 CL | UPPER .95 CL |
|---|---|---|---|---|---|---|
| 1 | 16.6000000000 | 2.11660 | 7.84276 | .000 | 11.98832 | 21.21168 |

TREAT(1)

| PARAMETER | COEFF. | STD. ERR. | T-VALUE | SIG. OF T | LOWER .95 CL | UPPER .95 CL |
|---|---|---|---|---|---|---|
| 2 | 2.2000000000 | 1.72820 | 1.27300 | ② .227 | -1.56542 | 5.96542 |

TREAT(2)

| PARAMETER | COEFF. | STD. ERR. | T-VALUE | SIG. OF T | LOWER .95 CL | UPPER .95 CL |
|---|---|---|---|---|---|---|
| 3 | 1.8000000000 | 1.72820 | 1.04155 | ② .318 | -1.96542 | 5.56542 |

Note: The annotations for this page can be found in SPSS (MANOVA) (2-1).

① Repeated contrasts one frequently used in repeated measures profile analyses.

② The first contrast between the first and second cell means is not significant (p = .227 > .05), and the second contrast between the second and third cell means is also not significant (p = .318 > .05).

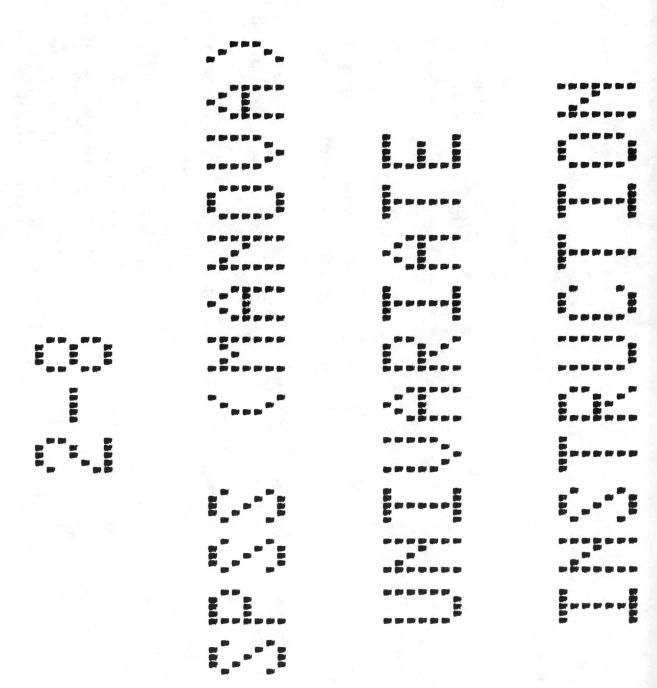

```
0000000000111111111122222222223333333333444444444455555555556666666666777777777 8
1234567890123456789012345678901234567890123456789012345678901234567890123456789 0
```

```
RUN NAME        ONE-WAY (ANOVA):  SPECIAL CONTRASTS, EQUAL N
VARIABLE LIST   TREAT,CREDBY
INPUT FORMAT    FREEFIELD
MANOVA          CREDBY BY TREAT(1,3)/
                PRINT=CELLINFC(MEANS)
                HOMOGENEITY(BARTLETT,COCHRAN)
                POBS/
                PLOT = CELLPLOTS,BOXPLOTS,STEMLEAF,POBS/
①DESIGN = TREAT/
                METHOD = SSTYPE(UNIQUE)/
                PARTITION(TREAT)/
②CONTRAST(TREAT) = SPECIAL(1 1 2 -1 -1 0 1 -1)/
                DESIGN = TREAT(1),TREAT(2)/
READ INPUT DATA
1 10
1  4
1 10
1  4
1 10
2  8
2  4
2  2
2  9
3  3
3  5
3  5
3  4
3  1
END INPUT DATA
```

```
0000000000111111111122222222223333333333444444444455555555556666666666777777777 8
1234567890123456789012345678901234567890123456789012345678901234567890123456789 0
```

Note: This is an 'instruction' program.  It illustrates ANOVA results with special contrasts and equal n's.

Note: Most of these input cards have been annotated in SPSS(MANOVA) (2-1), but with unequal n's.

① The DESIGN subcommand set at TREAT requests SPSS to print an overall ANOVA.

② The CONTRAST (TREAT) subcommand specifies the use of SPECIAL contrasts.  The SPECIAL specification requires the user to place contrast coefficients in parentheses.  Here the '1 1 1' is the grand mean contrast;  '2 -1 -1' contrasts the first treatment with the average of the other two;  and, '0 1 -1' contrasts the second and third treatments.  (Note: there will usually be as many contrasts as cells with data.)

121

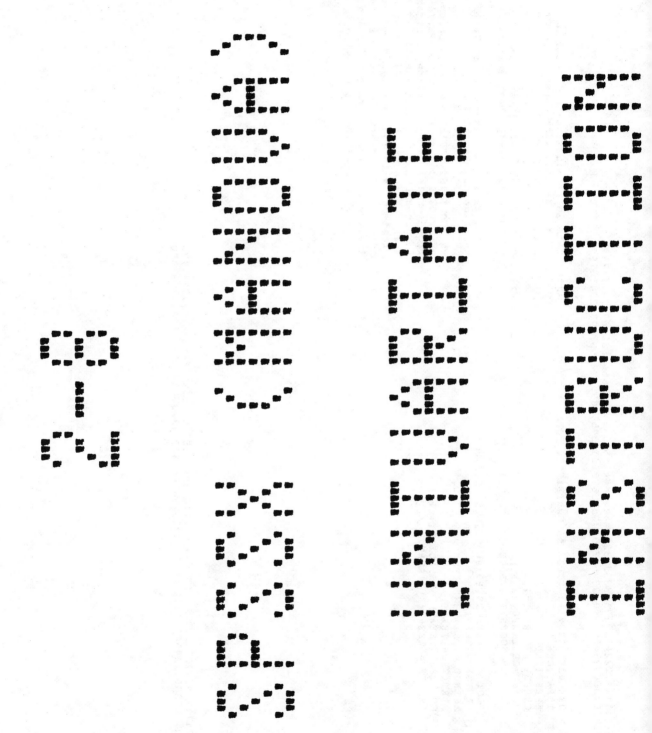

Note: The SPSSX input annotations provided here are of value for most problems of this type. Consult your SPSSX manual for more general information.

① These are column identifiers and are not part of the program content.

Note: SPSSX command keywords begin in column 1; specifications, separated by at least one blank, follow the command keywords. Specifications which continue beyond the first card must be indented by at least one column, and may continue for as many cards as is necessary.

② The TITLE card (optional) allows the user to specify a title for the analysis; it is limited to 60 characters.

③ The DATA LIST card (required) provides SPSSX with the names of the variables. The variables must be listed in the order in which they are being read by the format specification. Here the LIST format specification was used. This input specification indicates that the scores for each case will be found on one card (record). The LIST input specification requires that the scores be separated by at least one blank or comma.

④ The BEGIN DATA card (required) signals that the data begins with the next card.

⑤ The END DATA card (required) signals the end of the data.

```
②TITLE   ONE-WAY (ANOVA):   SPECIAL CONTRASTS,  EQUAL N
③DATA LIST LIST/ TREAT,CREDBY
 MANOVA       CREDBY BY TREAT(1,3)/
              PRINT=CELLINFO(MEANS)
              HOMOGENEITY(BARTLETT,COCHRAN)
              POBS/
           PLOT = CELLPLOTS,BOXPLOTS,STEMLEAF,POBS/
           DESIGN = TREAT/
           METHOD = SSTYPE(UNIQUE)/
           PARTITION(TREAT)/
           CONTRAST(TREAT) = SPECIAL(1 1 1 2 -1 -1 0 1 -1)/
           DESIGN = TREAT(1),TREAT(2)/
④BEGIN DATA
  1 10
  1 4
  1 10
  1 4
  1 10
  2 8
  2 4
  2 4
  2 2
  2 9
  2 3
  3 3
  3 5
  3 5
  3 4
  3 1
⑤END DATA
```

123

ONE-WAY (ANOVA): SPECIAL CONTRASTS, EQUAL N          02/03/83          PAGE  12

* * * * * * * * * * * * * * * * A N A L Y S I S   O F   V A R I A N C E * * * * * * * * * * * * * * * * * * *

TESTS OF SIGNIFICANCE FOR CREDBY USING UNIQUE SUMS OF SQUARES

| SOURCE OF VARIATION | SUM OF SQUARES | DF | MEAN SQUARE | F | SIG. OF F |
|---|---|---|---|---|---|
| WITHIN CELLS | 89.60000 | 12 | 7.46667 | | |
| CONSTANT | 459.26667 | 1 | 459.26667 | 61.50893 | 0-0 |
| TREAT(1) | 32.03333 | 1 | 32.03333 | 4.29018 | .061 |
| TREAT(2) | 8.10000 | 1 | 8.10000 | 1.08482 | .318 |

ESTIMATES FOR CREDBY

CONSTANT

| PARAMETER | COEFF. | STD. ERR. | T-VALUE | SIG. OF T | LOWER .95 CL | UPPER .95 CL |
|---|---|---|---|---|---|---|
| 1 | 5.5333333333 | .70553 | 7.84276 | .000 | 3.99611 | 7.07056 |

TREAT(1)

| PARAMETER | COEFF. | STD. ERR. | T-VALUE | SIG. OF T | LOWER .95 CL | UPPER .95 CL |
|---|---|---|---|---|---|---|
| 2 | 6.2000000000 | 2.99333 | 2.07127 | (1) .061 | -.32190 | 12.72190 |

TREAT(2)

| PARAMETER | COEFF. | STD. ERR. | T-VALUE | SIG. OF T | LOWER .95 CL | UPPER .95 CL |
|---|---|---|---|---|---|---|
| 3 | 1.8000000000 | 1.72820 | 1.04155 | (1) .318 | -1.96542 | 5.56542 |

Note: The output for this program is similar to that found for the previous runs of the SPSS subprogram MANOVA, and was eliminated here to save space. The only page of output presented focuses on the special contrasts.

Note: The annotations for this page can be found in SPSS(MANOVA) (2-1).

(1) The reader may have noted that the special contrasts that we used were the same as the Helmert contrasts used in this chapter. As with the unequal n case, we find no significant differences (alpha=.05) with these contrasts.

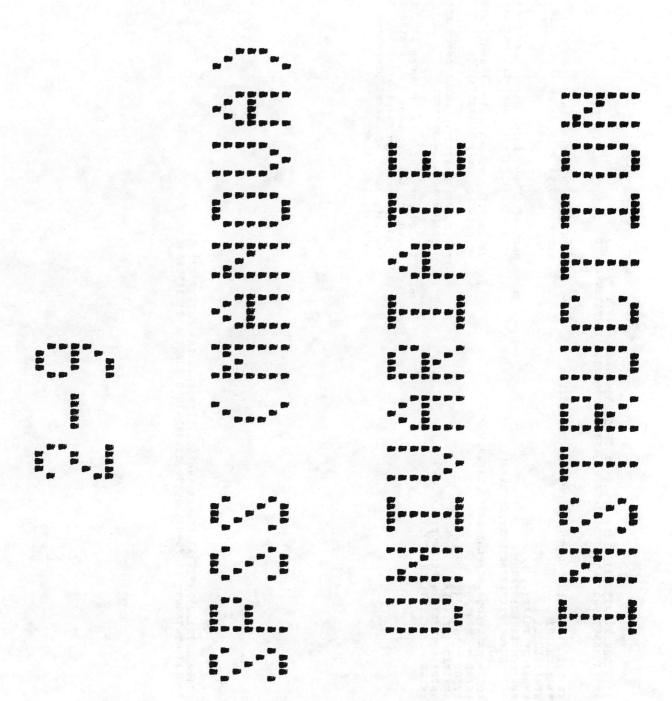

```
0000000001111111111222222222233333333334444444444555555555566666666667777777778
1234567890123456789012345678901234567890123456789012345678901234567890123456789 0

RUN NAME        ONE-WAY (ANOVA):  POLYNOMIAL CONTRASTS, EQUAL N
VARIABLE LIST   TREAT,CREDBY
INPUT FORMAT    FREEFIELD
MANOVA          CREDBY BY TREAT(1,3)/
                PRINT=CELLINFO(MEANS)
                  HOMOGENEITY(BARTLETT,COCHRAN)
                  POBS/
                PLOT = CELLPLOTS,BOXPLOTS,STEMLEAF,POBS/
①               DESIGN = TREAT/
                METHOD = SSTYPE(UNIQUE)/
                PARTITION(TREAT)/
②               CONTRAST(TREAT) = PCLYNOMIAL/
                DESIGN = TREAT(1),TREAT(2)/
READ INPUT DATA
   1 10
   1  4
   1 10
   1  4
   1 10
   2  8
   2  4
   2  4
   2  2
   2  9
   3  3
   3  5
   3  5
   3  4
   3  1
END INPUT DATA

0000000001111111111222222222233333333334444444444555555555566666666667777777778
1234567890123456789012345678901234567890123456789012345678901234567890123456789 0
```

Note: This is an 'instruction' program.  It illustrates ANOVA results with polynomial contrasts and equal n's.

Note: Most of these input cards have been annotated in SPSS(MANOVA) (2-1), but with unequal n's.

① The DESIGN subcommand set at TREAT requests SPSS to print an overall ANOVA.

② The CONTRAST (TREAT) subcommand specifies the use of PCLYNOMIAL contrasts.

Note: The output for this program is similar to that found for the previous runs of the SPSS subprogram MANOVA, and was eliminated here to save space. The only page of output presented focuses on the polynomial contrasts.

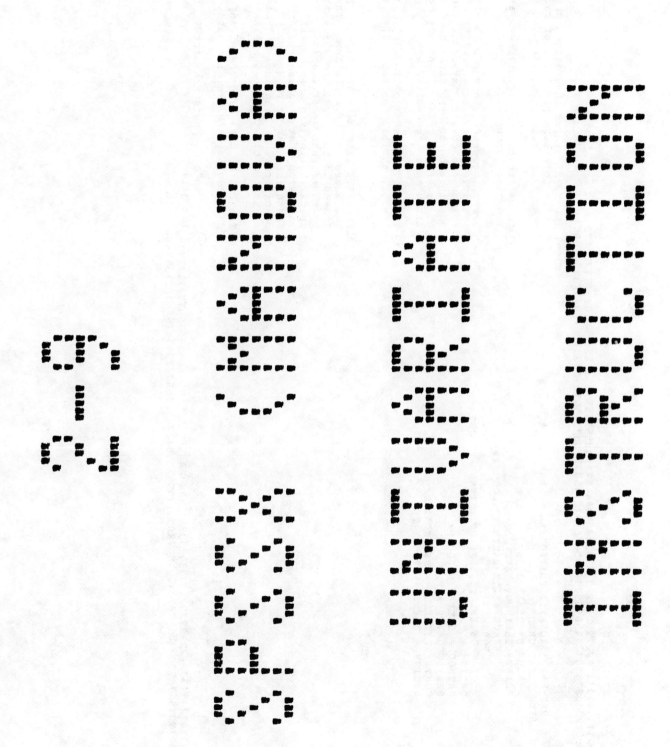

Note: The SPSSX input annotations provided here are of value for most problems of this type. Consult your SPSSX manual for more general information.

① These are column identifiers and are not part of the program content.

Note: SPSSX command keywords begin in column 1; specifications, separated by at least one blank, follow the command keywords. Specifications which continue beyond the first card must be indented by at least one column, and may continue for as many cards as is necessary.

```
② TITLE    ONE-WAY (ANOVA):  POLYNOMIAL CONTRASTS, EQUAL N
③ DATA LIST LIST/ TREAT,CREDBY
MANOVA     CREDBY BY TREAT(1,3)/
           PRINT=CELLINFO(MEANS)
                POBS/
           PLOT = CELLPLOTS,BOXPLOTS,STEMLEAF,POBS/
           DESIGN = TREAT/
           METHOD = SSTYPE(UNIQUE)/
           PARTITION(TREAT)/
           CONTRAST(TREAT) = PCLYNOMIAL/
           DESIGN = TREAT(1),TREAT(2)/
```

② The TITLE card (optional) allows the user to specify a title for the analysis; it is limited to 60 characters.

③ The DATA LIST card (required) provides SPSSX with the names of the variables. The variables must be listed in the order in which they are being read by the format specification. Here the LIST format specification was used. This input specification indicates that the scores for each case will be found on one card (record). The LIST input specification requires that the scores be separated by at least one blank or comma.

```
④ BEGIN DATA
   1 10
   1  4
   1 10
   1  4
   1 10
   2  8
   2  4
   2  2
   2  9
   2  3
   3  3
   3  5
   3  5
   3  4
   3  1
⑤ END DATA
```

④ The BEGIN DATA card (required) signals that the data begins with the next card.

⑤ The END DATA card (required) signals the end of the data.

ONE-WAY (ANOVA): POLYNOMIAL CONTRASTS, EQUAL N        02/28/83        PAGE  12

* * * * * * * * * * * * * * * A N A L Y S I S   O F   V A R I A N C E * * * * * * * * * * * * * * * *

TESTS OF SIGNIFICANCE FOR CREDBY USING UNIQUE SUMS OF SQUARES

| SOURCE OF VARIATION | SUM OF SQUARES | DF | MEAN SQUARE | F | SIG. OF F |
|---|---|---|---|---|---|
| WITHIN CELLS | 89.60000 | 12 | 7.46667 | | |
| CONSTANT | 459.26667 | 1 | 459.26667 | 61.50893 | 0.0 |
| TREAT(1) | 40.00000 | 1 | 40.00000 | 5.35714 | .039 |
| TREAT(2) | .13333 | 1 | .13333 | .01786 | .896 |

ESTIMATES FOR CREDBY

CONSTANT

| PARAMETER | COEFF. | STD. ERR. | T-VALUE | SIG. OF T | LOWER .95 CL | UPPER .95 CL |
|---|---|---|---|---|---|---|
| 1 | 5.5333333333 | .70553 | 7.84276 | .000 | 3.99611 | 7.07056 |

TREAT(1) (1)

| PARAMETER | COEFF. | STD. ERR. | T-VALUE | SIG. OF T | LOWER .95 CL | UPPER .95 CL |
|---|---|---|---|---|---|---|
| 2 | -2.8284271247 | 1.22202 | -2.31455 | (2) .039 | -5.49098 | -.16587 |

TREAT(2) (1)

| PARAMETER | COEFF. | STD. ERR. | T-VALUE | SIG. OF T | LOWER .95 CL | UPPER .95 CL |
|---|---|---|---|---|---|---|
| 3 | .1632993162 | 1.22202 | .13363 | (2) .896 | -2.49925 | 2.82585 |

(1) Polynomial contrasts allow one to test for trends (e.g. linear, quadratic) across the cell means.

(2) At alpha=.05 there is a significant linear trend, the cell means are: 7.6, 5.4, 3.6, across the cells, and there is no quadratic trend (p<.895).

129

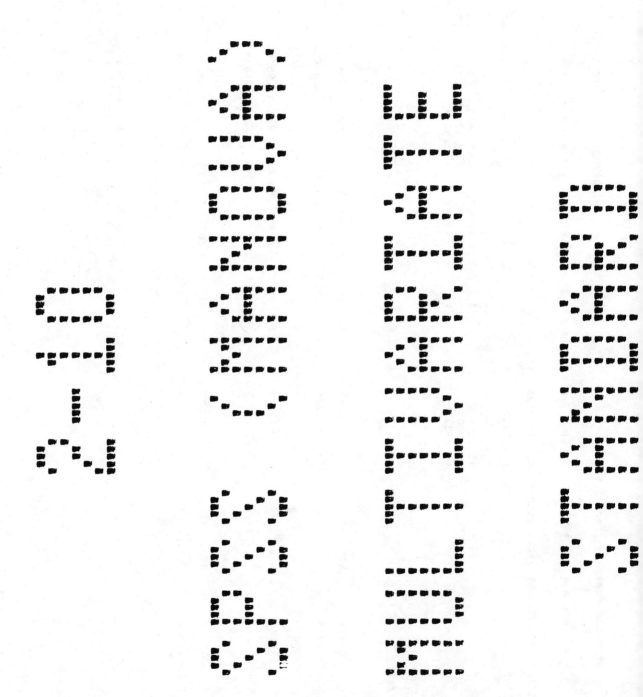

```
000000000111111111122222222223333333333444444444455555555556666666666777777777 8
123456789012345678901234567890123456789012345678901234567890123456789012345678 90
```

Note: The SPSS input annotations provided here are of value for most problems of this type. Consult your SPSS manual for more general information.

① These are column identifiers and are not part of the program content.

Note: SPSS control words are punched between columns 1-15, and specifications are placed in columns 16-80 on the first and all succeeding cards necessary to complete the specifications.

② The TASK NAME card (optional) allows the user to specify a title for different tasks within a given run; it is limited to 64 characters.

③ The VARIABLE LIST card (required) provides SPSS with the names of the variables. The variables must be listed in the order in which they are being read by the FORMAT statement.

④ The INPUT FORMAT card (required) specifies FREEFIELD which indicates that the data must be separated by blanks and that two or more cases may occupy the same card (see also input number 2-17). The FREEFIELD format specification is not recommended by SPSS, especially in large data sets, because of the potential for errors if a value is accidentally omitted.

⑤ The control word MANOVA (required) indicates the subprogram to be executed. The specification CREDBY BY TREAT (1,3) indicates CREDBY is the dependent variable and TREAT is the factor name with levels 1 through 3. The slash informs SPSS that the specification is ended and that another one may follow.

```
RUN NAME        ONE-WAY (MANOVA)
TASK NAME       PLANNED COMPARISONS, UNEQUAL N
VARIABLE LIST   TREAT,CREDBY,EFFECT
INPUT FORMAT    FREEFIELD
MANOVA          CREDBY,EFFECT BY TREAT(1,3)/
                PRINT=CELLINFO(MEANS,SSCP,COV,COR)
                HOMOGENEITY(BARTLETT,COCHRAN,BOXM)
                SIGNIF(HYPOTH,STEPDOWN)
                DISCRIM(RAW,STAN,ESTIM,COR,ROTATE(VARIMAX),ALPHA(1-0))
                ERROR(SSCP,COV,CCR,STDV)
                POBS/
                PLOT = CELLPLOTS,FOXPLOTS,STEMLEAF,POBS/
                METHOD = SSTYPE(UNIQUE)/
                PARTITION(TREAT)/
                CONTRAST(TREAT) = HELMERT/
                DESIGN = TREAT(1),TREAT(2)/
READ INPUT DATA
1 10 16
1 10 10
1 10 18
2  8 12
2  4  8
2  4  6
2  2  6
2  9 14
3  3 10
3  5 16
3  4 14
3  1  9
END INPUT DATA
TASK NAME       OVERALL ANALYSIS, UNEQUAL N
MANOVA          CREDBY,EFFECT BY TREAT(1,3)/
                PRINT=SIGNIF(HYPOTH,STEPDOWN)
                DISCRIM(RAW,STAN,ESTIM,COR,ROTATE(VARIMAX) ALPHA(1-0))/
                DESIGN=TREAT/
```

```
000000000111111111122222222223333333333444444444455555555556666666666777777777 8
123456789012345678901234567890123456789012345678901234567890123456789012345678 90
```

131

⑥ The PRINT subcommand (optional) requests that the following be printed:

⑦ cell means, standard deviations and counts, through the specification CELL INFO(MEANS);

⑧ the Bartlett-Box, Cochran's C, and Box's M tests, through the specification HOMOGENEITY (BARTLETT, COCHRAN, BOXM);

⑨ the hypothesis sums of squares and cross-products, SSCP, and the Roy-Bargmann stepdown F tests, through the specification SIGNIF(HYPOTH,STEPDOWN);

⑩ the raw and standardized canonical discriminant function (CDF) coefficients, the discriminant CDF effect estimates, the discriminant structure coefficients, the varimax rotation of the discriminant structure coefficients, and all discriminant functions, through the specification DISCRIM (RAW,STAN,ESTIM,COR, ROTATE(VARIMAX), ALPHA (1.0));

⑪ the error sums of squares and cross-products matrix, variance-covariance matrix, and the correlation matrix with standard deviations on the diagonal, through the specification ERROR (SSCP,COV,COR,STDV); and,

⑫ the observed value of each dependent variable, its predicted value, raw residual (observed-predicted), and standardized residual, through the specification POBS.

⑬ The PLOT subcommand (optional) requests plots of the following:

⑭ the cell means versus cell variances, cell means versus cell standard deviations, and a histogram of cell means through the specification CELLPLOTS;

⑮ box plots through the specification BOXPLOTS;

⑯ a stem-and-leaf display through the specification STEMLEAF; and,

⑰ observed versus standardized residuals, cell means versus standardized residuals, case number versus standardized residuals, a normal probability plot, and a detrended normal probability for the standardized residuals through the specification POBS. (Note: the plots requested by POBS will not be produced unless POBS also appears in the PRINT subcommand).

⑱ The METHOD subcommand requests the method of weighted squares of means analysis (see Appendix A) through the specification SSTYPE(UNIQUE).

⑲ The PARTITION subcommand allows for single degree of freedom partitioning of the between groups sums of squares on the independent variable TREAT.

⑳ The CONTRAST subcommand requests HELMERT contrasts for the independent variable TREAT. This subcommand interacts with the PARTITION subcommand to yield the planned comparisons desired in Chapter 2.

㉑ The DESIGN subcommand specifies the between-subjects model to be analyzed. Here TREAT (1) and TREAT (2) refer to the first and second partitions of TREAT as previously specified in the PARTITION subcommand.

㉒ The READ INPUT DATA card (required) signals that the data begins with the next card.

㉓ The END INPUT DATA card (required) signals the end of the data. This card is required here because the number of cases was not specified.

㉔ The overall one-way MANOVA could have been requested using a separate program, however, to save space, we included it here as part of this run. This allowed us not to have to repeat some of the print specifications which remain the same regardless of whether you perform planned comparisons or an overall analysis. To perform only an overall analysis one would replace the first task's DESIGN subcommand with the second task's DESIGN subcommand and remove the METHOD, PARTITION, and CONTRAST cards from the first task.

㉕ In SPSS a data set may be re-analysed by the same or other subprograms by listing the subprogram specifications following the data.

㉖ Here the control word MANOVA and the PRINT subcommand are as annotated above. Note that of the PRINT specifications listed above only SIGNIF and DISCRIM must be repeated here because they will yield different output for the overall analysis.

㉗ The DESIGN subcommand with specification TREAT indicates that an overall MANOVA is desired.

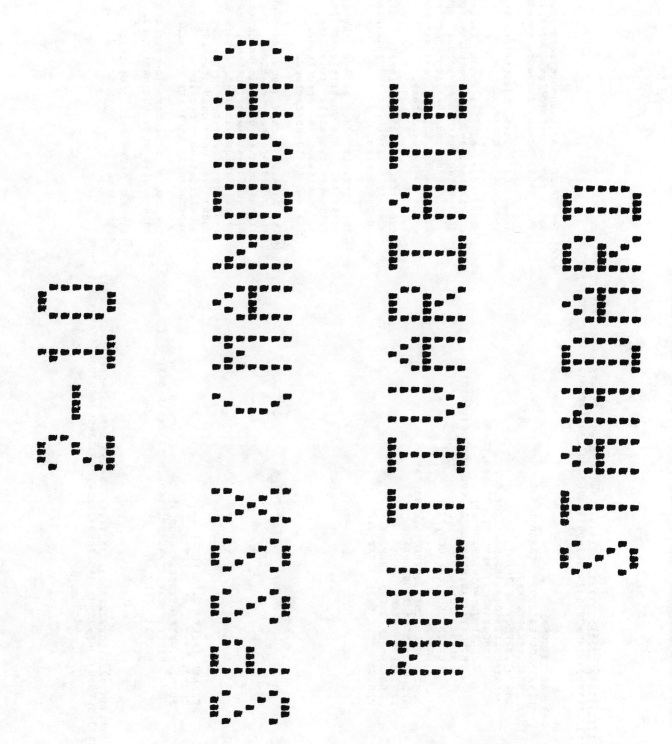

```
000000000111111111122222222223333333333444444444455555555556666666666777777777 8
123456789012345678901234567890123456789012345678901234567890123456789012345678 90
```

① 
② TITLE     ONE-WAY (MANOVA)
③ SUBTITLE  PLANNED COMPARISONS, UNEQUAL N
④ DATA LIST LIST/ TREAT,CREDBY,EFFECT
  MANOVA    CREDBY,EFFECT BY TREAT(1,3)/
            PRINT=CELLINFO(MEANS,SSCP,COV,COR)
            HOMOGENEITY(BARTLETT,COCHRAN,BOXM)
            SIGNIF(HYPOTH,STEPDOWN)
            DISCRIM(RAW,STAN,ESTIM,COR,ROTATE(VARIMAX),
            ALPHA(1.0))
            ERROR(SSCP,COV,COR,STDV)
            POBS/
            PLOT = CELLPLOTS,BOXPLOTS,STEMLEAF,POBS/
            METHOD = SSTYPE(UNIQUE)/
            PARTITION(TREAT)/
            CONTRAST (TREAT) = HELMERT/
            DESIGN = TREAT(1),TREAT(2)/

⑤ BEGIN DATA
  1 10 16
  1  4 10
  1 10 18
  2  8 12
  2  4  8
  2  4  6
  2  2  6
  2  9 14
  3  3 10
  3  5 16
  3  4 14
  3  1  9
⑥ END DATA
③ SUBTITLE  OVERALL ANALYSIS, UNEQUAL N
  MANOVA    CREDBY,EFFECT BY TREAT(1,3)/
            PRINT=SIGNIF(HYPOTH,STEPDOWN)
            DISCRIM(RAW,STAN,ESTIM,COR,ROTATE(VARIMAX)
            ALPHA(1.0))/
            DESIGN=TREAT/
```

```
000000000111111111122222222223333333333444444444455555555556666666666777777777 8
123456789012345678901234567890123456789012345678901234567890123456789012345678 90
```

Note: The SPSSX input annotations provided here are of value for most problems of this type. Consult your SPSSX manual for more general information.

① These are column identifiers and are not part of the program content.

Note: SPSSX command keywords begin in column 1; specifications, separated by at least one blank, follow the command keywords. Specifications which continue beyond the first card must be indented by at least one column, and may continue for as many cards as is necessary.

② The TITLE card (optional) allows the user to specify a title for the analysis; it is limited to 60 characters.

③ The SUBTITLE card allows the user to specify a subtitle. The subtitle is printed on the line following the title (this line is left blank when no subtitle is specified). The subtitle is limited to 60 characters.

④ The DATA LIST card (required) provides SPSSX with the names of the variables. The variables must be listed in the order in which they are being read by the format specification. Here the LIST format specification was used. This input specification indicates that the scores for each case will be found on one card (record). The LIST input specification requires that the scores be separated by at least one blank or comma.

⑤ The BEGIN DATA card (required) signals that the data begins with the next card.

⑥ The END DATA card (required) signals the end of the data.
```

SPSS FOR OS/360, VERSION H, RELEASE 9.1, FEBRUARY 1, 1982

CURRENT DOCUMENTATION FOR THE SPSS BATCH SYSTEM

ORDER FROM MCGRAW-HILL:   SPSS, 2ND ED. (PRINCIPAL TEXT)       ORDER FROM SPSS INC.:    SPSS STATISTICAL ALGORITHMS
                          SPSS UPDATE 7-9 (USE W/SPSS,2ND FOR REL. 7, 8, 9)       KEYWORDS: THE SPSS INC. NEWSLETTER
                          SPSS POCKET GUIDE, RELEASE 9
                          SPSS INTRODUCTORY GUIDE:  BASIC STATISTICS AND OPERATIONS
                          SPSS PRIMER (BRIEF INTRO TO SPSS)

DEFAULT SPACE ALLOCATION.-      ALLOWS FOR.-       102  TRANSFORMATIONS
WORKSPACE     71680 BYTES                          409  RECODE VALUES + LAG VARIABLES
TRANSPACE     10240 BYTES                         1641  IF/COMPUTE OPERATIONS

(1)

```
 1  RUN NAME        ONE-WAY (MANOVA)
 2  TASK NAME       PLANNED COMPARISONS, UNEQUAL N
 3  VARIABLE LIST   TREAT,CREDBY,EFFECT
 4  INPUT FORMAT    FREEFIELD
 5  MANOVA          CREDBY,EFFECT BY TREAT(1,3)/
 6                  PRINT=CELLINFO(MEANS,SSCP,COV,COR)
 7                       HOMOGENEITY(BARTLETT,COCHRAN,BOXM)
 8                       SIGNIF(HYPOTH,STEPDOWN)
 9                       DISCRIM(RAW,STAN,ESTIM,COR,ROTATE(VARIMAX),ALPHA(1.0))
10                       ERROR(SSCP,COV,COR,STDV)
11                       POBS/
12                  PLOT = CELLPLOTS,BOXPLOTS,STEMLEAF,POBS/
13                  METHOD = SSTYPE(UNIQUE)/
14                  PARTITION(TREAT)/
15                  CONTRAST(TREAT) = HELMERT/
16                  DESIGN = TREAT(1),TREAT(2)/
17  READ INPUT DATA
```

APTER READING    12  CASES FROM SUBFILE NONAME  ,  END OF DATA WAS ENCOUNTERED ON LOGICAL UNIT # 5

(1) SPSS provides a listing of program control cards.
    This listing should be checked for input accuracy.

* * * * * * * * * * * * * * * * * * * * * A N A L Y S I S   O F   V A R I A N C E * * * * * * * * * * * * * * * * * * * * * * * *

CELL MEANS AND STANDARD DEVIATIONS

VARIABLE -- CREDBY

| FACTOR (4) | CODE | (5) MEAN | STD. DEV. | N | (2) 95 PERCENT CONF. INTERVAL | |
|---|---|---|---|---|---|---|
| TREAT | 1 | 8.00000 | 3.46410 | 3 | -.60540 | 16.60540 |
| TREAT | 2 | 5.40000 | 2.96648 | 5 | 1.71669 | 9.08331 |
| TREAT | 3 | 3.25000 | 1.70783 | 4 | .53251 | 5.96749 |
| FOR ENTIRE SAMPLE | | 5.33333 | 3.11400 | 12 | 3.35480 | 7.31187 |

VARIABLE -- EFFECT

| FACTOR (4) | CODE | (5) MEAN | STD. DEV. | N | 95 PERCENT CONF. INTERVAL | |
|---|---|---|---|---|---|---|
| TREAT | 1 | 14.66667 | 4.16333 | 3 | 4.32426 | 25.00907 |
| TREAT | 2 | 9.20000 | 3.63318 | 5 | 4.68888 | 13.71112 |
| TREAT | 3 | 12.25000 | 3.30404 | 4 | 6.99261 | 17.50739 |
| FOR ENTIRE SAMPLE | | 11.58333 | 4.03301 | 12 | 9.02088 | 14.14578 |

UNIVARIATE HOMOGENEITY OF VARIANCE TESTS

VARIABLE -- CREDBY

(8) COCHRANS C(3,3) =                    .50597, P = .417 (APPROX.) (7)
(3) BARTLETT-BOX F(2,152) =              .56321, P = .571

VARIABLE -- EFFECT

COCHRANS C(3,3) =                        .41817, P = .644 (APPROX.)
BARTLETT-BOX F(2,152) =                  .05606, P = .946

---

(4) The input data check should include: identification of the variable names, factor levels, number of subjects per cell, and the total number of subjects.

(5) Cell means may be used in a priori or post hoc analyses. The user may calculate these means by hand to further check on input accuracy and program execution.

(6) Cell standard deviations should be approximately equal (a check on the assumption of homogeneity of variance). This check is particularly important when the cells have unequal n's.

(7) The tests for homogeneity of variance are not significant, which indicates that the homogeneity of variance assumption has been met. However, with small n, these tests are unreliable.

(8) Cochran's C test is found as the largest variance divided by the sum of all of the variances. Here the sum of the variances is: 12.0000 + 8.8000 + 2.9167 = 23.7167. Therefore, Cochran's C = 12.0000/23.7167 = .50597. Critical values for Cochran's C are available in Dixon and Massey...

(2) The 95% confidence interval provides the researcher with an idea of the possible mean (cell and overall) values.

(3) The Bartlett-Box test was developed by Bartlett (1937) for the univariate case and was extended by Box (1949) for the multivariate case. The test used here is based on Box's extension, but the calculations are done for one dependent variable. The formulas for this test are complex, but are...

136

* * * * * * * * * * * * * * * * * A N A L Y S I S   O F   V A R I A N C E * * * * * * * * * * * * * * * * * * * * * *

CELL NUMBER .. 1

SUM OF SQUARES AND CROSS-PRODUCTS MATRIX

|  | CREDBY | EFFECT |
|---|---|---|
| **(9)** CREDBY | 24.00000 |  |
| EFFECT | 28.00000 | 34.66667 |

VARIANCE-COVARIANCE MATRIX

|  | CREDBY | EFFECT |
|---|---|---|
| **(10)** CREDBY | 12.00000 |  |
| EFFECT | 14.00000 | 17.33333 |

CORRELATION MATRIX WITH STANDARD DEVIATIONS ON DIAGONAL

|  | CREDBY | EFFECT |
|---|---|---|
| **(11)** CREDBY | 3.46410 |  |
| **(12)** EFFECT | .97073 | 4.16333 |

DETERMINANT OF VARIANCE-COVARIANCE MATRIX =   **(13)** 12.00000
LOG(DETERMINANT) =                                  2.48491

- - - - - - - - - -

CELL NUMBER .. 2

SUM OF SQUARES AND CROSS-PRODUCTS MATRIX

|  | CREDBY | EFFECT |
|---|---|---|
| **(9)** CREDBY | 35.20000 |  |
| EFFECT | 41.60000 | 52.80000 |

**(9)** The cell sums of squares and cross-products matrix is used as a base to calculate the following matrices (e.g. if you multiply this matrix by 1/(cell size -1), the result is the cell variance-covariance matrix).

**(10)** The cell variance-covariance matrices should be approximately equal (a check on the assumption on homogeneity of variance-covariance matrices). This check is particularly important when the cells have unequal n's. The cell variance-covariance matrices presented here appear to satisfy the assumption of homogeneity.

**(11)** The correlation matrix with standard deviations on the diagonal allow you to observe the cell standard deviation on each variable (these should be approximately equal across cells) and the intercorrelation among the variables in a cell.

**(12)** In this data one can see that across cells there is a high correlation between the credibility and effectiveness measures.

**(13)** These values are used in Box's M test. They should be approximately equal across cells.

137

ONE-WAY (MANOVA)
PLANNED COMPARISONS, UNEQUAL N
* * * * * * * * * * * * * * * A N A L Y S I S   O F   V A R I A N C E * * * * * * * * * * * * * * * * * * * * * * * *

02/28/83      PAGE   4

CELL NUMBER -- 2      (CONT.)

VARIANCE-COVARIANCE MATRIX

|  | CREDBY | EFFECT |
|---|---|---|
| ⑩ |  |  |
| CREDBY | 8.80000 |  |
| EFFECT | 10.40000 | 13.20000 |

CORRELATION MATRIX WITH STANDARD DEVIATIONS ON DIAGONAL

|  | CREDBY | EFFECT |
|---|---|---|
| ⑪ |  |  |
| CREDBY | 2.96648 |  |
| EFFECT | .96495 | 3.63318 |

DETERMINANT OF VARIANCE-COVARIANCE MATRIX =      8.00000
LOG(DETERMINANT) =      2.07944

- - - - - - -

CELL NUMBER -- 3

SUM OF SQUARES AND CROSS-PRODUCTS MATRIX

|  | CREDBY | EFFECT |
|---|---|---|
| ⑨ |  |  |
| CREDBY | 8.75000 |  |
| EFFECT | 15.75000 | 32.75000 |

VARIANCE-COVARIANCE MATRIX

|  | CREDBY | EFFECT |
|---|---|---|
| ⑩ |  |  |
| CREDBY | 2.91667 |  |
| EFFECT | 5.25000 | 10.91667 |

138

CELL NUMBER .. 3        (CONT.)
CORRELATION MATRIX WITH STANDARD DEVIATIONS ON DIAGONAL

                CREDBY          EFFECT

CREDBY      (11) 1.70783
EFFECT           .93040      3.30404

DETERMINANT OF VARIANCE-COVARIANCE MATRIX =          4.27778
LOG(DETERMINANT) =                                   1.45343

POOLED WITHIN-CELLS VARIANCE-COVARIANCE MATRIX

                CREDBY          EFFECT

CREDBY      (14) 7.55000
EFFECT           9.48333     13.35741

DETERMINANT OF POOLED VARIANCE-COVARIANCE MATRIX     10.91481
LOG(DETERMINANT) =                                    2.39012

MULTIVARIATE TEST FOR HOMOGENEITY OF DISPERSION MATRICES

BOXS M =    (15) 3.86321
F WITH (6,578) DF =      .41114, P =    .872 (APPROX.)
CHI-SQUARE WITH 6 DF =  2.50691, P =    .868 (APPROX.)

(16)  12 CASES ACCEPTED.
       0 CASES REJECTED BECAUSE OF OUT-OF-RANGE FACTOR VALUES.
       0 CASES REJECTED BECAUSE OF MISSING DATA.
       3 NON-EMPTY CELLS.

(14) This matrix contains the variance and covariance of the dependent variables with the effects of the independent variable removed. The error (within groups) sums of squares and cross products matrix shown in Tables 2.6 and 2.7 can be found by multiplying this matrix by its degrees of freedom (9).

(15) This is Box's test of homogeneity of the variance-covariance matrices from each treatment level (see Cooley and Lohnes, 1971, p. 229). The test results given here indicate that the variance-covariance matrices are homogeneous because the significance probabilities are .872 (for F) or .868 (for chi-square) which are larger than our a priori level of significance of .05. The reader should be warned that this test is often ignored by researchers for two reasons: 1. MANOVA is robust with respect to modest violations of this assumption, and 2. the test is too sensitive to violations of multivariate normality.

(16) The number of cases accepted/rejected, and the number of cells with data should be reviewed as part of the data check.

Note: In SPSSX the output on accepted/rejected cases, i.e., annotation number 16, was deleted.

139

* * * * * * * * * * * * * * * * * A N A L Y S I S   O F   V A R I A N C E * * * * * * * * * * * * * * * * * * * * * *

(17) MEANS VS. VARIANCES FOR EFFECT

CELL MEANS

(18) MEANS VS. STD. DEVS. FOR EFFECT

CELL MEANS

DISTRIBUTION OF CELL MEANS FOR EFFECT

| FREQUENCY | 0 | 1 | 0 | 0 | 0 | 1 | 0 | 1 | 0 | 1 | 0 |
|-----------|---|---|---|---|---|---|---|---|---|---|---|
|     1     |   | * |   |   |   | * |   | * |   | * |   |
| INTERVAL : | 8.400 | | 10.000 | | 11.600 | | 13.200 | | 14.800 | |
| MID-POINTS: | 9.200 | | 10.800 | | 12.400 | | 14.000 | | 15.600 |

(17) If the assumption of homogeneity of variance was
met, all of the points in the 'mean vs. variances'
and the 'means vs. std. devs.' plots would fall on
a horizontal line.

Note: SPSS page 6 of this output, which contains mean
versus variance and mean versus standard deviation
plots for CREDBY, is exactly the same as SPSS page
3 in SPSS(MANOVA) (2-1); therefore, it was
eliminated to save space.

Note: SPSS page 7 contained no information and was
deleted.

(18) The cell means appear to be spread out, but the
differences are not significant at the .05 level
of significance (shown later in this output).

Note: SPSS page 9 contained no information and was
deleted.

(19) The box-plots, more descriptively called by Tukey(1977, p.39) the 'box-and-whisker plots', picture the range, median, and hinges (similar to quartiles) of the scores in each cell. They provide the user with further information with which to check statistical assumptions, and a visual comparison of the differences among the cells and their scores.

(20) The first box-plot pictures the scores, i.e., 10,10,4, from the Oral/Visual treatment. In this plot the vertical I's represent the distance from the highest score of 10 to the lowest score of 4. (The double column of I's usually represent the distance between the 'hinges,' but in this data set the hinges and the extremes are the same.) The * at the top of this plot indicates that 10 is the median, middle score, of this set of scores. At this point one would observe that this treatment contains a score, 4, that might require further study (see the discussion in Chapter 2).

(21) The second box-plot pictures the scores from the visual treatment, i.e., 9,8,4,2. The extremes, denoted by Y's, are at 9 and 2; these scores are found at the end of Tukey's 'whiskers,' i.e., the single column of I's. The vertical lines, dashes with a + sign between them, represent 'hinges.' A hinge is a score that falls half-way between an extreme and the median. In this treatment the hinges are at 8 and 4. The median, represented by an *, is the middle score of 4.

(22) In the third set of data, the Oral treatment, the scores are: 5,4,3,1. Here the extremes are at 5 and 1; the hinges are at 4 and 3; and, the median is at 3.5.

(23) The box-plots for both variables across the cells indicate considerable overall variance among the scores; one might expect there to be no univariate significant differences.

BOX-PLOTS FOR VARIABLE -- CREDEY

```
          (20)              (22)  X
   10 . --*--                    -+--
      .  I  I                  I  I  I
      .  I  I   (21) X         I  *  I
      .  I  I        I         I  I  I
      .  I  I      -+---       I  I  I
      .  I  I       I  I       I  I  I
      .  I  I       I  I       ----+--
      .  --+--      *  I       X
      .  I  I       I  I
      .  I  I       I  I
      .  X          X
      .
    1 .
```

BOX-PLOTS FOR VARIABLE -- EFFECT

```
   18 . -+--
      .  I  I           X
      .  I  I           I
      . I*I           -+--
      .  I  I           I  I
      .  I  I          I  *  I
      .  I  I       X   I  I  I
      .  I  I      -+--  I  I  I
      .  -+--       I  I  I  I  I
      .  I  I      I  *  I  ---+--
      .  I  I       I  I  X
      .  I  I       -+--
      .
    6 .
```

141

ONE-WAY (MANOVA)
PLANNED COMPARISONS, UNEQUAL N
* * * * * * * * * * * * * * * * * * * * * * A N A L Y S I S   O F   V A R I A N C E * * * * * * * * * * * * * * * * * * * * * *

(24) A stem-and-leaf display is used to provide information, like that found in a frequency distribution--only more--of the type and distribution of scores found in a design. The basic idea ' is to give part of the information at the start of each line', i.e. at the stem, 'and then give the rest of the information in the line', i.e., in the leaves(Tukey, 1977, p. 8). Here the values in the stem for CREDBY are given at even integers and the values in the leaves are those found in the first position after the decimal point. Since all of the CREDBY scores in this design are whole numbers, e.g., 1.0, the computer listed zeros to represent each number. The leaf for the stem 0 represents the scores 1.0, the leaves for the stem 2 represent the scores 2.0 and 3.0, etc.

STEM-AND-LEAF DISPLAY FOR VARIABLE -- CREDBY

```
 0 . 0
 2 . 00
 4 . 00000         (26)
 6 . 00
 8 . 00
10 . 00
```

(25) Some of the scores for EFFECT have two digits so the program listed the first digit, '0', of the scores 6,8,9 (considered as 06,08,09) and split those scores whose first digit was one into two sets, those whose second digit was less than five and those whose second digit was greater than or equal to 5.

STEM-AND-LEAF DISPLAY FOR VARIABLE -- EFFECT

```
(25)  0 . 6689
      1 . 00244
      1 . 668
```

(26) We recommend this as a standard part of the output in order to provide further discriptive information on the data. If significant differences were found among the groups we might expect two or three distinct groups of scores.

CORRESPONDENCE BETWEEN EFFECTS AND COLUMNS OF BETWEEN-SUBJECTS DESIGN

| STARTING COLUMN | ENDING COLUMN | EFFECT NAME |
|---|---|---|
| (27) | | |
| 1 | 1 | CONSTANT |
| 2 | 2 | TREAT(1) |
| 3 | 3 | TREAT(2) |

(27) The between-subjects design matrix is made up of three columns: one for the constant, grand mean, one for the first contrast on TREAT, and one for the second contrast on TREAT. This output should be checked to see that you have correctly specified your design.

WITHIN CELLS CORRELATIONS WITH STD. DEVS. ON DIAGONAL

| | CREDBY | EFFECT |
|---|---|---|
| CREDBY | 2.74773 | |
| EFFECT | .94434 | 3.65478 |

DETERMINANT = .10823
BARTLETT TEST OF SPHERICITY = 16.67623 WITH 1 D. F.
SIGNIFICANCE = .000

F (MAX) CRITERION = 1.76919 WITH (2,9) D. F.

142

WITHIN CELLS VARIANCES AND COVARIANCES

|        | CREDBY   | EFFECT   |
|--------|----------|----------|
| CREDBY | 7.55000  |          |
| EFFECT | 9.48333  | 13.35741 |

WITHIN CELLS SUM-OF-SQUARES AND CROSS-PRODUCTS

|        | CREDBY    | EFFECT     |
|--------|-----------|------------|
| CREDBY | 67.95000  |            |
| EFFECT | 85.35000  | 120.21667  |

143

ONE-WAY (MANOVA)
PLANNED COMPARISONS, UNEQUAL N

* * * * * * * * * * * * * * * * * * * A N A L Y S I S   O F   V A R I A N C E * * * * * * * * * * * * * * * * * * *

EFFECT .. (27) (28) TREAT(2)

ADJUSTED HYPOTHESIS SUM-OF-SQUARES AND CROSS-PRODUCTS

|        | CREDBY    | EFFECT    |
|--------|-----------|-----------|
| CREDBY | 10.27222  |           |
| EFFECT | -14.57222 | 20.67222  |

(30)

MULTIVARIATE TESTS OF SIGNIFICANCE (S = 1, M = 0, N = 3)

| TEST NAME (31) | VALUE   | APPROX. F | HYPOTH. DF | ERROR DF | SIG. OF F |
|----------------|---------|-----------|------------|----------|-----------|
| PILLAIS        | .85292  | 23.19669  | 2.00       | 8.00     | .000      |
| HOTELLINGS     | 5.79917 | 23.19669  | 2.00       | 8.00     | .000      |
| WILKS          | .14708  | 23.19669  | 2.00       | 8.00     | .000      |
| ROYS           | .85292  |           |            |          |           |

EIGENVALUES AND CANONICAL CORRELATIONS

| ROOT NO. | EIGENVALUE (34) | PCT. (35)  | CUM. PCT. | CANON. CCR. (32) |
|----------|-----------------|------------|-----------|------------------|
| 1        | 5.79917         | 100.00000  | 100.00000 | .92354           |

DIMENSION REDUCTION ANALYSIS

| ROOTS   | WILKS LAMBDA    | F        | HYPOTH. DF | ERROR DF | SIG. OF F |
|---------|-----------------|----------|------------|----------|-----------|
| 1 TO 1  | (33) .14708     | 23.19669 | 2.00       | 8.00     | .000      |

(27) (28) The program outputs the statistical tests of the effects in the DESIGN statement starting with the last effect and proceding to the first effect, see the effects listed above.

(29) Here TREAT(2) represents our second contrast between the visual presentation and the oral presentation.

(30) The sums-of-squares and cross-product matrix is needed for the planned comparisons source table (see Table 2.6).

(31) These are the four most popular multivariate statistical tests. They all indicate that there is a significant difference between the treatment (Oral versus Visual) mean vectors (p<.05). That is, there is a difference between these treatment groups when message credibility and effectiveness are considered together. These tests are discussed further in Appendix B.

(32) The canonical correlation is the correlation between the canonical discriminant function and a linear function of the grouping variable. (The grouping variable is the independent variable coded as a set of dummy variables, see Kerlinger and Pedhazur, 1973.) In this manner the canonical correlation reflects the relationship between the independent variable and a canonical discriminant function. The canonical correlation may be calculated as the square root of the ratio of an eigenvalue to one plus the eigenvalue, e.g., SQUARE ROOT (5.79917/(1+5.79917)) =.92354.

(33) Wilks' lambda and its associated F statistic indicate that there is a significant multivariate

(34) With a single contrast, where you are comparing two things, there is only one eigenvalue. It is an indicator of the discriminatory power of the corresponding canonical discriminant function. To see this, note that the eigenvalue is the same as Hotelling's T² statistic reported above.

(35) The percent of variance accounted for by the first discriminant function is 100, as is the cumulative percent, because there is only one eigenvector.

* * * * * * * * * * * * * * * * A N A L Y S I S   O F   V A R I A N C E * * * * * * * * * * * * * * * * * * * *

EFFECT -- TREAT(2) (36) (CONT.)

UNIVARIATE F-TESTS WITH (1,9) D. F

| VARIABLE | HYPOTH. SS | ERROR SS | HYPOTH. MS | ERROR MS | (37) F | SIG. OF F |
|---|---|---|---|---|---|---|
| CREDBY | 10.27222 | 67.95000 | 10.27222 | 7.55000 | 1.36056 | .273 |
| EFFECT | 20.67222 | 120.21667 | 20.67222 | 13.35741 | 1.54762 | .245 |

(38) ROY-BARGMAN STEPDOWN F - TESTS

| VARIABLE | HYPOTH. MS | ERROR MS | STEP-DOWN F | HYPOTH. DF | ERROR DF | SIG. OF F |
|---|---|---|---|---|---|---|
| CREDBY | 10.27222 | 7.55000 | 1.36056 | 1 | 9 | .273 |
| EFFECT | 63.83603 | 1.62638 | 39.25038 | 1 | 8 | .000 |

RAW DISCRIMINANT FUNCTION COEFFICIENTS

FUNCTION NO.

| VARIABLE | (39) 1 |
|---|---|
| CREDBY | -1.08972 |
| EFFECT | .82079 |

STANDARDIZED DISCRIMINANT FUNCTION COEFFICIENTS

FUNCTION NO.

| VARIABLE | (40) 1 |
|---|---|
| CREDBY | -2.99426 |
| EFFECT | 2.99979 |

(36) Because the multivariate tests are significant, the univariate tests are considered next (see Table 2.6).

(37) The univariate tests indicate that neither variable by itself is able to differentiate between the groups (i.e. both tests are not significant, $p > .05$).

(38) The Roy-Bargman stepdown F tests require an a priori ordering of the dependent variables. Since this was not done here these tests are ignored (see Appendix C).

(39) The raw canonical discriminant function coefficients are difficult to interpret with respect to variable importance because they are affected by the scale of measurement of the variable with which they are associated, and by the intercorrelations among the variables.

(40) The standardized discriminant function coefficients aid in interpreting the contribution of each variable to group differentiation. Here the large coefficients indicate that both variables contribute to group differentiation, but that they appear to be measuring opposite ends of a single construct.

145

\* \* \* \* \* \* \* \* \* \* \* \* \* \* \* \* \* \* \* A N A L Y S I S   O F   V A R I A N C E \* \* \* \* \* \* \* \* \* \* \* \* \* \* \* \* \* \* \*

EFFECT .. TREAT(2)      (CONT.)

ESTIMATES OF EFFECTS FOR CANONICAL VARIABLES

CANONICAL VARIABLE

PARAMETER    (41)      1

    3           -4.84630

---

CORRELATIONS BETWEEN DEPENDENT AND CANONICAL VARIABLES

CANONICAL VARIABLE

VARIABLE    (42)      1

CREDBY      -.16146
EFFECT       .17220

(41) The estimate of effect for this contrast is found
by evaluating the mean scores for each group using
the raw discriminant coefficients, and then
substituting the resultant canonical discriminant
functions evaluated at the group means into the
contrast of interest.  The result here indicates
that the Oral treatment yielded a larger canonical
discriminant function mean score than did the
Visual treatment, and the multivariate tests
indicate that this difference is significant.

(42) The correlations between the scores from canonical
discriminant functions and the dependent variables
aid in interpreting the importance of each
variable to group differentiation.  Here the low
variable function-variable correlations indicate
that the canonical discriminant function is not
strongly related to either variable by itself.

PLANNED COMPARISONS, UNEQUAL N

\* \* \* \* \* \* \* \* \* \* \* \* \* \* \* \* \* \* \* \* A N A L Y S I S   O F   V A R I A N C E \* \* \* \* \* \* \* \* \* \* \* \* \* \* \* \* \* \* \* \* \*
\*

EFFECT .. TREAT(1) (43)

(43) Here TREAT(1) represents the first contrast between the Oral/Visual treatment and the average of the Oral and Visual treatments.

ADJUSTED HYPOTHESIS SUM-OF-SQUARES AND CROSS-PRODUCTS

(44) The sums-of-squares and cross-products matrix is needed for the planned comparisons source table (see Table 2.6).

|  | CREDBY | EFFECT |
|---|---|---|
| (44) | | |
| CREDBY | 30.29299 | |
| EFFECT | 32.49112 | 34.84875 |

---

MULTIVARIATE TESTS OF SIGNIFICANCE (S = 1, M = 0, N = 3)

| TEST NAME | VALUE | APPROX. F | HYPOTH. DF | ERROR DF | SIG. OF F |
|---|---|---|---|---|---|
| PILLAIS | .34393 | 2.09687 | 2.00 | 8.00 | (45) .185 |
| HOTELLINGS | .52422 | 2.09687 | 2.00 | 8.00 | .185 |
| WILKS | .65607 | 2.09687 | 2.00 | 8.00 | .185 |
| ROYS | .34393 | | | | |

(45) The MANOVA planned comparison null hypothesis that there was no difference between the oral-visual group mean vector and the average of the visual and oral groups mean vectors was not rejected (p<.185).

---

EIGENVALUES AND CANONICAL CORRELATIONS

| ROOT NO. | EIGENVALUE | PCT. | CUM. PCT. | CANON. COR. |
|---|---|---|---|---|
| 1 | (46) .52422 | 100.00000 | 100.00000 | .58645 |

(46) The preceding nonsignificant multivariate result is reflected in the small eigenvalue. However, the canonical correlation is reasonably high suggesting that with a larger sample size significant results may be found. (Compare these values with those found for TREAT(2)).

---

DIMENSION REDUCTION ANALYSIS

| ROOTS | WILKS LAMBDA | F | HYPOTH. DF | ERROR DF | SIG. OF F |
|---|---|---|---|---|---|
| 1 TO 1 | (47) .65607 | 2.09687 | 2.00 | 8.00 | .185 |

(47) Wilks' lambda and its associated F-statistic indicate that there is not a significant multivariate difference between the Oral/Visual and the average of the Oral and Visual treatments on the canonical discriminant function (p<.185).

ONE-WAY (MANOVA)
PLANNED COMPARISONS, UNEQUAL N

* * * * * * * * * * * * * * * * * * A N A L Y S I S   O F   V A R I A N C E * * * * * * * * * * * * * * * * * * *

(48) EFFECT .. TREAT(1)    (CONT.)

UNIVARIATE F-TESTS WITH (1,9) D. F.

| VARIABLE | HYPOTH. SS | ERROR SS | HYPOTH. MS | ERROR MS | F | SIG. OF F |
|---|---|---|---|---|---|---|
| CREDBY | 30.29299 | 67.95000 | 30.29299 | 7.55000 | 4.01232 | .076 |
| EFFECT | 34.84875 | 120.21667 | 34.84875 | 13.35741 | 2.60895 | .141 |

ROY-BARGMAN STEPDOWN F - TESTS

| VARIABLE | HYPOTH. MS | ERROR MS | STEP-DOWN F | HYPOTH. DF | ERROR DF | SIG. OF F |
|---|---|---|---|---|---|---|
| CREDBY | 30.29299 | 7.55000 | 4.01232 | 1 | 9 | .076 |
| EFFECT | .70557 | 1.62638 | .43383 | 1 | 8 | .529 |

RAW DISCRIMINANT FUNCTION COEFFICIENTS
FUNCTION NO.

| VARIABLE | 1 |
|---|---|
| CREDBY | .73963 |
| EFFECT | -.32165 |

STANDARDIZED DISCRIMINANT FUNCTION COEFFICIENTS
FUNCTION NO.

| VARIABLE | 1 |
|---|---|
| CREDBY | 2.03230 |
| EFFECT | -1.17555 |

(48) Consideration of the output should stop here because the multivariate tests were not significant. Further interpretation of the univariate tests, especially when one of them is significant, is often very tempting, but must be considered to be hazardous to your research (i.e. you have a good chance of making a Type I error). If however you find a result in the following output that you feel you must follow-up on, do so in another experiment. These results would be part of the planned comparisons MANOVA table, see Table 2.6.

Note: Pages 19-22 of this output contained results for the CONSTANT effect which tests the multivariate hypothesis that the grand mean vector is equal to a null vector. Because this output was not of interest in this design we dropped it to save space.

Note: We also dropped pages 23-27, which contained information on the observed, predicted, raw residuals, standardized residuals, and their plots, because we already annotated these results in SPSS(MANOVA) (2-1) on that program's SPSS pages 8-11.

* * * * * * * * * * * * * * * * * * * A N A L Y S I S   O F   V A R I A N C E * * * * * * * * * * * * * * * * * * * * * * * * *

OBSERVED AND PREDICTED VALUES FOR EACH CASE

DEPENDENT VARIABLE-- EFFECT

| CASE NO. (49) | OBSERVED (50) | PREDICTED (51) | RAW RESID. (52) | STD RESID. |
|---|---|---|---|---|
| 1 | 16.00000 | 14.66667 | 1.33333 | .36482 |
| 2 | 10.00000 | 14.66667 | -4.66667 | -1.27687 |
| 3 | 18.00000 | 14.66667 | 3.33333 | .91205 |
| 4 | 12.00000 | 9.20000 | 2.80000 | .76612 |
| 5 | 8.00000 | 9.20000 | -1.20000 | -.32834 |
| 6 | 6.00000 | 9.20000 | -3.20000 | -.87557 |
| 7 | 6.00000 | 9.20000 | -3.20000 | -.87557 |
| 8 | 14.00000 | 9.20000 | 4.80000 | 1.31335 |
| 9 | 10.00000 | 12.25000 | -2.25000 | -.61563 |
| 10 | 16.00000 | 12.25000 | 3.75000 | 1.02605 |
| 11 | 14.00000 | 12.25000 | 1.75000 | .47883 |
| 12 | 9.00000 | 12.25000 | -3.25000 | -.88925 |

(49) The observed scores for each cell should be proofread to ensure that the correct observations have entered the analysis.

(50) The predicted score for each observation in a cell will be the cell mean.

(51) The raw residual for each observation is the difference between it and its cell mean (i.e., for case no. 1, 16.00000-14.66667=1.33333).

(52) The standardized residual is the raw residual divided by the standard error of the mean (i.e., the square root of the mean square within cell). In the first case the standardized residual is 1.33333/3.65478=.36482, where 3.65478 is the square root of the variance of EFFECT. The value 3.65478 was taken from the diagonal of the pooled within-cells variance-covariance matrix found earlier in this output.

(52) standardized residuals that are larger than 3.0 or smaller than -3.0 should be considered as potential outliers; no such values appear in this data set.

149

PLOTS OF OBSERVED, PREDICTED, AND RESIDUAL CASE VALUES

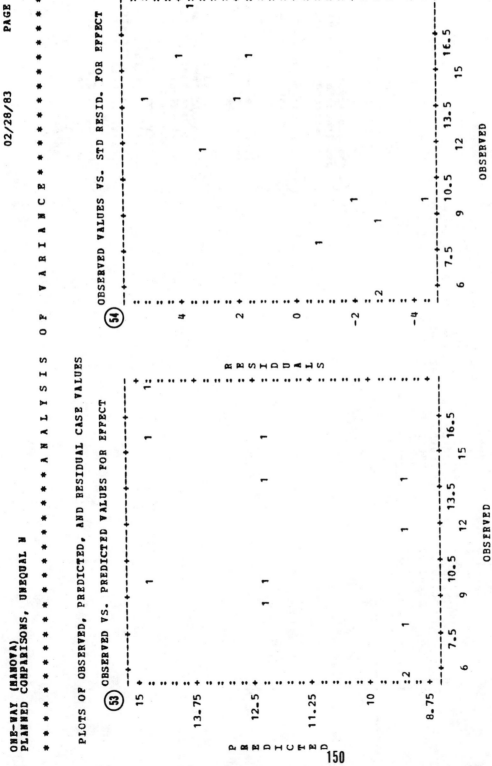

(53) OBSERVED VS. PREDICTED VALUES FOR EFFECT

(54) OBSERVED VALUES VS. STD RESID. FOR EFFECT

(53) Because the predicted value for each cell is the cell mean, the plot of the observed versus the predicted values for CREDBY displays the spread of the scores from each cell horizontally. This plot permits us to check for outliers and to check on the homogeneity of the cell variances. By viewing the scores vertically we can see that the scores overlapped across the cells—an indication of no significant treatment differences.

(54) In observing the plot of the observed values versus the standardized residuals for EFFECT we see that the low values were predicted to be higher, and that the high values were predicted to be lower. Since we expected a horizontal band of points around a residual of zero, this linear trend may indicate that another independent variable (e.g. personality type of the subjects) may help to explain the results. Of course, this plot may simply reflect the small sample size.

150

ONE-WAY (MANOVA)
PLANNED COMPARISONS, UNEQUAL N

02/28/83        PAGE    30

* * * * * * * * * * * * * * * * * * * A N A L Y S I S   O F   V A R I A N C E * * * * * * * * * * * * * * * * * * * * * * * * * * *
*

PLOTS OF OBSERVED, PREDICTED, AND RESIDUAL CASE VALUES (CONT.)

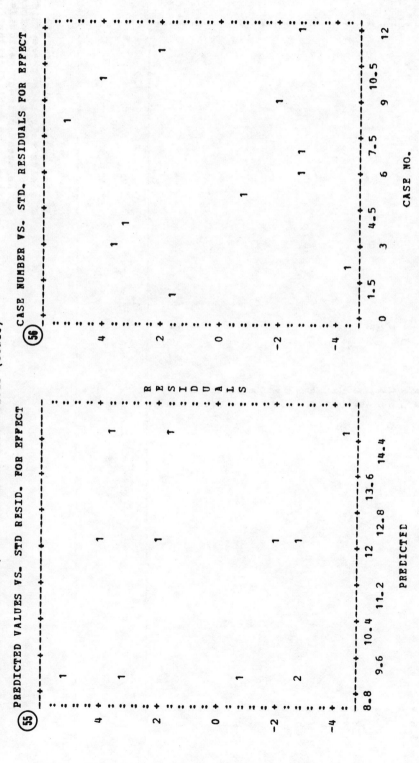

CASE NUMBER VS. STD. RESIDUALS FOR EFFECT

PREDICTED VALUES VS. STD RESID. FOR EFFECT

(55) The plot of the predicted values versus the standardized residuals yields information similar to that found in the plot of the observed versus the predicted value, only with the axes changed.

(56) The plot of the case numbers versus the standardized residuals indicates, through the more-or-less horizontal band of points, that there is no relationship between the standardized residuals and the case numbers.

151

PLOTS OF OBSERVED, PREDICTED, AND RESIDUAL CASE VALUES (CONT.)

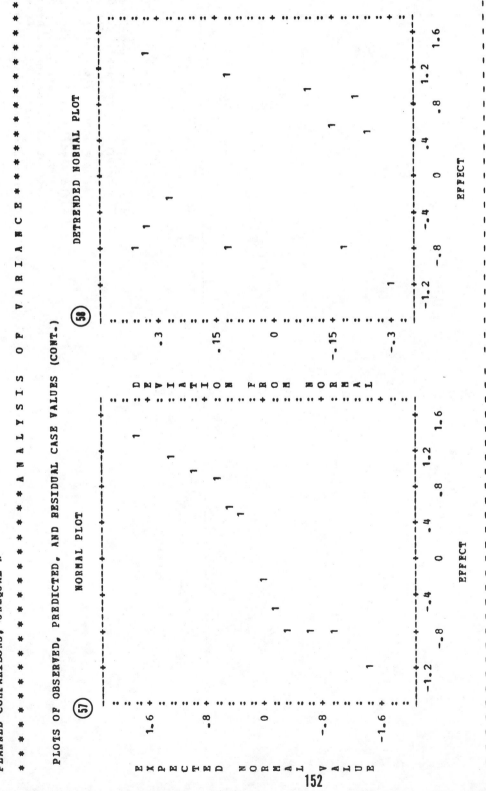

(57) The normal plot of the standardized residuals yields values that are fairly close to falling on a straight line. Therefore, we may conclude that the standardized residuals in this analysis come from a normal distribution. See SPSS(MANOVA) (2-1) for a further discussion of this plot.

(58) The detrended normal plot shows a band of points scattered around zero; indicating that the points probably come from a normal distribution.

ONE-WAY (MANOVA)
PLANNED COMPARISONS, UNEQUAL N

9128 BYTES OF WORKSPACE NEEDED FOR MANOVA EXECUTION.

CPU TIME REQUIRED..     5.55 SECONDS

(59)    18 TASK NAME     OVERALL ANALYSIS, UNEQUAL N
        19 MANOVA        CREDBI,EFFECT BY TREAT(1,3)/
        20               PRINT=SIGNIF(HYPOTH,STEPDOWN)
        21                  DISCRIM(RAW,STAN,ESTIM,COR,ROTATE(VARIMAX) ALPHA(1.0))/
        22               DESIGN=TREAT/

(59) Control cards which follow the data are listed
     prior to the analyses which they generate. They
     should be checked for input accuracy.

ONE-WAY (MANOVA),
OVERALL ANALYSIS, UNEQUAL N
FILE NONAME  (CREATION DATE = 02/28/83)

* * * * * * * * * * * * * * * * * * * A N A L Y S I S   O F   V A R I A N C E * * * * * * * * * * * * * * * * * * * *

   12 CASES ACCEPTED.
    0 CASES REJECTED BECAUSE OF OUT-OF-RANGE FACTOR VALUES.
    0 CASES REJECTED BECAUSE OF MISSING DATA.
    3 NON-EMPTY CELLS.

CORRESPONDENCE BETWEEN EFFECTS AND COLUMNS OF BETWEEN-SUBJECTS DESIGN

STARTING  ENDING
COLUMN    COLUMN    EFFECT NAME

   1        1       CONSTANT
   2        3       TREAT

* * * * * * * * * * * * * * * * * * A N A L Y S I S   O F   V A R I A N C E * * * * * * * * * * * * * * * * * * * * *

EFFECT .. TREAT (60)

(60) The following output contains the overall multivariate statistical results for the Type of Presentation Experiment.

ADJUSTED HYPOTHESIS SUM-OF-SQUARES AND CROSS-PRODUCTS

|  | CREDBY | EFFECT |
|---|---|---|
| (61) | | |
| CREDBY | 38.71667 | |
| EFFECT | 18.31667 | 58.70000 |

(61) The hypothesis sums-of-squares and cross-products matrix is needed for the MANOVA source table, see Tables 2.6 and 2.7.

MULTIVARIATE TESTS OF SIGNIFICANCE (S = 2, M = 1/2, N = 3)

| TEST NAME | VALUE | APPROX. F | HYPOTH. DF | ERROR DF | SIG. OF F |
|---|---|---|---|---|---|
| (62) | | | | | |
| PILLAIS | 1.12630 | 5.80105 | 4.00 | 18.00 | .004 |
| HOTELLINGS | 6.23956 | 10.91924 | 4.00 | 14.00 | .000 |
| WILKS | .10604 | 8.28377 | 4.00 | 16.00 | .001 |
| ROYS | .85436 | | | | |

(62) All four multivariate statistical tests indicate (although with different 'SIG. OF F' values, see Appendix B) that there is a multivariate significant difference between the treatments. Note that we use Wilks' lambda in Table 2.7.

EIGENVALUES AND CANONICAL CORRELATIONS

| ROOT NO. | EIGENVALUE | PCT. | CUM. PCT. | CANON. COR. |
|---|---|---|---|---|
| | (65) | (63) | (64) | (66) |
| 1 | 5.86604 | 94.01359 | 94.01359 | .92431 |
| 2 | .37353 | 5.98641 | 100.00000 | .52149 |

(63) The percent of variance is an indicator of the importance of a canonical discriminant function in discriminating among the treatment levels. It is the ratio of the variance (eigenvalue) of one canonical discriminant function to the total variance accounted for by all functions (see Table 2.8).

(64) CUM. PCT. is the cumulative percentage. It indicates how much of the variation accounted for by the eigenvalues has been accounted for up to a given eigenvalue.

DIMENSION REDUCTION ANALYSIS

| ROOTS | WILKS LAMBDA | F | HYPOTH. DF | ERROR DF | SIG. OF F |
|---|---|---|---|---|---|
| | (68) | (67) | | | |
| 1 TO 2 | .10604 | 8.28377 | 4.00 | 16.00 | .001 |
| 2 TO 2 | .72805 | 3.17497 | 1.00 | 8.50 | .113 |

(65) The size of an eigenvalue is an indication of the discriminatory power of its corresponding canonical discriminant function. To see this we notice that when an eigenvalue is multiplied by the degrees of freedom for error (within), the resultant number is the between sum of squares that one would find if the canonical discriminant function scores were placed in an ANOVA. (Note that the latter point assumes that the error variance is the ANOVA is 1.0, see Finn (1974, p. 360)). For this reason the eigenvalue is referred to as 'variance' in Table 2.8.

66 Wilks' lambda and its associated F statistic indicate that there is a significant multivariate difference between the treatments, and that the first discriminant function contributes to group differentiation significantly ($p<.001$). They also indicate that the second canonical discriminant function does not significantly ($p<.113$) contribute to group differentiation (see Table 2.8).

66 The canonical correlation is the correlation between canonical discriminant function and a linear function of the grouping variable. (The grouping variable is the independent variable coded as a set of dummy variables, see Kerlinger and Pedhazur, 1973). In this manner the canonical correlation reflects the relationship between the independent variable and a canonical discriminant function. The canonical correlation may be calculated as the square root of the ratio of an eigenvalue to one plus the eigenvalue, e.g., $5.86604/(1+5.86604) = 0.9243136$, see Table 2.8.

67 The canonical discriminant function tests of significance proceed in a step-wise fashion. The first test is the same as that used to determine if there is an overall difference among the group mean vectors (see Table 2.7); this test makes use of information from all the canonical discriminant functions. The second test is based on calculations with the information from the first canonical discriminant function removed.

EFFECT .. TREAT (CONT.)

69 UNIVARIATE F-TESTS WITH (2,9) D. F.

| VARIABLE | HYPOTH. SS | ERROR SS | HYPOTH. MS | ERROR MS | F | SIG. OF F |
|---|---|---|---|---|---|---|
| CREDBY | 38.71667 | 67.95000 | 19.35833 | 7.55000 | 2.56402 | .131 |
| EFFECT | 58.70000 | 120.21667 | 29.35000 | 13.35741 | 2.19728 | .167 |

70 ROY-BARGMAN STEPDOWN F - TESTS

| VARIABLE | HYPOTH. MS | ERROR MS | STEP-DOWN F | HYPOTH. DF | ERROR DF | SIG. OF F |
|---|---|---|---|---|---|---|
| CREDBY | 19.35833 | 7.55000 | 2.56402 | 2 | 9 | .131 |
| EFFECT | 32.57729 | 1.62638 | 20.03056 | 2 | 8 | .001 |

RAW DISCRIMINANT FUNCTION COEFFICIENTS

71 FUNCTION NO.

| VARIABLE | 1 | 2 |
|---|---|---|
| CREDBY | -1.09463 | .15990 |
| EFFECT | -.81670 | .15721 |

STANDARDIZED DISCRIMINANT FUNCTION COEFFICIENTS

72 FUNCTION NO.

| VARIABLE | 1 | 2 |
|---|---|---|
| CREDBY | -3.00775 | -.43937 |
| EFFECT | 2.98487 | .57458 |

156

69 Because the overall multivariate test was significant the univariate tests (see Table 2.7) may be considered. Here neither univariate test is significant (p>.05) which indicates that neither dependent variable by itself is capable of differentiating between the groups.

70 The Roy-Bargman stepdown F-tests require an a priori ordering of the dependent variables. Since this was not done here these tests are ignored (see Appendix C).

71 The raw canonical discriminant function coefficients are difficult to interpret, with respect to variable importance, because they are affected by the scale of measurement of the variable with which they are associated and by the intercorrelations among the variables.

72 The standardized discriminant function coefficients aid in interpreting the importance of each variable to group differentiation (see Table 2.8, and the discussion of canonical discriminant analysis).

* * * * * * * * * * * * * * * * * A N A L Y S I S   O F   V A R I A N C E * * * * * * * * * * * * * * * *

EFFECT .. TREAT (CONT.)

ESTIMATES OF EFFECTS FOR CANONICAL VARIABLES

CANONICAL VARIABLE

| PARAMETER (73) | 1 | 2 |
|---|---|---|
| 2 | -.53573 | -.80489 |
| 3 | -2.15434 | -.47030 |

(73) Here the estimates of effects are found for deviation contrasts. That is, the raw discriminant function coefficients are evaluated at the treatment means and on the unweighted treatment mean (the unweighted treatment means are 5.5500 for CREDBY and 12.0387 for EFFECT) and then the grand mean results are subtracted from the treatment mean results. For example the value -.53573 is the difference between the first canonical discriminant function evaluated on the first treatment group's means minus the canonical discriminant function evaluated on the unweighted grand means.

CORRELATIONS BETWEEN DEPENDENT AND CANONICAL VARIABLES

CANONICAL VARIABLE

| VARIABLE (74) | 1 | 2 |
|---|---|---|
| CREDBY | -.18903 | -.98197 |
| EFFECT | -.14455 | -.98950 |

(74) The correlations between the scores from canonical discriminant functions and the dependent variables aid in interpreting the importance of each variable to group differentiation (see Table 2.8, and the discussion of canonical discriminant analysis).

VARIMAX ROTATED CORRELATIONS BETWEEN CANONICAL AND DEPENDENT VARIATES

CAN. VAR.

| DEP. VAR. (75) | 1 | 2 |
|---|---|---|
| CREDBY | .57923 | .81516 |
| EFFECT | .81516 | .57923 |

(75) One may rotate the original canonical-variate correlations using the varimax solution to arrive at more readily interpretable canonical discriminant functions. Ideally, this method should yield high (greater than .40) canonical-variate correlations for one function per variable. As you can see, this rotation did not help us here as both variables still correlate strongly with both discriminant functions.

TRANSFORMATION MATRIX

| (76) | 1 | 2 |
|---|---|---|
| 1 | -.69098 | -.72288 |
| 2 | -.72288 | .69098 |

(76) This transformation matrix when pre-multiplied times the above rotated correlations yields the original correlation matrix.

Note: SPSS pages 37-39 consist of output concerned with the unweighted grand mean vector; since this output is of no interest for this problem, it was deleted.

ONE-WAY (MANOVA)
OVERALL ANALYSIS, UNEQUAL N

* * * * * * * * * * * * * * * * * * A N A L Y S I S   O F   V A R I A N C E * * * * * * * * * * * * * * * * * * * * * * * * *

ESTIMATES FOR EFFECT

CONSTANT

| PARAMETER | COEFF. | STD. ERR. | T-VALUE | SIG. OF T | LOWER .95 CL | UPPER .95 CL |
|-----------|--------|-----------|---------|-----------|--------------|--------------|
| 1 | 12.0388888889 | 1.07823 | 11.16537 | .000 | 9.59975 | 14.47802 |

TREAT

| PARAMETER | COEFF. | STD. ERR. | T-VALUE | SIG. OF T | LOWER .95 CL | UPPER .95 CL |
|-----------|--------|-----------|---------|-----------|--------------|--------------|
| 2 | 2.6277777778 | 1.62688 | 1.61522 | .141 | -1.05248 | 6.30804 |
| 3 | -2.8388888889 | 1.43286 | -1.98128 | .079 | -6.08024 | -.40246 |

ONE-WAY (MANOVA)
OVERALL ANALYSIS, UNEQUAL N

3752 BYTES OF WORKSPACE NEEDED FOR MANOVA EXECUTION.

CPU TIME REQUIRED..    1.66 SECONDS

(77) 23 FINISH        (SPSS GENERATED)

(78) NORMAL END OF JOB.
     23 CONTROL CARDS WERE PROCESSED.
      0 ERRORS WERE DETECTED.

(77) A FINISH card may follow the last card in an SPSS
     run; if one is not present (as is the case here)
     SPSS generates this card internally.

(78) This is the first place you might check after
     receiving your output. It tells you if you've had
     any errors and how many SPSS control cards were
     processed.  The control card count includes the
     FINISH card, but does not include the data cards.

FIG. 11-2

OSCILLOSCOPE SPS3

HEWLETT-PACKARD INSTRUMENT

STANDARD 3

```
00000000011111111112222222222333333333344444444445555555555666666666677777777778
12345678901234567890123456789012345678901234567890123456789012345678901234567890
```

② RUN NAME       SPIKER: ONE-WAY UNEQUAL N
③ DATA LIST      FIXED(1)/1 TREAT 3 CREDBY 4-6 EFFECT 7-9
④ N OF CASES     12
⑤ LIST CASES     CASES=12/VARIABLES = TREAT,CREDBY,EFFECT
⑦ DISCRIMINANT   GROUPS = TREAT (1,3)/VARIABLES = CREDBY,EFFECT/ ANALYSIS = CREDBY,EFFECT/
⑧ STATISTICS     ALL
⑨ OPTIONS        6,7,11
⑥ READ INPUT DATA
```
      1 10 16
      1  4 10
      1 10 18
      2  8 12
      2  4  8
      2  4  6
      2  2  6
      2  9 14
      3  5 16
      3  3 10
      3  5 16
      3  4 14
      3  1  9
```

Note: The SPSS input annotations provided here are of value for most problems of this type. Consult your SPSS manual for more general information.

① These are column identifiers and are not part of the program content.

Note: SPSS control words are punched between columns 1-15, and specifications are placed in columns 16-80 on the first and all succeeding cards necessary to complete the specifications.

② The RUN NAME card (optional) allows the user to specify a title for the analysis; it is limited to 64 characters.

③ The DATA LIST card (optional) can be used in place of the VARIABLE LIST and INPUT FORMAT CARDS (see the preceding input). Here, FIXED indicates that the variables are in the same position on each data card for each case. The '1' in the '(1)' indicates only one data card per case. The slash informs SPSS that this specification is ended and that another one may follow. The number '1' following the slash indicates the card on which the following variables are found. The first variable on the card is TREAT which is in column 3, the second variable is CREDBY which is in column 4-6, the third variable is EFFECT which is in column 8-9.

④ The N OF CASES card (optional) specifies the number of cases (subjects) in the problem run.

⑤ The LIST CASES card (optional) will cause cases to be listed as they are processed. This card is recommended as an aid in checking the input accuracy of the data. The specification CASES=12 indicates that all 12 cases are to be listed. The slash indicates that the specification is ended and that another one may follow. The variables to be listed are specified next.

⑥ The READ INPUT DATA card signals that the data begins with the next card.

```
00000000011111111112222222222333333333344444444445555555555666666666677777777778
12345678901234567890123456789012345678901234567890123456789012345678901234567890
```

⑦ The control word DISCRIMINANT (required) indicates the subprogram to be executed. The specification GROUPS = TREAT (1,3) indicates that TREAT is the factor name with levels 1 through 3. The slash informs SPSS that the specification is ended and another one follows. The VARIABLES specification indicates that CREDBY and EFFECT are dependent variables. The ANALYSIS specification indicates that both dependent variables are to be included in the analysis.

⑧ The STATISTICS card (optional) specifying ALL statistics is recommended as an aid in checking input accuracy and the validity of the MANOVA model assumptions.

⑨ Options 6,7, and 11 are recommended. Option 6 prints the canonical discriminant funtion scores. Option 7 prints either a histogram (for one discriminant funtion) or a scatterplot (for the first two discriminant functions) of the canonical discriminant function scores. Option 11 prints the unstandardized (raw) canonical discriminant function coefficients.

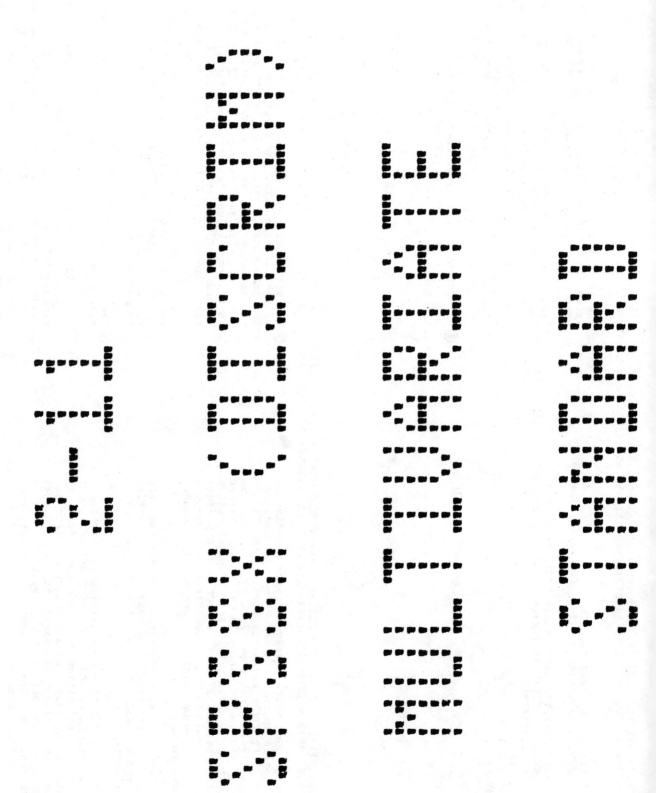

```
00000000011111111112222222222333333333344444444445555555555666666666677777777778
12345678901234567890123456789012345678901234567890123456789012345678901234567890
```

```
① ② TITLE    SPIKER: ONE-WAY UNEQUAL N
  ③ DATA LIST RECORD=1/1 TREAT 3 CREDBY 4-6 EFFECT 7-9
     DISCRIMINANT GROUPS = TREAT (1,3)/VARIABLES = CREDBY,EFFECT/
                  ANALYSIS = CREDBY,EFFECT/
     STATISTICS
     ALL
  ④ BEGIN DATA
     1 10 16
     1  4 10
     1 10 18
     2  8 12
     2  4  8
     2  4  6
     2  2  6
     2  9 14
     3  3 10
     3  5 16
     3  4 14
     3  1  9
  ⑤ END DATA
  ⑥ ⑦ LIST VARIABLES = TREAT,CREDBY,EFFECT
```

```
① 00000000011111111112222222222333333333344444444445555555555666666666677777777778
   12345678901234567890123456789012345678901234567890123456789012345678901234567890
```

163

Note: The SPSSX input annotations provided here are of value for most problems of this type. Consult your SPSSX manual for more general information.

① These are column identifiers and are not part of the program content.

Note: SPSSX command keywords begin in column 1; specifications, separated by at least one blank, follow the command keywords. Specifications which continue beyond the first card must be indented by at least one column, and may continue for as many cards as is necessary.

② The TITLE card (optional) allows the user to specify a title for the analysis; it is limited to 60 characters.

③ The DATA LIST card provides SPSSX with the names of the variables. When no input format specification is specified, the specification FIXED is implied. Here, FIXED indicates that the variables are in the same position on each data card for each case. The '1' in 'RECORD=1' indicates only one data card per case. The slash informs SPSSX that this specification is ended and that another one may follow. The number '1' following the slash indicates the card on which the following variables are found. The first variable on the card is TREAT which is in column 3, the second variable is CREDBY which is in columns 4-6.

Note: The OPTION and STATISTICS option numbers have changed from those found in SPSS. For example, OPTIONS 6,7, and 9 are now found as STATISTICS 11, 14 and 15, which we call for here by specifying STATISTICS ALL.

④ The BEGIN DATA card (required) signals that the data begins with the next card.

⑤ The END DATA card (required) signals the end of the data.

⑥ The LIST card (optional) will cause cases to be listed. This card is recomended as an aid in checking the input accuracy of the data. Here the scores for the variables listed will be printed for all of the cases.

⑦ In SPSSX we moved the LIST card after the discriminant analysis. Only one program (procedure) may precede the data.

SPSS FOR OS/360, VERSION H, RELEASE 9.1, FEBRUARY 1, 1982

```
                    CURRENT DOCUMENTATION FOR THE SPSS BATCH SYSTEM
ORDER FROM MCGRAW-HILL:  SPSS, 2ND ED. (PRINCIPAL TEXT)      SPSS STATISTICAL ALGORITHMS
                         SPSS UPDATE 7-9 (USE W/SPSS,2ND FOR REL. 7, 8, 9)    ORDER FROM SPSS INC.:
                         SPSS POCKET GUIDE, RELEASE 9              KEYWORDS: THE SPSS INC. NEWSLETTER
                         SPSS INTRODUCTORY GUIDE:  BASIC STATISTICS AND OPERATIONS
                         SPSS PRIMER (BRIEF INTRO TO SPSS)
                                                          (1) SPSS provides a listing  of program control cards.
                                                              This listing should be checked for input accuracy.

DEFAULT SPACE ALLOCATION..      ALLOWS FOR..      102 TRANSFORMATIONS
WORKSPACE    71680 BYTES                          409 RECODE VALUES + LAG VARIABLES
TRANSPACE    10240 BYTES                         1641 IF/COMPUTE OPERATIONS

     (1) 1 RUN NAME       SPIKER: ONE-WAY UNEQUAL N
         2 DATA LIST      FIXED(1)/1 TREAT 3 CREDBY 4-6 EFFECT 7-9

THE DATA LIST PROVIDES FOR  3 VARIABLES AND  1 RECORDS ('CARDS') PER CASE. A MAXIMUM OF   9 COLUMNS ARE USED ON A RECORD.

LIST OF THE CONSTRUCTED FORMAT STATEMENT..
     (2X,F1.0,2F3.0)

         3 N OF CASES        12
         4 LIST CASES        CASES=12/VARIABLES = TREAT,CREDBY,EFFECT
         5 DISCRIMINANT      GROUPS = TREAT (1,3)/VARIABLES = CREDBY,EFFECT/ ANALYSIS =
         6                   CREDBY,EFFECT/
         7 STATISTICS        ALL
         8 OPTIONS           6,7,11

THIS DISCRIMINANT ANALYSIS REQUIRES      4380  (      4.3K) BYTES OF WORKSPACE.
         9 READ INPUT DATA
```

164

FILE   NONAME   (CREATION DATE = 03/01/83)

(2) CASE-N    TREAT    CREDBY    EFFECT

| CASE-N | TREAT | CREDBY | EFFECT |
|---|---|---|---|
| 1 | 1. | 10. | 16. |
| 2 | 1. | 4. | 10. |
| 3 | 1. | 10. | 18. |
| 4 | 2. | 8. | 12. |
| 5 | 2. | 4. | 8. |
| 6 | 2. | 4. | 6. |
| 7 | 2. | 2. | 6. |
| 8 | 2. | 9. | 14. |
| 9 | 3. | 3. | 10. |
| 10 | 3. | 5. | 16. |
| 11 | 3. | 4. | 14. |
| 12 | 3. | 1. | 9. |

(2) The LIST CASES card produced this data list which should be proofread.

Note: In our SPSSX output the cases were not numbered, i.e., the CASE-N column was deleted.

Note: In SPSSX this output follows that for the discriminant analysis.

165

SPIKER: ONE-WAY UNEQUAL N

FILE   NONAME   (CREATION DATE = 03/01/83)

03/01/83      PAGE   3

- - - - - - - - - - - - - - - - - D I S C R I M I N A N T   A N A L Y S I S - - - - - - - - - - - - - - - - -

ON GROUPS DEFINED BY TREAT

    12 (UNWEIGHTED) CASES WERE PROCESSED.
    0 OF THESE WERE EXCLUDED FROM THE ANALYSIS.
    12 (UNWEIGHTED) CASES WILL BE USED IN THE ANALYSIS.

NUMBER OF CASES BY GROUP

③

| TREAT | NUMBER OF CASES UNWEIGHTED | WEIGHTED | LABEL |
|---|---|---|---|
| 1 | 3 | 3.0 | |
| 2 | 5 | 5.0 | |
| 3 | 4 | 4.0 | |
| TOTAL | 12 | 12.0 | |

GROUP MEANS

④

| TREAT | CREDBY | EFFECT |
|---|---|---|
| 1 | 8.00000 | 14.66667 |
| 2 | 5.40000 | 9.20000 |
| 3 | 3.25000 | 12.25000 |
| TOTAL | 5.33333 | 11.58333 |

GROUP STANDARD DEVIATIONS

⑤

| TREAT | CREDBY | EFFECT |
|---|---|---|
| 1 | 3.46410 | 4.16333 |
| 2 | 2.96648 | 3.63318 |
| 3 | 1.70783 | 3.30404 |
| TOTAL | 3.11400 | 4.03301 |

③ The input data check should include: identification of the factor levels, number of subjects per cell, and the total number of subjects.

④ Cell means may be used in a priori or post hoc analyses. The user may calculate these means by hand to further check on input accuracy and program execution.

⑤ Cell standard deviations should be approximately equal (a check on the assumption of homogeneity of variance). This check is particularly important when the cells have unequal n's.

POOLED WITHIN-GROUPS COVARIANCE MATRIX WITH        9 DEGREES OF FREEDOM

(6)   CREDBY       EFFECT

CREDBY    7.550000
EFFECT    9.483333    13.35741

POOLED WITHIN-GROUPS CORRELATION MATRIX

(7)   CREDBY       EFFECT

CREDBY    1.00000
EFFECT    0.94434     1.00000

CORRELATIONS WHICH CANNOT BE COMPUTED ARE PRINTED AS 99.0.

WILKS' LAMBDA (U-STATISTIC) AND UNIVARIATE F-RATIO
WITH  2 AND       9 DEGREES OF FREEDOM

| VARIABLE | WILKS' LAMBDA | F | SIGNIFICANCE |
| --- | --- | --- | --- |
| (8) CREDBY | 0.63703 | 2.564 | (9) 0.1314 |
| EFFECT | 0.67191 | 2.197 | 0.1671 |

COVARIANCE MATRIX FOR GROUP    1,

(10)  CREDBY       EFFECT

CREDBY    12.00000
EFFECT    14.00000    17.33333

(6) This matrix contains the variance and covariances
of the dependent variables with the effects of the
independent variable removed.   The error (within
groups) sums of squares and cross products matrix
shown in Tables 2.6 and 2.7 can be found by
multiplying this matrix by its degrees of freedom
(9).

(7) This matrix contains the correlations among   the
dependent variables with the   effects of   the
independent variable removed.   The partial
correlation is discussed further   in the SAS (GLM)
(2-3) multivariate output.

(8) Wilks' lambda (the ratio of the univariate error
sum of squares to the univariate total sum of
squares)   and its corresponding F-statistic   are
reported for the   univariate analysis on   each
dependent variable.

(9) These are the probabilities of   obtaining an F
ratio larger than the calculated values of 2.564
and 2.197.   Therefore,   if   the level of
significance, alpha, was .05, one would fail to
reject the overall null   hypothesis that the
treatment means are all equal for both dependent
variables that is, for the F or U (Wilks' lambda)
statistics   to   indicate   that   significant
differences are present, this obtained P value
must be less than the predetermined level of
significance.

(10) The cell variance-covariance   matrices should   be
approximately equal (a check   on the assumption on
homogeneity   of variance-covariance   matrices).
This check   is particularly   important when the
cells have   unequal n's.   The   cell   variance-
covariance matrices   presented   here   appear to
satisfy the assumption of homogeneity.

167

COVARIANCE MATRIX FOR GROUP      2,

                    CREDBY        EFFECT

⑩

CREDBY          8.800000
EFFECT         10.40000      13.20000


COVARIANCE MATRIX FOR GROUP      3,

                    CREDBY        EFFECT

⑩

CREDBY          2.916667
EFFECT          5.250000     10.91667


TOTAL COVARIANCE MATRIX WITH      11 DEGREES OF FREEDOM

                    CREDBY        EFFECT

⑪

CREDBY          9.696970
EFFECT          9.424242     16.26515


⑪ This is the total (adjusted for the grand mean)
variance-covariance matrix.   The total sums of
squares and cross products matrix shown in Tables
2.6 and 2.7 can be found by multiplying the matrix
by its degrees of freedom (11).

FILE   NONAME   (CREATION DATE = 03/01/83)

- - - - - - - - - - - -   D I S C R I M I N A N T   A N A L Y S I S   - - - - - - - - - - -

ON GROUPS DEFINED BY TREAT

ANALYSIS NUMBER     1

DIRECT METHOD:   ALL VARIABLES PASSING THE TOLERANCE TEST ARE ENTERED.

MINIMUM TOLERANCE LEVEL............... 0.00100

CANONICAL DISCRIMINANT FUNCTIONS

MAXIMUM NUMBER OF FUNCTIONS............. 2
MINIMUM CUMULATIVE PERCENT OF VARIANCE... 100.00
MAXIMUM SIGNIFICANCE OF WILKS' LAMBDA.... 1.0000

PRIOR PROBABILITY FOR EACH GROUP IS 0.33333

CANONICAL DISCRIMINANT FUNCTIONS

| FUNCTION | EIGENVALUE | PERCENT OF VARIANCE | CUMULATIVE PERCENT | CANONICAL CORRELATION | : AFTER FUNCTION | WILKS' LAMBDA | CHI-SQUARED | D.F. | SIGNIFICANCE |
|---|---|---|---|---|---|---|---|---|---|
| | | | | | : | | | | |
| 1* | (12) 5.86604 | (13) 94.01 | 94.01 | (14) 0.9243136 | (15) 0 : | (16) 0.1060369 | (17) 19.074 | 4 | 0.0008 |
| 2* | 0.37353 | 5.99 | 100.00 | 0.5214853 | 1 : | 0.7280531 | 2.6977 | 1 | 0.1005 |

* MARKS THE   2   CANONICAL DISCRIMINANT FUNCTION(S) TO BE USED IN THE REMAINING ANALYSIS.

STANDARDIZED CANONICAL DISCRIMINANT FUNCTION COEFFICIENTS

| | FUNC 1 | FUNC 2 |
|---|---|---|
| (18) | | |
| CREDBY | 3.00775 | 0.43937 |
| EFFECT | -2.98487 | 0.57458 |

(12) The size of an eigenvalue is an indication of the discriminatory power of its corresponding canonical discriminant function. To see this we notice that when an eigenvalue is multiplied by the degrees of freedom for error (within), the resultant number is the between sum of squares that one would find if the canonical discriminant function scores were placed in an ANOVA. (Note that the latter point assumes that the error variance in the ANOVA is 1.0, see Finn (1974, p. 360)). For this reason, the eigenvalue is referred to as 'Variance' in Table 2.8.

Note: In SPSSX following the Prior Probability For Each Group the classification function coefficients are printed. (See 2-8, BMDP7M, annotation number 20.)

(14) The canonical correlation is the correlation between the canonical discriminant funtion and a linear function of the grouping variable. (The grouping variable is the independent variable coded as a set of dummy variables, see Kerlinger and Pedhazur, 1973.) In this manner the canonical correlation reflects the relationship between the independent variable and a canonical discriminant function. The canonical correlation may be calculated as the square root of the ratio of an eigenvalue to one plus the eigenvalue, e.g., the square root of the quantity 5.8604/ (1+5.8604) = .924313, see Table 2.8.

(13) The percent of variance is an indicator of the importance of a canonical discriminant function in discriminating among the treatment levels. It is the ratio of the variance (eigenvalue) of one canonical discriminant function to the total variance accounted for by all functions (see Table 2.8).

169

15 In the column labeled 'After Function' the '0' indicates that the first test included information from all of the canonical discriminant functions, and the '1' indicates that information from the first canonical discriminant function was removed for the test results presented in this row.

16 The tests of significance proceed in a step-wise fashion. The first test is the same as that used to determine if there is an overall difference among the group mean vectors (see Table 2.7); this test makes use of information from all of the canonical discriminant functions. The second test is based on calculations with the information from the first canonical discriminant function removed.

17 Wilks' lambda and its associated chi-square value indicate that there is a significant multivariate difference between the treatments, and that the first discriminant function significantly (p<.0008) contributes to group differentiation. They also indicate that the second canonical discriminant function does not significantly (p<.1005) contribute to group differentiation (see Table 2.8).

18 The standardized discriminant function coefficients aid in interpreting the importance of each variable to group differentiation (see Table 2.8, and the discussion of canonical discriminant analysis).

POOLED WITHIN-GROUPS CORRELATIONS BETWEEN CANONICAL DISCRIMINANT FUNCTIONS AND DISCRIMINATING VARIABLES
VARIABLES ARE ORDERED BY THE FUNCTION WITH LARGEST CORRELATION AND THE MAGNITUDE OF THAT CORRELATION.

(19)
|        | FUNC 1   | FUNC 2   |
|--------|----------|----------|
| EFFECT | -0.14455 | 0.98950* |
| CREDBY | 0.18903  | 0.98197* |

UNSTANDARDIZED CANONICAL DISCRIMINANT FUNCTION COEFFICIENTS

(20)
|            | FUNC 1    | FUNC 2    |
|------------|-----------|-----------|
| CREDBY     | 1.094631  | 0.1599044 |
| EFFECT     | -0.816703 | 0.1572138 |
| (CONSTANT) | 3.622113  | -2.673884 |

CANONICAL DISCRIMINANT FUNCTIONS EVALUATED AT GROUP MEANS (GROUP CENTROIDS)

(21)
| GROUP | FUNC 1   | FUNC 2   |
|-------|----------|----------|
| 1     | 0.40085  | 0.91115  |
| 2     | 2.01945  | -0.36403 |
| 3     | -2.82495 | -0.22833 |

TEST OF EQUALITY OF GROUP COVARIANCE MATRICES USING BOX'S M

THE RANKS AND NATURAL LOGARITHMS OF DETERMINANTS PRINTED ARE THOSE
OF THE GROUP COVARIANCE MATRICES.

(22)
| GROUP LABEL | RANK | LOG DETERMINANT |
|-------------|------|-----------------|
| 1           | 2    | 2.484907        |
| 2           | 2    | 2.079442        |
| 3           | 2    | 1.453434        |
| POOLED WITHIN-GROUPS COVARIANCE MATRIX | 2 | 2.390121 |

| BOX'S M | APPROXIMATE F | DEGREES OF FREEDOM | SIGNIFICANCE |
|---------|---------------|--------------------|--------------|
| 3.8632  | 0.41114       | 6,      578.4      | 0.8718       |

(19) The correlations between the scores from canonical discriminant functions and the dependent variables aid in interpreting the importance of each variable to group differentiation (see Table 2.8, and the discussion of canonical discriminant analysis).

(20) The raw canonical discriminant function coefficients are difficult to interpret with respect to variable importance, because they are affected by the scale of measurement of the variable with which they are associated and by the intercorrelations among the variables.

(21) An extremely helpful aid in observing group differences is to plot the scores arrived at when the treatment level means are substituted into the canonical discriminant functions. In this program the canonical discriminant function equations are modified by a constant so that the mean of the canonical discriminant function scores is zero (this facilitates plotting the scores). The constant is found by substituting the grand mean into the function equation and then taking the negative value of the result. (Note that the raw (unstandardized) coefficients, discussed above, are used in these equations.) For example, to arrive at the group mean evaluated on the first canonical discriminant function, the following steps are taken:

   1. Evaluate the first canonical discriminant function at the grand mean--

   1.09463(5.33333) - .81670(11.58333) = -3.62211

   2. Take the negative of the value arrived at in step 1 and add it to the canonical discriminant function--

   3.62211 + 1.09463(CREDBY) - .81670(EFFECT)

   3. Substitute the group means into the equation arrived at in step 2--

   3.62211 + 1.09463(8.00000) - .81670(14.66667) = .40085.

(22) This is Box's M test of homogeneity of the variance-covariance matrices from each treatment level (see Cooley and Lohnes, 1971, p-229). The test results given here indicate that the variance-covariance matrices are homogeneous, because the significance probability is .8718 which is larger than our a priori level of significance of .05. The reader should be warned that this test is often ignored by researchers for two reasons: 1. MANOVA is robust with respect to modest violations of assumptions, and 2. the test is too sensitive to violations of multivariate normality.

171

| CASE SUBFILE SEQNUM | MIS VAL | SEL | ACTUAL GROUP | HIGHEST PROBABILITY GROUP | P(X/G) | P(G/X) | 2ND HIGHEST GROUP | P(G/X) | DISCRIMINANT SCORES | |
|---|---|---|---|---|---|---|---|---|---|---|
| | | | | ㉓ | | | ㉔ | | | |
| NONAME 1 | | | 1 | 1 | 0.4745 | 0.7344 | 2 | 0.2656 | 1.5012 | 1.4406 |
| NONAME 2 | | | 1 | 1 | 0.3316 | 0.7348 | 2 | 0.2023 | -0.1664 | -0.4621 |
| NONAME 3 | | | 1 | 1 | 0.6077 | 0.9772 | 2 | 0.0168 | -0.1322 | 1.7550 |
| NONAME 4 | | | 2 | 2 | 0.5929 | 0.8740 | 2 | 0.1260 | 2.5787 | 0.4919 |
| NONAME 5 | | | 2 | 2 | 0.7885 | 0.8525 | 1 | 0.1474 | 1.4670 | -0.7766 |
| NONAME 6 | | | 2 | 2 | 0.4281 | 0.9918 | 1 | 0.0082 | 3.1004 | -1.0910 |
| NONAME 7 | | | 2 | 2 | 0.3129 | 0.8397 | 1 | 0.1590 | 0.9112 | -1.4108 |
| NONAME 8 | | | 2 | 2 | 0.4127 | 0.6130 | 1 | 0.3870 | 2.0399 | 0.9662 |
| NONAME 9 | | | 3 | 3 | 0.2724 | 0.7685 | 1 | 0.2189 | -1.2610 | -0.6220 |
| NONAME 10 | | | 3 | 3 | 0.3550 | 0.9998 | 1 | 0.0002 | -3.9720 | 0.6411 |
| NONAME 11 | | | 3 | 3 | 0.7687 | 0.9994 | 1 | 0.0006 | -3.4332 | 0.1667 |
| NONAME 12 | | | 3 | 3 | 0.6721 | 0.9980 | 1 | 0.0020 | -2.6336 | -1.0991 |

SYMBOLS USED IN PLOTS

| SYMBOL | GROUP | LABEL |
|---|---|---|
| 1 | 1 | |
| 2 | 2 | |
| 3 | 3 | |
| * | | GROUP CENTROIDS |

172

Note: In SPSSX a territorial map of the discriminant functions is part of the standard output. This map follows the Symbols Used In Plots output.

Note: In SPSSX the probabilities and discriminant scores output follows the territorial map output.

㉓ This is part of the classification results. In this problem, all of the cases have been correctly classified. Classification is made on the basis of the largest probability.

㉔ Here each subject's discriminant function score is calculated using the raw discriminant function coefficients and the constant given earlier. For example, the first score in the oral-visual group for the first person on the first canonical discriminant function is 1.50 = 3.62211 + 1.09463(10) -.81670(16) - 1.09451(10). These scores and their group means are plotted in the next scatterplot.

ALL-GROUPS SCATTERPLOT - * INDICATES A GROUP CENTROID

CANONICAL DISCRIMINANT FUNCTION 1

```
                          -6        -4        -2         0         2         4         6    OUT
   OUT  X----+---------+---------+---------+---------+---------+---------+---------+---------X
        X                                                                                   X
      6 +                                                                                 + X  .
        .                                                                                   .
        .                                                                                   .
        .                                                                                   .
      4 +                                                                                   +
        .                                                                                   .
        .                                                                                   .
        .                                                                       2           .
      2 +                                                        1                           +
        .                                          *        2                                .
        .                                                 *                                   .
      0 +                          1         3   1                                           +
        .                               3   1                                                .
        .                      3   *                                                          .
     -2 +                        3                                                            +
        .                  3                                                                  .
        .              3                                                                      .
     -4 +                                                                                     +
        .                                                                                     .
        .                                                                                     .
     -6 +                                                                                     +
        .                                                                                     .
        X                                                                                 X
   OUT  X----+---------+---------+---------+---------+---------+---------+---------+---------X
                          -6        -4        -2         0         2         4         6    OUT
```

C A N O N I C A L   D I S C R I M I N A N T   F U N C T I O N   2

(25) This is a scatterplot of the preceding canonical discriminant function scores. Here '*' represents the mean coordinates in the oral-visual presentation, and each '1' represents the score coordinates for the subjects in this presentation; '*' represents the mean coordinates for the visual presentation, and each '2' represents the score coordinates for the subjects in this presentation; '*' represents the mean coordinates for the oral presentation, and each '3' represents the score coordinates for the subjects in this presentation. Note how well the scores are discriminated on the first canonical discriminant function (x-axis) and how poorly they are discriminated on the second function (y-axis).

Note: In SPSSX the following standard output follows the preceding scatterplot: a scatterplot on the canonical discriminant functions for each group, and a table of classification results (similar to BMDP7M, classification tables are shown in 2-8, annotation number 21, and in 2-6, SAS(DISCRIM), annotation number 38).

## CHAPTER 3

## TWO-WAY ANALYSIS OF VARIANCE
## by Robert S. Barcikowski

### Introduction

In this chapter we discuss two-way analysis of variance which is commonly used when a researcher manipulates two fixed independent variables (factors) in order to observe their effects on one (univariate) or more (multivariate) dependent variable(s). The primary purpose for doing this type of analysis over performing two one-way analyses, one for each independent variable, is that a two-way analysis considers both independent variables together, and allows the researcher to examine the effect that the interaction of the independent variables has on the dependent variable(s).

Two examples of two-way analyses are considered in this chapter. The first example is a 2x2 factorial, that is there are two treatments (levels) associated with each of two independent variables (factors), see Figure 3.1. In this first example no significant interaction effect of the independent variables on the dependent variable(s) is found, but depending on whether the analysis is planned or overall, significant main effects are or are not found. The second example is a 3x2 factorial with three treatment levels associated with the first factor and two treatment levels associated with the second factor, see Figure 3.4. In the second example, significant main effects and a significant interaction are found, but not for all variables in the multivariate case. A further discussion of two-way analysis may be found in Appendix A, and we continue our discussion of interactions in the next chapter on three-way analysis.

### Organization of the Programs

To illustrate several ways that data from a two-way analysis of variance design may be analyzed, 21 computer runs were made with the data from this chapter. All of these programs feature standard input so as to illustrate how to analyze the designs considered, including data accuracy checks and material required for most research reports. The differences between the I/O in this chapter and that in Chapter 2 are that here we annotate only input features that are different from those in Chapter 2, and we only include those parts of the program output needed to construct analysis of variance tables; other parts of the output, e.g. plots, data lists, were omitted to save space. In each program I/O we refer the reader to the appropriate program in Chapter 2 for an idea of what the complete program output would look like. The instruction I/O that could have been a part of this chapter was placed in

Appendix A, "Two-Way Nonorthogonal (Unequal N) Analysis", because it focused on a single important topic.

Table 3.1 contains the list of the programs run for this chapter in each volume and indicates their program numbers, whether they are univariate or multivariate, the page they start on, and their special features. The output from the standard runs is discussed in the succeeding analysis of variance sections.

## Analysis of Variance Presentations: (2x2) Example

In our first example the univariate and multivariate data were taken from Stevens and Barcikowski (1984). Their fictitious problem concerns the study of the effects of degree of examination difficulty and teaching method on student attitude and achievement. The problem and research hypotheses are stated in the question and answer format suggested by Kerlinger (1973, pp. 16-20).

Both the univariate and multivariate analyses are approached in two ways. First, the researcher is assumed to have knowledge based on theory and/or past research which supports an analysis with planned questions. This approach is discussed in sections concerned with what are known as "planned comparisons." Second, the researcher is assumed to be in an exploratory phase of analysis with little supporting research and/or theory. This type of analysis is discussed in sections concerned with overall tests and post hoc comparisons. A brief discussion of the nature of the problem follows.

### Problem

A researcher was interested in investigating the effects of test type (factor A) and method of instruction (factor B) on the attitudes held by third grade students towards arithmetic. A random sample of third grade students was selected from all such students in a large city. Each of these third graders was then randomly placed in one of four treatment conditions where the effects of instructional method (auditory or heuristic) and type of test (easy or difficult) were measured. The instruction and testing were conducted in such a manner that it could be assumed that attitude scores were independent of one another.

The test types were differentiated by the degree of difficulty of the items used to test the students on what they had learned. These arithmetic tests were given once a week over a three month period. An easy test was composed of items that had been answered correctly by 70% of past students and a difficult test was composed of items that had been answered correctly by 30% of past students. The auditory instructional method consisted primarily of verbal

Table 3.1
Descriptions of the Programs
Run on the Two Factor (Two-Way) Data from Chapter 3

| Program | Program Number | Mode[1] | Page | I/O Feature(s) |
|---------|----------------|---------|------|----------------|
| Volume 1: BMDP | | | | |
| BMDP7D | 3-1 | U | 178 | 2x2 analysis |
| BMDP2V | 3-2 | U | 181 | 2x2 analysis |
| BMDP4V | 3-3 | U | 184 | 2x2 analysis |
| BMDP4V | 3-4 | U | 189 | 3x2 planned and overall analysis |
| BMDP7D | 3-5 | U | 195 | 3x2 overall analysis |
| BMDP2V | 3-6 | U | 198 | 3x2 overall analysis |
| BMDP4V | 3-7 | M | 201 | 2x2 analysis |
| BMDP4V | 3-8 | M | 206 | 3x2 planned and overall analysis |
| Volume 2: SAS | | | | |
| SAS(GLM) | 3-1 | U | 176 | 2x2 analysis |
| SAS(GLM) | 3-2 | U | 180 | 3x2 planned analysis |
| SAS(GLM) | 3-3 | U | 185 | 3x2 overall analysis |
| SAS(GLM) | 3-4 | M | 191 | 2x2 analysis |
| SAS(GLM) | 3-5 | M | 202 | 3x2 planned univariate; overall multivariate analysis |

Table 3.1, continued

| Program | Program Number | Mode[1] | Page | I/O Feature(s) |
|---------|----------------|---------|------|----------------|
| | | Volume 3: SPSS and SPSSX | | |
| SPSS-SPSSX (ANOVA) | 3-1 | U | 214 | 2x2 analysis, option 9 |
| SPSS-SPSSX (MANOVA) | 3-2 | U | 219 | 2x2 analysis |
| SPSS-SPSSX (MANOVA) | 3-3 | U | 226 | 3x2 planned analysis, repeated and simple contrasts |
| SPSS-SPSSX (ANOVA) | 3-4 | U | 233 | 3x2 overall analysis |
| SPSS-SPSSX (MANOVA) | 3-5 | U | 238 | 3x2 overall analysis |
| SPSS-SPSSX (MANOVA) | 3-6 | M | 245 | 2x2 analysis |
| SPSS-SPSSX (MANOVA) | 3-7 | M | 262 | 3x2 planned analysis, special and simple contrasts |
| SPSS-SPSSX (MANOVA) | 3-8 | M | 277 | 3x2 overall analysis, special and simple contrasts |

[1]U = univariate, M = multivariate

178

presentations and discussions by both the teacher and the students. The heuristic method of instruction consisted of a series of lessons embedded in projects and games where knowledge of arithmetic was necessary for success. The theory and past research in this area indicated that the researcher could expect significant main effects, but was unclear as to what could be expected with respect to the interaction.

## Univariate Analysis: Planned Comparisons

We recommend that the reader consult other texts for further consideration of two-way ANOVA. Books available on this topic are listed in this section of Chapter 2.

### Problems.
(1) Does the difficulty level of a test affect student attitude towards the subject matter tested?

(2) Does the method of instruction affect student attitude towards a subject?

(3) Is there an interaction between the difficulty level of a test and the method of instruction which affects student attitude towards a subject?

Research Hypotheses. The research hypotheses were formulated on the basis of theory and previous research which were reviewed before the data were collected.

Research Hypothesis (1): Students who are given easy arithmetic tests will have more positive attitudes towards arithmetic than will those students who are given difficult tests.

Research Hypothesis (2): Students who are instructed in arithmetic using the heuristic method will have more positive attitudes towards arithmetic than will those students who are instructed under the auditory method.

Research Hypothesis (3): Test difficulty and method of instruction will interact so as to affect student attitude in a way that would not be predicted by test difficulty or method of instruction considered separately.

Statistical Hypotheses. The statistical hypotheses are written in symbolic form to match the research hypotheses. The symbol $u(i,j)$ represents the population mean for group $i,j$ ($i=1,2$), $j=1,2$): $H(0h)$ and $H(Ah)$ represent the null and alternate hypothesis for research hypothesis h ($h = 1,2,3$). Here (easy, auditory) is group 1,1; (easy, heuristic) is group 1,2; (difficult, auditory) is group 2,1; and (difficult, heuristic) is group 2,2.

Null Hypothesis (1), H(01):

$$\frac{u(1,1) + u(1,2)}{2} = \frac{u(2,1) + u(2,2)}{2}$$

Alternate Hypothesis (1), H(A1):

$$\frac{u(1,1) + u(1,2)}{2} > \frac{u(2,1) + u(2,2)}{2}$$

Null Hypothesis (2), H(02):

$$\frac{u(1,1) + u(2,1)}{2} = \frac{u(1,2) + u(2,2)}{2}$$

Alternate Hypothesis (2), H(A2):

$$\frac{u(1,2) + u(2,2)}{2} > \frac{u(1,1) + u(2,1)}{2}$$

Null Hypothesis (3), H(03):

$$u(1,1) - u(2,1) = u(1,2) - u(2,2)$$

Alternate Hypothesis (3), H(A3):

$$u(1,1) - u(2,1) \neq u(1,2) - u(2,2)$$

Each null hypothesis will be tested at the .05 level of significance[1].

Data. Although the study originally had 10 students in each cell, many students had to be eliminated after the study was under way because they were also found to be participating in a federally funded project to study mathematical problem solving ability. It was felt that this dual participation would confound the treatment effects. This, plus losses because students moved from the school district, yielded the cell sizes shown in Figure 3.1. It was assumed that the attrition of the subjects was not caused by treatment effects. (We realize that the resultant cell sizes are a bit bizarre, given random attrition, but the data were created to illustrate the program differences shown here and in Appendix A.)

In this presentation of the data we have deviated from the pattern you will find in the other chapters, i.e., all data present and then some data deleted to arrive at an unequal n design. The reason for this is that in Figure 3.1 we wanted to present summary statistics, and this would

Factor B
Instructional Method

| Factor A Test Type | Auditory | Heuristic | Mean |
|---|---|---|---|
| Easy | 6,4 <br> Cell 11, $\underline{n}$ = 2 <br> Mean = 5.00 <br> Variance = 2.00 | 5,7,8,6 <br> Cell 12, $\underline{n}$ = 4 <br> Mean = 6.50 <br> Variance = 1.67 | weighted 6.00 <br> unweighted 5.75 |
| Difficult | 3,3,2,4 <br> 6,5,2,2,1 <br> Cell 21, $\underline{n}$ = 9 <br> Mean = 3.11 <br> Variance = 2.61 | 6,5,4 <br> Cell 22, $\underline{n}$ = 3 <br> Mean = 5.00 <br> Variance = 1.00 | weighted 3.58 <br> unweighted 4.06 |
| Mean | weighted 3.45 <br> unweighted 4.06 | weighted 5.86 <br> unweighted 5.75 | |

Figure 3.1 Data and descriptive statistics from a two factor nonorthogonal, fixed effects experimental design, where the dependent variable was a measure of student attitude towards arithmetic.

be unwieldy if the data contained both equal and unequal n's. You are encouraged to consult Appendix A for the reason we have included both weighted and unweighted means in Figure 3.1.

Two-Way ANOVA Table. Table 3.2 is the planned comparison two-way ANOVA table (for unequal n's) which would appear in a research report on this experiment. The contents of this table could be drawn from all of the univariate program runs of this data, see Table 3.1.

The results in Table 3.2 indicate that the data from this experiment do not support the first two null hypotheses, but do support the interaction null hypothesis. Therefore, the first two research hypotheses were supported but the interaction research hypothesis was not supported. The researcher concluded that third grade students like those found in this study should be given easy (as opposed to difficult) exams and should be taught arithmetic using the heuristic method (as opposed to the auditory method) of instruction. He also conjectured (beyond the evidence of this study) that students with better attitudes would face further math courses with more optimism and confidence, and also be more likely to take elective math courses.

## Univariate Analysis: Overall Tests and Post Hoc Comparisons

If a researcher has no planned questions that he feels are appropriate (i.e. on the basis of theory or past research) to ask about his treatments, then he might conduct an overall test of significance. If the overall test is significant, then he would test differences among the treatment means using a post hoc test. In this case the problem statements would remain the same as in a planned comparison example, but the research hypotheses would change in that they would become less specific.

Problems.
(1)  Does the difficulty level of a test affect student attitude towards the subject matter tested?

(2)  Does the method of instruction affect student attitude towards a subject?

(3)  Is there an interaction between the difficulty level of a test and the method of instruction which affects student attitude towards a subject?

Research Hypothesis. In this case the researcher believes that differences will appear among his group means, but past research was inconclusive, and his theory is not formulated well enough for him to make specific

Table 3.2

Univariate Planned Comparisons Analysis of Variance for the
Test Type by Instructional Method Experiment.

| Source of Variation | Degrees of Freedom | Sum of Squares | Mean Square | t statistic | Prob |
|---|---|---|---|---|---|
| Test Type | 1 | 9.61 | 9.61 | 2.12 | .026[1] |
| Method | 1 | 9.61 | 9.61 | -2.12 | .026[1] |
| Interaction | 1 | .13 | .13 | .36 | .811[2] |
| Error (within groups) | 14 | 29.89 | 2.13 | | |
| Total (adjusted for grand mean) | 17 | 64.28 | | | |

[1]One-tailed test, significant p<.05
[2]Two-tailed test.

predictions.

Research Hypothesis (1): There will be a significant difference on mean attitude toward arithmetic between the students who are given easy tests and those students who were given difficult tests.

Research Hypothesis (2): There will be a significant difference on mean attitude between students who were instructed under the auditory method and those students instructed under the heuristic method.

Research Hypothesis (3): There will be a significant interaction between types of test and methods of instruction.

Statisical Hypotheses.

$$H(01): \frac{u(1,1) + u(1,2)}{2} = \frac{u(2,1) + u(2,2)}{2}$$

$$H(A1): \frac{u(1,1) + u(1,2)}{2} \neq \frac{u(2,1) + u(2,2)}{2}$$

$$H(02): \frac{u(1,1) + u(2,1)}{2} = \frac{u(1,2) + u(2,2)}{2}$$

$$H(A2): \frac{u(1,1) + u(2,1)}{2} \neq \frac{u(1,2) + u(2,2)}{2}$$

$$H(03): \quad u(1,1) - u(2,1) = u(1,2) - u(2,2)$$

$$H(A3): \quad u(1,1) - u(2,1) \neq u(1,2) - u(2,2)$$

Each null hypothesis will be tested at the .05 level of significance[1].

Data. The data are the unequal $n$ data presented in Figure 3.1.

Two-Way ANOVA Table. Table 3.3 is the two-way ANOVA source table that would appear in a research report on this experiment. The contents of this table could be derived from all of the univariate standard unequal $n$ program runs for this chapter. A similar table for an equal $n$ design could be constructed from all of these standard programs. The results in Table 3.3 indicate that the data from this experiment support all of the null hypotheses ($p < .0521$; $p < .0521$; $p < .8111$). Therefore, the research hypotheses are not supported. The results indicate that neither test type,

Table 3.3

Univariate Analysis of Variance for the Test Type by Method of
Instruction Experiment.

| Source of Variation | Degrees of Freedom | Sum of Squares | Mean Square | F-Ratio | Prob>F |
|---|---|---|---|---|---|
| Test type | 1 | 9.61 | 9.61 | 4.50 | .0521 |
| Method | 1 | 9.61 | 9.61 | 4.50 | .0521 |
| Interaction | 1 | .13 | .13 | .06 | .8111 |
| Error (within groups) | 14 | 29.89 | 2.13 | | |
| Total | 17 | 64.28 | | | |

instructional method, nor their interaction affect student attitude. Therefore the researcher decided to reconsider his theory. Note that if he were able to make predictions in advance, he would have found the significant main effects shown in Table 3.2.

Post Hoc Contrasts. In the latter example the overall test yielded no significant differences between the means for any of the sources of variation; therefore, no post hoc test would be done. Indeed, in the latter example, each main effect represented a contrast between two treatments so that a post hoc test would represent an academic exercise. When we consider the 3x2 example in this chapter, we will consider Fisher's LSD post hoc procedure.

## Multivariate Analysis: Planned Comparisons

We recommend that the reader consult other texts for further discussion of two-way MANOVA designs. Books available on this topic are listed in this section of Chapter 2.

The multivariate analysis presented here is an extension of the univariate planned comparisons analysis discussed earlier in this chapter. These contiguous presentations should allow readers who are unfamiliar with the multivariate model to compare it with the univariate model. In our MANOVA example, the design remains the same (i.e. two-way), but an additional dependent variable, student arithmetic achievement, is added. It was felt that student attitude and achievement are important dimensions of student learning. Here the researcher is interested in investigating the effects of two independent variables, degree of test difficulty and type of instructional method, on two dependent variables, student attitude and achievement.

Problems.
(1)   Does the difficulty level of a test affect student attitude towards and achievement in the subject matter?

(2)   Does the method of instruction affect student attitude towards and achievement in a subject?

(3)   Is there an interaction between the difficulty level of tests taken and the method of instruction received which affects student attitude towards and achievement in a subject?

Research Hypothesis. The research hypotheses were formulated on the basis of theory and previous research before the data were collected.

Research Hypothesis (1):   The students who are given

Factor B
Instruction Method

| Factor A Test Type | Auditory attitude | Auditory achievement | Heuristic attitude | Heuristic achievement | | |
|---|---|---|---|---|---|---|
| Easy | 6 | 10 | 5 | 13 | weighted means | |
| | 4 | 7 | 7 | 11 | 6.00  11.67 | |
| | | | 8 | 16 | unweighted | |
| | | | 6 | 13 | 5.75  10.88 | |
| | X̄=5.00 | X̄=8.50 | X̄=6.50 | X̄=13.25 | | |
| Difficult | 3 | 6 | 6 | 7 | weighted means | |
| | 3 | 3 | 5 | 11 | 3.58  5.08 | |
| | 2 | 1 | 4 | 9 | unweighted | |
| | 4 | 8 | | | 4.06  6.39 | |
| | 6 | 5 | | | | |
| | 5 | 4 | | | | |
| | 2 | 2 | | | | |
| | 2 | 2 | | | | |
| | 1 | 3 | | | | |
| | X̄=3.11 | X̄=3.78 | X̄=5.00 | X̄=9.00 | | |
| weighted means | 3.45 | 4.64 | 5.86 | 11.43 | | |
| unweighted means | 4.06 | 6.14 | 5.75 | 11.12 | | |

Figure 3.2  Data and means for a two factor nonorthogonal, fixed-effects experimental design, where the dependent variables are student attitude towards and achievement in arithmetic (from Stevens and Barcikowski, 1984).

easy arithmetic tests will differ on achievement and attitude from those students who are given difficult tests.

Research Hypothesis (2): The students who are instructed in arithmetic using the heuristic method will differ in attitude and achievement from those students who are instructed under the auditory method.

Research Hypothesis (3): Test difficulty and method of instruction will interact so as to affect student attitude and achievement in a way that would not be predicted by test difficulty or method of instruction considered separately.

Statistical Hypotheses. The statistical hypotheses are written in symbolic form to match the research hypotheses. Here the symbol $u(pij)$ represents the population mean for variable $p$ ($p = 1,2$) in group $i,j$ ($i = 1,2$), ($j = 1,2$), and the symbol $\underline{u}(ij)$ represents the vector of means containing both dependent variable means from treatment $i,j$. Here (easy, auditory) is group 1,1; (easy, heuristic) is group 1,2; (difficult, auditory) is group 2,1; and (difficult, heuristic) is group 2,2.

$$H(01): \quad \frac{\underline{u}(11) + \underline{u}(12)}{2} = \frac{\underline{u}(21) + \underline{u}(22)}{2}$$

$$H(A1): \quad \frac{\underline{u}(11) + \underline{u}(12)}{2} \neq \frac{\underline{u}(21) + \underline{u}(22)}{2}$$

$$H(02): \quad \frac{\underline{u}(11) + \underline{u}(21)}{2} = \frac{\underline{u}(12) + \underline{u}(22)}{2}$$

$$H(A2): \quad \frac{\underline{u}(11) + \underline{u}(21)}{2} \neq \frac{\underline{u}(12) + \underline{u}(22)}{2}$$

$$H(03): \quad \underline{u}(11) - \underline{u}(21) = \underline{u}(12) - \underline{u}(22)$$

$$H(A3): \quad \underline{u}(12) - \underline{u}(22) \neq \underline{u}(11) - \underline{u}(21)$$

Each null hypothesis was tested at the .05 level of significance[1].

Data. The data are presented in Figure 3.2 as a multivariate, unequal $\underline{n}$ problem. The design is the two-factor design that we considered in the univariate case, but here we have included a second dependent variable, arithmetic achievement.

Measures of each dependent variable were arrived at using Barth's attitude and achievement scales. The

188

subjects (third grade students) were randomly selected from a large city population and then were randomly assigned to the four treatment combinations. A further description of the treatments and the loss of subjects may be found in the univariate presentation at the beginning of this chapter.

Two-Way MANOVA Table. Table 3.4 is the planned comparison two-way MANOVA table that would appear in a research report on this experiment. The complete contents of this table can be drawn from all of the programs run on this data set, see Table 3.1. Note, however, that SAS (GLM) does not yield planned MANOVA comparisons; the reason this program provides results here is that there are only two levels with each factor.

The results in Table 3.4 indicate that the first two null hypotheses were rejected (H(01), p<.0094; H(02), p<.0046) and that the interaction null hypothesis was supported (p <.9686). Then, in order to help indicate what caused the multivariate tests to be significant, the researcher may turn to the univariate tests that are also reported in Table 3.4. Here we see that both the test type and method of instruction groups are, at the .05 level of significance, primarily differentiated on achievement (test type p<.0019; method of instruction p<.0008) and that neither group had significant mean differences on attitude (p<.0521 for both groups). When we observe the following group vector mean differences,

### Test Type

|             | Easy    | Difficult |      |       |
|-------------|---------|-----------|------|-------|
| Attitude    | 5.75    | 4.06      | =    | 1.69  |
| Achievement | 10.88   | 6.39      |      | 4.49  |

### Method of Instruction

|             | Auditory | Heuristic |      |        |
|-------------|----------|-----------|------|--------|
| Attitude    | 4.06     | 5.75      | =    | -1.69  |
| Achievement | 6.14     | 11.12     |      | -4.98  |

we see that: 1. students who had the easy tests had higher mean achievement on the Earth achievement test than students who had the difficult tests; 2. students who received instruction with the heuristic method had higher mean achievement than students who had the auditory method of instruction; 3. student attitude mean differences were in the same direction as the achievement means, but were

Table 3.4
Multivariate Planned Comparisons Analysis
of Variance for the Test by Method of Instruction Experiment

| Source of Variation | Sums of Squares and Products Attitude | Achievement | Multivariate Wilks' Lambda | Df | F(Probability) | Univariate Df | F (Probability) Attitude | F (Probability) Achievement |
|---|---|---|---|---|---|---|---|---|
| Test Type | [ 9.61 [25.46 | 25.46] 67.40] | .49 | 2 | 6.82* (.0094) | 1 | 4.50 (.0521) | 14.56* (.0019) |
| Method of Instruction | [ 9.61 [28.29 | 28.29] 83.26] | .44 | 2 | 8.36* (.0046) | 1 | 4.50 (.0521) | 17.99* (.0008) |
| Interaction (Test Type by Instruction) | [ .13 [ .15 | .15] .19] | 1.00 | 2 | .03 (.9686) | 1 | .06 (.8111) | .04 (.8437) |
| Error (within groups) | [29.89 [20.72 | 20.72] 64.81] | | 13 | | 14 | | |

* Significant at p<.05

not significantly different. In interpreting these results
a researcher may conclude that students will have higher
mean achievement when using the heuristic method with easy
tests (i.e., tests composed of items that were passed by
70% of past students) during the school term. Also, some
researchers may claim that the loss of 22 students severely
hurt the power of the statistical tests to discern attitude
differences, and that under replication they would expect
that attitude would also be higher in the heuristic group
with easy tests.

It is of interest to note that if the researcher had
predicted that mean attitude and achievement scores would
be larger for the easy test condition and for the heuristic
method of instruction, then he would have established (a
priori) one-tailed univariate tests to follow the
multivariate test. In this case both univariate tests
would have been significant (p<.0261, p <.0010,
respectively, for the attitude and achievement comparison
between the test types, and p<.0261, p<.0004,
respectively, for the comparison between the methods of
instruction). This result is modified, however, by the
fact that the step-down tests (shown in the SPSS(MANOVA)
output and discussed in Appendix C) indicate that attitude
with achievement partialled from it does not significantly
differentiate between either of the test types (p<.807) or
the instructional methods (p<.929), but that achievement
with attitude partialled from it (these results are not
shown) does significantly differentiate between both groups
(p<.019; p<.009). These step-down tests strongly indicate
that what is causing group differentiation is the
achievement variable and that including attitude does not
add much to this differentiation. This finding may
encourage the researcher to replicate this study and to use
the step-down procedure with the attitude variable ordered
last (tested first) in a step-down analysis as a means of
investigating this multivariate problem.

### Multivariate Analysis: Overall Tests and Post Hoc Comparisons

A researcher who has no planned questions that he
feels are appropriate (i.e., on the basis of theory or past
research) to ask about his treatments, might conduct an
overall test of significance for each main source of
variation, i.e., A, B, AXB. If these overall multivariate
tests are not significant, further testing is considered
inappropriate. This last statement is frequently difficult
for some researchers to practice, because in their computer
output univariate tests are automatically provided, and one
of them may be significant. The temptation is to interpret
this significant univariate test. However, if the study
has been properly composed, there is a good chance that one
or more significant univariate tests, following a
nonsignificant overall multivariate test, represent

spurious results. The best approach to this problem is for the researcher to conduct another study.

In the two-way design considered in this chapter we have only two levels with each factor; therefore, the problems, research hypotheses, statistical hypotheses, and results are exactly the same as those shown for the multivariate planned comparisons, and they will not be repeated here. This illustrates a fundamental difference in the use of planned comparisons in a multivariate analysis versus a univariate analysis. In a univariate analysis one may use planned comparisons to test directional questions, e.g., by indicating in the alternate hypothesis that one group's achievement mean will be larger than another group's achievement mean. However, in multivariate analysis one is concerned with making predictions about more than one correlated variable, and therefore, the alternate hypothesis is nondirectional. The function of planned comparisons in multivariate analysis is to ask if groups differ; it is left to step-down analysis (Appendix C) or discriminant analysis (Chapter 2) to test questions concerning individual variable potency and direction. That is, it is through step-down analysis and/or discriminant analysis that a researcher is able to indicate the direction of treatment differences on a variable, and/or whether a variable plays an important role in a construct that differentiates between one or more treatments.

## Roy-Bose Simultaneous Confidence Intervals (Post Hoc Tests)

In the preceding chapter on one-way analysis we followed a significant overall multivariate test with what would be considered a liberal (with respect to Type I experimentwise error rate) post hoc testing procedure, i.e., pairwise univariate tests. In this section we will present multivariate simultaneous confidence intervals (Morrison, 1967; Stevens, 1973) which represent a more conservative approach (with respect to Type I experimentwise error rate) to post hoc comparisons. This presentation is based on Morrison[2] (1967, pp. 182-186) and will be referred to as the Roy-Bose simultaneous confidence interval since it was first presented by Roy and Bose (1953). Morrison's presentation is modified here for use with the full rank general linear model (see Morrison p. 161, formula (9)).

The Roy-Bose simultaneous confidence interval procedure is used only after the multivariate null hypothesis has been rejected; it can be calculated using the following steps.

Step 1. State the general linear model for the design. The general linear model in full rank may be written as Y = XB + E where,

N = total number of units cf analysis (e.g., subjects) in the design,

P = the number of dependent variables,

L = the number of cells in the design,

Y is the N X P matrix of observed scores on the dependent variables (across all cells in the design),

X is the N X L design matrix which is composed of ones and zeros,

B is the L X P matrix of population cell means, and

E is the N X P matrix of errors (deviations of each score from its cell population mean).

Example. Our two-way multivariate general linear model may be written as:

$$
\begin{bmatrix} 6 & 10 \\ 4 & 7 \\ 5 & 13 \\ 7 & 11 \\ 8 & 16 \\ 6 & 13 \\ 3 & 6 \\ 3 & 3 \\ 2 & 1 \\ 4 & 8 \\ 6 & 5 \\ 5 & 4 \\ 2 & 2 \\ 2 & 2 \\ 1 & 3 \\ 6 & 7 \\ 5 & 11 \\ 4 & 9 \end{bmatrix}
=
\begin{bmatrix} 1 & 0 & 0 & 0 \\ 1 & 0 & 0 & 0 \\ 0 & 1 & 0 & 0 \\ 0 & 1 & 0 & 0 \\ 0 & 1 & 0 & 0 \\ 0 & 1 & 0 & 0 \\ 0 & 0 & 1 & 0 \\ 0 & 0 & 1 & 0 \\ 0 & 0 & 1 & 0 \\ 0 & 0 & 1 & 0 \\ 0 & 0 & 1 & 0 \\ 0 & 0 & 1 & 0 \\ 0 & 0 & 1 & 0 \\ 0 & 0 & 1 & 0 \\ 0 & 0 & 1 & 0 \\ 0 & 0 & 0 & 1 \\ 0 & 0 & 0 & 1 \\ 0 & 0 & 0 & 1 \end{bmatrix}
\begin{bmatrix} u(111) & u(211) \\ u(112) & u(212) \\ u(121) & u(221) \\ u(122) & u(222) \end{bmatrix}
+
\begin{bmatrix} e(1111) & e(2111) \\ e(1112) & e(2112) \\ e(1121) & e(2121) \\ e(1122) & e(2122) \\ e(1123) & e(2123) \\ e(1124) & e(2124) \\ e(1211) & e(2211) \\ e(1212) & e(2212) \\ e(1213) & e(2213) \\ e(1214) & e(2214) \\ e(1215) & e(2215) \\ e(1216) & e(2216) \\ e(1217) & e(2217) \\ e(1218) & e(2218) \\ e(1219) & e(2219) \\ e(1221) & e(2221) \\ e(1222) & e(2222) \\ e(1223) & e(2223) \end{bmatrix}
$$

Y          =          X                   B                +          E

Where u(pij) and e(pijk) are subscripted with: variable p, cell i, j, and within cell subject k.

Step 2. State the multivariate null hypothesis. The general form of the multivariate null hypothesis is: ABC' = D where,

G is the number of contrasts among the cell means that one decides tc investigate, G ≤ the between degrees of freedom from the source of variation under investigation.

L is the number of cells in the design,

P is the number of dependent variables,

M is the number of contrasts among the dependent variables that one decides to investigate, M ≤ P,

A is a G X L matrix of contrasts among treatment cell means,

B is a L X P matrix of unknown population cell

means on the dependent variables,
C' is a P X M matrix of contrasts among the
dependent variables, and
D is a G X M matrix of known population values.

Example. In the problem we have been considering we may state the multivariate null hypothesis of no test type effects as:

$$H(01) : [1/2 \quad 1/2 \quad -1/2 \quad -1/2] \begin{bmatrix} u(111) & u(211) \\ u(112) & u(212) \\ u(121) & u(221) \\ u(122) & u(222) \end{bmatrix} = [0 \quad 0]$$

$$\quad\quad\quad\quad\quad\quad\quad\quad A \quad\quad\quad\quad\quad\quad\quad\quad B \quad\quad\quad = \quad D$$

where C' (from the general form of the null hypothesis) is the identity matrix and is not needed in the hypothesis equation.

Step 3. Let a' represent a row of A for a contrast of interest. Calculate the constant b as:

$$b = \underline{a}' (X'X)^{-1} \underline{a}.$$

Example. Let Nij represent the number of subjects in cell i,j then, for our example problem we have:

$$(X'X)^{-1} = \begin{bmatrix} 1/2 & 0 & 0 & 0 \\ 0 & 1/4 & 0 & 0 \\ 0 & 0 & 1/9 & 0 \\ 0 & 0 & 0 & 1/3 \end{bmatrix}$$

Since there is only one row of contrasts in A, for the hypothesis of no test type effect, we have that A = a', and

$$A(X'X)^{-1}A' = \frac{1}{4} \begin{bmatrix} \dfrac{1}{2} + \dfrac{1}{4} + \dfrac{1}{9} + \dfrac{1}{3} \end{bmatrix} = .29861$$

so that, b = .29861.

Step 4. The Roy-Bose simultaneous confidence interval for the function a'Ec'r may be written as:

$$\underline{a}' (X'X)^{-1} X' Y C' \underline{r} - \sqrt{\frac{b \, H(alpha)}{1 - H(alpha)} \underline{r}' E \underline{r}}$$

$$\leq \underline{a}' B C' \underline{r} \leq$$

194

$$\underline{a}' (X' X)^{-1} X' Y C' \underline{r} + \sqrt{\frac{b\ H\ (alpha)}{1 - H\ (alpha)}\ \underline{r}'\ E\ \underline{r}}$$

where, $\underline{r}$ is an MX1 ncn null vector of real elements, and H (alpha) is the 100 (alpha) percentage point that is read from charts compiled by Heck (1960) (see Morrison, 1967, pp. 312-319). The parameters needed to find H (alpha) are:

s = min (G, p),
m = ( |G - p| - 1)/2,
n = (DFE - p - 1)/2,
DFE = degrees of freedom for error, i.e., where DFE = N - Q - 1, where Q is the total of the degrees of freedom for all factorial sources of variation in the design, and E is the error sums of squares and cross products matrix, E-SSCP. (Note that we also used E to represent the error matrix in the general model.)

Example. In our design we may desire to establish Roy-Bose simultaneous confidence intervals for the unweighted mean attitude and achievement differences found between the test type levels. To do this we must fill in the needed matrices and vectors in Step 4. Since C' is an identity matrix and may be dropped, we have that the simultaneous confidence interval becomes:

$$\underline{a}' (X' X)^{-1} X' Y \underline{r} - \sqrt{\frac{b\ H\ (alpha)}{1 - H\ (alpha)}\ \underline{r}'\ E\ \underline{r}}$$

$$\leq \underline{a}'\ B\ \underline{r} \leq$$

$$\underline{a}' (X' X)^{-1} X' Y \underline{r} + \sqrt{\frac{b\ H\ (alpha)}{1 - H\ (alpha)}\ \underline{r}'\ E\ \underline{r}}$$

Here we see that $\underline{a}'B$ (in the center of this inequality) =

$$\left[ \frac{u(111)+u(112)}{2} - \frac{u(121)+u(122)}{2} \quad \frac{u(211)+u(212)}{2} - \frac{u(221)+u(222)}{2} \right]$$

and that if we want a simultaneous confidence interval on the unweighted attitude means we select

$$\underline{r} = \begin{bmatrix} 0 \\ 1 \end{bmatrix}.$$

Now, $(X' X)^{-1} X'Y$ yields the L X P matrix of our

sample cell means, i.e.,

$$(X' X)^{-1} X'Y = \begin{bmatrix} 5.00 & 8.50 \\ 6.50 & 13.25 \\ 3.11 & 2.78 \\ 5.00 & 9.00 \end{bmatrix}$$

So that $\underline{a}'$ $(X' X)^{-1} X'Y$ yields the vector of unweighted cell mean differences, i.e.,

$$\underline{a}' (X' X)^{-1} X'Y = \begin{bmatrix} 1.695 & 4.985 \end{bmatrix} .$$

H(.05) with s = 1, m = 0, n = 5.5 is not available from the Heck charts, but may be found using (Morrison, p. 167)

$$H(alpha) = \frac{(m + 1) F (alpha)}{(n + 1) + (m + 1) F (alpha)}$$

where F (alpha) is Fisher's F (the 1-alpha percentile) with 2m + 2 and 2n + 2 degrees of freedom. In our case F (.05; 2, 13) = 3.81 and H (alpha) = 3.81/ (6.5 + 3.81) = .37. The value of E, is (from Table 3.4)

$$E = \begin{bmatrix} 29.89 & 20.72 \\ 20.72 & 64.81 \end{bmatrix}$$

Then, setting $\underline{r} = \begin{bmatrix} 1 \\ 0 \end{bmatrix}$,

and substituting the preceding values into the Roy-Bose simultaneous confidence interval, we have:

$$1.695 - \sqrt{((.29861 \times .37)/(1-.37))}\ 29.89$$

$$\leq u(11.) - u(12.) \leq$$

$$1.695 + \sqrt{((.29861 \times .37)/(1-.37))}\ 29.89$$

where u(pi.) is the unweighted mean of factor A, for variable p and treatment level i; the dot notation indicates that we summed across the j levels of Factor B. The final calculations yield:

$$-.59 \leq u(11.) - u(12.) \leq 3.97$$

The preceding interval contains zero and therefore no significant difference is indicated between the attitudes of those students who had different test types.

Setting $r = \begin{bmatrix} 0 \\ 1 \end{bmatrix}$ ,

we have the following simultaneous confidence interval for the unweighted achievement mean differences for factor A:

$$1.13 \leq u(21_.) - u(22_.) \leq 7.87.$$

This interval does not contain zero and therefore a significant difference was found between the achievement of those students who had easy tests and those students who had difficult tests.

The reader should note that the Roy-Bose simultaneous confidence intervals are similar to the confidence intervals found in univariate analysis with the Scheffe technique (discussed in Chapter 7). Both procedures require an overall test to be significant before they may be used by the researcher to help discern what caused this overall significance. Also, both yield confidence intervals such that the probability is 1-alpha that all such possible intervals are simultaneously true. This causes their per comparison error rates to be much less than alpha, and therefore, they may be most appropriate as a follow-up procedure when large sample sizes are used. Hummel and Sligo (1971) discuss the conservative nature of the Roy-Bose intervals.

## Analysis of Variance Presentations: (3 x 2) Example

In our second example the univariate and multivariate data were created especially for this text, but the idea for the problem was taken from an article by Williams and Ware (1977). The focus of this presentation is on the interaction that is found both in the univariate and multivariate analyses. The format is the same as that found in the preceding (2 x 2) example, i.e., univariate planned and overall analyses, followed by multivariate planned and overall analyses. A brief discussion of the nature of the problem follows. (Readers who are unfamiliar with what an interaction is should find the discussion at the beginning of Chapter 4 helpful.)

### Problem

A researcher was curious about the effects of the amount of content covered by a lecturer and the expressiveness of the lecturer on a measure of student subject matter interest. He was interested in this problem because of past research by Ware and Williams (1975) where an actor was hired to perform six lecture types using all combinations of three content coverages (high, medium, low) and two levels of lecturer expressiveness (low, high). Their findings indicated that students had higher

197

achievement under the highly expressive lecturer and when they were exposed to high content coverage. However, when a measure of student ratings of the lecturer was used as the dependent variable "Mean student ratings were not sensitive to either variations in content coverage or group achievement when lectures were highly expressive (Williams and Ware, 1977, p. 450)." Ware and Williams (1975) labeled this interaction the "Dr. Fox effect," and this effect was replicated by Williams and Ware (1977) after students were repeatedly exposed to the lectures.

In the present study the six treatment conditions noted by Ware and Williams were created for use with ninth graders who were studying a science section on astronomy. An actor was hired to create six videotaped astronomy lectures. In the lectures "verbatim scripts were used to insure control of content coverage (Williams and Ware, 1977, p. 451)". The medium content lecture covered 50% less material than did the high content lecture, and the low content lecture covered 15% of the material in the high content lecture. "Levels of expressiveness were associated with differences in vocal inflection, friendliness, charisma, humor, and 'personality' (Williams and Ware, 1977, p. 451)." Twenty four schools were randomly selected from the population of schools in a large city school system. Within each school, one ninth grade class was randomly sampled and randomly placed within one of the six treatment conditions. This process left four classrooms within each treatment combination, however a teacher strike in three of the schools (which was unrelated to the study) caused them to be eliminated from the analysis. In this design the unit of analysis is the classroom and the dependent variable is measured through the mean classroom interest ratings (see Barcikowski (1981) for a discussion of power when an aggregate is used as the unit of analysis). Since the researcher was interested in an affective variable that was similar to the lecturer ratings used in the studies by Ware and Williams, he expected to find an interaction effect. (See the next chapter for a further discussion of interactions from two- and three-way analyses).

## Univariate Analysis: Planned Comparisons

In this analysis the researcher is interested in determining if the "Dr. Fox effect" exists when the dependent variable is class interest.

Problem. Is class interest insensitive to content coverage when an expressive lecture is given, but sensitive to content coverage when an inexpressive lecture is given?

Research Hypothesis. Classrooms exposed to a highly expressive lecture will not differ in subject matter interest, while classrooms exposed to a low expressive

198

lecture will vary according to the amount of content covered in the lecture.

Statistical Hypothesis. In the analysis of the design considered here, the source of variation for the interaction has two degrees of freedom. Here each statistical hypothesis is associated with a simple interaction effect having one degree of freedom. The symbol $u(ij)$ represents the population mean for group $i,j$ ($i = 1,2,3$), ($j = 1,2$); $H(Ch)$ and $H(Ah)$ represent the null and alternate hypotheses for simple interaction effect h (h = 1,2). Here (high content, low expressiveness) is group 1,1; (high content, high expressiveness) is group 1,2; (medium content, low expressiveness) is group 2,1; (medium content, high expressiveness) is group 2,2; (low content, low expressiveness) is group 3,1; and (low content, high expressiveness) is group 3,2.

$$H(01): \quad u(11) - u(21) = u(12) - u(22)$$

$$H(A1): \quad u(11) - u(21) > u(12) - u(22)$$

$$H(02): \quad u(21) - u(31) = u(22) - u(32)$$

$$H(A2): \quad u(21) - u(31) > u(22) - u(32)$$

Figure 3.3 illustrates how a plot of the means from each cell is expected to look. Each null hypothesis will be tested at the .05 level of significance.

Data. The data are presented in Figure 3.4.

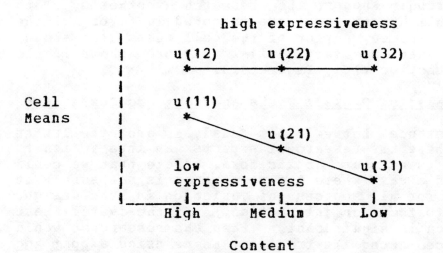

Figure 3.3   Expected interaction plot of the population cell class interest means, given the research hypothesis, and past research results.

199

Low                High

Content

High

| | Low | High |
|---|---|---|

131          140
126          145
134          141
$\bar{X}(11)=130.33$    142
                    $\bar{X}(12)=142.00$

$\bar{X}(1.)=136.17$

Medium

104          140
105          144
102          $\bar{X}(22)=142.00$
102
$\bar{X}(21)=103.25$

$\bar{X}(2.)=122.63$

Low

74          142
71          138
69          144
67          146
$\bar{X}(31)=70.25$    $\bar{X}(32)=142.50$

$\bar{X}(3.)=106.38$

$\bar{X}(.1)=101.28$    $\bar{X}(.2)=142.17$

Figure 3.4    Data and unweighted means from a two
              factor nonorthogonal, fixed effects
              experimental design, where the scores
              are class interest means.

Two-Way ANOVA Table.    Table 3.5 is the table which
would appear in a research report on this experiment.    The
contents of this table could be drawn from BMDP4V,
SAS(GLM), or SPSS(MANOVA).    The results from this
experiment strongly support the research hypothesis; both
interaction null hypotheses were rejected in favor of the
alternatives.    Indeed, a plot of the cell means (not shown)
yields reults that are very similar to those shown in the
expected interaction plct, Figure 3.3.

Univariate Analysis: Overall Tests and Post Hoc Comparisons

The difference between this analysis and the latter
one is that here the researcher expects an interaction to
occur, but he is not sure of its form. (Note that we could
have presented a case where the researcher is not sure what
would happen for all sources of variation in the design,
but we chose to focus on interaction.) If the overall test
for interaction is significant, then the researcher would
test differences among the treatment means using a post hoc
test. Here the prcblem is stated in less specific form
than in the previous analysis.

Problem.    Is there an interaction between the amount
of subject content in a lecture and the expressiveness of
the lecturer that will affect a class's interest in the

Table 3.5

Univariated Planned Comparisons Analysis of Variance
for the Content by Expressiveness Experiment

| Source of Variation | Degrees of Freedom | Sum of Squares | Mean Square | t Statistic | Prob[1] |
|---|---|---|---|---|---|
| Content (C) | 2 | 3301.61 | | | |
| Expressiveness | 1 | 8207.52 | | | |
| C X E | 2 | 3418.10 | | | |
| Comparisons | | | | | |
| C1 X E | 1 | 550.13 | 550.13 | 8.19* | .0000 |
| C2 X E | 1 | 897.80 | 897.80 | 10.46* | .0000 |
| Error (within groups) | 15 | 123.17 | 8.21 | | |
| Total (adjusted for grand mean) | 20 | 16386.95 | | | |

[1]The programs do not report probabilities to more than four places;
SAS(GLM) reports .0001 as its smallest value.
*significant at p<.05.

201

subject matter?

Research Hypothesis. There will be a significant interaction between amount of subject matter content in a lecture and the expressiveness of the lecturer that will affect a class's interest in the subject matter.

Statistical Hypothesis. There are a variety of ways in which the interaction hypothesis can be specified, but when the interaction research hypothesis is not specific (as is the case here), a simple approach makes use of the equation used to represent an observation, i.e., $Y(ijk) = u + a(i) + b(j) + g(ij) + e(ijk)$. Here Y is the score of observation k in cell (i,j); u is the population grand mean of all observations; a represents the treatment effect for treatment i of factor A; b represents the treatment effect for treatment j of factor B; g represents the interaction between treatment i of factor A and treatment j of factor B; and, e(ijk) is that part of Y that is not accounted for by the other sources of variation in the equation. Then we have the following overall interaction hypothesis:

$H(0)$: $g(ij) = 0$ for all $i,j$

$H(A)$: $g(ij) \neq 0$ for some $i,j$.

The overall hypothesis will be tested at the .05 level of significance.

Data. The data are the unequal $n$ data shown in Figure 3.4.

Two-Way ANOVA Table. Table 3.6 is the two-way ANOVA source table that would appear in a research report on this experiment. The contents of this table could be derived from all of the univariate standard unequal $n$ program runs for this chapter. The results in Table 3.6 indicate that the interaction null hypothesis is to be rejected (p<.0000). (The results also show that the main effects null hypotheses would be rejected, but these results were not of major interest in this study which is focused on the interaction.) Since an overall interaction was found in the study, the researcher decided to follow the overall test with Fisher's LSD post hoc contrasts (here we use the same contrasts that we used for the planned comparisons). A discussion of this approach follows.

Fisher's (LSD) Post Hoc Contrasts. Kirk (1968) indicates that the LSD test "has been widely used in research but is not generally recommended by statisticians (p.87)." The reason for its poor recommendation is due to the generally poor control of experimentwise Type I error provided by this test. However, Carmer and Swanson[3] (1973) indicate that although Fisher's LSD may provide poor protection against Type I error, it is excellent at detecting real mean differences when they do exist. On

Table 3.6

Univariate Analysis of Variance for the
Content by Expressiveness Experiment

| Source of Variation | Degrees of Freedom | Sum of Squares | Mean Square | F Statistic | Prob[1] |
|---|---|---|---|---|---|
| Content (C) | 2 | 3301.61 | 1650.81 | 201.05* | .0000 |
| Expressiveness (E) | 1 | 8207.52 | 8207.52 | 999.56* | .0000 |
| Interaction: C X E | 2 | 3418.10 | 1709.05 | 208.14* | .0000 |
| Error (within groups) | 15 | 123.17 | 8.21 | | |
| Total (adjusted for the grand mean) | 20 | 16386.95 | | | |

[1]The programs do not report probabilities to more than four digits; SAS(GLM) does not report values less than .0001.
*Significant at p<.05.

203

this basis they recommended Fisher's LSD over eight other pairwise multiple comparison techniques (they found one other technique, the Waller-Duncan Bayes exact test, that had similar characteristics to Fisher's LSD, but recommended LSD because of its ease of computation). The following steps indicate how Fisher's LSD may be calculated in general and for the interaction contrast $u(1,1) - u(2,1) = u(1,2) - u(2,2)$ that the researcher decided to test after the overall significant interaction was found in the content by expressiveness experiment.

Step 1. Calculate Fisher's LSD for each mean comparison as:

$$LSD\ (1) = \sqrt{(F)\ (MSE)\left[\frac{(C(ij))^2}{n(ij)} + \frac{(C(ij)')^2}{n(ij)'} + \ldots + \frac{(C(ij)'')^2}{n(ij)''}\right]}$$

Here l is the number of the contrast of interest; F is the F statistic with the same level of significance as the overall test, with 1 and DFE degrees of freedom; DFE = the error degrees of freedom in the overall test; MSE = mean square error; $C(ij)$, $C(ij)'$ ... $C(ij)''$ are the coefficients that are multiplied times the cell means in order to form the contrast of interest; and, $n(ij)$, $n(ij)'$ ... $n(ij)''$ are the cell sample sizes for the cell means being compared.

Example. From our 3 x 2 example problem we decided to illustrate Fisher's LSD with the interaction contrast $u(1,1) - u(2,1) - u(1,2) + u(2,2) = 0$. Therefore, the coefficients that are multiplied times the cell means are:

    C (11) =  1
    C (12) = -1
    C (21) = -1
    C (22) =  1

2.  The cell sample sizes are:

    n (11) = 3
    n (12) = 4
    n (21) = 4
    n (22) = 2

3.  F (05: 1, 15) = 4.54

4.  MSE = 8.21

5.  Then, Fisher's LSD is found as:

$$LSD\ (1) = \sqrt{(4.54)\ (8.21)\ \left[1/3 + 1/4 + 1/4 + 1/2\right]}$$

    LSD (1) = 7.05

Step 2. Calculate the observed mean differences for the contrasts of interest.

<u>Example.</u>   For our example we decided  to illustrate
only one contrast, and it is:

130.33 - 142.00 - 103.25 + 142.00 = 27.08.

<u>Step 3.</u>   Compare the contrast(s) found in Step 2 with
the (their) associated LSD(1)  value(s).   If a contrast is
larger than its  associated LSD (1)   then a  significant
difference  has  been  found,   if not,   no  significant
difference has been found.

<u>Example.</u>   In our example problem we have that

contrast value > LSD (1)

27.08 > 7.05

Therefore,  there is a significant interaction between
content and expressiveness  in the first four  cells of the
design.

<u>Equal n.</u>   The formula for LSD (1)  given above is most
profitably  used  when  there  are  an  unequal  number  of
subjects per cell.   When $n(ij)$  are all equal we will have
only one  value for LSD,  and  may drop the  1 designation.
Here LSD becomes

$$LSD = \sqrt{(F) \ (MSE) \ (2K) \ (i/n)}$$

where,  F,  MSE,  and  n are defined as above and  K is the
number  of  cell means  that  are  in  the  contrast.   The
contrast on the  cell means is then calculated  as with the
unequal n case,  where a  significant contrast is one whose
sample value is larger than the value of LSD.

## Multivariate Analysis: Planned Comparisons

The  multivariate   analysis  presented  here   is  an
extension  of  the univariate  planned comparisons  analysis
discussed earlier for the 3 x 2 factorial design.    In this
MANOVA example we  have added  two  additional  dependent
measures,  an instructor  rating form which focuses  on the
lecturer's organization and preparation,   and a measure of
student achievement in astronomy.    Here the researcher is
interested in investigating the  effects of two independent
variables, subject matter content and the expressiveness of
the lecturer,   on three  dependent variables,   instructor
rating, class interest, and class achievement.

<u>Problem.</u>   Is a class's  instructor rating,  interest,
and  achievement insensitive  to content  coverage when  an
expressive lecture  is  given,  but sensitive to  content
coverage when an expressive lecture is given?

<u>Research Hypothesis.</u>    Classes  exposed  to  a  highly

expressive lecturer will not differ in instructor rating,
subject interest, and achievement, while classes exposed to
a low expressive lecture will vary on all three of the
measures according to the amount of content covered in the
lecture.

Statistical Hypotheses. The statistical hypotheses
are those associated with the two simple interactions
discussed earlier. Here the symbol u(pij) represents the
population mean for variable $p$ ($p$ = 1,2,3) in group i,j (i =
1,2,3; j = 1,2), and the symbol $\underline{u}$(ij) represents the vector
of means containing all three dependent variable means from
treatment i,j. The symbols H(Oh) and H(Ah) represent the
null and alternate hypotheses for simple interaction effect
h (h = 1,2). Here (high content, low expressiveness) is
group 1,1; (high content, high expressiveness) is group
1,2; (medium content, low expressiveness) is group 2,1;
(medium content, high expressiveness) is group 2,2; (low
content, low expressiveness) is group 3,1; and (low
content, high expressiveness) is group 3,2.

$$H(01): \underline{u}(11) - \underline{u}(21) = \underline{u}(12) - \underline{u}(22)$$

$$H(A1): \underline{u}(11) - \underline{u}(21) \neq \underline{u}(12) - \underline{u}(22)$$

$$H(02): \underline{u}(21) - \underline{u}(31) = \underline{u}(22) - \underline{u}(32)$$

$$H(A2): \underline{u}(21) - \underline{u}(31) \neq \underline{u}(22) - \underline{u}(32)$$

Figure 3.3 illustrates how a plot of each of the
dependent variable cell means is expected to look. Each
null hypothesis will be tested at the .05 level of
significance.

Data. The data are presented in Figure 3.5.

Two-Way MANOVA Table. Table 3.7 is the planned
comparison two-way MANOVA which would appear in a research
report describing this experiment. The contents of this
table can be drawn from the output from BMDP4V and
SPSS(MANOVA). The results of this experiment strongly
support the research hypothesis for the affective
variables, instructor rating and student interest, but fail
to support the research hypothesis for the cognitive
variable, student achievement. That is both simple
interaction effects were significant at the multivariate
level (p<.000 for both simple interactions), and the
corresponding univariate tests were significant for
instructor rating (p<.001 for the first simple interaction;
p<.001 for the second simple interaction), and student
interest in the subject (p<.000 for both simple
interactions), but the univariate tests were not
significant for the achievement measure (p<.411 for the
first simple interaction; p<.415 for the second simple
interaction). In reviewing the study the researcher found

Expressiveness

Content

|  | Low Expressiveness | | | High Expressiveness | | | | | |
|---|---|---|---|---|---|---|---|---|---|
|  | Rating | Interest | Achiev | Rating | Interest | Achiev |  |  |  |
| **High** | 50 | 131 | 34 | 51 | 140 | 36 | $\bar{X}(R) =$ | 50.96 |  |
|  | 56 | 126 | 28 | 44 | 145 | 37 | $\bar{X}(I) =$ | 136.20 |  |
|  | 52 | 134 | 33 | 52 | 141 | 30 | $\bar{X}(A) =$ | 32.83 |  |
|  |  |  |  | 50 | 142 | 33 |  |  |  |
|  | X=52.67 | 130.3 | 31.67 | 49.25 | 142.00 | 34.00 |  |  |  |
| **Medium** | 41 | 104 | 36 | 54 | 140 | 31 | $\bar{X}(R) =$ | 45.88 |  |
|  | 44 | 105 | 31 | 46 | 144 | 35 | $\bar{X}(I) =$ | 122.60 |  |
|  | 40 | 102 | 33 |  |  |  | $\bar{X}(A) =$ | 32.38 |  |
|  | 42 | 102 | 27 |  |  |  |  |  |  |
|  | X=41.75 | 103.30 | 31.75 | 50.00 | 142.00 | 33.00 |  |  |  |
| **Low** | 30 | 74 | 35 | 52 | 142 | 33 | $\bar{X}(B) =$ | 40.50 |  |
|  | 32 | 71 | 30 | 50 | 138 | 28 | $\bar{X}(I) =$ | 106.40 |  |
|  | 29 | 69 | 27 | 50 | 144 | 28 | $\bar{X}(A) =$ | 31.38 |  |
|  | 28 | 67 | 29 | 53 | 146 | 41 |  |  |  |
|  | X=29.75 | 70.25 | 30.25 | 51.25 | 142.5 | 32.50 |  |  |  |

$\bar{X}(R) =$ 41.39  $\bar{X}(I) =$ 101.30  $\bar{X}(A) =$ 31.22  $\bar{X}(B) =$ 50.17  $\bar{X}(I) =$ 142.2  $\bar{X}(A) =$ 33.17

Figure 3.5 Data and unweighted means for a two factor nonorthogonal, fixed-effects experimental design, where the dependent variables are lecturer rating, student subject matter interest, and student achievement.

Table 3.7
Multivariate Planned Comparisons Analysis
of Variance for the Content by Expressiveness Experiment

| Source of Variation | Multivariate[1] | | | Univariate | | | |
| --- | --- | --- | --- | --- | --- | --- | --- |
| | Wilks' Lambda | Df | F(Probability) | Df | t(one-tailed probability) | | |
| | | | | | Rating | Interest | Achievement |
| Content (C) | | | | | | | |
| Expressiveness (E) | | | | | | | |
| C X E | | | | | | | |
| Comparisons | | | | | | | |
| C1 X E | .09 | 3,13 | 44.85*(-.0000) | 1 | 3.67*(-.0012) | 8.19*(-.0000) | -.23(-.4106) |
| C2 X E | .06 | 3,13 | 68.10*(-.0000) | 1 | 4.31*(-.0003) | 10.46*(-.0000) | .22(-.4147) |
| Error (within groups) | | | | 15 | | | |

[1]The sums-of-squares and cross-products matrices were too large to be included here, but should be in an appendix of a report.
*Significant at p<.05; the programs do not report probabilities to more than 4 places.

that a Hawthorne effect may have existed among the classrooms chosen. Apparently, the students were so pleased to be studying astronomy that they did much extra work in the form of outside reading on the topic. Therefore, they were unaffected by the treatments on the achievement variable because they were all well prepared for the achievement test. However, the researcher did find evidence for the "Dr. Fox effect" with the affective variables.

## Multivariate Analysis: Overall Test and Post Hoc Comparisons

As in the parallel univariate discussion of this problem, here the researcher expects an interaction to occur but he is not able to predict its form as he was in the preceding presentation.

**Problem.** Is there an interaction between the amount of subject content in a lecture and the expressiveness of the lecturer that will affect a class's rating of the lecturer, interest in the subject, and achievement?

**Statistical Hypothesis.** In the parallel univariate presentation of this problem we defined $g(ij)$ to represent the interaction effect of treatments i and j on the dependent variable. Here we extend this notation and let $g(pij)$ represent the interaction of treatments i and j on variable p. Then, $\underline{g}(ij)$ is the vector of interactions containing all three interaction effects (one for each dependent variable), and we have the following overall interaction hypotheses:

$H(0): \underline{g}(ij) = \underline{0}$ for all ij

$H(A): \underline{g}(ij) \neq \underline{0}$ for some ij

Here $\underline{0}$ is the null vector, i.e., a column vector with zeros as elements. This null hypothesis will be tested at the .05 level of significance.

**Data.** The data are the unequal $\underline{n}$ data shown in Figure 3.5.

**Two-Way MANOVA Table.** Table 3.8 is the two-way MANOVA source table that would appear in a research report on this experiment. The contents of this table could be derived from all of the multivariate standard program runs of this chapter. The results in Table 3.8 indicate that there is a significant multivariate interaction between amount of content coverage and lecturer expressiveness (p<.000) and that this interaction is present at the univariate level for the class ratings (p<.000) and interest (p<.000), but not for class achievement (p<.969). Here we have used overall univariate tests as the follow up approach after the overall multivariate test; these univariate tests might

Table 3.8
Multivariate Analysis of Variance for
the Content by Expressiveness Experiment

| Source of Variation | Multivariate[1] | | | Df | Univariate | | |
|---|---|---|---|---|---|---|---|
| | Wilks' Lambda | Df | F(Probability) | | F(Probability) | | |
| | | | | | Rating | Interest | Achievement |
| Content (C) | .018 | 6,26 | 28.22*(-.0000) | 2 | 26.72*(-.0000) | 201.05*(-.0000) | -.25(-.7827) |
| Expressiveness(E) | .008 | 3,13 | 549.14*(-.0000) | 1 | 49.91*(-.0000) | 999.56*(-.0000) | 1.12(-.3072) |
| Interaction: C X E | .016 | 6,26 | 30.05*(-.0000) | 2 | 38.01*(-.0000) | 208.14*(-.0000) | -.03(-.9685) |
| Error (within groups) | | | | 15 | | | |

[1]The sums-of-squares and crossproducts matrices were too large to be included here, but should be in an appendix of a report.

*Significant at p<.05; the programs used do not report probabilities to more than four places.

then be followed by LSD contrasts (one for each dependent variable) such as the one shown with the simple interaction contrast of the univariate discussion for this type of analysis. However, another approach would be to use the Roy-Bose simultaneous confidence intervals presented earlier immediately following the overall multivariate test. The results of this approach are presented in the next section.

Results of the Roy-Bose Simultaneous Confidence Interval. In this section we fill in the needed matrices and vectors for Step 4 of the Roy-Bose simultaneous confidence interval presented earlier. Here, as with the LSD procedure discussed earlier, we decided to illustrate this procedure using the two planned multivariate interaction contrasts (but remember that they are used here after the fact). Then A, our matrix of contrasts (one contrast in each row), is

$$A = \begin{bmatrix} 1 & -1 & -1 & 1 & 0 & 0 \\ 0 & 0 & 1 & -1 & -1 & 1 \end{bmatrix} ,$$

and if we let $\underline{a}'$ be the first row of A, then

$$b = 1.3333.$$

Now $\underline{a}'(X'X)^{-1}X'Y$ is a vector of our three contrasts:

$$\underline{a}'(X'X)^{-1}X'Y = \begin{bmatrix} 11.67 & 27.08 & -1.08 \end{bmatrix}, \text{ and}$$

H(alpha) is found with

$$s = 2, \ m = 0, \ n = 5.5.$$

Again (as in the example for step 4) we find H(alpha), using the F (.05; 2, 12) = 3.89, as H(alpha) = .3744.

Now if we select $\underline{r}$ as

$$\underline{r} = \begin{bmatrix} 1 \\ 0 \\ 0 \end{bmatrix} ,$$

then

$$11.67 \pm \sqrt{((1.3333 \times .3744) / (1 - .3744)) (113.67)}$$

will yield the following 95% confidence interval for the first interaction contrast on lecturer rating.

rating: $2.15 \leq u(11) - u(12) - u(21) + u(22) \leq 21.19$.

If we let c(1) equal the first interaction contrast, then the 95% confidence intervals for interest and achievement are, respectively:

211

$$\text{interest:} \quad 17.15 \leq c(1) \leq 37.01,$$
$$\text{achievement:} \quad -16.86 \leq c(1) \leq 14.70.$$

Here we have that the first two confidence intervals do not contain zero, so that these interaction contrasts are significant. The last interval does contain zero; therefore, the first interaction contrast is not significant on the achievement variable.

For the second interaction contrast, $u(21) - u(22) - u(31) + u(32)$, denoted by $c(2)$, we have the following 95% simultaneous confidence intervals on each dependent variable:

$$\text{rating:} \quad 4.03 \leq c(2) \leq 22.47$$
$$\text{interest:} \quad 23.90 \leq c(2) \leq 43.10$$
$$\text{achievement:} \quad -12.65 \leq c(2) \leq 14.65$$

Therefore, on the second interaction contrast we also have that class rating and interest are significant and class achievement is not. Note that these are the same conclusions that we would arrive at if we had used the overall univariate tests followed by the LSD procedure, but here we are sure that our overall error rate is .05.

## Summary

In this chapter we have discussed two two-way designs a (2 x 2) and a (3 x 2) with both planned and overall approaches to univariate and multivariate analyses. In the 2 x 2 design we found no significant interaction but significant main effects when the analysis was planned and univariate or multivariate; no significant effects when the analysis was overall univariate, but significant main effects and no interaction when the analysis was multivariate. In the 3 x 2 design the focus was on the interaction which was significant regardless of the analysis, and the unit of analysis was class mean. For the 2 x 2 and 3 x 2 multivariate designs, we illustrated the use of Roy-Bose simultaneous confidence intervals as a post hoc procedure, and for the 3 x 2 univariate design we illustrated Fisher's LSD post hoc analysis.

This chapter is integrally related to Appendix A and the next chapter, Chapter 4. In Appendix A we further illustrate other approaches to analyzing two-way designs and in Chapter 4 we discuss the meaning of first and second order interactions and then consider a significant interaction in three-way analyses.

<u>Notes</u>

[1]A researcher might desire to hold the experimentwise error rate at .05, in this case he could divide .05 by 3 (about .0167) and use the result as his level of significance for each hypothesis. Of course, if the hypotheses were not of equal importance, he could designate levels of significance to each hypothesis test so that their sum was .05. For example the first hypothesis might be tested at .03; the second and third at .01.

[2]Timm (1975, pp. 312-313) indicates that the multivariate test statistic used in the Roy-Bose simultaneous confidence interval should be the same one that was used for the overall multivariate test, see Appendix B. Here, we used Roy's largest root to illustrate the Roy-Bose process because it is what Morrison (1967) illustrated. Timm (p. 313) presents the modifications necessary for use of the Roy-Bose simultaneous confidence interval with other multivariate test statistics.

[3]Carmer and Swanson (1973) discuss the use of Fisher's LSD in two ways, with and without prior significance of the overall F test. The latter approach they call Fisher's significant difference test, FSD, and it is this test that we are referring to here as LSD (i.e., our LSD = their FSD).

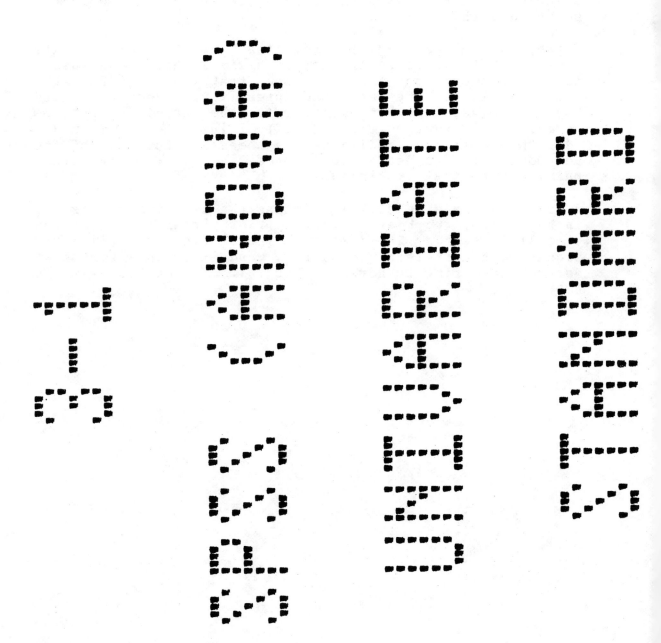

Note: The SPSS input annotations provided here are of
value for most problems of this type, consult your
SPSS manual for more general information.

① These are column identifiers and are not part of
the program content.

Note: Further annotations for this input and output can
be found in the program input for SPSS(ANOVA) in
Chapter 2, program 2-4.

② Here option 9 was specified so as to yield the
method of weighted squares of means (see Appendix
A).

③ Here we have two independent variables, TESTTYPE
and METHOD, and one dependent variable, ATTITUDE.

```
RUN NAME       CHAPTER 3:  TWO-WAY UNIVARIATE ANALYSIS
DATA LIST      FIXED(1)/1 TESTTYPE 2 METHOD 4 ATTITUDE 6
N OF CASES     18
LIST CASES     CASES=18/VARIABLES=TESTTYPE, METHOD, ATTITUDE
③ANOVA         ATTITUDE BY TESTTYPE(1,2),METHOD(1,2)
STATISTICS     ALL
②OPTIONS        9
READ INPUT DATA
       1 1 6
       1 4
       1 2 5
       1 2 7
       1 2 8
       1 2 6
       2 1 3
       2 1 3
       2 1 2
       2 1 4
       2 1 6
       2 1 5
       2 1 2
       2 1 2
       2 1 1
       2 2 6
       2 2 5
       2 2 4
```

215

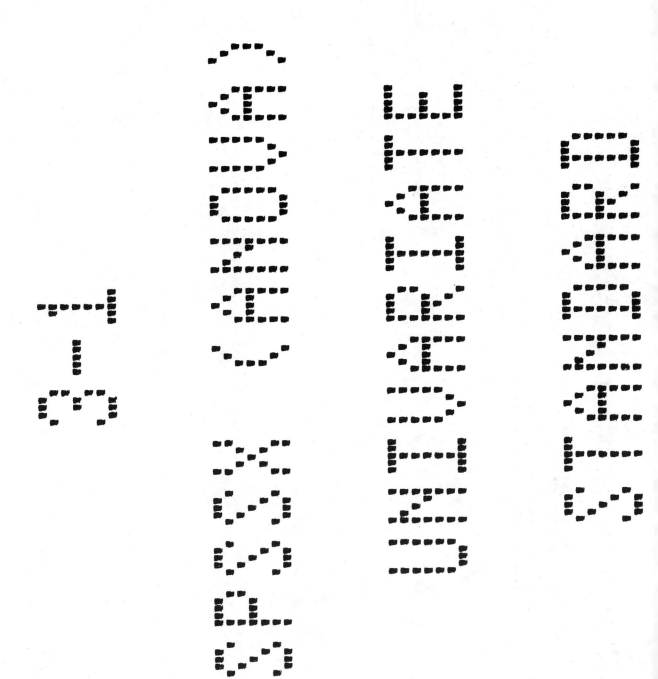

```
0000000000111111111122222222223333333333444444444455555555556666666666777777777 8
1234567890123456789012345678901234567890123456789012345678901234567890123456789 0

TITLE       CHAPTER 3:   TWO-WAY UNIVARIATE ANALYSIS
DATA LIST   RECORD = 1/1 TESTTYPE 2 METHOD 4 ATTITUDE 6
BEGIN DATA
1 1 6
1 1 4
1 2 5
1 2 7
1 2 8
1 2 6
2 1 3
2 1 3
2 1 2
2 1 4
2 1 6
2 1 5
2 1 2
2 1 1
2 2 6
2 2 5
2 2 4
END DATA
LIST        VARIABLES=TESTTYPE, METHOD, ATTITUDE
ANOVA       ATTITUDE BY TESTTYPE(1,2),METHOD(1,2)
STATISTICS  ALL
OPTIONS     9

0000000000111111111122222222223333333333444444444455555555556666666666777777777 8
1234567890123456789012345678901234567890123456789012345678901234567890123456789 0
```

FILE  NONAME   (CREATION DATE = 02/02/83)

①②  ***** A N A L Y S I S   O F   V A R I A N C E *****
         ATTITUDE
    BY  TESTTYPE
        METHOD

| SOURCE OF VARIATION | SUM OF SQUARES | DF | MEAN SQUARE | ④ F | SIGNIF OF F |
|---|---|---|---|---|---|
| MAIN EFFECTS | 31.803 | 2 | 15.902 | 7.448 | 0.006 |
| TESTTYPE | 9.615 | 1 | 9.615 | 4.504 | 0.052 ③⑤ |
| METHOD | 9.615 | 1 | 9.615 | 4.504 | 0.052 |
| 2-WAY INTERACTIONS | 0.127 | 1 | 0.127 | 0.059 | 0.811 |
| TESTTYPE METHOD | 0.127 | 1 | 0.127 | 0.059 | 0.811 |
| EXPLAINED | 34.389 | 3 | 11.463 | 5.369 | 0.011 |
| RESIDUAL | 29.889 | 14 | 2.135 | | |
| TOTAL | 64.278 | 17 | 3.781 | | |

18 CASES WERE PROCESSED.
0 CASES ( 0.0 PCT) WERE MISSING.

① This information would be found in an ANOVA source table (see Tables 3.2 and 3.3 of this chapter).

② This table serves as the source table for both the univariate planned and overall analyses because there are only two treatments in each factor.

③ For the planned analysis discussed in this chapter we divide the tail probability associated with the main effects in half (.0521/2 = .02605) to find the tail probability associated with a one tailed test. Then, if our level of significance is .05 for each test, we find that there is a significant difference between test types and methods of instruction.

④ For the planned analysis the t-statistic found in Table 3.2 is the square root of the F-value reported here.

⑤ For the overall analysis we find no significant differences for any of the sources of variation reported here because all of the tail probabilities are larger than our level of significance, .05.

218

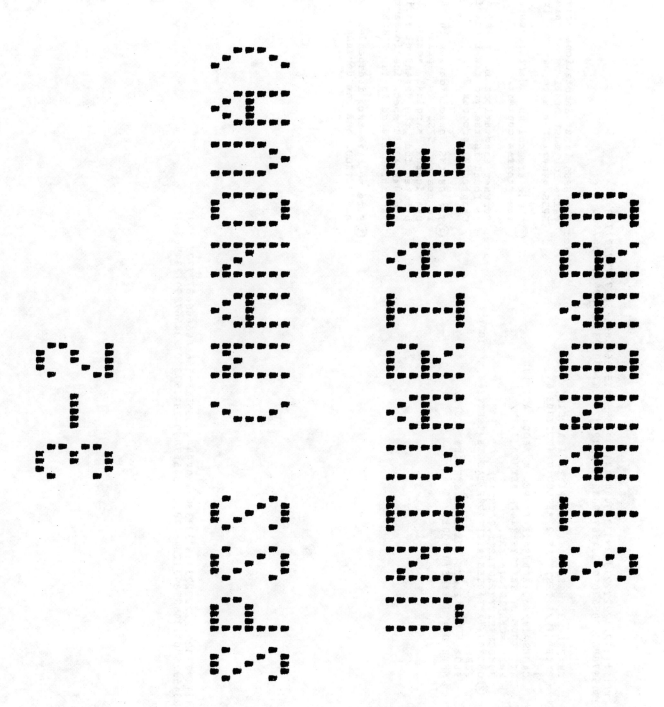

RUN NAME        CHAPTER 3:   TWO-WAY UNIVARIATE ANALYSIS
DATA LIST       FIXED(1)/1 TESTTYPE 2 METHOD 4 ATTITUDE 6
N OF CASES      18
LIST CASES      CASES=18/VARIABLES=TESTTYPE, METHOD, ATTITUDE
MANOVA          ATTITUDE BY TESTTYPE(1,2) METHOD(1,2)/
                PRINT=CELLINFO(MEANS)
                HOMOGENEITY(BARTLETT,COCHRAN)
                OMEANS(VARIABLES(ATTITUDE) TABLES(TESTTYPE,METHOD))
                POBS/
                PLOT = CELLPLOTS,BOXPLOTS,STEMLEAF,POBS/
                METHOD = SSTYPE(UNIQUE)/

READ INPUT DATA
1 1 6
1 1 4
1 2 5
1 2 7
1 2 8
1 2 6
2 1 3
2 1 3
2 1 4
2 1 6
2 1 5
2 1 2
2 1 1
2 2 6
2 2 5
2 2 4

Note:   The SPSS input annotations provided here are of
        value for most problems of this type, consult your
        SPSS manual for more general information.

① These are column identifiers and are not part of
   the program content.

Note:   Further annotations for this input and output can
        be found in the program input for SPSS(MANOVA) in
        Chapter 2, program 2-1.

② The OMEANS specification in the PRINT subcommand
   requests SPSS to print both weighted and
   unweighted marginal means. These means are
   printed for the dependent variable(s) listed in
   the VARIABLES specification across the independent
   variables listed in the TABLES specification.

③ Here we have two independent variables, TESTTYPE
   and METHOD, and one dependent variable, ATTITUDE.

00000000011111111112222222222333333333344444444445555555555666666666677777777778
1234567890123456789012345678901234567890123456789012345678901234567890

220

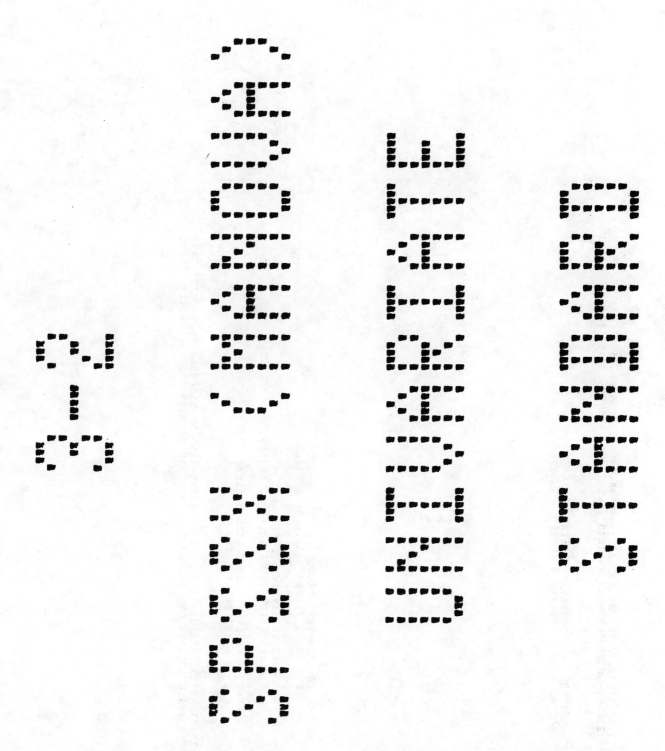

```
TITLE        CHAPTER 3:    TWO-WAY UNIVARIATE ANALYSIS
DATA LIST    RECORD = 1/1 TESTTYPE 2 METHOD 4 ATTITUDE 6
BEGIN DATA
1 1 6
1 1 4
1 2 5
1 2 7
1 2 8
1 2 6
2 1 3
2 1 3
2 1 2
2 1 4
2 1 6
2 1 5
2 1 2
2 1 2
2 1 1
2 2 6
2 2 5
2 2 4
END DATA
LIST         VARIABLES=TESTTYPE, METHOD, ATTITUDE
MANOVA       ATTITUDE BY TESTTYPE(1,2) METHOD (1,2)/
             PRINT=CELLINFO(MEANS)
             HOMOGENEITY(BARTLETT,COCHRAN)
             OMEANS(VARIABLES(ATTITUDE) TABLES(TESTTYPE,METHOD))
             POBS/
             PLOT = CELLPLOTS,BOXPLOTS,STEMLEAF,POBS/
             METHOD = SSTYPE (UNIQUE)/
```

0000000000111111111122222222223333333333444444444455555555556666666666777777777 8
1234567890123456789012345678901234567890123456789012345678901234567890123456789 0

222

* * * * * * * * * * * * * * * * * * A N A L Y S I S   O F   V A R I A N C E * * * * * * * * * * * * * * * * * * * * * * * *

CELL MEANS AND STANDARD DEVIATIONS

VARIABLE -- ATTITUDE

| FACTOR | CODE | MEAN | STD. DEV. | N | 95 PERCENT CONF. INTERVAL | |
|---|---|---|---|---|---|---|
| TESTTYPE | 1 | | | | | |
| METHOD | 1 | 5.00000 | 1.41421 | 2 | -7.70620 | 17.70620 |
| METHOD | 2 | 6.50000 | 1.29099 | 4 | 4.44577 | 8.55423 |
| TESTTYPE | 2 | | | | | |
| METHOD | 1 | 3.11111 | 1.61589 | 9 | 1.86903 | 4.35320 |
| METHOD | 2 | 5.00000 | 1.00000 | 3 | 2.51583 | 7.48417 |
| FOR ENTIRE SAMPLE | | 4.38889 | 1.94449 | 18 | 3.42192 | 5.35586 |

---

UNIVARIATE HOMOGENEITY OF VARIANCE TESTS

VARIABLE -- ATTITUDE

COCHRANS C(4,4) =                 .35878, P =  .657 (APPROX.)
BARTLETT-BOX F(3,114) =           .19332, P =  .901

---

18 CASES ACCEPTED.
 0 CASES REJECTED BECAUSE OF OUT-OF-RANGE FACTOR VALUES.
 0 CASES REJECTED BECAUSE OF MISSING DATA.
 4 NON-EMPTY CELLS.

---

CHAPTER 3:  TWO-WAY UNIVARIATE ANALYSIS

* * * * * * * * * * * * * * * * A N A L Y S I S   O F   V A R I A N C E * * * * * * * * * * * * * * * * * * * * * * *

COMBINED OBSERVED MEANS FOR TESTTYPE

VARIABLE -- ATTITUDE

TESTTYPE

    1       WGT.    6.00000
      ①UNWGT.  5.75000

    2       WGT.    3.58333
      ①UNWGT.  4.05556

COMBINED OBSERVED MEANS FOR METHOD

VARIABLE -- ATTITUDE

METHOD

    1       WGT.    3.45455
      ①UNWGT.  4.05556

    2       WGT.    5.85714
      ①UNWGT.  5.75000

CORRESPONDENCE BETWEEN EFFECTS AND COLUMNS OF BETWEEN-SUBJECTS DESIGN

STARTING  ENDING
COLUMN    COLUMN    EFFECT NAME

  1      1    CONSTANT
  2      2    TESTTYPE
  3      3    METHOD
  4      4    TESTTYPE BY METHOD

① Our hypotheses are based on linear contrasts of the unweighted means, labeled here as UNWGT (see Figure 3.1).

224

* * * * * * * * * * A N A L Y S I S   O F   V A R I A N C E * * * * * * * * * *

(2) TESTS OF SIGNIFICANCE FOR ATTITUDE USING UNIQUE SUMS OF SQUARES

(2) This information would be found in an ANOVA source table (see Tables 3.2 and 3.3 of this chapter).

(3) SOURCE OF VARIATION

| SOURCE OF VARIATION | SUM OF SQUARES | DF | MEAN SQUARE | F | SIG. OF F |
|---|---|---|---|---|---|
| WITHIN CELLS | 29.88889 | 14 | 2.13492 | | |
| CONSTANT | 321.98708 | 1 | 321.98708 | 150.81923 | 0.0 |
| TESTTYPE | 9.61499 | 1 | 9.61499 | 4.50367 | .052 (4)(6) |
| METHOD | 9.61499 | 1 | 9.61499 | 4.50367 | .052 |
| TESTTYPE BY METHOD | .12661 | 1 | .12661 | .05931 | .811 |

(5)

ESTIMATES FOR ATTITUDE

(7) CONSTANT

| PARAMETER | COEFF. | STD. ERR. | T-VALUE | SIG. OF T | LOWER .95 CL | UPPER .95 CL |
|---|---|---|---|---|---|---|
| 1 | 4.9027777778 | .39922 | 12.28085 | 0.0 | 4.04653 | 5.75902 |

(8) TESTTYPE

| PARAMETER | COEFF. | STD. ERR. | T-VALUE | SIG. OF T | LOWER .95 CL | UPPER .95 CL |
|---|---|---|---|---|---|---|
| 2 | .8472222222 | .39922 | 2.12219 | .052 | -.00902 | 1.70347 |

(8) METHOD

| PARAMETER | COEFF. | STD. ERR. | T-VALUE | SIG. OF T | LOWER .95 CL | UPPER .95 CL |
|---|---|---|---|---|---|---|
| 3 | -.8472222222 | .39922 | -2.12219 | .052 | -1.70347 | -.00902 |

(9) TESTTYPE BY METHOD

| PARAMETER | COEFF. | STD. ERR. | T-VALUE | SIG. OF T | LOWER .95 CL | UPPER .95 CL |
|---|---|---|---|---|---|---|
| 4 | .0972222222 | .39922 | .24353 | .811 | -.75902 | .95347 |

225

(3) This table serves as the source table for both the univariate planned and overall analyses because there are only two treatments in each factor.

(4) For the planned analysis discussed in this chapter we divide the tail probability associated with the main effects in half (.0521/2 =.02605) to find the tail probability associated with a one tailed test. Then, if our level of significance is .05 for each test, we find that there is a significant difference between test types and methods of instruction.

(5) For the planned analysis the t-statistic found in Table 3.2 is the square root of the F-value reported here.

(6) For the overall analysis we find no significant differences for any of the sources of variation reported here because all of the tail probabilities are larger than our level of significance, .05.

(7) This is the unweighted grand mean.

(8) These are estimates of the treatment effects, i.e. the differences of the unweighted grand mean from the unweighted marginal means.

(9) This is the estimate of the interaction contrast $c = u(11) - u(21) - u(12) + u(22)$ divided by 4, the number of cells in the contrast.

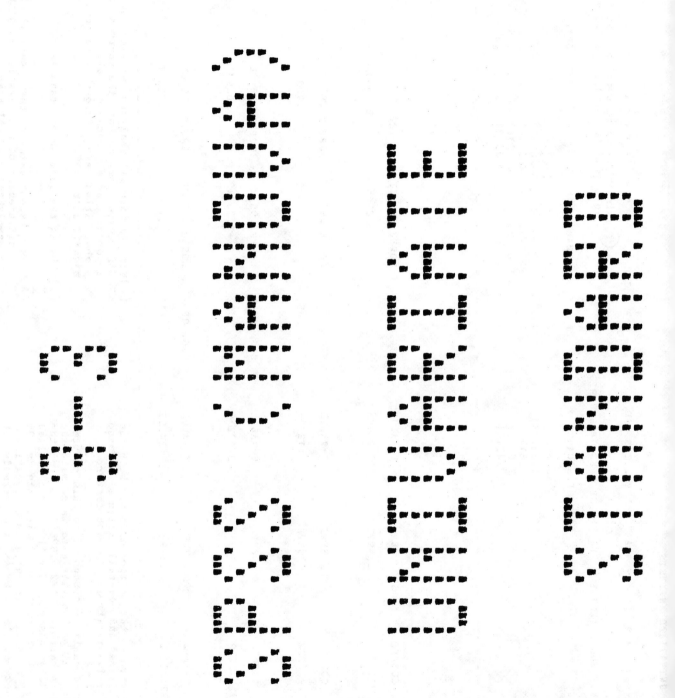

| | |
|---|---|
| RUN NAME | TWO-WAY ANOVA (3 X 2) |
| DATA LIST | FIXED(1)/ 1 CONTENT 1 EXPRESS 2 INTEREST 9-11 |
| N OF CASES | 21 |
| LIST CASES | CASES=21/VARIABLES=CONTENT EXPRESS INTEREST |
| MANOVA | INTEREST BY CONTENT(1,3) EXPRESS(1,2)/ |
| | PRINT=CELLINFO(MEANS) |
| | HOMOGENEITY(BARTLETT,COCHRAN) |

② OMEANS(VARIABLES(INTEREST) TABLES(CONTENT,EXPRESS))
POBS/
PLOT = CELLPLOTS,BOXPLOTS,STEMLEAF,POBS/
METHOD = SSTYPE(UNIQUE)/
CONTRAST(CONTENT) = REPEATED/
CONTRAST(EXPRESS) = SIMPLE/
PARTITION(CONTENT)/
PARTITON(EXPRESS)/
DESIGN = CONTENT,EXPRESS,CONTENT(1) BY EXPRESS(1),
CONTENT(2) BY EXPRESS(1)/

READ INPUT DATA.

| | |
|---|---|
| 11 | 131 |
| 11 | 126 |
| 11 | 134 |
| 12 | 140 |
| 12 | 145 |
| 12 | 141 |
| 12 | 142 |
| 21 | 104 |
| 21 | 105 |
| 21 | 102 |
| 21 | 102 |
| 22 | 140 |
| 22 | 144 |
| 31 | 74 |
| 31 | 71 |
| 31 | 69 |
| 31 | 67 |
| 32 | 142 |
| 32 | 138 |
| 32 | 144 |
| 32 | 146 |

Note: The SPSS input annotations provided here are of value for most problems of this type, consult your SPSS manual for more general information.

① These are column identifiers and are not part of the program content.

Note: Further annotations for this input and output can be found in the program input for SPSS(MANOVA) in Chapter 2, program 2-1.

② The OMEANS specification in the PRINT subcommand requests SPSS to print both weighted and unweighted marginal means. These means are printed for the dependent variable(s) listed in the VARIABLES specification across the independent variables listed in the TABLES specification.

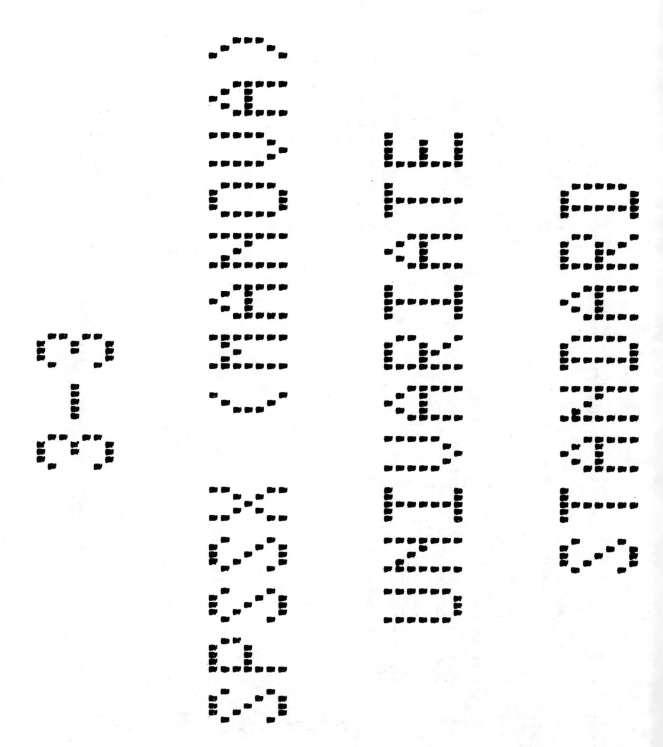

```
TITLE      TWO-WAY ANOVA (3 X 2)
DATA LIST   RECORD = 1/ 1 CONTENT 1 EXPRESS 2 INTEREST 9-11
BEGIN DATA
11      131
11      126
11      134
12      140
12      145
12      141
12      142
21      104
21      105
21      102
21      102
22      140
22      144
31      74
31      71
31      69
31      67
32      142
32      138
32      144
32      146
END DATA
LIST     VARIABLES=CONTENT EXPRESS INTEREST
MANOVA   INTEREST BY CONTENT(1,3) EXPRESS(1,2) /
         PRINT=CELLINFO(MEANS)
         HOMOGENEITY(BARTLETT,COCHRAN)
         OMEANS(VARIABLES(INTEREST) TABLES(CONTENT,EXPRESS))
         POBS/
         PLOT = CELLPLOTS,BOXPLOTS,STEMLEAF,POBS/
         METHOD = SSTYPE(UNIQUE)/
         CONTRAST(CONTENT) = REPEATED/
         CONTRAST(EXPRESS) = SIMPLE/
         PARTITION(CONTENT)/
         PARTITON(EXPRESS)/
         DESIGN = CONTENT,EXPRESS,CONTENT(1) BY EXPRESS(1),
                  CONTENT(2) BY EXPRESS(1)/
```

0000000000111111111122222222223333333333444444444455555555556666666666777777777 8
1234567890123456789012345678901234567890123456789012345678901234567890123456789 0

229

* * * * * * * * * * * * * * * * * * * * * A N A L Y S I S   O F   V A R I A N C E * * * * * * * * * * * * * * * * * * * * * * * *

CELL MEANS AND STANDARD DEVIATIONS

VARIABLE .. INTEREST

| FACTOR | CODE | MEAN | STD. DEV. | N | 95 PERCENT CONF. INTERVAL |
|--------|------|------|-----------|---|----------------------------|
| CONTENT | 1 | | | | |
| EXPRESS | 1 | 130.33333 | 4.04145 | 3 | 120.29370   140.37297 |
| EXPRESS | 2 | 142.00000 | 2.16025 | 4 | 138.56262   145.43738 |
| CONTENT | 2 | | | | |
| EXPRESS | 1 | 103.25000 | 1.50000 | 4 | 100.86320   105.63680 |
| EXPRESS | 2 | 142.00000 | 2.82843 | 2 | 116.58760   167.41240 |
| CONTENT | 3 | | | | |
| EXPRESS | 1 | 70.25000 | 2.98608 | 4 | 65.49855    75.00145 |
| EXPRESS | 2 | 142.50000 | 3.41565 | 4 | 137.06502   147.93498 |
| FOR ENTIRE SAMPLE | | 119.38095 | 28.62425 | 21 | 106.35135   132.41055 |

UNIVARIATE HOMOGENEITY OF VARIANCE TESTS

VARIABLE .. INTEREST

COCHRANS C(3,6) =               .31511,  P =  .594 (APPROX.)
BARTLETT-BOX F(5,206) =         .48909,  P =  .784

21 CASES ACCEPTED.
 0 CASES REJECTED BECAUSE OF OUT-OF-RANGE FACTOR VALUES.
 0 CASES REJECTED BECAUSE OF MISSING DATA.
 6 NON-EMPTY CELLS.

\* \* \* \* \* \* \* \* \* \* \* \* \* \* \* A N A L Y S I S   O F   V A R I A N C E \* \* \* \* \* \* \* \* \* \* \* \* \* \* \* \* \* \* \* \* \*

COMBINED OBSERVED MEANS FOR CONTENT

VARIABLE -- INTEREST

CONTENT

| | | | |
|---|---|---|---|
| 1 | | WGT. | 137.00000 |
| | (1) | UNWGT. | 136.16667 |
| 2 | | WGT. | 116.16667 |
| | (1) | UNWGT. | 122.62500 |
| 3 | | WGT. | 106.37500 |
| | (1) | UNWGT. | 106.37500 |

(1) Our hypotheses are based on linear contrasts of the unweighted means, labeled here as UNWGT (see Figure 3.4).

COMBINED OBSERVED MEANS FOR EXPRESS

VARIABLE -- INTEREST

EXPRESS

| | | | |
|---|---|---|---|
| 1 | | WGT. | 98.63636 |
| | (1) | UNWGT. | 101.27778 |
| 2 | | WGT. | 142.20000 |
| | (1) | UNWGT. | 142.16667 |

CORRESPONDENCE BETWEEN EFFECTS AND COLUMNS OF BETWEEN-SUBJECTS DESIGN

| STARTING COLUMN | ENDING COLUMN | EFFECT NAME |
|---|---|---|
| 1 | 1 | CONSTANT |
| 2 | 3 | CONTENT |
| 4 | 4 | EXPRESS |
| 5 | 5 | CONTENT(1) BY EXPRESS(1) |
| 6 | 6 | CONTENT(2) BY EXPRESS(1) |

231

* * * * * * * * * * * * * * * * * * * A N A L Y S I S   O F   V A R I A N C E * * * * * * * * * * * * * * * * * * * *

(2) This information would be found in an ANOVA source table (see Tables 3.5 and 3.6).

TESTS OF SIGNIFICANCE FOR INTEREST USING UNIQUE SUMS OF SQUARES

| SOURCE OF VARIATION | SUM OF SQUARES | DF | MEAN SQUARE | F | SIG. OF F |
|---|---|---|---|---|---|
| WITHIN CELLS | 123.16667 | 15 | 8.21111 | | |
| CONSTANT | 290938.24242 | 1 | 290938.24242 | 35432.26227 | 0.0 |
| CONTENT | 3301.61164 | 2 | 1650.80582 | 201.04536 | 0.0 |
| EXPRESS | 8207.51515 | 1 | 8207.51515 | 999.56206 | 0.0 |
| CONTENT(1) BY EXPRESS(1) | 550.13021 | 1 | 550.13021 | 66.99827 | 0.0 |
| CONTENT(2) BY EXPRESS(1) | 897.80000 | 1 | 897.80000 | 109.33965 | 0.0 |

ESTIMATES FOR INTEREST

(3) The interaction contrasts are significant and provide evidence for the 'Dr. Fox effect'--see the discussion in this chapter.

CONSTANT

| PARAMETER | COEFF. | STD. ERR. | T-VALUE | SIG. OF T | LOWER .95 CL | UPPER .95 CL |
|---|---|---|---|---|---|---|
| 1 | 365.16666667 | 1.93996 | 188.23459 | 0.0 | 361.03175 | 369.30158 |

CONTENT

| PARAMETER | COEFF. | STD. ERR. | T-VALUE | SIG. OF T | LOWER .95 CL | UPPER .95 CL |
|---|---|---|---|---|---|---|
| 2 | 13.5416666667 | 1.65440 | 8.18525 | .000 | 10.01540 | 17.06794 |
| 3 | 16.2500000000 | 1.60187 | 10.14442 | .000 | 12.83571 | 19.66429 |

EXPRESS

| PARAMETER | COEFF. | STD. ERR. | T-VALUE | SIG. OF T | LOWER .95 CL | UPPER .95 CL |
|---|---|---|---|---|---|---|
| 4 | -122.666666667 | 3.87991 | -31.61585 | 0.0 | -130.93650 | -114.39683 |

CONTENT(1) BY EXPRESS(1)

| PARAMETER | COEFF. | STD. ERR. | T-VALUE | SIG. OF T | LOWER .95 CL | UPPER .95 CL |
|---|---|---|---|---|---|---|
| 5 | 27.0833333333 | 3.30880 | 8.18525 | .000 | 20.03080 | 34.13587 |

* * * * * * * * * * * * * * * * * * * A N A L Y S I S   O F   V A R I A N C E * * * * * * * * * * * * * * * * * * * *

ESTIMATES FOR INTEREST    (CONT.)

CONTENT(2) BY EXPRESS(1)

| PARAMETER | COEFF. | STD. ERR. | T-VALUE | SIG. OF T | LOWER .95 CL | UPPER .95 CL |
|---|---|---|---|---|---|---|

232

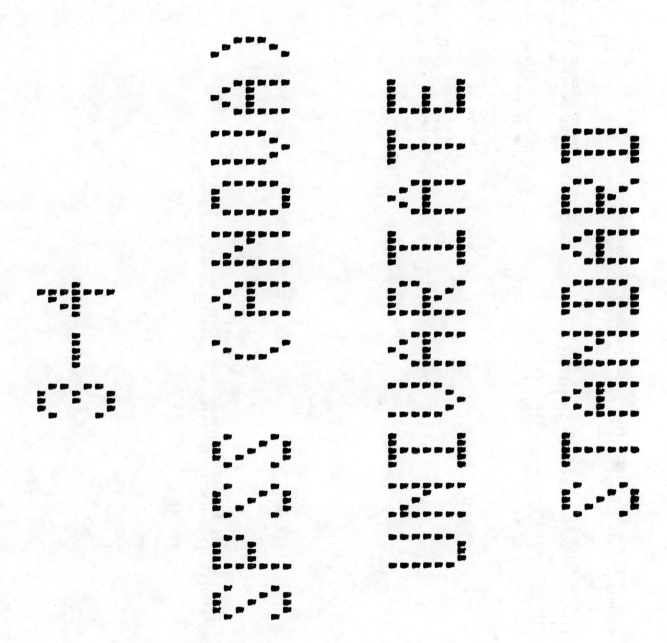

① 

**Note:** The SPSS input annotations provided here are of value for most problems of this type, consult your SPSS manual for more general inforation.

① These are column identifiers and are not part of the program content.

**Note:** Further annotations for this input and output can be found in the program input for SPSS(ANOVA) in Chapter 2, program 2-4.

② Here option 9 was specified so as to yield the method of weighted squares of means analysis (see Appendix A).

```
RUN NAME       TWO-WAY ANOVA (3 x 2)
DATA LIST      FIXED(1)/ 1 CONTENT 1 EXPRESS 2 INTEREST 9-11
N CF CASES     21
LIST CASES     CASES=21/VARIABLES=CONTENT EXPRESS INTEREST
ANOVA          INTEREST BY CONTENT(1,3) EXPRESS(1,2)
STATISTICS     ALL
② OPTIONS      9
READ INPUT DATA
   11   131
   11   126
   11   134
   12   140
   12   145
   12   141
   12   142
   21   104
   21   105
   21   102
   21   102
   22   140
   22   144
   31    74
   31    71
   31    69
   31    67
   32   142
   32   138
   32   144
   32   146
```

234

①

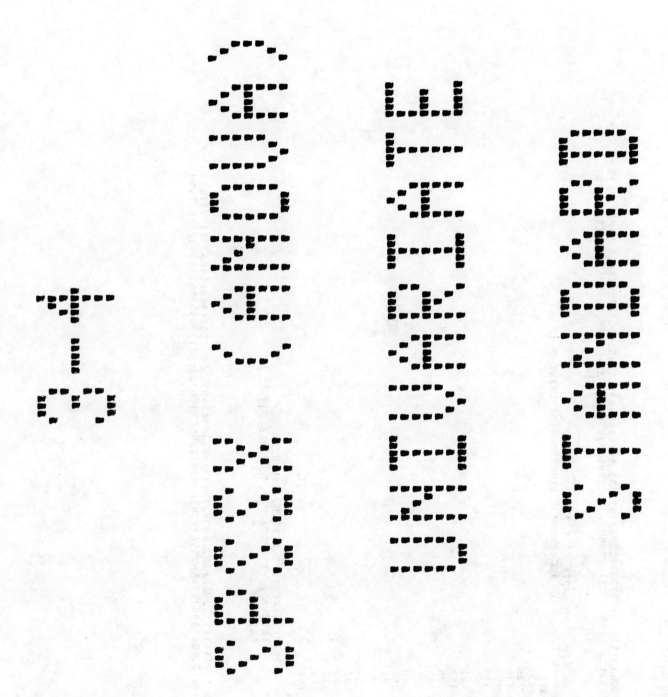

```
0000000001111111111222222222233333333334444444444555555555566666666667777777778
1234567890123456789012345678901234567890123456789012345678901234567890

TITLE      TWO-WAY ANOVA (3 X 2)
DATA LIST   RECORD = 1/ 1 CONTENT 1 EXPRESS 2 INTEREST 9-11
BEGIN DATA
11     131
11     126
11     134
12     140
12     145
12     141
12     142
21     104
21     105
21     102
21     102
22     140
22     144
31      74
31      71
31      69
31      67
32     142
32     138
32     144
32     146
END DATA
LIST       VARIABLES=CONTENT EXPRESS INTEREST
ANOVA      INTEREST BY CONTENT (1,3) EXPRESS (1,2)
STATISTICS  ALL
OPTIONS     9

0000000001111111111222222222233333333334444444444555555555566666666667777777778
1234567890123456789012345678901234567890123456789012345678901234567890
```

236

TWO-WAY ANOVA (3 X 2)                                                      02/03/83        PAGE    3

FILE   NONAME   (CREATION DATE = 02/03/83)

* * * * * * * * * * * * A N A L Y S I S   O F   V A R I A N C E * * * * * * * * * * * * * * * * * *
*           INTEREST
*        BY CONTENT
*           EXPRESS
* * * * * * * * * * * * * * * * * * * * * * * * * * * * * * * * * * * * * * * * * * * * * * * * * * *

|                      | SUM OF   |    | MEAN     |         | SIGNIF |
| SOURCE OF VARIATION  | SQUARES  | DF | SQUARE   | F       | OF F   |
|----------------------|----------|----|----------|---------|--------|
| MAIN EFFECTS         | 12374.309| 3  | 4124.770 | 502.398 | 0.000  |
|   CONTENT            | 3301.612 | 2  | 1650.806 | 201.069 | 0.000  |
|   EXPRESS            | 8207.516 | 1  | 8207.516 | 999.678 | 0.000  |
|                      |          |    |          |         |        |
| 2-WAY INTERACTIONS   | 3418.102 | 2  | 1709.051 | 208.163 | 0.000 ①|
|   CONTENT EXPRESS    | 3418.102 | 2  | 1709.051 | 208.163 | 0.000  |
|                      |          |    |          |         |        |
| EXPLAINED            | 16263.785| 5  | 3252.757 | 396.187 | 0.000  |
|                      |          |    |          |         |        |
| RESIDUAL             | 123.152  | 15 | 8.210    |         |        |
|                      |          |    |          |         |        |
| TOTAL                | 16386.938| 20 | 819.347  |         |        |

21 CASES WERE PROCESSED.
0 CASES ( 0.0 PCT) WERE MISSING.

① The overall analysis indicates that there is a
  significant interaction (see the discussion in
  this chapter, and Table 3.6).

237

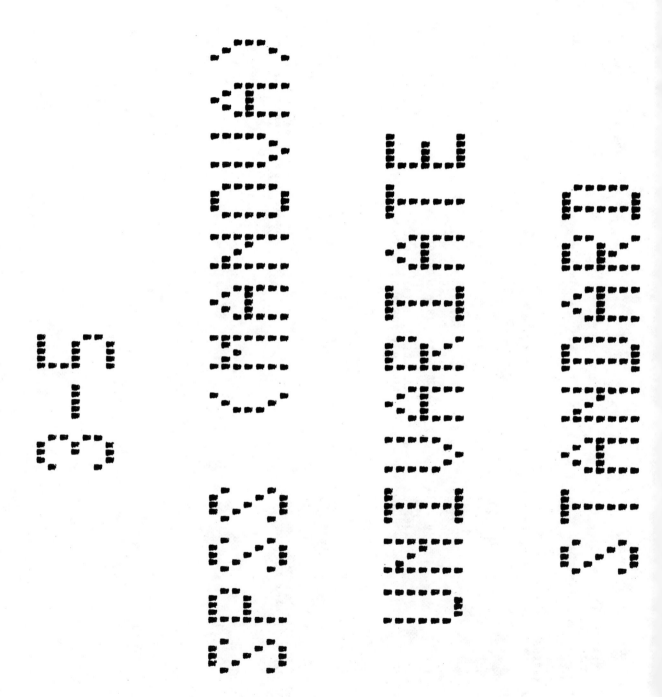

```
RUN NAME       TWO-WAY ANOVA (3 X 2)
DATA LIST      FIXED(1)/ 1 CONTENT 1 EXPRESS 2 INTEREST 9-11
N OF CASES     21
LIST CASES     CASES=21/VARIABLES=CONTENT EXPRESS INTEREST
MANOVA         INTEREST BY CONTENT(1,3) EXPRESS(1,2) /
               PRINT=CELLINFO(MEANS)
               HOMOGENEITY(BARTLETT,COCHRAN)
②              OMEANS(VARIABLES(INTEREST) TABLES(CONTENT,EXPRESS))
               POBS/
               PLOT = CELLPLOTS,BOXPLOTS,STEMLEAF,POBS/
               METHOD = SSTYPE(UNIQUE) /

READ INPUT DATA
   11   131
   11   126
   11   134
   12   140
   12   145
   12   141
   12   142
   21   104
   21   105
   21   102
   21   102
   22   140
   22   144
   31    74
   31    71
   31    69
   31    67
   32   142
   32   138
   32   144
   32   146
```

Note:   The SPSS input annotations provided here are of
        value for most problems of this type, consult your
        SPSS manual for more general information.

① These are column identifiers and are not   part of
   the program content.

Note:   Further annotations for this input and output can
        be found in the program input for SPSS(MANOVA) in
        Chapter 2, program 2-5.

② The OMEANS specification in the PRINT subcommand
   requests  SPSS  to  print  both  weighted  and
   unweighted  marginal  means.   These  means  are
   printed for  the dependent variable(s)  listed in
   the VARIABLES specification across the independent
   variables listed in the TABLES specification.

① 00000000011111111112222222222333333333344444444445555555555666666666677777777778
   1234567890123456789012345678901234567890123456789012345678901234567890

239

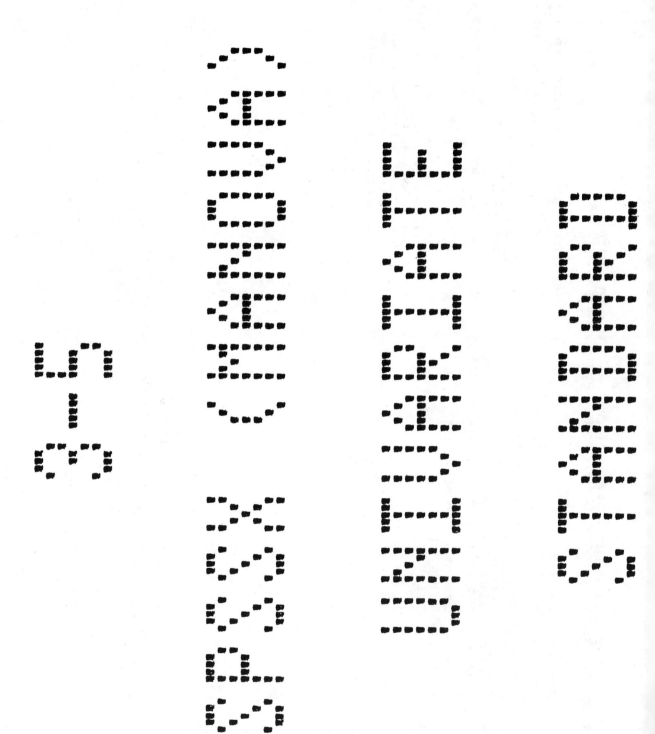

```
0000000000111111111122222222223333333333444444444455555555556666666666777777777 8
1234567890123456789012345678901234567890123456789012345678901234567890123456789 0

TITLE        TWO-WAY ANOVA (3 X 2)
DATA LIST     RECORD = 1/ 1 CONTENT 1 EXPRESS 2 INTEREST 9-11
BEGIN DATA
     11       131
     11       126
     11       134
     12       140
     12       145
     12       141
     12       142
     21       104
     21       105
     21       102
     21       102
     22       140
     22       144
     31        74
     31        71
     31        69
     31        67
     32       142
     32       138
     32       144
     32       146
END DATA
LIST       VARIABLES=CONTENT EXPRESS INTEREST
MANOVA       INTEREST BY CONTENT(1,3) EXPRESS(1,2) /
             PRINT=CELLINFO(MEANS)
             HOMOGENEITY(BARTLETT,COCHRAN)
             OMEANS(VARIABLES(INTEREST) TABLES(CONTENT,EXPRESS))
             POBS/
             PLOT = CELLPLOTS,BOXPLOTS,STEMLEAF,POBS/
             METHOD = SSTYPE(UNIQUE)/
```

```
0000000000111111111122222222223333333333444444444455555555556666666666777777777 8
1234567890123456789012345678901234567890123456789012345678901234567890123456789 0
```

241

TWO-WAY ANOVA (3 X 2)

FILE   NONAME   (CREATION DATE = 02/02/83)

02/02/83          PAGE   3

* * * * * * * * * * * * * * * * * * * * * A N A L Y S I S   O F   V A R I A N C E * * * * * * * * * * * * * * * * * * * * * * * * * *

CELL MEANS AND STANDARD DEVIATIONS

VARIABLE .. INTEREST

| FACTOR | CODE | MEAN | STD. DEV. | N | 95 PERCENT CONF. INTERVAL | |
|---|---|---|---|---|---|---|
| CONTENT | 1 | | | | | |
| EXPRESS | 1 | 130.33333 | 4.04145 | 3 | 120.29370 | 140.37297 |
| EXPRESS | 2 | 142.00000 | 2.16025 | 4 | 138.56262 | 145.43738 |
| CONTENT | 2 | | | | | |
| EXPRESS | 1 | 103.25000 | 1.50000 | 4 | 100.86320 | 105.63680 |
| EXPRESS | 2 | 142.00000 | 2.82843 | 2 | 116.58760 | 167.41240 |
| CONTENT | 3 | | | | | |
| EXPRESS | 1 | 70.25000 | 2.98608 | 4 | 65.49855 | 75.00145 |
| EXPRESS | 2 | 142.50000 | 3.41565 | 4 | 137.06502 | 147.93498 |
| FOR ENTIRE SAMPLE | | 119.38095 | 28.62425 | 21 | 106.35135 | 132.41055 |

UNIVARIATE HOMOGENEITY OF VARIANCE TESTS

VARIABLE .. INTEREST

COCHRANS C(3,6) =           .31511, P =    .594 (APPROX.)
BARTLETT-BOX F(5,206) =     .48909, P =    .784

21  CASES ACCEPTED.
 0  CASES REJECTED BECAUSE OF OUT-OF-RANGE FACTOR VALUES.
 0  CASES REJECTED BECAUSE OF MISSING DATA.
 6  NON-EMPTY CELLS.

242

* * * * * * * * * * * * * * * * * * * A N A L Y S I S   O F   V A R I A N C E * * * * * * * * * * * * * * * * * * * * * * * * *

COMBINED OBSERVED MEANS FOR CONTENT

VARIABLE -- INTEREST

CONTENT

1   WGT.        137.00000
  (1)UNWGT.     136.16667

2   WGT.        116.16667
  (1)UNWGT.     122.62500

3   WGT.        106.37500
  (1)UNWGT.     106.37500

COMBINED OBSERVED MEANS FOR EXPRESS

VARIABLE -- INTEREST

EXPRESS

1   WGT.         98.63636
  (1)UNWGT.     101.27778

2   WGT.        142.20000
  (1)UNWGT.     142.16667

(1) Our hypotheses are based on linear contrasts of the unweighted means, labeled here as UNWGT (see Figure 3.4).

CORRESPONDENCE BETWEEN EFFECTS AND COLUMNS OF BETWEEN-SUBJECTS DESIGN

| STARTING COLUMN | ENDING COLUMN | EFFECT NAME |
|---|---|---|
| 1 | 1 | CONSTANT |
| 2 | 3 | CONTENT |
| 4 | 4 | EXPRESS |
| 5 | 6 | CONTENT BY EXPRESS |

243

* * * * * * * * * * * * * * * * * * * * A N A L Y S I S   O F   V A R I A N C E * * * * * * * * * * * * * * * * * * *

TESTS OF SIGNIFICANCE FOR INTEREST USING UNIQUE SUMS OF SQUARES

| SOURCE OF VARIATION | SUM OF SQUARES | DF | MEAN SQUARE | F | SIG. OF F |
|---|---|---|---|---|---|
| WITHIN CELLS | 123.16667 | 15 | 8.21111 | | |
| CONSTANT | 290938.24242 | 1 | 290938.24242 | 35432.26227 | 0.0 |
| CONTENT | 3301.61164 | 2 | 1650.80582 | 201.04536 | 0.0 |
| EXPRESS | 8207.51515 | 1 | 8207.51515 | 999.56206 | 0.0 |
| (2) CONTENT BY EXPRESS | 3418.10220 | 2 | 1709.05110 | 208.13883 | 0.0 |

ESTIMATES FOR INTEREST

CONSTANT

| PARAMETER | COEFF. | STD. ERR. | T-VALUE | SIG. OF T | LOWER .95 CL | UPPER .95 CL |
|---|---|---|---|---|---|---|
| (3) 1 | 121.7222222222 | .64665 | 188.23459 | 0.0 | 120.34392 | 123.10053 |

CONTENT

| PARAMETER | COEFF. | STD. ERR. | T-VALUE | SIG. OF T | LOWER .95 CL | UPPER .95 CL |
|---|---|---|---|---|---|---|
| (4) 2 | 14.4444444444 | .90405 | 15.97745 | 0.0 | 12.51750 | 16.37139 |
| 3 | -.9027777778 | .96507 | -.93546 | .364 | -1.15421 | 2.95977 |

EXPRESS

| PARAMETER | COEFF. | STD. ERR. | T-VALUE | SIG. OF T | LOWER .95 CL | UPPER .95 CL |
|---|---|---|---|---|---|---|
| (4) 4 | -20.4444444444 | .64665 | -31.61585 | 0.0 | -21.82275 | -19.06614 |

CONTENT BY EXPRESS

| PARAMETER | COEFF. | STD. ERR. | T-VALUE | SIG. OF T | LOWER .95 CL | UPPER .95 CL |
|---|---|---|---|---|---|---|
| (5) 5 | 14.6111111111 | .90405 | 16.16181 | 0.0 | 12.68417 | 16.53805 |
| 6 | 1.0694444444 | .96507 | 1.10816 | .285 | -.98755 | 3.12643 |

(2) The overall analysis indicates that there is a significant interaction (see the discussion in this chapter, and Table 3.6).

(3) This is the unweighted grand mean.

(4) These are estimates of the treatment effects, i.e. the differences between the unweighted grand mean and the unweighted marginal means.

(5) The interaction contrast coefficients are not of much interest here because they are based on

244

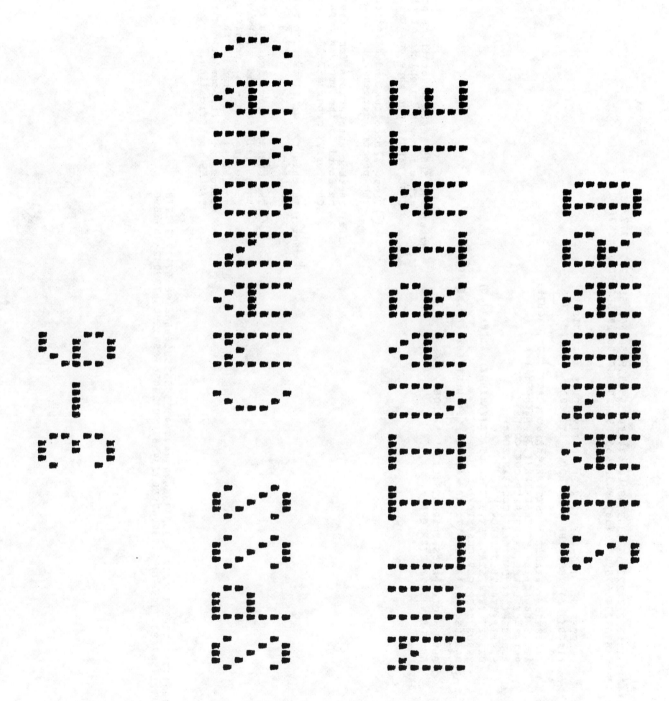

① `000000000011111111112222222222333333333344444444445555555555666666666677777777778`
`1234567890123456789012345678901234567890123456789012345678901234567890123456789 0`

```
RUN NAME        CHAPTER 3:  TWO-WAY (2 X 2) MULTIVARIATE ANALYSIS
DATA LIST       FIXED(1)/1 TESTTYPE 2 METHOD 4 ATTITUDE 6 ACHIEV 7-8
N OF CASES      18
LIST CASES      CASES=18/VARIABLES=TESTTYPE, METHOD, ATTITUDE, ACHIEV
MANOVA          ATTITUDE ACHIEV BY TESTTYPE(1,2), METHOD(1,2)/
                PRINT=CELLINFO(MEANS,SSCP,COV,COR)
                HOMOGENEITY(BARTLETT,COCHRAN,BOXM)
                SIGNIF(HYPOTH,STEPDOWN)
                DISCRIM(RAW,STAN,ESTIM,COR,ROTATE(VARIMAX) ALPHA(1.0))
                ERROR(SSCP,COV,COR,STDV)
②              OMEANS(VARIABLES(ATTITUDE ACHIEV) TABLES(TESTTYPE,METHOD))
                POBS/
                PLOT = CELLPLOTS,BOXPLOTS,STEMLEAF,POBS/
                METHOD = SSTYPE(UNIQUE)/

READ INPUT DATA
1 1 610
1 1 4 7
1 2 513
1 2 711
1 2 816
1 2 613
2 1 3 6
2 1 3 3
2 1 2 1
2 1 4 8
2 1 6 5
2 1 5 4
2 1 2 2
2 1 2 2
2 1 1 3
2 2 6 7
2 2 511
2 2 4 9
```

Note: The SPSS input annotations provided here are of value for most problems of this type, consult your SPSS manual for more general information.

① These are column identifiers and are not part of the program content.

Note: Further annotations for this input and output can be found in the program input for SPSS(MANOVA) in Chapter 2, program 2-10.

Note: In this I/O we illustrate both overall and planned analyses.

② The OMEANS specification requests SPSS to print both weighted and unweighted marginal means. These means are printed for the dependent variable(s) listed in the VARIABLES specification across the independent variables listed in the TABLES specification.

① `000000000011111111112222222222333333333344444444445555555555666666666677777777778`
`1234567890123456789012345678901234567890123456789012345678901234567890123456789 0`

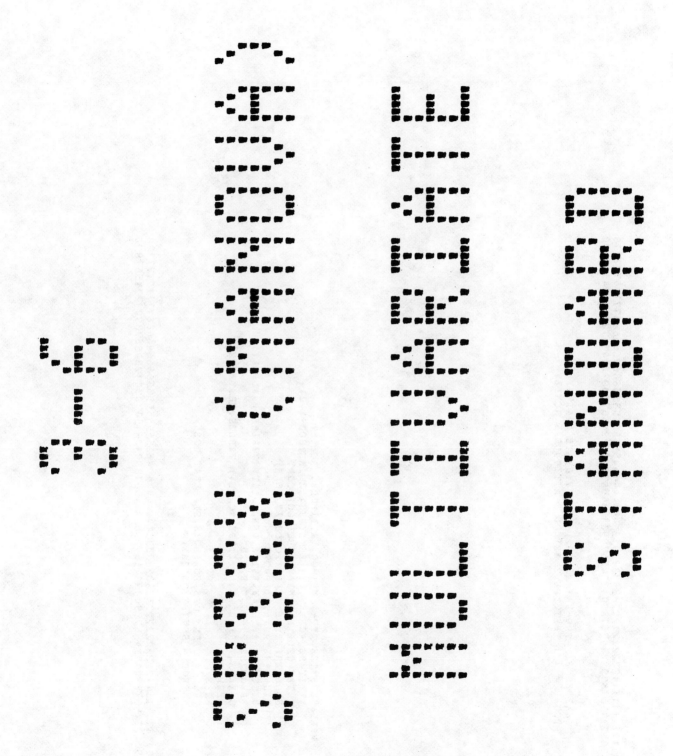

```
0000000000111111111122222222223333333333444444444455555555556666666666777777777 8
1234567890123456789012345678901234567890123456789012345678901234567890123456789 0

TITLE       CHAPTER 3:  TWO-WAY (2 X 2) MULTIVARIATE ANALYSIS
DATA LIST   RECORD = 1/1 TESTTYPE 2 METHOD 4 ATTITUDE 6 ACHIEV 7-8
BEGIN DATA
 1 1 610
 1 1 4 7
 1 2 513
 1 2 711
 1 2 816
 1 2 613
 2 1 3 6
 2 1 3 3
 2 1 2 1
 2 1 4 8
 2 1 6 5
 2 1 5 4
 2 1 2 2
 2 1 2 2
 2 1 1 3
 2 2 6 7
 2 2 511
 2 2 4 9
END DATA
LIST
MANOVA    VARIABLES=TESTTYPE, METHOD, ATTITUDE, ACHIEV
          ATTITUDE ACHIEV BY TESTTYPE(1,2),METHOD(1,2)/
          PRINT=CELLINFO(MEANS,SSCP,COV,COR)
          HOMOGENEITY(BARTLETT,COCHRAN,BOXM)
          SIGNIF(HYPOTH,STEPDOWN)
          DISCRIM(RAW,STAN,ESTIM,CGR,ROTATE(VARIMAX) ALPHA(1-0))
          ERROR(SSCP,COV,COR,STDV)
          OMEANS(VARIABLES(ATTITUDE ACHIEV) TABLES(TESTTYPE,
          METHOD))
          POBS/
          PLOT = CELLPLOTS,BOXPLOTS,STEMLEAF,POBS/
          METHOD = SSTYPE(UNIQUE)/

0000000000111111111122222222223333333333444444444455555555556666666666777777777 8
1234567890123456789012345678901234567890123456789012345678901234567890123456789 0
```

248

CELL MEANS AND STANDARD DEVIATIONS

VARIABLE -- ATTITUDE

| FACTOR | CODE | MEAN | STD. DEV. | N | 95 PERCENT CONF. INTERVAL | |
|---|---|---|---|---|---|---|
| TESTTYPE | 1 | | | | | |
| METHOD | 1 | 5.00000 | 1.41421 | 2 | -7.70620 | 17.70620 |
| METHOD | 2 | 6.50000 | 1.29099 | 4 | 4.44577 | 8.55423 |
| TESTTYPE | 2 | | | | | |
| METHOD | 1 | 3.11111 | 1.61589 | 9 | 1.86903 | 4.35320 |
| METHOD | 2 | 5.00000 | 1.00000 | 3 | 2.51583 | 7.48417 |
| FOR ENTIRE SAMPLE | | 4.38889 | 1.94449 | 18 | 3.42192 | 5.35586 |

VARIABLE -- ACHIEV

| FACTOR | CODE | MEAN | STD. DEV. | N | 95 PERCENT CONF. INTERVAL | |
|---|---|---|---|---|---|---|
| TESTTYPE | 1 | | | | | |
| METHOD | 1 | 8.50000 | 2.12132 | 2 | -10.55930 | 27.55930 |
| METHOD | 2 | 13.25000 | 2.06155 | 4 | 9.96966 | 16.53034 |
| TESTTYPE | 2 | | | | | |
| METHOD | 1 | 3.77778 | 2.22361 | 9 | 2.06856 | 5.48699 |
| METHOD | 2 | 9.00000 | 2.00000 | 3 | 4.03167 | 13.96833 |
| FOR ENTIRE SAMPLE | | 7.27778 | 4.40328 | 18 | 5.08808 | 9.46748 |

UNIVARIATE HOMOGENEITY OF VARIANCE TESTS

COMBINED OBSERVED MEANS FOR TESTTYPE

VARIABLE -- ATTITUDE

    TESTTYPE

    1    WGT-      6.00000
      (1) UNWGT-   5.75000

    2    WGT-      3.58333
      (1) UNWGT-   4.05556

VARIABLE -- ACHIEV

    TESTTYPE

    1    WGT-      11.66667
      (1) UNWGT-   10.87500

    2    WGT-      5.08333
      (1) UNWGT-   6.38889

COMBINED OBSERVED MEANS FOR METHOD

VARIABLE -- ATTITUDE

    METHOD

    1    WGT-      3.45455
      (1) UNWGT-   4.05556

    2    WGT-      5.85714
      (1) UNWGT-   5.75000

(1) Our hypotheses are based on linear contrasts of the unweighted means, labeled here as UNWGT (see Figure 3.2).

250

VARIABLE -- ACHIEV

VARIABLE -- ACHIEV     (CONT.)

METHOD

| | | |
|---|---|---|
| 1 | WGT. | 4.63636 |
| | UNWGT. | 6.13889 |
| 2 | WGT. | 11.42857 |
| | UNWGT. | 11.12500 |

CORRESPONDENCE BETWEEN EFFECTS AND COLUMNS OF BETWEEN-SUBJECTS DESIGN

| STARTING COLUMN | ENDING COLUMN | EFFECT NAME |
|---|---|---|
| 1 | 1 | CONSTANT |
| 2 | 2 | TESTTYPE |
| 3 | 3 | METHOD |
| 4 | 4 | TESTTYPE BY METHOD |

WITHIN CELLS CORRELATIONS WITH STD. DEVS. ON DIAGONAL

| | ATTITUDE | ACHIEV |
|---|---|---|
| ATTITUDE | 1.46114 | |
| ACHIEV | .47084 | 2.15150 |

DETERMINANT =                          .77831
BARTLETT TEST OF SPHERICITY =     3.13292 WITH 1 D. F.
SIGNIFICANCE =                          .077

F(MAX) CRITERION =          2.16822 WITH (2,14) D. F.

② These sums of squares and cross products matrices
   would be found in a MANOVA source table (see Table
   3.4 of this chapter).

WITHIN CELLS VARIANCES AND COVARIANCES

|          | ATTITUDE | ACHIEV |
|----------|----------|--------|
| ATTITUDE | 2.13492  |        |
| ACHIEV   | 1.48016  | 4.62897 |

- - - - - - - - - - - - - - - - - - - - - - - - - - - - - - - - - - - - -

WITHIN CELLS SUM-OF-SQUARES AND CROSS-PRODUCTS

② 

|          | ATTITUDE | ACHIEV |
|----------|----------|--------|
| ATTITUDE | 29.88889 |        |
| ACHIEV   | 20.72222 | 64.80556 |

- - - - - - - - - - - - - - - - - - - - - - - - - - - - - - - - - - - - -

CHAPTER 3:  TWO-WAY (2 X 2) MULTIVARIATE ANALYSIS

* * * * * * * * * * * * * * * * * * * A N A L Y S I S   O F   V A R I A N C E * * * * * * * * * * * * * * * * * * * *

EFFECT .. TESTTYPE BY METHOD
ADJUSTED HYPOTHESIS SUM-OF-SQUARES AND CROSS-PRODUCTS

Note: These multivariate source tables serve as the
      source tables for both the multivariate planned
      and overall analyses because there are only two
      treatments in each factor.

          ATTITUDE      ACHIEV

ATTITUDE  .12661
ACHIEV    .15375       .18669

③ Here no significant multivariate interaction was
  found.

MULTIVARIATE TESTS OF SIGNIFICANCE (S = 1, M = 0, N = 5 1/2)

| TEST NAME | VALUE | APPROX. F | HYPOTH. DF | ERROR DF | SIG. OF F |
|-----------|-------|-----------|------------|----------|-----------|
| PILLAIS     | .00489 | .03196 | 2.00 | 13.00 | .969 |
| HOTELLINGS ③ | .00492 | .03196 | 2.00 | 13.00 | .969 |
| WILKS       | .99511 | .03196 | 2.00 | 13.00 | .969 |
| RCYS        | .00489 |        |      |       |      |

EIGENVALUES AND CANONICAL CORRELATIONS

| ROOT NO. | EIGENVALUE | PCT. | CUM. PCT. | CANCN. COR. |
|----------|------------|------|-----------|-------------|
| 1 | .00492 | 100.00000 | 100.00000 | .06995 |

DIMENSION REDUCTION ANALYSIS

| ROOTS | WILKS LAMBDA | F | HYPOTH. DF | ERROR DF | SIG. OF F |
|-------|--------------|---|------------|----------|-----------|
| 1 TO 1 | .99511 | .03196 | 2.00 | 13.00 | .969 |

253

CHAPTER 3: TWO-WAY (2 X 2) MULTIVARIATE ANALYSIS

* * * * * * * * * * * * * * * * * * A N A L Y S I S  O F  V A R I A N C E * * * * * * * * * * * * * * * * * * * * * * * * * *    02/02/83    PAGE    19

EFFECT -- TESTTYPE BY METHOD    (CONT.)

UNIVARIATE F-TESTS WITH (1,14) D. F.

| VARIABLE | HYPOTH. SS | ERROR SS | HYPOTH. MS | ERROR MS | F | SIG. OF F |
|----------|-----------|----------|-----------|----------|---|-----------|
| ATTITUDE | .12661 | 29.88889 | .12661 | 2.13492 | .05931 | .811 |
| ACHIEV | .18669 | 64.80556 | .18669 | 4.62897 | .04033 | .844 |

ROY-BARGMAN STEPDOWN F - TESTS

| VARIABLE | HYPOTH. MS | ERROR MS | STEP-DOWN F | HYPOTH. DF | ERROR DF | SIG. OF F |
|----------|-----------|----------|-------------|-----------|----------|-----------|
| ATTITUDE | .12661 | 2.13492 | .05931 | 1 | 14 | .811 |
| ACHIEV | .03422 | 3.87990 | .00882 | 1 | 13 | .927 |

RAW DISCRIMINANT FUNCTION COEFFICIENTS

FUNCTION NO.

| VARIABLE | 1 |
|----------|---|
| ATTITUDE | .49926 |
| ACHIEV | .19610 |

STANDARDIZED DISCRIMINANT FUNCTION COEFFICIENTS

FUNCTION NO.

| VARIABLE | 1 |
|----------|---|
| ATTITUDE | .72948 |
| ACHIEV | .42192 |

* * * * * * * * * * * * * * * * * * * A N A L Y S I S   O F   V A R I A N C E * * * * * * * * * * * * * * * * * * * * *

EFFECT .. TESTTYPE BY METHOD      (CONT.)

ESTIMATES OF EFFECTS FOR CANCNICAL VARIABLES

       CANONICAL VARIABLE

   PARAMETER        1

       4          .07169

CORRELATIONS BETWEEN DEPENDENT AND CANONICAL VARIABLES

       CANONICAL VARIABLE

   VARIABLE         1

   ATTITUDE       .92814
   ACHIEV         .76539

* * * * * * * * * * * * * * * * A N A L Y S I S　O F　V A R I A N C E * * * * * * * * * * * * * * * * * * * * * * * * *

EFFECT .. METHOD

④ Here a multivariate significant difference was found between the two methods of instruction levels.

ADJUSTED HYPOTHESIS SUM-OF-SQUARES AND CROSS-PRODUCTS

|  | ATTITUDE | ACHIEV |
|---|---|---|
| ATTITUDE | 9.61499 | |
| ACHIEV | 28.29328 | 83.25646 |

MULTIVARIATE TESTS OF SIGNIFICANCE (S = 1, M = 0, N = 5 1/2)

| TEST NAME | VALUE | APPROX. F | HYPOTH. DF | ERROR DF | SIG. OF F |
|---|---|---|---|---|---|
| PILLAIS | .56258 | 8.36000 | 2.00 | 13.00 | .005 |
| HOTELLINGS | 1.28615 | 8.36000 | 2.00 | 13.00 | .005 |
| WILKS | .43742 | 8.36000 | 2.00 | 13.00 | .005 |
| ROYS | .56258 | | | | |

④

EIGENVALUES AND CANONICAL CORRELATIONS

| ROOT NO. | EIGENVALUE | PCT. | CUM. PCT. | CANON. COR. |
|---|---|---|---|---|
| 1 | 1.28615 | 100.00000 | 100.00000 | .75006 |

DIMENSION REDUCTION ANALYSIS

| ROOTS | WILKS LAMBDA | F | HYPOTH. DF | ERROR DF | SIG. OF F |
|---|---|---|---|---|---|
| 1 TO 1 | .43742 | 8.36000 | 2.00 | 13.00 | .005 |

* * * * * * * * * * * * * * * A N A L Y S I S   O F   V A R I A N C E * * * * * * * * * * * * * * * * * * *

EFFECT .. METHOD    (CONT.)

(5) A significant univariate result was found between the two methods of instruction on achievemnt, but not on attitude.

UNIVARIATE F-TESTS WITH (1,14) D. F.

| VARIABLE | HYPOTH. SS | ERROR SS | HYPOTH. MS | ERROR MS | F | SIG. OF F |
|---|---|---|---|---|---|---|
| ATTITUDE | 9.61499 | 29.88889 | 9.61499 | 2.13492 | 4.50367 | .052 (5) |
| ACHIEV | 83.25646 | 64.80556 | 83.25646 | 4.62897 | 17.98596 | .001 |

ROY-BARGMAN STEPDOWN F - TESTS

| VARIABLE | HYPOTH. MS | ERROR MS | STEP-DOWN F | HYPCTH. DF | ERROR DF | SIG. OF F |
|---|---|---|---|---|---|---|
| ATTITUDE | 9.61499 | 2.13492 | 4.50367 | 1 | 14 | .052 |
| ACHIEV | 36.80604 | 3.87990 | 9.48634 | 1 | 13 | .009 |

RAW DISCRIMINANT FUNCTION COEFFICIENTS

FUNCTION NO.

| VARIABLE | 1 |
|---|---|
| ATTITUDE | -.02598 |
| ACHIEV | .45622 |

STANDARDIZED DISCRIMINANT FUNCTICN COEFFICIENTS

FUNCTION NO.

| VARIABLE | 1 |
|---|---|
| ATTITUDE | -.03795 |
| ACHIEV | .98157 |

CHAPTER 3: TWO-WAY (2 X 2) MULTIVARIATE ANALYSIS

* * * * * * * * * * * * * * * * * * A N A L Y S I S   O F   V A R I A N C E * * * * * * * * * * * * * * * * * * * * * *

EFFECT .. METHOD     (CONT.)

ESTIMATES OF EFFECTS FCR CANCNICAL VARIABLES

     CANONICAL VARIABLE

  PARAMETER              1

      3            -1.15940

- - - - - - - - - - - - - - - - - - - - - - - - - - - - - -

CORRELATIONS BETWEEN DEPENDENT AND CANONICAL VARIABLES

     CANONICAL VARIABLE

  VARIABLE               1

  ATTITUDE           .50012
  ACHIEV             .99944

- - - - - - - - - - - - - - - - - - - - - - - - - - - - - -

* * * * * * * * * * * * * * * * * A N A L Y S I S   O F   V A R I A N C E * * * * * * * * * * * * * * * * * * * * * * *

EFFECT -- TESTTYPE

ADJUSTED HYPOTHESIS SUM-OF-SQUARES AND CROSS-PRODUCTS

|          | ATTITUDE | ACHIEV   |
|----------|----------|----------|
| ATTITUDE | 9.61499  |          |
| ACHIEV   | 25.45607 | 67.39599 |

⑥ Here a multivariate significant difference was found between the two levels of test type.

MULTIVARIATE TESTS OF SIGNIFICANCE (S = 1, M = 0, N = 5 1/2)

| TEST NAME  | VALUE    | APPROX. F | HYPOTH. DF | ERROR DF | SIG. OF F |
|------------|----------|-----------|------------|----------|-----------|
| PILLAIS    | .51212   | 6.82306   | 2.00       | 13.00    | .009      |
| HOTELLINGS ⑥ | 1.04970 | 6.82306  | 2.00       | 13.00    | .009      |
| WILKS      | .48788   | 6.82306   | 2.00       | 13.00    | .009      |
| ROYS       | .51212   |           |            |          |           |

EIGENVALUES AND CANONICAL CORRELATIONS

| ROOT NO. | EIGENVALUE | PCT.      | CUM. PCT. | CANON. COR. |
|----------|------------|-----------|-----------|-------------|
| 1        | 1.04970    | 100.00000 | 100.00000 | .71563      |

DIMENSION REDUCTION ANALYSIS

| ROOTS  | WILKS LAMBDA | F       | HYPOTH. DF | ERROR DF | SIG. OF F |
|--------|--------------|---------|------------|----------|-----------|
| 1 TO 1 | .48788       | 6.82306 | 2.00       | 13.00    | .009      |

\* \* \* \* \* \* \* \* \* \* \* \* \* \* \* \* \* \* \* \* \* A N A L Y S I S   O F   V A R I A N C E \* \* \* \* \* \* \* \* \* \* \* \* \* \* \* \* \* \* \*

EFFECT .. TESTTYPE        (CONT.)

① A significant univariate result was found between the levels of test type on achievement, but not on attitude.

UNIVARIATE F-TESTS WITH (1,14) D. F.

| VARIABLE | HYPOTH. SS | ERROR SS | HYPOTH. MS | ERROR MS | F | SIG. OF F |
|---|---|---|---|---|---|---|
| ATTITUDE | 9.61499 | 29.88889 | 9.61499 | 2.13492 | 4.50367 | .052 |
| ACHIEV | 67.39599 | 64.80556 | 67.39599 | 4.62897 | 14.55961 | ① .002 |

ROY-BARGMAN STEPDOWN F - TESTS

| VARIABLE | HYPOTH. MS | ERROR MS | STEP-DOWN F | HYPOTH. DF | ERROR DF | SIG. OF F |
|---|---|---|---|---|---|---|
| ATTITUDE | 9.61499 | 2.13492 | 4.50367 | 1 | 14 | .052 |
| ACHIEV | 27.78249 | 3.87990 | 7.16063 | 1 | 13 | .019 |

RAW DISCRIMINANT FUNCTION COEFFICIENTS

FUNCTION NO.        1

VARIABLE

| | |
|---|---|
| ATTITUDE | -.07468 |
| ACHIEV | .43875 |

STANDARDIZED DISCRIMINANT FUNCTION COEFFICIENTS

FUNCTION NO.        1

VARIABLE

| | |
|---|---|
| ATTITUDE | -.10912 |
| ACHIEV | .94397 |

CHAPTER 3: TWO-WAY (2 X 2) MULTIVARIATE ANALYSIS

* * * * * * * * * * * * * * * * * * * A N A L Y S I S   O F   V A R I A N C E * * * * * * * * * * * * * * * * * * * * * 02/02/83    PAGE    26

EFFECT .. TESTTYPE    (CONT.)

ESTIMATES OF EFFECTS FOR CANCNICAL VARIABLES

CANONICAL VARIABLE

PARAMETER        1

2      1.04742

CORRELATIONS BETWEEN DEPENDENT AND CANONICAL VARIABLES

CANONICAL VARIABLE

VARIABLE         1

ATTITUDE       .55359
ACHIEV         .99536

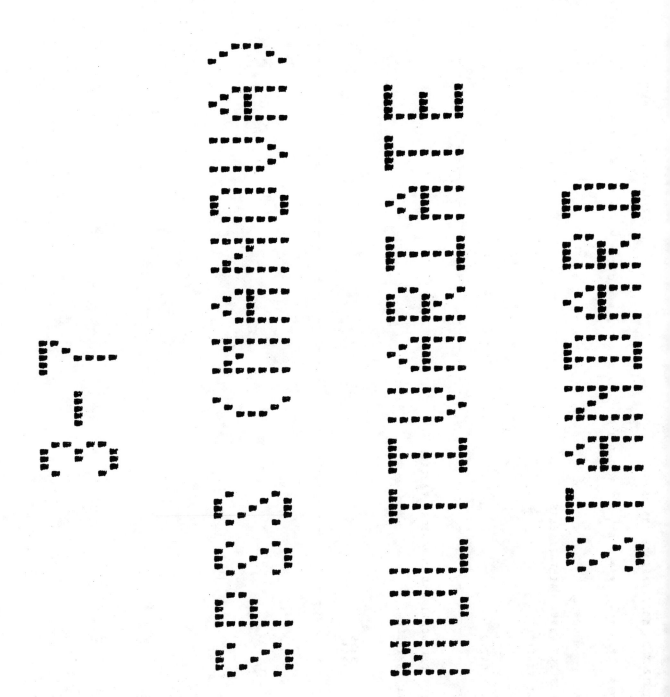

```
RUN NAME        TWO-WAY MANOVA (3 X 2)
DATA LIST       FIXED(1) / 1 CONTENT 1 EXPRESS 2 RATING 5-6 INTEREST 9-11
                ACHIEV 14-15
N OF CASES      21
LIST CASES
MANOVA          CASES=21/VARIABLES=CONTENT EXPRESS RATING INTEREST ACHIEV
                RATING INTEREST ACHIEV BY CONTENT(1,3),EXPRESS(1,2)/
                PRINT=CELLINFO(MEANS,SSCP,COV,COR)
                HOMOGENIETY(BARTLETT,COCHRAN,BOXM)
                SIGNIF(HYPOTH,STEPDOWN)
                DISCRIM(RAW,STAN,ESTIM,COR,ROTATE(VARIMAX) ALPHA(1.0))
                ERROR(SSCP,COV,COR,STDV)
        ②      OMEANS(TABLES(CONTENT,EXPRESS))
                POBS/
                PLOT = CELLPLOTS,BOXPLOTS,STEMLEAF,POBS/
                METHOD = SSTYPE(UNIQUE)/
        ③      CONTRAST(CONTENT) = SPECIAL(1 1 1 -1 0 0 1 -1)/
                CONTRAST(EXPRESS) = SIMPLE/
                PARTITION(CONTENT)/
                PARTITON(EXPRESS)/
                DESIGN = CONTENT,EXPRESS,CONTENT(1) BY EXPRESS(1),
                         CONTENT(2) BY EXPRESS(1)/

READ INPUT DATA
11 50 131 34
11 56 126 28
11 52 134 33
12 51 140 36
12 44 145 37
12 52 141 30
12 50 142 33
21 41 104 36
21 44 105 31
21 40 102 33
21 42 102 27
22 54 140 31
22 46 144 35
31 30 74 35
31 32 71 30
31 29 69 27
31 28 67 29
32 52 142 33
32 50 138 28
32 50 144 28
32 53 146 41
```

Note: The SPSS input annotations provided here are of value for most problems of this type, consult your SPSS manual for more general information.

① These are column identifiers and are not part of the program content.

Note: Further annotations for this input and output can be found in the program input for SPSS(MANOVA) in Chapter 2, program 2-10.

② The OMEANS specification in the PRINT subcommand requests SPSS to print both weighted and unweighted marginal means. When no variables are specified (e.g. in the previous I/O they were) means are printed for all of the dependent variables across the independent variables listed in the TABLES specification.

③ The SPECIAL contrast was used to create contrasts that could have been created by the REPEATED contrast.

① 0000000000111111111122222222223333333333444444444455555555556666666666777777777 8
  1234567890123456789012345678901234567890123456789012345678901234567890123456789 0

263

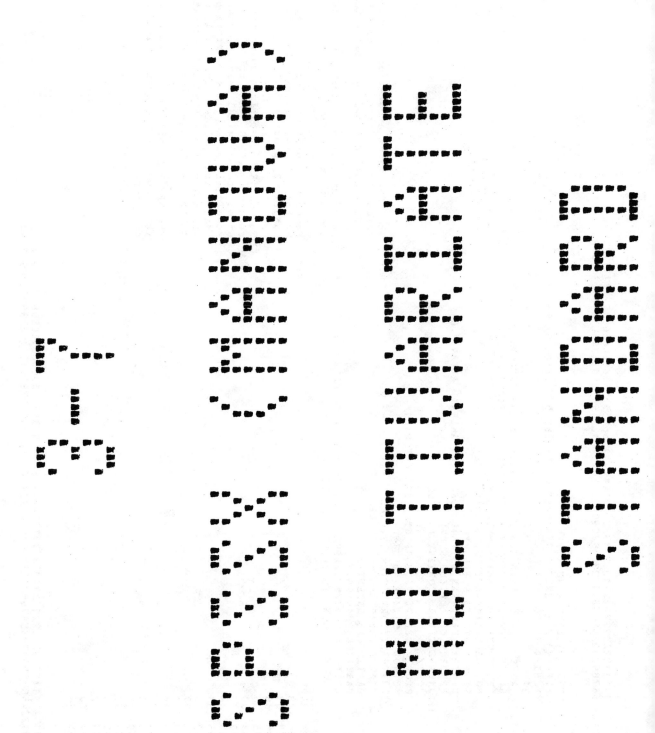

```
TITLE      TWO-WAY MANOVA (3 X 2)
DATA LIST  RECORD = 1/ 1 CONTENT 1 EXPRESS 2 RATING 5-6 INTEREST 9-11
           ACHIEV 14-15

BEGIN DATA
11 50 131 34
11 56 126 28
11 52 134 33
12 51 140 36
12 44 145 37
12 52 141 30
12 50 142 33
21 41 104 36
21 44 105 31
21 40 102 33
21 42 102 27
22 54 140 31
22 46 144 35
31 30 74 35
31 32 71 30
31 29 69 27
31 28 67 29
32 52 142 33
32 50 138 28
32 50 144 28
32 53 146 41
END DATA
LIST
MANOVA     VARIABLES=CONTENT EXPRESS RATING INTEREST ACHIEV
           RATING INTEREST ACHIEV BY CONTENT(1,3),EXPRESS(1,2)/
           PRINT=CELLINFO(MEANS,SSCP,COV,COR)
           HOMOGENIETY(BARTLETT,COCHRAN,BOXM)
           SIGNIF(HYPOTH,STEPDOWN)
           DISCRIM(RAW,STAN,ESTIM,COR,ROTATE(VARIMAX) ALPHA(1.0))
           ERROR(SSCP,COV,COR,STDV)
           OMEANS(TABLES(CONTENT,EXPRESS))
           POBS/
           PLOT = CELLPLOTS,BOXPLOTS,STEMLEAF,POBS/
           METHOD = SSTYPE(UNIQUE)/
           CONTRAST(CONTENT) = SPECIAL(1 1 1 -1 0 0 1 -1)/
           CONTRAST(EXPRESS) = SIMPLE/
           PARTITION(CONTENT)/
           PARTITON(EXPRESS)/
           DESIGN = CONTENT,EXPRESS,CONTENT(1) BY EXPRESS(1),
                    CONTENT(2) BY EXPRESS(1)/
```

FILE   NONAME   (CREATION DATE = 02/02/83)

* * * * * * * * * * * * * * * * * A N A L Y S I S   O F   V A R I A N C E * * * * * * * * * * * * * * * * * * * * *

CELL MEANS AND STANDARD DEVIATIONS

VARIABLE .. RATING

| FACTOR | CODE | MEAN | STD. DEV. | N | 95 PERCENT CONF. INTERVAL | |
|---|---|---|---|---|---|---|
| CONTENT | 1 | | | | | |
| EXPRESS | 1 | 52.66667 | 3.05505 | 3 | 45.07742 | 60.25592 |
| EXPRESS | 2 | 49.25000 | 3.59398 | 4 | 43.53126 | 54.96874 |
| CONTENT | 2 | | | | | |
| EXPRESS | 1 | 41.75000 | 1.70783 | 4 | 39.03251 | 44.46749 |
| EXPRESS | 2 | 50.00000 | 5.65685 | 2 | -.82480 | 100.82480 |
| CONTENT | 3 | | | | | |
| EXPRESS | 1 | 29.75000 | 1.70783 | 4 | 27.03251 | 32.46749 |
| EXPRESS | 2 | 51.25000 | 1.50000 | 4 | 48.86320 | 53.63680 |
| FOR ENTIRE SAMPLE | | 45.04762 | 8.77768 | 21 | 41.05207 | 49.04317 |

VARIABLE .. INTEREST

| FACTOR | CODE | MEAN | STD. DEV. | N | 95 PERCENT CONF. INTERVAL | |
|---|---|---|---|---|---|---|
| CONTENT | 1 | | | | | |
| EXPRESS | 1 | 130.33333 | 4.04145 | 3 | 120.29370 | 140.37297 |
| EXPRESS | 2 | 142.00000 | 2.16025 | 4 | 138.56262 | 145.43738 |
| CONTENT | 2 | | | | | |
| EXPRESS | 1 | 103.25000 | 1.50000 | 4 | 100.86320 | 105.63680 |
| EXPRESS | 2 | 142.00000 | 2.82843 | 2 | 116.58760 | 167.41240 |
| CONTENT | 3 | | | | | |
| EXPRESS | 1 | 70.25000 | 2.98608 | 4 | 65.49855 | 75.00145 |
| EXPRESS | 2 | 142.50000 | 3.41565 | 4 | 137.06502 | 147.93498 |
| FOR ENTIRE SAMPLE | | 119.38095 | 28.62425 | 21 | 106.35135 | 132.41055 |

VARIABLE .. ACHIEV

| FACTOR | CODE | MEAN | STD. DEV. | N | 95 PERCENT CONF. INTERVAL |
|---|---|---|---|---|---|

\* \* \* \* \* \* \* \* \* \* \* \* \* \* \* \* \* \* \* \* \* A N A L Y S I S   O F   V A R I A N C E \* \* \* \* \* \* \* \* \* \* \* \* \* \* \* \* \* \* \* \* \* \*

CELL MEANS AND STANDARD DEVIATIONS (CONT.)

VARIABLE -- ACHIEV

| FACTOR | CODE | MEAN | STD. DEV. | N | 95 PERCENT CONF. INTERVAL | |
|--------|------|------|-----------|---|---------------------------|---|
| CONTENT | 1 | | | | | |
| EXPRESS | 1 | 31.66667 | 3.21455 | 3 | 23.68119 | 39.65214 |
| EXPRESS | 2 | 34.00000 | 3.16228 | 4 | 28.96818 | 39.03182 |
| CONTENT | 2 | | | | | |
| EXPRESS | 1 | 31.75000 | 3.77492 | 4 | 25.74335 | 37.75665 |
| EXPRESS | 2 | 33.00000 | 2.82843 | 2 | 7.58760 | 58.41240 |
| CONTENT | 3 | | | | | |
| EXPRESS | 1 | 30.25000 | 3.40343 | 4 | 24.83446 | 35.66554 |
| EXPRESS | 2 | 32.50000 | 6.13732 | 4 | 22.73430 | 42.26570 |
| FOR ENTIRE SAMPLE | | 32.14286 | 3.74547 | 21 | 30.43794 | 33.84778 |

UNIVARIATE HOMOGENEITY OF VARIANCE TESTS

VARIABLE -- RATING

    COCHRANS C(3,6) =          .51337, P = .055 (APPROX.)
    BARTLETT-BOX F(5,206) =    .99992, P = .419

VARIABLE -- INTEREST

    COCHRANS C(3,6) =          .31511, P = .594 (APPROX.)
    BARTLETT-BOX F(5,206) =    .48909, P = .784

VARIABLE -- ACHIEV

    COCHRANS C(3,6) =          .41016, P = .214 (APPROX.)
    BARTLETT-BOX F(5,206) =    .38112, P = .861

* * * * * * * * * * * * * A N A L Y S I S   O F   V A R I A N C E * * * * * * * * * * * * * * * * * * *

COMBINED OBSERVED MEANS FOR CONTENT

VARIABLE -- RATING

CONTENT

| | | |
|---|---|---|
| 1 | WGT. | 50.71429 |
| | (1) UNWGT. | 50.95833 |
| 2 | WGT. | 44.50000 |
| | (1) UNWGT. | 45.87500 |
| 3 | WGT. | 40.50000 |
| | (1) UNWGT. | 40.50000 |

(1) Our hypothese are based on linear contrasts of the unweighted means, labeled here as UNWGT (see Figure 3.5).

VARIABLE -- INTEREST

CONTENT

| | | |
|---|---|---|
| 1 | WGT. | 137.00000 |
| | (1) UNWGT. | 136.16667 |
| 2 | WGT. | 116.16667 |
| | (1) UNWGT. | 122.62500 |
| 3 | WGT. | 106.37500 |
| | (1) UNWGT. | 106.37500 |

VARIABLE -- ACHIEV

CONTENT

| | | |
|---|---|---|
| 1 | WGT. | 33.00000 |
| | (1) UNWGT. | 32.83333 |
| 2 | WGT. | 32.16667 |
| | (1) UNWGT. | 32.37500 |

* * * * * * * * * * * * * * * A N A L Y S I S   O F   V A R I A N C E * * * * * * * * * * * * * * * * * * * * * * * * * *

VARIABLE -- ACHIEV    (CONT.)

            3     WGT.     31.37500
               (1)UNWGT.  31.37500

- - - - - - - - - - - - - - - - - - - - - - - - - - - - - - - - - - - - - - - - - - - - - - -

COMBINED OBSERVED MEANS FOR EXPRESS

VARIABLE -- RATING

    EXPRESS

            1     WGT.     40.36364
               (1)UNWGT.  41.38889

            2     WGT.     50.20000
               (1)UNWGT.  50.16667

- - - - - - - - - - - - - - - - - - - - - - - - - - - - - - - - - - - - - - - - - - - - - - -

VARIABLE -- INTEREST

    EXPRESS

            1     WGT.     98.63636
               (1)UNWGT. 101.27778

            2     WGT.    142.20000
               (1)UNWGT. 142.16667

- - - - - - - - - - - - - - - - - - - - - - - - - - - - - - - - - - - - - - - - - - - - - - -

VARIABLE -- ACHIEV

    EXPRESS

            1     WGT.     31.18182
               (1)UNWGT.  31.22222

            2     WGT.     33.20000

TWO-WAY MANOVA (3 X 2)

* * * * * * * * * * * * * * * * * * * A N A L Y S I S   O F   V A R I A N C E * * * * * * * * * * * * * * * * * * * * * * * * * * * *

VARIABLE .. ACHIEV (CONT.)
              (1) UNWGT.   33.16667

CORRESPONDENCE BETWEEN EFFECTS AND COLUMNS OF BETWEEN-SUBJECTS DESIGN

| STARTING COLUMN | ENDING COLUMN | EFFECT NAME |
|---|---|---|
| 1 | 1 | CONSTANT |
| 2 | 3 | CONTENT |
| 4 | 4 | EXPRESS |
| 5 | 5 | CONTENT(1) BY EXPRESS(1) |
| 6 | 6 | CONTENT(2) BY EXPRESS(1) |

WITHIN CELLS CORRELATIONS WITH STD. DEVS. ON DIAGONAL

|  | RATING | INTEREST | ACHIEV |
|---|---|---|---|
| RATING | 2.75278 |  |  |
| INTEREST | -.27608 | 2.86550 |  |
| ACHIEV | -.21292 | -.65265 | 4.07567 |

DETERMINANT =                       .52922
BARTLETT TEST OF SPHERICITY =     8.37864 WITH 3 D. F.
SIGNIFICANCE =                      -.039

F(MAX) CRITERION =                2.19208 WITH (3,15) D. F.

WITHIN CELLS VARIANCES AND COVARIANCES

|  | RATING | INTEREST | ACHIEV |
|---|---|---|---|
| RATING | 7.57778 |  |  |
| INTEREST | -2.17778 | 8.21111 |  |
| ACHIEV | -2.38889 | 7.62222 | 16.61111 |

270

**********ANALYSIS OF VARIANCE**************************************

WITHIN CELLS SUM-OF-SQUARES AND CROSS-PRODUCTS

② 

|         | RATING     | INTEREST   | ACHIEV    |
|---------|------------|------------|-----------|
| RATING  | 113.66667  |            |           |
| INTEREST| -32.66667  | 123.16667  |           |
| ACHIEV  | -35.83333  | 114.33333  | 249.16667 |

② These sums of squares and cross product matrices would be found in a MANOVA table such as Table 3.7.

---

TWO-WAY MANOVA (3 X 2)                                    02/02/83    PAGE   25

**********ANALYSIS OF VARIANCE**************************************

③ 

EFFECT .. CONTENT(2) BY EXPRESS(1)

③ The hypotheses tested by MANOVA are output in the reverse order of input of the sources of variation in the DESIGN statement.

ADJUSTED HYPOTHESIS SUM-OF-SQUARES AND CROSS-PRODUCTS

|         | RATING     | INTEREST   | ACHIEV   |
|---------|------------|------------|----------|
| RATING  | 140.45000  |            |          |
| INTEREST| 355.10000  | 897.80000  |          |
| ACHIEV  | 10.60000   | 26.80000   | .80000   |

④ This is a test of our second interaction null hypothesis in the planned comparison analysis. Here we find a significant result.

---

MULTIVARIATE TESTS OF SIGNIFICANCE (S = 1, M = 1/2, N = 5 1/2)

| TEST NAME  | VALUE    | APPROX. F | HYPOTH. DF | ERROR DF | SIG. OF F |
|------------|----------|-----------|------------|----------|-----------|
| PILLAIS    | .94017   | 68.09736  | 3.00       | 13.00    | .000      |
| HOTELLINGS | 15.71478 | 68.09736  | 3.00       | 13.00    | .000      |
| WILKS      | .05983   | 68.09736  | 3.00       | 13.00    | .000      |
| RCYS       | .94017   |           |            |          |           |

④

---

EIGENVALUES AND CANONICAL CORRELATIONS

| RCOT NO. | EIGENVALUE | PCT.      | CUM. PCT. | CANON. COR. |
|----------|------------|-----------|-----------|-------------|
| 1        | 15.71478   | 100.00000 | 100.00000 | .96963      |

---

DIMENSION REDUCTION ANALYSIS

| ROOTS   | WILKS LAMBDA | F        | HYPOTH. DF | ERROR DF | SIG. OF F |
|---------|--------------|----------|------------|----------|-----------|
| 1 TO 1  | .05983       | 68.09736 | 3.00       | 13.00    | .000      |

271

\* \* \* \* \* \* \* \* \* \* \* \* \* \* \* \* \* \* A N A L Y S I S   O F   V A R I A N C E \* \* \* \* \* \* \* \* \* \* \* \* \* \* \* \* \* \* \*

EFFECT .. CONTENT(2) BY EXPRESS(1)       (CONT.)

⑤ The univariate tests on the second interaction are
   significant for student rating and interest, but
   not for achievement.

UNIVARIATE F-TESTS WITH (1,15) D. F.

| VARIABLE | HYPOTH. SS | ERROR SS | HYPOTH. MS | ERROR MS | F | SIG. OF F |
|---|---|---|---|---|---|---|
| RATING | 140.45000 | 113.66667 | 140.45000 | 7.57778 | 18.53446 | .001 |
| INTEREST | 897.80000 | 123.16667 | 897.80000 | 8.21111 | 109.33965 | ⑤ .000 |
| ACHIEV | .80000 | 249.16667 | .80000 | 16.61111 | .04816 | .829 |

ROY-BARGMAN STEPDOWN F - TESTS

| VARIABLE | HYPOTH. MS | ERROR MS | STEP-DOWN F | HYPOTH. DF | ERROR DF | SIG. OF F |
|---|---|---|---|---|---|---|
| RATING | 140.45000 | 7.57778 | 18.53446 | 1 | 15 | .001 |
| INTEREST | 498.07184 | 8.12704 | 61.28574 | 1 | 14 | .000 |
| ACHIEV | 55.71634 | 10.98031 | 5.07420 | 1 | 13 | .042 |

RAW DISCRIMINANT FUNCTION COEFFICIENTS

    FUNCTION NO.

| VARIABLE | 1 |
|---|---|
| RATING | -.17492 |
| INTEREST | -.44851 |
| ACHIEV | .17714 |

STANDARDIZED DISCRIMINANT FUNCTION COEFFICIENTS

    FUNCTION NO.

| VARIABLE | 1 |
|---|---|
| RATING | -.48151 |
| INTEREST | -1.28519 |
| ACHIEV | .72197 |

272

TWO-WAY MANOVA (3 X 2)

* * * * * * * * * * * * * * * * * * * * A N A L Y S I S   O F   V A R I A N C E * * * * * * * * * * * * * * * * * * * * * * * * * * * * *

EFFECT .. CONTENT(2) BY EXPRESS(1)    (CONT.)

ESTIMATES OF EFFECTS FOR CANCNICAL VARIABLES

　　CANONICAL VARIABLE

PARAMETER        1

　　6        -17.16543

CORRELATIONS BETWEEN DEPENDENT AND CANONICAL VARIABLES

　　CANONICAL VARIABLE

VARIABLE        1

RATING        -.28041
INTEREST      -.68107
ACHIEV        -.01429

TWO-WAY MANOVA (3 X 2)

* * * * * * * * * * * * * * * * * * * * * A N A L Y S I S   O F   V A R I A N C E * * * * * * * * * * * * * * * * * * * * * *

⑥ EFFECT .. CONTENT(1) BY EXPRESS(1)

⑥ This is a test of our first interaction null hypothesis.

⑦ A significant multivariate result is indicated for the first interaction planned contrast.

ADJUSTED HYPOTHESIS SUM-OF-SQUARES AND CROSS-PRODUCTS

|          | RATING    | INTEREST   | ACHIEV   |
|----------|-----------|------------|----------|
| RATING   | 102.08333 |            |          |
| INTEREST | 236.97917 | 550.13021  |          |
| ACHIEV   | -9.47917  | -22.00521  | .88021   |

MULTIVARIATE TESTS OF SIGNIFICANCE (S = 1, M = 1/2, N = 5 1/2)

| TEST NAME  | VALUE    | APPROX. F | HYPOTH. DF | ERROR DF | SIG. OF F |
|------------|----------|-----------|------------|----------|-----------|
| PILLAIS    | .91190   | 44.85169  | 3.00       | 13.00    | .000      |
| HOTELLINGS | 10.35039 | 44.85169  | 3.00       | 13.00  ⑦| .000      |
| WILKS      | .08810   | 44.85169  | 3.00       | 13.00    | .000      |
| ROYS       | .91190   |           |            |          |           |

EIGENVALUES AND CANONICAL CORRELATIONS

| ROOT NO. | EIGENVALUE | PCT.      | CUM. PCT. | CANON. COR. |
|----------|------------|-----------|-----------|-------------|
| 1        | 10.35039   | 100.00000 | 100.00000 | .95493      |

DIMENSION REDUCTION ANALYSIS

| ROOTS  | WILKS LAMBDA | F        | HYPOTH. DF | ERROR DF | SIG. OF F |
|--------|--------------|----------|------------|----------|-----------|
| 1 TO 1 | .08810       | 44.85169 | 3.00       | 13.00    | .000      |

* * * * * * * * * * * * * * * A N A L Y S I S   O F   V A R I A N C E * * * * * * * * * * * * * * * * * * * * * * * * * * * *

EFFECT .. CONTENT(1) BY EXPRESS(1)      (CONT.)           ⑧ The univariate tests on the first interaction
UNIVARIATE F-TESTS WITH (1,15) D. F.                       contrast are significant for student rating and
                                                           interest, but not achievement.

| VARIABLE | HYPOTH. SS | ERROR SS | HYPOTH. MS | ERROR MS | F | SIG. OF F |
|----------|-----------|----------|-----------|----------|---|-----------|
| RATING   | 102.08333 | 113.66667 | 102.08333 | 7.57778 | 13.47141 | .002 |
| INTEREST | 550.13021 | 123.16667 | 550.13021 | 8.21111 | 66.99827 | ⑧ .000 |
| ACHIEV   | .88021    | 249.16667 | .88021    | 16.61111 | .05299 | .821 |

ROY-BARGMAN STEPDOWN F - TESTS

| VARIABLE | HYPOTH. MS | ERROR MS | STEP-DOWN F | HYPOTH. DF | ERROR DF | SIG. OF F |
|----------|-----------|----------|-------------|------------|----------|-----------|
| RATING   | 102.08333 | 7.57778  | 13.47141    | 1          | 15       | .002 |
| INTEREST | 366.03695 | 8.12704  | 45.03938    | 1          | 14       | .000 |
| ACHIEV   | 59.66846  | 10.98031 | 5.43413     | 1          | 13       | .036 |

RAW DISCRIMINANT FUNCTION COEFFICIENTS

       FUNCTION NO.

| VARIABLE | 1 |
|----------|---|
| RATING   | -.17749 |
| INTEREST | -.44741 |
| ACHIEV   | .18431 |

STANDARDIZED DISCRIMINANT FUNCTION COEFFICIENTS

       FUNCTION NO.

| VARIABLE | 1 |
|----------|---|
| RATING   | -.48858 |
| INTEREST | -1.28206 |
| ACHIEV   | .75118 |

275

TWO-WAY MANOVA (3 X 2)

* * * * * * * * * * * * * * * * * * * * * * A N A L Y S I S   O F   V A R I A N C E * * * * * * * * * * * * * * * * * * * * * * * * * * *

EFFECT .. CONTENT(1) BY EXPRESS(1)    (CONT.)

ESTIMATES OF EFFECTS FCR CANCNICAL VARIABLES

CANONICAL VARIABLE

PARAMETER           1

5           -14.38777

CORRELATIONS BETWEEN DEPENDENT AND CANONICAL VARIABLES

CANONICAL VARIABLE

VARIABLE            1

RATING          -.29457
INTEREST        -.65691
ACHIEV           .01847

Note: Because the interactions were both significant,
      the tests of the main effects are not provided
      here—see the next program I/O.

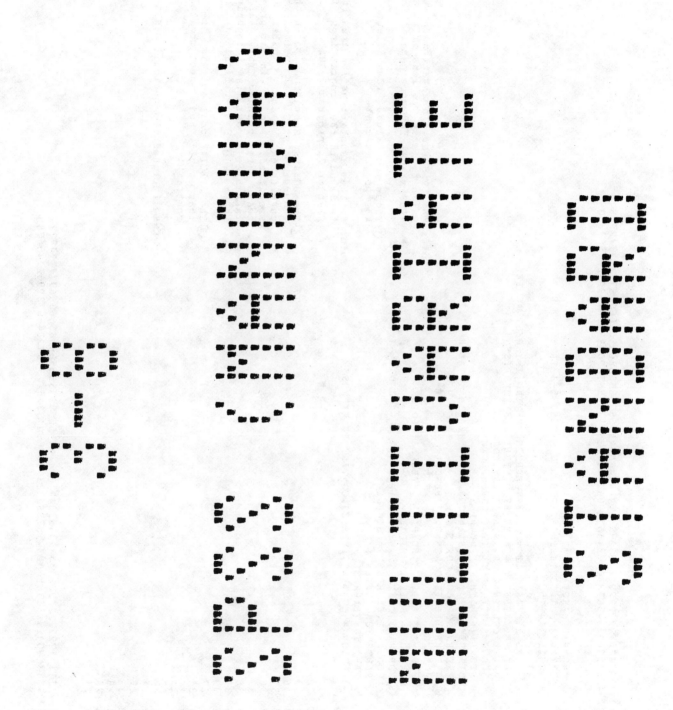

```
RUN NAME        TWO-WAY MANOVA  (3 X 2)
DATA LIST       FIXED(1) / 1 CONTENT 1 EXPRESS 2 RATING 5-6 INTEREST 9-11
                ACHIEV 14-15
N OF CASES      21
LIST CASES      CASES=21/VARIABLES=CONTENT EXPRESS RATING INTEREST ACHIEV
MANOVA          RATING INTEREST ACHIEV BY CONTENT(1,3),EXPRESS(1,2)/
                PRINT=CELLINFO(MEANS,SSCP,COV,COR)
                HOMOGENEITY(BARTLETT,CCCHBAN,BOXM)
                SIGNIF(HYPOTH,STEPDOWN)
                DISCRIM(RAW,STAN,ESTIM,COR,ROTATE(VARIMAX) ALPHA(1.0))
                ERROR(SSCP,COV,COR,STDV)
②             OMEANS(TABLES(CONTENT,EXPRESS))
                POBS/
                PLOT = CELLPLOTS,BOXPLOTS,STEMLEAP,POBS/
                METHOD = SSTYPE(UNIQUE)/
③             CONTRAST(CONTENT) = SPECIAL(1 1 1 -1 0 0 1 -1)/
                CONTRAST(EXPRESS) = SIMPLE/
                PARTITION(CONTENT)/
                PARTITON(EXPRESS)/
④             DESIGN = CONTENT,EXPRESS,CONTENT BY EXPRESS/
READ INPUT DATA
11 50 131 34
11 56 126 28
11 52 134 33
12 51 140 36
12 44 145 37
12 52 141 30
12 50 142 33
21 41 104 36
21 44 105 31
21 40 102 33
21 42 102 27
22 54 140 31
22 46 144 35
31 30  74 35
31 32  71 30
31 29  69 27
31 28  67 29
32 52 142 33
32 50 138 28
32 50 144 28
32 53  146 41
```

Note: The SPSS input annotations provided here are of value for most problems of this type, consult your SPSS manual for more general information.

① These are column identifiers and are not part of the program content.

Note: Further annotations for this input and output can be found in the program input for SPSS(MANOVA) in Chapter 2, program 2-10.

② The OMEANS specification in the PRINT subcommand requests SPSS to print both weighted and unweighted means. When no variables are specified, e.g., in the previous I/O they are, means are printed for all of the dependent variables across the independent variables listed in the TABLES specification.

③ The SPECIAL contrast was used to create contrasts that could have been created by the REPEATED contrast.

④ We included the optional DESIGN statement here.

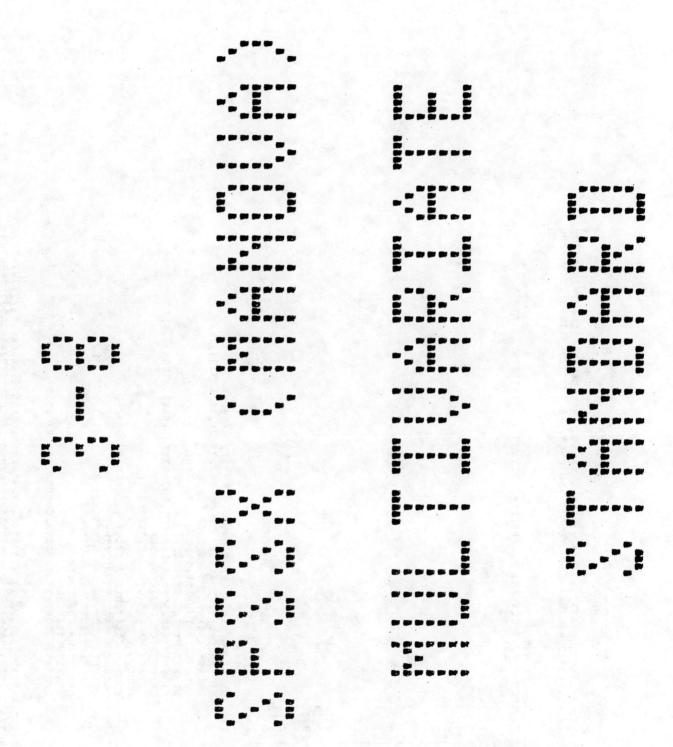

```
TITLE       TWO-WAY MANOVA (3 X 2)
DATA LIST   RECORD = 1/ 1 CONTENT 1 EXPRESS 2 RATING 5-6 INTEREST 9-11
            ACHIEV 14-15

BEGIN DATA
11 50 131 34
11 56 126 28
11 52 134 33
12 51 140 36
12 44 145 37
12 52 141 30
12 50 142 33
21 41 104 36
21 44 105 31
21 40 102 33
21 42 102 27
22 54 140 31
22 46 144 35
31 30 74 35
31 32 71 30
31 29 69 27
31 28 67 29
32 52 142 33
32 50 138 28
32 50 144 28
32 53 146 41
END DATA
LIST
MANOVA      VARIABLES=CONTENT EXPRESS RATING INTEREST ACHIEV
            RATING INTEREST ACHIEV BY CONTENT(1,3),EXPRESS(1,2)/
            PRINT=CELLINFO(MEANS,SSCP,COV,COR)
            HOMOGENEITY(BARTLETT,COCHRAN,BOXM)
            SIGNIF(HYPOTH,STEPDOWN)
            DISCRIM(RAW,STAN,ESTIM,COR,ROTATE(VARIMAX) ALPHA(1-0)
            ERROR(SSCP,COV,COR,STDV)
            OMEANS(TABLES(CONTENT,EXPRESS))
            POBS/
            PLOT = CELLPLOTS,BOXPLOTS,STEMLEAF,POBS/
            METHOD = SSTYPE(UNIQUE)/
            CONTRAST(CONTENT) = SPECIAL(1 1 1 -1 0 0 1 -1)/
            CONTRAST(EXPRESS) = SIMPLE/
            PARTITION(CONTENT)/
            PARTITON(EXPRESS)/
            DESIGN = CONTENT,EXPRESS,CONTENT BY EXPRESS/
```

FILE   NONAME    (CREATION DATE = 02/02/83)

* * * * * * * * * * * A N A L Y S I S   O F   V A R I A N C E * * * * * * * * * * * * * * * * * *

CELL MEANS AND STANDARD DEVIATIONS

VARIABLE -- RATING

| FACTOR | CODE | MEAN | STD. DEV. | N | 95 PERCENT CONF. INTERVAL | |
|---|---|---|---|---|---|---|
| CONTENT | 1 | | | | | |
| EXPRESS | 1 | 52.66667 | 3.05505 | 3 | 45.07742 | 60.25592 |
| EXPRESS | 2 | 49.25000 | 3.59398 | 4 | 43.53126 | 54.96874 |
| CONTENT | 2 | | | | | |
| EXPRESS | 1 | 41.75000 | 1.70783 | 4 | 39.03251 | 44.46749 |
| EXPRESS | 2 | 50.00000 | 5.65685 | 2 | -.82480 | 100.82480 |
| CONTENT | 3 | | | | | |
| EXPRESS | 1 | 29.75000 | 1.70783 | 4 | 27.03251 | 32.46749 |
| EXPRESS | 2 | 51.25000 | 1.50000 | 4 | 48.86320 | 53.63680 |
| FOR ENTIRE SAMPLE | | 45.04762 | 8.77768 | 21 | 41.05207 | 49.04317 |

281

VARIABLE -- INTEREST

| FACTOR | CODE | MEAN | STD. DEV. | N | 95 PERCENT CONF. INTERVAL | |
|---|---|---|---|---|---|---|
| CONTENT | 1 | | | | | |
| EXPRESS | 1 | 130.33333 | 4.04145 | 3 | 120.29370 | 140.37297 |
| EXPRESS | 2 | 142.00000 | 2.16025 | 4 | 138.56262 | 145.43738 |
| CONTENT | 2 | | | | | |
| EXPRESS | 1 | 103.25000 | 1.50000 | 4 | 100.86320 | 105.63680 |
| EXPRESS | 2 | 142.00000 | 2.82843 | 2 | 116.58760 | 167.41240 |
| CONTENT | 3 | | | | | |
| EXPRESS | 1 | 70.25000 | 2.98608 | 4 | 65.49855 | 75.00145 |
| EXPRESS | 2 | 142.50000 | 3.41565 | 4 | 137.06502 | 147.93498 |
| FOR ENTIRE SAMPLE | | 119.38095 | 28.62425 | 21 | 106.35135 | 132.41055 |

VARIABLE -- ACHIEV

| FACTOR | CODE | MEAN | STD. DEV. | N | 95 PERCENT CONF. INTERVAL |
|---|---|---|---|---|---|

\* \* \* \* \* \* \* \* \* \* \* \* \* \* \* \* \* \* A N A L Y S I S   O F   V A R I A N C E \* \* \* \* \* \* \* \* \* \* \* \* \* \* \* \* \* \* \* \*

CELL MEANS AND STANDARD DEVIATIONS  (CONT.)

VARIABLE -- ACHIEV

| FACTOR | CODE | MEAN | STD. DEV. | N | 95 PERCENT CONF. INTERVAL |
|--------|------|------|-----------|---|---------------------------|
| CONTENT | 1 | | | | |
| EXPRESS | 1 | 31.66667 | 3.21455 | 3 | 23.68119   39.65214 |
| EXPRESS | 2 | 34.00000 | 3.16228 | 4 | 28.96818   39.03182 |
| CONTENT | 2 | | | | |
| EXPRESS | 1 | 31.75000 | 3.77492 | 4 | 25.74335   37.75665 |
| EXPRESS | 2 | 33.00000 | 2.82843 | 2 | 7.58760    58.41240 |
| CONTENT | 3 | | | | |
| EXPRESS | 1 | 30.25000 | 3.40343 | 4 | 24.83446   35.66554 |
| EXPRESS | 2 | 32.50000 | 6.13732 | 4 | 22.73430   42.26570 |
| FOR ENTIRE SAMPLE | | 32.14286 | 3.74547 | 21 | 30.43794   33.84778 |

UNIVARIATE HOMOGENEITY OF VARIANCE TESTS

VARIABLE -- RATING

    COCHRANS C(3,6) =            .51337, P =   .055 (APPROX.)
    BARTLETT-BOX F(5,206) =      .99992, P =   .419

VARIABLE -- INTEREST

    COCHRANS C(3,6) =            .31511, P =   .594 (APPROX.)
    BARTLETT-BOX F(5,206) =      .48909, P =   .784

VARIABLE -- ACHIEV

    COCHRANS C(3,6) =            .41016, P =   .214 (APPROX.)
    BARTLETT-BOX F(5,206) =      .38112, P =   .861

\* \* \* \* \* \* \* \* \* \* \* \* \* \* \* \* \* \* \* A N A L Y S I S　O F　V A R I A N C E \* \* \* \* \* \* \* \* \* \* \* \* \* \* \* \* \* \* \* \* \* \*

COMBINED OBSERVED MEANS FOR CONTENT

VARIABLE -- RATING

CONTENT

```
1    ①WGT.     50.71429
     ①UNWGT.   50.95833

2    ①WGT.     44.50000
     ①UNWGT.   45.87500

3    ①WGT.     40.50000
     ①UNWGT.   40.50000
```

VARIABLE -- INTEREST

CONTENT

```
1    ①WGT.     137.00000
     ①UNWGT.   136.16667

2    ①WGT.     116.16667
     ①UNWGT.   122.62500

3    ①WGT.     106.37500
     ①UNWGT.   106.37500
```

VARIABLE -- ACHIEV

CONTENT

```
1    ①WGT.     33.00000
     ①UNWGT.   32.83333

2    ①WGT.     32.16667
     ①UNWGT.   32.37500
```

① Our hypotheses are based on linear contrasts of the unweighted means, labeled here as UNWGT (see Figure 3.5).

283

TWO-WAY MANOVA (3 X 2)

\* \* \* \* \* \* \* \* \* \* \* \* \* \* \* \* \* A N A L Y S I S   O F   V A R I A N C E \* \* \* \* \* \* \* \* \* \* \* \* \* \* \* \* \* \* \* \* \* \* \*

VARIABLE -- ACHIEV    (CONT.)

    3      WGT.      31.37500
        (1) UNWGT.   31.37500

COMBINED OBSERVED MEANS FOR EXPRESS

VARIABLE -- RATING

    EXPRESS

        1       WGT.      40.36364
            (1) UNWGT.    41.38889

        2       WGT.      50.20000
            (1) UNWGT.    50.16667

VARIABLE -- INTEREST

    EXPRESS

        1       WGT.      98.63636
            (1) UNWGT.   101.27778

        2       WGT.     142.20000
            (1) UNWGT.   142.16667

VARIABLE -- ACHIEV

    EXPRESS

        1       WGT.      31.18182
            (1) UNWGT.    31.22222

        2       WGT.      33.20000

284

TWO-WAY MANOVA (3 X 2)

\* \* \* \* \* \* \* \* \* \* \* \* \* \* \* \* \* \* A N A L Y S I S   O F   V A R I A N C E \* \* \* \* \* \* \* \* \* \* \* \* \* \* \* \* \* \* \* \* \* \* \*   02/02/83   PAGE   23

VARIABLE -- ACHIEV (CONT.)

(1) UNWGT. 33.16667

----

CORRESPONDENCE BETWEEN EFFECTS AND COLUMNS OF BETWEEN-SUBJECTS DESIGN

| STARTING COLUMN | ENDING COLUMN | EFFECT NAME |
|---|---|---|
| 1 | 1 | CONSTANT |
| 2 | 3 | CONTENT |
| 4 | 4 | EXPRESS |
| 5 | 6 | CONTENT BY EXPRESS |

----

WITHIN CELLS CORRELATIONS WITH STD. DEVS. ON DIAGONAL

|  | RATING | INTEREST | ACHIEV |
|---|---|---|---|
| RATING | 2.75278 | | |
| INTEREST | -.27608 | 2.86550 | |
| ACHIEV | -.21292 | .65265 | 4.07567 |

----

DETERMINANT = .52922
BARTLETT TEST OF SPHERICITY = 8.37864 WITH 3 D. F.
SIGNIFICANCE = .039

----

F(MAX) CRITERION = 2.19208 WITH (3,15) D. F.

----

WITHIN CELLS VARIANCES AND COVARIANCES

|  | RATING | INTEREST | ACHIEV |
|---|---|---|---|
| RATING | 7.57778 | | |
| INTEREST | -2.17778 | 8.21111 | |
| ACHIEV | -2.38889 | 7.62222 | 16.61111 |

----

285

\* \* \* \* \* \* \* \* \* \* \* \* \* \* \* \* A N A L Y S I S   O F   V A R I A N C E \* \* \* \* \* \* \* \* \* \* \* \* \* \* \* \* \*

WITHIN CELLS SUM-OF-SQUARES AND CROSS-PRODUCTS

②

|  | RATING | INTEREST | ACHIEV |
|---|---|---|---|
| RATING | 113.66667 | | |
| INTEREST | -32.66667 | 123.16667 | |
| ACHIEV | -35.83333 | 114.33333 | 249.16667 |

② These sums of squares and cross product matrices are needed for Table 3.8.

\* \* \* \* \* \* \* \* \* \* \* \* \* \* \* \* A N A L Y S I S   O F   V A R I A N C E \* \* \* \* \* \* \* \* \* \* \* \* \* \* \* \* \*

④

EFFECT .. CONTENT BY EXPRESS

ADJUSTED HYPOTHESIS SUM-OF-SQUARES AND CROSS-PRODUCTS

②

|  | RATING | INTEREST | ACHIEV |
|---|---|---|---|
| RATING | 576.08805 | | |
| INTEREST | 1402.92610 | 3418.10220 | |
| ACHIEV | -.13365 | .98270 | 1.06447 |

③ Selected parts of this output would be found in a MANOVA table such as Table 3.8.

④ The hypotheses tested by MANOVA are output in the reverse order of input of the sources of variation in the DESIGN statement.

⑤ A significant interaction is found, see the discussion in this chapter.

MULTIVARIATE TESTS OF SIGNIFICANCE (S = 2, M = 0, N = 5 1/2)

| TEST NAME | | VALUE | APPROX. F | HYPOTH. DF | ERROR DF | SIG. OF F |
|---|---|---|---|---|---|---|
| PILLAIS | | .98854 | 4.56090 | 6.00 | 28.00 | .002 |
| HOTELLINGS | ⑤ | 61.69826 | 123.39653 | 6.00 | 24.00 | 0.0 |
| WILKS | | -.01588 | 30.05499 | 6.00 | 26.00 | 0.0 |
| ROYS | | .98405 | | | | |

EIGENVALUES AND CANONICAL CORRELATIONS

| ROOT NO. | EIGENVALUE | PCT. | CUM. PCT. | CANON. COR. |
|---|---|---|---|---|
| 1 | 61.69376 | 99.99269 | 99.99269 | .99199 |
| 2 | .00451 | .00731 | 100.00000 | .06699 |

DIMENSION REDUCTION ANALYSIS

| ROOTS | WILKS LAMBDA | F | HYPOTH. DF | ERROR DF | SIG. OF F |
|---|---|---|---|---|---|
| 1 TO 2 | .01588 | 30.05499 | 6.00 | 26.00 | 0.0 |
| 2 TC 2 | .99551 | .03043 | 2.00 | 13.50 | .970 |

* * * * * * * * * * * * * * * * A N A L Y S I S   O F   V A R I A N C E * * * * * * * * * * * * * * * * * * *

EFFECT .. CONTENT BY EXPRESS    (CONT.)

(6) The overall univariate tests indicate a significant interaction on student ratings and interest, but not on achievement.

UNIVARIATE F-TESTS WITH (2,15) D. F.

| VARIABLE | HYPOTH. SS | ERROR SS | HYPOTH. MS | ERROR MS | F | SIG. OF F |
|---|---|---|---|---|---|---|
| RATING | 576.08805 | 113.66667 | 288.04403 | 7.57778 | 38.01167 | .000 |
| INTEREST | 3418.10220 | 123.16667 | 1709.05110 | 8.21111 | 208.13883 (6) | 0-0 |
| ACHIEV | 1.06447 | 249.16667 | .53223 | 16.61111 | .03204 | .969 |

ROY-BARGMAN STEPDOWN F - TESTS

| VARIABLE | HYPOTH. MS | ERROR MS | STEP-DOWN F | HYPOTH. DF | ERROR DF | SIG. OF F |
|---|---|---|---|---|---|---|
| RATING | 288.04403 | 7.57778 | 38.01167 | 2 | 15 | .000 |
| INTEREST | 352.67368 | 8.12704 | 43.39508 | 2 | 14 | .000 |
| ACHIEV | 31.51348 | 10.98031 | 2.87000 | 2 | 13 | .093 |

RAW DISCRIMINANT FUNCTION COEFFICIENTS

FUNCTION NO.

| VARIABLE | 1 | 2 |
|---|---|---|
| RATING | -.17606 | -.07671 |
| INTEREST | -.44809 | -.03146 |
| ACHIEV | -.18028 | -.21337 |

STANDARDIZED DISCRIMINANT FUNCTION COEFFICIENTS

FUNCTION NO.

| VARIABLE | 1 | 2 |
|---|---|---|
| RATING | -.48465 | -.21116 |
| INTEREST | -1.28401 | -.09016 |
| ACHIEV | .73476 | -.86961 |

287

TWO-WAY MANOVA (3 X 2)

EFFECT .. CONTENT BY EXPRESS     (CONT.)

ESTIMATES OF EFFECTS FOR CANONICAL VARIABLES

CANONICAL VARIABLE

| PARAMETER | 1 | 2 |
|---|---|---|
| 5 | -14.38516 | -.27394 |
| 6 | -17.16360 | -.25101 |

CORRELATIONS BETWEEN DEPENDENT AND CANONICAL VARIABLES

CANONICAL VARIABLE

| VARIABLE | 1 | 2 |
|---|---|---|
| RATING | -.28660 | -.42122 |
| INTEREST | -.67067 | -.71601 |
| ACHIEV | -.00006 | -.97342 |

VARIMAX ROTATED CORRELATIONS BETWEEN CANONICAL AND DEPENDENT VARIATES

CAN. VAR.

| DEP. VAR. | 1 | 2 |
|---|---|---|
| RATING | -.02910 | -.50864 |
| INTEREST | .94345 | -.26903 |
| ACHIEV | .50078 | -.83473 |

TRANSFORMATION MATRIX

| | 1 | 2 |
|---|---|---|
| 1 | -.85755 | -.51440 |
| 2 | -.51440 | -.85755 |

* * * * * * * * * * * * * * * * * * * * * A N A L Y S I S   O F   V A R I A N C E * * * * * * * * * * * * * * * * * * * * * *

EFFECT .. CONTENT BY EXPRESS       (CONT.)

EFFECT .. EXPRESS ①

ADJUSTED HYPOTHESIS SUM-OF-SQUARES AND CROSS-PRODUCTS

|          | RATING     | INTEREST   | ACHIEV   |
|----------|------------|------------|----------|
| RATING   | 378.24242  |            |          |
| INTEREST | 1761.93939 | 8207.51515 |          |
| ACHIEV   | 83.78788   | 390.30303  | 18.56061 |

① These are the main effect multivariate tests for differences between the levels of expressiveness. They are given less emphasis because of the significant interaction.

MULTIVARIATE TESTS OF SIGNIFICANCE (S = 1, M = 1/2, N = 5 1/2)

| TEST NAME  | VALUE     | APPROX. F | HYPOTH. DF | ERROR DF | SIG. OF F |
|------------|-----------|-----------|------------|----------|-----------|
| PILLAIS    | .99217    | 549.14290 | 3.00       | 13.00    | 0.0       |
| HOTELLINGS | 126.72528 | 549.14290 | 3.00       | 13.00    | 0.0       |
| WILKS      | .00783    | 549.14290 | 3.00       | 13.00    | 0.0       |
| RCYS       | .99217    |           |            |          |           |

EIGENVALUES AND CANONICAL CORRELATIONS

| ROOT NO. | EIGENVALUE | PCT.      | CUM. PCT. | CANON. COR. |
|----------|------------|-----------|-----------|-------------|
| 1        | 126.72528  | 100.00000 | 100.00000 | .99608      |

DIMENSION REDUCTION ANALYSIS

| ROOTS  | WILKS LAMBDA | F         | HYPOTH. DF | ERROR DF | SIG. OF F |
|--------|--------------|-----------|------------|----------|-----------|
| 1 TO 1 | .00783       | 549.14290 | 3.00       | 13.00    | 0.0       |

* * * * * * * * * * * * * * * * * * * * * A N A L Y S I S   O F   V A R I A N C E * * * * * * * * * * * * * * * * * * * * *

EFFECT .. EXPRESS      (CONT.)

UNIVARIATE F-TESTS WITH (1,15) D. F.

| VARIABLE | HYPOTH. SS | ERROR SS | HYPOTH. MS | ERROR MS | F | SIG. OF F |
|---|---|---|---|---|---|---|
| RATING | 378.24242 | 113.66667 | 378.24242 | 7.57778 | 49.91469 | .000 |
| INTEREST | 8207.51515 | 123.16667 | 8207.51515 | 8.21111 | 999.56206 | 0.0 |
| ACHIEV | 18.56061 | 249.16667 | 18.56061 | 16.61111 | 1.11736 | .307 |

ROY-BARGMAN STEPDOWN F - TESTS

| VARIABLE | HYPOTH. MS | ERROR MS | STEP-DOWN F | HYPOTH. DF | ERROR DF | SIG. OF F |
|---|---|---|---|---|---|---|
| RATING | 378.24242 | 7.57778 | 49.91469 | 1 | 15 | .000 |
| INTEREST | 2137.76336 | 8.12704 | 263.04322 | 1 | 14 | 0.0 |
| ACHIEV | 70.15009 | 10.98031 | 6.38871 | 1 | 13 | .025 |

RAW DISCRIMINANT FUNCTION COEFFICIENTS

FUNCTION NO.

| VARIABLE | 1 |
|---|---|
| RATING | -.13265 |
| INTEREST | -.46166 |
| ACHIEV | .13681 |

STANDARDIZED DISCRIMINANT FUNCTION COEFFICIENTS

FUNCTION NO.

| VARIABLE | 1 |
|---|---|
| RATING | -.36515 |
| INTEREST | -1.32288 |
| ACHIEV | .76139 |

\* \* \* \* \* \* \* \* \* \* \* \* \* \* \* \* \* \* \* A N A L Y S I S   O F   V A R I A N C E \* \* \* \* \* \* \* \* \* \* \* \* \* \* \* \* \* \* \* \*

EFFECT -. EXPRESS     (CONT-)

ESTIMATES OF EFFECTS FCR CANCNICAL VARIABLES

    CANONICAL VARIABLE

    PARAMETER          1

         4        19.67781

- - - - - - - - - - - - - - - - - - -

CORRELATIONS BETWEEN DEPENDENT AND CANONICAL VARIABLES

    CANONICAL VARIABLE

VARIABLE                1

RATING           -.16205
INTEREST         -.72515
ACHIEV           -.02424

291

* * * * * * * * * * * * * * * * * * * * * A N A L Y S I S   O F   V A R I A N C E * * * * * * * * * * * * * * * * * * * * * * * * * * *

EFFECT .. CONTENT ⑧

ADJUSTED HYPOTHESIS SUM-OF-SQUARES AND CROSS-PRODUCTS

|  | RATING | INTEREST | ACHIEV |
|---|---|---|---|
| RATING | 405.03145 | | |
| INTEREST | 1155.79403 | 3301.61164 | |
| ACHIEV | 57.01730 | 163.62421 | 8.27201 |

⑧ These are the main effects multivariate tests for differences between the levels of content.

MULTIVARIATE TESTS OF SIGNIFICANCE (S = 2, M = 0, N = 5 1/2)

| TEST NAME | VALUE | APPROX. F | HYPOTH. DF | ERROR DF | SIG. OF F |
|---|---|---|---|---|---|
| PILLAIS | .98506 | 4.52926 | 6.00 | 28.00 | .003 |
| HOTELLINGS | 55.28631 | 110.57262 | 6.00 | 24.00 | 0.0 |
| WILKS | .01772 | 28.22236 | 6.00 | 26.00 | 0.0 |
| ROYS | .98223 | | | | |

EIGENVALUES AND CANONICAL CORRELATIONS

| ROOT NO. | EIGENVALUE | PCT. | CUM. PCT. | CANON. COR. |
|---|---|---|---|---|
| 1 | 55.28347 | 99.99487 | 99.99487 | .99108 |
| 2 | .00283 | .00513 | 100.00000 | .05316 |

DIMENSION REDUCTION ANALYSIS

| ROOTS | WILKS LAMBDA | F | HYPOTH. DF | ERROR DF | SIG. OF F |
|---|---|---|---|---|---|
| 1 TO 2 | .01772 | 28.22236 | 6.00 | 26.00 | 0.0 |
| 2 TO 2 | .99717 | .01913 | 2.00 | 13.50 | .981 |

292

\* \* \* \* \* \* \* \* \* \* \* \* \* \* \* \* \* \* \* \* \* A N A L Y S I S   O F   V A R I A N C E \* \* \* \* \* \* \* \* \* \* \* \* \* \* \* \* \* \* \* \* \*

EFFECT .. CONTENT     (CONT.)

UNIVARIATE F-TESTS WITH (2,15) D. F.

| VARIABLE | HYPOTH. SS | ERROR SS | HYPOTH. MS | ERROR MS | F | SIG. OF F |
|----------|-----------|----------|-----------|----------|---|-----------|
| RATING   | 405.03145 | 113.66667 | 202.51572 | 7.57778  | 26.72495  | .000 |
| INTEREST | 3301.61164 | 123.16667 | 1650.80582 | 8.21111 | 201.04536 | 0.0  |
| ACHIEV   | 8.27201   | 249.16667 | 4.13601   | 16.61111 | .24899    | .783 |

ROY-BARGMAN STEPDOWN F - TESTS

| VARIABLE | HYPOTH. MS | ERROR MS | STEP-DOWN F | HYPOTH. DF | ERROR DF | SIG. OF F |
|----------|-----------|----------|------------|-----------|----------|-----------|
| RATING   | 202.51572 | 7.57778  | 26.72495   | 2 | 15 | .000 |
| INTEREST | 439.55648 | 8.12704  | 54.08566   | 2 | 14 | .000 |
| ACHIEV   | 29.78941  | 10.98031 | 2.71298    | 2 | 13 | .104 |

RAW DISCRIMINANT FUNCTION COEFFICIENTS

            FUNCTION NO.

| VARIABLE | 1 | 2 |
|----------|---|---|
| RATING   | -.16609 | -.29605 |
| INTEREST | -.45181 | -.10199 |
| ACHIEV   | .17748  | -.03369 |

STANDARDIZED DISCRIMINANT FUNCTION COEFFICIENTS

            FUNCTION NO.

| VARIABLE | 1 | 2 |
|----------|---|---|
| RATING   | -.45721  | -.81496 |
| INTEREST | -1.29466 | -.29226 |
| ACHIEV   | .72337   | -.13733 |

293

TWO-WAY MANOVA (3 X 2)

\* \* \* \* \* \* \* \* \* \* \* \* \* \* \* A N A L Y S I S   O F   V A R I A N C E \* \* \* \* \* \* \* \* \* \* \* \* \* \* \* \* \* \* \* \* \* \*

EFFECT .. CONTENT     (CONT.)

ESTIMATES OF EFFECTS FCR CANCNICAL VARIABLES

CANONICAL VARIABLE

| PARAMETER | 1 | 2 |
|---|---|---|
| 2 | -6.88117 | -.10835 |
| 3 | -8.05712 | -.09977 |

CORRELATIONS BETWEEN DEPENDENT AND CANCNICAL VARIABLES

CANONICAL VARIABLE

| VARIABLE | 1 | 2 |
|---|---|---|
| RATING | -.25379 | -.92489 |
| INTEREST | -.69632 | -.60688 |
| ACHIEV | -.02424 | -.50159 |

VARIMAX ROTATED CORRELATIONS BETWEEN CANONICAL AND DEPENDENT VARIATES

CAN. VAR.

| DEP. VAR. | 1 | 2 |
|---|---|---|
| RATING | .93614 | -.20853 |
| INTEREST | -.21048 | -.89937 |
| ACHIEV | -.43194 | -.25615 |

TRANSFORMATION MATRIX

| | 1 | 2 |
|---|---|---|
| 1 | -.46796 | -.88375 |
| 2 | .88375 | -.46796 |

294

\* \* \* \* \* \* \* \* \* \* \* \* \* \* \* \* \* A N A L Y S I S   O F   V A R I A N C E \* \* \* \* \* \* \* \* \* \* \* \* \* \* \* \* \* \* \* \* \* \*

EFFECT .. CONSTANT     (CONT.)

ESTIMATES OF EFFECTS FOR CANONICAL VARIABLES

CANONICAL VARIABLE

| PARAMETER | 1 |
|---|---|
| 1 | -57.38586 |

CORRELATIONS BETWEEN DEPENDENT AND CANONICAL VARIABLES

CANONICAL VARIABLE

| VARIABLE | 1 |
|---|---|
| RATING | -.28979 |
| INTEREST | -.74023 |
| ACHIEV | -.13765 |

ESTIMATES FOR RATING (9)

CONSTANT

| PARAMETER | COEFF. | STD. ERR. | T-VALUE | SIG. OF T | LOWER .95 CL | UPPER .95 CL |
|---|---|---|---|---|---|---|
| 1 | 45.7777777778 | .62121 | 73.69098 | 0.0 | 44.45369 | 47.10186 |

CONTENT

| PARAMETER | COEFF. | STD. ERR. | T-VALUE | SIG. OF T | LOWER .95 CL | UPPER .95 CL |
|---|---|---|---|---|---|---|
| 2 | 5.0833333333 | 1.58932 | 3.19844 | .006 | 1.69579 | 8.47088 |
| 3 | 5.3750000000 | 1.53885 | 3.49287 | .003 | 2.09502 | 8.65498 |

(9) We have shown the estimates of our contrasts here because: 1) they provide us with a univariate estimate of the contrasts for each of our null hypotheses; 2) they provide us with a comparison of the contrasts on the interest variable given for the univariate overall results.

295

TWO-WAY MANOVA (3 X 2)

\* \* \* \* \* \* \* \* \* \* \* \* \* \* \* \* A N A L Y S I S   O F   V A R I A N C E \* \* \* \* \* \* \* \* \* \* \* \* \* \* \* \* \*

ESTIMATES FOR RATING      (CONT.)

EXPRESS

| PARAMETER | COEFF. | STD. ERR. | T-VALUE | SIG. OF T | LOWER .95 CL | UPPER .95 CL |
|---|---|---|---|---|---|---|
| 4 | -8.7777777778 | 1.24243 | -7.06503 | .000 | -11.42595 | -6.12961 |

CONTENT BY EXPRESS

| PARAMETER | COEFF. | STD. ERR. | T-VALUE | SIG. OF T | LOWER .95 CL | UPPER .95 CL |
|---|---|---|---|---|---|---|
| 5 | 11.666666667 | 3.17863 | 3.67034 ⑩ | .002 | 4.89157 | 18.44176 |
| 6 | 13.2500000000 | 3.07770 | 4.30517 | .001 | 6.69004 | 19.80996 |

ESTIMATES FOR INTEREST

CONSTANT

| PARAMETER | COEFF. | STD. ERR. | T-VALUE | SIG. OF T | LOWER .95 CL | UPPER .95 CL |
|---|---|---|---|---|---|---|
| 1 | 121.7222222222 | .64665 | 188.23459 | 0.0 | 120.34392 | 123.10053 |

CONTENT

| PARAMETER | COEFF. | STD. ERR. | T-VALUE | SIG. OF T | LOWER .95 CL | UPPER .95 CL |
|---|---|---|---|---|---|---|
| 2 | 13.541666667 | 1.65440 | 8.18525 | .000 | 10.01540 | 17.06794 |
| 3 | 16.2500000000 | 1.60187 | 10.14442 | .000 | 12.83571 | 19.66429 |

EXPRESS

| PARAMETER | COEFF. | STD. ERR. | T-VALUE | SIG. OF T | LOWER .95 CL | UPPER .95 CL |
|---|---|---|---|---|---|---|
| 4 | -40.8888888889 | 1.29330 | -31.61585 | 0.0 | -43.64550 | -38.13228 |

CONTENT BY EXPRESS

| PARAMETER | COEFF. | STD. ERR. | T-VALUE | SIG. OF T | LOWER .95 CL | UPPER .95 CL |
|---|---|---|---|---|---|---|
| 5 | 27.0833333333 | 3.30880 | 8.18525 ⑩ | .000 | 20.03080 | 34.13587 |
| 6 | 33.5000000000 | 3.20373 | 10.45656 | .000 | 26.67141 | 40.32859 |

296

⑩ Here we find large interaction effects on RATING
and INTEREST, but not on ACHIEV.

TWO-WAY MANOVA (3 X 2)

02/02/83      PAGE  38

\* \* \* \* \* \* \* \* \* \* \* \* \* \* \* \* \* \* \* \* \* \*\*\* A N A L Y S I S   O F   V A R I A N C E \*\*\* \* \* \* \* \* \* \* \* \* \* \* \* \* \* \* \* \* \* \* \* \* \*

ESTIMATES FOR ACHIEV

CONSTANT

| PARAMETER | COEFF. | STD. ERR. | T-VALUE | SIG. OF T | LOWER .95 CL | UPPER .95 CL |
|---|---|---|---|---|---|---|
| 1 | 32.1944444444 | .91975 | 35.00355 | 0.0 | 30.23405 | 34.15484 |

CONTENT

| PARAMETER | COEFF. | STD. ERR. | T-VALUE | SIG. OF T | LOWER .95 CL | UPPER .95 CL |
|---|---|---|---|---|---|---|
| 2 | .4583333333 | 2.35309 | .19478 | .848 | -4.55716 | 5.47383 |
| 3 | 1.0000000000 | 2.27837 | .43891 | .667 | -3.85623 | 5.85623 |

EXPRESS

| PARAMETER | COEFF. | STD. ERR. | T-VALUE | SIG. OF T | LOWER .95 CL | UPPER .95 CL |
|---|---|---|---|---|---|---|
| 4 | -1.9444444444 | 1.83950 | -1.05705 | .307 | -5.86524 | 1.97635 |

CONTENT BY EXPRESS

| PARAMETER | COEFF. | STD. ERR. | T-VALUE | SIG. OF T | LOWER .95 CL | UPPER .95 CL |
|---|---|---|---|---|---|---|
| 5 | -1.0833333333 | 4.70618 | -.23019 | .821 | -11.11432 | 8.94766 |
| 6 | 1.0000000000 | 4.55674 | .21946 (10) | .829 | -8.71246 | 10.71246 |

297

CHAPTER 4

THREE-WAY ANALYSIS OF VARIANCE
by James D. Brodzinski

## Introduction

There are a number of advantages to using factorial designs (more than one independent factor). First, since several independent variables are manipulated simultaneously, a "more accurate" reflection of the "real" world can be obtained. Second, since the variables under study are examined simultaneously, a savings of time is attained. Third, within the factorial framework, the researcher can examine the effects variables have when they interact.

This chapter extends the discussion begun in Chapter 3 on the third advantage of the factorial design, the interaction. Readers interested in a discussion of main effects should refer to Chapter 2 and the first example in Chapter 3.

## Interaction

Consider a simple experiment with two independent variables: Car Model (coded 1,2) and Gasoline Type (coded 1,2). Assume that one of the cars gets more miles per gallon (mpg) than the other. If the mean difference in mpg between the car models is the same regardless of the gasoline used, then there is no interaction between the two variables. Figure 4.1 graphically displays this "zero" interaction.

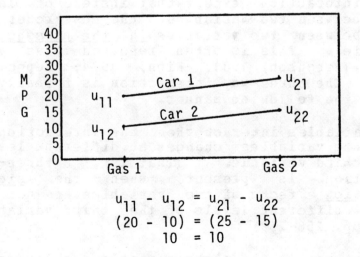

$$u_{11} - u_{12} = u_{21} - u_{22}$$
$$(20 - 10) = (25 - 15)$$
$$10 = 10$$

Figure 4.1   Example of two-way design, no interaction.

In this example, the difference in mpg between Car 1 and Car 2 is 10 mpg using Gas 1. Although the mpg for both cars is greater with Gas 2, the difference between Car 1 and Car 2 remains 10 mpg. If, however, one of the cars gets relatively more mpg with one type of gasoline than the other, then the two variables are said to interact. Figure 4.2 displays this interaction.

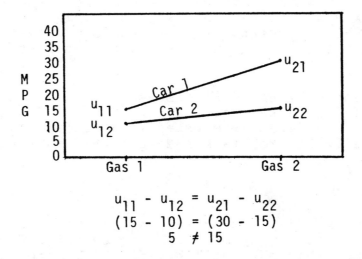

$$u_{11} - u_{12} = u_{21} - u_{22}$$
$$(15 - 10) = (30 - 15)$$
$$5 \neq 15$$

Figure 4.2    Example of two-way interaction.

In this case, the difference in mpg between Car 1 and Car 2 with Gas 1 is 5 mpg. However, with Gas 2, this difference is 15 mpg, indicating an interaction between the two variables, Car Model and Gasoline Type.

The three-way interaction is a logical extension of the two-way interaction except that instead of looking at differences between two variables, the researcher looks at differences between two variables in the presence of the third variable. This is often referred to as a "simple interaction" (Ferguson, 1981; Finn, 1974; Keppel, 1973; Kirk, 1968). The three-way interaction is formally defined by Keppel in the following manner.

Three variables interact when the interaction of two of the variables changes at different levels of the third variable. (That is), a three-way interaction is present when the simple interaction effects of two variables are not the same at different levels of the third variable. (1973, pp. 258-259)

Let's return to the above example problem and add a third variable, Transmission Type (Automatic, Manual). Figure 4.3 displays no three-way interaction.

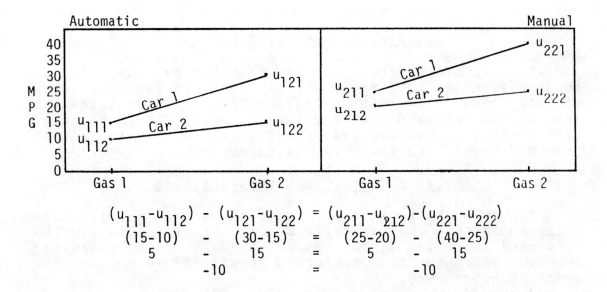

$$(u_{111}-u_{112}) - (u_{121}-u_{122}) = (u_{211}-u_{212})-(u_{221}-u_{222})$$
$$(15-10) \quad - \quad (30-15) \quad = \quad (25-20) \quad - \quad (40-25)$$
$$5 \quad - \quad 15 \quad = \quad 5 \quad - \quad 15$$
$$-10 \quad = \quad -10$$

Figure 4.3    Example of three-way design, no interaction.

The interaction of the Car Type and the Gasoline Type is the same in both Transmission conditions.

Another way to view the three-way interaction is to ask: Is there a difference between the simple interaction patterns at different levels of the third variable? Figure 4.4 shows a three-way interaction. In this case, the interaction pattern changes over the levels of the variable Transmission Type.

The remainder of this chapter presents a specific three-way ANOVA problem, with emphasis placed on the analysis and interpretation of the second order (i.e. triple) interactions.

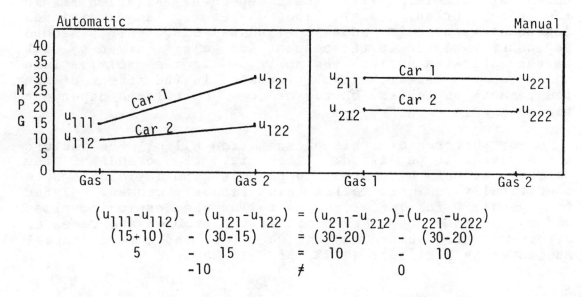

$$(u_{111}-u_{112}) - (u_{121}-u_{122}) = (u_{211}-u_{212})-(u_{221}-u_{222})$$
$$(15+10) \quad - \quad (30-15) \quad = (30-20) \quad - \quad (30-20)$$
$$5 \quad - \quad 15 \quad = 10 \quad - \quad 10$$
$$-10 \quad \neq \quad 0$$

Figure 4.4    Example of three-way interaction.

## Organization of the Programs

To illustrate the use of computer packages for a three-way analysis of variance, 12 computer runs were made with the data from this chapter. Table 4.1 contains the list of the programs run for this chapter, their numbers, whether they are univariate or multivariate, their initial page reference, and their I/O features.

## Analysis of Variance Presentations

The presentation of the univariate and multivariate analyses in this chapter employs data taken from a problem discussed in Fryer (1966, pp. 346-347). The following section presents the rationale used to formulate the research hypotheses.

In the univariate problem, a poultry scientist wishes to study the effects of three variables on the monthly egg yield of chickens. The first variable consists of three chicken breeds, White Rock, White Leghorn, and Rhode Island Red. The second variable consists of two diets fed to the chickens, one containing a high level of a protein supplement and one consisting of a medium level of the same protein supplement. The third variable, artificial daylength, exposes the chickens to three artificially created daylengths, short (six hours), medium (12 hours), and long (18 hours).

The objectives of the univariate analysis are to determine whether the independent variables, in combination, interact to influence monthly egg yield.

The multivariate example is an extension of the univariate problem. While the independent variables remain the same, breed, diet, and daylength, an additional dependent measure is added to the analysis. This second dependent variable is the percent of weight gained by each of the chickens during the month. In the multivariate analysis, the researcher is interested in the effect of the independent variables on two or more correlated dependent variables.

For purposes of this presentation all of the factors are assumed to be fixed. That is, the breeds of the chicken, amounts of protein supplement, and daylengths were specifically assigned rather than randomly chosen. Refer to Appendix D for guidelines to follow when employing mixed and random models. The format of the problem and research hypotheses are stated in the question and answer format suggested by Kerlinger (1973, pp. 16-20).

Table 4.1
Descriptions of the Programs Run on the
Three Factor (Three-Way) Data From Chapter 4

| Program | Program Number | Mode[1] | Type[2] | Page | I/O Features |
|---|---|---|---|---|---|
| | | | Volume 1: BMDP | | |
| BMDP4V | 4-1 | U | S | 243 | Planned and overall analysis |
| BMDP2V | 4-2 | U | S | 249 | Overall analysis |
| BMDP4V | 4-3 | U | I | 252 | Tests of a single degree of freedom second order interaction, simple effects and simple-simple effects. |
| BMDP4V | 4-4 | M | S | 256 | Planned and overall analysis |
| | | | Volume 2: SAS | | |
| SAS(GLM) | 4-1 | U | S | 241 | Planned and overall analysis, use of '1' in MODEL statement |
| SAS(ANOVA) | 4-2 | U | S | 248 | Overall analysis, equal n |
| SAS(GLM) | 4-3 | U | I | 255 | Tests of a single degree of freedom second order interaction, simple effects and simple-simple effects. |
| SAS(GLM) | 4-4 | M | S | 263 | Planned and overall analysis |

Table 4.1, continued

| Program | Program Number | Mode[1] | Type[2] | Page | I/O Features |
|---|---|---|---|---|---|
| | | | | | |
| Volume 3: SPSS and SPSSX | | | | | |
| | | | | | |
| SPSS-SPSSX (MANOVA) | 4-1 | U | S | 325 | Planned analysis |
| SPSS-SPSSX (ANOVA) & | 4-2 | U | S | 337 | Overall analysis, use of VAR LABELS, VALUE LABELS, and MISSING VALUES control statements. |
| (MANOVA) | | | | | Overall analysis |
| SPSS-SPSSX (MANOVA) | 4-3 | U | I | 348 | Tests of a single degree of freedom second order interaction, simple effects and simple-simple effects. |
| SPSS-SPSSX (MANOVA) | 4-4 | M | S | 363 | Planned and overall analysis |

[1]Mode is coded U for univariate or M for multivariate.
[2]Type is coded S for standard or I for instruction.

## Past Research

A review of the literature on poultry production has led this researcher to hypothesize that many variables have a direct impact on the egg yield of chickens. Furthermore, this review has shown that the effect of these variables, examined simultaneously, has been neglected. Therefore, the following paragraphs summarize the literature and point to several planned comparisons.

### Main Effects

Parnell (1957) classified three breeds of chicken based on egg production, the Rhode Island Red and White Rock breeds were considered average egg producers and the White Leghorn breed was considered an excellent egg producer. Research confirmed these yield classifications, that is, chicken breed does affect egg yield, and, more specifically, the White Leghorn breed outproduces both the Rhode Island Red and White Rock breeds.

Another variable studied by poultry researchers is the content of the diet fed to the chickens. The protein content in the diet of the chickens has ranged from a low of 10 percent to a ceiling of 16-17 percent in earlier studies. Egg yield has been shown to vary as a result of this difference in protein content (Titus, 1949). High protein diets (17 percent) have resulted in a greater egg yield than low protein diets (10 percent).

Finally, the length of daylight has been examined in relation to the egg yield of chickens. In general, short (6 hours) and long (18 hours) daylengths result in decreased yield when compared to medium (12 hours) daylengths.

### First-Order Interactions

Early research generally examined each of the above variables while holding the others constant. That is, "main effects" models were employed. A closer examination of this research suggests several possible interactions. First we will look at one of the three possible first-order interactions, "Breed x Diet."

In several experiments all chickens were fed a single protein diet, regardless of breed. This was done to control for diet while examining the "Breed" effect. The following conclusions could be drawn from those experiments. First, the mean egg yield in the studies where the chickens were fed high protein diets was greater than the yield in studies where chickens were fed low protein diets. Second, in those studies where high protein diets were ingested, the White Rock and White Leghorn breeds had higher egg yields than the Rhode Island Red breed. However, in the studies using low protein diets, the Rhode Island Red breed had significantly higher egg yields than the other two breeds. These results suggest that the variables chicken breed and diet may interact to affect egg yield.

There are two other first-order interactions that can be examined in this three-way design, "Breed x Daylength" and "Diet x Daylength," however, the researcher soon became interested in the second order interaction which is discussed in the following section.

## Second-Order Interactions

The a priori comparisons concerning the second-order interaction (three-way interaction) in this example are based on the following information assumed to be from previous research.

In short daylength conditions the White Leghorn breed has outproduced the White Rock and Rhode Island Red breeds when high protein diets were ingested, but was outproduced by the White Rock and Rhode Island Red breeds in low diet conditions. In research employing medium daylength conditions, the White Rock breed had a higher egg yield than the White Leghorn and Rhode Island Red breeds with high protein diets, but was outproduced by the White Leghorn and Rhode Island Red breeds in low diet conditions. Finally, when long daylengths were employed, Rhode Island Red and White Leghorn breeds outproduced the White Rock breed in high diet conditions, but the White Rock breed outproduced the White Leghorn and the Rhode Island Red breeds in low diet conditions.

A major poultry products producer has asked this poultry scientist to recommend the combination of breed, diet, and daylength which will maximize the producer's profit, i.e., result in the greatest egg yield.

The following section describes the research and statistical hypotheses associated with univariate planned comparisons.

## Univariate Analysis: Planned Comparisons

Stating questions in terms of a priori comparisons among means requires a considerable knowledge of the problem and of past research on the part of the researcher. The planned comparisons are designed to reflect both what has been drawn from past research and the logical conclusions drawn from theory involving the variables employed.

The planned comparisons that follow are stated in such a way as to be able to be tested with the contrasts readily available in BMDP4V, SPSS(MANOVA), and SAS(GLM). These programs readily permit the testing of planned comparisons for factorial designs.

As mentioned earlier, this chapter focuses on the analysis of the three-way interactions. Therefore, the statement of the problem and following hypotheses and analyses only refer to the interactions.

Problem. Is the monthly egg production of chickens dependent on the interactions among breed of chicken, the diet fed to the chickens, and the length of artificial daylight in which the chickens exist?

Research Hypotheses. The research hypotheses were based on theory and the previous research mentioned earlier. These hypotheses were formulated before the data were collected. Because these hypotheses are difficult to conceptualize, the second-order interaction hypotheses (1), (2), (3), and (4) are presented graphically in Figure 4.5

Given a high protein diet, the figure for the first research hypothesis predicts that as daylength goes from short to medium the White Rock will yield more eggs but that the White Leghorn will produce fewer eggs. Note that the plot looks the same under a low diet, but here the White Rock yields fewer eggs and the White Leghorn more as daylength goes from short to medium. In the second research hypothesis the latter patterns reverse themselves as daylength goes from medium to long. Given a high diet, the third research hypothesis predicts that the egg yield of the White Leghorn will decrease as daylength goes from short to medium, but that the egg yield of the Rhode Island Red will increase. Under the low diet condition the Rhode Island Red produces more eggs as daylength increases and the White Leghorn also produces more eggs. In the fourth research hypothesis reversal interaction patterns similar to those in the first research hypothesis are thought to be present, but not significantly so.

Research Hypothesis (1): Given a high protein diet, the first order interaction found on egg yield between chicken breeds (White Rock and White Leghorn) and daylength (short and medium) will be less than the first order interaction found on egg yield with low protein diet.

Research Hypothesis (2): Given a high protein diet, the first order interaction found on egg yield between chicken breeds (White Rock and White Leghorn) and daylength (medium and long) will be less than the first order interction found on egg yield with low protein diet.

Research Hypothesis (3): Given a high protein diet, the first order interaction found on egg yield between chicken breeds (White Leghorn and Rhode Island) and

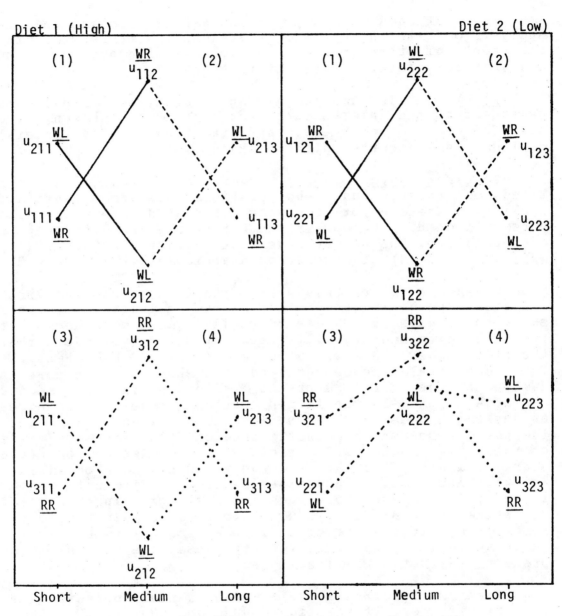

Figure 4.5    Hypothesized (Breed by Diet by Daylength)
Second-Order (Triple) Interactions.

daylength (short and medium) will be less than the first order interaction found on egg yield with low protein diet.

Research Hypothesis (4): Given a high protein diet, the first order interaction found on egg yield between chicken breeds (White Leghorn and Rhode Island) and daylength (medium and long) will not differ from the first order interaction found on egg yield with low protein diet.

Statistical Hypotheses. The statistical hypotheses are written in symbolic form to match the research hypotheses. The following symbols are employed for the population means:

u(ijk): Breed*Diet*Daylength, $\underline{i}$=1,2,3; $\underline{j}$=1,2; $\underline{k}$=1,2,3.

H(Oh) represents the null and H(Ah) the alternate hypotheses ($\underline{h}$ = 1,2,3,4).

H(O1):  (u(111)-u(211)) - (u(112)-u(212)) =
        (u(121)-u(221)) - (u(122)-u(222))

H(A1):  (u(111)-u(211)) - (u(112)-u(212)) <
        (u(121)-u(221)) - (u(122)-u(222))

H(O2):  (u(212)-u(112)) - (u(213)-u(113)) =
        (u(222)-u(122)) - (u(223)-u(123))

H(A2):  (u(212)-u(112)) - (u(213)-u(113)) <
        (u(222)-u(122)) - (u(223)-u(123))

H(O3):  (u(311)-u(211)) - (u(312)-u(212)) =
        (u(321)-u(221)) - (u(322)-u(222))

H(A3):  (U(311)-U(211)) - (U(312)-U(212)) <
        (u(321)-u(221)) - (u(322)-u(222))

H(O4):  (u(212)-u(312)) - (u(213)-u(313)) =
        (u(222)-u(322)) - (u(223)-u(323))

H(A4):  (u(212)-u(312)) - (u(213)-u(313)) $\neq$
        (u(222)-u(322)) - (u(223)-u(323))

Each null hypothesis will be tested at the .05 level of significance.

Data. The data are presented in Table 4.2 as a univariate, equal $\underline{n}$ problem. The design has three factors, Breed with three levels, Diet with two levels, and Daylength with three levels. This would commonly be written as a 3 x 2 x 3 factorial analysis of variance. The dependent variable is the number of eggs produced by each chicken during the experimental time period. Eight

Table 4.2
Data¹, Cell Identification, and Cell Means For
a Three-Way Design

| Breed | White Rock(1) | | White Leghorn(2) | | Rhode Island(3) | |
|---|---|---|---|---|---|---|
| Diet | High(1) | Low(2) | High(1) | Low(2) | High(1) | Low(2) |
| **Daylength** | | | | | | |
| **Short(1)** | 12 | 13 | 16* | 8 | 10 | 15 |
| | 8 | 16 | 19 | 11 | 12 | 11 |
| | 14(111) | 10(121) | 12(211) | 6(221) | 10(311) | 19(321) |
| | 11 | 9 | 15 | 10 | 8 | 14 |
| | 15 | 13 | 18 | 5 | 10 | 16 |
| | X̄=12.00 | X̄=13.00 | X̄=16.00 | X̄=8.00 | X̄=10.00 | X̄=15.00 |
| | *X̄=12.00 | *X̄=13.00 | *X̄=16.00 | *X̄=8.00 | *X̄=10.00 | *X̄=15.00 |
| **Medium(2)** | 17* | 10 | 11 | 15 | 12 | 15 |
| | 13* | 6 | 14 | 21 | 9 | 11* |
| | 21(112) | 13(122) | 10(212) | 17(222) | 13(312) | 18(322) |
| | 19 | 11 | 9 | 10 | 11 | 12 |
| | 15 | 10 | 11 | 12 | 15 | 19 |
| | X̄=17.00 | X̄=10.00 | X̄=11.00 | X̄=15.00 | X̄=12.00 | X̄=15.00 |
| | *X̄=18.33 | *X̄=10.00 | *X̄=11.00 | *X̄=15.00 | *X̄=12.00 | *X̄=16.00 |
| **Long(3)** | 11 | 14 | 12 | 13 | 15 | 9 |
| | 8 | 10 | 16 | 16 | 11 | 5 |
| | 15(113) | 12(123) | 9*(213) | 14(223) | 18(313) | 13(323) |
| | 10 | 18 | 11* | 10 | 12 | 10 |
| | 11 | 16* | 12* | 12 | 19 | 8 |
| | X̄=11.00 | X̄=14.00 | X̄=12.00 | X̄=13.00 | X̄=15.00 | X̄=9.00 |
| | *X̄=11.00 | *X̄=13.50 | *X̄=14.00 | *X̄=13.00 | *X̄=15.00 | *X̄=9.00 |

¹ The data were taken from Fryer (1966, p.346); "*" scores were removed to create an unequal n problem.

subjects were dropped (represented by *) for most of the computer runs to demonstrate the effects of unequal n 's. If this were an actual experiment the researcher would have to check to be sure that these subjects were not absent because of the treatment effects (e.g., a chicken might have died before the completion of the experiment as a result of the diet manipulation). The analysis that follows is based on the unequal n data.

Three-Way ANOVA Table. Table 4.3 is the planned comparison three-way ANOVA table which would appear in a research report on this experiment. The contents of this table could be drawn from the univariate output of the programs: BMDP4V, SAS(GLM) and SPSS(MANOVA).

The results in Table 4.3 indicate that the data from this experiment reject null hypotheses one, two, and three (p<.0000; p<.0001; p<.0004), and support null hypothesis four (p<.2091). Consequently, we find that Figure 4.5 does well in illustrating the obtained interaction patterns.

Given these results, a poultry producer, if high protein diets were used, would choose the White Leghorn over the White Rock and Rhode Island Red if short daylengths were employed; the White Rock over the White Leghorn and Rhode Island Red when medium daylengths were employed; and either the White Leghorn or the Rhode Island Red over the White Rock when the daylength was long. If the producer decided to feed the chickens low protein diets, the Rhode Island Red or the White Rock would be used when short daylengths are employed; the Rhode Island Red or White Leghorn would be used when medium daylengths are employed; and the White Rock or White Leghorn would be used when long daylengths are employed.

## Univariate Analysis: Overall Tests and Post Hoc Comparisons

If the researcher did not have a detailed body of research from which to formulate planned questions, or if the research was exploratory, overall tests of significance would be appropriate. Then, if significant effects were obtained, an appropriate post hoc test could follow the initial analysis to determine where the significant differences occur. In this example the problem statement is the same as in the case of the planned comparisons.

Problem. Is the monthly egg production of chickens dependent on the interaction of the Breed of chicken, the Diet fed to the chickens, and the amount of daylight to which the chickens are exposed?

Reasearch Hypotheses. In this case the researcher believes that an overall significant interaction will appear among group means but past research was

Table 4.3

Univariate Planned Comparisons Analysis
of variance for the Poultry Production Experiment

| Source of Variation | Degrees of Freedom | Sum of Squares | Mean Square | t Statistic | Prob[1] |
|---|---|---|---|---|---|
| Breed (Br) | 2 | .33 | | | |
| Diet (Di) | 1 | 11.16 | | | |
| Daylength (Da) | 2 | 29.10 | | | |
| Br*Di | 2 | 31.61 | | | |
| Br*Da | 4 | 16.46 | | | |
| Di*Da | 2 | 5.96 | | | |
| Br*Di*Da | 4 | 470.37 | | | |
| Comparisons | | | | | |
| 1 | 1 | 255.20 | 255.20 | -5.66* | .0000 |
| 2 | 1 | 120.33 | 120.33 | -3.89** | .0001 |
| 3 | 1 | 99.41 | 99.41 | -3.53* | .0004 |
| 4 | 1 | 12.82 | 12.82 | 1.27 | .2091 |
| Error (within) | 64 | 509.67 | 7.96 | | |
| Total | 81 | 1063.28 | | | |

[1]all probabilities are for one-tailed tests except
comparison 4 which is two-tailed.
*significant at p<.05; the programs do not report
probabilities to more than four decimal places.

312

inconclusive, and theory is not formulated well enough to make more specific predictions.

Research Hypothesis: Breeds will respond differently to different diet and daylength combinations.

Statistical Hypotheses. The statistical hypotheses are written in symbolic form to match the research hypotheses. Here we take the same approach as was developed in Chapter 3 for the 3 x 2 design, i.e. by specifying an observation as:

$$Y(ijkl) = u + a(i) + b(j) + c(k) + ab(ij) + ac(ik) + bc(jk) + abc(ijk) + e(ijkl).$$

Where Y is the score of observation l in cell ijk; u is the population grand mean of all observations; a represents the treatment effect for treatment i of factor A; b represents the treatment effect for treatment j of factor B; c represents the treatment effect for treatment k of factor C; ab represents the first order interaction between treatment i of factor A and treatment j of factor B; ac represents the first order interaction between treatment i of factor A and treatment k of factor C; bc represents the first order interaction between treatment j of factor B and treatment k of factor C; abc represents the second order interaction between treatments i, j and k of factors A, B, and C, respectively; and, e(ijkl) is that part of Y that is not accounted for by the other sources of variation in the design. Then, for this problem, we have the following overall interaction hypothesis:

H(0): abc(ijk) = 0 for all ijk

H(A): abc(ijk) $\neq$ 0 for some ijk

ijk: Breed*Diet*Daylength, $i$=1,2,3; $j$=1,2; $k$=1,2,3.

This null hypothesis will be tested at the .05 level of significance.

Data. The data are the unequal $n$ data presented in Table 4.2.

Three-Way ANOVA Table. Table 4.4 is the three-way ANOVA table that would appear in a research report on this experiment. The contents of this table could be derived from all of the unequal $n$ program runs for this chapter. A similar table for the equal $n$ design could be constructed from our instruction program SAS(ANOVA), program numbered 4-2.

The results of Table 4.4 indicate a significant second order interaction (p<.0001) is present in the data. Since a significant triple interaction has been attained, post hoc comparisons are in order to determine significant mean differences among the treatment means.

Table 4.4
Analysis of Variance
for the Poultry Production Experiment

| Source of Variation | Degrees of Freedom | Sum of Squares | Mean Square | F-Ratio | Prob > F |
|---|---|---|---|---|---|
| Breed (Br) | 2 | .33 | .17 | .02 | .9792 |
| Diet (Di) | 1 | 11.16 | 11.16 | 1.40 | .2409 |
| Daylength (Da) | 2 | 29.10 | 14.55 | 1.83 | .1691 |
| Br*Di | 2 | 31.61 | 15.80 | 1.98 | .1458 |
| Br*Da | 4 | 16.46 | 4.12 | .52 | .7236 |
| Di*Da | 2 | 5.96 | 2.98 | .37 | .6892 |
| Br*Di*Da | 4 | 470.37 | 117.59 | 14.77* | .0000 |
| Error (Within) | 64 | 509.67 | 7.96 | | |
| Total | 81 | 1074.66 | | | |

*Significant at $p < .05$; the programs do not report probabilities to more than four decimal places.

## Post-Hoc Analyses: Simple Effects

In this section we consider approaches to the three-way analysis under two conditions: 1. a significant triple interaction has been found; 2. no significant triple interaction has been found. In both conditions one faces the possiblity of using tests of what are known as "simple effects" or "simple-simple effects" (see Keppel, 1973, pp. 283-307). There is considerable controversy surrounding the analysis of simple effects, however, and the reader would be well advised to consult the relevant literature before deciding to employ simple effect analyses. (See Betz & Gabriel, 1978; Games, 1973; Levin & Marascuilo, 1973; Marascuilo & Levin, 1970, 1976; for a variety of positions on the post hoc analyses of interaction effects).

Simple Effects. What is a simple effect? Perhaps the easiest way to describe a simple effect is to consider a two-way analysis. The 2 x 2 analysis of car models and gasoline type described at the beginning of this chapter provides us with a good example. After we found a significant interaction, as depicted in Figure 4.2, we might decide to test the differences between the two car model means for a given level of gasoline; if we did this, we would be testing for what is known as a "simple effect." That is, a simple effect test occurs in a factorial experiment when one tests for mean differences over the levels of other factors in the design while holding constant one factor. In the preceding example we would consider the difference between the types of cars for a given type of gasoline. In a three-way analysis we would consider the simple interaction effects holding constant one factor. For example, in the data we are considering here we might consider the four possible simple interactions when diet is fixed at high protein. Then, a "simple-simple" effects test occurs when one tests for mean differences while holding constant two factors. In our three-way design a simple-simple effects test would occur if we held diet and daylength constant (e.g. at high and short, respectively) and then tested for differences among the chicken breeds. The following discussion of when to use these tests is primarily based on Keppel's (1973, pp. 283-307) presentation of this topic.

No significant Triple Interaction. When one encounters no significant triple interaction, the next set of tests to consider are the first order interactions. When the first order interactions are significant, one could use tests of simple main effects. However, if the first order interaction test is not significant, then one should test the overall main effects.

Significant Triple Interaction. When one encounters a significant overall triple interaction the next step would be to consider the single degree of freedom triple interaction effects in order to help discover what caused the overall interaction. (Keppel does not include this step in his discussion.) Tests of simple interaction effects might follow the latter tests, and could in turn be followed by tests of simple-simple main effects. We use this approach with our three-way data in the discussion that follows.

An Example. In the problem we have been considering we found a significant overall second-order interaction. Our next step would be to consider the single degree of freedom second-order interactions. Let's consider one of them with the understanding that the same pattern of analysis would be used for the others. The single degree of freedom second order interaction we chose to consider here is given in the following contrast:

$$u(111)-u(211)-u(112)+u(212)-u(121)+u(221)+u(122)-u(222)=0$$

(Note that this is the same contrast that we considered earlier as a planned comparison in $H(01)$.) When the observed cell means are substituted into this contrast we find that it equals -21.33 (i.e., 12.00-16.00-18.33-+11.00-13.00+8.00+10.00-15.00 = -21.33). In the following paragraph we discuss Table 4.5 which contains the statistical test of this contrast and the tests of the simple, and simple-simple effects that follow it. All tests were conducted at the .005 level because of their post hoc nature.

Table 4.5
An Example of One Set of Statistical Tests
That Could Follow An Overall
Significant Second-Order Interaction

| Source of Variation | Sample Contrast | Degrees of Freedom | Mean Square | F-Ratio | Prob>F |
|---|---|---|---|---|---|
| Single Df Second-Order Interaction | -21.33 | 1 | 255.20 | 32.05* | .0000 |
| Simple Effects | | | | | |
| 1:u(111)-u(211)-u(112)+u(212) | -11.33 | 1 | 130.62 | 16.40* | .0001 |
| 2:u(121)-u(221)-u(122)+u(222) | 10.00 | 1 | 125.00 | 15.70* | .0002 |
| Simple-Simple Effects | | | | | |
| 1:u(111)-u(211) | -4.00 | 1 | 35.56 | 4.46 | .0385 |
| 2:u(112)-u(212) | 7.33 | 1 | 100.83 | 12.66* | .0007 |
| 3:u(121)-u(221) | 5.00 | 1 | 62.50 | 7.85 | .0067 |
| 4:u(122)-u(222) | -5.00 | 1 | 62.50 | 7.85 | .0067 |
| Error | | 64 | 7.96 | | |

*Significant at p<.005.

316

In Table 4.5 we find that the preceding single degree of freedom second order interaction contrast is significantly different from zero (p<.0000). From this result we may conclude that the first-order interaction found under a high diet is less than the first-order interaction found under a low diet when the chicken breeds, White Rock and White Leghorn, and the daylengths short and medium are considered. The test of these simple interactions considered individually, i.e. under each diet, indicates that they are both significantly different from zero. The simple effect sample contrast under high diet being -11.33 (p<.0001) and the simple effect contrast under low diet being 10.00 (p<.0002). The first two simple-simple effects in Table 4.5 indicate that there is no significant difference between the White Rock and White Leghorn breeds given high protein diets and short daylengths (p<.0385), but that these breeds do differ (with White Rock producing more eggs) under a high protein diet with medium daylength (p<.0007). The tests of simple-simple effects three and four indicate that given low diet and short or medium daylength there is no significant different between the White Rock and White Leghorn (p<.0067, in both cases). The results found in Table 4.5 may be gathered from programs BMDP4V (4-3), SAS(GLM) (4-3) and SPSS(MANOVA) (4-3).

## Multivariate Analysis: Planned Comparisons

The multivariate analysis presented here is an extension of the univariate planned comparisons analysis discussed earlier in this chapter. In our MANOVA example, the design remains the same, but an additional dependent variable, weight gain, is added. This variable shares a common conceptual meaning with egg production, since both have been used as criteria for poultry production in past experiments (Cook & Juergenson, 1955; Gregory, 1938; Heuser, 1955; Parnell, 1957; Titus, 1949). Parnell (1957) has reported that the makeup of a chicken's diet directly effects weight gain, and that the gain has been shown to vary from breed to breed. Thus the two dependent variables, egg production and weight gain can be considered as dimensions of poultry production; the researcher in this case is interested in testing the effects of the different treatments on the two dependent variables considered together.

Problem. Is the monthly egg production and weight gain dependent on the interaction of breed of chicken, the diet fed to the chickens, and the length of daylight in which the chickens exist?

Research Hypotheses. Since past research has frequently studied the effects of different breeds of chicken, diets, and daylength on egg production and weight gain (see above), several planned comparisons can be set forth that are of interest. The following research hypotheses, which are extensions of our univariate presentation, reflect four such comparisons.

Research Hypothesis (1): Given a high protein diet, the first order interaction found on egg yield and weight gain between chicken breeds (White Rock and White Leghorn) and daylength (short and medium) will not equal the first order interaction found on egg yield and weight gain with low protein diet.

Research Hypothesis (2): Given a high protein diet, the first order interaction found on egg yield and weight gain between chicken breeds (White Rock and White Leghorn) and daylength (medium and long) will not equal the first order interaction found on egg yield and weight gain with low protein diet.

Research Hypothesis (3): Given a high protein diet, the first order interaction found on egg yield and weight gain between chicken breeds (White Leghorn and Rhode Island) and daylength (short and medium) will not equal the first order interaction found on egg yield and weight gain with low protein diet.

Research Hypothesis (4): Given a high protein diet, the first order interaction found on egg yield and weight gain between chicken breeds (White Leghorn and Rhode Island) and daylength (medium and long) will not differ from the first order interaction found on egg yield and weight gain with low protein diet.

Statistical Hypotheses. The statistical hypotheses are written in symbolic form to match the research hypotheses. The following symbols are employed for the population mean vectors: $\underline{u}(ijk)$: Breed * Diet * Daylength, $\underline{i}=1,2,3$; $\underline{j}=1,2$; $\underline{k}=1,2,3$. These symbols represent the vector of means containing both dependent variable means for the respective factor levels. $H(Oh)$ represents the null and $H(Ah)$ the alternate hypotheses ($\underline{h} = 1,2,3,4$).

$H(01)$: $(\underline{u}(111)-\underline{u}(211)) - (\underline{u}(112)-\underline{u}(212)) =$
$(\underline{u}(121)-\underline{u}(221)) - (\underline{u}(122)-\underline{u}(222))$

$H(A1)$: $(\underline{u}(111)-\underline{u}(211)) - (\underline{u}(112)-\underline{u}(212)) \neq$
$(\underline{u}(121)-\underline{u}(221)) - (\underline{u}(122)-\underline{u}(222))$

$H(02)$: $(\underline{u}(212)-\underline{u}(112)) - (\underline{u}(213)-\underline{u}(113)) =$
$(\underline{u}(222)-\underline{u}(122)) - (\underline{u}(223)-\underline{u}(123))$

$H(A2)$: $(\underline{u}(212)-\underline{u}(112)) - (\underline{u}(213)-\underline{u}(113)) \neq$
$(\underline{u}(222)-\underline{u}(122)) - (\underline{u}(223)-\underline{u}(123))$

$$H(03): \quad (\underline{u}(311) - \underline{u}(211)) - (\underline{u}(312) - \underline{u}(212)) =$$
$$(\underline{u}(321) - \underline{u}(221)) - (\underline{u}(322) - \underline{u}(222))$$

$$H(A3): \quad (\underline{u}(311) - \underline{u}(211)) - (\underline{u}(312) - \underline{u}(212)) \neq$$
$$(\underline{u}(321) - \underline{u}(221)) = (\underline{u}(322) - \underline{u}(222))$$

$$H(04): \quad (\underline{u}(212) - \underline{u}(312)) - (\underline{u}(213) - \underline{u}(313)) =$$
$$(\underline{u}(222) - \underline{u}(322)) - (\underline{u}(223) - \underline{u}(323))$$

$$H(A4): \quad (\underline{u}(212) - \underline{u}(312)) - (\underline{u}(213) - \underline{u}(313)) \neq$$
$$(\underline{u}(222) - \underline{u}(322)) - (\underline{u}(223) - \underline{u}(323))$$

Each null hypothesis will be tested at the .05 level of significance.

Data. The data are presented in Table 4.6 as a multivariate, equal $\underline{n}$ problem. Eight observations were dropped (represented by *) from the computer runs to demonstrate the effects of unequal $\underline{n}$'s. The analysis that follows is based on the unequal $\underline{n}$ data.

Three-Way MANOVA Table. Table 4.7 is the planned comparison three-way MANOVA table which would appear in a research report on this experiment. The contents of this table could be drawn from the BMDP4V (4-4) and SPSS(MANOVA) (4-4).

The results in Table 4.7 indicate that the first three multivariate null hypotheses were rejected ($p < .0000$; $p < .0000$, $p < .0028$), and that the fourth null hypothesis was supported ($p < .4547$). Since a number of the multivariate tests were significant, their corresponding univariate tests were examined (Hummel & Sligo, 1971). An examination of the univariate tests included in Table 4.7 indicate that the significant F's appear to be caused by both dependent variables. The reader may consider the previous chapters or our discussion of simple effects in the last section, for other analyses following significant multivariate results.

## Multivariate Analysis: Overall Tests and Post Hoc Comparisons

Often a researcher is interested in examining experimental effects in an exploratory manner, with no planned comparisons in mind. This is frequently the case in pilot testing prior to running a complete experiment. When this is the case, overall tests of significance are computed. The results of the overall analysis may be treated in the following manner. First, if the overall multivariate test for a treatment effect is not significant, no further analysis is warranted. If the effect is significant, then the univariate tests and/or discriminant analysis results can be examined (standard output with multivariate programs). Finally, a researcher

## Table 4.6
## Data[1] For a Three-Way MANOVA Design

| Breed | White Rock(1) | | | | White Leghorn(2) | | | | Rhode Island(3) | | | |
|---|---|---|---|---|---|---|---|---|---|---|---|---|
| Diet | High(1) | | Low(2) | | High(1) | | Low(2) | | High(1) | | Low(2) | |
| | Egg[2] | Wgt[2] | Egg | Wgt | Egg | Wgt | Egg | Wgt | Egg | Wgt | Egg | Wgt |
| **Daylength Short(1)** | 12 | 12 | 13 | 8 | 16* | 14* | 8 | 10 | 10 | 11 | 15 | 7 |
| | 8 | 16 | 16 | 10 | 19 | 16 | 11 | 7 | 12 | 14 | 11 | 4 |
| | 14 | 10 | 9 | 7 | 12 | 11 | 6 | 12 | 10 | 9 | 19 | 10 |
| | 11 | 9 | 19 | 9 | 15 | 13 | 10 | 11 | 8 | 10 | 14 | 8 |
| | 15 | 13 | 13 | 6 | 18 | 16 | 5 | 10 | 10 | 12 | 16 | 5 |
| **Medium(2)** | 17* | 13* | 10 | 10 | 11 | 17 | 15 | 9 | 12 | 13 | 15 | 9 |
| | 13* | 15* | 6 | 12 | 14 | 12 | 21 | 13 | 9 | 9 | 11* | 11* |
| | 21 | 9 | 13 | 7 | 10 | 15 | 17 | 7 | 13 | 17 | 18 | 7 |
| | 19 | 11 | 11 | 11 | 9 | 18 | 10 | 9 | 11 | 14 | 12 | 10 |
| | 15 | 14 | 10 | 8 | 11 | 17 | 12 | 11 | 15 | 13 | 19 | 9 |
| **Long(3)** | 11 | 19 | 14 | 11 | 12 | 18 | 13 | 14 | 15 | 17 | 9 | 11 |
| | 8 | 23 | 10 | 14 | 16 | 21 | 16 | 16 | 11 | 21 | 5 | 8 |
| | 15 | 20 | 12 | 8 | 9* | 14* | 14 | 10 | 18 | 13 | 13 | 15 |
| | 10 | 16 | 18 | 12 | 11* | 15* | 10 | 12 | 12 | 16 | 10 | 12 |
| | 11 | 15 | 16* | 12* | 12* | 16* | 12 | 16 | 19 | 16 | 8 | 9 |

[1]The data were taken from Fryer (1966, pp. 346-347); note that the data taken from p. 346 for Wgt were rearranged.
[2]The two dependent variables are Egg (monthly egg production) and Wgt (weight gained).

Table 4.7
Multivariate Planned Comparisons Analysis
of Variance for the Poultry Production Experiment

| Source of Variation | Sums of Squares and Products | | Multivariate | | | Univariate | | |
|---|---|---|---|---|---|---|---|---|
| | Eggs | Weight | Wilks' Lambda | Df | F(Probability) | Df | F(Probability) Eggs | F(Probability) Weight |
| Comparisons | | | | | | | | |
| 1 | [ 255.20<br>[ 195.99 | 195.99 ]<br>150.51 ] | .62 | 2,63 | 18.98*(.0000) | 1 | 32.05*(.0000) | 23.97*(.0000) |
| 2 | [ 120.33<br>[ 122.61 | 122.61 ]<br>124.94 ] | .73 | 2,63 | 11.85*(.0000) | 1 | 15.11*(.0002) | 19.90*(.0002) |
| 3 | [ 99.41<br>[ 58.50 | 58.50 ]<br>34.43 ] | .83 | 2,63 | 6.45*(.0028) | 1 | 12.48*(.0008) | 5.48*(.0223) |
| 4 | [ 12.82<br>[ 6.15 | 6.15 ]<br>2.95 ] | .98 | 2,63 | .80(.4547) | 1 | 1.61(.2091) | .47(.4952) |
| Error (Within) | [ 509.67<br>[ 210.67 | 210.67 ]<br>401.82 ] | | | | 64 | | |

*Significant at p<.05; the programs do not report probabilities to more than four decimal places.

321

might conclude by conducting univariate post hoc comparisons.

Problem. Is the monthly egg production and weight gain of the chickens dependent on the interaction of the breed of the chicken, the diet fed to chickens, and the amount of daylight to which the chickens are exposed?

Research Hypothesis. In this case the researcher believes that an overall significant interaction will appear among group vectors, but past research was inconclusive, and theory is not formulated well enough to make predictions.

Research Hypothesis: Breeds will respond differentially to diffferent diet and daylength combinations.

Statistical Hypotheses. The statistical hypotheses are written in symbolic form to match the research hypothesis. In the parallel univariate presentation of this problem we defined abc(ijk) to represent the second-order interaction of treatments i, j and k. Here we extend this notation and let abc(pijk) represent the univariate interactions of the specified treatments on variable p. Then, abc(ijk) is the vector containing the two second-order interaction effects (one effect for each dependent variable). We have the following overall interaction hypotheses:

H(O1):   abc(ijk) = 0 for all ijk
H(A1):   abc(ijk) $\neq$ 0 for some ijk

ijk: Breed*Diet*Daylength, i=1,2,3; j=1,2; k=1,2,3.

This null hypothesis will be tested at the .05 level of significance.

Data. The data are the unequal n data presented in Table 4.6.

Table 4.8 shows the results of the overall three-way MANOVA in the format that would be appropriate for a research report. The results shown here could be drawn from BMDP4V (4-4), SAS(GLM) (4-4) and SPSS(MANOVA) (4-4). The results of Table 4.8 show that the overall multivariate interaction null hypothesis was rejected (p<.0000).

Post Hoc Analyses. Since a significant multivariate F was attained for the Breed*Diet*Daylength interaction, the overall univariate tests were examined. This examination showed that the significant interaction effects were accounted for only by both dependent variables (p<.0000, for both variables). Further post hoc tests may be computed at this point, such as the tests for simple

322

Table 4.8
Multivariate Analysis of Variance
for the Poultry Production Experiment

| Source of Variation | Sums of Squares and Products | | Multivariate | | | | Univariate | | |
|---|---|---|---|---|---|---|---|---|---|
| | Eggs | Weight | Wilks' Lambda | Df | F(Probability) | Df | F(Probability) Eggs | Weight | |
| Breed (Br) | .33 | .02 | | | | | | | |
| | .02 | 50.51 | .86 | 4,126 | 2.43 (.0511) | 2 | .02 (.9792) | 3.99* (.0232) | |
| Diet (Di) | 11.16 | 66.62 | | | | | | | |
| | 66.62 | 397.60 | .47 | 2, 63 | 35.16* (.0000) | 1 | 1.40 (.2408) | 63.33* (.0000) | |
| Day Length (Da) | 29.10 | 34.76 | | | | | | | |
| | 34.76 | 42.66 | .89 | 4,126 | 1.80 (.1336) | 2 | 1.83 (.1691) | 3.40* (.0396) | |
| Br*Di | 31.61 | -2.35 | | | | | | | |
| | -2.35 | .91 | .92 | 4,126 | 1.36 (.2507) | 2 | 1.98 (.1458) | .07 (.9300) | |
| Br*Da | 16.46 | -8.09 | | | | | | | |
| | -8.09 | 22.60 | .88 | 8,126 | 1.04 (.4109) | 4 | .52 (.7236) | .90 (.4693) | |
| Di*Da | 5.96 | 3.04 | | | | | | | |
| | 3.04 | 4.51 | .98 | 4,126 | .34 (.8539) | 2 | .37 (.6892) | .36 (.6999) | |
| Br*Di*Da | 470.37 | 362.25 | | | | | | | |
| | 362.25 | 292.85 | .45 | 8,126 | 7.60* (.0000) | 4 | 14.77* (.0000) | 11.66* (.0000) | |
| Error (Within) | 509.67 | 210.67 | | | | 64 | | | |
| | 210.67 | 401.82 | | | | | | | |

*Significant at p<.05; the programs do not report probabilities to more than four decimal places.

effects on each variable (see the univariate discussion of this topic presented earlier in this chapter).

## Summary

In this chapter we continued our discussion of interaction, begun in Chapter 3, by focusing on the second-order interaction found in a three-way analysis of variance. This second-order (triple interaction) was examined through a set of data which enabled us to illustrate both planned and overall analyses. In the univariate overall analysis we discussed a significant overall triple interaction which we further interpreted using tests of simple interaction effects and simple-simple effects. The latter set of tests were featured in the instruction programs for this chapter.

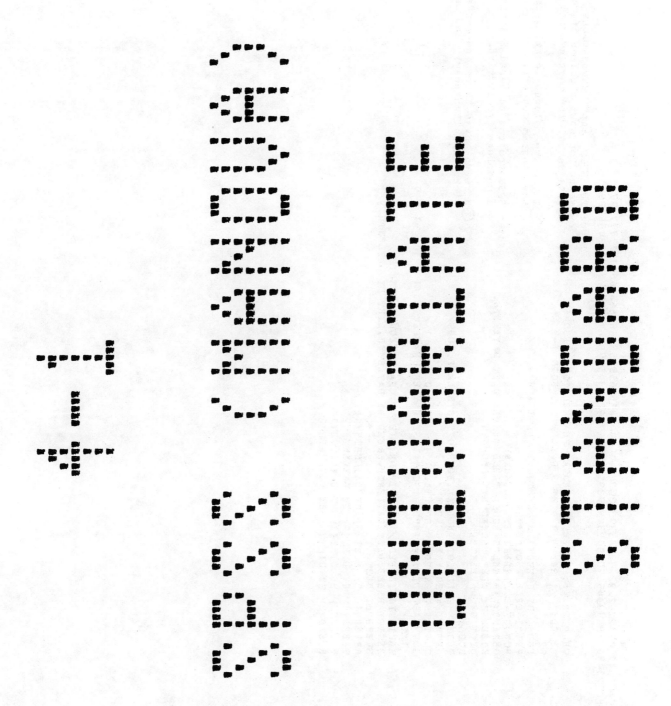

① 

Note: The SPSS input annotations provided here are of
value for most problems of this type. Consult the
SPSS manual for more general information.

```
RUN NAME       CHAPTER 4:   THREE-WAY ANOVA (PLANNED COMPARISONS)
DATA LIST      FIXED(1)/1 BREED 1 DIET 3 DAYLENTH 5 EGGS 7-8
N OF CASES     82
②MANOVA        EGGS  BY BREED(1,3),DIET(1,2),DAYLENTH(1,3)/
               PRINT=CELLINFO(MEANS)
               HOMOGENEITY(BARTLETT,COCHRAN)
               OMEANS(VARIABLES(EGGS) TABLES(BREED,DIET,DAYLENTH,
               BREED BY DIET, BREED BY DAYLENTH,
               DIET BY DAYLENTH))
               POBS/
               PLOT = CELLPLOTS,NORMAL,BOXPLOTS,STEMLEAF,POBS/
               METHOD = SSTYPE(UNIQUE)/
               CONTRAST(BREED) = SPECIAL(1 1 1 -1 0 0 -1 1)/
               CONTRAST(DIET)=SIMPLE/   CONTRAST(DAYLENTH)=SPECIAL(1 1 1 -1 0 0
               -1 1)/
               PARTITION(BREED)/  PARTITION(DIET)/  PARTITION(DAYLENTH)/
               DESIGN=BREED,DIET,DAYLENTH,BREED BY DAYLENTH,DIET BY DAYLENTH,
               BREED BY DIET,
               BREED(1)  BY DIET(1)  BY DAYLENTH(1),
               BREED(1)  BY DIET(1)  BY DAYLENTH(2),
               BREED(2)  BY DIET(1)  BY DAYLENTH(1),
               BREED(2)  BY DIET(1)  BY DAYLENTH(2)/
```

① Note: The SPSS program numbered 2-1 provides annotations for
a complete I/O listing.

② Here we have three independent variables (Breed,
Diet, and Lenthday) and one dependent variable
Eggs.

```
READ INPUT DATA
1 1 1 12
1 1 1  8
1 1 1 14
1 1 1 11
1 1 1 15
1 1 2 21
1 1 2 19
1 1 2 15
1 1 3 11
1 1 3  8
1 1 3 15
1 1 3 10
1 1 3 11
1 2 1 13
1 2 1 16
1 2 1  9
1 2 1 14
1 2 1 13
1 2 2 10
1 2 2  6
1 2 2 13
1 2 2 11
1 2 2 10
1 2 3 14
1 2 3 10
1 2 3 12
1 2 3 18
2 1 1 19
2 1 1 12
2 1 1 15
2 1 1 18
```

326

```
2 1 2 10
2 1 2 9
2 1 2 11
2 1 3 12
2 1 3 16
2 2 1 8
2 2 1 11
2 2 1 16
2 2 1 10
2 2 2 15
2 2 2 21
2 2 2 17
2 2 2 10
2 2 3 12
2 2 3 13
2 2 3 16
2 2 3 14
2 3 1 10
2 3 1 12
3 1 1 10
3 1 1 8
3 1 1 10
3 1 1 12
3 1 1 9
3 1 2 13
3 1 2 11
3 1 2 15
3 1 3 15
3 1 3 18
3 1 3 12
3 1 3 19
3 1 3 15
3 2 1 11
3 2 1 19
3 2 1 14
3 2 1 16
3 2 2 15
3 2 2 18
3 2 2 12
3 2 2 19
3 2 3 9
3 2 3 5
3 2 3 13
3 2 3 10
3 2 3 8
```

```
          1111111111222222222233333333334444444444555555555566666666667777777778
01234567890123456789012345678901234567890123456789012345678901234567890123456789
```

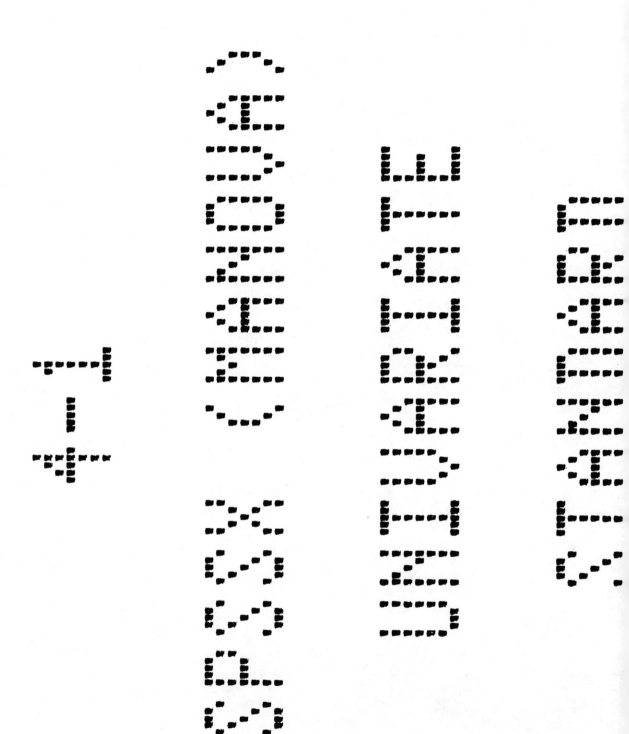

```
0000000000111111111122222222223333333333444444444455555555556666666666777777777 8
1234567890123456789012345678901234567890123456789012345678901234567890123456789 0
```

① UNNUMBERED
TITLE      CHAPTER 4:   THREE-WAY ANOVA (PLANNED COMPARISONS)
DATA LIST RECORD=1/1 BREED 1 DIET 3 DAYLENTH 5 EGGS 7-8
MANOVA     EGGS  BY BREED(1,3),DIET(1,2),DAYLENTH(1,3)/
           PRINT=CELLINFO(MEANS)
           HOMOGENEITY(BARTLETT,COCHRAN)
           OMEANS(VARIABLES(EGGS) TABLES(BREED,DIET,DAYLENTH,
           BREED BY DIET, BREED BY DAYLENTH,
           DIET BY DAYLENTH)
           POBS/
           PLOT = CELLPLOTS,NORMAL,BOXPLOTS,STEMLEAF,POBS/
           METHOD = SSTYPE(UNIQUE)/
           CONTRAST(BREED) = SPECIAL(1 1 1 -1 0 0 -1 1)/
           CONTRAST(DIET)=SIMPLE/  CONTRAST(DAYLENTH)=SPECIAL(1 1 1 -1 0 0
           -1 1)/
           PARTITION(BREED)/  PARTITION(DIET)/  PARTITION(DAYLENTH)/
           DESIGN=BREED,DIET,DAYLENTH,BREED BY DAYLENTH,DIET BY DAYLENTH,
           BREED BY DIET,
           BREED(1)  BY DIET(1)  BY DAYLENTH(1),
           BREED(1)  BY DIET(1)  BY DAYLENTH(2),
           BREED(2)  BY DIET(1)  BY DAYLENTH(1),
           BREED(2)  BY DIET(1)  BY DAYLENTH(2)/

BEGIN DATA

②

END DATA
```
0000000000111111111122222222223333333333444444444455555555556666666666777777777 8
1234567890123456789012345678901234567890123456789012345678901234567890123456789 0
```

① At our installation the default (NUMBERED)
instruction allowed SPSSX to read only 72 columns.
We therefore used the UNNUMBERED command to allow
SPSSX to read all 80 columns. The default may
vary by installation.

② The data go here.

329

CELL MEANS AND STANDARD DEVIATIONS

VARIABLE -- EGGS

| FACTOR | CODE | MEAN | STD. DEV. | N | 95 PERCENT CONF. INTERVAL | |
|---|---|---|---|---|---|---|
| BREED | 1 | | | | | |
| DIET | 1 | | | | | |
| DAYLENTH | 1 | 12.00000 | 2.73861 | 5 | 8.59962 | 15.40038 |
| DAYLENTH | 2 | 18.33333 | 3.05505 | 3 | 10.74408 | 25.92258 |
| DAYLENTH | 3 | 11.00000 | 2.54951 | 5 | 7.83442 | 14.16558 |
| DIET | 2 | | | | | |
| DAYLENTH | 1 | 13.00000 | 2.54951 | 5 | 9.83442 | 16.16558 |
| DAYLENTH | 2 | 10.00000 | 2.54951 | 5 | 6.83442 | 13.16558 |
| DAYLENTH | 3 | 13.50000 | 3.41565 | 4 | 8.06502 | 18.93498 |
| BREED | 2 | | | | | |
| DIET | 1 | | | | | |
| DAYLENTH | 1 | 16.00000 | 3.16228 | 4 | 10.96818 | 21.03182 |
| DAYLENTH | 2 | 11.00000 | 1.87083 | 5 | 8.67710 | 13.32290 |
| DAYLENTH | 3 | 14.00000 | 2.82843 | 2 | -11.41240 | 39.41240 |
| DIET | 2 | | | | | |
| DAYLENTH | 1 | 8.00000 | 2.54951 | 5 | 4.83442 | 11.16558 |
| DAYLENTH | 2 | 15.00000 | 4.30116 | 5 | 9.65949 | 20.34051 |
| DAYLENTH | 3 | 13.00000 | 2.23607 | 5 | 10.22360 | 15.77640 |
| BREED | 3 | | | | | |
| DIET | 1 | | | | | |
| DAYLENTH | 1 | 10.00000 | 1.41421 | 5 | 8.24405 | 11.75595 |
| DAYLENTH | 2 | 12.00000 | 2.23607 | 5 | 9.22360 | 14.77640 |
| DAYLENTH | 3 | 15.00000 | 3.53553 | 5 | 10.61013 | 19.38987 |
| DIET | 2 | | | | | |
| DAYLENTH | 1 | 15.00000 | 2.91548 | 5 | 11.38002 | 18.61998 |
| DAYLENTH | 2 | 16.00000 | 3.16228 | 4 | 10.96818 | 21.03182 |
| DAYLENTH | 3 | 9.00000 | 2.91548 | 5 | 5.38002 | 12.61998 |
| FOR ENTIRE SAMPLE | | 12.62195 | 3.62311 | 82 | 11.82587 | 13.41804 |

CHAPTER 4: THREE-WAY ANOVA (PLANNED COMPARISONS)

* * * * * * * * * * * * * * * * * A N A L Y S I S   O F   V A R I A N C E * * * * * * * * * * * * * * * * * * * * * * * * *     02/02/83     PAGE     9

COMBINED OBSERVED MEANS FOR BREED

VARIABLE -- EGGS

    BREED

        1         WGT.    12.55556
                  UNWGT.  12.97222

        2         WGT.    12.57692
                  UNWGT.  12.83333

        3         WGT.    12.72414
                  UNWGT.  12.83333

- - - - - - - - - - - - - - - - - - -

CCOMBINED OBSERVED MEANS FOR DIET

VARIABLE -- EGGS

    DIET

        1         WGT.    12.87179
                  UNWGT.  13.25926

        2         WGT.    12.39535
                  UNWGT.  12.50000

- - - - - - - - - - - - - - - - - - -

COMBINED OBSERVED MEANS FOR DAYLENTH

VARIABLE -- EGGS

    DAYLENTH

        1         WGT.    12.20690
                  UNWGT.  12.33333

        2         WGT.    13.29630

CHAPTER 4: THREE-WAY ANOVA (PLANNED COMPARISONS)

* * * * * * * * * * * * * * * * * A N A L Y S I S   O F   V A R I A N C E * * * * * * * * * * * * * * * * * * * * *          02/02/83          PAGE   10

COMBINED OBSERVED MEANS FOR DAYLENTH     (CONT.)

VARIABLE -- EGGS

|   |        | (CONT.)  |
|---|--------|----------|
|   | UNWGT. | 13.72222 |
| 3 | WGT.   | 12.38462 |
|   | UNWGT. | 12.58333 |

COMBINED OBSERVED MEANS FOR BREED BY DIET

VARIABLE -- EGGS

| DIET | BREED  | 1        | 2        | 3        |
|------|--------|----------|----------|----------|
| 1    | WGT.   | 13.07692 | 13.36364 | 12.33333 |
|      | UNWGT. | 13.77778 | 13.66667 | 12.33333 |
| 2    | WGT.   | 12.07143 | 12.00000 | 13.14286 |
|      | UNWGT. | 12.16667 | 12.00000 | 13.33333 |

COMBINED OBSERVED MEANS FOR BREED BY DAYLENTH

VARIABLE -- EGGS

| DAYLENTH | BREED  | 1        | 2        | 3        |
|----------|--------|----------|----------|----------|
| 1        | WGT.   | 12.50000 | 11.55556 | 12.50000 |
|          | UNWGT. | 12.50000 | 12.00000 | 12.50000 |
| 2        | WGT.   | 13.12500 | 13.00000 | 13.77778 |
|          | UNWGT. | 14.16667 | 13.00000 | 14.00000 |
| 3        | WGT.   | 12.11111 | 13.28571 | 12.00000 |
|          | UNWGT. | 12.25000 | 13.50000 | 12.00000 |

CHAPTER 4: THREE-WAY ANOVA (PLANNED COMPARISONS)

* * * * * * * * * * * * * * * * * A N A L Y S I S   O F   V A R I A N C E * * * * * * * * * * * * * * * * * * * * * * * * * * * *     02/02/83     PAGE 11

COMBINED OBSERVED MEANS FOR DIET BY DAYLENTH

VARIABLE -- EGGS

| DAYLENTH | DIET | 1 | 2 |
|---|---|---|---|
| 1 | WGT- | 12.42857 | 12.00000 |
|   | UNWGT- | 12.66667 | 12.00000 |
| 2 | WGT- | 13.07692 | 13.50000 |
|   | UNWGT- | 13.77778 | 13.66667 |
| 3 | WGT- | 13.16667 | 11.71429 |
|   | UNWGT- | 13.33333 | 11.83333 |

CORRESPONDENCE BETWEEN EFFECTS AND COLUMNS OF BETWEEN-SUBJECTS DESIGN

| STARTING COLUMN | ENDING COLUMN | EFFECT NAME |
|---|---|---|
| 1 | 1 | CONSTANT |
| 2 | 3 | BREED |
| 4 | 4 | DIET |
| 5 | 6 | DAYLENTH |
| 7 | 10 | BREED BY DAYLENTH |
| 11 | 12 | DIET BY DAYLENTH |
| 13 | 14 | BREED BY DIET |
| 15 | 15 | BREED(1) BY DIET(1) BY DAYLENTH(1) |
| 16 | 16 | BREED(1) BY DIET(1) BY DAYLENTH(2) |
| 17 | 17 | BREED(2) BY DIET(1) BY DAYLENTH(1) |
| 18 | 18 | BREED(2) BY DIET(1) BY DAYLENTH(2) |

* * * * * * * * * * * * * * * * * * * A N A L Y S I S  O F  V A R I A N C E * * * * * * * * * * * * * * * * * * *

TESTS OF SIGNIFICANCE FOR EGGS USING UNIQUE SUMS OF SQUARES

| SOURCE OF VARIATION | SUM OF SQUARES | DF | MEAN SQUARE | F | SIG. OF F |
|---|---|---|---|---|---|
| WITHIN CELLS | 509.66667 | 64 | 7.96354 | | |
| CONSTANT | 12847.81541 | 1 | 12847.81541 | 1613.32934 | 0.0 |
| BREED | .33462 | 2 | .16731 | .02101 | .979 |
| DIET | 11.16202 | 1 | 11.16202 | 1.40164 | .241 |
| DAYLENTH | 29.10416 | 2 | 14.55208 | 1.82734 | .169 |
| BREED BY DAYLENTH | 16.46249 | 4 | 4.11562 | .51681 | .724 |
| DIET BY DAYLENTH | 5.96348 | 2 | 2.98174 | .37442 | .689 |
| BREED BY DIET | 31.60954 | 2 | 15.80477 | 1.98464 | .146 |
| BREED(1) BY DIET(1) BY DAYLENTH(1) | 255.20249 | 1 | 255.20249 | 32.04636 | 0.0 |
| BREED(1) BY DIET(1) BY DAYLENTH(2) | 120.33333 | 1 | 120.33333 | 15.11053 | .000 |
| BREED(2) BY DIET(1) BY DAYLENTH(1) | 99.41176 | 1 | 99.41176 | 12.48336 | .001 |
| BREED(2) BY DIET(1) BY DAYLENTH(2) | 12.82051 | 1 | 12.82051 | 1.60990 | .209 |

ESTIMATES FOR EGGS

CONSTANT

| PARAMETER | COEFF. | STD. ERR. | T-VALUE | SIG. OF T | LOWER .95 CL | UPPER .95 CL |
|---|---|---|---|---|---|---|
| 1 | 12.8796296296 | .32066 | 40.16627 | 0.0 | 12.23904 | 13.52022 |

BREED

| PARAMETER | COEFF. | STD. ERR. | T-VALUE | SIG. OF T | LOWER .95 CL | UPPER .95 CL |
|---|---|---|---|---|---|---|
| 2 | -.1388888889 | .80553 | -.17242 | .864 | -1.47035 | 1.74812 |
| 3 | 0.0 | .78701 | 0.0 | 1.000 | -1.57224 | 1.57224 |

DIET

| PARAMETER | COEFF. | STD. ERR. | T-VALUE | SIG. OF T | LOWER .95 CL | UPPER .95 CL |
|---|---|---|---|---|---|---|
| 4 | -.7592592593 | .64132 | 1.18391 | .241 | -.52192 | 2.04043 |

(1) This output is found in the planned comparison analysis of variance Table 4.3.

(2) The single degree of freedom contrasts provide 95% confidence intervals for the contrasts of interest.

* * * * * * * * * * * * * * * * * * * * A N A L Y S I S   O F   V A R I A N C E * * * * * * * * * * * * * * * * * *

ESTIMATES FOR EGGS

DAYLENTH

| PARAMETER | COEFF. | STD. ERR. | T-VALUE | SIG. OF T | LOWER .95 CL | UPPER .95 CL |
|---|---|---|---|---|---|---|
| 5 | -1.3888888889 | .76323 | -1.81975 | .073 | -2.91361 | -.13584 |
| 6 | -1.1388888889 | .80553 | -1.41384 | .162 | -2.74812 | -.47035 |

BREED BY DAYLENTH

| PARAMETER | COEFF. | STD. ERR. | T-VALUE | SIG. OF T | LOWER .95 CL | UPPER .95 CL |
|---|---|---|---|---|---|---|
| 7 | -.6666666667 | 1.88425 | -.35381 | .725 | -4.43090 | 3.09756 |
| 8 | -2.4166666667 | 2.03658 | -1.18663 | .240 | -6.48521 | 1.65188 |
| 9 | -.5000000000 | 1.83970 | -.27178 | .787 | -4.17523 | 3.17523 |
| 10 | -2.5000000000 | 1.97034 | -1.26882 | .209 | -6.43620 | 1.43620 |

DIET BY DAYLENTH

| PARAMETER | COEFF. | STD. ERR. | T-VALUE | SIG. OF T | LOWER .95 CL | UPPER .95 CL |
|---|---|---|---|---|---|---|
| 11 | -.5555555556 | 1.52646 | -.36395 | .717 | -2.49389 | 3.60501 |
| 12 | 1.3888888889 | 1.61106 | -.86209 | .392 | -1.82958 | 4.60736 |

BREED BY DIET

| PARAMETER | COEFF. | STD. ERR. | T-VALUE | SIG. OF T | LOWER .95 CL | UPPER .95 CL |
|---|---|---|---|---|---|---|
| 13 | -.0555555556 | 1.61106 | -.03448 | .973 | -3.27402 | 3.16291 |
| 14 | -2.6666666667 | 1.57402 | -1.69417 | .095 | -5.81114 | -.47780 |

BREED(1) BY DIET(1) BY DAYLENTH(1)

| PARAMETER | COEFF. | STD. ERR. | T-VALUE | SIG. OF T | LOWER .95 CL | UPPER .95 CL |
|---|---|---|---|---|---|---|
| 15 | -21.3333333333 | 3.76851 | -5.66095 | .000 | -28.86179 | -13.80487 |

BREED(1) BY DIET(1) BY DAYLENTH(2)

| PARAMETER | COEFF. | STD. ERR. | T-VALUE | SIG. OF T | LOWER .95 CL | UPPER .95 CL |
|---|---|---|---|---|---|---|
| 16 | -15.8333333333 | 4.07317 | -3.88723 | .000 | -23.97043 | -7.69624 |

335

* * * * * * * * * * * * * * * * * A N A L Y S I S   O F   V A R I A N C E * * * * * * * * * * * * * * * * * * * * * * *

ESTIMATES FOR EGGS          (CONT.)

BREED(2) BY DIET(1) BY DAYLENTH(1)

| PARAMETER | COEFF. | STD. ERR. | T-VALUE | SIG. OF T | LOWER .95 CL | UPPER .95 CL |
|-----------|--------|-----------|---------|-----------|--------------|--------------|
| 17 | -13.0000000000 | 3.67940 | -3.53318 | .001 | -20.35046 | -5.64954 |

BREED(2) BY DIET(1) BY DAYLENTH(2)

| PARAMETER | COEFF. | STD. ERR. | T-VALUE | SIG. OF T | LOWER .95 CL | UPPER .95 CL |
|-----------|--------|-----------|---------|-----------|--------------|--------------|
| 18 | 5.0000000000 | 3.94067 | 1.26882 | .209 | -2.87240 | 12.87240 |

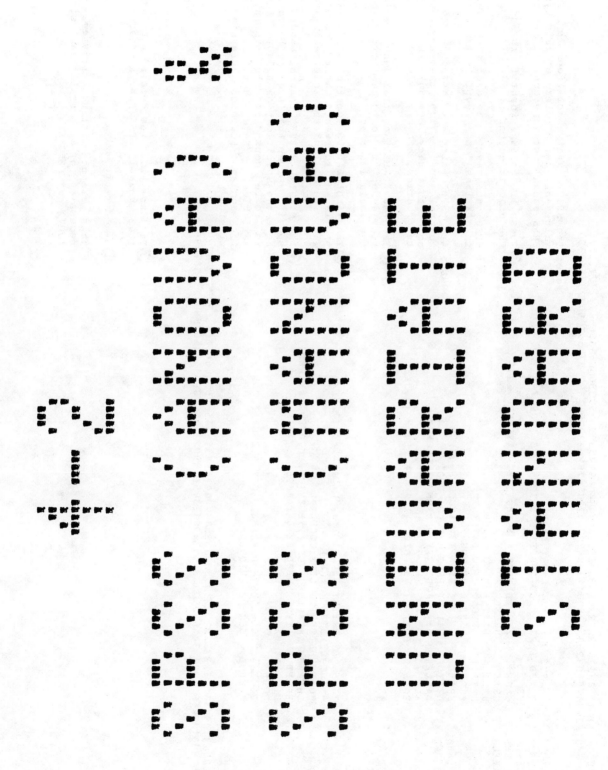

① These are column identifiers and are not part of the program content.

Note: SPSS programs numbered 2-4 and 2-5 provide annotations for a complete I/O listing.

Note: At this point we introduce some further SPSS control words which the user may find useful. Note that they are not necessary to run these subprograms, but may be of use in SPSS programs.

② The VAR LABELS control words allow the user to provide up to forty characters to further define the variables read.

③ The VALUE LABELS control words allow the user to provide up to twenty characters to name the values (here levels) of the independent variables.

④ The MISSING VALUES control words allow the user to specify values that are to be considered missing. Here the specification All(0) indicates that zero is to be considered the missing value for all variables. (Note that this is purely presented for academic purposes here since no values are missing.)

⑤ The data list was deleted here but is exactly as that shown in SPSS(MANOVA) program numbered 4-1.

⑥ The data go here.

⑦ This input listing provides the statements necessary for an overall analysis for subprograms ANOVA and MANOVA.

```
① 0000000000111111111122222222223333333333444444444455555555556666666666777777778
  1234567890123456789012345678901234567890123456789012345678901234567890123456789 0

RUN NAME          CHAPTER 4:  THREE-WAY ANOVA
DATA LIST         FIXED(1)/1 BREED 1 DIET 3 DAYLENTH 5 EGGS 7-8
N OF CASES        82
LIST CASES        CASES = 82/VARIABLES = BREED DIET DAYLENTH EGGS
②VAR LABELS       BREED    BREED OF BREED/
                  DIET     DIET FED TO BREED/
                  DAYLENTH EXPOSURE TO DAYLIGHT/
                  EGGS     NUMBER OF EGGS/
③VALUE LABELS     BREED    (1) WH ROCK (2) LEGHORN (3) R IS RED/
                  DIET     (1) HI PROT (2) LOW PROT/
                  DAYLENTH (1) SHORT (2) MEDIUM (3) LONG/
④MISSING VALUES   ALL (0)
ANOVA             EGGS BY BREED (1,3) DIET (1,2) DAYLENTH (1,3)
OPTIONS           9
STATISTICS        ALL
READ INPUT DATA
⑤ ⑥
⑦MANOVA          EGGS  BY BREED(1,3),DIET(1,2),DAYLENTH(1,3)/
                  PRINT=CELLINFO(MEANS)
                  HOMOGENEITY(BARTLETT,COCHRAN)
                  OMEANS(VARIABLES(EGGS) TABLES(BREED,DIET,DAYLENTH,
                  BREED BY DIET, BREED BY DAYLENTH,
                  DIET BY DAYLENTH))
                  POBS/
                  PLOT = CELLPLOTS,NORMAL,BOXPLOTS,STEMLEAF,POBS/
                  METHOD = SSTYPE(UNIQUE)/

① 0000000000111111111122222222223333333333444444444455555555556666666666777777778
  1234567890123456789012345678901234567890123456789012345678901234567890123456789 0
```

338

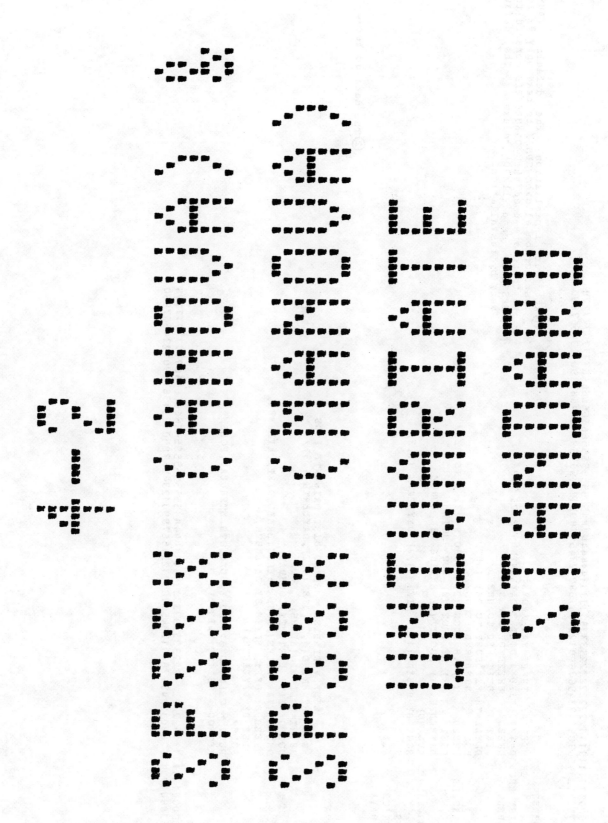

```
00000000011111111112222222222333333333344444444445555555555666666666677777777778
12345678901234567890123456789012345678901234567890123456789012345678901234567890
```

① UNNUMBERED
TITLE        CHAPTER 4:  THREE-WAY ANOVA
DATA LIST RECORD=1/1 BREED 1 DIET 3 DAYLENTH 5 EGGS 7-8
VAR LABELS    BREED    BREED OF BRFED/
              DIET     DIET FED TO BREED/
              DAYLENTH EXPOSURE TO DAYLIGHT/
              EGGS     NUMBER OF EGGS/
VALUE LABELS  BREED    (1) WH ROCK (2) LEGHORN (3) R IS RED/
              DIET     (1) HI PROT (2) LOW PROT/
              DAYLENTH (1) SHORT (2) MEDIUM (3) LONG/
MISSING VALUES ALL (0)
ANOVA         EGGS BY BREED (1,3) DIET (1,2) DAYLENTH (1,3)
OPTIONS       9
STATISTICS    ALL
BEGIN DATA
②                                                    ② The data go here.

END DATA
MANOVA            LIST VARIABLES = BREED DIET DAYLENTH EGGS
              EGGS BY BREED(1,3),DIET(1,2),DAYLENTH(1,3)/
              PRINT=CELLINFO(MEANS)
              HOMOGENEITY(BARTLETT,COCHRAN)
              OMEANS(VARIABLES(EGGS) TABLES(BREED,DIET,DAYLENTH,
              BREED BY DIET, BREED BY DAYLENTH,
              DIET BY DAYLENTH))
              POBS/
              PLOT = CELLPLOTS,NORMAL,BOXPLOTS,STEMLEAF,POBS/
              METHOD = SSTYPE(UNIQUE)/
```

① At our installation the default (NUMBERED)
instruction allowed SPSSX to read only 72 columns.
We therefore used the UNNUMBERED command to allow
SPSSX to read all 80 columns.  The default may
vary by installation.

```
00000000011111111112222222222333333333344444444445555555555666666666677777777778
12345678901234567890123456789012345678901234567890123456789012345678901234567890
```
```

CHAPTER 4: THREE-WAY ANOVA

FILE   NONAME   (CREATION DATE = 02/02/83)

02/02/83    PAGE   4

* * * * * * * A N A L Y S I S   O F   V A R I A N C E * * * * * * * * * * * * * *
(1)  BY BREED    BREED OF BREED
         EGGS       NUMBER OF EGGS
         DIET       DIET FED TO BREED
         DAYLENTH   DAYLENGTH EXPOSURE TO DAYLIGHT
* * * * * * * * * * * * * * * * * * * * * * * * * * * * * * * * *

(1) This output is from subprogram ANOVA and may be found in Table 4.4.

| SOURCE OF VARIATION | SUM OF SQUARES | DF | MEAN SQUARE | F | SIGNIF OF F |
|---|---|---|---|---|---|
| MAIN EFFECTS | 40.698 | 5 | 8.140 | 1.022 | 0.412 |
| BREED | 0.335 | 2 | 0.167 | 0.021 | 0.979 |
| DIET | 11.162 | 1 | 11.162 | 1.402 | 0.241 |
| DAYLENTH | 29.104 | 2 | 14.552 | 1.827 | 0.169 |
| 2-WAY INTERACTIONS | 46.310 | 8 | 5.789 | 0.727 | 0.667 |
| BREED DIET | 31.610 | 2 | 15.805 | 1.985 | 0.146 |
| BREED DAYLENTH | 16.462 | 4 | 4.116 | 0.517 | 0.724 |
| DIET DAYLENTH | 5.963 | 2 | 2.982 | 0.374 | 0.689 |
| 3-WAY INTERACTIONS | 470.371 | 4 | 117.593 | 14.767 | 0.000 |
| BREED DIET DAYLENTH | 470.371 | 4 | 117.593 | 14.767 | 0.000 |
| EXPLAINED | 553.614 | 17 | 32.566 | 4.089 | 0.000 |
| RESIDUAL | 509.659 | 64 | 7.963 | | |
| TOTAL | 1063.273 | 81 | 13.127 | | |

82 CASES WERE PROCESSED.
0 CASES ( 0.0 PCT) WERE MISSING.

341

CELL MEANS AND STANDARD DEVIATIONS

VARIABLE -- EGGS          NUMBER OF EGGS

| FACTOR | CODE | MEAN | STD. DEV. | N | 95 PERCENT CONF. INTERVAL | |
|---|---|---|---|---|---|---|
| BREED | WH ROCK | | | | | |
| DIET | HI PROT | | | | | |
| DAYLENTH | SHORT | 12.00000 | 2.73861 | 5 | 8.59962 | 15.40038 |
| DAYLENTH | MEDIUM | 18.33333 | 3.05505 | 3 | 10.74408 | 25.92258 |
| DAYLENTH | LONG | 11.00000 | 2.54951 | 5 | 7.83442 | 14.16558 |
| DIET | LOW PROT | | | | | |
| DAYLENTH | SHORT | 13.00000 | 2.54951 | 5 | 9.83442 | 16.16558 |
| DAYLENTH | MEDIUM | 10.00000 | 2.54951 | 5 | 6.83442 | 13.16558 |
| DAYLENTH | LONG | 13.50000 | 3.41565 | 4 | 8.06502 | 18.93498 |
| BREED | LEGHORN | | | | | |
| DIET | HI PROT | | | | | |
| DAYLENTH | SHORT | 16.00000 | 3.16228 | 4 | 10.96818 | 21.03182 |
| DAYLENTH | MEDIUM | 11.00000 | 1.87083 | 5 | 8.67710 | 13.32290 |
| DAYLENTH | LONG | 14.00000 | 2.82843 | 2 | -11.41240 | 39.41240 |
| DIET | LOW PROT | | | | | |
| DAYLENTH | SHORT | 8.00000 | 2.54951 | 5 | 4.83442 | 11.16558 |
| DAYLENTH | MEDIUM | 15.30000 | 4.30116 | 5 | 9.65949 | 20.34051 |
| DAYLENTH | LONG | 13.00000 | 2.23607 | 5 | 10.22360 | 15.77640 |
| BREED | R IS RED | | | | | |
| DIET | HI PROT | | | | | |
| DAYLENTH | SHORT | 10.00000 | 1.41421 | 5 | 8.24405 | 11.75595 |
| DAYLENTH | MEDIUM | 12.00000 | 2.23607 | 5 | 9.22360 | 14.77640 |
| DAYLENTH | LONG | 15.00000 | 3.53553 | 5 | 10.61013 | 19.38987 |
| DIET | LOW PROT | | | | | |
| DAYLENTH | SHORT | 15.00000 | 2.91548 | 5 | 11.38002 | 18.61998 |
| DAYLENTH | MEDIUM | 16.00000 | 3.16228 | 4 | 10.96818 | 21.03182 |
| DAYLENTH | LONG | 9.00000 | 2.91548 | 5 | 5.38002 | 12.61998 |
| FOR ENTIRE SAMPLE | | 12.62195 | 3.62311 | 82 | 11.82587 | 13.41804 |

* * * * * * * * * * * * * * * *ANALYSIS  OF  VARIANCE* * * * * * * * * * * * * * * * * * * * * * * *

COMBINED OBSERVED MEANS FOR BREED

VARIABLE -- EGGS

BREED

WH ROCK    WGT.      12.55556
           UNWGT.    12.97222

LEGHORN    WGT.      12.57692
           UNWGT.    12.83333

R IS RED   WGT.      12.72414
           UNWGT.    12.83333

COMBINED OBSERVED MEANS FOR DIET

VARIABLE -- EGGS

DIET

HI PROT    WGT.      12.87179
           UNWGT.    13.25926

LOW PROT   WGT.      12.39535
           UNWGT.    12.50000

COMBINED OBSERVED MEANS FOR DAYLENTH

VARIABLE -- EGGS

DAYLENTH

SHORT      WGT.      12.20690
           UNWGT.    12.33333

MEDIUM     WGT.      13.29630

CHAPTER 4:  THREE-WAY ANOVA

* * * * * * * * * * * * * * * * * A N A L Y S I S   O F   V A R I A N C E * * * * * * * * * * * * * * * * * * * * *       02/02/83       PAGE   14

COMBINED OBSERVED MEANS FOR DAYLENTH       (CONT.)

VARIABLE -- EGGS

| LONG | UNWGT. | 13.72222 |
|------|--------|----------|
|      | WGT.   | 12.38462 |
|      | UNWGT. | 12.58333 |

---

COMBINED OBSERVED MEANS FOR BREED BY DIET

VARIABLE -- EGGS

| DIET | BREED | WH ROCK | LEGHORN | R IS RED |
|------|-------|---------|---------|----------|
| HI PROT | WGT.   | 13.07692 | 13.36364 | 12.33333 |
|         | UNWGT. | 13.77778 | 13.66667 | 12.33333 |
| LOW PROT | WGT.   | 12.07143 | 12.00000 | 13.14286 |
|          | UNWGT. | 12.16667 | 12.00000 | 13.33333 |

---

COMBINED OBSERVED MEANS FOR BREED BY DAYLENTH

VARIABLE -- EGGS

| DAYLENTH | BREED | WH ROCK | LEGHORN | R IS RED |
|----------|-------|---------|---------|----------|
| SHORT  | WGT.   | 12.50000 | 11.55556 | 12.50000 |
|        | UNWGT. | 12.50000 | 12.00000 | 12.50000 |
| MEDIUM | WGT.   | 13.12500 | 13.00000 | 13.77778 |
|        | UNWGT. | 14.16667 | 13.00000 | 14.00000 |
| LONG   | WGT.   | 12.11111 | 13.28571 | 12.00000 |
|        | UNWGT. | 12.25000 | 13.50000 | 12.00000 |

---

CHAPTER 4: THREE-WAY ANOVA

* * * * * * * * * * * * * * * A N A L Y S I S   O F   V A R I A N C E * * * * * * * * * * * * * * * * * * * * * *   02/02/83      PAGE   15

COMBINED OBSERVED MEANS FOR DIET BY DAYLENTH

VARIABLE -- EGGS

| DAYLENTH | | DIET | HI PROT | LOW PROT |
|---|---|---|---|---|
| SHORT | | WGT. | 12.42857 | 12.00000 |
| | | UNWGT. | 12.66667 | 12.00000 |
| MEDIUM | | WGT. | 13.07692 | 13.50000 |
| | | UNWGT. | 13.77778 | 13.66667 |
| LONG | | WGT. | 13.16667 | 11.71429 |
| | | UNWGT. | 13.33333 | 11.83333 |

CORRESPONDENCE BETWEEN EFFECTS AND COLUMNS OF BETWEEN-SUBJECTS DESIGN

| STARTING COLUMN | ENDING COLUMN | EFFECT NAME |
|---|---|---|
| 1 | 1 | CONSTANT |
| 2 | 3 | BREED |
| 4 | 4 | DIET |
| 5 | 6 | DAYLENTH |
| 7 | 8 | BREED BY DIET |
| 9 | 12 | BREED BY DAYLENTH |
| 13 | 14 | DIET BY DAYLENTH |
| 15 | 18 | BREED BY DIET BY DAYLENTH |

* * * * * * * * * * * * * * * * * * * A N A L Y S I S  O F  V A R I A N C E * * * * * * * * * * * * * * * * * * * * *

TESTS OF SIGNIFICANCE FOR EGGS USING UNIQUE SUMS OF SQUARES

| ② SOURCE OF VARIATION | SUM OF SQUARES | DF | MEAN SQUARE | F | SIG. OF F |
|---|---|---|---|---|---|
| WITHIN CELLS | 509.66667 | 54 | 7.96354 | | |
| CONSTANT | 12847.81541 | 1 | 12847.81541 | 1613.32934 | 0.0 |
| BREED | .33462 | 2 | .16731 | .02101 | .979 |
| DIET | 11.16202 | 1 | 11.16202 | 1.40164 | .241 |
| DAYLENTH | 29.10416 | 2 | 14.55208 | 1.82734 | .169 |
| BREED BY DIET | 31.60954 | 2 | 15.80477 | 1.98464 | .146 |
| BREED BY DAYLENTH | 16.46249 | 4 | 4.11562 | .51681 | .724 |
| DIET BY DAYLENTH | 5.96348 | 2 | 2.98174 | .37442 | .689 |
| BREED BY DIET BY DAYLENTH | 470.37092 | 4 | 117.59273 | 14.76639 | 0.0 |

② This output is from subprogram MANOVA and may be found in Table 4.4.

ESTIMATES FOR EGGS

CONSTANT

| PARAMETER | COEFF. | STD. ERR. | T-VALUE | SIG. OF T | LOWER -95 CL | UPPER -95 CL |
|---|---|---|---|---|---|---|
| 1 | 12.8796296296 | .32066 | 40.16627 | 0.0 | 12.23904 | 13.52022 |

BREED

| PARAMETER | COEFF. | STD. ERR. | T-VALUE | SIG. OF T | LOWER -95 CL | UPPER -95 CL |
|---|---|---|---|---|---|---|
| 2 | -.0925925926 | .45257 | -.20459 | .839 | -.81153 | .99671 |
| 3 | -.0462962963 | .46595 | -.09936 | .921 | -.97715 | .88455 |

DIET

| PARAMETER | COEFF. | STD. ERR. | T-VALUE | SIG. OF T | LOWER -95 CL | UPPER -95 CL |
|---|---|---|---|---|---|---|
| 4 | .3796296296 | .32066 | 1.18391 | .241 | -.26096 | 1.02022 |

DAYLENTH

| PARAMETER | COEFF. | STD. ERR. | T-VALUE | SIG. OF T | LOWER -95 CL | UPPER -95 CL |
|---|---|---|---|---|---|---|
| 5 | -.5462962963 | .44158 | -1.23714 | .221 | -1.42845 | .33586 |
| 6 | .8425925926 | .45257 | 1.86178 | .067 | -.06153 | 1.74671 |

* * * * * * * * * * * * * * * *ANALYSIS OF VARIANCE* * * * * * * * * * * * * * * * * *

ESTIMATES FOR EGGS      (CONT.)

BREED BY DIET

| PARAMETER | COEFF. | STD. ERR. | T-VALUE | SIG. OF T | LOWER .95 CL | UPPER .95 CL |
|---|---|---|---|---|---|---|
| 7 | -.4592592259 | .45257 | -.94112 | .350 | -.47820 | 1.33005 |
| 8 | -.4537037037 | .46595 | -.97371 | .334 | -.47715 | 1.38455 |

BREED BY DAYLENTH

| PARAMETER | COEFF. | STD. ERR. | T-VALUE | SIG. OF T | LOWER .95 CL | UPPER .95 CL |
|---|---|---|---|---|---|---|
| 9 | -.0740740741 | .62087 | -.11931 | .905 | -1.16625 | 1.31440 |
| 10 | -.3518518519 | .65177 | -.53984 | .591 | -.95021 | 1.65391 |
| 11 | -.2870370370 | .63940 | -.44892 | .655 | -1.56438 | .99030 |
| 12 | -.6759259259 | .63843 | -1.05872 | .294 | -1.95135 | .59949 |

DIET BY DAYLENTH

| PARAMETER | COEFF. | STD. ERR. | T-VALUE | SIG. OF T | LOWER .95 CL | UPPER .95 CL |
|---|---|---|---|---|---|---|
| 13 | -.0462962963 | .44158 | -.10484 | .917 | -.92845 | .83586 |
| 14 | -.3240740741 | .45257 | -.71607 | .477 | -1.22820 | .58005 |

BREED BY DIET BY DAYLENTH

| PARAMETER | COEFF. | STD. ERR. | T-VALUE | SIG. OF T | LOWER .95 CL | UPPER .95 CL |
|---|---|---|---|---|---|---|
| 15 | -1.2592592593 | .62087 | -2.02822 | .047 | -2.49959 | -.01893 |
| 16 | 3.6851851852 | .65177 | 5.65412 | .000 | 2.38312 | 4.98725 |
| 17 | 3.2129629630 | .63940 | 5.02499 | .000 | 1.93562 | 4.49030 |
| 18 | -2.5092592593 | .63843 | -3.93033 | .000 | -3.78468 | -1.23384 |

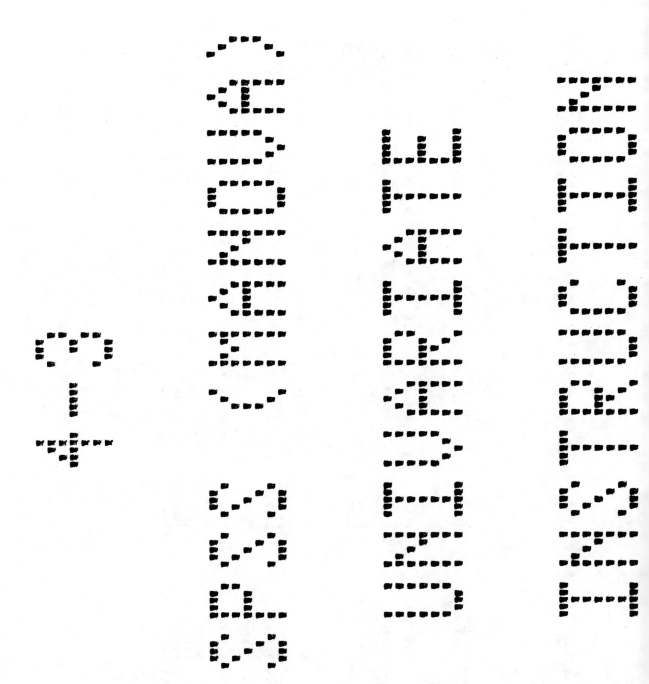

Note: The SPSS input annotations provided here are of value for most problems of this type. Consult the SPSS manual for more general information.

① These are column identifiers and are not part of the program content.

Note: This is an instruction program which illustrates how one might perform tests of a single second-order degree of freedom interaction test and its associated simple and simple-simple effects.

② The user must take great care to be sure that the appropriate cell means are being contrasted.

③ The data list was deleted here but is exactly as that shown in SPSS(MANOVA) program numbered 4-1.

④ The data goes here.

⑤ Here we used the TASK NAME cards to indicate what tests could be found in a given analysis.

⑥ To obtain the tests of simple effects the model must be changed with breed and day length crossed and nested within diet. Here the term BREED WITHIN DIET indicates that breed is nested within diet. (For further discussion of nested designs see Chapter 6).

⑦ In this statement the breed by diet contrast is being tested at the first level of diet. That is, the (1)'s following breed and daylength refer to the first contrasts and the (1) following diet refers to the high diet condition.

⑧ To obtain the tests of simple-simple effects we must have a completely nested design with day length nested within diet and breed nested within day length.

```
RUN NAME       CHAPTER 4: THREE-WAY ANOVA
TASK NAME      TEST OF SINGLE DEGREE OF FREEDOM TRIPLE INTERACTION
DATA LIST      FIXED(1)/1 BREED 1 DIET 3 DAYLENTH 5 EGGS 7-8
N OF CASES     82
LIST CASES     CASES = 82/VARIABLES = BREED DIET DAYLENTH EGGS
MANOVA         EGGS BY BREED(1,3),DIET(1,2),DAYLENTH(1,3)/
               PRINT =CELLINFO(MEANS)
               OMEANS(VARIABLES(EGGS) TABLES(BREED,DIET,DAYLENTH,
               BREED BY DIET, BREED BY DAYLENTH,
               DIET BY DAYLENTH))/
               METHOD = SSTYPE(UNIQUE)/
②              CONTRAST(BREED) = SPECIAL(1 1 1 -1 0 0 -1 1)/
               CONTRAST(DIET)=SIMPLE/ CONTRAST(DAYLENTH)=SPECIAL(1 1 1 -1 0 0
               -1 1)/
               PARTITION(BREED)/  PARTITION(DIET)/  PARTITION(DAYLENTH)/
               DESIGN=BREED,DIET,DAYLENTH,BREED BY DAYLENTH,DIET BY DAYLENTH,
               BREED BY DIET,
               BREED(1) BY DIET(1) BY DAYLENTH(1),
               BREED(1) BY DIET(1) BY DAYLENTH(2),
               BREED(2) BY DIET(1) BY DAYLENTH(1),
               BREED(2) BY DIET(1) BY DAYLENTH(2)/
READ INPUT DATA
③ ④
⑤ TASK NAME    TEST OF SIMPLE INTERACTION EFFECTS
  MANOVA       EGGS BY BREED(1,3),DIET(1,2),DAYLENTH(1,3)/
               METHOD = SSTYPE(UNIQUE)/
               CONTRAST(BREED) = SPECIAL(1 1 1 -1 0 0 -1 1)/
               CONTRAST(DIET)=SIMPLE/ CONTRAST(DAYLENTH)=SPECIAL(1 1 1 -1 0 0
               -1 1)/
               PARTITION(BREED)/  PARTITION(DIET)/  PARTITION(DAYLENTH)/
⑥              DESIGN DIET,BREED WITHIN DIET,DAYLENTH WITHIN DIET,
⑦              BREED(1) BY DAYLENTH(1) WITHIN DIET(1),
               BREED(1) BY DAYLENTH(1) WITHIN DIET(2),
               BREED(1) BY DAYLENTH(2) WITHIN DIET(1),
               BREED(1) BY DAYLENTH(2) WITHIN DIET(2),
               BREED(2) BY DAYLENTH(1) WITHIN DIET(1),
               BREED(2) BY DAYLENTH(1) WITHIN DIET(2),
               BREED(2) BY DAYLENTH(2) WITHIN DIET(1),
               BREED(2) BY DAYLENTH(2) WITHIN DIET(1)/
               TEST OF SIMPLE-SIMPLE MAIN EFFECTS
⑤ TASK NAME    EGGS BY BREED(1,3),DIET(1,2),DAYLENTH(1,3)/
  MANOVA       METHOD = SSTYPE(UNIQUE)/
               CONTRAST(BREED) = SPECIAL(1 1 1 -1 0 0 -1 1)/
               CONTRAST(DIET)=SIMPLE/ CONTRAST(DAYLENTH)=SPECIAL(1 1 1 -1 0 0
               -1 1)/
⑧              PARTITION(BREED)/  PARTITION(DIET)/  PARTITION(DAYLENTH)/
               DESIGN=DIET,DAYLENTH,DIET WITHIN DAYLENTH,
               BREED(1) WITHIN DAYLENTH(1) WITHIN DIET(1),
               BREED(1) WITHIN DAYLENTH(1) WITHIN DIET(2),
               BREED(1) WITHIN DAYLENTH(2) WITHIN DIET(1),
               BREED(1) WITHIN DAYLENTH(2) WITHIN DIET(2),
               BREED(1) WITHIN DAYLENTH(3) WITHIN DIET(1),
               BREED(1) WITHIN DAYLENTH(3) WITHIN DIET(2),
               BREED(2) WITHIN DAYLENTH(1) WITHIN DIET(1),
```

```
BREED(2) WITHIN DAYLENTH(1) WITHIN DIET(2),
BREED(2) WITHIN DAYLENTH(2) WITHIN DIET(1),
BREED(2) WITHIN DAYLENTH(2) WITHIN DIET(2),
BREED(2) WITHIN DAYLENTH(3) WITHIN DIET(1),
BREED(2) WITHIN DAYLENTH(3) WITHIN DIET(2)/
①00000000011111111112222222222333333333344444444445555555555666666666677777777778
  12345678901234567890123456789012345678901234567890123456789012345678901234567890
```

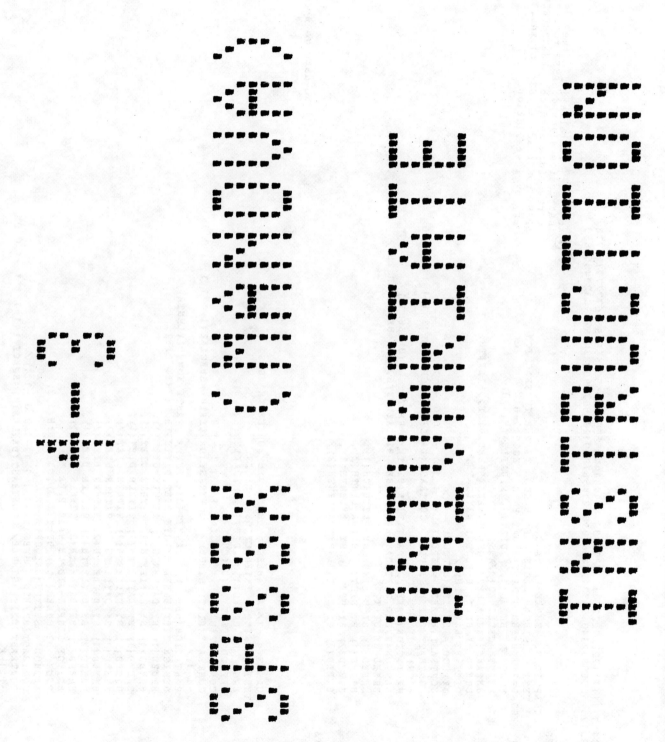

```
000000000011111111112222222222333333333344444444445555555555666666666677777777778   (NUMBERED)
1234567890123456789012345678901234567890123456789012345678901234567890123456789012
```

① At our installation the default instruction allowed SPSSX to read only 72 columns. We therefore used the UNNUMBERED command to allow SPSSX to read all 80 columns. The default may vary by installation.

```
① UNNUMBERED
TITLE       CHAPTER 4:  THREE-WAY ANOVA
SUBTITLE    TEST OF SINGLE DEGREE OF FREEDOM TRIPLE INTERACTION
DATA LIST RECORD=1/1 BREED 1 DIET 3 DAYLENTH 5 EGGS 7-8
MANOVA      EGGS BY BREED(1,3),DIET(1,2),DAYLENTH(1,3)/
            PRINT =CELLINFO(MEANS)
            OMEANS(VARIABLES(EGGS) TABLES(BREED,DIET,DAYLENTH,
            BREED BY DIET, BREED BY DAYLENTH,
            DIET BY DAYLENTH))/
            METHOD = SSTYPE(UNIQUE)/
            CONTRAST(BREED) = SPECIAL(1 1 1 -1 0 0 -1 1)/
            CONTRAST(DIET)=SIMPLE/   CONTRAST(DAYLENTH)=SPECIAL(1 1 1 -1 0 0
            -1 1)/
            PARTITION(BREED)/   PARTITION(DIET)/   PARTITION(DAYLENTH)/
            DESIGN=BREED,DIET,DAYLENTH,BREED BY DAYLENTH,DIET BY DAYLENTH,
            BREED BY DIET,
            BREED(1) BY DIET(1) BY DAYLENTH(1),
            BREED(1) BY DIET(1) BY DAYLENTH(2),
            BREED(2) BY DIET(1) BY DAYLENTH(1),
            BREED(2) BY DIET(1) BY DAYLENTH(2)/

BEGIN DATA
②  ② The data go here.

END DATA
LIST CASES  CASES = 82/VARIABLES = BREED DIET DAYLENTH EGGS
SUBTITLE    TEST OF SIMPLE INTERACTION EFFECTS
MANOVA      EGGS BY BREED(1,3),DIET(1,2),DAYLENTH(1,3)/
            METHOD = SSTYPE(UNIQUE)/
            CONTRAST(BREED) = SPECIAL(1 1 1 -1 0 0 -1 1)/
            CONTRAST(DIET)=SIMPLE/   CONTRAST(DAYLENTH)=SPECIAL(1 1 1 -1 0 0
            -1 1)/
            PARTITION(BREED)/   PARTITION(DIET)/   PARTITION(DAYLENTH)/
            DESIGN DIET, BREED WITHIN DIET,DAYLENTH WITHIN DIET,
            BREED(1) BY DAYLENTH(1) WITHIN DIET(1),
            BREED(1) BY DAYLENTH(1) WITHIN DIET(2),
            BREED(1) BY DAYLENTH(2) WITHIN DIET(1),
            BREED(2) BY DAYLENTH(1) WITHIN DIET(2),
            BREED(2) BY DAYLENTH(2) WITHIN DIET(2),
            BREED(1) BY DAYLENTH(2) WITHIN DIET(2),
            BREED(2) BY DAYLENTH(1) WITHIN DIET(1),
            BREED(2) BY DAYLENTH(2) WITHIN DIET(1)/
SUBTITLE    TEST OF SIMPLE-SIMPLE MAIN EFFECTS
MANOVA      EGGS BY BREED(1,3),DIET(1,2),DAYLENTH(1,3)/
            METHOD = SSTYPE(UNIQUE)/
            CONTRAST(BREED) = SPECIAL(1 1 1 -1 0 0 -1 1)/
            CONTRAST(DIET)=SIMPLE/   CONTRAST(DAYLENTH)=SPECIAL(1 1 1 -1 0 0
            -1 1)/
            PARTITION(BREED)/   PARTITION(DIET)/   PARTITION(DAYLENTH)/
            DESIGN=DIET,DAYLENTH,DIET WITHIN DAYLENTH,
            BREED(1) WITHIN DAYLENTH(1) WITHIN DIET(1),
            BREED(1) WITHIN DAYLENTH(1) WITHIN DIET(2),
            BREED(1) WITHIN DAYLENTH(2) WITHIN DIET(1),
            BREED(1) WITHIN DAYLENTH(2) WITHIN DIET(2),
```

```
BREED(2) WITHIN DAYLENTH(1) WITHIN DIET(1),
BREED(2) WITHIN DAYLENTH(1) WITHIN DIET(2),
BREED(2) WITHIN DAYLENTH(2) WITHIN DIET(1),
BREED(2) WITHIN DAYLENTH(2) WITHIN DIET(2),
BREED(2) WITHIN DAYLENTH(3) WITHIN DIET(1),
BREED(2) WITHIN DAYLENTH(3) WITHIN DIET(2)/
0000000001111111111222222222233333333334444444444555555555566666666667777777778
1234567890123456789012345678901234567890123456789012345678901234567890123456789 0
```

* * * * * * * * * * * * * * *ANALYSIS OF VARIANCE* * * * * * * * * * * * * * *

CELL MEANS AND STANDARD DEVIATIONS

VARIABLE .. EGGS

| FACTOR | CODE | MEAN | STD. DEV. | N | 95 PERCENT CONF. INTERVAL | |
|---|---|---|---|---|---|---|
| BREED | 1 | | | | | |
| DIET | 1 | | | | | |
| DAYLENTH | 1 | 12.00000 | 2.73861 | 5 | 8.59962 | 15.40038 |
| DAYLENTH | 2 | 18.33333 | 3.05505 | 3 | 10.74408 | 25.92258 |
| DAYLENTH | 3 | 11.00000 | 2.54951 | 5 | 7.83442 | 14.16558 |
| DIET | 2 | | | | | |
| DAYLENTH | 1 | 13.00000 | 2.54951 | 5 | 9.83442 | 16.16558 |
| DAYLENTH | 2 | 10.00000 | 2.54951 | 5 | 6.83442 | 13.16558 |
| DAYLENTH | 3 | 13.50000 | 3.41565 | 4 | 8.06502 | 18.93498 |
| BREED | 2 | | | | | |
| DIET | 1 | | | | | |
| DAYLENTH | 1 | 16.00000 | 3.16228 | 4 | 10.96818 | 21.03182 |
| DAYLENTH | 2 | 11.00000 | 1.87083 | 5 | 8.67710 | 13.32290 |
| DAYLENTH | 3 | 14.00000 | 2.82843 | 2 | -11.41240 | 39.41240 |
| DIET | 2 | | | | | |
| DAYLENTH | 1 | 8.00000 | 2.54951 | 5 | 4.83442 | 11.16558 |
| DAYLENTH | 2 | 15.00000 | 4.30116 | 5 | 9.65949 | 20.34051 |
| DAYLENTH | 3 | 13.00000 | 2.23607 | 5 | 10.22360 | 15.77640 |
| BREED | 3 | | | | | |
| DIET | 1 | | | | | |
| DAYLENTH | 1 | 10.00000 | 1.41421 | 5 | 8.24405 | 11.75595 |
| DAYLENTH | 2 | 12.00000 | 2.23607 | 5 | 9.22360 | 14.77640 |
| DAYLENTH | 3 | 15.00000 | 3.53553 | 5 | 10.61013 | 19.38987 |
| DIET | 2 | | | | | |
| DAYLENTH | 1 | 15.00000 | 2.91548 | 5 | 11.38002 | 18.61998 |
| DAYLENTH | 2 | 16.00000 | 3.16228 | 4 | 10.96818 | 21.03182 |
| DAYLENTH | 3 | 9.00000 | 2.91548 | 5 | 5.38002 | 12.61998 |
| FOR ENTIRE SAMPLE | | 12.62195 | 3.62311 | 82 | 11.82587 | 13.41804 |

82 CASES ACCEPTED.
0 CASES REJECTED BECAUSE OF OUT-OF-RANGE FACTOR VALUES.
0 CASES REJECTED BECAUSE OF MISSING DATA.
18 NON-EMPTY CELLS.

354

* * * * * * * * * * * * * * * * * * * A N A L Y S I S   O F   V A R I A N C E * * * * * * * * * * * * * * * * * * * * * * * *

COMBINED OBSERVED MEANS FOR BREED

VARIABLE -- EGGS

```
BREED

   1        WGT.     12.55556
            UNWGT.   12.97222

   2        WGT.     12.57692
            UNWGT.   12.83333

   3        WGT.     12.72414
            UNWGT.   12.83333
```

COMBINED OBSERVED MEANS FOR DIET

VARIABLE -- EGGS

```
DIET

   1        WGT.     12.87179
            UNWGT.   13.25926

   2        WGT.     12.39535
            UNWGT.   12.50000
```

COMBINED OBSERVED MEANS FOR DAYLENTH

VARIABLE -- EGGS

```
DAYLENTH

   1        WGT.     12.20690
            UNWGT.   12.33333

   2        WGT.     13.29630
```

COMBINED OBSERVED MEANS FOR DAYLENTH          (CONT.)

VARIABLE -- EGGS     (CONT.)
                     UNWGT.  13.72222

         3    WGT.   12.38462
              UNWGT. 12.58333

COMBINED OBSERVED MEANS FOR BREED BY DIET

VARIABLE -- EGGS

| DIET BREED | | 1 | 2 | 3 |
|---|---|---|---|---|
| 1 | WGT. | 13.07692 | 13.36364 | 12.33333 |
|   | UNWGT. | 13.77778 | 13.66667 | 12.33333 |
| 2 | WGT. | 12.07143 | 12.00000 | 13.14286 |
|   | UNWGT. | 12.16667 | 12.00000 | 13.33333 |

COMBINED OBSERVED MEANS FOR BREED BY DAYLENTH

VARIABLE -- EGGS

| DAYLENTH BREED | | 1 | 2 | 3 |
|---|---|---|---|---|
| 1 | WGT. | 12.50000 | 11.55556 | 12.50000 |
|   | UNWGT. | 12.50000 | 12.00000 | 12.50000 |
| 2 | WGT. | 13.12500 | 13.00000 | 13.77778 |
|   | UNWGT. | 14.16667 | 13.00000 | 14.00000 |
| 3 | WGT. | 12.11111 | 13.28571 | 12.00000 |
|   | UNWGT. | 12.25000 | 13.50000 | 12.00000 |

356

COMBINED OBSERVED MEANS FOR DIET BY DAYLENTH

VARIABLE .. EGGS

| DAYLENTH | DIET | 1 | 2 |
|---|---|---|---|
| 1 | WGT. | 12.42857 | 12.00000 |
|   | UNWGT. | 12.66667 | 12.00000 |
| 2 | WGT. | 13.07692 | 13.50000 |
|   | UNWGT. | 13.77778 | 13.66667 |
| 3 | WGT. | 13.16667 | 11.71429 |
|   | UNWGT. | 13.33333 | 11.83333 |

CORRESPONDENCE BETWEEN EFFECTS AND COLUMNS OF BETWEEN-SUBJECTS DESIGN

| STARTING COLUMN | ENDING COLUMN | EFFECT NAME |
|---|---|---|
| 1 | 1 | CONSTANT |
| 2 | 3 | BREED |
| 4 | 4 | DIET |
| 5 | 6 | DAYLENTH |
| 7 | 10 | BREED BY DAYLENTH |
| 11 | 12 | DIET BY DAYLENTH |
| 13 | 14 | BREED BY DIET |
| 15 | 15 | BREED(1) BY DIET(1) BY DAYLENTH(1) |
| 16 | 16 | BREED(1) BY DIET(1) BY DAYLENTH(2) |
| 17 | 17 | BREED(2) BY DIET(1) BY DAYLENTH(1) |
| 18 | 18 | BREED(2) BY DIET(1) BY DAYLENTH(2) |

357

\* \* \* \* \* \* \* \* \* \* \* \* \* \* \* \* \* \* \* \* A N A L Y S I S   O F   V A R I A N C E \* \* \* \* \* \* \* \* \* \* \* \* \* \* \* \* \* \*

(1) This output yields the results for the single
     degree of freedom interaction shown in Table 4.5.

(1) TESTS OF SIGNIFICANCE FOR EGGS USING UNIQUE SUMS OF SQUARES

| SOURCE OF VARIATION | SUM OF SQUARES | DF | MEAN SQUARE | F | SIG. OF F |
|---|---|---|---|---|---|
| WITHIN CELLS | 509.66667 | 64 | 7.96354 | | |
| CONSTANT | 12847.81541 | 1 | 12847.81541 | 1613.32934 | 0.0 |
| BREED | .33462 | 2 | .16731 | .02101 | .979 |
| DIET | 11.16202 | 1 | 11.16202 | 1.40164 | .241 |
| DAYLENTH | 29.10416 | 2 | 14.55208 | 1.82734 | .169 |
| BREED BY DAYLENTH | 16.46249 | 4 | 4.11562 | .51681 | .724 |
| DIET BY DAYLENTH | 5.96348 | 2 | 2.98174 | .37442 | .689 |
| BREED BY DIET | 31.60954 | 2 | 15.80477 | 1.98464 | .146 |
| BREED(1) BY DIET(1) BY DAYLENTH(1) | 255.20249 | 1 | 255.20249 | 32.04636 | 0.0 |
| BREED(1) BY DIET(1) BY DAYLENTH(2) | 120.33333 | 1 | 120.33333 | 15.11053 | .000 |
| BREED(2) BY DIET(1) BY DAYLENTH(1) | 99.41176 | 1 | 99.41176 | 12.48336 | .001 |
| BREED(2) BY DIET(1) BY DAYLENTH(2) | 12.82051 | 1 | 12.82051 | 1.60990 | .209 |

ESTIMATES FOR EGGS

CONSTANT

| PARAMETER | COEFF. | STD. ERR. | T-VALUE | SIG. OF T | LOWER .95 CL | UPPER .95 CL |
|---|---|---|---|---|---|---|
| 1 | 12.8796296296 | .32066 | 40.16627 | 0.0 | 12.23904 | 13.52022 |

BREED

| PARAMETER | COEFF. | STD. ERR. | T-VALUE | SIG. OF T | LOWER .95 CL | UPPER .95 CL |
|---|---|---|---|---|---|---|
| 2 | -.1388888889 | .80553 | -.17242 | .864 | -1.47035 | 1.74812 |
| 3 | 0.0 | .78701 | 0.0 | 1.000 | -1.57224 | 1.57224 |

DIET

| PARAMETER | COEFF. | STD. ERR. | T-VALUE | SIG. OF T | LOWER .95 CL | UPPER .95 CL |
|---|---|---|---|---|---|---|
| 4 | .7592592593 | .64132 | 1.18391 | .241 | -.52192 | 2.04043 |

* * * * * * * * * * * * * * * * A N A L Y S I S   O F   V A R I A N C E * * * * * * * * * * * * * * * * *

ESTIMATES FOR EGGS          (CONT.)

DAYLENTH

| PARAMETER | COEFF. | STD. ERR. | T-VALUE | SIG. OF T | LOWER .95 CL | UPPER .95 CL |
|---|---|---|---|---|---|---|
| 5 | -1.3888888889 | .76323 | -1.81975 | .073 | -2.91361 | .13584 |
| 6 | -1.1388888889 | .80553 | -1.41384 | .162 | -2.74812 | .47035 |

BREED BY DAYLENTH

| PARAMETER | COEFF. | STD. ERR. | T-VALUE | SIG. OF T | LOWER .95 CL | UPPER .95 CL |
|---|---|---|---|---|---|---|
| 7 | -.6666666667 | 1.88425 | -.35381 | .725 | -4.43090 | 3.09756 |
| 8 | -2.4166666667 | 2.03658 | -1.18663 | .240 | -6.48521 | 1.65188 |
| 9 | -.5000000000 | 1.83970 | -.27178 | .787 | -4.17523 | 3.17523 |
| 10 | -2.5000000000 | 1.97034 | -1.26882 | .209 | -6.43620 | 1.43620 |

DIET BY DAYLENTH

| PARAMETER | COEFF. | STD. ERR. | T-VALUE | SIG. OF T | LOWER .95 CL | UPPER .95 CL |
|---|---|---|---|---|---|---|
| 11 | -.5555555556 | 1.52646 | -.36395 | .717 | -2.49389 | 3.60501 |
| 12 | 1.3888888889 | 1.61106 | .86209 | .392 | -1.82958 | 4.60736 |

BREED BY DIET

| PARAMETER | COEFF. | STD. ERR. | T-VALUE | SIG. OF T | LOWER .95 CL | UPPER .95 CL |
|---|---|---|---|---|---|---|
| 13 | -.0555555556 | 1.61106 | -.03448 | .973 | -3.27402 | 3.16291 |
| 14 | -2.6666666667 | 1.57402 | -1.69417 | .095 | -5.81114 | .47780 |

BREED(1) BY DIET(1) BY DAYLENTH(1)

| PARAMETER | COEFF. | STD. ERR. | T-VALUE | SIG. OF T | LOWER .95 CL | UPPER .95 CL |
|---|---|---|---|---|---|---|
| 15 | -21.3333333333 | 3.76851 | -5.66095 | .000 | -28.86179 | -13.80487 |

BREED(1) BY DIET(1) BY DAYLENTH(2)

| PARAMETER | COEFF. | STD. ERR. | T-VALUE | SIG. OF T | LOWER .95 CL | UPPER .95 CL |
|---|---|---|---|---|---|---|
| 16 | -15.8333333333 | 4.07317 | -3.88723 | .000 | -23.97043 | -7.69624 |

* * * * * * * * * * * * * * * * * * A N A L Y S I S   O F   V A R I A N C E * * * * * * * * * * * * * * * * * * * * * * * *

ESTIMATES FOR EGGS          (CONT.)

BREED(2) BY DIET(1) BY DAYLENTH(1)

| PARAMETER | COEFF. | STD. ERR. | T-VALUE | SIG. OF T | LOWER .95 CL | UPPER .95 CL |
|-----------|--------|-----------|---------|-----------|--------------|--------------|
| 17 | -13.0000000000 | 3.67940 | -3.53318 | .001 | -20.35046 | -5.64954 |

BREED(2) BY DIET(1) BY DAYLENTH(2)

| PARAMETER | COEFF. | STD. ERR. | T-VALUE | SIG. OF T | LOWER .95 CL | UPPER .95 CL |
|-----------|--------|-----------|---------|-----------|--------------|--------------|
| 18 | 5.0000000000 | 3.94067 | 1.26882 | .209 | -2.87240 | 12.87240 |

* * * * * * * * * * * * * * * * A N A L Y S I S   O F   V A R I A N C E * * * * * * * * * * * * * * * *

02/02/83        PAGE  14

(2) This output yields the results for the simple effects shown in Table 4.5.

TESTS OF SIGNIFICANCE FOR EGGS USING UNIQUE SUMS OF SQUARES

(2) SOURCE OF VARIATION

| | SUM OF SQUARES | DF | MEAN SQUARE | F | SIG. OF F |
|---|---|---|---|---|---|
| WITHIN CELLS | 509.66667 | 64 | 7.96354 | | |
| CONSTANT | 12847.81541 | 1 | 12847.81541 | 1613.32934 | 0.0 |
| DIET | 11.16202 | 1 | 11.16202 | 1.40164 | .241 |
| BREED WITHIN DIET | 32.26259 | 4 | 8.06565 | 1.01282 | .408 |
| DAYLENTH WITHIN DIET | 36.92549 | 4 | 9.23137 | 1.15920 | .337 |
| BBREED(1) BY DAYLENTH(1) WITHIN DIET(1) | 130.62147 | 1 | 130.62147 | 16.40243 | .000 |
| BREED(1) BY DAYLENTH(1) WITHIN DIET(2) | 125.00000 | 1 | 125.00000 | 15.69653 | .000 |
| BREED(1) BY DAYLENTH(2) WITHIN DIET(1) | 86.57658 | 1 | 86.57658 | 10.87162 | .002 |
| BREED(1) BY DAYLENTH(2) WITHIN DIET(2) | 42.35294 | 1 | 42.35294 | 5.31835 | .024 |
| BREED(2) BY DAYLENTH(1) WITHIN DIET(2) | 29.41176 | 1 | 29.41176 | 3.69330 | .059 |
| BREED(2) BY DAYLENTH(2) WITHIN DIET(2) | 35.58824 | 1 | 35.58824 | 4.46890 | .038 |
| BREED(2) BY DAYLENTH(1) WITHIN DIET(1) | 57.64706 | 1 | 57.64706 | 7.23887 | .009 |
| BREED(2) BY DAYLENTH(2) WITHIN DIET(1) | 0.0 | 1 | 0.0 | 0.0 | 1.000 |

ESTIMATES FOR EGGS

CONSTANT

| PARAMETER | COEFF. | STD. ERR. | T-VALUE | SIG. OF T | LOWER .95 CL | UPPER .95 CL |
|---|---|---|---|---|---|---|
| 1 | 12.8796296296 | .32066 | 40.16627 | 0.0 | 12.23904 | 13.52022 |

DIET

| PARAMETER | COEFF. | STD. ERR. | T-VALUE | SIG. OF T | LOWER .95 CL | UPPER .95 CL |
|---|---|---|---|---|---|---|
| 2 | .7592592593 | .64132 | 1.18391 | .241 | -.52192 | 2.04043 |

BREED WITHIN DIET

| PARAMETER | COEFF. | STD. ERR. | T-VALUE | SIG. OF T | LOWER .95 CL | UPPER .95 CL |
|---|---|---|---|---|---|---|
| 3 | -.1111111111 | 1.22044 | -.09104 | .928 | -2.32700 | 2.54922 |
| 4 | -.1666666667 | 1.05169 | -.15848 | .875 | -1.93432 | 2.26765 |
| 5 | -1.3333333333 | 1.17111 | -1.13852 | .259 | -3.67289 | 1.00623 |
| 6 | 1.3333333333 | 1.05169 | 1.26780 | .209 | -.76765 | 3.43432 |

361

* * * * * * * * * * * * * * * * * * A N A L Y S I S   O F   V A R I A N C E * * * * * * * * * * * * * * * * * * * *

ESTIMATES FOR EGGS   (CONT.)

DAYLENTH WITHIN DIET

| PARAMETER | COEFF. | STD. ERR. | T-VALUE | SIG. OF T | LOWER -95 CL | UPPER -95 CL |
|---|---|---|---|---|---|---|
| 7 | -1.11111111 | 1.10636 | -1.00430 | .319 | -3.32131 | 1.09909 |
| 8 | -.44444444 | 1.20218 | -.36970 | .713 | -2.84607 | 1.95719 |
| 9 | -1.66666667 | 1.05169 | -1.58475 | .118 | -3.76765 | .43432 |
| 10 | -1.83333333 | 1.07252 | -1.70938 | .092 | -3.97593 | .30926 |

BREED(1) BY DAYLENTH(1) WITHIN DIET(1)

| PARAMETER | COEFF. | STD. ERR. | T-VALUE | SIG. OF T | LOWER -95 CL | UPPER -95 CL |
|---|---|---|---|---|---|---|
| 11 | -11.33333333 | 2.79836 | -4.04999 | .000 | -16.92370 | -5.74297 |

BREED(1) BY DAYLENTH(1) WITHIN DIET(2)

| PARAMETER | COEFF. | STD. ERR. | T-VALUE | SIG. OF T | LOWER -95 CL | UPPER -95 CL |
|---|---|---|---|---|---|---|
| 12 | 10.00000000 | 2.52405 | 3.96189 | .000 | 4.95763 | 15.04237 |

BREED(1) BY DAYLENTH(2) WITHIN DIET(1)

| PARAMETER | COEFF. | STD. ERR. | T-VALUE | SIG. OF T | LOWER -95 CL | UPPER -95 CL |
|---|---|---|---|---|---|---|
| 13 | -10.33333333 | 3.13396 | -3.29721 | .002 | -16.59414 | -4.07253 |

BREED(2) BY DAYLENTH(1) WITHIN DIET(2)

| PARAMETER | COEFF. | STD. ERR. | T-VALUE | SIG. OF T | LOWER -95 CL | UPPER -95 CL |
|---|---|---|---|---|---|---|
| 14 | 6.00000000 | 2.60173 | 2.30616 | .024 | .80244 | 11.19756 |

BREED(2) BY DAYLENTH(2) WITHIN DIET(2)

| PARAMETER | COEFF. | STD. ERR. | T-VALUE | SIG. OF T | LOWER -95 CL | UPPER -95 CL |
|---|---|---|---|---|---|---|
| 15 | -5.00000000 | 2.60173 | -1.92180 | .059 | -10.19756 | .19756 |

ESTIMATES FOR EGGS      (CONT.)

BREED(1) BY DAYLENTH(2) WITHIN LIET(2)

| PARAMETER | COEFF. | STD. ERR. | T-VALUE | SIG. OF T | LOWER .95 CL | UPPER .95 CL |
|---|---|---|---|---|---|---|
| 16 | 5.500000000 | 2.60173 | 2.11398 | .038 | .30244 | 10.69756 |

BREED(2) BY DAYLENTH(1) WITHIN DIET(1)

| PARAMETER | COEFF. | STD. ERR. | T-VALUE | SIG. OF T | LOWER .95 CL | UPPER .95 CL |
|---|---|---|---|---|---|---|
| 17 | -7.000000000 | 2.60173 | -2.69052 | .009 | -12.19756 | -1.80244 |

BREED(2) BY DAYLENTH(2) WITHIN DIET(1)

| PARAMETER | COEFF. | STD. ERR. | T-VALUE | SIG. OF T | LOWER .95 CL | UPPER .95 CL |
|---|---|---|---|---|---|---|
| 18 | 0.0 | 2.95971 | 0.0 | 1.000 | -5.91270 | 5.91270 |

* * * * * * * * * * * * * * * * * * * * * * A N A L Y S I S   O F   V A R I A N C E * * * * * * * * * * * * * * * * * * * * * *

③ This output yields the results for the simple-
simple effects shown in Table 4.5.

③ TESTS OF SIGNIFICANCE FOR EGGS USING UNIQUE SUMS OF SQUARES

| SOURCE OF VARIATION | SUM OF SQUARES | DF | MEAN SQUARE | F | SIG. OF F |
|---|---|---|---|---|---|
| WITHIN CELLS | 509.66667 | 64 | 7.96354 | | |
| CONSTANT | 12847.81541 | 1 | 12847.81541 | 1613.32934 | 0.0 |
| DIET | 13.06452 | 1 | 13.06452 | 1.64054 | .205 |
| DAYLENTH | 29.10416 | 2 | 14.55208 | 1.82734 | .169 |
| DIET WITHIN DAYLENTH | 5.96348 | 2 | 2.98174 | .37442 | .689 |
| BREED(1) WITHIN DAYLENTH(1) WITHIN DIET( 1) | 35.55556 | 1 | 35.55556 | 4.46479 | .039 |
| BREED(1) WITHIN DAYLENTH(2) WITHIN DIET( 2) | 62.50000 | 1 | 62.50000 | 7.84827 | .007 |
| BREED(1) WITHIN DAYLENTH(2) WITHIN DIET( 1) | 100.83333 | 1 | 100.83333 | 12.66187 | .001 |
| BREED(1) WITHIN DAYLENTH(2) WITHIN DIET( 2) | 62.50000 | 1 | 62.50000 | 7.84827 | .007 |
| BREED(1) WITHIN DAYLENTH(3) WITHIN DIET( 1) | 12.85714 | 1 | 12.85714 | 1.61450 | .208 |
| BREED(1) WITHIN DAYLENTH(3) WITHIN DIET( 2) | .55556 | 1 | .55556 | .06976 | .793 |
| BREED(2) WITHIN DAYLENTH(1) WITHIN DIET( 1) | 80.00000 | 1 | 80.00000 | 10.04578 | .002 |
| BREED(2) WITHIN DAYLENTH(1) WITHIN DIET( 1) | 122.50000 | 1 | 122.50000 | 15.38260 | .000 |
| BREED(2) WITHIN DAYLENTH(2) WITHIN DIET( 1) | 2.50000 | 1 | 2.50000 | .31393 | .577 |
| BREED(2) WITHIN DAYLENTH(2) WITHIN DIET( 1) | 2.22222 | 1 | 2.22222 | .27905 | .599 |
| BREED(2) WITHIN DAYLENTH(3) WITHIN DIET( 1) | 1.42857 | 1 | 1.42857 | .17939 | .673 |
| BREED(2) WITHIN DAYLENTH(3) WITHIN DIET( 2) | 40.00000 | 1 | 40.00000 | 5.02289 | .028 |

ESTIMATES FOR EGGS

CONSTANT

| PARAMETER | COEFF. | STD. ERR. | T-VALUE | SIG. OF T | LOWER .95 CL | UPPER .95 CL |
|---|---|---|---|---|---|---|
| 1 | 12.8796296296 | .32066 | 40.16627 | 0.0 | 12.23904 | 13.52022 |

* * * * * * * * * * * * * * A N A L Y S I S   O F   V A R I A N C E * * * * * * * * * * * * * * * * * *

ESTIMATES FOR EGGS        (CONT.)

DIET

| PARAMETER | COEFF. | STD. ERR. | T-VALUE | SIG. OF T | LOWER .95 CL | UPPER .95 CL |
|---|---|---|---|---|---|---|
| 2 | 1.5000000000 | 1.17111 | 1.28084 | .205 | -.83956 | 3.83956 |

DAYLENTH

| PARAMETER | COEFF. | STD. ERR. | T-VALUE | SIG. OF T | LOWER .95 CL | UPPER .95 CL |
|---|---|---|---|---|---|---|
| 3 | -1.3888888889 | .76323 | -1.81975 | .073 | -2.91361 | .13584 |
| 4 | -1.1388888889 | .80553 | -1.41384 | .162 | -2.74812 | .47035 |

DIET WITHIN DAYLENTH

| PARAMETER | COEFF. | STD. ERR. | T-VALUE | SIG. OF T | LOWER .95 CL | UPPER .95 CL |
|---|---|---|---|---|---|---|
| 5 | -.8333333333 | 1.57402 | -.52943 | .598 | -3.97780 | 2.31114 |
| 6 | -1.3888888889 | 1.61106 | -.86209 | .392 | -4.60736 | 1.82958 |
| 7 | 0.0 | | | | | |

BREED(1) WITHIN DAYLENTH(1) WITHIN DIET(1)

| PARAMETER | COEFF. | STD. ERR. | T-VALUE | SIG. OF T | LOWER .95 CL | UPPER .95 CL |
|---|---|---|---|---|---|---|
| 8 | -4.0000000000 | 1.89304 | -2.11301 | .039 | -7.78178 | -.21822 |

BREED(1) WITHIN DAYLENTH(1) WITHIN DIET(2)

| PARAMETER | COEFF. | STD. ERR. | T-VALUE | SIG. OF T | LOWER .95 CL | UPPER .95 CL |
|---|---|---|---|---|---|---|
| 9 | 5.0000000000 | 1.78477 | 2.80148 | .007 | 1.43450 | 8.56550 |

BREED(1) WITHIN DAYLENTH(2) WITHIN DIET(1)

| PARAMETER | COEFF. | STD. ERR. | T-VALUE | SIG. OF T | LOWER .95 CL | UPPER .95 CL |
|---|---|---|---|---|---|---|
| 10 | 7.3333333333 | 2.06088 | 3.55835 | .001 | 3.21625 | 11.45041 |

* * * * * * * * * * * * * * * * * * A N A L Y S I S   O F   V A R I A N C E * * * * * * * * * * * * * * * * * * *

ESTIMATES FOR EGGS     (CONT.)

BREED(1) WITHIN DAYLENTH(2) WITHIN DIET(2)

| PARAMETER | COEFF. | STD. ERR. | T-VALUE | SIG. OF T | LOWER .95 CL | UPPER .95 CL |
|---|---|---|---|---|---|---|
| 11 | -5.0000000000 | 1.78477 | -2.80148 | .007 | -8.56550 | -1.43450 |

BREED(1) WITHIN DAYLENTH(3) WITHIN DIET(1)

| PARAMETER | COEFF. | STD. ERR. | T-VALUE | SIG. OF T | LOWER .95 CL | UPPER .95 CL |
|---|---|---|---|---|---|---|
| 12 | -3.0000000000 | 2.36103 | -1.27063 | .208 | -7.71671 | 1.71671 |

BREED(1) WITHIN DAYLENTH(3) WITHIN DIET(2)

| PARAMETER | COEFF. | STD. ERR. | T-VALUE | SIG. OF T | LOWER .95 CL | UPPER .95 CL |
|---|---|---|---|---|---|---|
| 13 | -.5000000000 | 1.89304 | -.26413 | .793 | -3.28178 | 4.28178 |

BREED(2) WITHIN DAYLENTH(1) WITHIN DIET(1)

| PARAMETER | COEFF. | STD. ERR. | T-VALUE | SIG. OF T | LOWER .95 CL | UPPER .95 CL |
|---|---|---|---|---|---|---|
| 14 | -6.0000000000 | 1.89304 | -3.16951 | .002 | -9.78178 | -2.21822 |

BREED(2) WITHIN DAYLENTH(1) WITHIN DIET(2)

| PARAMETER | COEFF. | STD. ERR. | T-VALUE | SIG. OF T | LOWER .95 CL | UPPER .95 CL |
|---|---|---|---|---|---|---|
| 15 | 7.0000000000 | 1.78477 | 3.92207 | .000 | 3.43450 | 10.56550 |

BREED(2) WITHIN DAYLENTH(2) WITHIN DIET(1)

| PARAMETER | COEFF. | STD. ERR. | T-VALUE | SIG. OF T | LOWER .95 CL | UPPER .95 CL |
|---|---|---|---|---|---|---|
| 16 | 1.0000000000 | 1.78477 | .56030 | .577 | -2.56550 | 4.56550 |

BREED(2) WITHIN DAYLENTH(2) WITHIN DIET(2)

| PARAMETER | COEFF. | STD. ERR. | T-VALUE | SIG. OF T | LOWER .95 CL | UPPER .95 CL |
|---|---|---|---|---|---|---|
| 17 | 1.0000000000 | 1.89304 | .52825 | .599 | -2.78178 | 4.78178 |

* * * * * * * * * * * * * * * * * * A N A L Y S I S   O F   V A R I A N C E * * * * * * * * * * * * * * * * * * * * * * * * *

ESTIMATES FOR EGGS    (CONT.)

BREED(2) WITHIN DAYLENTH(3) WITHIN DIET(1)

| PARAMETER | COEFF. | STD. ERR. | T-VALUE | SIG. OF T | LOWER .95 CL | UPPER .95 CL |
|-----------|--------|-----------|---------|-----------|--------------|--------------|
| 18 | 1.0000000000 | 2.36103 | .42354 | .673 | -3.71671 | 5.71671 |

BREED(2) WITHIN DAYLENTH(3) WITHIN DIET(2)

| PARAMETER | COEFF. | STD. ERR. | T-VALUE | SIG. OF T | LOWER .95 CL | UPPER .95 CL |
|-----------|--------|-----------|---------|-----------|--------------|--------------|
| 19 | -4.0000000000 | 1.78477 | -2.24118 | .028 | -7.56550 | -.43450 |

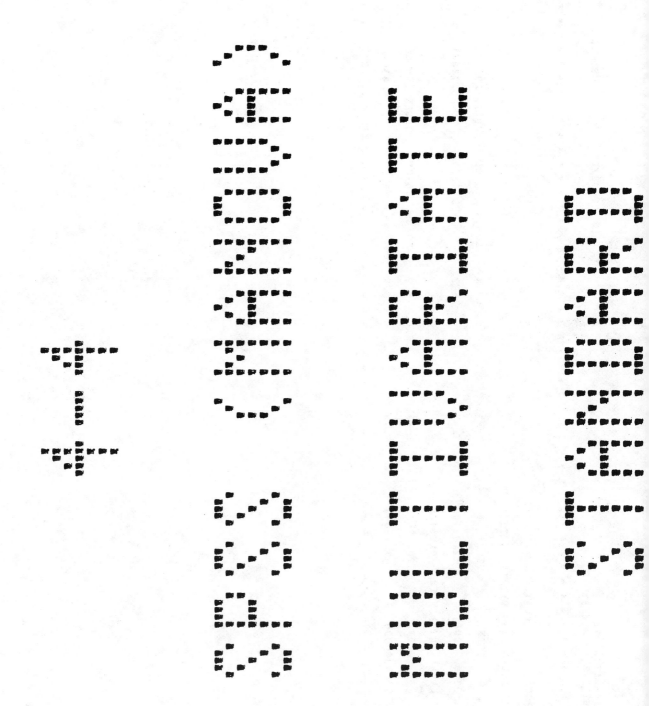

```
RUN NAME        CHAPTER 4:  THREE-WAY MANOVA
DATA LIST       FIXED(1)/1 BREED 1 DIET 3 DAYLENTH 5 EGGS 7-8 WEIGHT 10-11
N OF CASES      82
② MANOVA        EGGS WEIGHT BY BREED(1,3),DIET(1,2),DAYLENTH(1,3)/
                PRINT=CELLINFO(MEANS,SSCP,COV,COR)
                HOMOGENEITY(BARTLETT,COCHRAN,BOXM)
                SIGNIF(HYPOTH,STEPDOWN)
                DISCRIM(RAW,STAN,ESTIM,COR,ROTATE(VARIMAX)  ALPHA(1.0))
                ERROR(SSCP,COV,COR,STDV)
                OMEANS(VARIABLES(EGGS WEIGHT) TABLES(BREED,DIET,DAYLENTH,
                BREED BY DIET, BREED BY DAYLENTH,
                DIET BY DAYLENTH))
                POBS/
                PLOT = CELLPLOTS,NORMAL,BOXPLOTS,STEMLEAF,ZCORR,POBS/
                METHOD = SSTYPE(UNIQUE)/
                CONTRAST(BREED) = SPECIAL(1 1 1 -1 0 0 -1 1)/
                CONTRAST(DIET)=SIMPLE/  CONTRAST(DAYLENTH)=SPECIAL(1 1 1 -1 0 0
                -1 1)/
                PARTITION(BREED)/  PARTITION(DIET)/  PARTITION(DAYLENTH)/
                DESIGN=BREED,DIET,DAYLENTH,BREED BY DAYLENTH,DIET BY DAYLENTH,
                BREED BY DIET,
                BREED(1) BY DIET(1) BY DAYLENTH(1),
                BREED(1) BY DIET(1) BY DAYLENTH(2),
                BREED(2) BY DIET(1) BY DAYLENTH(1),
                BREED(2) BY DIET(1) BY DAYLENTH(2)/
READ INPUT DATA
1 1 1 12  9
1 1 1  8 12
1 1 1 14 13
1 1 1 15 10
1 1 1 15 16
1 1 2 21 23
1 1 2 19 20
1 2 1 15 15
1 2 1 15 15
1 3 1 11 11
1 3 1  8 13
1 3 1 15 15
1 3 1 10  9
1 3 1 11 14
1 2 1 13  8
1 2 1 16 12
1 2 1  9 10
1 2 1 14  7
1 2 1 13 11
1 2 2 10  9
1 2 2  6  8
1 2 2 13 10
1 2 2 12  7
1 2 2 10  6
1 2 3 14  9
1 2 3 10 16
1 2 3 12 12
1 2 3 18 11
2 1 1 19 21
2 1 1 12 18
2 1 1 15 14
```

Note: The SPSS input annotations provided here are of value for most problems of this type. Consult the SPSS manual for more general information.

① These are column identifiers and are not part of the program content.

Note: SPSS program numbered 2-10 provides annotations for a complete I/O listing.

② This is the planned comparisons MANOVA.

③ This is the overall MANOVA.

```
2 1 1 18 16
2 1 1 11 13
2 1 2 14 16
2 1 2 10 14
2 1 2  9 11
2 1 2 11 16
2 1 2 12 12
2 1 3 16 18
2 1 3  8 11
2 2 1 11 13
2 2 1  6  9
2 2 1 10  7
2 2 1  5  9
2 2 2 15 16
2 2 2 21 16
2 2 2 17 14
2 2 2 10 10
2 2 2 12 14
2 2 3 13 10
2 2 3 16 12
2 2 3 14 10
2 2 3 10  7
2 2 3 12 10
3 1 1 10 10
3 1 1 12 11
3 1 1  8  9
3 1 1 10 12
3 1 2 12  9
3 1 2 13 13
3 1 2 13 14
3 1 3 11 13
3 1 3 15 17
3 1 3 16 16
3 1 3 11 17
3 1 3 18 16
3 1 3 19 13
3 2 1 16 21
3 2 1 11  9
3 2 1 19 11
3 2 1 14  7
3 2 1 16  9
3 2 2  9 12
3 2 2 18  8
3 2 2 12 15
3 2 3 12  9
3 2 3 19 15
3 2 3  9  8
3 2 3 13  7
3 2 3 10 10
3 2 3  8  5
```

③ MANOVA

```
EGGS WEIGHT BY BREED(1,3),DIET(1,2),DAYLENTH(1,3)/
   PRINT=SIGNIF(HYPOTH)/
   METHOD = SSTYPE(UNIQUE)/
```

```
0000000000 111111111122222222223333333333444444444455555555556666666666777777777778
```

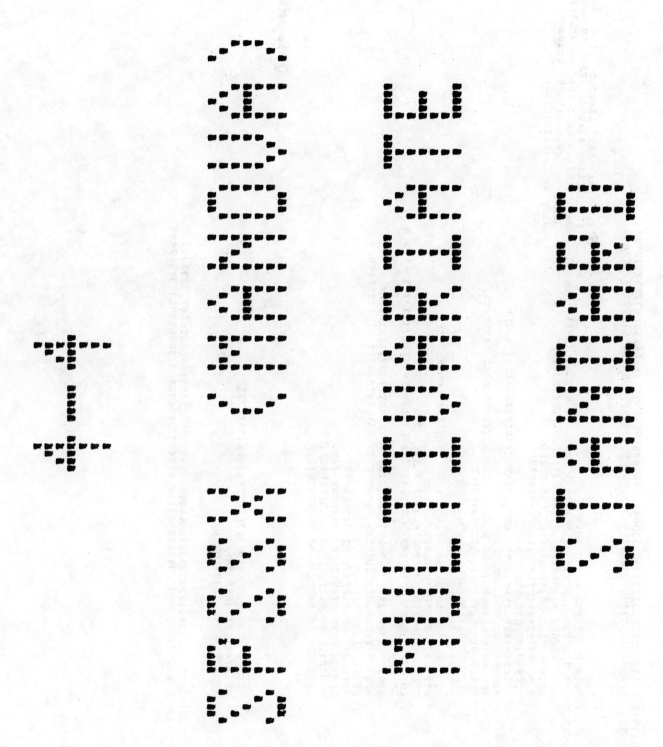

```
00000000011111111112222222222333333333344444444445555555555666666666677777777778
12345678901234567890123456789012345678901234567890123456789012345678901234567890
```

① At our installation the default (NUMBERED)
instruction allowed SPSSX to read only 72 columns.
We therefore used the UNNUMBERED command to allow
SPSSX to read all 80 columns.  The default may
vary by installation.

② The data go here.

```
① UNNUMBERED
  TITLE     CHAPTER 4:  THREE-WAY MANOVA
  DATA LIST RECORD=1/1 BREED 1 DIET 3 DAYLENTH 5 EGGS 7-8 WEIGHT 10-11
  MANOVA    EGGS WEIGHT BY BREED(1,3),DIET(1,2),DAYLENTH(1,3)/
            PRINT=CELLINFO(MEANS,SSCP,COV,COR)
            HOMOGENEITY(BARTLETT,COCHRAN,BOXM)
            SIGNIF(HYPOTH,STEPDOWN)
            DISCRIM(RAW,STAN,ESTIM,COR,ROTATE(VARIMAX) ALPHA(1.0))
            ERROR(SSCP,COV,COR,STDV)
            OMEANS(VARIABLES(EGGS WEIGHT) TABLES(BREED,DIET,DAYLENTH,
            BREED BY DIET, BREED BY DAYLENTH,
            DIET BY DAYLENTH)
            POBS/
            PLOT = CELLPLOTS,NORMAL,BCXPLOTS,STEMLEAF,ZCORR,POBS/
            METHOD = SSTYPE(UNIQUE)/
            CONTRAST(BREED) = SPECIAL(1 1 1 -1 0 0 -1 1)/
            CONTRAST(DIET)=SIMPLE/  CONTRAST(DAYLENTH)=SPECIAL(1 1 1 -1 0 0
            -1 1)/
            PARTITION(BREED)/  PARTITION(DIET)/  PARTITION(DAYLENTH)/
            DESIGN=BREED,DIET,DAYLENTH,BREED BY DAYLENTH,DIET BY DAYLENTH,
            BREED BY DIET,
            BREED(1) BY DIET(1) BY DAYLENTH(1),
            BREED(1) BY DIET(1) BY DAYLENTH(2),
            BREED(2) BY DIET(1) BY DAYLENTH(1),
            BREED(2) BY DIET(1) BY DAYLENTH(2)/
  BEGIN DATA
②
  END DATA
  MANOVA    EGGS WEIGHT BY BREED(1,3),DIET(1,2),DAYLENTH(1,3) /
            PRINT=SIGNIF(HYPOTH)/
            METHOD = SSTYPE(UNIQUE)/
```

```
00000000011111111112222222222333333333344444444445555555555666666666677777777778
12345678901234567890123456789012345678901234567890123456789012345678901234567890
```

************** A N A L Y S I S  O F  V A R I A N C E ************************

CELL MEANS AND STANDARD DEVIATIONS

VARIABLE -- EGGS

| FACTOR | CODE | MEAN | STD. DEV. | N | 95 PERCENT CONF. INTERVAL | |
|---|---|---|---|---|---|---|
| BREED | 1 | | | | | |
| DIET | 1 | | | | | |
| DAYLENTH | 1 | 12.00000 | 2.73861 | 5 | 8.59962 | 15.40038 |
| DAYLENTH | 2 | 18.33333 | 3.05505 | 3 | 10.74408 | 25.92258 |
| DAYLENTH | 3 | 11.00000 | 2.54951 | 5 | 7.83442 | 14.16558 |
| DIET | 2 | | | | | |
| DAYLENTH | 1 | 13.00000 | 2.54951 | 5 | 9.83442 | 16.16558 |
| DAYLENTH | 2 | 10.00000 | 2.54951 | 5 | 6.83442 | 13.16558 |
| DAYLENTH | 3 | 13.50000 | 3.41565 | 4 | 8.06502 | 18.93498 |
| BREED | 2 | | | | | |
| DIET | 1 | | | | | |
| DAYLENTH | 1 | 16.00000 | 3.16228 | 4 | 10.96818 | 21.03182 |
| DAYLENTH | 2 | 11.00000 | 1.87083 | 5 | 8.67710 | 13.32290 |
| DAYLENTH | 3 | 14.00000 | 2.82843 | 2 | -11.41240 | 39.41240 |
| DIET | 2 | | | | | |
| DAYLENTH | 1 | 8.00000 | 2.54951 | 5 | 4.83442 | 11.16558 |
| DAYLENTH | 2 | 15.00000 | 4.30116 | 5 | 9.65949 | 20.34051 |
| DAYLENTH | 3 | 13.00000 | 2.23607 | 5 | 10.22360 | 15.77640 |
| BREED | 3 | | | | | |
| DIET | 1 | | | | | |
| DAYLENTH | 1 | 10.00000 | 1.41421 | 5 | 8.24405 | 11.75595 |
| DAYLENTH | 2 | 12.00000 | 2.23607 | 5 | 9.22360 | 14.77640 |
| DAYLENTH | 3 | 15.00000 | 3.53553 | 5 | 10.61013 | 19.38987 |
| DIET | 2 | | | | | |
| DAYLENTH | 1 | 15.00000 | 2.91548 | 5 | 11.38002 | 18.61998 |
| DAYLENTH | 2 | 16.00000 | 3.16228 | 4 | 10.96818 | 21.03182 |
| DAYLENTH | 3 | 9.00000 | 2.91548 | 5 | 5.38002 | 12.61998 |
| FOR ENTIRE SAMPLE | | 12.62195 | 3.62311 | 82 | 11.82587 | 13.41804 |

VARIABLE -- WEIGHT

| FACTOR | CODE | MEAN | STD. DEV. | N | 95 PERCENT CONF. INTERVAL |
|---|---|---|---|---|---|

373

\* \* \* \* \* \* \* \* \* \* \* \* A N A L Y S I S   O F   V A R I A N C E \* \* \* \* \* \* \* \* \* \* \* \* \* \* \* \* \*

CELL MEANS AND STANDARD DEVIATIONS  (CONT.)

VARIABLE .. WEIGHT

| FACTOR | CODE | MEAN | STD. DEV. | N | 95 PERCENT CONF. INTERVAL | |
|---|---|---|---|---|---|---|
| BREED | 1 | | | | | |
| DIET | 1 | | | | | |
| DAYLENTH | 1 | 12.00000 | 2.73861 | 5 | 8.59962 | 15.40038 |
| DAYLENTH | 2 | 19.33333 | 4.04145 | 3 | 9.29370 | 29.37297 |
| DAYLENTH | 3 | 12.40000 | 2.40832 | 5 | 9.40973 | 15.39027 |
| DIET | 2 | | | | | |
| DAYLENTH | 1 | 9.60000 | 2.07364 | 5 | 7.02527 | 12.17473 |
| DAYLENTH | 2 | 8.00000 | 1.58114 | 5 | 6.03679 | 9.96321 |
| DAYLENTH | 3 | 12.00000 | 2.94392 | 4 | 7.31563 | 16.68437 |
| BREED | 2 | | | | | |
| DIET | 1 | | | | | |
| DAYLENTH | 1 | 17.25000 | 2.98608 | 4 | 12.49855 | 22.00145 |
| DAYLENTH | 2 | 14.00000 | 2.12132 | 5 | 11.36608 | 16.63392 |
| DAYLENTH | 3 | 15.00000 | 4.24264 | 2 | -23.11860 | 53.11860 |
| DIET | 2 | | | | | |
| DAYLENTH | 1 | 9.80000 | 2.28035 | 5 | 6.96862 | 12.63138 |
| DAYLENTH | 2 | 14.00000 | 2.44949 | 5 | 10.95861 | 17.04139 |
| DAYLENTH | 3 | 9.80000 | 1.78885 | 5 | 7.57888 | 12.02112 |
| BREED | 3 | | | | | |
| DIET | 1 | | | | | |
| DAYLENTH | 1 | 11.20000 | 1.92354 | 5 | 8.81165 | 13.58835 |
| DAYLENTH | 2 | 13.20000 | 2.86356 | 5 | 9.64447 | 16.75553 |
| DAYLENTH | 3 | 16.60000 | 2.88097 | 5 | 13.02286 | 20.17714 |
| DIET | 2 | | | | | |
| DAYLENTH | 1 | 9.20000 | 1.48324 | 5 | 7.35834 | 11.04166 |
| DAYLENTH | 2 | 11.00000 | 3.16228 | 4 | 5.96818 | 16.03182 |
| DAYLENTH | 3 | 6.80000 | 2.38747 | 5 | 3.83562 | 9.76438 |
| FOR ENTIRE SAMPLE | | 11.97561 | 3.82318 | 82 | 11.13557 | 12.81565 |

\* \* \* \* \* \* \* \* \* \* \* \* \* \* \* \* \* A N A L Y S I S   O F   V A R I A N C E \* \* \* \* \* \* \* \* \* \* \* \* \* \* \* \* \* \*

COMBINED OBSERVED MEANS FOR BREED

VARIABLE -- EGGS

```
        BREED

            1       WGT.      12.55556
                    UNWGT.    12.97222

            2       WGT.      12.57692
                    UNWGT.    12.83333

            3       WGT.      12.72414
                    UNWGT.    12.83333
```

VARIABLE -- WEIGHT

```
        BREED

            1       WGT.      11.70370
                    UNWGT.    12.22222

            2       WGT.      12.96154
                    UNWGT.    13.30833

            3       WGT.      11.34483
                    UNWGT.    11.33333
```

COMBINED OBSERVED MEANS FOR DIET

VARIABLE -- EGGS

```
        DIET

            1       WGT.      12.87179
                    UNWGT.    13.25926

            2       WGT.      12.39535
```

CHAPTER 4: THREE-WAY MANOVA

/02/83      PAGE  29

* * * * * * * * * * * * A N A L Y S I S   O F   V A R I A N C E * * * * * * * * * * * * * * * * * * * *

COMBINED OBSERVED MEANS FOR DIET      (CONT.)
VARIABLE .. EGGS    UNWGT.    12.5C000
                    (CONT.)

VARIABLE .. WEIGHT

DIET

1    WGT.    14.20513
     UNWGT.  14.5537C

2    WGT.     9.95349
     UNWGT.  10.02222

COMBINED CBSERVED MEANS FOR DAYLENTH
VARIABLE .. EGGS

DAYLENTH

1    WGT.    12.20690
     UNWGT.  12.33333

2    WGT.    13.29€30
     UNWGI.  13.72222

3    WGT.    12.38462
     UNWGT.  12.58333

VARIABLE .. WEIGHT

DAYLENTH

1    WGT.    11.31034

376

VARIABLE -- WEIGHT (CONT.)

UNWGT.  11.50833

2    WGT.    12.88889
     UNWGT.  13.25556

3    WGT.    11.76923
     UNWGT.  12.10000

COMBINED OBSERVED MEANS FOR BREED BY DIET

VARIABLE -- EGGS

| DIET | BREED | 1 | 2 | 3 |
|---|---|---|---|---|
| 1 | WGT. | 13.07692 | 13.36364 | 12.33333 |
|   | UNWGT. | 13.77778 | 13.66667 | 12.33333 |
| 2 | WGT. | 12.07143 | 12.00000 | 13.14286 |
|   | UNWGT. | 12.16667 | 12.00000 | 13.33333 |

VARIABLE -- WEIGHT

| DIET | BREED | 1 | 2 | 3 |
|---|---|---|---|---|
| 1 | WGT. | 13.84615 | 15.36364 | 13.66667 |
|   | UNWGT. | 14.57778 | 15.41667 | 13.66667 |
| 2 | WGT. | 9.71429 | 11.20000 | 8.85714 |
|   | UNWGT. | 9.86667 | 11.20000 | 9.00000 |

\* \* \* \* \* \* \* \* \* \* \* \* \* \* \* \* \* \* A N A L Y S I S   O F   V A R I A N C E \* \* \* \* \* \* \* \* \* \* \* \* \* \* \* \* \* \* \* \* \* \*

COMBINED OBSERVED MEANS FOR BREED BY DAYLENTH

VARIABLE -- EGGS

COMBINED OBSERVED MEANS FOR BREED BY DAYLENTH    (CONT.)

VARIABLE -- EGGS      (CONT.)

| DAYLENTH | BREED | 1 | 2 | 3 |
|---|---|---|---|---|
| 1 | WGT. | 12.50000 | 11.55556 | 12.50000 |
|   | UNWGT. | 12.50000 | 12.00000 | 12.50000 |
| 2 | WGT. | 13.12500 | 13.00000 | 13.77778 |
|   | UNWGT. | 14.16667 | 13.00000 | 14.00000 |
| 3 | WGT. | 12.11111 | 13.28571 | 12.00000 |
|   | UNWGT. | 12.25000 | 13.50000 | 12.00000 |

VARIABLE -- WEIGHT

| DAYLENTH | BREED | 1 | 2 | 3 |
|---|---|---|---|---|
| 1 | WGT. | 10.80000 | 13.11111 | 10.20000 |
|   | UNWGT. | 10.80000 | 13.52500 | 10.20000 |
| 2 | WGT. | 12.25000 | 14.00000 | 12.22222 |
|   | UNWGT. | 13.66667 | 14.00000 | 12.10000 |
| 3 | WGT. | 12.22222 | 11.28571 | 11.70000 |
|   | UNWGT. | 12.20000 | 12.40000 | 11.70000 |

* * * * * * * * * * * * * * * * * * * * A N A L Y S I S   O F   V A R I A N C E * * * * * * * * * * * * * * * * * * * * * *

COMBINED OBSERVED MEANS FOR DIET BY DAYLENTH

VARIABLE -- EGGS

COMBINED OBSERVED MEANS FOR DIET BY DAYLENTH     (CONT.)

VARIABLE -- EGGS     (CONT.)

| DAYLENTH | | DIET 1 | 2 |
|---|---|---|---|
| 1 | WGT. | 12.42857 | 12.00000 |
|   | UNWGT. | 12.66667 | 12.00000 |
| 2 | WGT. | 13.07692 | 13.50000 |
|   | UNWGT. | 13.77778 | 13.66667 |
| 3 | WGT. | 13.16667 | 11.71429 |
|   | UNWGT. | 13.33333 | 11.83333 |

VARIABLE -- WEIGHT

| DAYLENTH | | DIET 1 | 2 |
|---|---|---|---|
| 1 | WGT. | 13.21429 | 9.53333 |
|   | UNWGT. | 13.48333 | 9.53333 |
| 2 | WGT. | 14.92308 | 11.00000 |
|   | UNWGT. | 15.51111 | 11.00000 |
| 3 | WGT. | 14.58333 | 9.35714 |
|   | UNWGT. | 14.66667 | 9.53333 |

379

* * * * * * * * * * * * * * * * * A N A L Y S I S   O F   V A R I A N C E * * * * * * * * * * * * * * * * * *

(1) SPSS tests the sources of variation in reverse of the order listed for input.

WITHIN CELLS SUM-OF-SQUARES AND CROSS-PRODUCTS

(2a)          EGGS          WEIGHT

(2a) This is the error (within) sum of squares and products matrix used in Tables 4.7 and 4.8.

EGGS          509.66667
WEIGHT        210.66667     401.81667

---

* * * * * * * * * * * * * * * * * A N A L Y S I S   O F   V A R I A N C E * * * * * * * * * * * * * * * * * *

(1) EFFECT -- BREED(2) BY DIET(1) BY DAYLENTH(2)

ADJUSTED HYPOTHESIS SUM-OF-SQUARES AND CROSS-PRODUCTS

(2b)          EGGS          WEIGHT

(2b) This is the value of the sum of products found in Table 4.7 for the fourth comparison.

EGGS          12.82051
WEIGHT        6.15385       2.95385

(3) This is the value of Wilks' lambda found in Table 4.7 for the fourth comparison.

MULTIVARIATE TESTS OF SIGNIFICANCE (S = 1, M = 0, N = 30 1/2)

| TEST NAME | VALUE | APPROX. F | HYPOTH. DF | ERROR DF | SIG. OF F |
|-----------|-------|-----------|------------|----------|-----------|
| PILLAIS | .02471 | .79807 | 2.00 | 63.00 | .455 |
| HOTELLINGS | .02534 | .79807 | 2.00 | 63.00 | .455 |
| WILKS (3) | .97529 | .79807 | 2.00 | 63.00 | .455 |
| ROYS | .02471 | | | | |

EIGENVALUES AND CANONICAL CORRELATIONS

| ROOT NO. | EIGENVALUE | PCT. | CUM. PCT. | CANON. COR. |
|----------|------------|------|-----------|-------------|
| 1 | .02534 | 100.00000 | 100.00000 | .15719 |

DIMENSION REDUCTION ANALYSIS

| ROOTS | WILKS LAMBDA | F | HYPOTH. DF | ERROR DF | SIG. OF F |
|-------|--------------|---|------------|----------|-----------|
| | .97529 | .79807 | 2.00 | 63.00 | .455 |

* * * * * * * * * * * * * * * * * * * A N A L Y S I S   O F   V A R I A N C E * * * * * * * * * * * * * * * * * * * * * * * *

EFFECT .. BREED(2) BY DIET(1) BY LAYLENTH(2)    (CNT.)          ④ These are  the univariate F-ratios found  in Table
UNIVARIATE F-TESTS WITH (1,64) D. F.                               4.7 for the fourth comparison.

| VARIABLE | HYPOTH. SS | ERROR SS | HYPOTH. MS | ERROR MS | F | SIG. OF F |
|----------|-----------|----------|-----------|----------|---|-----------|
| EGGS     | 12.82051  | 509.66667 | 12.82051  | 7.96354  | 1.60990 | .209 |
| WEIGHT   | 2.95385   | 401.81667 | 2.95385   | 6.27839  | .47048  | .495 |

ROY-BARGMAN STEPDOWN F - TESTS

| VARIABLE | HYPOTH. MS | ERROR MS | STEP-DOWN F | HYPOTH. DF | ERROR DF | SIG. OF F |
|----------|-----------|----------|-------------|-----------|----------|-----------|
| EGGS     | 12.82051  | 7.96354  | 1.60990     | 1         | 64       | .209 |
| WEIGHT   | .05557    | 4.99586  | .01112      | 1         | 63       | .916 |

RAW DISCRIMINANT FUNCTION COEFFICIENTS

    FUNCTION NO.            1

VARIABLE

EGGS           -.33734
WEIGHT         -.03811

STANDARDIZED DISCRIMINANT FUNCTION COEFFICIENTS

    FUNCTION NO.            1

VARIABLE

EGGS           .95196
WEIGHT         .09550

* * * * * * * * * * * * * * * * * A N A L Y S I S   O F   V A R I A N C E * * * * * * * * * * * * * * * * * *

EFFECT -- BREED(2) BY DIET(1) BY LAYLENTH(1)
ADJUSTED HYPOTHESIS SUM-OF-SQUARES AND CROSS-PRODUCTS

(5) This is the value of the sum of squares and products found in Table 4.7 for the third comparison.

(6) This is the value of Wilks' lambda found in Table 4.7 for the third comparison.

|        | (5) EGGS   | WEIGHT   |
|--------|------------|----------|
| EGGS   | 99.41176   |          |
| WEIGHT | 58.50000   | 34.42500 |

MULTIVARIATE TESTS OF SIGNIFICANCE (S = 1, M = 0, N = 30 1/2)

| TEST NAME  | VALUE  | APPROX. F | HYPOTH. DF | ERROR DF | SIG. OF F |
|------------|--------|-----------|------------|----------|-----------|
| PILLAIS    | .16994 | 6.44927   | 2.00       | 63.00    | .003      |
| HOTELLINGS | .20474 | 6.44927   | 2.00       | 63.00    | .003      |
| WILKS      | (6) .83006 | 6.44927 | 2.00     | 63.00    | .003      |
| ROYS       | .16994 |           |            |          |           |

EIGENVALUES AND CANONICAL CORRELATIONS

| ROOT NO. | EIGENVALUE | PCT.      | CUM. PCT. | CANON. COR. |
|----------|------------|-----------|-----------|-------------|
| 1        | .20474     | 100.00000 | 100.00000 | .41224      |

DIMENSION REDUCTION ANALYSIS

| ROOTS    | WILKS LAMBDA | F       | HYPOTH. DF | ERROR DF | SIG. OF F |
|----------|--------------|---------|------------|----------|-----------|
| 1 TO 1   | .83006       | 6.44927 | 2.00       | 63.00    | .003      |

382

* * * * * * * * * * * * * * * * A N A L Y S I S   O F   V A R I A N C E * * * * * * * * * * * * * * * * * * *

①These are the univariate F-ratios found in Table
4.7 for the third comparison.

EFFECT .. BREED(2) BY DIET(1) BY LAYLENTH(1)    (CONT.)

UNIVARIATE F-TESTS WITH (1,64) D. F.

| VARIABLE | HYPOTH. SS | ERROR SS | HYPOTH. MS | ERROR MS | F | SIG. OF F |
|----------|-----------|----------|-----------|----------|---|-----------|
| EGGS | 99.41176 | 509.66667 | 99.41176 | 7.96354 | 12.48336 | .001 |
| WEIGHT | 34.42500 | 401.81667 | 34.42500 | 6.27839 | 5.48310 | .022 |

ROY-BARGMAN STEPDOWN F - TESTS

| VARIABLE | HYPOTH. MS | ERROR MS | STEP-DOWN F | HYPOTH. DF | ERROR DF | SIG. OF F |
|----------|-----------|----------|-------------|-----------|----------|-----------|
| EGGS | 99.41176 | 7.96354 | 12.48336 | 1 | 64 | .001 |
| WEIGHT | 2.55105 | 4.99586 | .51063 | 1 | 63 | .478 |

RAW DISCRIMINANT FUNCTION COEFFICIENTS

| VARIABLE | FUNCTION NO. 1 |
|----------|----------------|
| EGGS | .30534 |
| WEIGHT | .09808 |

STANDARDIZED DISCRIMINANT FUNCTION COEFFICIENTS

| VARIABLE | FUNCTION NO. 1 |
|----------|----------------|
| EGGS | .36165 |
| WEIGHT | .24576 |

CHAPTER 4:  THREE-WAY MANOVA

* * * * * * * * * * * * * * * * * * * * A N A L Y S I S   O F   V A R I A N C E * * * * * * * * * * * * * * * * * * * * * * * * * *

EFFECT -- BREED(1) BY DIET(1) BY LAYLENTH(2)
ADJUSTED HYPOTHESIS SUM-OF-SQUARES AND CROSS-PRODUCTS

**(8)** This is the value of the sum of squares and
products found in Table 4.7 for the second
comparison.

**(9)** This is the value of Wilks' lambda found in Table
4.7 for the second comparison.

            EGGS        WEIGHT

EGGS     120.33333
WEIGHT   122.61333   124.93653

----------------------------------------------------------------------------------------------------------------

MULTIVARIATE TESTS OF SIGNIFICANCE (S = 1, M = 0, N = 30 1/2)

TEST NAME         VALUE      APPROX. F      HYPOTH. DF      ERROR DF      SIG. OF F

PILLAIS          .27343      11.85419          2.00          63.00         .000
HOTELLINGS       .37632      11.85419          2.00          63.00         .000
WILKS      **(9)** .72657    11.85419          2.00          63.00         .000
RCYS             .27343

----------------------------------------------------------------------------------------------------------------

EIGENVALUES AND CANONICAL CORRELATIONS

RCCT NO.     EIGENVALUE        PCT.        CUM. PCT.      CANON. COR.

   1           .37632       100.00000     100.00000        .52290

----------------------------------------------------------------------------------------------------------------

DIMENSION REDUCTION ANALYSIS

BCOTS      WILKS LAMBDA          F        HYPOTH. DF      ERROR DF      SIG. OF F

1 TO 1        .72657        11.85419         2.00          63.00         .000

----------------------------------------------------------------------------------------------------------------

384

* * * * * * * * * * * * * * * * * * * A N A L Y S I S   O F   V A R I A N C E * * * * * * * * * * * * * * * * * * * * * * * *
*

EFFECT .. BREED(1) BY DIET(1) BY LAYLENTH(2)   (CONT.)          ⑩ These are the univariate F-ratios found   in Table
UNIVARIATE F-TESTS WITH (1,64) D. F.                              4.7 for the second comparison.

| VARIABLE | HYPOTH. SS | ERROR SS | HYPOTH. MS | ERROR MS | ⑩ F | SIG. OF F |
|---|---|---|---|---|---|---|
| EGGS | 120.33333 | 509.66667 | 120.33333 | 7.96354 | 15.11053 | .000 |
| WEIGHT | 124.93653 | 401.81667 | 124.93653 | 6.27839 | 19.89947 | .000 |

ROY-BARGMAN STEPDOWN F - TESTS

| VARIABLE | HYPOTH. MS | ERROR MS | STEP-DOWN F | HYPOTH. DF | ERROR DF | SIG. OF F |
|---|---|---|---|---|---|---|
| EGGS | 120.33333 | 7.96354 | 15.11053 | 1 | 64 | .000 |
| WEIGHT | 35.70352 | 4.99586 | 7.14662 | 1 | 63 | .010 |

RAW DISCRIMINANT FUNCTION COEFFICIENTS

FUNCTION NO.        1

| VARIABLE | |
|---|---|
| EGGS | .16691 |
| WEIGHT | .27526 |

STANDARDIZED DISCRIMINANT FUNCTION COEFFICIENTS

FUNCTION NO.        1

| VARIABLE | |
|---|---|
| EGGS | .47101 |
| WEIGHT | .68971 |

* * * * * * * * * * * * * * * A N A L Y S I S   O F   V A R I A N C E * * * * * * * * * * * * * * * *

EFFECT -- BREED(1) BY DIET(1) BY LAYLENTH(1)

ADJUSTED HYPOTHESIS SUM-OF-SQUARES AND CROSS-PRODUCTS

⑪ This is the value of the sum of squares and products found in Table 4.7 for the first comparison.

⑫ This is the value of Wilks' lambda found in Table 4.7 for the first comparison.

|        | EGGS       | WEIGHT    |
|--------|------------|-----------|
| EGGS   | ⑪ 255.20249 |           |
| WEIGHT | 195.98754  | 150.51231 |

MULTIVARIATE TESTS OF SIGNIFICANCE (S = 1, M = 0, N = 30 1/2)

| TEST NAME  | VALUE  | APPROX. F | HYPOTH. DF | ERROR DF | SIG. OF F |
|------------|--------|-----------|------------|----------|-----------|
| PILLAIS    | .37605 | 18.98490  | 2.00       | 63.00    | .000      |
| HOTELLINGS | .60270 | 18.98490  | 2.00       | 63.00    | .000      |
| WILKS      | ⑫ .62395 | 18.98490 | 2.00       | 63.00    | .000      |
| ROYS       | .37605 |           |            |          |           |

EIGENVALUES AND CANONICAL CORRELATIONS

| ROOT NO. | EIGENVALUE | PCT.      | CUM. PCT. | CANON. COR. |
|----------|------------|-----------|-----------|-------------|
| 1        | .60270     | 100.00000 | 100.00000 | .61323      |

DIMENSION REDUCTION ANALYSIS

| ROOTS  | WILKS LAMBDA | F        | HYPOTH. DF | ERROR DF | SIG. OF F |
|--------|--------------|----------|------------|----------|-----------|
| 1 TO 1 | .62395       | 18.98490 | 2.00       | 63.00    | .000      |

**\* \* \* \* \* \* \* \* \* \* \* \* \* A N A L Y S I S   O F   V A R I A N C E \* \* \* \* \* \* \* \* \* \* \* \* \* \* \* \* \* \* \* \***

EFFECT .. BREED(1) BY DIET(1) BY LAYLENTH(1)     (CONT.)
UNIVARIATE F-TESTS WITH (1,64) D. F.

| VARIABLE | HYPOTH. SS | ERROR SS | HYPOTH. MS | ERROR MS | F | SIG. OF F |
|---|---|---|---|---|---|---|
| EGGS | 255.20249 | 509.66667 | 255.20249 | 7.96354 | 32.04636 | .000 |
| WEIGHT | 150.51231 | 401.81667 | 150.51231 | 6.27839 | 23.97309 | .000 |

(13) These are the univariate F-ratios found in Table 4.7 for the first comparison.

ROY-BARGMAN STEPDOWN F - TESTS

| VARIABLE | HYPOTH. MS | ERROR MS | STEP-DOWN F | HYPOTH. DF | ERROR DF | SIG. OF F |
|---|---|---|---|---|---|---|
| EGGS | 255.20249 | 7.96354 | 32.04636 | 1 | 64 | .000 |
| WEIGHT | 21.38587 | 4.99586 | 4.28072 | 1 | 63 | .043 |

RAW DISCRIMINANT FUNCTION COEFFICIENTS

FUNCTION NO.          1

| VARIABLE | |
|---|---|
| EGGS | .24633 |
| WEIGHT | .18548 |

STANDARDIZED DISCRIMINANT FUNCTION COEFFICIENTS

FUNCTION NO.          1

| VARIABLE | |
|---|---|
| EGGS | .69513 |
| WEIGHT | .46476 |

Note: The first analysis also prints statistical tests for the other sources of variation listed in the DESIGN statement. These tests were not shown here because they are exactly the same as the tests from the overall analysis, which we show next.

* * * * * * * * * * * * * * * * * A N A L Y S I S   O F   V A R I A N C E * * * * * * * * * * * * * * * * * * * * * * * * * *

EFFECT .. BREED BY DIET BY DAYLENTH

ADJUSTED HYPOTHESIS SUM-OF-SQUARES AND CROSS-PRODUCTS

|        | EGGS | WEIGHT |
|--------|------|--------|
| EGGS   | (14) 470.37092 | |
| WEIGHT | 362.24699 | 292.84952 |

(14) This is the value of the sum of squares and products found in Table 4.8 for Br * Di * Da.

(15) This is the value of Wilks' lambda found in Table 4.8 for Br * Di * Da.

MULTIVARIATE TESTS OF SIGNIFICANCE (S = 2, M = 1/2, N = 30 1/2)

| TEST NAME | VALUE | APPROX. F | HYPOTH. DF | ERROR DF | SIG. OF F |
|-----------|-------|-----------|------------|----------|-----------|
| PILLAIS    | .56353       | 6.27677 | 8.00 | 128.00 | .000 |
| HOTELLINGS | 1.15722      | 8.96844 | 8.00 | 124.00 | 0.0  |
| WILKS      | (15) .45498  | 7.59984 | 8.00 | 126.00 | .000 |
| ROYS       | .52851       |         |      |        |      |

EIGENVALUES AND CANONICAL CORRELATIONS

| ROOT NO. | EIGENVALUE | PCT. | CUM. PCT. | CANON. COR. |
|----------|-----------|------|-----------|-------------|
| 1 | 1.12093 | 96.86418 | 96.86418 | .72699 |
| 2 | .03629  | 3.13582  | 100.00000 | .18713 |

DIMENSION REDUCTION ANALYSIS

| ROOTS | WILKS LAMBDA | F | HYPOTH. DF | ERROR DF | SIG. OF F |
|-------|--------------|---|------------|----------|-----------|
| 1 TO 2 | .45498 | 7.59984 | 8.00 | 126.00 | .000 |
| 2 TO 2 | .96498 | .76425 | 3.00 | 127.50 | .516 |

388

* * * * * * * * * * * * * * * * * * * A N A L Y S I S   O F   V A R I A N C E * * * * * * * * * * * * * * * * * * * *

EFFECT .. BREED BY DIET BY DAYLENTH       (CONT.)                (16) These are  the univariate F-ratios found  in Table
                                                                      4.8 for Br * Di * Da.

UNIVARIATE F-TESTS WITH (4,64) D. F.

| VARIABLE | HYPOTH. SS | ERROR SS | HYPOTH. MS | ERROR MS | (16) F | SIG. OF F |
|----------|-----------|----------|-----------|----------|--------|-----------|
| EGGS   | 470.37092 | 509.66667 | 117.59273 | 7.96354 | 14.76639 | .000 |
| WEIGHT | 292.84952 | 401.81667 | 73.21238  | 6.27839 | 11.66102 | .000 |

* * * * * * * * * * * * * * * * A N A L Y S I S   O F   V A R I A N C E * * * * * * * * * * * * * * * * * * * *

EFFECT.. DIET BY DAYLENTH

ADJUSTED HYPOTHESIS SUM-OF-SQUARES AND CROSS-PRODUCTS

(17)    EGGS        WEIGHT

EGGS      5.96348
WEIGHT    3.03755     4.50557

(17) This is the value of the sum of squares and products found in Table 4.8 for Di * Da.

(18) This is the value of Wilks' lambda found in Table 4.8 for Di * Da.

MULTIVARIATE TESTS OF SIGNIFICANCE (S = 2, M = 1/2, N = 30 1/2)

| TEST NAME | VALUE | APPROX. F | HYPOTH. DF | ERROR DF | SIG. OF F |
|---|---|---|---|---|---|
| PILLAIS | .02104 | .34030 | 4.00 | 128.00 | .850 |
| HOTELLINGS | .02127 | .32976 | 4.00 | 124.00 | .858 |
| WILKS (18) | .97906 | .33503 | 4.00 | 126.00 | .854 |
| RCYS | .01227 | | | | |

EIGENVALUES AND CANONICAL CORRELATIONS

| ROOT NO. | EIGENVALUE | PCT. | CUM. PCT. | CANON. COR. |
|---|---|---|---|---|
| 1 | .01242 | 58.37478 | 58.37478 | .11076 |
| 2 | .00886 | 41.62522 | 100.00000 | .09369 |

DIMENSION REDUCTION ANALYSIS

| ROOTS | WILKS LAMBDA | F | HYPOTH. DF | ERROR DF | SIG. OF F |
|---|---|---|---|---|---|
| 1 TO 2 | .97906 | .33503 | 4.00 | 126.00 | .854 |
| 2 TO 2 | .99122 | .56234 | 1.00 | 63.50 | .456 |

* * * * * * * * * * * * * * * * * * A N A L Y S I S   O F   V A R I A N C E * * * * * * * * * * * * * * * * * * * * * * * * * * * *

EFFECT .. DIET BY DAYLENTH    (CONT.)

UNIVARIATE F-TESTS WITH (2,64) D. F.

(19) These are the univariate F-ratios found  in Table
     4.8 for Di * Da.

| VARIABLE | HYPOTH. SS | ERROR SS | HYPOTH. MS | ERROR MS | (19) F | SIG. OF F |
|----------|-----------|----------|-----------|----------|--------|-----------|
| EGGS   | 5.96348 | 509.66667 | 2.98174 | 7.96354 | .37442 | .689 |
| WEIGHT | 4.50557 | 401.81667 | 2.25278 | 6.27839 | .35882 | .700 |

* * * * * * * * * * * * * * * * * * * * * A N A L Y S I S   O F   V A R I A N C E * * * * * * * * * * * * * * * * * * * * * * * *

EFFECT .. BREED BY DAYLENTH

ADJUSTED HYPOTHESIS SUM-OF-SQUARES AND CROSS-PRODUCTS

**(20)** This is the value of the sum of squares and products found in Table 4.8 for Br * Da.

**(21)** This is the value of Wilks' lambda found in Table 4.8 for Br * Da.

|  | EGGS | WEIGHT |
|---|---|---|
| **(20)** |  |  |
| EGGS | 16.46249 |  |
| WEIGHT | -8.09225 | 22.60485 |

---

MULTIVARIATE TESTS OF SIGNIFICANCE (S = 2, M = 1/2, N = 30 1/2)

| TEST NAME | VALUE | APPROX. F | HYPOTH. DF | ERROR DF | SIG. OF F |
|---|---|---|---|---|---|
| PILLAIS | .12157 | 1.03554 | 8.00 | 128.00 | .413 |
| HOTELLINGS | .13431 | 1.04092 | 8.00 | 124.00 | .409 |
| WILKS | **(21)** .88011 | 1.03853 | 8.00 | 126.00 | .411 |
| ROYS | .10565 |  |  |  |  |

---

EIGENVALUES AND CANONICAL CORRELATIONS

| ROOT NO. | EIGENVALUE | PCT. | CUM. PCT. | CANON. COR. |
|---|---|---|---|---|
| 1 | .11813 | 87.95174 | 87.95174 | .32504 |
| 2 | .01618 | 12.04826 | 100.00000 | .12619 |

---

DIMENSION REDUCTION ANALYSIS

| ROOTS | WILKS LAMBDA | F | HYPOTH. DF | ERROR DF | SIG. OF F |
|---|---|---|---|---|---|
| 1 TO 2 | .88011 | 1.03853 | 8.00 | 126.00 | .411 |
| 2 TO 2 | .98408 | .34249 | 3.00 | 127.50 | .795 |

---

* * * * * * * * * * * * * * * * * * * * * A N A L Y S I S  O F  V A R I A N C E * * * * * * * * * * * * * * * * * * * * * *

EFFECT -- BREED BY DAYLENTH   (CONT.)

UNIVARIATE F-TESTS WITH (4,64) D. F.

| VARIABLE | HYPOTH. SS | ERROR SS | HYPOTH. MS | ERROR MS | F | SIG. OF F |
|----------|-----------|----------|-----------|----------|---|-----------|
| EGGS | 16.46249 | 509.66667 | 4.11562 | 7.96354 | .51681 | .724 |
| WEIGHT | 22.60485 | 401.81667 | 5.65121 | 6.27839 | .90011 | .469 |

(22) These are the univariate F-ratios found in Table 4.8 for Br * Da.

\* \* \* \* \* \* \* \* \* \* \* \* \* \* \* \* \* \* \* A N A L Y S I S   O F   V A R I A N C E \* \* \* \* \* \* \* \* \* \* \* \* \* \* \* \* \* \* \* \* \* \* \* \* \* \*

EFFECT .. BREED BY DIET

\* \* \* \* \* \* \* \* \* \* \* \* \* \* \* \* \* \* \* \* \* \* \* \* \* \*

ADJUSTED HYPOTHESIS SUM-OF-SQUARES AND CROSS-PRODUCTS

(23) This is the value of the sum of squares and products found in Table 4.8 for Br * Di.

(24) This is the value of Wilks' lambda found in Table 4.8 for Br * Di.

|        | EGGS      | WEIGHT   |
|--------|-----------|----------|
| EGGS   | (23) 31.60954 |          |
| WEIGHT | -2.34564  | .91192   |

MULTIVARIATE TESTS OF SIGNIFICANCE (S = 2, M = 1/2, N = 30 1/2)

| TEST NAME  | VALUE   | APPROX. F | HYPOTH. DF | ERROR DF | SIG. OF F |
|------------|---------|-----------|------------|----------|-----------|
| PILLAIS    | .08134  | 1.35660   | 4.00       | 128.00   | .253      |
| HOTELLINGS | .08824  | 1.36769   | 4.00       | 124.00   | .249      |
| WILKS      | (24) .91879 | 1.36256 | 4.00       | 126.00   | .251      |
| ROYS       | .07966  |           |            |          |           |

EIGENVALUES AND CANONICAL CORRELATIONS

| ROOT NO. | EIGENVALUE | PCT.      | CUM. PCT.  | CANON. CCR. |
|----------|------------|-----------|------------|-------------|
| 1        | .08656     | 98.09630  | 98.09630   | .28224      |
| 2        | .00168     | 1.90370   | 100.00000  | .04095      |

DIMENSION REDUCTION ANALYSIS

| ROOTS   | WILKS LAMBDA | F       | HYPOTH. DF | ERROR DF | SIG. OF F |
|---------|--------------|---------|------------|----------|-----------|
| 1 TO 2  | .91879       | 1.36256 | 4.00       | 126.00   | .251      |
| 2 TO 2  | .99832       | .10667  | 1.00       | 63.50    | .745      |

02/02/83     PAGE  92

* * * * * * * * * * * * * * * * * A N A L Y S I S   O F   V A R I A N C E * * * * * * * * * * * * * * * * *

EFFECT .. BREED BY DIET (CONT.)

(25) These are the univariate F-ratios found in Table 4.8 for Br * Di.

UNIVARIATE F-TESTS WITH (2,64) D. F.

| VARIABLE | HYPOTH. SS | ERROR SS | HYPOTH. MS | ERROR MS | (25) F | SIG. OF F |
|---|---|---|---|---|---|---|
| EGGS | 31.60954 | 509.66667 | 15.80477 | 7.96354 | 1.98464 | .146 |
| WEIGHT | .91192 | 401.81667 | .45596 | 6.27839 | .07262 | .930 |

* * * * * * * * * * * * * * * * * * A N A L Y S I S   O F   V A R I A N C E * * * * * * * * * * * * * * * * * *

EFFECT -- DAYLENTH

ADJUSTED HYPOTHESIS SUM-OF-SQUARES AND CROSS-PRODUCTS

(26)    EGGS         WEIGHT

| | EGGS | WEIGHT |
|---|---|---|
| EGGS | 29.10416 | |
| WEIGHT | 34.76235 | 42.65615 |

(26) This is the value of the sum of squares and products found in Table 4.8 for Day Length (Da).

(27) This is the value of Wilks' lambda found in Table 4.8 for Day Length (Da).

MULTIVARIATE TESTS OF SIGNIFICANCE (S = 2, M = 1/2, N = 30 1/2)

| TEST NAME | VALUE | APPROX. F | HYPOTH. DF | ERROR DF | SIG. OF F |
|---|---|---|---|---|---|
| PILLAIS | .10520 | 1.77657 | 4.00 | 128.00 | .138 |
| HOTELLINGS | .11713 | 1.81545 | 4.00 | 124.00 | .130 |
| WILKS (27) | .89499 | 1.79674 | 4.00 | 126.00 | .134 |
| ROYS | .10341 | | | | |

EIGENVALUES AND CANONICAL CORRELATIONS

| RCCI NO. | EIGENVALUE | PCT. | CUM. PCT. | CANON. CCR. |
|---|---|---|---|---|
| 1 | .11534 | 98.47484 | 98.47484 | .32158 |
| 2 | .00179 | 1.52516 | 100.00000 | .04223 |

DIMENSION REDUCTION ANALYSIS

| ROOTS | WILKS LAMBDA | F | HYPOTH. DF | ERROR DF | SIG. OF F |
|---|---|---|---|---|---|
| 1 TO 2 | .89499 | 1.79674 | 4.00 | 126.00 | .134 |
| 2 TO 2 | .99822 | .11343 | 1.00 | 63.50 | .737 |

* * * * * * * * * * * * * * * * * * A N A L Y S I S   O F   V A R I A N C E * * * * * * * * * * * * * * * * * * * * * *

EFFECT .. DAYLENTH     (CONT.)                    (28) These are the univariate F-ratios found  in Table
                                                       4.8 for Day Length (Da).
UNIVARIATE F-TESTS WITH (2,64) D. F.

| VARIABLE | HYPOTH. SS | ERROR SS | HYPOTH. MS | ERROR MS | (28) F | SIG. OF F |
|----------|-----------|----------|-----------|----------|--------|-----------|
| EGGS     | 29.10416  | 509.66667 | 14.55208  | 7.96354  | 1.82734 | .169 |
| WEIGHT   | 42.65615  | 401.81667 | 21.32807  | 6.27839  | 3.39706 | .040 |

* * * * * * * * * * * * * * * * * A N A L Y S I S  O F  V A R I A N C E * * * * * * * * * * * * * * * * * * *

EFFECT -- DIET

ADJUSTED HYPOTHESIS SUM-OF-SQUARES AND CROSS-PRODUCTS

|  | EGGS | WEIGHT |
|---|---|---|
| (29) | | |
| EGGS | 11.16202 | |
| WEIGHT | 66.61819 | 397.59688 |

(29) This is the value of the sum of squares and products found in Table 4.8 for Diet (Di).

(30) This is the value of Wilks' lambda found in Table 4.8 for Diet (Di).

MULTIVARIATE TESTS OF SIGNIFICANCE (S = 1, M = 0, N = 30 1/2)

| TEST NAME | VALUE | APPROX. F | HYPOTH. DF | ERROR DF | SIG. OF F |
|---|---|---|---|---|---|
| PILLAIS | .52746 | 35.16157 | 2.00 | 63.00 | 0.0 |
| HOTELLINGS | 1.11624 | 35.16157 | 2.00 | 63.00 | 0.0 |
| WILKS | (30) .47254 | 35.16157 | 2.00 | 63.00 | 0.0 |
| ROYS | .52746 | | | | |

EIGENVALUES AND CANONICAL CORRELATIONS

| ROOT NO. | EIGENVALUE | PCT. | CUM. PCT. | CANON. COR. |
|---|---|---|---|---|
| 1 | 1.11624 | 100.00000 | 100.00000 | .72627 |

DIMENSION REDUCTION ANALYSIS

| ROOTS | WILKS LAMBDA | F | HYPOTH. DF | ERROR DF | SIG. OF F |
|---|---|---|---|---|---|
| 1 TO 1 | .47254 | 35.16157 | 2.00 | 63.00 | 0.0 |

* * * * * * * * * * * * * * * * * * * A N A L Y S I S   O F   V A R I A N C E * * * * * * * * * * * * * * * * * * * * * * * *

EFFECT .. DIET  (CONT.)                          (31) These are the univariate F-ratios found in Table
                                                      4.8 for Diet (Di).

UNIVARIATE F-TESTS WITH (1,64) D. F.

| VARIABLE | HYPOTH. SS | ERROR SS | HYPOTH. MS | ERROR MS | F | SIG. OF F |
|----------|------------|----------|------------|----------|---|-----------|
| EGGS   | 11.16202  | 509.66667 | 11.16202  | 7.96354 | 1.40164  | .241 |
| WEIGHT | 397.59688 | 401.81667 | 397.59688 | 6.27839 | 63.32789 | 0.0  |

(31) appears at the F column.

\* \* \* \* \* \* \* \* \* \* \* \* \* \* \* \* \* \* A N A L Y S I S   O F   V A R I A N C E \* \* \* \* \* \* \* \* \* \* \* \* \* \* \* \* \* \* \* \* \* \*

EFFECT .. BREED

ADJUSTED HYPOTHESIS SUM-OF-SQUARES AND CROSS-PRODUCTS

|        | EGGS    | WEIGHT   |
|--------|---------|----------|
| EGGS   | (32) .33462 |          |
| WEIGHT | .01733  | 50.15179 |

(32) This is the value of the sum of squares and products found in Table 4.8 for Breed (Br).

(33) This is the value of Wilks' lambda found in Table 4.8 for Breed (Br).

MULTIVARIATE TESTS OF SIGNIFICANCE (S = 2, M = 1/2, N = 30 1/2)

| TEST NAME  | VALUE   | APPROX. F | HYPOTH. DF | ERROR DF | SIG. OF F |
|------------|---------|-----------|------------|----------|-----------|
| PILLAIS    | .13820  | 2.37534   | 4.00       | 128.00   | .055      |
| HOTELLINGS | .16014  | 2.48212   | 4.00       | 124.00   | .047      |
| WILKS      | (33) .86189 | 2.43007   | 4.00       | 126.00   | .051      |
| ROYS       | .13754  |           |            |          |           |

EIGENVALUES AND CANONICAL CORRELATIONS

| ROOT NO. | EIGENVALUE | PCT.      | CUM. PCT. | CANON. COR. |
|----------|------------|-----------|-----------|-------------|
| 1        | .15948     | 99.59036  | 99.59036  | .37087      |
| 2        | .00066     | .40964    | 100.00000 | .02560      |

DIMENSION REDUCTION ANALYSIS

| ROOTS   | WILKS LAMBDA | F       | HYPOTH. DF | ERROR DF | SIG. OF F |
|---------|--------------|---------|------------|----------|-----------|
| 1 TO 2  | .86189       | 2.43007 | 4.00       | 126.00   | .051      |
| 2 TO 2  | .99934       | .04165  | 1.00       | 63.50    | .839      |

400

CHAPTER 4: THREE-WAY MANOVA 02/02/83 PAGE 98

\* \* \* \* \* \* \* \* \* \* \* \* \* \* \* \* \* A N A L Y S I S   O F   V A R I A N C E \* \* \* \* \* \* \* \* \* \* \* \* \* \* \* \* \* \* \* \* \* \* \* \* \* \* \*

EFFECT -- BREED (CONT.)        (34) These are the univariate F-ratios found in Table
                                    4.8 for Breed (Br).

UNIVARIATE F-TESTS WITH (2,64) D. F.

| VARIABLE | HYPOTH. SS | ERROR SS | HYPOTH. MS | ERROR MS | F (34) | SIG. OF F |
|----------|-----------|----------|------------|----------|---|-----------|
| EGGS   | .33462  | 509.66667 | .16731   | 7.96354 | .02101  | .979 |
| WEIGHT | 50.15179 | 401.81667 | 25.07590 | 6.27839 | 3.99400 | .023 |

401

# CHAPTER 5

## ANALYSIS OF COVARIANCE
### by Charles Kufs

### Introduction

In Chapter 2, a one-way analysis of variance, ANOVA, was considered where the model was

$$y(i) = u + a(i) + e(i)$$

with

$y(i)$ = the observed value of the dependent variable in cell i,

$u$ = the grand mean,
$a(i)$ = the effect of treatment i, and
$e(i)$ = the error in cell i.

In the analysis of covariance, ANCOVA, the precision of the mean comparisons is increased by reducing systematic errors. This is accomplished by removing the effects of a "distractor" variable, or covariate, from the error term, such that

$$e(i) = b(x(i) - \bar{x}) + e'(i))$$

where $b(x(i) - \bar{x})$ is the effect attributable to the covariate. Here, "x" represents the covariate; "$\bar{x}$" represents the grand mean (either weighted or unweighted) on the covariate and "b" is the pooled regression coefficient found by pooling the coefficients from the regression of y on x in each cell. A covariate is a variable which is related to the treatment factor and/or the dependent variable such that it obscures group differences on the treatments. If $b(x(i) - \bar{x})$ is substantial, $e'(i)$ will be much smaller than $e(i)$ and more sensitive statistical tests will result. The ANCOVA model, then is

$$y(i) = u + a(i) + b(x(i) - \bar{x}) + e'(i).$$

This relationship is commonly rewritten as

$$y(i) - b(x(i) - \bar{x}) = u + a(i) + e'(i)$$

where the term $y(i) - b(x(i) - \bar{x})$ is called an adjusted score. The analysis of covariance, then, is simply an analysis of variance on adjusted scores, which are the residuals of the regression of y on x, given the independent variable(s). Thus, while ANOVA deals with qualitative factors and regression analysis deals with quantitative variables, ANCOVA represents the linking of the two approaches. Information on the computational procedure can be found in Huitema (1980), Kerlinger and Pedhazur (1973, Chapter 10) and Winer (1971, Chapter 10).

The primary purpose of ANCOVA (i.e. the reduction of error variance) is identical to that of blocking in ANOVA, but is an indirect, or statistical method of doing so. Randomized blocking, in fact, proceeds much the same way as ANCOVA, only the covariate is a categorical factor. From theoretical considerations, Cochran (1957, p. 262-263) concluded that the correlation between y and x, (p), had to be greater than 0.3 in absolute value for covariance analysis to have a substantially greater precision. Cox (1957), in studying true and apparent imprecision, determined that (p) should exceed 0.6, or better, 0.8, for ANCOVA to be more precise. Should (p) be less than 0.4, he considered blocking preferable. Feldt (1958) also studied experimental imprecision and basically agreed with Cox.

Because ANCOVA results in a loss of only one degree of freedom per covariate from the error term, the method provides for more powerful tests than do block designs having more than two levels on the blocking factor. Furthermore, if the number of treatments is large, it may be difficult to construct homogeneous blocks. Other considerations are given by Elashoff (1969, p. 399).

ANCOVA has other uses besides reducing the error variance. Cochran (1957, p. 262-267) describes several ways in which the technique can be applied, including to provide information on the nature of treatment effects, to fit regressions in multiple classifications, and to analyze data when some observations are missing. In addition, ANCOVA can be useful where intact groups are unavoidable. This point is discussed by Cook and Campbell (1979, Chapter 4) and Kerlinger and Pedhazur (1973, p. 366).

Analysis of covariance should, then, appear to be a panacea to researchers plagued by systematic errors that cannot be experimentally controlled. But ANCOVA has its costs as well as its benefits. Overall and Woodward (1977, p. 171) state, "In spite of strong statistical sanction, the important method has been so maligned in the psychological literature that many substantive researchers are afraid to use it except in the most conventional circumstances." Here, psychology is typical of most experimental research. The reason for this avoidance, the cost of ANCOVA, is the rigorous assumptions which are necessitated by the technique.

## Assumptions

In addition to the statistical requirements of the ANOVA model, ANCOVA demands that:

   1) Subjects are randomly assigned to treatments, or at worst, that treatments are randomly assigned to intact groups;

   2) Within each treatment, y scores have a linear regression on x scores; and finally

   3) The covariate is not influenced by the treatments, such that the slope of the regression of y on x is the same for all treatments (termed the 'homogeneity of regressions' or 'parallelism' assumption).

Kahneman (1965) and Lord (1960) present a case for also requiring that the covariate be measured without error. However, Overall and Woodward (1977) show, through Monte Carlo simulation, that this assumption is not essential so long as assignment to treatments is either random or is dependent in some way on the observed covariate scores.

   The random assignment of subjects and/or treatments can sometimes be the most restrictive of the ANCOVA assumptions. This is because it excludes attribute factors (i.e. conditions innate to the subject of the analysis) such as rock type, species, sex, or socioeconomic class. In cases where a small number of intact groups, such as classrooms or sample localities are to be examined, treatments should be randomly assigned. When a larger number of intact groups is available, the unit of analysis should be the group, and groups should be randomly assigned to treatments. Where subjects and treatments occur naturally together, as in attribute factors, covariance analysis can be misleading. This topic is discussed further by Evans and Anastasio (1968) and Elashoff (1969, p. 386-388).

   Assumptions concerning the regression of y on x are treated extensively in many textbooks on experimental design. Linearity is necessary if the regression term in the model is to adequately adjust y scores. Examining the scatter plots of y versus x for each treatment group is a simple yet effective way to assess linearity. Where nonlinear relationships obtain, transformations can usually correct this situation. Hoerl (1954) discusses the selection of functions for correcting violations of this assumption.

More difficult to evaluate and correct is the violation of the parallelism hypothesis. Because the model includes only one regression coefficient to adjust the y scores, the relationship between x and y must have the same slope (i.e. must be parallel) in all the cells. Studies by Peckham (1968) and Atiqulla (1964) suggest that as the degree of heterogeneity of the slopes increases, ANCOVA becomes more conservative with respect to making Type I errors. However, as Glass, Peckham, and Sanders (1972, p. 279) note, further investigation into the power of ANCOVA when slopes are unequal is still needed.

Consequences of violating ANCOVA assumptions are reviewed by Elashoff (1969). In summary, she states "...violations of the assumptions of linearity, homogeneity of regressions, normality or homogeneity of variances will be less serious if individuals have been assigned to treatments at random and the x variable has a normal distribution" (p. 396). Thus, where the necessary conditions apply, covariance analysis is a potent technique for increasing the precision of statistical tests.

## Organization of Programs

To illustrate the use of the computer packages for ANCOVA, a fictitious problem was designed and appropriate data were generated. Nineteen computer runs follow which show One- and Two-way designs having one or two covariates in both univariate and multivariate situations. These programs and their features are described in Table 5.1. Only fixed effects designs are considered. More information on other topics of interest can be found in the appendices and in the earlier chapters of this book.

The programs considered in this chapter include BMDP1V, BMDP2V, BMDP4V, SAS(GLM), SPSS(ANCVA), and SPSS(MANOVA). While several of the regression analysis programs, such as the SPSS subprogram REGRESSION, can also perform the analysis of covariance, they require the user to either input or generate the coded vectors for the grouping variables. Only those programs which were written primarily for ANOVA and/or MANOVA have been considered.

## Analysis of Covariance Presentations

The example conceived to demonstrate the use of ANCOVA reflects a real situation involving groundwater quality, water well design, and environmental influences. More specifically, it focuses on the influences of faulty well construction and fertilizer use on the concentration of certain contaminants in drinking water.

Table 5.1
Descriptions of the Programs Run on the
Analysis of Covariance Examples in Chapter 5

| Program | Program Number | Mode[1] | Page | I/O Features |
|---|---|---|---|---|
| | | | | |
| | | Volume 1: BMDP | | |
| | | | | |
| BMDP1V | 5-1 | U | 279 | One-Way, two treatments, one covariate |
| BMDP2V | 5-2 | U | 302 | One-Way, two treatments, one covariate |
| BMDP4V | 5-3 | U | 306 | One-Way, two treatments, one covariate |
| BMDP2V | 5-4 | U | 309 | Two-Way, (3x2), one covariate |
| BMDP4V | 5-5 | U | 314 | Two-Way, (3x2), one covariate |
| BMDP2V | 5-6 | U | 318 | Two-Way, (3x2), two covariates |
| BMDP4V | 5-7 | U | 323 | Two-Way, (3x2), two covariates |
| BMDP4V | 5-8 | M | 327 | One-Way, two treatments, three dependent variables, one covariate |
| BMDP4V | 5-9 | M | 332 | Two-Way, (3x2), three dependent variables, two covariates |
| | | | | |
| | | Volume 2: SAS | | |
| | | | | |
| SAS(GLM) | 5-1 | U | 309 | One-Way, two treatments one covariate |
| SAS(GLM) | 5-2 | U | 315 | Two-Way, (3x2), one covariate |
| SAS(GLM) | 5-3 | U | 321 | Two-Way, (3x2), two covariates |

Table 5.1, continued

| Program | Program Number | Mode[1] | Page | I/O Features |
|---------|---------|------|------|--------------|
| SAS(GLM) | 5-4 | M | 327 | One-Way, two treatments, three dependent variables, one covariate |
| SAS(GLM) | 5-5 | M | 338 | Two-Way, (3x2), three dependent variables, two covariates |

Volume 3: SPSS and SPSSX

| Program | Program Number | Mode[1] | Page | I/O Features |
|---------|---------|------|------|--------------|
| SPSS-SPSSX (ANOVA) & (MANOVA) | 5-1 | U | 427 | One-Way, two treatments, one covariate, use of PRINT FORMATS and ERROR(W) |
| SPSS-SPSSX (ANOVA) & (MANOVA) | 5-2 | U | 437 | Two-Way, (3x2), one covariate, use of '+' sign to lump sources of variation |
| SPSS-SPSSX (ANOVA) & (MANOVA) | 5-3 | U | 450 | Two-Way, (3x2), two covariates, use of '+' sign to lump sources of variation and use of the CONTIN specification |
| SPSS-SPSSX (MANOVA) | 5-4 | U | 464 | One-Way, two treatments, three dependent variables, one covariate |
| SPSS-SPSSX (MANOVA) | 5-5 | M | 477 | Two-Way, (3x2), three dependent variables, two covariates, use of '+' sign to lump sources of variation and use of CONTIN specification |

[1]Mode is coded U for univariate or M for multivariate.

The main pollutant considered by this study is the nitrate ion, $NO_3$. Nitrates have been implicated in cases of methemaglobinemia, or 'blue babies' disease, in children under six months of age. Drinking water commonly has less than 45 parts per million (ppm) of nitrate. This pollutant is particularly important because it is very expensive to remove.

Well design can play an important part in water quality, especially in places where thick soil layers are sealed off, or cased, to prevent contamination. In these situations, it is common for water to flow down the outside of the well casing rather than through the soil where it might be purified. When this happens, the security of the seal, where the casing meets bedrock, is critical. If the casing is cemented, or grouted to the bedrock, no unfiltered water can enter the well (see Figure 5.1). All too often, however, well drillers will merely hammer the casing into the bedrock, thus leaving gaps (see Figure 5.2). This latter construction could, then, be more susceptable to pollution.

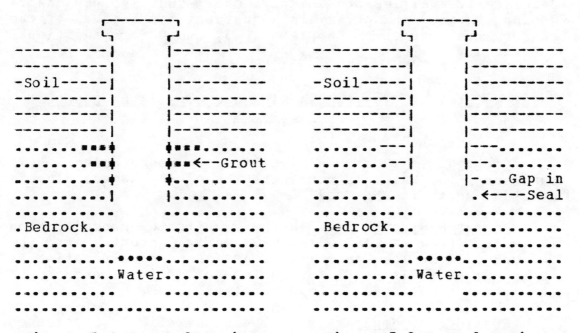

Figure 5.1 Grouted Casing          Figure 5.2 Jammed Casing

The purpose of this hypothetical study is to assess the effects that well construction and the nearby use of different types of fertilizers will have on the concentration of the nitrate ion. It was recognized, however, that the depth to the bedrock/casing seal and the total amount of ions in the water could disrupt the test. Hence, these effects had to be removed prior to testing mean differences.

The experiment involved drilling an observation well on the land of sixty-nine farmers who were each randomly assigned one of three different brands of fertilizer. Wells were situated so that there was no contamination between them. Each well's casing was, randomly, either grouted or jammed into bedrock. All the farmers agreed to plant the same crop, use equivalent amounts of their respective fertilizers, irrigate within designated limits, and in general, hold all other factors constant. All farms experienced roughly the same crop yield.

The wells were classed as to whether their casing was grouted or not (SEAL), and as to which fertilizer (FERT), A, B, or C, was used nearby. Measurements were taken of the total dissolved solids (TDS) content of each well's water and the depth to the bedrock seal (DEPTH) before the spring planting. The nitrate concentration (NO3) was measured after the fall harvest. In summary, there was one dependent variable, NO3, two factors, SEAL and FERT, and two covariates, DEPTH and TDS. Examples of different designs utilizing some or all of these components follow. Because the examples are simply One- and Two-way ANOVA designs (once the covariate adjustment has been made) the reader should refer to Chapters 2, 3, and 4 for additional information.

## Univariate, One-Way ANCOVA With One Covariate: Planned Comparisons

Problem. Does a well's bedrock/casing seal influence the nitrate concentration of the water, given a constant depth to the seal?

Research Hypothesis. The mean nitrate concentration in water from wells with the casing grouted into the bedrock will be less than the mean nitrate concentration in water from wells with the casing jammed into bedrock, if the depth to the seal is held constant.

Statistical Hypotheses. The statistical hypotheses are written in symbolic form to match the research hypotheses.

Null Hypothesis        H(0): u(grouted) = u(jammed)
Alternate Hypothesis H(A): u(grouted) < u(jammed)

This null hypothesis will be tested at the .05 level of significance.

Data. The data are presented in Table 5.2 as a univariate, one covariate, unequal n problem.

One-Way ANCOVA Table. Table 5.3 is the ANCOVA table for the One-way experiment. These results indicate that the type of seal does influence the amount of nitrate contamination of the well's water, and that the use of the covariate was appropriate to increase the precision of the experiment. Further discussion of the example can be found on the annotated computer output.

Table 5.2
Data for the One-Way ANCOVA Example

-------------------------------------------------------------
| | Grouted | | | | | Jammed | | | |
| NO3 | Depth | NO3 | Depth | | NO3 | Depth | NO3 | Depth |
|------|-------|------|-------|---|------|-------|------|-------|
| 48 | 48 | 37 | 59 | | 51 | 45 | 41.5 | 59 |
| 38 | 59 | 37 | 53 | | 55.5 | 50 | 44 | 52 |
| 36 | 67 | 30 | 67 | | 51 | 59 | 55.5 | 53 |
| 51 | 50 | 37 | 54 | | 58 | 52 | 50 | 51 |
| 34 | 59 | 42 | 49 | | 58.5 | 55 | 40.5 | 53 |
| 41.5 | 58 | 38.5 | 58 | | 51 | 51 | 61 | 60 |
| 45.5 | 57 | 50 | 54 | | 55.5 | 45 | 45.5 | 61 |
| 44 | 61 | 49 | 52 | | 60 | 52 | 61 | 44 |
| 47 | 62 | 45 | 64 | | 60 | 46 | 58 | 49 |
| 45 | 50 | 33.5 | 67 | | 46 | 48 | 37.5 | 62 |
| 45 | 51 | 57 | 43 | | 51 | 54 | 58 | 56 |
| 40.5 | 61 | 41.5 | 61 | | 53.5 | 56 | 47 | 58 |
| 37.5 | 58 | 48 | 54 | | 48 | 53 | 49 | 49 |
| 38 | 48 | 39.5 | 51 | | 43 | 64 | | |
| 36 | 49 | 37.5 | 63 | | 47 | 60 | | |
| 38 | 52 | 47 | 57 | | 59 | 57 | | |
| 38.5 | 67 | 45.5 | 49 | | 57 | 56 | | |
| 33.5 | 65 | 37 | 61 | | 51 | 51 | | |
| 34 | 57 | | | | 54.5 | 47 | | |

-------------------------------------------------------------

Univariate, Two-Way ANCOVA (3x2) With One Covariate:
Overall Test and Post Hoc Comparisons

Problem. Does a well's bedrock/casing seal or the type of fertilizer used nearby influence the nitrate concentration of its water, given a constant depth to the seal?

Table 5.3
One-Way ANCOVA Summary Table

| Source of Variation | Degrees of Freedom | Sum of Squares | Mean Square | t Statistic | Prob |
|---|---|---|---|---|---|
| Parallelism | 1 | 0.16 | 0.16 | -.07 | .9427 |
| Error | 65 | 2013.78 | 30.98 | | |
| DEPTH (cov) | 1 | 585.80 | 585.80 | -4.38* | .0001 |
| SEAL | 1 | 1306.66 | 1306.66 | -6.54* | .0000[1] |
| Error | 66 | 2013.94 | 30.51 | | |

[1]One-tailed
*Significant at p<.05


### Research Hypotheses.

Research Hypothesis (1): The mean nitrate concentration in water from wells with the casing grouted into the bedrock will differ from the mean nitrate concentration in water from wells with the casing jammed into bedrock if the depth to the seal is held constant.

Research Hypothesis (2): The mean nitrate concentration of well water will be dependent on the type of fertilizer used nearby, if the depth to the bedrock/casing seal is held constant.

### Statistical Hypotheses.

Null Hypothesis (1)        H(01): u(grouted) = u(jammed)
Alternate Hypothesis (1) H(A1): u(grouted) ≠ u(jammed)

Null Hypothesis (2)        H(02): u(A) = u(B) = u(C)
Alternate Hypothesis (2) H(A2): u(A) ≠ u(B) ≠ u(C)

These null hypotheses will be tested at the .05 level of significance.

Data. The data are the unequal $n$ data presented in Table 5.4.

Two-Way ANCOVA Table. Table 5.5 is the ANCOVA table for the Two-way experiment. These results indicate that both of the treatments, SEAL and FERT, have a significant effect on the nitrate concentration. At this point, the researcher could test for individual differences between means on the FERT factor.

Table 5.4
Data for the Two-Way ANCOVA Example

| FERT | Grouted NO3 | Depth | NO3 | Depth | Jammed NO3 | Depth | NO3 | Depth |
|------|------|-------|-----|-------|------------|-------|-----|-------|
| | 48 | 48 | 45.5 | 57 | 51 | 45 | 55.5 | 45 |
| | 38 | 59 | 44 | 61 | 55.5 | 50 | 60 | 52 |
| A | 36 | 67 | 47 | 62 | 51 | 59 | 60 | 46 |
| | 51 | 50 | 45 | 50 | 58 | 52 | 46 | 48 |
| | 34 | 59 | 45 | 51 | 58.5 | 55 | 51 | 54 |
| | 41.5 | 58 | 40.5 | 61 | 51 | 51 | | |
| | 37.5 | 58 | 34 | 57 | 53.5 | 56 | 51 | 51 |
| | 38 | 48 | 37 | 59 | 48 | 53 | 54.5 | 47 |
| B | 36 | 49 | 37 | 53 | 43 | 64 | 41.5 | 59 |
| | 38 | 52 | 30 | 67 | 47 | 60 | 44 | 52 |
| | 38.5 | 67 | 37 | 54 | 59 | 57 | 55.5 | 53 |
| | 33.5 | 65 | 42 | 49 | 57 | 56 | | |
| | 38.5 | 58 | 48 | 54 | 50 | 51 | 58 | 56 |
| | 50 | 54 | 39.5 | 51 | 40.5 | 53 | 47 | 58 |
| | 49 | 52 | 37.5 | 63 | 61 | 60 | 49 | 49 |
| C | 45 | 64 | 47 | 57 | 45.5 | 61 | | |
| | 33.5 | 67 | 45.5 | 49 | 61 | 44 | | |
| | 57 | 43 | 37 | 61 | 58 | 49 | | |
| | 41.5 | 61 | | | 37.5 | 62 | | |

Table 5.5
Two-Way ANCOVA Summary Table

| Source of Variation | Degrees of Freedom | Sum of Squares | Mean Square | F-Ratio | Prob > F |
|---------------------|--------------------|----------------|-------------|---------|----------|
| Parallelism | 5 | 113.44 | 22.69 | .87 | .5076 |
| Error | 57 | 1487.89 | 26.10 | | |
| DEPTH (cov) | 1 | 511.74 | 511.74 | 19.81* | .0000 |
| SEAL | 1 | 1332.75 | 1332.75 | 51.60* | .0000 |
| FERT | 2 | 229.23 | 114.61 | 4.44 | .0158 |
| SEAL x FERT | 2 | 156.84 | 78.42 | 3.04 | .0552 |
| Error | 62 | 1601.33 | 25.83 | | |

Note: The parallelism test for higher order designs is found in SSPS(MANOVA) (5-2).
*Significant at p<.05

413

If a specific research hypothesis was constructed prior to the experiment, planned comparisons could be used. These are described in Chapter 2. In the absence of any specific hypotheses, post hoc tests can be used. Several of these tests are described in other chapters. The Bonferroni test will be demonstrated here.

Bonferroni Test. The Bonferroni test (sometimes called Dunn's test) is computationally similiar to the Scheffe test described in Chapter 7. However, whereas the Scheffe test provides for a Type I error rate of no more than alpha for each of the possible post hoc comparisons, the Bonferroni test sets the Type I error rate for the complete set of relevant contrasts at no more than alpha. In other words, the experimentwise risk of Type I error will be less than or equal to the sum of the individual comparison risks. This is done by dividing the alpha level for the experiment among each of the individual contrasts. In fact, one of the most desirable properties of the Bonferroni test is that the researcher can set different alpha levels for each of the mean contrasts. In addition, as long as the number of desired contrasts is kept small, the Bonferroni test will be more powerful than the Scheffe test.

The computations for the Bonferroni test have been given by Kirk (1968, p. 79-81) and by Games (1971, p. 550-551). As with the Scheffe test, this comparison has two components, the difference statistic given by

$$D = C(1)\overline{Y}(1) + C(2)\overline{Y}(2) + \ldots + C(j)\overline{Y}(j)$$

where $C(j)$ is the coefficient by which a given mean, $\overline{Y}(j)$, is to be multiplied (which is the mean contrast to be tested) and the B statistic given by

$$B = t(b) \sqrt{MSR \left( \sum [C^2(j) / n(j)] \right)}$$

where   $t(b)$ = the t value for $(N - j - 1)$ degrees of freedom and the appropriate alpha level,
        $MSR$ = the mean square residual, and
        $n(j)$ = the sample size of cell j.
When $|D|$ exceeds B, the contrast is significant.

Three comparisons between means on the NO3 variable for the FERT treatment are relevant to this study. These comparisons are:

1)   $u(A) - u(B)$,
2)   $u(A) - u(C)$, and
3)   $u(B) - u(C)$.

The D statistics are given by:

$$D(1) = (1)(47.99) + (-1)(43.82) = 4.17,$$
$$D(2) = (1)(47.99) + (-1)(47.39) = .60, \text{ and}$$
$$D(3) = (1)(43.82) + (-1)(47.39) = -3.57.$$

[Note that the preceeding adjusted means were taken from SAS(GLM) (5-2), and that the same results would be found using the adusted means from SPSS(MANOVA) (5-2).]

because all the cells have the same number of observations and all the contrasts have the same coefficients, the B statistics for all the comparisons are given by:

$$B = t(b) \sqrt{(25.8279)(2/23)} = 1.4986 \ t(b).$$

However, a previous study has shown a significant difference between the mean nitrate values in water from farms using fertilizers A and B (viz. contrast 1). Hence, a more stringent alpha level was desired for this test, so the .01 level was chosen. The remaining contrasts were each assigned alpha levels of .02. This is an especially convenient partition since any good table of t values can be used to obtain t. Where nonstandard alpha levels are selected, special tables provided by Kirk (1968, p. 551) must be used. Thus, the B statistic for the first comparison is given by:

$$B(1) = 1.4986 \ t(b) = (1.4986)(2.660) = 3.986$$

and the B statistic for the second and third contrasts is given by:

$$B(2) = B(3) = 1.4986 \ t(b) = (1.4986)(2.390) = 3.582.$$

Therefore, only the first comparison, u(A) - u(B), is significant. However, the D statistic for the third contrast, u(B) - u(C), is close to the value of B. Had a less conservative post hoc test been chosen, this comparison might have been significant. While many statisticians agree that special circumstances dictate the use of certain post hoc tests (e.g. Dunnett's test for comparison to a control group), opinions diverge where more than one test could be used. Miller (1966) suggests that there is nothing wrong with calculating the critical values for each of the tests and selecting the test having the smallest values, so long as the choice is independent of the observed data. In any case, researchers should also consider whether or not the differences are theoretically meaningful before making conclusions and recommendations.

## Univariate Two-Way ANCOVA (3x2), Two Covariates: Overall Test

Problem. Does a well's bedrock/casing seal or the type of fertilizer used nearby influence the nitrate concentration of its water, given a constant depth to the seal and a constant amount of ions in the water.

### Research Hypotheses.

Research Hypothesis (1):The mean nitrate concentration in water from wells with the casing grouted into the bedrock will differ from the mean nitrate concentration in water from wells with the casing jammed into bedrock if the depth to the seal and the total amount of ions in the water are held constant.

Research Hypothesis (2): The mean nitrate concentration of well water will depend on the type of fertilizer used nearby, if the depth to the bedrock/casing seal and the total amount of ions in the water are held constant.

### Statistical Hypotheses.

Null Hypothesis (1)      H(01): u(grouted) = u(jammed)
Alternate Hypothesis (1) H(A1): u(grouted) ≠ u(jammed)

Null Hypothesis (2)      H(02): u(A) = u(B) = u(C)
Alternate Hypothesis (2) H(A2): u(A) ≠ u(B) ≠ u(C)

These hypotheses will be tested at the .05 level of significance.

Data. The data are the unequal n data presented in Table 5.6.

Two-Way, Two Covariate ANCOVA Table. Table 5.7 is the ANCOVA table for the Two-way experiment with two covariates. Both the parallelism test and the interaction effect are not significant, as expected. Bonferroni tests for the three contrasts (discussed previously) yielded:

$$D(1) = (1)(47.92) + (-1)(44.06) = 3.86$$
$$D(2) = (1)(47.92) + (-1)(47.27) = .65$$
$$D(3) = (1)(44.06) + (-1)(47.27) = -3.21$$

and
$$B(1) = 2.660 \sqrt{(22.25)(2/23)} = 3.70$$
$$B(2) = B3 = 2.390 \sqrt{(22.25)(2/23)} = 3.32.$$

Once again, only the first comparison is statistically

significant.

## Table 5.6
### Data for the Two Covariate, Two-Way ANCOVA Example

| SEAL | FERT A NO3 | A Depth | A TDS | FERT B NO3 | B Depth | B TDS | FERT C NO3 | C Depth | C TDS |
|---|---|---|---|---|---|---|---|---|---|
| | 48 | 48 | 750 | 37.5 | 58 | 500 | 38.5 | 58 | 375 |
| | 38 | 59 | 400 | 38 | 48 | 875 | 50 | 54 | 700 |
| | 36 | 67 | 425 | 36 | 49 | 650 | 49 | 52 | 850 |
| G | 51 | 50 | 850 | 38 | 52 | 575 | 45 | 64 | 575 |
| R | 34 | 59 | 300 | 38.5 | 67 | 275 | 33.5 | 67 | 300 |
| O | 41.5 | 58 | 650 | 33.5 | 65 | 450 | 57 | 43 | 800 |
| U | 45.5 | 57 | 575 | 34 | 57 | 350 | 41.5 | 61 | 625 |
| T | 44 | 61 | 475 | 37 | 59 | 350 | 48 | 54 | 725 |
| E | 47 | 62 | 400 | 37 | 53 | 650 | 39.5 | 51 | 575 |
| D | 45 | 50 | 650 | 30 | 67 | 350 | 37.5 | 63 | 475 |
| | 45 | 51 | 875 | 37 | 54 | 675 | 47 | 57 | 450 |
| | 40.5 | 61 | 375 | 42 | 49 | 675 | 45.5 | 49 | 775 |
| | | | | | | | 37 | 61 | 375 |
| | 51 | 45 | 775 | 53.5 | 56 | 625 | 50 | 51 | 625 |
| | 55.5 | 50 | 675 | 48 | 53 | 675 | 40.5 | 53 | 400 |
| J | 51 | 59 | 700 | 43 | 64 | 400 | 61 | 60 | 650 |
| A | 58 | 52 | 550 | 47 | 60 | 300 | 45.5 | 61 | 400 |
| M | 58.5 | 55 | 600 | 59 | 57 | 750 | 61 | 44 | 675 |
| M | 51 | 51 | 625 | 57 | 56 | 675 | 58 | 49 | 700 |
| E | 55.5 | 45 | 675 | 51 | 51 | 525 | 37.5 | 62 | 500 |
| D | 60 | 52 | 650 | 54.5 | 47 | 575 | 58 | 56 | 575 |
| | 60 | 46 | 800 | 41.5 | 59 | 475 | 47 | 58 | 625 |
| | 46 | 48 | 525 | 44 | 52 | 700 | 49 | 49 | 675 |
| | 51 | 54 | 700 | 55.5 | 53 | 650 | | | |

## Multivariate Analysis

Commercial fertilizers generally contain other components besides nitrates, most commonly, potassium and phosphate. In order to more fully assess the effects of fertilizer pollution of groundwater, the potassium content (K) and the phosphate content (PO4) were added as dependent variables. As with nitrates, potassium and phosphate can be injurious if in high concentrations, and are expensive to remove from water supplies. Ordinarily, groundwater has less than 10 ppm of potassium and less than 1 ppm of phosphate, but higher values have been found in agricultural areas. In summary, then, the multivariate example has three dependent variables (NO3, K, and PO4), two factors (SEAL and FERT), and two covariates (DEPTH and

TDS).

## Table 5.7
### Two Covariate, Two-Way ANCOVA Summary Table

| Source of Variation | Degrees of Freedom | Sum of Squares | Mean Square | F-Ratio | Prob > F |
|---|---|---|---|---|---|
| Parallelism | 10 | 247.33 | 24.73 | 1.14 | .3548 |
| Error | 51 | 1109.96 | 21.76 | | |
| Regression | 2 | 755.78 | 377.89 | 16.98* | .0000 |
| SEAL | 1 | 1386.72 | 1386.72 | 62.32* | .0000 |
| FERT | 2 | 191.54 | 95.77 | 4.30* | .0178 |
| SEAL x FERT | 2 | 110.42 | 55.21 | 2.48 | .0920 |
| Error | 61 | 1357.29 | 22.25 | | |

Note: The parallelism test for higher order designs is found in SSPS(MANCVA) (5-3).
*Significant at p<.05

## Multivariate One-Way MANCOVA With One Covariate: Overall Test

Problem. Does a well's bedrock/casing seal influence the nitrate, potassium, and phosphate content of its water, given a constant depth to the seal?

Research Hypothesis. The mean nitrate, potassium, and phosphate concentrations in water from wells with the casing grouted into bedrock will differ from the mean concentrations in water from wells with the casing jammed into the bedrock, if the depth to the seal is held constant.

Statistical Hypotheses.

$$
\text{Null Hypothesis} \quad H(01): \begin{bmatrix} u(NO3) \\ u(K) \\ u(PO4) \end{bmatrix}_{grouted} = \begin{bmatrix} u(NO3) \\ u(K) \\ u(PO4) \end{bmatrix}_{jammed}
$$

i.e., $H(01): \underline{u}(grouted) = \underline{u}(jammed)$

```
Alternate           ┌ u(NO3) ┐        ┌ u(NO3) ┐
Hypothesis   H(A1):  │ u(K)   │   ≠    │ u(K)   │
                     │ u(PO4) │        │ u(PO4) │
                     └        ┘grouted └        ┘jammed
```

i.e.,    H(A1):  u(grouted) ≠ u(jammed)

This null hypothesis will be tested at the .05 level of significance.

Data. The data are presented in Table 5.8 as a multivariate, unequal n problem, with one covariate (DEPTH), and three dependent variables (NO3, K, PO4).

One-Way MANCOVA Table. Table 5.9 is the MANCOVA table for the one-way experiment. The results indicate that the type of seal affects the concentration of all three ions, but that the use of the covariate, DEPTH, to reduce the error variance was probably not appropriate in the case of the K and PO4 dependent variables.

## Multivariate, Two-Way MANCOVA (3x2), With Two Covariates: Overall Test

Problem. Does a well's bedrock/casing seal or the type of fertilizer used nearby influence the nitrate, potassium, and phosphate concentrations of its water, if the depth to the seal and the total amount of ions in the water are held constant?

## Research Hypotheses.

Research Hypothesis (1): The mean nitrate, potassium, and phosphate concentrations in water from wells with the casing grouted into bedrock will differ from the mean concentrations in water from wells with the casing jammed into the bedrock if the depth to the seal and the total amount of ions are held constant.

Research Hypothesis (2): The mean nitrate, potassium, and phosphate concentrations in water from wells will depend on what type of fertilizer is used nearby, if the depth to the well's bedrock/casing seal and the total amount of ions in the water are held constant.

## Table 5.8
### Data for the One-Way MANCOVA Example

SEAL

| | Grouted | | | | Jammed | | |
|-----|------|------|-------|------|------|------|-------|
| NO3 | K | PO4 | Depth | NO3 | K | PO4 | Depth |
| 48 | 17.7 | .88 | 48 | 51 | 21.8 | .89 | 45 |
| 38 | 14.1 | .88 | 59 | 55.5 | 21.2 | .91 | 50 |
| 36 | 13.9 | .84 | 67 | 51 | 22 | .89 | 59 |
| 34 | 17.9 | .87 | 59 | 58 | 14.4 | .90 | 52 |
| 41.5 | 19.3 | .85 | 58 | 58.5 | 13.1 | .91 | 55 |
| 45.5 | 13.6 | .89 | 57 | 51 | 13.8 | .91 | 51 |
| 44 | 13.8 | .85 | 61 | 55.5 | 22.8 | .93 | 45 |
| 47 | 17.9 | .89 | 62 | 60 | 18.8 | .88 | 52 |
| 45 | 13.8 | .81 | 50 | 60 | 20.7 | .90 | 46 |
| 45 | 17.7 | .81 | 51 | 46 | 15.4 | .90 | 48 |
| 40.5 | 13.6 | .87 | 61 | 51 | 13.8 | .96 | 54 |
| 37.5 | 14 | .88 | 58 | 53.5 | 13.4 | .88 | 56 |
| 38 | 14.9 | .88 | 48 | 48 | 14.4 | .93 | 53 |
| 36 | 14.7 | .89 | 49 | 43 | 16.8 | .88 | 64 |
| 38 | 10.7 | .84 | 52 | 47 | 13.4 | .87 | 60 |
| 38.5 | 13.5 | .83 | 67 | 59 | 21.8 | .85 | 57 |
| 33.5 | 14.6 | .80 | 65 | 57 | 22.9 | .85 | 56 |
| 34 | 15.2 | .86 | 57 | 51 | 18 | .93 | 51 |
| 37 | 10.5 | .83 | 59 | 54.5 | 16.6 | .90 | 47 |
| 37 | 13.4 | .90 | 53 | 41.5 | 14.4 | .90 | 59 |
| 30 | 15.4 | .80 | 67 | 44 | 19.4 | .88 | 52 |
| 37 | 14.4 | .86 | 54 | 55.5 | 21.8 | .96 | 53 |
| 42 | 15.2 | .86 | 49 | 50 | 21.8 | .94 | 51 |
| 38.5 | 13.6 | .85 | 58 | 40.5 | 14.4 | .96 | 53 |
| 50 | 19 | .86 | 54 | 61 | 15.4 | .95 | 60 |
| 49 | 18.8 | .88 | 52 | 45.5 | 15.4 | .89 | 61 |
| 45 | 13.6 | .91 | 64 | 61 | 15.4 | .91 | 44 |
| 33.5 | 14.6 | .89 | 67 | 58 | 18 | .88 | 49 |
| 57 | 17.5 | .84 | 43 | 37.5 | 13.8 | .91 | 62 |
| 41.5 | 13.9 | .86 | 61 | 58 | 22.8 | .93 | 56 |
| 48 | 19.9 | .91 | 54 | 47 | 22.8 | .90 | 58 |
| 39.5 | 16.5 | .86 | 51 | 49 | 18 | .94 | 49 |
| 37.5 | 14.9 | .83 | 63 | | | | |
| 47 | 18.8 | .89 | 57 | | | | |
| 45.5 | 18.8 | .92 | 49 | | | | |
| 37 | 20.9 | .89 | 61 | | | | |
| 51 | 16.5 | .89 | 50 | | | | |

Table 5.9

One-Way MANCOVA Summary Table

| Source of Variation | Sums of Squares and Products | | | Multivariate Wilks' Lambda | Df | F(prob) | Univariate F(Probability) | | |
|---|---|---|---|---|---|---|---|---|---|
| | NO3 | K | PO4 | | | | NO3 | K | PO4 |
| PARLLSM | -.16 | -.44 | -.00 | .997 | 3, 63 | .05 (.983) | .01 (.943) | .13 (.715) | .00 (.963) |
| | -.44 | 1.20 | -.00 | | | | | | |
| | -.00 | -.00 | -.00 | | | | | | |
| Error | 2013.78 | 317.93 | -.20 | | | | | | |
| | 317.93 | 579.75 | -.21 | | | | | | |
| | -.20 | -.21 | .06 | | | | | | |
| REGRSSN | 585.80 | 134.64 | 1.20 | .75 | 3, 64 | 7.11* (.000) | 19.20* (.000) | 3.52 (.065) | 2.72 (.104) |
| | 134.65 | 30.95 | -.28 | | | | | | |
| | 1.20 | -.28 | -.00 | | | | | | |
| SEAL | 1306.66 | 258.95 | 5.78 | .49 | 3, 64 | 22.64* (.000) | 42.82* (.000) | 5.83* (.019) | 28.34* (.000) |
| | 258.95 | 51.32 | 1.14 | | | | | | |
| | 5.78 | 1.14 | .03 | | | | | | |
| Error | 2913.94 | 317.49 | -.20 | | | | | | |
| | 317.49 | 580.95 | -.21 | | | | | | |
| | -.20 | -.21 | .06 | | | | | | |

Note: The parallelism test shown here is found in SSPS(MANOVA) (5-4).

*Significant at p<.05

## Statistical Hypotheses.

Null
Hypothesis (1) H(01): 
$$\begin{bmatrix} u(NO3) \\ u(K) \\ u(PO4) \end{bmatrix}_{grouted} = \begin{bmatrix} u(NO3) \\ u(K) \\ u(PO4) \end{bmatrix}_{jammed}$$

i.e.,    H(01): $\underline{u}$(grouted) = $\underline{u}$(jammed)


Alternate
Hypothesis (1) H(A1): 
$$\begin{bmatrix} u(NO3) \\ u(K) \\ u(PO4) \end{bmatrix}_{grouted} \neq \begin{bmatrix} u(NO3) \\ u(K) \\ u(PO4) \end{bmatrix}_{jammed}$$

i.e.,    H(A1): $\underline{u}$(grouted) $\neq$ $\underline{u}$(jammed)


Null
Hypothesis (2) H(02): 
$$\begin{bmatrix} u(NO3) \\ u(K) \\ u(PO4) \end{bmatrix}_A = \begin{bmatrix} u(NO3) \\ u(K) \\ u(PO4) \end{bmatrix}_B = \begin{bmatrix} u(NO3) \\ u(K) \\ u(PO4) \end{bmatrix}_C$$

i.e.,    H(02): $\underline{u}$(A) = $\underline{u}$(B) = $\underline{u}$(C)


Alternate
Hypothesis (2) H(A2): 
$$\begin{bmatrix} u(NO3) \\ u(K) \\ u(PO4) \end{bmatrix}_A \neq \begin{bmatrix} u(NO3) \\ u(K) \\ u(PO4) \end{bmatrix}_B \neq \begin{bmatrix} u(NO3) \\ u(K) \\ u(PO4) \end{bmatrix}_C$$

i.e.,    H(A2): $\underline{u}$(A) $\neq$ $\underline{u}$(B) $\neq$ $\underline{u}$(C)

These null hypotheses will be tested at the .05 level of significance.

Data. The data are presented in Table 5.10 as a multivariate, unequal $\underline{n}$ problem with two covariates (DEPTH, TDS), and three dependent variables (NO3, K, PO4).

Table 5.10
Data for the Two-Way, Two Covariate MANCOVA Example

| FERT | SEAL Grouted | | | | | SEAL Jammed | | | | |
|---|---|---|---|---|---|---|---|---|---|---|
| | NO3 | K | PO4 | Depth | TDS | NO3 | K | PO4 | Depth | TDS |
| | 48 | 17.7 | .88 | 48 | 750 | 51 | 21.8 | .89 | 45 | 775 |
| | 38 | 14.1 | .88 | 59 | 400 | 55.5 | 21.2 | .91 | 50 | 675 |
| | 36 | 13.9 | .84 | 67 | 425 | 51 | 22 | .89 | 59 | 700 |
| | 51 | 13.5 | .89 | 50 | 850 | 58 | 14.4 | .90 | 52 | 550 |
| | 34 | 17.9 | .87 | 59 | 300 | 58.5 | 13.1 | .91 | 55 | 600 |
| A | 41.5 | 19.3 | .85 | 58 | 650 | 51 | 13.8 | .91 | 51 | 625 |
| | 45.5 | 13.6 | .89 | 57 | 575 | 55.5 | 22.8 | .93 | 45 | 675 |
| | 44 | 13.8 | .85 | 61 | 475 | 60 | 18.8 | .88 | 52 | 650 |
| | 47 | 17.9 | .89 | 62 | 400 | 60 | 20.7 | .90 | 46 | 800 |
| | 45 | 13.8 | .81 | 50 | 650 | 46 | 15.4 | .90 | 48 | 525 |
| | 45 | 17.7 | .81 | 51 | 875 | 51 | 13.8 | .96 | 54 | 700 |
| | 40.5 | 13.6 | .87 | 61 | 375 | | | | | |
| | | | | | | | | | | |
| | 37.5 | 14 | .88 | 58 | 500 | 53.5 | 13.4 | .88 | 56 | 625 |
| | 38 | 14.9 | .88 | 48 | 875 | 48 | 14.4 | .93 | 53 | 675 |
| | 36 | 14.7 | .89 | 49 | 650 | 43 | 16.8 | .88 | 64 | 400 |
| | 38 | 10.7 | .84 | 52 | 575 | 47 | 13.4 | .87 | 60 | 300 |
| | 38.5 | 13.5 | .83 | 67 | 275 | 59 | 21.8 | .85 | 57 | 750 |
| B | 33.5 | 14.6 | .80 | 65 | 450 | 57 | 22.9 | .85 | 56 | 675 |
| | 34 | 15.2 | .86 | 57 | 350 | 51 | 18 | .93 | 51 | 525 |
| | 37 | 10.5 | .83 | 59 | 350 | 54.5 | 16.6 | .90 | 47 | 575 |
| | 37 | 13.4 | .90 | 53 | 650 | 41.5 | 14.4 | .90 | 59 | 475 |
| | 30 | 15.4 | .80 | 67 | 350 | 44 | 19.4 | .88 | 52 | 700 |
| | 37 | 14.4 | .86 | 54 | 675 | 55.5 | 21.8 | .96 | 53 | 650 |
| | 42 | 15.2 | .86 | 49 | 675 | | | | | |
| | | | | | | | | | | |
| | 38.5 | 13.6 | .85 | 58 | 375 | 50 | 21.8 | .94 | 51 | 625 |
| | 50 | 19 | .86 | 54 | 700 | 40.5 | 14.4 | .96 | 53 | 400 |
| | 49 | 18.8 | .88 | 52 | 850 | 61 | 15.4 | .95 | 60 | 650 |
| | 45 | 13.6 | .91 | 64 | 575 | 45.5 | 15.4 | .89 | 61 | 400 |
| | 33.5 | 14.6 | .89 | 67 | 300 | 61 | 15.4 | .91 | 44 | 675 |
| C | 57 | 17.5 | .84 | 43 | 800 | 58 | 18 | .88 | 49 | 700 |
| | 41.5 | 13.9 | .86 | 61 | 625 | 37.5 | 13.8 | .91 | 62 | 500 |
| | 48 | 19.9 | .91 | 54 | 725 | 58 | 22.8 | .93 | 56 | 575 |
| | 39.5 | 16.5 | .86 | 51 | 575 | 47 | 22.8 | .90 | 58 | 625 |
| | 37.5 | 14.9 | .83 | 63 | 475 | 49 | 18 | .94 | 49 | 675 |
| | 47 | 18.8 | .89 | 57 | 450 | | | | | |
| | 45.5 | 18.8 | .92 | 49 | 775 | | | | | |
| | 37 | 20.9 | .89 | 61 | 375 | | | | | |

Two-Way, Two Covariate MANCOVA Table. Table 5.11 is the MANCOVA table for the Two-way design with two covariates. The results indicate that all three ions are affected by the type of seal but only NO3 and PO4 are influenced by the type of fertilizer used nearby. Neither covariate, DEPTH or TDS, was appropriate for removing error from the PO4 model and only the NO3 model's error was reduced significantly by the DEPTH covariate.

## Summary: Error Reduction

Table 5.12 is a summary of the reduction in the error mean squares for the designs discussed in this chapter and for the analogous MANOVA designs. While the error in the NO3 model is continually reduced by the addition of either the second factor or the covariates, the K model's error is reduced more by either the second factor or the TDS covariate than by the DEPTH covariate. The PO4 model shows a much greater reduction in error when the second factor is used than when either covariate is used. The correlations between the dependent variables and the covariates show that the limits suggested by Cochran (1957) and Cox (1957) are fairly good rules of thumb for selecting blocking over covariance analysis, all other things being equal. A more complete discussion of the example problems follows in the annotated computer output.

## Table 5.11
### Two-Way, Two Covariate MANCOVA Summary Table

| Source of Variation | Sums of Squares and Products | | | Multivariate Wilks' | | | Univariate F(Probability) | | | |
|---|---|---|---|---|---|---|---|---|---|---|
| | NO3 | K | PO4 | Lambda | Df | F(prob) | Df | NO3 | K | PO4 |
| PARLLSM | 247.33 | 34.59 | -.62 | | | | | | | |
| | 34.59 | 88.34 | -.39 | .55 | 30,144 | 1.10 (.338) | 10,51 | 1.14 (.355) | 1.16 (.339) | 1.17 (.331) |
| | -.62 | -.39 | -.01 | | | | | | | |
| Error | 1109.96 | 34.70 | .09 | | | | | | | |
| | 34.70 | 388.60 | .21 | | | | | | | |
| | .09 | .21 | .04 | | | | | | | |
| REGRSSN | 755.78 | 226.15 | .87 | | | | | | | |
| | 226.15 | 72.67 | -.15 | .57 | 6,118 | 6.39* (.000) | 2,61 | 16.98* (.000) | 4.65* (.013) | 1.40 (.254) |
| | -.87 | -.18 | -.00 | | | | | | | |
| SEAL | 1386.72 | 283.08 | 6.03 | | | | | | | |
| | 283.08 | 57.79 | 1.23 | .37 | 3, 59 | 33.51* (.000) | 1,61 | 62.32* (.000) | 7.39* (.009) | 30.80* (.000) |
| | 6.03 | 1.23 | .03 | | | | | | | |
| FERT | 191.54 | 56.00 | .80 | | | | | | | |
| | 56.00 | 24.56 | -.42 | .74 | 6,118 | 3.24* (.006) | 2,61 | 4.30* (.018) | 1.57 (.216) | 4.36* (.017) |
| | -.80 | -.42 | .01 | | | | | | | |
| SEAL x FERT | 110.42 | 45.26 | -.03 | | | | | | | |
| | 45.26 | 18.58 | -.01 | .90 | 6,118 | 1.07 (.384) | 2,61 | 2.48 (.092) | 1.19 (.312) | .01 (.991) |
| | -.03 | -.01 | -.00 | | | | | | | |
| Error | 1357.29 | 69.29 | -.52 | | | | | | | |
| | 69.29 | 476.94 | -.18 | | | | | | | |
| | -.52 | -.18 | .05 | | | | | | | |

*Significant at p<.05

425

Table 5.12
Comparison of Error Mean Squares

| Design | NO3 | K | PO4 |
|---|---|---|---|
| One-Way MANOVA | 38.80 | 9.13 | .00092 |
| Two-Way MANOVA | 33.54 | 8.72 | .00086 |
| One-Way MANCOVA One Covariate | 30.51 | 8.80 | .00090 |
| Two-Way MANCOVA One Covariate | 25.83 | 8.38 | .00084 |
| One-Way MANCOVA Two Covariates | 25.78 | 8.05 | .00091 |
| Two-Way MANCOVA Two Covariates | 22.25 | 7.82 | .00085 |

| Correlation with: | | | |
|---|---|---|---|
| Depth | -.4921 | -.2345 | -.2022 |
| TDS | .5868 | .3627 | .1015 |

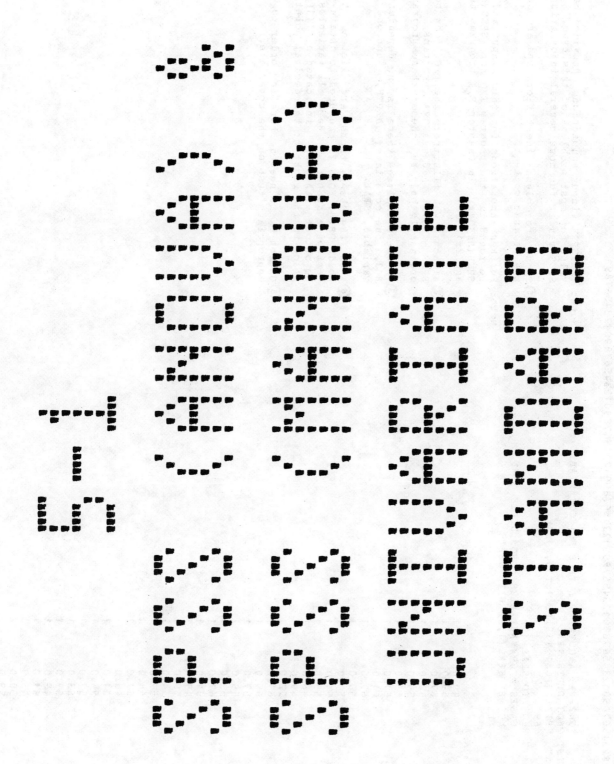

```
     RUN NAME      ONE-WAY ANCOVA (2 LEVELS & 1 COVARIATE)
     VARIABLE LIST NO3 DEPTH SEAL
③    INPUT FORMAT  FIXED(F6.1,T19,F5.1,T30,F1.0)
     N OF CASES    69
④    PRINT FORMATS NO3 TO SEAL (1)
     LIST CASES    CASES = 69/VARIABLES = NO3 DEPTH SEAL
③ ②  ANOVA         NO3 BY SEAL(1,2) WITH DEPTH
     STATISTICS    ALL
⑤    OPTIONS       9
     READ INPUT DATA
                   48.0
     38.0          48.0          1
                   59.0          1
                   67.0          1
                   50.0          1
     34.0          59.0          1
     41.5          58.0          1
     45.5          57.0          1
     44.0          61.0          1
     47.0          62.0          1
     45.0          50.0          1
     45.0          51.0          1
     40.5          61.0          1
     37.5          58.0          1
     38.0          48.0          1
     36.0          49.0          1
     38.5          52.0          1
     38.5          67.0          1
     33.5          65.0          1
     34.0          57.0          1
     37.0          59.0          1
     37.0          53.0          1
     30.0          67.0          1
     37.0          54.0          1
     42.0          49.0          1
     38.5          58.0          1
     50.0          54.0          1
     49.0          52.0          1
     45.0          64.0          1
     33.5          67.0          1
     57.0          43.0          1
     41.5          61.0          1
     48.0          54.0          1
     39.5          51.0          1
     37.5          63.0          1
     47.0          57.0          1
     45.5          49.0          1
     37.0          61.0          1
     45.0          45.0          2
     51.0          50.0          2
     55.5          59.0          2
     58.0          52.0          2
     58.5          55.0          2
     51.0          51.0          2
```

Note: The SPSS input annotations provided here are of value for most problems of this type. Consult the SPSS manual for more general information.

① These are column identifiers and are not part of the program content.

Note: Further annotations for this input and output can be found in the program I/O for SPSS(ANOVA) and SPSS(MANOVA) in Chapter 2, programs numbered 2-4 and 2-1.

② Although we illustrate the I/O from both of the SPSS ANCVA and MANOVA programs, one would ordinarily only run one of these programs.

③ In these analyses there is one dependent variable, NO3, one covariate, DEPTH, and one independent variable, SEAL.

④ When the observations are listed, the control words PRINT FORMATS are used to obtain the decimal part of a number. Here all variables input will be output with one, indicated by '(1)', decimal place to the right of the decimal point.

⑤ Option 9 is needed here in order to obtain the appropriate test on the covariate.

⑥ In the subprogram MANOVA the specification that describes the design uses the word WITH to indicate the covariate, here DEPTH.

⑦ The PRINT subcommand (optional) requests that the observed cell means, adjusted (for the covariate) cell means, estimated cell means, average raw residual, and the average standardized residual be printed through the specification PMEANS. Here the specification ERROR(W) must be included in PMEANS and POBS to obtain output from PMEANS and POBS, both here and in the PLOT subcommand.

⑧ The PMEANS specification in the PLOT subcommand requests that the observed, adjusted, and estimated means be plotted. Note that the ERROR(W) specification must also be used with PMEANS in the PRINT subcommand to obtain this plot.

⑨ The test of the homogeneity of the within cell regression coefficients may be found by re-specifying the design with the covariate considered as a dependent variable.

⑩ The ANALYSIS specification indicates that NO3 is the dependent variable to be analysed.

⑪ The test of the homogeneity of the within cell regression coefficients is found as the DEPTH BY SEAL interaction.

```
          46.0            48.0   2
          51.0            54.0   2
          53.5            56.0   2
          48.0            53.0   2
          43.0            64.0   2
          47.0            60.0   2
          59.0            57.0   2
          57.0            56.0   2
          56.0            51.0   2
          51.0            47.0   2
          54.5            54.5   2
          41.5            41.5   2
          52.0            52.0   2
          53.0            53.0   2
          51.0            51.0   2
          40.5            40.5   2
          53.0            53.0   2
          60.0            60.0   2
          61.0            61.0   2
          45.5            45.5   2
          44.0            44.0   2
          49.0            49.0   2
          58.0            58.0   2
          37.5            37.5   2
          62.0            62.0   2
          56.0            56.0   2
          58.0            58.0   2
          47.0            47.0   2
          49.0            49.0   2
```

```
② ⑥ MANOVA   NO3 BY SEAL(1,2) WITH DEPTH /
    ⑦ PRINT = CELLINFO(MEANS)
              HOMOGENEITY(BARTLETT,COCHRAN)
    ⑧        PMEANS(ERROR(W))/
              POBS(ERROR(W)) /
            PLOT = BOXPLOTS STEMLEAF PMEANS POBS/
            TEST OF WITHIN CELL REGRESSION
② ⑨ MANOVA   NO3 DEPTH BY SEAL(1,2) /
            METHOD = SSTYPE(UNIQUE) /
    ⑩ ANALYSIS = NO3/
    ⑪ DESIGN = DEPTH, SEAL, DEPTH BY SEAL/

   TASK NAME
   MANOVA
```

① 
```
00000000011111111112222222222333333333344444444445555555555666666666677777777778
12345678901234567890123456789012345678901234567890123456789012345678901234567890
```

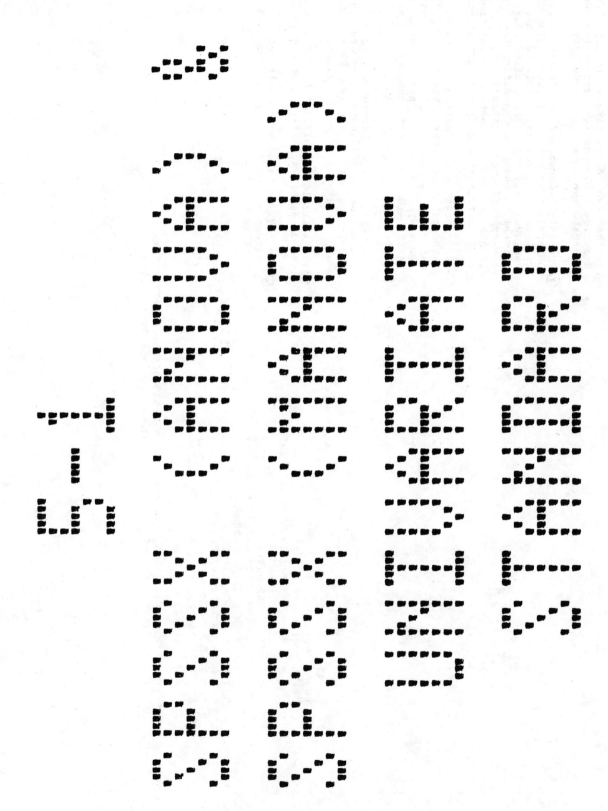

```
00000000011111111112222222222333333333344444444445555555555666666666677777777778
12345678901234567890123456789012345678901234567890123456789012345678901234567890
```

① UNNUMBERED
TITLE       ONE-WAY ANCOVA (2 LEVELS & 1 COVARIATE)
DATA LIST/  NO3 DEPTH SEAL
  (F6.1,T19,F5.1,T30,F1.0)
ANOVA       NO3 BY SEAL(1,2) WITH DEPTH
STATISTICS  ALL
OPTIONS     9
BEGIN DATA
②

END DATA
LIST        VARIABLES = NO3 DEPTH SEAL
MANOVA      NO3 BY SEAL(1,2) WITH DEPTH /
  PRINT = CELLINFO(MEANS)
        HOMOGENEITY(BARTLETT,COCHRAN)
        PMEANS(ERROR(W))
        POBS(ERROR(W))/
  PLOT = BOXPLOTS STEMLEAF PMEANS POBS/
SUBTITLE    TEST OF WITHIN CELL REGRESSION
MANOVA      NO3 DEPTH BY SEAL(1,2)/
  METHOD = SSTYPE(UNIQUE)/
  ANALYSIS = NO3/
  DESIGN = DEPTH, SEAL, DEPTH BY SEAL/

```
00000000011111111112222222222333333333344444444445555555555666666666677777777778
12345678901234567890123456789012345678901234567890123456789012345678901234567890
```

① At our installation the default (NUMBERED) instruction allowed SPSSX to read only 72 columns. We therefore used the UNNUMBERED command to allow SPSSX to read all 80 columns. The default may vary by installation.

② The data go here.

431

ONE-WAY ANCOVA (2 LEVELS & 1 COVARIATE)

FILE NONAME (CREATION DATE = 02/02/83)

02/02/83   PAGE   4

① NO3
BY SEAL
WITH DEPTH

* * * * * * * A N A L Y S I S   O F   V A R I A N C E * * * * * * * * * * * * * *

②

| SOURCE OF VARIATION | SUM OF SQUARES | DF | MEAN SQUARE | F | SIGNIF OF F |
|---|---|---|---|---|---|
| ③ COVARIATES | 585.800 | 1 | 585.800 | 19.198 | 0.000 |
| DEPTH | 585.800 | 1 | 585.800 | 19.198 | 0.000 |
| ④ MAIN EFFECTS | 1306.657 | 1 | 1306.657 | 42.821 | 0.000 |
| SEAL | 1306.657 | 1 | 1306.657 | 42.821 | 0.000 ⑤ |
| EXPLAINED | 2543.627 | 2 | 1271.813 | 41.680 | 0.000 |
| RESIDUAL | 2013.932 | 66 | 30.514 | | |
| TOTAL | 4557.559 | 68 | 67.023 | | |

COVARIATE    RAW REGRESSION COEFFICIENT
DEPTH  ⑥  -0.500

69 CASES WERE PROCESSED.
0 CASES ( 0.0 PCT) WERE MISSING.

① SPSS(ANOVA) will provide a separate analysis for each dependent variable but does not have multivariate capabilities.

② SPSS(ANOVA) prints the hypothesis tests in the traditional ANOVA format including sums of squares, degrees of freedom, mean squares, F values, and the exact probability of the test (see Table 5.3).

③ The first test is the test of significance for the covariate (test for zero slope or no effect). Here we find that the covariate is significantly related to the dependent variable.

④ The second test is a test of the main effect (equality of the adjusted cell means).

⑤ The one-tailed statistical test (half of the SIGNIF OF F shown here) indicates that the nitrate concentration of the wells with grouted casings is significantly less than the nitrate concentration of the wells with jammed casings.

⑥ The estimated pooled within cell regression coefficient is printed.

432

ONE-WAY ANCOVA (2 LEVELS & 1 COVARIATE)

FILE   NONAME   (CREATION DATE = 02/02/83)                                                    02/02/83                    PAGE   6

* * * * * * * * * * * * * * * * * * A N A L Y S I S   O F   V A R I A N C E * * * * * * * * * * * * * * * * * * * * * * * * * * * *

CELL MEANS AND STANDARD DEVIATIONS

VARIABLE -- NO3

| FACTOR | CODE | MEAN | STD. DEV. | N | 95 PERCENT CONF. INTERVAL | |
|--------|------|------|-----------|---|---------------------------|---|
| SEAL | 1 | 41.16216 | 5.96524 | 37 | 39.17325 | 43.15107 |
| SEAL | 2 | 51.84375 | 6.52222 | 32 | 49.49224 | 54.19526 |
| FOR ENTIRE SAMPLE | | 46.11594 | 8.18677 | 69 | 44.14927 | 48.08262 |

VARIABLE -- DEPTH

| FACTOR | CODE | MEAN | STD. DEV. | N | 95 PERCENT CONF. INTERVAL | |
|--------|------|------|-----------|---|---------------------------|---|
| SEAL | 1 | 56.62162 | 6.36986 | 37 | 54.49781 | 58.74544 |
| SEAL | 2 | 53.37500 | 5.32644 | 32 | 51.45461 | 55.29539 |
| FOR ENTIRE SAMPLE | | 55.11594 | 6.08889 | 69 | 53.65323 | 56.57865 |

UNIVARIATE HOMOGENEITY OF VARIANCE TESTS

VARIABLE -- NO3

CCHRANS C(34,2) =     .54451,  P =  .303  (APPROX.)
BARTLETT-BOX F(1,13268) =     .26232,  P =  .609

VARIABLE -- DEPTH

COCHRANS C(34,2) =     .58850,  P =  .151  (APPROX.)
BARTLETT-BOX F(1,13268) =    1.03565,  P =  .309

69  CASES ACCEPTED.
 0  CASES REJECTED BECAUSE OF CUT-OF-RANGE FACTOR VALUES.
 0  CASES REJECTED BECAUSE OF MISSING DATA.
 2  NON-EMPTY CELLS.

433

ONE-WAY ANCOVA (2 LEVELS & 1 COVARIATE)                02/02/83          PAGE   11

\* \* \* \* \* \* \* \* \* \* \* \* \* \* \* \* \* \* \* \* A N A L Y S I S   O F   V A R I A N C E \* \* \* \* \* \* \* \* \* \* \* \* \* \* \* \* \* \* \* \* \* \*

(1) TESTS OF SIGNIFICANCE FOR NO3 USING SEQUENTIAL SUMS OF SQUARES

| SOURCE OF VARIATION | SUM OF SQUARES | DF | MEAN SQUARE | F | SIG. OF F |
|---|---|---|---|---|---|
| WITHIN CELLS | 2013.94148 | 66 | 30.51426 | | |
| (2) REGRESSION | 585.80430 | 1 | 585.80430 | 19.19772 | .000 |
| (3) CONSTANT | 4137.26856 | 1 | 4137.26856 | 135.58474 | 0.0 |
| SEAL | 1306.65739 | 1 | 1306.65739 | 42.82120 | 0.0 (4) |

ESTIMATES FOR NO3 ADJUSTED FOR 1 COVARIATE

CONSTANT

| PARAMETER | COEFF. | STD. ERR. | T-VALUE | SIG. OF T | LOWER .95 CL | UPPER .95 CL |
|---|---|---|---|---|---|---|
| 1 | 74.0198170204 | 6.31550 | 11.72033 | 0.0 | 61.41051 | 86.62913 |

SEAL

| PARAMETER | COEFF. | STD. ERR. | T-VALUE | SIG. OF T | LOWER .95 CL | UPPER .95 CL |
|---|---|---|---|---|---|---|
| 2 | -4.5286159232 | .69205 | -6.54379 | 0.0 | -5.91033 | -3.14690 |

REGRESSION ANALYSIS FOR WITHIN CELLS ERROR TERM
DEPENDENT VARIABLE ..NO3

| COVARIATE (5) | B | (6) BETA | STD. ERR. | T-VALUE | SIG. OF T | LOWER .95 CL | UPPER .95 CL |
|---|---|---|---|---|---|---|---|
| DEPTH | -.5003219287 | -.4746908229 | .11419 | -4.38152 | .000 | -.72831 | -.27234 |

434

(1) SPSS(MANOVA) prints the hypothesis tests in the traditional ANOVA format including sums of squares, degrees of freedom, mean squares, F values, and the exact probability of the test (see Table 5.3).

(2) This test is a test of the significance of the covariate (test for zero slope or no effect).

(3) This test is a test of the main effects (equality of the adjusted cell means).

(4) The one-tailed statistical test (half of the SIG. OF F shown here) indicates that the nitrate concentration of the wells with grouted casings is

(5) This is an estimate of the pooled within cell regression coefficient. Note that the t test given here is equivalent to the F test for REGRESSION given above.

(6) This is an estimate of the standardized pooled regression coefficient.

ONE-WAY ANCOVA (2 LEVELS & 1 COVARIATE)

* * * * * * * * * * * * * * * A N A L Y S I S   O F   V A R I A N C E * * * * * * * * * * * * * * * * * *

ADJUSTED AND ESTIMATED MEANS

VARIABLE -- NO3

⑦ The OBS.MEAN (observed mean)   is   the cell mean on the dependent variable.

| FACTOR | CODE | ⑦ OBS. MEAN | ⑧⑨ ADJ. MEAN | ⑩⑨ EST. MEAN | ⑪ RAW RESID. | ⑫ STD. RESID. |
|--------|------|-------------|--------------|--------------|--------------|---------------|
| SEAL | 1 | 41.16216 | 41.97434 | 41.22102 | -.05885 | -.01065 |
| SEAL | 2 | 51.84375 | 51.03157 | 51.90260 | -.05885 | -.01065 |

PLOT OF OBSERVED(O), ADJUSTED(A), AND ESTIMATED(E) MEANS

VARIABLE -- NO3

```
      +
   1  I         OE   A
      +
   2  I
      +
      I
      +----+----------+---------+---------+---------+----------+
   40.56000      42.95999    45.35999   47.75999   50.15999    52.559
```
98

⑧ The ADJ.MEAN (adjusted mean) is the observed mean adjusted for the covariate.   It can be found using:

$$\bar{Y}(adj) = \bar{Y} - b(\bar{X}-GM)$$

where, $\bar{Y}(adj)$ = the adjusted mean,

$\bar{Y}$ = the observed mean on the dependent variable for cell i,

$b$ = the pooled regression coefficient,

$\bar{X}$ = the observed mean on the covariate for cell i, and

$GM$ = the unweighted grand mean on the covariate.

Note that BMDP and SAS use the weighted grand mean on the covariate in the above equation. The important result, however, is that the difference between the $\bar{Y}(adj)$'s from the packages is the same (i.e. -9.05723), and therefore, all of these packages yield the same statistical test on the adjusted means.

⑨ Finn (1974, p.376) describes the ADJ.MEAN and the EST.MEAN values shown here.

⑩ The EST.MEAN (estimated mean) is the mean estimated from the covariance model used by this program.

⑪ The RAW RESID. (raw residual) is the difference between the OBS.MEAN minus the EST.MEAN. It can be used to spot outliers in the data.

⑫ The STD.RESID. (standardized residual) is the RAW RESID. divided by the square root of the preceding WITHIN CELLS MEAN SQUARE.

ONE-WAY ANCOVA (2 LEVELS & 1 COVARIATE)
TEST OF WITHIN CELL REGRESSION

\* \* \* \* \* \* \* \* \* \* \* \* \* \* \* \* \* A N A L Y S I S   O F   V A R I A N C E \* \* \* \* \* \* \* \* \* \* \* \* \* \* \* \* \* \* \*

TESTS OF SIGNIFICANCE FOR NO3 USING UNIQUE SUMS OF SQUARES

| SOURCE OF VARIATION | SUM OF SQUARES | DF | MEAN SQUARE | F | SIG. OF F |
|---|---|---|---|---|---|
| WITHIN+RESIDUAL | 2013.78024 | 65 | 30.98123 | | |
| CONSTANT | 3979.12957 | 1 | 3979.12957 | 128.43677 | 0.0 |
| DEPTH | 545.00537 | 1 | 545.00537 | 17.59147 | .000 |
| SEAL | 12.00949 | 1 | 12.00949 | .38764 | .536 |
| ⑬ DEPTH BY SEAL | .16124 | 1 | .16124 | .00520 | .943 |

ESTIMATES FOR NO3.

CONSTANT

| PARAMETER | COEFF. | STD. ERR. | T-VALUE | SIG. OF T | LOWER .95 CL | UPPER .95 CL |
|---|---|---|---|---|---|---|
| 1 | 73.916821369 | 6.52226 | 11.33299 | 0.0 | 60.89084 | 86.94253 |

DEPTH

| PARAMETER | COEFF. | STD. ERR. | T-VALUE | SIG. OF T | LOWER .95 CL | UPPER .95 CL |
|---|---|---|---|---|---|---|
| 2 | -.4981937722 | .11878 | -4.19422 | .000 | -.73542 | -.26097 |

SEAL

| PARAMETER | COEFF. | STD. ERR. | T-VALUE | SIG. OF T | LOWER .95 CL | UPPER .95 CL |
|---|---|---|---|---|---|---|
| 3 | -4.060790859 | 6.52226 | -.62261 | .536 | -17.08663 | 8.96505 |

DEPTH BY SEAL

| PARAMETER | COEFF. | STD. ERR. | T-VALUE | SIG. OF T | LOWER .95 CL | UPPER .95 CL |
|---|---|---|---|---|---|---|
| 4 | -.0085689854 | .11878 | -.07214 | .943 | -.24579 | .22865 |

⑬ The test of homogeneity of the within cell
regression coefficients is found in the re-
specified model's interaction. This test
indicates that we do have homogeneous regression
coefficients.

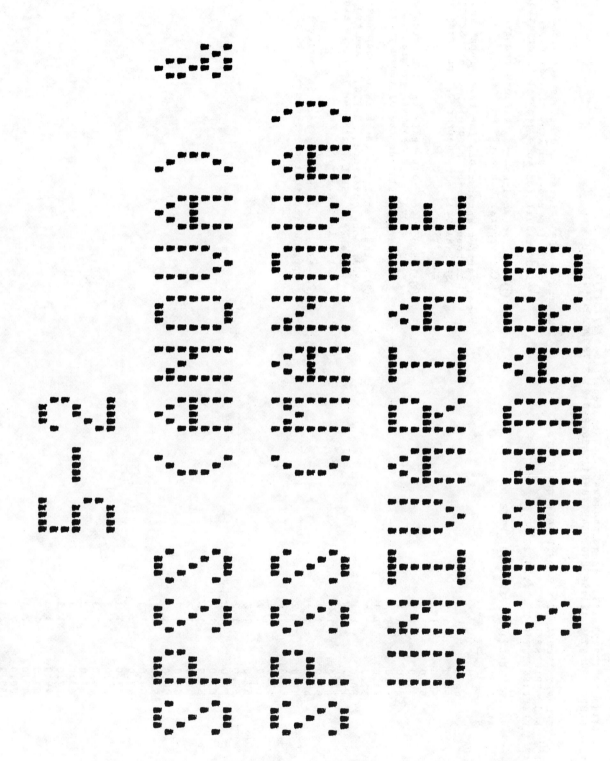

```
00000000011111111112222222222333333333344444444445555555555666666666677777777778
12345678901234567890123456789012345678901234567890123456789012345678901234567890
```

①

```
RUN NAME        TWO-WAY ANCOVA (2 X 3) WITH ONE COVARIATE
③ VARIABLE LIST    NO3 DEPTH SEAL FERT
INPUT FORMAT    FIXED(F6.1,T19,F5.1,T29,2F2.0)
N OF CASES      69
② ANOVA           NO3 BY SEAL(1,2),FERT(1,3) WITH DEPTH
STATISTICS      ALL
④ OPTIONS         9
READ INPUT DATA
48.0                  1 1
38.0                  1 1
36.0                  1 1
51.0                  1 1
34.0                  1 1
41.5                  1 1
45.5                  1 1
44.0                  1 1
47.0                  1 1
50.0                  1 1
45.0                  1 1
61.0                  1 1
58.0                  1 2
48.0                  1 2
49.0                  1 2
52.0                  1 2
67.0                  1 2
65.0                  1 2
57.0                  1 2
59.0                  1 2
53.0                  1 2
67.0                  1 2
54.0                  1 2
49.0                  1 2
58.0                  1 3
54.0                  1 3
52.0                  1 3
64.0                  1 3
67.0                  1 3
43.0                  1 3
61.0                  1 3
54.0                  1 3
51.0                  1 3
63.0                  1 3
57.0                  1 3
49.0                  1 3
61.0                  1 3
45.0                  2 1
50.0                  2 1
59.0                  2 1
52.0                  2 1
55.5                  2 1
51.0                  2 1
58.0                  2 1
58.5                  2 1
51.0                  2 1
55.5                  2 1
60.0                  2 1
```

Note: The SPSS input annotations provided here are of value for most problems of this type. Consult the SPSS manual for more general information.

① These are column identifiers and are not part of the program content.

Note: Further annotations for this input and output can be found in the program I/O for SPSS(ANOVA) and SPSS(MANOVA) in Chapter 2, programs numbered 2-4 and 2-1.

② Although we illustrate the I/O from both of the SPSS ANOVA and MANOVA programs, one would ordinarily only run one of these programs.

③ In these analyses there is one dependent variable, NO3, one covariate, DEPTH, and two independent variables, SEAL with two levels, and FERT with three levels.

④ Option 9 is needed here in order to obtain the appropriate test on the covariate.

⑤ In the subprogram MANOVA the specification that describes the design uses the word WITH to indicate the covariate, here DEPTH.

⑥ The PRINT subcommand (optional) requests that the observed cell means, adjusted (for the covariate) cell means, estimated cell means, average raw residual, and the average standardized residual be printed through the specification PMEANS. Here the specification ERROR(W) must be included in PMEANS and POBS to obtain output from PMEANS and POBS, both here and in the PLOT subcommand. The subspecification TABLES indicates that unweighted adjusted marginal means are to be printed for SEAL and FERT, and the unweighted adjusted cell means are to be printed for SEAL BY FERT.

⑦ The PMEANS specification in the PLOT subcommand requests that the observed, adjusted, and estimated means be plotted. Note that the ERROR(W) specification must also be used with PMEANS in the PRINT subcommand to obtain this plot.

⑧ This METHOD specification is needed to obtain the method of weighted squares of means analysis described in Appendix A.

⑨ The test of the homogeneity of the within cell regression coefficients may be found by re-specifying the design with the covariate considered as a dependent variable.

⑩ The ANALYSIS specification indicates that NO3 is the dependent variable to be analysed.

⑪ The test of the homogeneity of the within cell regression coefficients is found as the sum of the interaction effects between DEPTH and the other sources of variation in the design. Here the '+' sign lumps these sources into a single term.

```
53.5    56.0    2 2
48.0    53.0    2 2
43.0    64.0    2 2
47.0    60.0    2 2
59.0    57.0    2 2
57.0    56.0    2 2
51.0    51.0    2 2
54.5    47.0    2 2
41.5    59.0    2 2
44.0    52.0    2 2
55.5    53.0    2 2
50.5    51.0    2 3
40.5    53.0    2 3
61.0    60.0    2 3
45.5    61.0    2 3
61.0    44.0    2 3
58.0    49.0    2 3
37.5    62.0    2 3
58.0    56.0    2 3
47.0    58.0    2 3
49.0    49.0    2 3
```

```
② ⑤ MANOVA
     NO3 BY SEAL(1,2),FERT(1,3) WITH DEPTH /
  ⑥ PRINT = CELLINFO(MEANS)
       HOMOGENEITY(BARTLETT,COCHRAN)
       PMEANS(TABLES(SEAL,FERT,SEAL BY FERT) ERROR(W))
       POBS(ERROR(W))/
  ⑦ PLOT = BOXPLOTS STEMLEAF PMEANS POBS/
  ⑧ METHOD = SSTYPE(UNIQUE)/

   TASK NAME
② ⑨ MANOVA
     TEST OF HOMOGENEITY OF WITHIN CELL REGRESSION
     NO3 DEPTH BY SEAL(1,2),FERT(1,3) /
     METHOD = SSTYPE(UNIQUE)/
  ⑩ ANALYSIS = NO3/
  ⑪ DESIGN = DEPTH, SEAL, FERT, SEAL BY FERT, DEPTH BY SEAL + DEPTH
     BY FERT + DEPTH BY SEAL BY FERT/
```

```
①
0000000000111111111122222222223333333333444444444455555555556666666666777777777778
1234567890123456789012345678901234567890123456789012345678901234567890123456789012
```

```
0000000000111111111122222222223333333333444444444455555555556666666666777777777778
1234567890123456789012345678901234567890123456789012345678901234567890123456789012345678 90
```

① UNNUMBERED
TITLE      TWO-WAY ANCOVA  (2 X 3) WITH ONE COVARIATE
DATA LIST/ NO3 DEPTH SEAL FERT
           (F6.1,T19,F5.1,T29,2F2.0)
ANOVA      NO3 BY SEAL(1,2),FERT(1,3) WITH DEPTH
STATISTICS ALL
OPTIONS    9
BEGIN DATA
② 

END DATA
MANOVA     NO3 BY SEAL(1,2),FERT(1,3) WITH DEPTH /
           PRINT = CELLINFO(MEANS)
                   HOMOGENEITY(BARTLETT,COCHRAN)
                   PMEANS(TABLES(SEAL,FERT,SEAL BY FERT) ERROR(W))
                   POBS(ERROR(W))/
           PLOT = BOXPLOTS STEMLEAF PMEANS POBS/
           METHOD = SSTYPE(UNIQUE)/
SUBTITLE   TEST OF HOMOGENEITY OF WITHIN CELL REGRESSION
MANOVA     NO3 DEPTH BY SEAL(1,2),FERT(1,3) /
           METHOD = SSTYPE(UNIQUE)/
           ANALYSIS = NO3/
           DESIGN = DEPTH, SEAL, FERT, SEAL BY FERT, DEPTH BY SEAL + DEPTH
           BY FERT + DEPTH BY SEAL BY FERT/
```

```
0000000000111111111122222222223333333333444444444455555555556666666666777777777778
1234567890123456789012345678901234567890123456789012345678901234567890123456789012345678 90
```

① At our installation the default (NUMBERED) instruction allowed SPSSx to read only 72 columns. We therefore used the UNNUMBERED command to allow SPSSx to read all 80 columns. The default may vary by installation.

② The data go here.

441
```

TWO-WAY ANCOVA (2 X 3) WITH ONE COVARIATE

FILE   NONAME   (CREATION DATE = 02/02/83)

* * * * * * * * * * * * A N A L Y S I S   O F   V A R I A N C E * * * * * * * * * * * * * * * * *

(1) NO3
      BY SEAL
         FERT
      WITH DEPTH

(2)

| SOURCE OF VARIATION | SUM OF SQUARES | DF | MEAN SQUARE | F | SIGNIF OF F |
|---|---|---|---|---|---|
| (3) COVARIATES | 511.739 | 1 | 511.739 | 19.814 | 0.000 |
| DEPTH | 511.739 | 1 | 511.739 | 19.814 | 0.000 |
| (4) MAIN EFFECTS | 1511.907 | 3 | 503.969 | 19.513 | 0.000 |
| SEAL | 1332.750 | 1 | 1332.750 | 51.602 | 0.000 |
| FERT | 229.229 | 2 | 114.614 | 4.438 | 0.016 |
| (5) 2-WAY INTERACTIONS | 156.840 | 2 | 78.420 | 3.036 | 0.055 |
| SEAL    FERT | 156.840 | 2 | 78.420 | 3.036 | 0.055 |
| EXPLAINED | 2956.239 | 6 | 492.706 | 19.077 | 0.000 |
| RESIDUAL | 1601.320 | 62 | 25.828 | | |
| TOTAL | 4557.559 | 68 | 67.023 | | |

COVARIATE   RAW REGRESSION COEFFICIENT

DEPTH   (6)   -0.481

69 CASES WERE PROCESSED.
0 CASES ( 0.0 PCT) WERE MISSING.

442

(1) SPSS(ANOVA) will provide a separate analysis for each dependent variable but does not have multivariate capabilities.

(2) SPSS(ANOVA) prints the hypothesis tests in the traditional ANOVA format including sums of squares, degrees of freedom, mean squares, F values, and the exact probability of the test (see Table 5.5).

(3) The first test is the test of significance for the covariate (test for zero slope or no effect). Here we find that the covariate is significantly related to the dependent variable.

(4) The second test is a test of the main effect (equality of the adjusted cell means).

(5) The third test is a test of the interaction between the two independent variables.

(6) The estimated pooled within cell regression coefficient is printed.

**** * * * * * * * * * * * * * * * * * * * * * * * * A N A L Y S I S   O F   V A R I A N C E * * * * * * * * * * * * * * * * * * * * * *

CELL MEANS AND STANDARD DEVIATIONS

VARIABLE .. NO3

| FACTOR | CODE | MEAN | STD. DEV. | N | 95 PERCENT CONF. INTERVAL |
|---|---|---|---|---|---|
| SEAL | 1 | | | | |
| FERT | 1 | 42.95833 | 5.07874 | 12 | 39.73146  46.18521 |
| FERT | 2 | 36.54167 | 2.98830 | 12 | 34.64299  38.44034 |
| FERT | 3 | 43.76923 | 6.55622 | 13 | 39.80735  47.73111 |
| SEAL | 2 | | | | |
| FERT | 1 | 54.31818 | 4.60040 | 11 | 51.22760  57.40877 |
| FERT | 2 | 50.36364 | 6.02117 | 11 | 46.31856  54.40872 |
| FERT | 3 | 50.75000 | 8.44015 | 10 | 44.71228  56.78772 |
| FOR ENTIRE SAMPLE | | 46.11594 | 8.18677 | 69 | 44.14927  48.08262 |

VARIABLE .. DEPTH

| FACTOR | CODE | MEAN | STD. DEV. | N | 95 PERCENT CONF. INTERVAL |
|---|---|---|---|---|---|
| SEAL | 1 | | | | |
| FERT | 1 | 56.91667 | 5.88462 | 12 | 53.17776  60.65558 |
| FERT | 2 | 56.50000 | 6.90849 | 12 | 52.11055  60.88945 |
| FERT | 3 | 56.46154 | 6.78989 | 13 | 52.35845  60.56463 |
| SEAL | 2 | | | | |
| FERT | 1 | 50.63636 | 4.43334 | 11 | 47.65800  53.61472 |
| FERT | 2 | 55.27273 | 4.73478 | 11 | 52.09186  58.45360 |
| FERT | 3 | 54.30000 | 6.03784 | 10 | 49.98079  58.61921 |
| FOR ENTIRE SAMPLE | | 55.11594 | 6.08889 | 69 | 53.65323  56.57865 |

# TWO-WAY ANCOVA (2 X 3) WITH ONE COVARIATE

02/02/83     PAGE     9

* * * * * * * * * * * * * * * A N A L Y S I S   O F   V A R I A N C E * * * * * * * * * * * * * * * * * * * * * *

**(7)** TESTS OF SIGNIFICANCE FOR NO3 USING UNIQUE SUMS OF SQUARES

| SOURCE OF VARIATION | SUM OF SQUARES | DF | MEAN SQUARE | F | SIG. OF F |
|---|---|---|---|---|---|
| WITHIN CELLS | 1601.32951 | 62 | 25.82790 | | |
| **(8)** REGRESSION | 511.74334 | 1 | 511.74334 | 19.81359 | .000 |
| CONSTANT | 3839.88570 | 1 | 3839.88570 | 148.67203 | 0-0 |
| SEAL | 1332.74991 | 1 | 1332.74991 | 51.60118 | 0-0 |
| **(9)** FERT | 229.22856 | 2 | 114.61428 | 4.43762 | .016 |
| **(10)** SEAL BY FERT | 156.84016 | 2 | 78.42008 | 3.03626 | .055 |

ESTIMATES FOR NO3 ADJUSTED FOR 1 COVARIATE

CONSTANT

| PARAMETER | COEFF. | STD. ERR. | T-VALUE | SIG. OF T | LOWER .95 CL | UPPER .95 CL |
|---|---|---|---|---|---|---|
| 1 | 72.9355793815 | 5.98170 | 12.19311 | 0.0 | 60.97833 | 84.89283 |

SEAL

| PARAMETER | COEFF. | STD. ERR. | T-VALUE | SIG. OF T | LOWER .95 CL | UPPER .95 CL |
|---|---|---|---|---|---|---|
| 2 | -4.5846049468 | .63822 | -7.18340 | 0.0 | -5.86039 | -3.30882 |

FERT

| PARAMETER | COEFF. | STD. ERR. | T-VALUE | SIG. OF T | LOWER .95 CL | UPPER .95 CL |
|---|---|---|---|---|---|---|
| 3 | 1.5920615759 | .87744 | 1.81443 | .074 | -.16192 | 3.34604 |
| 4 | -2.5778097138 | .87228 | -2.95527 | .004 | -4.32147 | -.83415 |

SEAL BY FERT

| PARAMETER | COEFF. | STD. ERR. | T-VALUE | SIG. OF T | LOWER .95 CL | UPPER .95 CL |
|---|---|---|---|---|---|---|
| 5 | -.4164295826 | .88279 | -.47172 | .639 | -1.34823 | 2.18109 |
| 6 | -2.0309597349 | .87386 | -2.32414 | .023 | -3.77777 | -.28415 |

REGRESSION ANALYSIS FOR WITHIN CELLS ERROR TERM

**(7)** SPSS(MANOVA) prints the hypothesis tests in the traditional ANOVA format including sums of squares, degrees of freedom, mean squares, F values, and the exact probability of the test (see Table 5.5).

**(8)** The first test is the test of significance for the covariate (test for zero slope of no effect).

**(9)** These are the tests on the main effects.

**(10)** This is the test of the interaction between the two independent variables.

444

TWO-WAY ANCOVA (2 X 3) WITH CNE COVARIATE

02/02/83      PAGE  10

* * * * * * * * * * * * A N A L Y S I S   O F   V A R I A N C E * * * * * * * * * * * * * * * *

REGRESSION ANALYSIS FOR WITHIN CELLS ERROR TERM      (CONT.)

(11) This is an estimate of the pooled within cell regression coefficient. Note that the t test given here is equivalent to the F test for REGRESSION given above.

DEPENDENT VARIABLE ..NO3

| CCVARIATE | (11) B | (12) BETA | STD. ERR. | T-VALUE | SIG. OF T | LOWER .95 CL | UPPER .95 CL |
|---|---|---|---|---|---|---|---|
| DEPTH | -.4814254570 | -.4921175624 | .10816 | -4.45125 | .000 | -.69762 | -.26523 |

(12) This is an estimate of the standardized pooled regression coefficient.

ADJUSTED AND ESTIMATED MEANS

VARIABLE .. NO3

| FACTOR | CODE | (13) OBS. MEAN | (14)(19) ADJ. MEAN | (15)(16) EST. MEAN | (17) RAW RESID. | (18) STD. RESID. |
|---|---|---|---|---|---|---|
| SEAL | 1 | | | | | |
| FERT | 1 | 42.95833 | 43.87406 | 43.00715 | -.04881 | -.00960 |
| FERT | 2 | 36.54167 | 37.25680 | 36.59048 | -.04881 | -.00960 |
| FERT | 3 | 43.76923 | 44.46585 | 43.81804 | -.04881 | -.00960 |
| SEAL | 2 | | | | | |
| FERT | 1 | 54.31818 | 52.21041 | 54.36699 | -.04881 | -.00960 |
| FERT | 2 | 50.36364 | 50.48793 | 50.41245 | -.04881 | -.00960 |
| FERT | 3 | 50.75000 | 50.40600 | 50.79881 | -.04881 | -.00960 |

(13) The OBS.MEAN (observed mean) is the cell mean on the dependent variable.

PLOT OF OBSERVED(O), ADJUSTED(A), AND ESTIMATED(E) MEANS

VARIABLE .. NO3

```
        35.39998        43.39998        47.39998           55.399
      +-------+-------+-------+-------+-------+-------+-------+
    1 I                    E  A
      +
    2 I              E A
      +
    3 I                E A
      +
    4 I                                        A              E
      +
    5 I                                   E
      +
    6 I                                     A E
      +-------+-------+-------+-------+-------+-------+-------+
        35.39999        43.39998        51.39998
```

445

98

TWO-WAY ANCOVA (2 X 3) WITH ONE COVARIATE

* * * * * * * * * * * * * * * * * * * A N A L Y S I S   O F   V A R I A N C E * * * * * * * * * * * * * * * * * * * * * * * * * * *   02/02/83       PAGE   11

ADJUSTED AND ESTIMATED MEANS (CONT.)

VARIABLE -- NO3

(14) The ADJ.MEAN (adjusted mean) is the observed mean adjusted for the covariate. It can be found using:

$$\bar{Y}(adj) = \bar{Y} - b(\bar{X}-GM)$$

where, $\bar{Y}(adj)$ = the adjusted mean,

$\bar{Y}$ = the observed mean on the dependent variable for cell i,

b = the pooled regression coefficient,

$\bar{X}$ = the observed mean on the covariate for cell i, and

GM = the unweighted grand mean on the covariate.

(15) Finn (1974, p.376) describes the ADJ.MEAN and the EST.MEAN values shown here.

(16) The EST.MEAN (estimated mean) is the mean estimated from the covariance model used by this program.

(17) The RAW RESID. (raw residual) is the difference between the OBS.MEAN minus the EST.MEAN. It can be used to spot outliers in the data.

(18) The STD.RESID. (standardized residual) is the RAW RESID. divided by the square root of the preceding WITHIN CELLS MEAN SQUARE.

(19) The UNWGT. (unweighted) marginal adjusted and adjusted cell means may be used in post hoc analyses.

446

* * * * * * * * * * * * * * * * * * * * A N A L Y S I S   O F   V A R I A N C E * * * * * * * * * * * * * * * * * * * *

COMBINED ESTIMATED MEANS FOR SEAL

VARIABLE -- NO3

   SEAL (19)

      1     UNWGT.    41.86557

      2     UNWGT.    51.03478

---

COMBINED ESTIMATED MEANS FOR FERT

VARIABLE -- NO3

   FERT (19)

      1     UNWGT.    48.04224

      2     UNWGT.    43.87237

      3     UNWGT.    47.43592

---

COMBINED ESTIMATED MEANS FOR SEAL EY FERT

VARIABLE -- NO3

   FERT (19)    SEAL          1              2

      1     UNWGT.    43.87406       52.21041

      2     UNWGT.    37.25680       50.48793

      3     UNWGT.    44.46585       50.40600

---

447

TWO-WAY ANCOVA (2 X 3) WITH ONE COVARIATE
TEST OF HOMOGENEITY OF WITHIN CELL REGRESSION

\* \* \* \* \* \* \* \* \* \* \* \* \* \* \* A N A L Y S I S   O F   V A R I A N C E \* \* \* \* \* \* \* \* \* \* \* \* \* \* \* \* \* \* \*

TESTS OF SIGNIFICANCE FOR NO3 USING UNIQUE SUMS OF SQUARES

| SOURCE OF VARIATION | SUM OF SQUARES | DF | MEAN SQUARE | F | SIG. OF F |
|---|---|---|---|---|---|
| WITHIN+RESIDUAL | 1487.89354 | 57 | 26.10340 | | |
| CONSTANT | 3230.99217 | 1 | 3230.99217 | 123.77670 | 0.0 |
| DEPTH | 374.75200 | 1 | 374.75200 | 14.35645 | .000 |
| SEAL | .76865 | 1 | .76865 | .02945 | .864 |
| FERT | 61.43640 | 2 | 30.71820 | 1.17679 | .316 |
| SEAL BY FERT | 55.84848 | 2 | 27.92424 | 1.06976 | .350 |
| DEPTH BY SEAL + DEPTH BY FERT + DEPTH BY SEAL BY FERT | 113.43597 | 5 | 22.68719 | .86913 | .508 |

--------------------------------------------------

ESTIMATES FOR NO3

CONSTANT

| PARAMETER | COEFF. | STD. ERR. | T-VALUE | SIG. OF T | LOWER .95 CL | UPPER .95 CL |
|---|---|---|---|---|---|---|
| 1 | 71.2304623981 | 6.40245 | 11.12550 | 0.0 | 58.40977 | 84.05115 |

DEPTH

| PARAMETER | COEFF. | STD. ERR. | T-VALUE | SIG. OF T | LOWER .95 CL | UPPER .95 CL |
|---|---|---|---|---|---|---|
| 2 | -.4439576753 | .11717 | -3.78899 | .030 | -.67859 | -.20933 |

SEAL

| PARAMETER | COEFF. | STD. ERR. | T-VALUE | SIG. OF T | LOWER .95 CL | UPPER .95 CL |
|---|---|---|---|---|---|---|
| 3 | -1.0986605442 | 6.40245 | -.17160 | .864 | -13.91935 | 11.72203 |

FERT

| PARAMETER | COEFF. | STD. ERR. | T-VALUE | SIG. OF T | LOWER .95 CL | UPPER .95 CL |
|---|---|---|---|---|---|---|
| 4 | -6.4262813062 | 9.39403 | -.68408 | .497 | -25.23751 | 12.38495 |
| 5 | -6.7122142230 | 9.17830 | -.73131 | .468 | -25.09144 | 11.66702 |

(20) The test of homogeneity of the within cell regression coefficients is found in the re-specified model's interaction. This test indicates that we do have homogeneous regression coefficients.

448

TWO-WAY ANCOVA (2 X 3) WITH CNE COVARIATE
TEST OF HOMOGENEITY OF WITHIN CELL REGRESSION

* * * * * * * * * * * * * * * * * * * * * A N A L Y S I S   O F   V A R I A N C E * * * * * * * * * * * * * * * * * * * * * * *

ESTIMATES FOR NO3          (CONT.)

SEAL BY FERT

| PARAMETER | COEFF. | STD. ERR. | T-VALUE | SIG. OF T | LOWER .95 CL | UPPER .95 CL |
|---|---|---|---|---|---|---|
| 6 | 11.0108434864 | 9.39403 | 1.17211 | .246 | -7.80038 | 29.82207 |
| 7 | -12.7529209643 | 9.17830 | -1.38946 | .170 | -31.13215 | 5.62631 |

DEPTH BY SEAL + DEPTH BY FERT + DEPTH BY SEAL BY FERT

| PARAMETER | COEFF. | STD. ERR. | T-VALUE | SIG. OF T | LOWER .95 CL | UPPER .95 CL |
|---|---|---|---|---|---|---|
| 8 | -.0688551880 | .11717 | -.58765 | .559 | -.30348 | .16577 |
| 9 | -.1593045328 | .17466 | -.91207 | .366 | -.19045 | .50906 |
| 10 | -.0656121765 | .16606 | -.39511 | .694 | -.26691 | .39814 |
| 11 | -.2044658546 | .17466 | -1.17063 | .247 | -.55422 | .14529 |
| 12 | .1972006868 | .16606 | 1.18754 | .240 | -.13533 | .52973 |

449

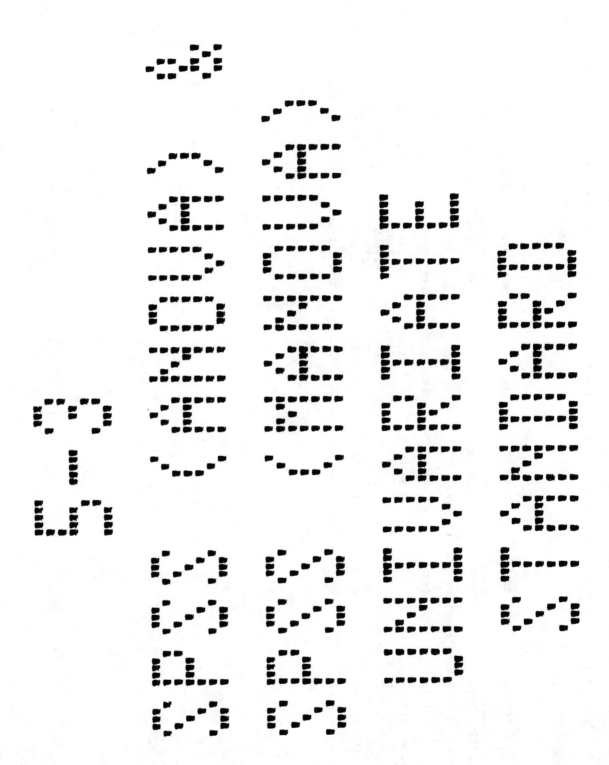

```
000000000011111111112222222222333333333344444444445555555555666666666677777777778
123456789012345678901234567890123456789012345678901234567890123456789012345678 90
```

RUN NAME         TWO-WAY ANCOVA WITH TWO COVARIATES
VARIABLE LIST    NO3 DEPTH TDS SEAL FERT
INPUT FORMAT     FIXED(F6.1,11X,F6.1,F5.0,T29,2F2.0)
N OF CASES       69
ANOVA            NO3 BY SEAL(1,2),FERT(1,3) WITH DEPTH TDS
STATISTICS       ALL
OPTIONS          9
READ INPUT DATA

```
48.0    750 1 1
59.0    400 1 1
67.0    425 1 1
51.0    850 1 1
34.0    300 1 1
41.5    650 1 1
45.5    575 1 1
61.0    475 1 1
47.0    400 1 1
50.0    650 1 1
51.0    875 1 1
40.5    375 1 1
61.0    500 1 2
58.0    500 1 2
48.0    875 1 2
49.0    650 1 2
52.0    575 1 2
67.0    275 1 2
65.0    450 1 2
57.0    350 1 2
59.0    350 1 2
53.0    650 1 2
67.0    350 1 2
54.0    675 1 2
49.0    675 1 2
58.0    375 1 3
50.0    700 1 3
52.0    850 1 3
45.0    575 1 3
64.0    575 1 3
67.0    300 1 3
43.0    800 1 3
61.0    625 1 3
54.0    725 1 3
39.5    575 1 3
37.5    475 1 3
47.0    450 1 3
49.0    775 1 3
61.0    375 1 3
45.0    775 2 1
55.5    675 2 1
51.0    700 2 1
58.5    550 2 1
55.0    600 2 1
51.0    625 2 1
45.5    675 2 1
52.0    650 2 1
46.0    800 2 1
48.0    525 2 1
54.0    700 2 1
```

① Note: The SPSS input annotations provided here are of value for most problems of this type. Consult the SPSS manual for more general information.

① These are column identifiers and are not part of the program content.

Note: Further annotations for this input and output can be found in the program I/O for SPSS(ANOVA) and SPSS(MANOVA) in Chapter 2, programs numbered 2-4 and 2-1.

② Although we illustrate the I/O from both of the SPSS ANOVA and MANOVA programs, one would ordinarily only run one of these programs.

③ In these analyses there is one dependent variable, NO3, two covariates, DEPTH and TDS, and two independent variables, SEAL with two levels, and FERT with three levels.

④ Option 9 is needed here in order to obtain the appropriate test on the covariate.

⑤ In the subprogram MANOVA the specification that describes the design uses the word WITH to indicate the covariates, here DEPTH and TDS.

⑥ The PRINT subcommand (optional) requests that the observed cell means, adjusted (for the covariate) cell means, estimated cell means, average raw residual, and the average standardized residual be printed through the specification PMEANS. Here the specification ERROR(W) must be included in PMEANS and POBS to obtain output from PMEANS and POBS, both here and in the PLOT subcommand. The subspecification TABLES indicates that unweighted adjusted marginal means are to be printed for SEAL and FERT, and the unweighted adjusted cell means are to be printed for SEAL BY FERT.

⑦ The PMEANS specification in the PLOT subcommand requests that the observed, adjusted, and estimated means be plotted. Note that the ERROR(W) specification must also be used with PMEANS in the PRINT subcommand to obtain this plot.

⑪ In the DESIGN specification the use of CONTIN allows you to consider the effects of several interval variables (i.e. covariates) together, and is therefore more convenient to write. For example, here

     CONTIN (DEPTH, TDS) BY SEAL

replaces

     DEPTH BY SEAL + TDS BY SEAL.

⑫ The test of homogeneity of the within cell regression coefficients is found as the sum of the interaction effects between DEPTH and TDS, and the other sources of variation in the design. Here the '+' sign lumps these sources into a single term.

```
        53.5    56.0    625   2 2
        48.0    53.0    675   2 2
        43.0    64.0    400   2 2
        47.0    60.0    300   2 2
        59.0    57.0    750   2 2
        57.0    56.0    675   2 2
        51.0    51.0    525   2 2
        54.5    47.0    575   2 2
        41.5    59.0    475   2 2
        44.0    52.0    700   2 2
        55.5    53.0    650   2 2
        50.0    51.0    625   2 3
        40.5    53.0    400   2 3
        61.0    60.0    650   2 3
        45.5    61.0    400   2 3
        61.0    44.0    675   2 3
        58.0    49.0    700   2 3
        37.5    58.0    500   2 3
        58.0    56.0    575   2 3
        47.0    58.0    625   2 3
        49.0    49.0    675   2 3
```

```
② ⑤ MANOVA   NO3 BY SEAL(1,2) FERT(1,3) WITH DEPTH TDS/
      ⑥ PRINT = CELLINFO(MEANS)
               HOMOGENEITY(BARTLETT,COCHRAN)
               PMEANS
               (VARIABLES(NO3) TABLES(SEAL,FERT,SEAL BY FERT) ERROR(W))
               POBS(ERROR(W))/
      ⑦ PLOT = BOXPLOTS STEMLEAF PMEANS POBS/
      ⑧ METHOD = SSTYPE(UNIQUE)/
      ⑨ TEST OF HOMOGENEITY OF WITHIN CELL REGRESSION
         NO3 DEPTH TDS BY SEAL(1,2) FERT(1,3)/
      ⑩ METHOD = SSTYPE(UNIQUE)/
         ANALYSIS = NO3/
      ⑪ DESIGN = DEPTH, TDS, SEAL, FERT, SEAL BY FERT,
      ⑫ CONTIN(DEPTH,TDS) BY SEAL + CONTIN(DEPTH,TDS) BY
         FERT + CONTIN(DEPTH,TDS) BY SEAL BY FERT/
```

```
TASK NAME
② MANOVA
```

```
① 0000000001111111111222222222233333333334444444444555555555566666666667777777778
   1234567890123456789012345678901234567890123456789012345678901234567890123456789 0
```

⑧ This METHOD specification is needed to obtain the method of weighted squares of means analysis described in Appendix A.

⑨ The test of the homogeneity of the within cell regression coefficients may be found by re-specifying the design with the covariate considered as a dependent variable.

⑩ The ANALYSIS specification indicates that NO3 is the dependent variable to be analysed.

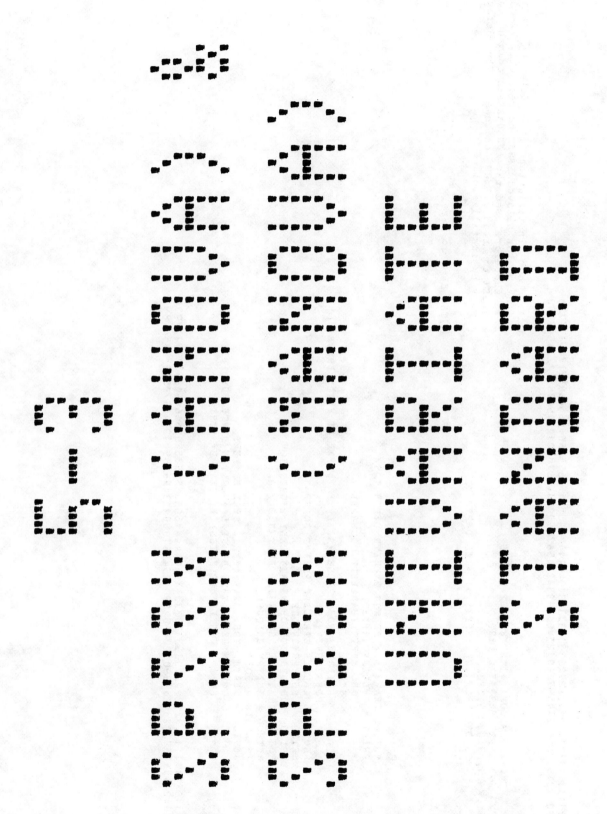

```
0000000001111111111222222222233333333334444444444555555555566666666667777777778
1234567890123456789012345678901234567890123456789012345678901234567890123456789 0
```

① UNNUMBERED
TITLE       TWO-WAY ANCOVA WITH TWO COVARIATES
DATA LIST/   NO3 DEPTH TDS SEAL FERT
            (F6.1,11X,F6.1,F5.0,T29,2F2.0)
ANOVA        NO3 BY SEAL(1,2),FERT(1,3) WITH DEPTH TDS
STATISTICS   ALL
OPTIONS      9
BEGIN DATA

②

END DATA
MANOVA       NO3 BY SEAL(1,2) FERT(1,3) WITH DEPTH TDS/
             PRINT = CELLINFO(MEANS)
                     HOMOGENEITY(BARTLETT,COCHRAN)
                     PMEANS
                     (VARIABLES(NO3) TABLES(SEAL,FERT,SEAL BY FERT) ERROR(W))
                     POBS(ERROR(W))/
             PLOT = BOXPLOTS STEMLEAF PMEANS POBS/
             METHOD = SSTYPE(UNIQUE)/
TEST OF HOMOGENEITY OF WITHIN CELL REGRESSION
SUBTITLE     NO3 DEPTH TDS BY SEAL(1,2) FERT(1,3)/
MANOVA       METHOD = SSTYPE(UNIQUE)/
             ANALYSIS = NO3/
             DESIGN = DEPTH, TDS, SEAL, FERT, SEAL BY FERT,
                      CONTIN(DEPTH,TDS) BY SEAL + CONTIN(DEPTH,TDS) BY
                      FERT + CONTIN(DEPTH,TDS) BY SEAL BY FERT/
```
0000000001111111111222222222233333333334444444444555555555566666666667777777778
1234567890123456789012345678901234567890123456789012345678901234567890123456789 0
```

① At our installation the default (NUMBERED)
instruction allowed SPSSX to read only 72 columns.
We therefore used the UNNUMBERED command to allow
SPSSX to read all 80 columns. The default may
vary by installation.

② The data go here.

454

TWO-WAY ANCOVA WITH TWO COVARIATES

FILE  NONAME  (CREATION DATE = 02/02/83)

* * * * * * * * * A N A L Y S I S  O F  V A R I A N C E * * * * * * * * * * * * * * *

(1)    NO3
    BY SEAL
       FERT
    WITH DEPTH
       TDS

* * * * * * * * * * * * * * * * * * * * * * * * * * * * * * * * * * *

(2)

| SOURCE OF VARIATION | SUM OF SQUARES | DF | MEAN SQUARE | F | SIGNIF OF F |
|---|---|---|---|---|---|
| (3) COVARIATES | 755.783 | 2 | 377.892 | 16.984 | 0.000 |
| (4) DEPTH | 28.092 | 1 | 28.092 | 1.263 | 0.266 |
| TDS | 244.044 | 1 | 244.044 | 10.968 | 0.002 |
| (5) MAIN EFFECTS | 1535.821 | 3 | 511.940 | 23.008 | 0.000 |
| SEAL | 1386.717 | 1 | 1386.717 | 62.323 | 0.000 |
| FERT | 191.542 | 2 | 95.771 | 4.304 | 0.018 |
| (6) 2-WAY INTERACTIONS | 110.422 | 2 | 55.211 | 2.481 | 0.092 |
| SEAL FERT | 110.422 | 2 | 55.211 | 2.481 | 0.092 |
| EXPLAINED | 3200.283 | 7 | 457.183 | 20.547 | 0.000 |
| RESIDUAL | 1357.275 | 61 | 22.250 | | |
| TOTAL | 4557.559 | 68 | 67.023 | | |

| COVARIATE | RAW REGRESSION COEFFICIENT |
|---|---|
| DEPTH (7) | -0.157 |
| TDS | 0.018 |

69 CASES WERE PROCESSED.
0 CASES ( 0.0 PCT) WERE MISSING.

(1) SPSS(ANOVA) will provide a separate analysis for each dependent variable but does not have multivariate capabilities.

(2) SPSS(ANOVA) prints the hypothesis tests in the traditional ANOVA format including sums of squares, degrees of freedom, mean squares, F values, and the exact probability of the test (see Table 5.7).

(3) The first test is the test of significance for the covariates (test of zero slope or no effect). Here we find that both covariates are significantly related to the dependent variable.

(4) These are the individual tests for each covariate given the other. Here we find that when TDS is partialed from DEPTH, what is left of DEPTH is not significantly related to NO3 (p<.266). However, when DEPTH is partialed from TDS what remains of TDS is significantly related to NO3 (p<.002).

(5) These are the tests on the main effects.

(6) This is the test of the interaction between the two independent variables.

(7) The estimated pooled within cell regression coefficients are printed next.

455

* * * * * * * * * * * * * * * A N A L Y S I S   O F   V A R I A N C E * * * * * * * * * * * * * * * * * * * *

CELL MEANS AND STANDARD DEVIATIONS

VARIABLE -- NO3

| FACTOR | CODE | MEAN | STD. DEV. | N | 95 PERCENT CONF. INTERVAL | |
|---|---|---|---|---|---|---|
| SEAL | 1 | | | | | |
| FERT | 1 | 42.95833 | 5.07874 | 12 | 39.73146 | 46.18521 |
| FERT | 2 | 36.54167 | 2.98830 | 12 | 34.64299 | 38.44034 |
| FERT | 3 | 43.76923 | 6.55622 | 13 | 39.80735 | 47.73111 |
| SEAL | 2 | | | | | |
| FERT | 1 | 54.31818 | 4.60040 | 11 | 51.22760 | 57.40877 |
| FERT | 2 | 50.36364 | 6.02117 | 11 | 46.31856 | 54.40872 |
| FERT | 3 | 50.75000 | 8.44015 | 10 | 44.71228 | 56.78772 |
| FOR ENTIRE SAMPLE | | 46.11594 | 8.18677 | 69 | 44.14927 | 48.08262 |

VARIABLE -- DEPTH

| FACTOR | CODE | MEAN | STD. DEV. | N | 95 PERCENT CONF. INTERVAL | |
|---|---|---|---|---|---|---|
| SEAL | 1 | | | | | |
| FERT | 1 | 56.91667 | 5.88462 | 12 | 53.17776 | 60.65558 |
| FERT | 2 | 56.50000 | 6.90849 | 12 | 52.11055 | 60.88945 |
| FERT | 3 | 56.46154 | 6.78989 | 13 | 52.35845 | 60.56463 |
| SEAL | 2 | | | | | |
| FERT | 1 | 50.63636 | 4.43334 | 11 | 47.65800 | 53.61472 |
| FERT | 2 | 55.27273 | 4.73478 | 11 | 52.09186 | 58.45360 |
| FERT | 3 | 54.30000 | 6.03784 | 10 | 49.98079 | 58.61921 |
| FOR ENTIRE SAMPLE | | 55.11594 | 6.08889 | 69 | 53.65323 | 56.57865 |

VARIABLE -- TDS

| FACTOR | CODE | MEAN | STD. DEV. | N | 95 PERCENT CONF. INTERVAL |
|---|---|---|---|---|---|

\* \* \* \* \* \* \* \* \* \* \* \* \* \* \* \* A N A L Y S I S   O F   V A R I A N C E \* \* \* \* \* \* \* \* \* \* \* \* \* \* \* \* \*

CELL MEANS AND STANDARD DEVIATIONS  (CONT.)

VARIABLE -- TDS

| FACTOR | CODE | MEAN | STD. DEV. | N | 95 PERCENT CONF. INTERVAL | |
|--------|------|------|-----------|---|---------------------------|--|
| SEAL | 1 | | | | | |
| FERT | 1 | 560.41667 | 194.07658 | 12 | 437.10631 | 683.72702 |
| FERT | 2 | 531.25000 | 181.25980 | 12 | 416.08304 | 646.41696 |
| FERT | 3 | 584.61538 | 179.56500 | 13 | 476.10535 | 693.12542 |
| SEAL | 2 | | | | | |
| FERT | 1 | 661.36364 | 84.67854 | 11 | 604.47584 | 718.25144 |
| FERT | 2 | 577.27273 | 138.94898 | 11 | 483.92556 | 670.61989 |
| FERT | 3 | 582.50000 | 111.83445 | 10 | 502.49849 | 662.50151 |
| FOR ENTIRE SAMPLE | | 581.88406 | 155.58736 | 69 | 544.50789 | 619.26022 |

UNIVARIATE HOMOGENEITY OF VARIANCE TESTS

VARIABLE -- NO3

```
COCHRANS C(11,6)    =           .34520, P = .044 (APPROX.)
BARTLETT-BOX F(5,5015) =       2.22315, P = .050
```

VARIABLE -- DEPTH

```
COCHRANS C(11,6)    =           .23058, P = .794 (APPROX.)
BARTLETT-BOX F(5,5015) =        .64425, P = .666
```

VARIABLE -- TDS

```
COCHRANS C(11,6)    =           .26572, P = .373 (APPROX.)
BARTLETT-BOX F(5,5015) =       1.79886, P = .110
```

69  CASES ACCEPTED.
 0  CASES REJECTED BECAUSE OF OUT-OF-RANGE FACTOR VALUES.
 0  CASES REJECTED BECAUSE OF MISSING DATA.
 6  NON-EMPTY CELLS.

TWO-WAY ANCOVA WITH TWO COVARIATES

02/02/83     PAGE   11

* * * * * * * * * * * * * * * * A N A L Y S I S   O F   V A R I A N C E * * * * * * * * * * * * * * * * *

(8) TESTS OF SIGNIFICANCE FOR NO3 USING UNIQUE SUMS OF SQUARES

| SOURCE OF VARIATION | SUM OF SQUARES | DF | MEAN SQUARE | F | SIG. OF F |
|---|---|---|---|---|---|
| WITHIN CELLS | 1357.28966 | 61 | 22.25065 | | |
| (9) REGRESSION | 755.78319 | 2 | 377.89159 | 16.98340 | 0.0 |
| CONSTANT | 436.42733 | 1 | 436.42733 | 19.61414 | .000 |
| (10) SEAL | 1386.71589 | 1 | 1386.71589 | 62.32249 | 0.0 |
| FERT | 191.54240 | 2 | 95.77120 | 4.30420 | .018 |
| (11) SEAL BY FERT | 110.42327 | 2 | 55.21164 | 2.48135 | .092 |

ESTIMATES FOR NO3 ADJUSTED FOR 2 COVARIATES

CONSTANT

| PARAMETER | COEFF. | STD. ERR. | T-VALUE | SIG. OF T | LOWER .95 CL | UPPER .95 CL |
|---|---|---|---|---|---|---|
| 1 | 44.8696139334 | 10.13136 | 4.42879 | .000 | 24.61071 | 65.12852 |

SEAL

| PARAMETER | COEFF. | STD. ERR. | T-VALUE | SIG. OF T | LOWER .95 CL | UPPER .95 CL |
|---|---|---|---|---|---|---|
| 2 | -4.6822991232 | .59311 | -7.89446 | 0.0 | -5.86830 | -3.49630 |

FERT

| PARAMETER | COEFF. | STD. ERR. | T-VALUE | SIG. OF T | LOWER .95 CL | UPPER .95 CL |
|---|---|---|---|---|---|---|
| 3 | 1.5011984200 | .81488 | 1.84224 | .070 | -.12825 | 3.13064 |
| 4 | -2.3568111921 | .81237 | -2.90117 | .005 | -3.98124 | -.73239 |

SEAL BY FERT

| PARAMETER | COEFF. | STD. ERR. | T-VALUE | SIG. OF T | LOWER .95 CL | UPPER .95 CL |
|---|---|---|---|---|---|---|
| 5 | -.3840536389 | .81943 | -.46868 | .641 | -1.25450 | 2.02261 |
| 6 | -1.7275940653 | .81624 | -2.11652 | .038 | -3.35977 | -.09542 |

REGRESSION ANALYSIS FOR WITHIN CELLS ERROR TERM

(8) SPSS(MANOVA) prints the hypothesis tests in the traditional ANOVA format including sums of squares, degrees of freedom, mean squares, F values, and the exact probability of the test (see Table 5.7).

(9) The first test is the test of significance for the covariates (test of zero slope or no effect). Here we find that both covariates are significantly related to the dependent variable.

(10) These are the tests on the main effects.

458

\* \* \* \* \* \* \* \* \* \* \* \* \* \* \* \* \* \* \*A N A L Y S I S  O F  V A R I A N C E\* \* \* \* \* \* \* \* \* \* \* \* \* \* \* \* \* \* \*

REGRESSION ANALYSIS FOR WITHIN CELLS ERROR TERM    (CONT.)

DEPENDENT VARIABLE .. NO3

| COVARIATE | (12) B | (13) BETA | STD. ERR. | (14) T-VALUE | SIG. OF T | LOWER .95 CL | UPPER .95 CL |
|---|---|---|---|---|---|---|---|
| DEPTH | -.1574951219 | -.1609929728 | .14016 | -1.12369 | .266 | -.43776 | .12277 |
| TDS | .0175759652 | .4744828755 | .00531 | 3.31176 | .002 | -.00696 | .02819 |

ADJUSTED AND ESTIMATED MEANS

VARIABLE .. NO3

| FACTOR | CODE | (15) OBS. MEAN | (16) ADJ. MEAN | (17) (18) EST. MEAN | (19) RAW RESID. | (20) STD. RESID. |
|---|---|---|---|---|---|---|
| SEAL | 1 | | | | | |
| FERT | 1 | 42.95833 | 43.65313 | 42.99221 | -.03388 | -.00718 |
| FERT | 2 | 36.54167 | 37.68347 | 36.57555 | -.03388 | -.00718 |
| FERT | 3 | 43.76923 | 43.96703 | 43.80311 | -.03388 | -.00718 |
| SEAL | 2 | | | | | |
| FERT | 1 | 54.31818 | 52.24962 | 54.35206 | -.03388 | -.00718 |
| FERT | 2 | 50.36364 | 50.50326 | 50.39752 | -.03388 | -.00718 |
| FERT | 3 | 50.75000 | 50.64455 | 50.78388 | -.03388 | -.00718 |

PLOT OF OBSERVED(O), ADJUSTED(A), AND ESTIMATED(E) MEANS

VARIABLE .. NO3

```
 1    +
      I     +         E   A
 2    I  +  E  A
      I  +
 3    I  +        EA
      I  +
 4    I       +                                    A       E
      I  +
 5    I  +                              AE
      I  +
 6    I  +
      +----------+----------+----------+----------+----------+
   35.39999  39.39998  43.39998  47.39998  51.39998  55.399
```

98

459

---

(12) The estimated pooled within cell regression coefficients are printed next.

(13) The column headed BETA contains the standardized regression coefficients.

(14) These are the individual tests for each covariate given the other. Here we find that when TDS is partialed from DEPTH, what is left of DEPTH is not significantly related to NO3 (p<.266). However, when DEPTH is partialed from TDS what remains of TDS is significantly related to NO3 (p<.002).

TWO-WAY ANCOVA WITH TWO COVARIATES

* * * * * * * * * * * * * * * * * * * * A N A L Y S I S   O F   V A R I A N C E * * * * * * * * * * * * * * * * * * * * * * * * *          02/02/83          PAGE    13

ADJUSTED AND ESTIMATED MEANS (CONT.)

VARIABLE .. NO3

(15) The OBS.MEAN (observed mean) is the cell mean on the dependent variable.

(16) The ADJ.MEAN (adjusted mean) is the observed mean adjusted for the covariate. It can be found using:

$$\overline{Y}(adj) = \overline{Y} - b(\overline{X}-GM)$$

where, $\overline{Y}(adj)$ = the adjusted mean,

$\overline{Y}$ = the observed mean on the dependent variable for cell i,
 b = the pooled regression coefficient,

$\overline{X}$ = the observed mean on the covariate for cell i, and
GM = the unweighted grand mean on the covariate.

(17) Finn (1974, p.376) describes the ADJ.MEAN and the EST.MEAN values shown here.

(18) The EST.MEAN (estimated mean) is the mean estimated from the covariance model used by this program.

(19) The RAW RESID. (raw residual) is the difference between the OBS.MEAN minus the EST.MEAN. It can be used to spot outliers in the data.

(20) The STD.RESID. (standardized residual) is the RAW RESID. divided by the square root of the preceding WITHIN CELLS MEAN SQUARE.

460

TWO-WAY ANCOVA WITH TWO COVARIATES

* * * * * * * * * * * * * * * * * * A N A L Y S I S   O F   V A R I A N C E * * * * * * * * * * * * * * * * * * * * * * * * * *

02/02/83      PAGE   19

COMBINED ESTIMATED MEANS FOR SEAL

VARIABLE .. NO3

SEAL (21)

| | | |
|---|---|---|
| 1 | UNWGT. | 41.76788 |
| 2 | UNWGT. | 51.13247 |

(21) The UNWGT. (unweighted) marginal adjusted and adjusted cell means may be used in post hoc analyses.

COMBINED ESTIMATED MEANS FOR FERT

VARIABLE .. NO3

FERT (21)

| | | |
|---|---|---|
| 1 | UNWGT. | 47.95137 |
| 2 | UNWGT. | 44.09336 |
| 3 | UNWGT. | 47.30579 |

COMBINED ESTIMATED MEANS FOR SEAL BY FERT

VARIABLE .. NO3

FERT (21)

| SEAL | | 1 | 2 |
|---|---|---|---|
| 1 | UNWGT. | 43.65313 | 52.24962 |
| 2 | UNWGT. | 37.68347 | 50.50326 |
| 3 | UNWGT. | 43.96703 | 50.64455 |

TWO-WAY ANCOVA WITH TWO COVARIATES
TEST OF HOMOGENEITY OF WITHIN CELL REGRESSION

\* \* \* \* \* \* \* \* \* \* \* \* \* \* \* \* \* \* \* A N A L Y S I S   O F   V A R I A N C E \* \* \* \* \* \* \* \* \* \* \* \* \* \* \* \* \* \* \*     02/02/83     PAGE  23

TESTS OF SIGNIFICANCE FOR NO3 USING UNIQUE SUMS OF SQUARES

| SOURCE OF VARIATION | SUM OF SQUARES | DF | MEAN SQUARE | F | SIG. OF F |
|---|---|---|---|---|---|
| WITHIN+RESIDUAL | 1109.96106 | 51 | 21.76394 | | |
| CONSTANT | 398.21519 | 1 | 398.21519 | 18.29702 | .000 |
| DEPTH | 29.85257 | 1 | 29.85257 | 1.37165 | .247 |
| TDS | 230.41067 | 1 | 230.41067 | 10.58681 | .002 |
| SEAL | 4.27342 | 1 | 4.27342 | .19635 | .660 |
| FERT | 6.32270 | 2 | 3.16135 | .14526 | .865 |
| SEAL BY FERT | 5.62024 | 2 | 2.81012 | .12912 | .879 |
| (22) CONTIN(DEPTH TDS) BY SEAL + CONTIN(DEPTH TDS) BY FERT + CONTIN(DEPTH TDS) BY SEAL BY FERT | 247.32860 | 10 | 24.73286 | 1.13641 | .355 |

ESTIMATES FOR NO3

CONSTANT

| PARAMETER | COEFF. | STD. ERR. | T-VALUE | SIG. OF T | LOWER .95 CL | UPPER .95 CL |
|---|---|---|---|---|---|---|
| 1 | 44.7177668692 | 10.45418 | 4.27750 | .000 | 23.73012 | 65.70541 |

DEPTH

| PARAMETER | COEFF. | STD. ERR. | T-VALUE | SIG. OF T | LOWER .95 CL | UPPER .95 CL |
|---|---|---|---|---|---|---|
| 2 | -.1699442594 | .14511 | -1.17118 | .247 | -.46126 | .12137 |

TDS

| PARAMETER | COEFF. | STD. ERR. | T-VALUE | SIG. OF T | LOWER .95 CL | UPPER .95 CL |
|---|---|---|---|---|---|---|
| 3 | .0192564611 | .00592 | 3.25374 | .002 | .00738 | .03114 |

SEAL

| PARAMETER | COEFF. | STD. ERR. | T-VALUE | SIG. OF T | LOWER .95 CL | UPPER .95 CL |
|---|---|---|---|---|---|---|
| 4 | 4.6324298858 | 10.45418 | .44312 | .660 | -16.35521 | 25.62607 |

(22) The test of homogeneity of the within cell regression coefficients is found in the re-specified model's interaction. This test indicates that we do have homogeneous regression coefficients.

462

* * * * * * * * * * * A N A L Y S I S   O F   V A R I A N C E * * * * * * * * * * * * * * * * * *

ESTIMATES FOR NO3          (CONT.)

FERT

| PARAMETER | COEFF. | STD. ERR. | T-VALUE | SIG. OF T | LOWER .95 CL | UPPER .95 CL |
|---|---|---|---|---|---|---|
| 5 | -.4648896353 | 15.12441 | -.03074 | .976 | -30.82841 | 29.89863 |
| 6 | 6.9682632802 | 15.15807 | .45971 | .648 | -23.46284 | 37.39936 |

SEAL BY FERT

| PARAMETER | COEFF. | STD. ERR. | T-VALUE | SIG. OF T | LOWER .95 CL | UPPER .95 CL |
|---|---|---|---|---|---|---|
| 7 | -5.6118003504 | 15.12441 | -.37104 | .712 | -35.97532 | 24.75172 |
| 8 | -1.1199176244 | 15.15807 | -.07388 | .941 | -31.55102 | 29.31118 |

CONTIN(DEPTH TDS) BY SEAL + CONTIN(DEPTH TDS) BY FERT + CONTIN(DEPTH TDS) BY SEAL BY FERT

| PARAMETER | COEFF. | STD. ERR. | T-VALUE | SIG. OF T | LOWER .95 CL | UPPER .95 CL |
|---|---|---|---|---|---|---|
| 9 | -.0892138157 | .14511 | -.61482 | .541 | -.38053 | .20210 |
| 10 | -.0081796905 | .00592 | -1.38211 | .173 | -.02006 | .00370 |
| 11 | -.1142858023 | .21256 | -.53767 | .593 | -.31244 | .54101 |
| 12 | -.0752250157 | .21134 | -.35595 | .723 | -.49950 | .34905 |
| 13 | -.0064846357 | .00868 | -.74748 | .458 | -.02391 | .01094 |
| 14 | -.0098194360 | .00813 | -1.20764 | .233 | -.02614 | .00650 |
| 15 | -.0087670315 | .21256 | -.04125 | .967 | -.43549 | .41796 |
| 16 | .0279195486 | .21134 | .13211 | .895 | -.39636 | .45220 |
| 17 | -.0104514872 | .00868 | 1.20433 | .234 | -.00697 | .02787 |
| 18 | -.0037828604 | .00813 | -.46523 | .644 | -.02011 | .01254 |

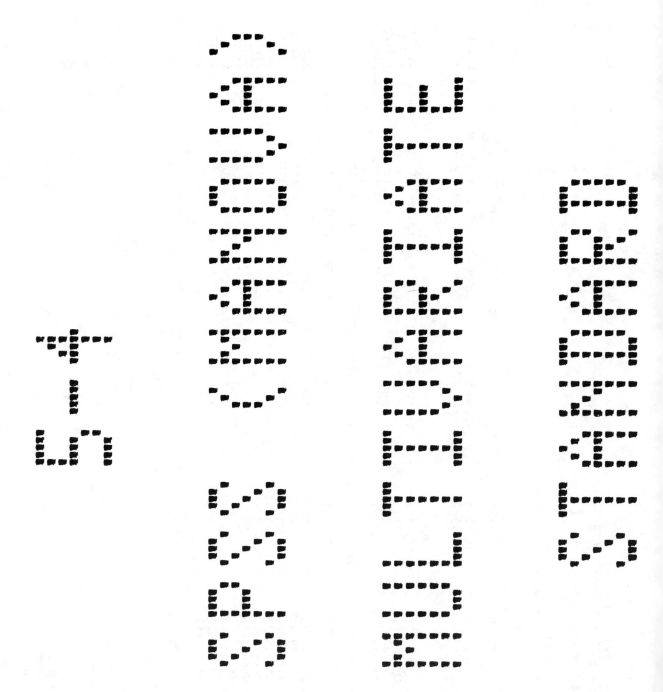

① 

② VARIABLE LIST

③ MANOVA

Note: The SPSS input annotations provided here are of value for most problems of this type. Consult your SPSS manual for more general information.

① These are column identifiers and are not part of the program content.

Note: Further annotations for this input and output can be found in the program I/O for SPSS(MANOVA) in Chapter 2, program numbered 2-10.

② In these analyses there are three dependent variables, NO3, K and PO4, one covariate, DEPTH, and one independent variable, SEAL.

③ In the subprogram MANOVA the specification that describes the design uses the word WITH to indicate the covariate, here DEPTH.

④ The PRINT subcommand (optional) requests that the hypothesis sum-of-squares and cross-products be printed through the specification SIGNIF(HYPOTH) and that the observed cell means, adjusted (for the covariate) cell means, estimated cell means, average raw residual, and the average standardized residual be printed through the specification PMEANS. Here the specification ERROR(W) must be included in PMEANS and POBS to obtain output from PMEANS and POBS, both here and in the PLOT subcommand.

⑤ The PMEANS specification in the PLOT subcommand requests that the observed, adjusted, and estimated means be plotted. Note that the specification must also be used with ERROR(W) in the PRINT subcommand to obtain this plot.

```
RUN NAME           CHAPTER 5:   MANCOVA ONE-WAY(2 LEVELS) WITH 1 COVARIATE
VARIABLE LIST      NO3 K PO4 DEPTH SEAL
N OF CASES         UNKNOWN
INPUT FORMAT       FREEFIELD
MANOVA             NO3 K PO4 BY SEAL(1,2) WITH DEPTH /
   PRINT = CELLINFO(MEANS)
           HOMOGENEITY(BARTLETT,COCHRAN)
           SIGNIF(HYPOTH) ERROR(SSCP) PMEANS(ERROR(W))
           POBS(ERROR(W))/
   PLOT = BOXPLOTS STEMLEAF PMEANS POBS/

READ INPUT DATA
48.0 17.7 0.880 48.0 1
38.0 14.1 0.880 59.0 1
36.0 13.9 0.840 67.0 1
51.0 16.5 0.890 50.0 1
34.0 17.9 0.870 59.0 1
41.5 19.3 0.850 58.0 1
45.5 13.6 0.890 57.0 1
44.0 13.8 0.850 61.0 1
47.0 17.9 0.890 62.0 1
45.0 13.8 0.810 50.0 1
45.0 17.7 0.810 51.0 1
40.5 13.6 0.870 61.0 1
37.5 14.0 0.880 58.0 1
38.0 14.9 0.880 48.0 1
36.0 14.7 0.890 49.0 1
38.0 10.7 0.840 52.0 1
38.5 13.5 0.830 67.0 1
33.5 14.6 0.800 65.0 1
34.0 15.2 0.860 57.0 1
37.0 10.5 0.830 59.0 1
37.0 13.4 0.900 53.0 1
30.0 15.4 0.800 67.0 1
37.0 14.4 0.860 54.0 1
42.0 15.2 0.860 49.0 1
38.5 13.6 0.850 58.0 1
50.0 19.0 0.860 54.0 1
49.0 18.8 0.880 52.0 1
45.0 13.6 0.910 64.0 1
33.5 14.6 0.890 67.0 2
57.0 17.5 0.840 43.0 2
41.5 13.9 0.860 61.0 2
48.0 15.9 0.910 54.0 2
39.5 16.5 0.860 51.0 2
37.5 14.9 0.830 63.0 2
47.0 18.8 0.890 57.0 2
45.5 18.8 0.920 49.0 1
37.0 20.9 0.890 61.0 1
51.0 21.8 0.910 45.0 2
55.5 21.2 0.910 50.0 2
51.0 22.0 0.890 59.0 2
58.0 14.4 0.900 52.0 2
58.5 13.1 0.910 55.0 2
51.0 13.8 0.910 51.0 2
55.5 22.8 0.930 45.0 2
60.0 18.8 0.880 52.0 2
```

```
        60.0  20.7  0.900  46.0   2
        46.0  15.4  0.900  48.0   2
        51.0  13.8  0.960  54.0   2
        53.5  13.4  0.880  56.0   2
        48.0  14.4  0.930  53.0   2
        43.0  16.8  0.880  64.0   2
        47.0  13.4  0.870  60.0   2
        59.0  21.8  0.850  57.0   2
        57.0  22.9  0.850  56.0   2
        51.0  18.0  0.930  51.0   2
        54.5  16.6  0.930  47.0   2
        41.5  14.4  0.900  59.0   2
        44.0  19.4  0.880  52.0   2
        55.5  21.8  0.960  53.0   2
        50.0  21.8  0.910  51.0   2
        40.5  14.4  0.960  53.0   2
        61.0  15.4  0.950  60.0   2
        45.5  15.4  0.890  61.0   2
        61.0  15.0  0.910  44.0   2
        58.0  18.0  0.880  49.0   2
        37.5  13.8  0.910  62.0   2
        58.0  22.8  0.930  56.0   2
        47.0  22.8  0.900  58.0   2
        49.0  18.0  0.940  49.0   2
END INPUT DATA
TASK NAME    TEST OF WITHIN CELL REGRESSION
⑦ MANOVA       NO3 K PO4 DEPTH  BY SEAL(1,2) /
             PRINT=SIGNIF(HYPOTH)
             ERROR(SSCP)/
⑥ METHOD = SSTYPE(UNIQUE)/
⑧ ANALYSIS = NO3 K PO4/
⑨ DESIGN = DEPTH, SEAL, DEPTH  BY  SEAL/
```

```
0000000000111111111122222222223333333333444444444455555555556666666666777777777778
1234567890123456789012345678901234567890123456789012345678901234567890123456789012345678901234567890
```

⑥ This METHOD specification is needed to obtain the method of weighted squares of means analysis described in Appendix A.

⑦ The test of the homogeneity of the within cell regression coefficients may be found by re-specifying the design with the covariate considered as a dependent variable.

⑧ The ANALYSIS specification indicates that NO3, K, and PO4 are the dependent variables to be analysed.

⑨ The test of the homogeneity of the within cell regression coefficients is found as the DEPTH BY SEAL interaction.

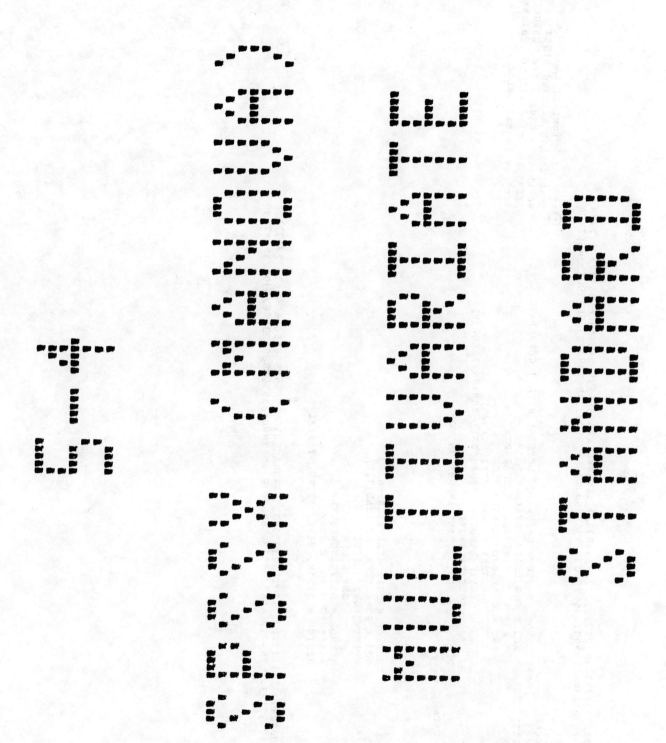

① UNNUMBERED
```
TITLE        CHAPTER 5:   MANCOVA ONE-WAY(2 LEVELS) WITH 1 COVARIATE
DATA LIST LIST/   NO3 K PO4 DEPTH SEAL
MANOVA            NO3 K PO4 BY SFAL(1,2) WITH DEPTH /
             PRINT = CELLINFO(MEANS)
                     HOMOGENEITY(BARTLETT,COCHRAN)
                     SIGNIF(HYPOTH) ERROR(SSCP) PMEANS(ERROR(W))
                     POBS(ERROR(W))/
             PLOT = BOXPLOTS STEMLEAF PMEANS POBS/

BEGIN DATA
```
②
```
END DATA
SUBTITLE     TEST OF WITHIN CELL REGRESSION
MANOVA       NO3 K PO4 DEPTH BY SEAL(1,2) /
             PRINT=SIGNIF(HYPOTH)
                   ERROR(SSCP)/
             METHOD = SSTYPE(UNIQUE)/
             ANALYSIS = NO3 K PO4/
             DESIGN = DEPTH, SEAL, DEPTH BY SEAL/
```

① At our installation the default (NUMBERED) instruction allowed SPSSX to read only 72 columns. We therefore used the UNNUMBERED command to allow SPSSX to read all 80 columns. The default may vary by installation.

② The data go here.

468

* * * * * * * * * * * * * * * * * A N A L Y S I S   O F   V A R I A N C E * * * * * * * * * * * * * * * * * *

CELL MEANS AND STANDARD DEVIATIONS

VARIABLE -- NO3

| FACTOR | CODE | MEAN | STD. DEV. | N | 95 PERCENT CONF. INTERVAL | |
|---|---|---|---|---|---|---|
| SEAL | 1 | 41.16216 | 5.96524 | 37 | 39.17325 | 43.15107 |
| SEAL | 2 | 51.84375 | 6.52222 | 32 | 49.49224 | 54.19526 |
| FOR ENTIRE SAMPLE | | 46.11594 | 8.18677 | 69 | 44.14927 | 48.08262 |

VARIABLE -- K

| FACTOR | CODE | MEAN | STD. DEV. | N | 95 PERCENT CONF. INTERVAL | |
|---|---|---|---|---|---|---|
| SEAL | 1 | 15.59729 | 2.50061 | 37 | 14.76355 | 16.43104 |
| SEAL | 2 | 17.76562 | 3.53230 | 32 | 16.49209 | 19.03915 |
| FOR ENTIRE SAMPLE | | 16.60290 | 3.19139 | 69 | 15.83624 | 17.36955 |

VARIABLE -- PO4

| FACTOR | CODE | MEAN | STD. DEV. | N | 95 PERCENT CONF. INTERVAL | |
|---|---|---|---|---|---|---|
| SEAL | 1 | .86351 | .03102 | 37 | .85317 | .87386 |
| SEAL | 2 | .90687 | .02967 | 32 | .89618 | .91757 |
| FOR ENTIRE SAMPLE | | .88362 | .03722 | 69 | .87468 | .89256 |

VARIABLE -- DEPTH

| FACTOR | CODE | MEAN | STD. DEV. | N | 95 PERCENT CONF. INTERVAL | |
|---|---|---|---|---|---|---|
| SEAL | 1 | 56.62162 | 6.36986 | 37 | 54.49781 | 58.74544 |
| SEAL | 2 | 53.37500 | 5.32644 | 32 | 51.45461 | 55.29539 |
| FOR ENTIRE SAMPLE | | 55.11594 | 6.08889 | 69 | 53.65323 | 56.57865 |

469

CHAPTER 5:  MANCOVA ONE-WAY(2 LEVELS) WITH 1 COVARIATE

* * * * * * * * * * * A N A L Y S I S   O F   V A R I A N C E * * * * * * * * * * * * * * * * ①

① This section displays the analysis of the three dependent measures regressed on the covariate.

② These matrices are needed for the MANCOVA summary table (see Table 5.9).

ADJUSTED WITHIN CELLS SUM-OF-SQUARES AND CROSS-PRODUCTS

② 

|      | NO3        | K         | PO4    |
|------|------------|-----------|--------|
| NO3  | 2013.94148 |           |        |
| K    | 317.49468  | 580.95099 |        |
| PC4  | .19587     | .20968    | .05948 |

CHAPTER 5:  MANCOVA ONE-WAY(2 LEVELS) WITH 1 COVARIATE

* * * * * * * * * * A N A L Y S I S   O F   V A R I A N C E * * * * * * * * * * * * * * * * *

③ The multivariate tests indicate that there is a significant relationship between the dependent variables and the covariate (p<.000).

EFFECT .. WITHIN CELLS REGRESSION
ADJUSTED HYPOTHESIS SUM-OF-SQUARES AND CROSS-PRODUCTS

② 

|      | NO3       | K        | PO4 |
|------|-----------|----------|-----|
| NO3  | 585.80430 |          |     |
| K    | 134.64923 | 30.94961 |     |
| PC4  | 1.19743   | .27523   | 0.0 |

MULTIVARIATE TESTS OF SIGNIFICANCE (S = 1, M = 1/2, N = 31)

| TEST NAME  | VALUE   | APPROX. F | HYPOTH. DF | ERROR DF | SIG. OF F |
|------------|---------|-----------|------------|----------|-----------|
| ③          |         |           |            |          |           |
| PILLAIS    | .24985  | 7.10560   | 3.00       | 64.00    | .000      |
| HOTELLINGS | .33307  | 7.10560   | 3.00       | 64.00    | .000      |
| WILKS      | .75015  | 7.10560   | 3.00       | 64.00    | .000      |
| ROYS       | .24985  |           |            |          |           |

EIGENVALUES AND CANONICAL CORRELATIONS

| ROOT NO. | EIGENVALUE | PCT.      | CUM. PCT. | CANON. COR. | SQUARED COR. |
|----------|------------|-----------|-----------|-------------|--------------|
| 1        | .33307     | 100.00000 | 100.00000 | .49985      | .24985       |

DIMENSION REDUCTION ANALYSIS

| ROOTS | WILKS LAMBDA | F | HYPOTH. DF | ERROR DF | SIG. OF F |
|-------|--------------|---|------------|----------|-----------|

* * * * * * * * * * * * * * * * * * *A N A L Y S I S   O F   V A R I A N C E* * * * * * * * * * * * * * * * * * * * * * * *

EFFECT .. WITHIN CELLS REGRESSION          (CONT.)

(4)

UNIVARIATE F-TESTS WITH (1,66) D. F.

| VARIABLE | SQ. MUL. R | MUL. R | ADJ. R-SQ. | HYPOTH MS | ERROR MS | F | SIG. OF F |
|---|---|---|---|---|---|---|---|
| NO3 | .22533 | .47469 | .20186 | 585.80430 | 30.51426 | 19.19772 | .000 |
| K | .05058 | .22490 | .02181 | 30.94961 | 8.80229 | 3.51609 | .065 |
| PO4 | .03952 | .19880 | .01042 | -.00245 | .00090 | 2.71578 | .104 |

(5)     (6)

REGRESSION ANALYSIS FOR WITHIN CELLS ERROR TERM

DEPENDENT VARIABLE ..NO3

| COVARIATE | B | EETA | STD. ERR. | T-VALUE | SIG. OF T | LOWER .95 CL | UPPER .95 CL |
|---|---|---|---|---|---|---|---|
| DEPTH | -.5003219287 | -.4746908229 | .11419 | -4.38152 | .000 | -.72831 | -.27234 |

DEPENDENT VARIABLE ..K

| COVARIATE | B | BETA | STD. ERR. | T-VALUE | SIG. OF T | LOWER .95 CL | UPPER .95 CL |
|---|---|---|---|---|---|---|---|
| DEPTH | -.1150007988 | -.2248980084 | .06133 | -1.87512 | .065 | -.23745 | .00745 |

DEPENDENT VARIABLE ..PO4

| COVARIATE | B | EETA | STD. ERR. | T-VALUE | SIG. OF T | LOWER .95 CL | UPPER .95 CL |
|---|---|---|---|---|---|---|---|
| DEPTH | -.0010226938 | -.1988012734 | .00062 | -1.64796 | .104 | -.00226 | .00022 |

(4) This table contains the results of the simple regression of each dependent variable on the covariate. Here we see that in the univariate analysis NO3 has the highest partial multiple correlation (.47469) with DEPTH. Note that this correlation is based on the pooled error sums-of-squares and cross-products matrix, and therefore, is the absolute value of the correlation between NO3 and DEPTH with the effects of the independent variable (SEX) held constant.

(5) These are the univariate estimates of and tests on the regression coefficients. Note that since there is only one covariate, the standardized regression coefficients (BETA) equal, except for their signs, the multiple regression coefficients (MUL. R.) given above.

(6) The ADJ.R-SQ. (adjusted squared multiple correlation coefficient) is an estimate of the squared population multiple correlation coefficient. It can be found using the formula:

$$Rho^2 = 1 - (N-1/Dfe)\ (1-R^2)$$

where, $Rho^2$ = the squared population multiple correlation coefficient,

$N$ = the total number of observations, here 69,

$Dfe$ = the error degrees of freedom, here 66, and

$R^2$ = the estimated squared multiple correlation, here found in the column labeled SQ. MUL. R.

471

* * * * * * * * * * * * * * * * * * * * * A N A L Y S I S   O F   V A R I A N C E * * * * * * * * * * * * * * * * * * * * *

EFFECT .. SEAL

(7) This section contains the MANCOVA results.

(8) This matrix is needed for the MANCOVA summary table (see Table 5.9).

ADJUSTED HYPOTHESIS SUM-OF-SQUARES AND CROSS-PRODUCTS

|        | NO3        | K         | PO4    |
|--------|------------|-----------|--------|
| (8) NO3 | 1306.65739 |           |        |
| K      | 258.95326  | 51.31934  |        |
| PO4    | 5.77661    | 1.14481   | .02554 |

MULTIVARIATE TESTS OF SIGNIFICANCE (S = 1, M = 1/2, N = 31)

| TEST NAME  | VALUE   | APPROX. F | HYPOTH. DF | ERROR DF | SIG. OF F |
|------------|---------|-----------|------------|----------|-----------|
| PILLAIS    | .51491  | 22.64432  | 3.00       | 64.00    | 0.0       |
| HOTELLINGS | 1.06145 | 22.64432  | 3.00       | 64.00    | 0.0       |
| WILKS      | .48509  | 22.64432  | 3.00       | 64.00    | 0.0       |
| ROYS       | .51491  |           |            |          |           |

(9)

EIGENVALUES AND CANONICAL CORRELATIONS

| ROOT NO. | EIGENVALUE | PCT.      | CUM. PCT. | CANON. CCR. |
|----------|------------|-----------|-----------|-------------|
| 1        | 1.06145    | 100.00000 | 100.00000 | .71757      |

DIMENSION REDUCTION ANALYSIS

| ROOTS  | WILKS LAMBDA | F        | HYPOTH. DF | ERROR DF | SIG. OF F |
|--------|--------------|----------|------------|----------|-----------|
| 1 TO 1 | .48509       | 22.64432 | 3.00       | 64.00    | 0.0       |

(9) The multivariate tests indicate that there is a significant difference between the groups on the three dependent variables after adjustment for the covariate.

* * * * * * * * * * * * * * * * * * * * * * * A N A L Y S I S   O F   V A R I A N C E * * * * * * * * * * * * * * * * * * * * * * * *

EFFECT .. SEAL   (CONT.)

UNIVARIATE F-TESTS WITH (1,66) D. F.

| VARIABLE | HYPOTH. SS | ERROR SS | HYPOTH. MS | ERROR MS | ⑩ F | SIG. OF F |
|----------|------------|----------|------------|----------|--------|-----------|
| NO3 | 1306.65739 | 2013.94148 | 1306.65739 | 30.51426 | 42.82120 | .000 |
| K | 51.31934 | 580.95099 | 51.31934 | 8.80229 | 5.83023 | .019 |
| PC4 | .02554 | .05948 | .02554 | .00090 | 28.33576 | .000 |

⑩ The univariate tests indicate that group differences would be found with each adjusted dependent variable considered by itself, if the level of significance was .05.

* * * * * * * * * * * * * * * * * * * A N A L Y S I S   O F   V A R I A N C E * * * * * * * * * * * * * * * * * * *

ADJUSTED AND ESTIMATED MEANS (CONT.)

VARIABLE -- K

| FACTOR | CODE | OBS. MEAN | ADJ. MEAN | EST. MEAN | RAW RESID. | STD. RESID. |
|---|---|---|---|---|---|---|
| SEAL | 1 | 15.59729 | 15.78398 | 15.61082 | -.01353 | -.00456 |
| SEAL | 2 | 17.76562 | 17.57894 | 17.77915 | -.01353 | -.00456 |

PLOT OF OBSERVED(O), ADJUSTED(A), AND ESTIMATED(E) MEANS

VARIABLE -- K

```
           +
        1  I         E   A
           +
        2  I                                                         A         E
           +----+---------------+---------------+---------------+---------------+
   00  15.45000           15.95000         16.45000         16.95000         17.45000         17.950
```

ADJUSTED AND ESTIMATED MEANS (CONT.)

VARIABLE -- PO4

| FACTOR | CODE | OBS. MEAN | ADJ. MEAN | EST. MEAN | RAW RESID. | STD. RESID. |
|---|---|---|---|---|---|---|
| SEAL | 1 | .86351 | .86517 | .86363 | -.00012 | -.00401 |
| SEAL | 2 | .90687 | .90521 | .90700 | -.00012 | -.00401 |

PLOT OF OBSERVED(O), ADJUSTED(A), AND ESTIMATED(E) MEANS

VARIABLE -- PO4

```
           +
        1  I    E   A
           +
        2  I                                                         A         E
           +----+---------------+---------------+---------------+---------------+
   00  .36000           .87000           .88000           .89000           .90000           .910
```

474

* * * * * * * * * * * * * * * * * * A N A L Y S I S   O F   V A R I A N C E * * * * * * * * * * * * * * * * * * * * * * * * * * *

WITHIN+RESIDUAL SUM-OF-SQUARES AND CROSS-PRODUCTS

|      | NO3        | K          | PO4    |
|------|------------|------------|--------|
| NO3  | 2013.78024 |            |        |
| K    | 317.93417  | 579.75305  |        |
| PC4  | .19643     | .20814     | .05948 |

- - - - - - - - - - - - - - - - - - - - - - - - - - - - - - - - - - - -

\* \* \* \* \* \* \* \* \* \* \* \* \* \* \* \* \* \* \* \* \* A N A L Y S I S   O F   V A R I A N C E \* \* \* \* \* \* \* \* \* \* \* \* \* \* \* \* \* \* \* \* \* \*

EFFECT -- DEPTH BY SEAL

ADJUSTED HYPOTHESIS SUM-OF-SQUARES AND CROSS-PRODUCTS

|      | NO3       | K        | PO4     |
|------|-----------|----------|---------|
| NO3  | .16124    |          |         |
| K    | -.43949   | 1.19794  |         |
| PC4  | -.00057   | -.00154  | .00000  |

MULTIVARIATE TESTS OF SIGNIFICANCE (S = 1, M = 1/2, N = 30 1/2)

| TEST NAME  |      | VALUE   | APPROX. F | HYPOTH. DF | ERROR DF | SIG. OF F |
|------------|------|---------|-----------|------------|----------|-----------|
| PILLAIS    | ⑪    | .00262  | .05525    | 3.00       | 63.00    | .983      |
| HOTELLINGS |      | .00263  | .05525    | 3.00       | 63.00    | .983      |
| WILKS      |      | .99738  | .05525    | 3.00       | 63.00    | .983      |
| ROYS       |      | .00262  |           |            |          |           |

EIGENVALUES AND CANONICAL CORRELATIONS

| ROOT NO. | EIGENVALUE | PCT.      | CUM. PCT. | CANCN. COR. |
|----------|------------|-----------|-----------|-------------|
| 1        | .00263     | 100.00000 | 100.00000 | .05122      |

DIMENSION REDUCTION ANALYSIS

| RCOTS  | WILKS LAMBDA | F      | HYPOTH. DF | ERROR DF | SIG. OF F |
|--------|--------------|--------|------------|----------|-----------|
| 1 TO 1 | .99738       | .05525 | 3.00       | 63.00    | .983      |

⑪ The multivariate tests of homogeneity of the
within cell regression coefficients is found in
the re-specified model's interaction. These tests
indicate that we do have homogeneous regression
coefficients.

Note: Since the multivariate tests were not significant

476

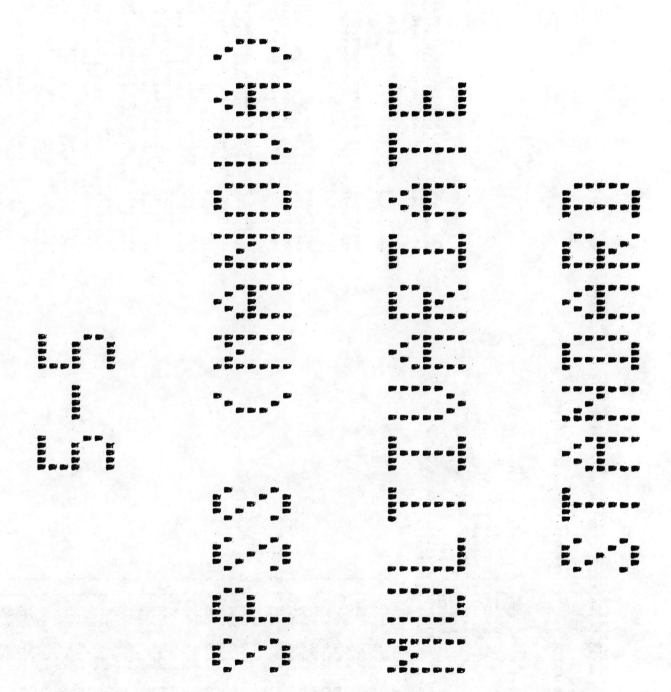

```
         00000000001111111111222222222233333333334444444444555555555566666666667777777777
         12345678901234567890123456789012345678901234567890123456789012345678901234567890
```

```
RUN NAME       CHAPTER 5:  2X3 MANCOVA WITH 2 COVARIATES
VARIABLE LIST  NO3 K PO4 DEPTH TDS SEAL FERT
N OF CASES     UNKNOWN
INPUT FORMAT   FREEFIELD
MANOVA         NO3 K PO4 BY SEAL(1,2) FERT(1,3) WITH DEPTH TDS/
  PRINT = CELLINFO(MEANS)
          HOMOGENEITY(BARTLETT,COCHRAN,BOXM)
          SIGNIF(HYPOTH) ERROR(SSCP) PMEANS
          (VARIABLES(NO3 K PO4) TABLES(SEAL,FERT,SEAL BY FERT)
          ERROR(W))
          PCBS(ERROR(W))/
  PLOT = BOXPLOTS STEMLEAF PMEANS POBS/
  METHOD = SSTYPE(UNIQUE)/
READ INPUT DATA
48.0 17.7 0.880 48.0 750 1 1
38.0 14.1 0.880 59.0 400 1 1
36.0 13.9 0.840 67.0 425 1 1
51.0 16.5 0.890 50.0 850 1 1
34.0 17.9 0.870 59.0 300 1 1
41.5 19.3 0.850 58.0 650 1 1
45.5 13.6 0.890 57.0 575 1 1
44.0 13.8 0.850 61.0 475 1 1
47.0 17.9 0.890 62.0 400 1 1
45.0 13.8 0.890 65.0 650 1 1
45.0 17.7 0.810 51.0 875 1 1
40.5 13.6 0.870 61.0 375 1 1
37.5 14.0 0.880 58.0 500 1 2
38.0 14.9 0.880 48.0 875 1 2
36.0 14.7 0.890 49.0 650 1 2
38.0 10.7 0.840 52.0 575 1 2
38.5 13.5 0.830 67.0 275 1 2
33.5 14.6 0.800 65.0 450 1 2
34.0 15.2 0.860 57.0 350 1 2
37.0 10.5 0.830 59.0 350 1 2
37.0 13.4 0.900 53.0 650 1 2
30.0 15.4 0.860 67.0 350 1 2
37.0 14.4 0.860 54.0 675 1 2
42.0 15.2 0.860 49.0 675 1 2
38.5 13.6 0.850 58.0 375 1 3
50.0 19.0 0.860 54.0 700 1 3
49.0 18.8 0.880 52.0 850 1 3
45.5 13.6 0.910 64.0 575 1 3
33.5 14.6 0.890 67.0 300 1 3
57.0 17.5 0.840 43.0 800 1 3
41.5 13.9 0.860 61.0 625 1 3
48.0 19.9 0.910 54.0 725 1 3
39.5 16.5 0.860 51.0 575 1 3
37.5 14.9 0.830 63.0 475 1 3
47.0 18.8 0.890 57.0 450 1 3
45.5 18.8 0.920 49.0 775 1 3
37.0 20.9 0.890 61.0 375 1 3
51.0 21.8 0.890 45.0 775 2 1
55.5 21.2 0.910 50.0 675 2 1
51.0      0.890 59.0 700 2 1
```

Note: The SPSS input annotations provided here are of value for most problems of this type. Consult the SPSS manual for more general information.

① These are column identifiers and are not part of the program content.

Note: Further annotations for the I/O can be found in the program I/O for SPSS(MANOVA) in Chapter 2, program numbered 2-10.

② In these analyses there are three dependent variables, NO3, K and PO4, two covariates, DEPTH and TDS, and two independent variables, SEAL with two levels, and FERT with three levels.

③ In the subprogram MANOVA the specification that describes the design uses the word WITH to indicate the covariates, here DEPTH and TDS.

④ The PRINT subcommand (optional) requests that the hypothesis sum-of-squares and cross-products be printed through the specification SIGNIF(HYPOTH) and that the observed cell means, adjusted (for the covariate) cell means, estimated cell means, average raw residual, and the average standardized residual be printed through the specification PMEANS. Here the specification ERROR(W) must be included in PMEANS and POBS to obtain output from PMEANS and POBS, both here and in the PLOT subcommand. The subspecification TABLES indicates that unweighted adjusted marginal means are to be printed for SEAL and FERT, and the unweighted adjusted cell means are to be printed for SEAL BY FERT.

⑤ The PMEANS specification in the PLOT subcommand requests that the observed, adjusted, and estimated means be plotted. Note that the specification ERROR(W) must also be used with PMEANS in the PRINT subcommand to obtain this plot.

```
51.0 13.8 0.910 51.0 625 2 1
55.5 22.8 0.930 45.0 675 2 1
60.0 18.8 0.880 52.0 650 2 1
60.0 20.7 0.900 46.0 800 2 1
46.0 15.4 0.900 48.0 525 2 1
51.0 13.8 0.960 54.0 700 2 1
53.5 13.4 0.880 56.0 625 2 2
48.0 14.4 0.930 53.0 675 2 2
43.0 16.8 0.880 64.0 400 2 2
47.0 13.4 0.870 60.0 300 2 2
59.0 21.8 0.850 57.0 750 2 2
57.0 22.9 0.850 56.0 675 2 2
51.0 18.0 0.930 51.0 525 2 2
54.5 16.6 0.900 47.0 575 2 2
41.5 14.4 0.900 59.0 475 2 2
44.0 19.4 0.880 52.0 700 2 2
55.5 21.8 0.960 53.0 650 2 2
50.0 21.8 0.940 51.0 625 2 3
40.5 14.4 0.960 53.0 400 2 3
61.0 15.4 0.950 60.0 650 2 3
45.5 15.4 0.890 61.0 400 2 3
61.0 15.4 0.910 44.0 675 2 3
58.0 18.0 0.880 49.0 700 2 3
37.5 13.8 0.910 62.0 500 2 3
58.0 22.8 0.930 56.0 575 2 3
47.0 22.8 0.900 58.0 625 2 3
49.0 18.0 0.940 49.0 675 2 3
     END INPUT DATA
     TASK NAME    TEST OF WITHIN CELL REGRESSION
(3)(7)MANOVA       NO3 K PO4 DEPTH TDS BY SEAL(1,2) FERT(1,3)/
                   PRINT = SIGNIF(HYPOTH) ERROR(SSCP)/
(6)                METHOD = SSTYPE(UNIQUE)/
(8)                ANALYSIS = NO3 K PO4/
(9)                DESIGN = DEPTH, TDS, SEAL, FERT, SEAL BY FERT,
(10)               CONTIN(DEPTH,TDS) BY SEAL + CONTIN(DEPTH,TDS) BY
                   FERT + CONTIN(DEPTH,TDS) BY SEAL BY FERT/
```

```
(1) 00000000011111111112222222222333333333344444444445555555555666666666677777777778
    12345678901234567890123456789012345678901234567890123456789012345678901234567890
```

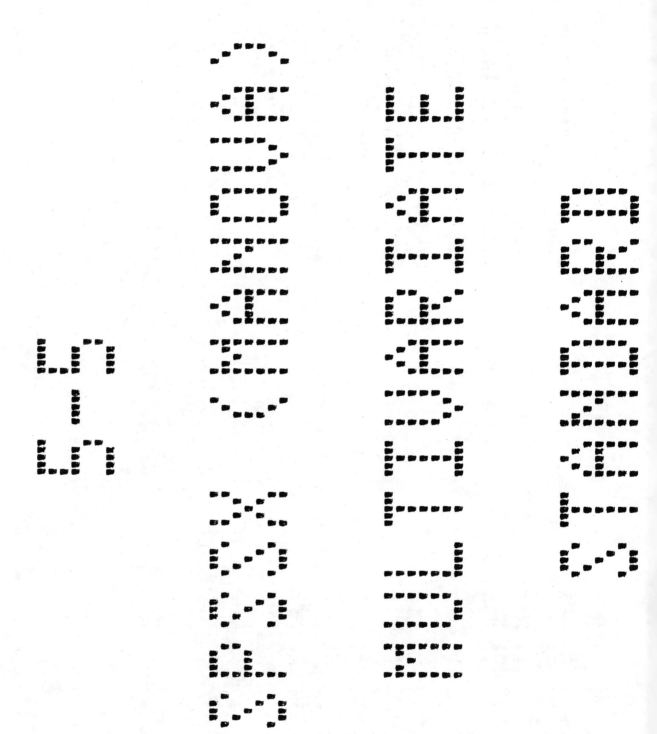

```
0000000000111111111122222222223333333333444444444455555555556666666666777777777778
1234567890123456789012345678901234567890123456789012345678901234567890123456789 0

① UNNUMBERED
  TITLE          CHAPTER 5:  2X3 MANCOVA WITH 2 COVARIATES
  DATA LIST LIST/ NO3 K PO4 DEPTH TDS SEAL FERT
  MANOVA         NO3 K PO4 BY SEAL(1,2) FERT(1,3)  WITH DEPTH TDS/
                 PRINT = CELLINFO(MEANS)
                         HOMOGENEITY(BARTLETT,COCHRAN,BOXM)
                         SIGNIF(HYPOTH) ERROR(SSCP) PMEANS
                         (VARIABLES(NO3 K PO4) TABLES(SEAL,FERT,SEAL BY FERT)
                         ERRCR(W))
                         POBS(ERROR(W))/
                 PLOT = BOXPLOTS STEMLEAF PMEANS POBS/
                 METHOD = SSTYPE(UNIQUE)/
  BEGIN DATA
②
  END DATA
  SUBTITLE       TEST OF WITHIN CELL REGRESSION
  MANOVA         NO3 K PO4 DEPTH TDS BY SEAL(1,2) FERT(1,3)/
                 PRINT = SIGNIF(HYPOTH) ERROR(SSCP)/
                 METHOD = SSTYPE(UNIQUE)/
                 ANALYSIS = NO3 K PO4/
                 DESIGN = DEPTH, TDS, SEAL, FERT, SEAL BY FERT,
                          CONTIN(DEPTH,TDS) BY SEAL + CONTIN(DEPTH,TDS) BY
                          FERT + CONTIN(DEPTH,TDS) BY SEAL BY FERT/

0000000000111111111122222222223333333333444444444455555555556666666666777777777778
1234567890123456789012345678901234567890123456789012345678901234567890123456789 0
```

① At our installation the default (NUMBERED) instruction allowed SPSSX to read only 72 columns. We therefore used the UNNUMBERED command to allow SPSSX to read all 80 columns. The default may vary by installation.

② The data go here.

481

* * * * * * * * * * * * * * * * A N A L Y S I S   O F   V A R I A N C E * * * * * * * * * * * * * * * * * * * * *

CELL MEANS AND STANDARD DEVIATIONS

VARIABLE .. NO3

| FACTOR | CODE | MEAN | STD. DEV. | N | 95 PERCENT CONF. INTERVAL | |
|---|---|---|---|---|---|---|
| SEAL | 1 | | | | | |
| FERT | 1 | 42.95833 | 5.07874 | 12 | 39.73146 | 46.18521 |
| FERT | 2 | 36.54167 | 2.98830 | 12 | 34.64299 | 38.44034 |
| FERT | 3 | 43.76923 | 6.55622 | 13 | 39.80735 | 47.73111 |
| SEAL | 2 | | | | | |
| FERT | 1 | 54.31818 | 4.60040 | 11 | 51.22760 | 57.40877 |
| FERT | 2 | 50.36364 | 6.02117 | 11 | 46.31856 | 54.40872 |
| FERT | 3 | 50.75000 | 8.44015 | 10 | 44.71228 | 56.78772 |
| FOR ENTIRE SAMPLE | | 46.11594 | 8.18677 | 69 | 44.14927 | 48.08262 |

VARIABLE .. K

| FACTOR | CODE | MEAN | STD. DEV. | N | 95 PERCENT CONF. INTERVAL | |
|---|---|---|---|---|---|---|
| SEAL | 1 | | | | | |
| FERT | 1 | 15.81666 | 2.19414 | 12 | 14.42258 | 17.21075 |
| FERT | 2 | 13.87500 | 1.65756 | 12 | 12.82184 | 14.92816 |
| FERT | 3 | 16.98461 | 2.59385 | 13 | 15.41716 | 18.55206 |
| SEAL | 2 | | | | | |
| FERT | 1 | 17.98181 | 3.88144 | 11 | 15.37422 | 20.58940 |
| FERT | 2 | 17.53636 | 3.52314 | 11 | 15.16948 | 19.90324 |
| FERT | 3 | 17.78000 | 3.51055 | 10 | 15.26870 | 20.29129 |
| FOR ENTIRE SAMPLE | | 16.60290 | 3.19139 | 69 | 15.83624 | 17.36955 |

VARIABLE .. PO4

| FACTOR | CODE | MEAN | STD. DEV. | N | 95 PERCENT CONF. INTERVAL |
|---|---|---|---|---|---|

* * * * * * * * * * * * * * * A N A L Y S I S   O F   V A R I A N C E * * * * * * * * * * * * * * * * 02/02/83     PAGE   3

CELL MEANS AND STANDARD DEVIATIONS (CCNT.)

VARIABLE -- PO4

| FACTOR | CODE | MEAN | STD. DEV. | N | 95 PERCENT CONF. INTERVAL | |
|---|---|---|---|---|---|---|
| SEAL | 1 | | | | | |
| FERT | 1 | .86083 | .02906 | 12 | .84237 | .87930 |
| FERT | 2 | .85250 | .03306 | 12 | .83149 | .87351 |
| FERT | 3 | .87615 | .02844 | 13 | .85897 | .89334 |
| SEAL | 2 | | | | | |
| FERT | 1 | .90727 | .02195 | 11 | .89253 | .92202 |
| FERT | 2 | .89364 | .03472 | 11 | .87031 | .91696 |
| FERT | 3 | .92100 | .02685 | 10 | .90179 | .94021 |
| FOR ENTIRE SAMPLE | | .88362 | .03722 | 69 | .87468 | .89256 |

VARIABLE -- DEPTH

| FACTOR | CODE | MEAN | STD. DEV. | N | 95 PERCENT CONF. INTERVAL | |
|---|---|---|---|---|---|---|
| SEAL | 1 | | | | | |
| FERT | 1 | 56.91667 | 5.89462 | 12 | 53.17776 | 60.65558 |
| FERT | 2 | 56.50000 | 6.90849 | 12 | 52.11055 | 60.88945 |
| FERT | 3 | 56.46154 | 6.78989 | 13 | 52.35845 | 60.56463 |
| SEAL | 2 | | | | | |
| FERT | 1 | 50.63636 | 4.43334 | 11 | 47.65800 | 53.61472 |
| FERT | 2 | 55.27273 | 4.73478 | 11 | 52.09186 | 58.45360 |
| FERT | 3 | 54.30000 | 6.03784 | 10 | 49.98079 | 58.61921 |
| FOR ENTIRE SAMPLE | | 55.11594 | 6.08889 | 69 | 53.65323 | 56.57865 |

VARIABLE -- TDS

| FACTOR | CODE | MEAN | STD. DEV. | N | 95 PERCENT CONF. INTERVAL |
|---|---|---|---|---|---|

CELL MEANS AND STANDARD DEVIATIONS   (CONT.)

VARIABLE -- TDS

| FACTOR | CODE | MEAN | STD. DEV. | N | 95 PERCENT CONF. INTERVAL | |
|---|---|---|---|---|---|---|
| SEAL | 1 | | | | | |
| FERT | 1 | 560.41667 | 194.07658 | 12 | 437.10631 | 683.72702 |
| FERT | 2 | 531.25000 | 181.25980 | 12 | 416.08304 | 646.41696 |
| FERT | 3 | 584.61538 | 179.56500 | 13 | 476.10535 | 693.12542 |
| SEAL | 2 | | | | | |
| FERT | 1 | 661.36364 | 84.67854 | 11 | 604.47584 | 718.25144 |
| FERT | 2 | 577.27273 | 138.94898 | 11 | 483.92556 | 670.61989 |
| FERT | 3 | 582.50000 | 111.83445 | 10 | 502.49849 | 662.50151 |
| FOR ENTIRE SAMPLE | | 581.88406 | 155.56736 | 69 | 544.50789 | 619.26022 |

UNIVARIATE HOMOGENEITY OF VARIANCE TESTS

VARIABLE -- NO3

COCHRANS C(11,6) =         .34520, P =    .044 (APPROX.)
BARTLETT-BOX F(5,5015) =   2.22315, P =    .050

VARIABLE -- K

COCHRANS C(11,6) =         .27852, P =    .275 (APPROX.)
BARTLETT-BOX F(5,5015) =   1.98151, P =    .078

VARIABLE -- PO4

COCHRANS C(11,6) =         .23383, P =    .744 (APPROX.)
BARTLETT-BOX F(5,5015) =   .48847, P =    .785

VARIABLE -- DEPTH

COCHRANS C(11,6) =         .23058, P =    .794 (APPROX.)
BARTLETT-BOX F(5,5015) =   .64425, P =    .666

**\* \* \* \* \* \* \* \* \* \* \* \* A N A L Y S I S   O F   V A R I A N C E \* \* \* \* \* \* \* \* \* \* \* \* \* \* \* \* \* \* \* \* \* \* \* \* \* \* \***

STEM-AND-LEAF DISPLAY FOR VARIABLE .. TDS

```
2 . 7
3 . 000555777
4 . 000000255777
5 . 0025777777
6 . 0222225555555577777777
7 . 000025577
8 . 005577
```

CORRESPONDENCE BETWEEN EFFECTS AND COLUMNS OF BETWEEN-SUBJECTS DESIGN

| STARTING COLUMN | ENDING COLUMN | EFFECT NAME |
|---|---|---|
| 1 | 1 | CONSTANT |
| 2 | 2 | SEAL |
| 3 | 4 | FERT |
| 5 | 6 | SEAL BY FERT |

ADJUSTED WITHIN CELLS SUM-OF-SQUARES AND CROSS-PRODUCTS

(1)

| | NO3 | K | PO4 |
|---|---|---|---|
| NO3 | 1357.28966 | | |
| K | 69.28891 | 476.93940 | |
| PO4 | -.52497 | -.17516 | .05200 |

Note: This section displays the analysis of the three dependent measures regressed on the covariates.

(1) This matrix is needed for the MANCOVA summary table (see Table 5.11).

485

* * * * * * * * * * * * * * * * * A N A L Y S I S  O F  V A R I A N C E * * * * * * * * * * * * * * * * * * * * * * * * * *

EFFECT .. WITHIN CELLS REGRESSION

ADJUSTED HYPOTHESIS SUM-OF-SQUARES AND CROSS-PRODUCTS

|       | NC3       | K         | PO4     |
|-------|-----------|-----------|---------|
| NC3   | 755.78319 |           |         |
| K     | 226.15368 | 72.67333  |         |
| PO4   | .86510    | .17518    | .00239  |

②  The multivariate tests indicate that there is a significant relationship between the dependent variables and the covariates (p<.000).

MULTIVARIATE TESTS OF SIGNIFICANCE (S = 2, M = 0, N = 28 1/2)

| TEST NAME | VALUE   | APPROX. F | HYPOTH. DF | ERROR DF | SIG. OF F |
|-----------|---------|-----------|------------|----------|-----------|
| PILLAIS ② | .44466  | 5.71777   | 6.00       | 120.00   | .000      |
| HOTELLINGS | .72961 | 7.05289   | 6.00       | 116.00   | .000      |
| WILKS     | .56980  | 6.38693   | 6.00       | 118.00   | .000      |
| ROYS      | .40933  |           |            |          |           |

EIGENVALUES AND CANONICAL CORRELATIONS

| ROOT NO. | EIGENVALUE | PCT.     | CUM. PCT.  | CANON. CCR. | SQUARED COR. |
|----------|------------|----------|------------|-------------|--------------|
| 1        | .69299     | 94.98081 | 94.98081   | .63979      | .40933       |
| 2        | .03662     | 5.01919  | 100.00000  | .18795      | .03533       |

DIMENSION REDUCTION ANALYSIS

| ROOTS   | WILKS LAMBDA | F       | HYPOTH. DF | ERROR DF | SIG. OF F |
|---------|--------------|---------|------------|----------|-----------|
| 1 TO 2  | .56930       | 6.38693 | 6.00       | 118.00   | .000      |
| 2 TO 2  | .96467       | 1.08946 | 2.00       | 59.50    | .343      |

* * * * * * * * * * * * * * * * * * * * * A N A L Y S I S   O F   V A R I A N C E * * * * * * * * * * * * * * * * * * * * * * * * * * * *

EFFECT -- WITHIN CELLS REGRESSION          (CONT.)

③ UNIVARIATE F-TESTS WITH (2,61) D. F.

| VARIABLE | SQ. MUL. R | MUL. R | ADJ. R-SQ. ④ | HYPOTH MS | ERROR MS | F | SIG. OF F |
|---|---|---|---|---|---|---|---|
| NO3 | .35767 | .59806 | .28396 | 377.89159 | 22.25065 | 16.98340 | .000 |
| K | .13223 | .36363 | .03265 | 36.33667 | 7.81868 | 4.64742 | .013 |
| PO4 | .04395 | .20965 | 0.0 | .00120 | .00085 | 1.40226 | .254 |

REGRESSION ANALYSIS FOR WITHIN CELLS ERROR TERM

DEPENDENT VARIABLE -- NO3 ⑤

| COVARIATE | B | EETA | STD. ERR. | T-VALUE | SIG. OF T | LOWER .95 CL | UPPER .95 CL |
|---|---|---|---|---|---|---|---|
| DEPTH | -.1574951219 | -.1609925728 | .14016 | -1.12369 | .266 | -.43776 | .12277 |
| TDS | -.0175759652 | .4744828755 | .00531 | 3.31176 | .002 | -.00696 | .02819 |

DEPENDENT VARIABLE -- K

| CCVARIATE | B | EETA | STD. ERR. | T-VALUE | SIG. OF T | LOWER .95 CL | UPPER .95 CL |
|---|---|---|---|---|---|---|---|
| DEPTH | -.0180744346 | .0362270836 | .08308 | -.21754 | .829 | -.14806 | .18421 |
| TDS | .0073296604 | .3879842100 | .00315 | 2.32985 | .023 | -.00104 | .01362 |

DEPENDENT VARIABLE -- PO4

| CCVARIATE | B | EETA | STD. ERR. | T-VALUE | SIG. OF T | LOWER .95 CL | UPPER .95 CL |
|---|---|---|---|---|---|---|---|
| DEPTH | -.0012713190 | -.2561554657 | .00087 | -1.46549 | .148 | -.00301 | .00046 |
| TDS | -.0000145264 | -.0772980906 | .00003 | -.44223 | .660 | -.00008 | .00005 |

⑤ These are the univariate estimates of and tests on the regression coefficients.

③ This table contains the results of the multiple regression of each dependent variable on the covariates. Here we see that in the univariate analysis NO3 has the highest partial multiple correlation (.59806) with the two covariates.

④ The ADJ. R-SQ. (adjusted squared multiple correlation coefficient) is an estimate of the multiple correlation coefficient. It can be found using the formula:

$Rho^2 = 1 - (N-1/Dfe)(1-R^2)$

where, $Rho^2$ = the squared population multiple correlation coefficients,

N = the total number of observations, here 69,

DFE = the error degrees of freedom, here 61, and

$R^2$ = the estimated squared multiple correlation, here found in the column labeled SQ. MUL. R.

EFFECT -- SEAL BY PERT

ADJUSTED HYPOTHESIS SUM-OF-SQUARES AND CROSS-PRODUCTS

Note: The following three sections contain the MANCOVA results for each source of variance in the design.

⑥ This matrix is needed for the MANCOVA summary table (see Table 5.11).

|      | NO3 | K | PO4 |
|------|-----|---|-----|
| NC3 ⑥ | 110.42327 | | |
| K | 18.57775 | 45.25691 | |
| PO4 | -.01023 | -.02619 | -.00001 |

MULTIVARIATE TESTS OF SIGNIFICANCE (S = 2, M = 0, N = 28 1/2)

| TEST NAME | VALUE | APPROX. F | HYPOTH. DF | ERROR DF | SIG. OF F |
|-----------|-------|-----------|------------|----------|-----------|
| ⑦ | | | | | |
| PILLAIS | .10057 | 1.05898 | 6.00 | 120.00 | .391 |
| HOTELLINGS | .11177 | 1.08042 | 6.00 | 116.00 | .378 |
| WILKS | .89945 | 1.07017 | 6.00 | 118.00 | .384 |
| RCYS | .10036 | | | | |

EIGENVALUES AND CANONICAL CORRELATIONS

| ROOT NO. | EIGENVALUE | PCT. | CUM. PCT. | CANON. CCR. |
|----------|-----------|------|-----------|-------------|
| 1 | .11155 | 99.80641 | 99.80641 | .31679 |
| 2 | .00022 | .19359 | 100.00000 | .01471 |

⑦ The multivariate tests indicate that there is no significant interaction between SEAL and PERT after adjustment for the covariates.

DIMENSION REDUCTION ANALYSIS

| ROOTS | WILKS LAMBDA | F | HYPOTH. DF | ERROR DF | SIG. OF F |
|-------|--------------|---|------------|----------|-----------|
| 1 TO 2 | .89945 | 1.07017 | 6.00 | 118.00 | .384 |
| 2 TO 2 | .99978 | .00644 | 2.00 | 59.50 | .994 |

CHAPTER 5:   2X3 MANCOVA WITH 2 COVARIATES

* * * * * * * * * * * * * * * * * * * * * * * A N A L Y S I S   O F   V A R I A N C E * * * * * * * * * * * * * * * * * * * * * * * * * *

EFFECT -- FERT

ADJUSTED HYPOTHESIS SUM-OF-SQUARES AND CROSS-PRODUCTS

(8)

|      | NO3       | K        | PO4     |
|------|-----------|----------|---------|
| NO3  | 191.54240 |          |         |
| K    | 55.99777  | 24.56225 |         |
| PO4  | .79870    | .41671   | -.00743 |

(8) This matrix is needed for the MANCOVA summary table (see Table 5.11).

(9) The multivariate tests indicate that there is a significant difference between the levels of fertilizers after adjustment for the covariates.

MULTIVARIATE TESTS OF SIGNIFICANCE (S = 2, M = 0, N = 28 1/2)

| TEST NAME  | VALUE   | APPROX. F | HYPOTH. DF | ERROR DF | SIG. OF F |
|------------|---------|-----------|------------|----------|-----------|
| PILLAIS    | .27328  | 3.16530   | 6.00       | 120.00   | .006      |
| HOTELLINGS | .34283  | 3.31405   | 6.00       | 116.00   | .005      |
| WILKS      | .73702  | 3.24150   | 6.00       | 118.00   | .006      |
| ROYS       | .22812  |           |            |          |           |

(9)

EIGENVALUES AND CANONICAL CORRELATIONS

| ROOT NO. | EIGENVALUE | PCT.     | CUM. PCT. | CANON. COR. |
|----------|------------|----------|-----------|-------------|
| 1        | .29554     | 86.20439 | 86.20439  | .47762      |
| 2        | .04730     | 13.79561 | 100.00000 | .21251      |

DIMENSION REDUCTION ANALYSIS

| ROOTS     | WILKS LAMBDA | F       | HYPOTH. DF | ERROR DF | SIG. OF F |
|-----------|--------------|---------|------------|----------|-----------|
| 1 TO 2    | .73702       | 3.24150 | 6.00       | 118.00   | .006      |
| 2 TO 2    | .95484       | 1.40705 | 2.00       | 59.50    | .253      |

* * * * * * * * * * * * * * * *A N A L Y S I S   O F   V A R I A N C E* * * * * * * * * * * * * * * * * * * * * * *

EFFECT .. FERT    (CONT.)

UNIVARIATE F-TESTS WITH (2,61) D. F.

| VARIABLE | HYPOTH. SS | ERROR SS | HYPOTH. MS | ERROR MS | F | SIG. OF F |
|----------|-----------|----------|-----------|----------|---|-----------|
| NO3 | 191.54240 | 1357.28966 | 95.77120 | 22.25065 | 4.30420 | .018 |
| K | 24.56225 | 476.93940 | 12.28113 | 7.81868 | 1.57074 | .216 |
| PC4 | .00743 | .05200 | .00371 | .00085 | 4.35725 | .017 |

* * * * * * * * * * * * * * * * * * * * * A N A L Y S I S   O F   V A R I A N C E * * * * * * * * * * * * * * * * * * * * * *

EFFECT .. SEAL

ADJUSTED HYPOTHESIS SUM-OF-SQUARES AND CROSS-PRODUCTS

(10)

|       | NO3        | K        | PO4    |
|-------|------------|----------|--------|
| NO3   | 1386.71589 |          |        |
| K     | 283.07712  | 57.78592 |        |
| PO4   | 6.03348    | 1.23164  | .02625 |

(10) This matrix is needed for the MANCOVA summary table (see Table 5.11).

MULTIVARIATE TESTS OF SIGNIFICANCE (S = 1, M = 1/2, N = 28 1/2)

| TEST NAME  | VALUE   | APPROX. F | HYPOTH. DF | ERROR DF | SIG. OF F |
|------------|---------|-----------|------------|----------|-----------|
| PILLAIS    | .63019  | 33.51341  | 3.00       | 59.00    | 0.0       |
| HOTELLINGS | 1.70407 | 33.51341  | 3.00       | 59.00    | 0.0       |
| WILKS      | .36981  | 33.51341  | 3.00       | 59.00    | 0.0       |
| ROYS       | .63019  |           |            |          |           |

(11) (positioned at TEST NAME level)

(11) The multivariate tests indicate that there is a significant difference between the levels of seals after adjustment for the covariates.

EIGENVALUES AND CANONICAL CORRELATIONS

| ROOT NO. | EIGENVALUE | PCT.      | CUM. PCT. | CANON. CCR. |
|----------|------------|-----------|-----------|-------------|
| 1        | 1.70407    | 100.00000 | 100.00000 | .79384      |

DIMENSION REDUCTION ANALYSIS

| ROOTS  | WILKS LAMBDA | F        | HYPOTH. DF | ERROR DF | SIG. OF F |
|--------|--------------|----------|------------|----------|-----------|
| 1 TO 1 | .36981       | 33.51341 | 3.00       | 59.00    | 0.0       |

**\* \* \* \* \* \* \* \* \* \* \* \* \* \* \* \*A N A L Y S I S   O F   V A R I A N C E\* \* \* \* \* \* \* \* \* \* \* \* \* \* \* \* \* \* \* \***

EFFECT .. SEAL   (CONT.)

UNIVARIATE F-TESTS WITH (1,61) D. F.

| VARIABLE | HYPOTH. SS | ERROR SS | HYPOTH. MS | ERROR MS | F | SIG. OF F |
|----------|-----------|----------|------------|----------|------|-----------|
| NC3 | 1386.71589 | 1357.28966 | 1386.71589 | 22.25065 | 62.32249 | 0.0 |
| K | 57.78592 | 476.93940 | 57.78592 | 7.81868 | 7.39075 | .009 |
| PO4 | .02625 | .05200 | .02625 | .00085 | 30.79665 | .000 |

492

**\* \* \* \* \* \* \* \* \* \* \* \* \* \* \* \* \* A N A L Y S I S   O F   V A R I A N C E \* \* \* \* \* \* \* \* \* \* \* \* \* \* \* \* \***

ESTIMATES FOR 204 ADJUSTED FOR 2 COVARIATES    (CONT.)

FERT

| PARAMETER | COEFF. | STD. ERR. | T-VALUE | SIG. OF T | LOWER .95 CL | UPPER .95 CL |
|-----------|--------|-----------|---------|-----------|--------------|--------------|
| 3 | -.0023470674 | .00504 | -.46535 | .643 | -.01243 | -.00774 |
| 4 | -.0114722383 | .00503 | -2.28163 | .026 | -.02153 | -.00142 |

SEAL BY FERT

| PARAMETER | COEFF. | STD. ERR. | T-VALUE | SIG. OF T | LOWER .95 CL | UPPER .95 CL |
|-----------|--------|-----------|---------|-----------|--------------|--------------|
| 5 | .0004115043 | .00507 | .08114 | .936 | -.00973 | -.01055 |
| 6 | .0002499418 | .00505 | .04947 | .961 | -.00985 | -.01035 |

ADJUSTED AND ESTIMATED MEANS

VARIABLE -- NO3

| FACTOR | CODE | OBS. MEAN | ADJ. MEAN | EST. MEAN | RAW RESID. | STD. RESID. |
|--------|------|-----------|-----------|-----------|------------|-------------|
| SEAL | 1 | | | | | |
| FERT | 1 | 42.95833 | 43.65313 | 42.99221 | -.03388 | -.00718 |
| FERT | 2 | 36.54167 | 37.68347 | 36.57555 | -.03388 | -.00718 |
| FERT | 3 | 43.76923 | 43.96703 | 43.80311 | -.03388 | -.00718 |
| SEAL | 2 | | | | | |
| FERT | 1 | 54.31818 | 52.24962 | 54.35206 | -.03388 | -.00718 |
| FERT | 2 | 50.36364 | 50.50326 | 50.39752 | -.03388 | -.00718 |
| FERT | 3 | 50.75000 | 50.64455 | 50.78388 | -.03388 | -.00718 |

493

\* \* \* \* \* \* \* \* \* \* \* \* \* \* \* \* \* \* \* A N A L Y S I S   O F   V A R I A N C E \* \* \* \* \* \* \* \* \* \* \* \* \* \* \* \* \* \* \*

ADJUSTED AND ESTIMATED MEANS (CONT.)

PLOT OF OBSERVED(O), ADJUSTEE(A), AND ESTIMATED(E) MEANS

VARIABLE -- NO3

```
         +
   1     I
   2     I        E    A
         I
   3     I           E   A
         I
   4     I                         F A
         I
   5     I                                      E A        A        E
         I
   6     I                                            AE
         +-------+---------+---------+---------+---------+
      35.39999  35.39998  43.39998  47.39998  51.39998  55.399
  98
```

ADJUSTED AND ESTIMATED MEANS (CONT.)

VARIABLE -- K

| FACTOR | CODE | OBS. MEAN | ADJ. MEAN | EST. MEAN | RAW RESID. | STD. RESID. |
|---|---|---|---|---|---|---|
| SEAL | 1 | | | | | |
| FERT | 1 | 15.81666 | 15.94710 | 15.82230 | -.00564 | -.00202 |
| FERT | 2 | 13.87500 | 14.22675 | 13.88064 | -.00564 | -.00202 |
| FERT | 3 | 16.98461 | 16.94591 | 16.99025 | -.00564 | -.00202 |
| SEAL | 2 | | | | | |
| FERT | 1 | 17.98181 | 17.48586 | 17.98745 | -.00564 | -.00202 |
| FERT | 2 | 17.53636 | 17.57296 | 17.54199 | -.00564 | -.00202 |
| FERT | 3 | 17.78000 | 17.79587 | 17.78563 | -.00564 | -.00202 |

* * * * * * * * * * * * * * * * A N A L Y S I S   O F   V A R I A N C E * * * * * * * * * * * * * * * * * * * * *

ADJUSTED AND ESTIMATED MEANS (CONT.)

PLOT OF OBSERVED(O), ADJUSTED(A), AND ESTIMATED(E) MEANS

VARIABLE -- K

```
                                              E  A
      1  +
         I
      2  I           OE      A
         +
      3  I
         I
      4  +                                          AE              A
         I                                                              E
      5  I                                                    E
         +                                                                    E
      6  I
     OO  +----------+----------+----------+----------+----------+----------+
        13.45000   14.45000   15.45000   16.45000   17.45000   18.45000
```

ADJUSTED AND ESTIMATED MEANS (CONT.)

VARIABLE -- PO4

| FACTOR | CODE | OBS. MEAN | ADJ. MEAN | EST. MEAN | RAW RESID. | STD. RESID. |
|--------|------|-----------|-----------|-----------|------------|-------------|
| SEAL   | 1    |           |           |           |            |             |
| FERT   | 1    | .86083    | .86292    | .86095    | -.00011    | -.00391     |
| FERT   | 2    | .85250    | .85364    | .85261    | -.00011    | -.00391     |
| FERT   | 3    | .87615    | .87802    | .87627    | -.00011    | -.00391     |
| SEAL   | 2    |           |           |           |            |             |
| FERT   | 1    | .90727    | .90285    | .90739    | -.00011    | -.00391     |
| FERT   | 2    | .89364    | .89388    | .89375    | -.00011    | -.00391     |
| FERT   | 3    | .92100    | .92009    | .92111    | -.00011    | -.00391     |

* * * * * * * * * * * * * * * * * * * * A N A L Y S I S   O F   V A R I A N C E * * * * * * * * * * * * * * * * * * * * * * *

ADJUSTED AND ESTIMATED MEANS (CONT.)

PLOT OF OBSERVED(O), ADJUSTED(A), AND ESTIMATED(E) MEANS

VARIABLE -- PO4

```
        +
  1     I                    E  A
        +
  2     I        EA
        +
  3     I                         E  A
        +
  4     I                                  A    E
        +
  5     I                         E
        +
  6     I                                              AE
        +-------+-------+-------+-------+-------+-------+
 40   .84640  .86240  .87840  .89440  .91040  .926
```

\*\*\*\*\*\*\*\*\*\*\*\*\*\*\*\*\*\*\*\*\*\*A N A L Y S I S   O F   V A R I A N C E\*\*\*\*\*\*\*\*\*\*\*\*\*\*\*\*\*\*\*\*\*\*\*\*\*\*\*\*\*\*

COMBINED ESTIMATED MEANS FOR SEAL

VARIABLE -- NO3

```
      SEAL

         1      UNWGT.    41.76788

         2      UNWGT.    51.13247
```

VARIABLE -- K

```
      SEAL

         1      UNWGT.    15.70659

         2      UNWGT.    17.61823
```

VARIABLE -- PO4

```
      SEAL

         1      UNWGT.     .86486

         2      UNWGT.     .90560
```

COMBINED ESTIMATED MEANS FOR FFRT

VARIABLE -- NO3

```
      FERT

         1      UNWGT.    47.95137
```

* * * * * * * * * * * * * * * * * A N A L Y S I S   O F   V A R I A N C E * * * * * * * * * * * * * * * * * * * * * * * * * * * *

COMBINED ESTIMATED MEANS FOR FERT     (CONT.)

VARIABLE -- NO3     (CONT.)

    2    UNWGT.    44.09336

    3    UNWGT.    47.30579

VARIABLE -- K

    FERT

    1    UNWGT.    16.71648

    2    UNWGT.    15.85986

    3    UNWGT.    17.37089

VARIABLE -- PO4

    FERT

    1    UNWGT.    .88289

    2    UNWGT.    .87376

    3    UNWGT.    .89905

COMBINED ESTIMATED MEANS FOR SEAL BY FERT

VARIABLE -- NO3

          SEAL       1       2

    FERT

\* \* \* \* \* \* \* \* \* \* \* \* \* \* \* \* \* \* \* A N A L Y S I S   O F   V A R I A N C E \* \* \* \* \* \* \* \* \* \* \* \* \* \* \* \* \* \* \* \* \*

COMBINED ESTIMATED MEANS FOR SEAL BY FERT     (CONT.)

VARIABLE -- NO3     (CONT.)

| | | 1 | 2 |
|---|---|---|---|
| 1 | UNWGT. | 43.65313 | 52.24962 |
| 2 | UNWGT. | 37.66347 | 50.50326 |
| 3 | UNWGT. | 43.96703 | 50.64455 |

- - - - - - - - - - - - - - - - - - - - - - - - - - - - -

VARIABLE -- K

| | SEAL | 1 | 2 |
|---|---|---|---|
| FERT | | | |
| 1 | UNWGT. | 15.94710 | 17.48586 |
| 2 | UNWGT. | 14.22675 | 17.57296 |
| 3 | UNWGT. | 16.94591 | 17.79587 |

- - - - - - - - - - - - - - - - - - - - - - - - - - - - -

VARIABLE -- PO4

| | SEAL | 1 | 2 |
|---|---|---|---|
| FERT | | | |
| 1 | UNWGT. | .86292 | .90285 |
| 2 | UNWGT. | .85364 | .89388 |
| 3 | UNWGT. | .87802 | .92009 |

- - - - - - - - - - - - - - - - - - - - - - - - - - - - -

************** A N A L Y S I S   O F   V A R I A N C E ***************************

02/02/83     PAGE    49

WITHIN+RESIDUAL SUM-OF-SQUARES AND CROSS-PRODUCTS

|      | NO3        | K          | PO4    |
|------|------------|------------|--------|
| NO3  | 1109.96106 |            |        |
| K    | 34.70212   | 388.60223  |        |
| PC4  | .09390     | .21458     | .04228 |

* * * * * * * * * * * * * * * * * A N A L Y S I S   O F   V A R I A N C E * * * * * * * * * * * * * * * * * * * * *

EFFECT -- CONTIN(DEPTH TDS) BY SEAL + CONTIN(DEPTH TDS) BY FERT + CONTIN(DEPTH TDS) BY SEAL BY FERT

ADJUSTED HYPOTHESIS SUM-OF-SQUARES AND CROSS-PRODUCTS

|  | NO3 | K | PO4 |
|---|---|---|---|
| NO3 | 247.32860 | | |
| K | 34.58679 | 88.33717 | |
| PO4 | -.61887 | -.38975 | .00972 |

MULTIVARIATE TESTS OF SIGNIFICANCE (S = 3, M = 3, N = 23 1/2)

| TEST NAME | VALUE | APPROX. F | HYPOTH. DF | ERROR DF | SIG. OF F |
|---|---|---|---|---|---|
| PILLAIS | .53792 | 1.11426 | 30.00 | 153.00 | .326 |
| HOTELLINGS | .68916 | 1.09500 | 30.00 | 143.00 | .351 |
| WILKS | .54533 | 1.10530 | 30.00 | 144.50 | .338 |
| ROYS | .28323 | | | | |

(12)

EIGENVALUES AND CANONICAL CORRELATIONS

| ROOT NO. | EIGENVALUE | PCT. | CUM. PCT. | CANON. COR. |
|---|---|---|---|---|
| 1 | .39516 | 57.33858 | 57.33858 | .53220 |
| 2 | .18214 | 26.42949 | 83.76807 | .39253 |
| 3 | .11186 | 16.23193 | 100.00000 | .31719 |

DIMENSION REDUCTION ANALYSIS

| ROOTS | WILKS LAMBDA | F | HYPOTH. DF | ERROR DF | SIG. OF F |
|---|---|---|---|---|---|
| 1 TO 3 | .54533 | 1.10530 | 30.00 | 144.50 | .338 |
| 2 TO 3 | .76081 | .80814 | 18.00 | 148.25 | .688 |
| 3 TO 3 | .89939 | .70154 | 8.00 | 150.72 | .690 |

(12) The multivariate tests of homogeneity of the
within cell regression coefficients is found in
the re-specified model's interaction. These tests
indicate that we do have homogeneous regression
coefficients.

Note: Since the multivariate tests were not significant
we would not consider the univariate tests so as
to avoid finding a spuriously significant result.

# CHAPTER 6

## ANALYSIS OF NESTED DESIGNS
by Tom D. Daniels

## General Introduction

Chapters 3 through 5 of this book are concerned with analysis of variance models involving fully-crossed, factorial designs. While the use of factorial designs is quite common, research studies may sometimes require designs with factors which are not fully-crossed. That is, each level of a given factor in the design occurs at one and only one level of another factor. Here, the former is said to be "nested" within the latter.

For example, suppose a researcher is interested in studying the effects of four levels of message organization (Messorg) upon recall of message information. Randomly formed groups of subjects are to be exposed to the four Messorg conditions, then tested for recall of message information, with an analysis of test scores for differences among Messorg levels. The researcher decides to use assistants as group proctors (Proctor) in each treatment condition to orient the subjects and monitor the treatments. Given the direct involvement of proctors, any differences in recall scores among levels of Messorg could be attributable to differences in proctors. Therefore, the researcher elects to include Proctor as a factor in the model.

In this case, the researcher uses eight proctors, with each proctor monitoring one group under one treatment condition (i.e., there are eight groups of subjects, each monitored by a proctor, with two groups per level of Messorg). Each level of Proctor occurs at one and only one level of Messorg, yielding what is generally described as an A, B(A) nested design. The "B(A)" notation indicates that Factor B (Proctor) is nested within Factor A (Messorg).

It should be emphasized that the researcher's major concern in the situation described above is with the Messorg factor. Keppel (1973, p.370) has argued that the utility of including a nested factor in a model lies in increasing the external validity of an experiment. Thus, the model is designed to assess the variance accounted for by the presence of Proctor, though the nested factor is not of primary interest.

The researcher should also be aware that the very act of nesting cne factor within another negates the possibility of assessing any interaction between those factors (Dayton, 1970, p.199). The effect of the nested factor is confounded with the interaction, i.e., the B(A) effect is confounded with the AB interaction.

Interpretation of significant effects in nested designs also requires caution. Given an A, B(A) model, interpretation of the A effect depends, in part, upon whether the levels of B occur randomly across levels of A. If not, any effect for A might be attributable to differences in levels of B (see Lindman, 1974, p.171). The F test for B(A) does not test for differences between levels of B(A) across levels of A, but, rather, for differences between levels of B(A) within levels of A. Thus, it follows from Keppel's argument above that interpretation cf significant A effect must be done in light of the B(A) effect, should the latter be significant.

The comments so far have been directed to the simplest form of nested design (A,B(A)). When additional factors are introduced in a model, there are various possibilities for crossing and nesting factors. In Appendix D we present further information cn designs having both fixed and random factors.

## Organization of the Programs

To illustrate the analysis of a nested design, ten computer runs are included with this chapter. Table 6.1 contains the list of the programs run for this chapter, their numbers, whether they are univariate or multivariate, whether they are standard or instructional, their initial page number, and their I/O features.

Table 6.1
Descriptions of the Programs Run on the
Nested Data From Chapter 6

| Program | Program Number | Mode[1] | Type[2] | Page | I/O Features |
|---------|---------|------|------|------|--------------|
| | | | | | |
| Volume 1: BMDP | | | | | |
| | | | | | |
| BMDP4V | 6-1 | U | S | 368 | test of the nested factor; cell means |
| BMDP4V | 6-2 | U | S | 373 | test of the main factor with the nested factor pooled with the error |
| BMDP8V | 6-3 | U | S | 377 | special program for designs with random and fixed factors |
| BMDP4V | 6-4 | M | S | 382 | test of the nested factor; cell means |
| BMDP4V | 6-5 | M | S | 389 | test of the main factor with the nested factor pooled with error |
| | | | | | |
| Volume 2: SAS | | | | | |
| | | | | | |
| SAS(GLM) | 6-1 | U | S | 384 | overall and planned comparisons analyses with all factors in the model, followed by overall and planned comparisons with the nested factor pooled with the error term |
| SAS (NESTED) | 6-2 | U | I | 392 | no statistical tests, but sums of squares and estimates of variance components |
| SAS(GLM) | 6-3 | M | S | 395 | test of the main factor with the nested factor pooled with error, but with multivariate tests only for the overall analyses |

---

| Program | Program Number | Mode[1] | Type[2] | Page | I/O Features |
|---------|---------|---------|---------|------|--------------|

---

Volume 3: SPSS and SPSSX

---

| | | | | | |
|---------|---------|---------|---------|------|--------------|
| SPSS-SPSSX (MANOVA) | 6-1 | U | S | 532 | overall and planned comparisons analyses with all factors in the model, followed by overall and planned comparisons with the nested factor pooled with the error term |
| SPSS-SPSSX (MANOVA) | 6-2 | M | S | 546 | overall and planned comparisons analyses with all factors in the model, followed by overall and planned comparisons with the nested factor pooled with the error term |

---

[1]Mode is coded U for univariate or M for multivariate.
[2]Type is coded S for standard or I for instruction.

## Special Analytical Note: Pooling

The example problem in this chapter involves a mixed model where one factor is fixed and the other is random. The fixed factor in such a model is normally tested against the random factor rather than the within-cell error term. However, use of an A, B(A) design where A is fixed and B(A) is random may permit testing of the fixed factor against a pooled term representing both the random factor and within-cell error.

Winer (1971, pp. 378-384) discusses general procedures for pooling certain terms in models involving random factors. Preliminary tests are conducted on interactions involving random factors, using a liberal alpha level (e.g., .20). Where such a test is nonsignificant, the sum of squares and degrees of freedom for the effect may be pooled with the sum of squares and degrees of freedom for within-cell error in conducting the next test. The procedure begins with higher-order interactions and continues through lower-order interactions. Interactions which are pooled with error are, in effect, dropped from the model. Once pooling is completed, the remaining terms in the model are tested with an appropriate alpha level (e.g., .05).

Kirk (1968, pp. 231-233) has specifically discussed this procedure in connection with the A, B(A) model where A is fixed and B(A) is random. In this case, the preliminary test discussed by Winer is applied to the random effect. If this test is non-significant, the sum of squares and degrees of freedom for the random effect are pooled with the sum of squares and degrees of freedom for the within-cell error term. This pooled term becomes the denominator for the F test of the fixed effect. Since the B(A) effect would generally be associated with few degrees of freedom, the pooled term may yield a lower denominator in the F test for the A effect. Kirk suggests pooling whenever the mean square for B(A) is based on fewer than 25-30 degrees of freedom. This procedure is employed in the analysis of variance presentations. However, it should also be noted that some writers (Keppel, 1973, p. 560; Scheffe, 1959, p. 126) express reservations about the appropriateness of pooling terms in analysis of variance models.

## Analysis of Variance Presentations

Four presentations follow which describe analyses of a nested design. The first two are univariate applications, one involving planned comparisons, the other using overall and _post_ _hoc_ tests. The other two are multivariate applications, again with a planned comparisons analysis, then overal analysis and _post_ _hoc_ tests. The data for these presentations were taken from a problem found in Timm (1975, p. 429). The nature of the problem and arrangement of the data in Timm were modified substantially for purposes of this chapter. The data have been tailored to fit the fictitious problem described in the Introduction.

A researcher is interested in examining the effects of four levels of message organization (Messorg) upon recall of message information. Several studies of message organization (Frase, 1969; Myers, Pezdek & Coulson, 1973; Perlmutter & Royer, 1973; Schultz & DiVesta, 1972; Whitman & Timmis, 1975) have employed messages which consist of sentences relating concepts to attributes of those concepts in terms of attribute values. These researchers have organized the messages by concept categories and/or attribute categories and by random sentence order, applying a category clustering index (Frase, 1969) to measure the degree of structure in the messages. The category clustering index is a function of the contiguous occurence of sentences involving the same concept or attribute. The concept and attribute arrangements in these studies have had category clustering indices of 100% (maximum categorical structure), while the random orders have had indices at or near 0%. The studies have consistently shown the high-structure (100%) versions to be superior to the random versions in effects upon recall. Figure 6.1 exhibits a high-structure (100%) concept order and a random order for the same message as an example of the materials used in these studies.

This researcher is interested in creating two additional levels of structure (75% and 50%) between the maximum (100%) and random structures and investigating the effects of these four levels upon recall of message information. The researcher develops a 50-sentence message using the sort of system described in Figure 6.1 and imposes three levels of structure having respective category clustering indices of 100%, 75% and 50%. A fourth level is created by randomly ordering the sentences. This fourth version turns out to have a category clustering index of 7% (even a random order would be expected to possess some measurable structure). These levels of message organization are labeled 100%, 75%, 50% and 7% in the program runs wherever such labeling is permitted.

Proctors are used to provide oral instructions and orientation to randomly formed groups of subjects and to monitor the treatments. The proctors are randomly selected from a pool of potential proctors and randomly assigned across levels of Messorg. Proctor is nested within Messorg. There are eight proctors, two in each level of Messorg, with eight groups of subjects, each assigned to a proctor.

After treatment administration, the subjects are to recall as much of the message information as possible in a free recall protocol. That is, the subjects are to regenerate as many message sentences as possible. The univariate analyses will be executed on free recall accuracy as a measure of recall of message information. The accuracy score is the number of sentences a subject correctly recalls. The multivariate analyses will be executed on accuracy and on the degree of clustering in free recall output. In this case, a subject's clustering score is obtained with a derivative of the category clustering index.

| Attribute | Education | Title | Previous Employment |
| --- | --- | --- | --- |

Concept

| | | | |
| --- | --- | --- | --- |
| B. Spiker | M.A. | Research Asst. | Used Car Salesman |
| J. Brodzinski | M.A. | Teaching Asst. | Tatoo Artist |
| T. Daniels | M.A. | Grad. Fellow | Faith Healer |

Concept Structure:

B. Spiker has an M.A. in government.
B. Spiker is now a research assistant.
B. Spiker was previously employed as a used car salesman.

J. Brodzinski has an M.A. in communication theory.
J. Brodzinski is now a teaching assistant.
J. Brodzinski  was previously employed as a tatoo artist.

T. Daniels has an M.A. in rhetoric.
T. Daniels is now a graduate fellow.
T. Daniels was previously employed as a faith healer.

Random Structure:

J. Brodzinski has an M.A. in communication theory.
T. Daniels was previously employed as a faith healer.
T. Daniels is now a graduate fellow.

B. Spiker was previously employed as a used car salesman.
J. Brodzinski is now a teaching assistant.
B. Spiker has an M.A. in government.

T. Daniels has an M.A. in rhetoric.
B. Spiker is now a research assistant.
J. Brodzinski was previously employed as a tatoo artist.

Figure 6.1 An example of a message with concept structure and
          random structure.

## Univariate Analysis: Planned Comparisons

Planned comparisons are contrasts among levels of a factor which are set up a *priori* as hypotheses. The researcher has some basis in previous theory or research for such contrasts and tests only the planned comparisons for a factor, rather than conducting overall tests on the factor.

In this section, only planned comparisons will be executed on the Messorg effect. The Proctor effect will be examined with an overall test; however, a researcher could conduct separate tests for a nested effect within each level of a treatment effect (see Winer, 1971, p. 360) or even planned comparisons if so desired.

### Problem

A. Is accuracy in the free recall of message information dependent upon the level of message organization?

B. Is accuracy in the free recall of message information dependent upon the proctor orienting the subjects and monitoring the treatments?

### Research Hypotheses

The research hypotheses are formulated to reflect planned comparisons for the Messorg factor. Having reviewed the studies previously cited, the researcher believes that recall accuracy is maximized under the 100% structure condition and predicts in the planned comparisons the degree of disorganization which must occur before accuracy is significantly reduced.

Research Hypothesis (1A): A message structure with a category clustering index of 100% will be superior to a message structure with a category clustering index of 75% in effects upon accuracy in the free recall of message information.

Research Hypothesis (2A): A message structure with a category clustering index of 100% will be superior to a message structure with a category clustering index of 50% in effects upon accuracy in the free recall of message information.

Research Hypothesis (3A): A message structure with a category clustering index of 100% will be superior to a message structure with a category clustering index of 7% in effects upon accuracy in the free recall of message information.

Research Hypothesis (4B): There will be no differences between proctors within levels of message organization in effects upon accuracy in the free recall of message information.

### Statistical Hypotheses

The statistical hypotheses are written in symbolic form. $H(A1)$, $H(A2)$, and $H(A3)$ reflect the actual research hypotheses for the Messorg factor. $H(04)$ reflects the research hypothesis for the Proctor factor. The symbol $u(i)$ represents the population mean for Messorg i (i = 1 - 4) and $u(ij)$ represents the population mean for Proctor j in Messorg i (j = 1, 2).

Null Hypothesis (1A) $H(01)$: $u(1) = u(2)$

Alternate Hypothesis (1A) $H(A1)$: $u(1) > u(2)$

Null Hypothesis (2A) $H(02)$: $u(1) = u(3)$

Alternate Hypothesis (2A) $H(A2)$: $u(1) > u(3)$

Null Hypothesis (3A) $H(03)$: $u(1) = u(4)$

Alternate Hypothesis (3A) $H(A3)$: $u(1) > u(4)$

Null Hypothesis (4B) $H(04)$: $u(i1) = u(i2)$ for each i

Alternate Hypothesis (4B) $H(A4)$: $u(i1) \neq u(i2)$ for one or more i's

Since the three planned comparisons are not orthogonal, the alpha level for the significance tests (in this case, .05) is not actually constant across comparisons. Where a number of non-orthogonal contrasts are involved, one might somehow split up the alpha level among the contrasts in order to maintain the overall alpha at a desired level. For example, one might divide the overall alpha level by the number of contrasts and use the quotient as the level for rejection of the null hypothesis on each contrast. Should such a procedure be applied in this problem, the alpha level for rejection of each null hypothesis in the planned comparisons would be .05/3 = .0167. However, the necessity of this procedure is open to some question where the number of contrasts is small. Therefore, we will use .05 for each contrast.

As noted earlier, this chapter will demonstrate the preliminary testing and pooling procedure described by Kirk. Because we wanted to demonstrate the pooling process, we tested the fourth hypothesis of no proctor effect at the .05 level of significance rather than the more liberal .20 level suggested by Kirk.

### Data

In this chapter we deviate from our other chapters in that we deal only with designs that have an equal number of subjects in each cell. This was done because of the general confusion that exists among statisticians on how to treat the unequal $n$ case for mixed designs. The reader interested in exploring this topic further should consult the 1981 BMDP manual and consider BMDP3V (pp. 413-426).

The data are presented in Table 6.2 as a univariate, equal $n$ problem. The design has two factors (Messorg with four levels and Proctor with two levels nested in each level of Messorg). The dependent variable is recall accuracy (labeled ACCURACY in the program runs) on a free recall protocol. Scores represent the number of correct sentence reproductions. A sentence does not have to be reproduced verbatim to be correct; the reproduction need only assert a correct concept/attribute value relationship.

### Analyses of Variance

No pooling. Table 6.3 summarizes the univariate planned comparison analysis of variance when Proctor and the error (within) sums of squares are not pooled.

Error and Proctor pooled. Table 6.4 summarizes the univariate planned comparison analysis of variance when Proctor and the error (within) sums of squares are pooled. Note that the degrees of freedom for error in the test of Messorg have increased from 4, in Table 6.3, to 28 in Table 6.4, and therefore, the F test in Table 6.4 is more powerful.

Table 6.2
Data[1] for a Two-Factor Univariate Nested Design

| Messorg: | 100% | | 75% | | 50% | | 7% | |
|---|---|---|---|---|---|---|---|---|
| Proctor: | 1 | 2 | 3 | 4 | 5 | 6 | 7 | 8 |
| | 19 | 44 | 38 | 35 | 18 | 11 | 3 | 14 |
| | 41 | 38 | 19 | 31 | 38 | 6 | 10 | 8 |
| | 28 | 39 | 44 | 26 | 24 | 6 | 14 | 7 |
| | 40 | 36 | 40 | 27 | 17 | 2 | 25 | 39 |

[1]These data are adapted from a set found in Timm (1975,p.429).
Here the factor and level names and nesting relationships have
been altered, and cell orders were changed.

Table 6.3
Univariate Planned Comparisons, No Pooling

| Source of Variation | Degrees of Freedom | Sum of Squares | Mean Square | F Statistic[1] | Prob[2] |
|---|---|---|---|---|---|
| Messorg Planned Comparisons | 3 | 2908.34 | | | |
| 100% V. 75% | 1 | 39.06 | 39.06 | .18 | .345 |
| 100% V. 50% | 1 | 1660.56 | 1660.56 | 7.85* | .024 |
| 100% V. 7% | 1 | 1701.56 | 1701.56 | 8.05* | .023 |
| Proctor (error term for planned comparisons) | 4 | 845.63 | 211.41 | 2.49 | .070 |
| Error(within) | 24 | 2035.75 | 84.82 | | |

[1]We reported F statistics, instead of t statistics, for the
planned comparisons so that the table would have an F value
for Proctor.
[2]All probabilities are for one-tailed tests (half of the values
reported in the programs) except that for Proctor which is
two-tailed.
*Significant at p<.05.

Table 6.4
Univariate Planned Comparisons, Error and
Proctor Pooled

| Source of Variation | Degrees of Freedom | Sum of Squares | Mean Square | t Statistic[1] | Prob[2] |
|---|---|---|---|---|---|
| Messorg | 3 | 2908.34 | | | |
| Planned Comparisons | | | | | |
| 100% V. 75% | 1 | 39.06 | 39.06 | .62 | .271 |
| 100% V. 50% | 1 | 1660.56 | 1660.56 | 4.02* | .000 |
| 100% V. 7% | 1 | 1701.56 | 1701.56 | 4.07* | .000 |
| Error (pooled) | 28 | 2881.38 | 102.91 | | |

[1]The t values reported in the programs are negative because in the contrasts tested we subtracted the 100% mean from the means of each of the other levels. We report these values as positive here to be consistent with our hypotheses.

[2]These are one-tailed probabilities (half of the values reported in the programs).

*Significant at $p < .05$.

Results. The results in Tables 6.3 and 6.4 call for rejection of null hypotheses two and three. Null hypotheses one and four are not rejected. Thus, support was found for research hypotheses two, three and four, while no support was found for research hypothesis one. The 100% structure condition is superior to the 50% and 7% conditions, but does not differ from the 75% condition. There are no differences between proctors within Messorg levels.

## Univariate Analysis: Overall and Post Hoc Tests

If a researcher has no planned comparisons that seem to be appropriate on the basis of previous theory or research, a common procedure is to conduct an overall significance test for an effect. Given a significant overall test, post hoc tests are executed to locate significant differences among the means for the levels of the factor. In this case, the problem statement may very well be the same as in the planned comparison example, but the hypotheses are stated in terms of overall effects, not a priori contrasts.

### Problem

A. Is accuracy in the free recall of message information dependent upon the level of message organization?

B. Is accuracy in the free recall of message information dependent upon the proctor orienting the subjects and monitoring the treatments?

### Research Hypotheses

Suppose this study represents an initial investigation of the problem, with little previous research or theory in the area. In this case, the researcher believes that differences will appear among the Messorg means, but has no particular basis for specific predictions.

Research Hypothesis (1A): the four levels of message organization (100%, 75%, 50% and 7%) will have differing effects upon accuracy in free recall of message information.

Research Hypothesis (2B): There will be no differences between proctors within levels of message organization in effects upon accuracy in the free recall of message information.

### Statistical Hypotheses

The symbolic statistical hypotheses follow, with H(A1) reflecting research hypothesis one and H(02) reflecting research hypothesis two. See the planned comparisons section for an explanation of the u subscripts.

Null
Hypothesis (1) H(01): $u(1) = u(2) = u(3) = u(4)$

Alternate
Hypothesis (1) H(A1): $u(i) \neq u(i)'$ $(i \neq i'; i,i'=1,2,3,4)$

Null
Hypothesis (2) H(02): u(i1) = u(i2) for each i

Alternate
Hypothesis (2) H(A2): u(i1) $\neq$ u(i2) for one or more i's

The Messorg hypothesis will be tested at the .05 level of significance. As in the planned comparison section, the preliminary test and pooling procedure (Kirk) discussed earlier is employed here, so the Proctor hypothesis will be tested at .05.

### Data

Data are the same as that used in the univariate planned comparison example (see Table 6.2).

### Analysis of Variance

No pooling. Table 6.5 summarizes the overall univariate analysis of variance when Proctor and the error (within) sums of squares are not pooled.

Error and Proctor pooled. Table 6.6 summarizes the overall univariate analysis of variance when Proctor and the error (within) sums of squares are pooled. Note that the degrees of freedom for error in the test cf Messorg have increased from 4, in Table 6.5 to 28 in Table 6.6 and therefore, the latter F test is more powerful.

Results. The results for the overall analysis depend on whether or not one pools. In Table 6.5 where no pooling has taken place, we find no significant effect, and support for only our second research hypothesis. However, in Table 6.6, where we have pooled the Proctor and error sums of squares, we find a significant effect for message organization and support for our first research hypothesis.

### Table 6.5
### Overall Analysis, No Pooling

| Source of Variation | Degrees of Freedom | Sum of Squares | Mean Square | F Statistic | Prob. |
|---|---|---|---|---|---|
| Messorg | 3 | 2908.34 | 969.45 | 4.59 | .088 |
| Proctor (error term for Messorg) | 4 | 845.63 | 211.41 | 2.49 | .070 |
| Error (within) | 24 | 2035.75 | 84.82 | | |

516

## Table 6.6
## Overall Analysis, Error and Proctor Pooled

| Source of Variation | Degrees of Freedom | Sum of Squares | Mean Square | F Statistic | Prob. |
|---|---|---|---|---|---|
| Messorg | 3 | 2908.34 | 969.45 | 9.42* | .000 |
| Error(pooled) | 28 | 2881.38 | 102.91 | | |

*Significant at p<.05.

Newman-Keuls Post Hoc Tests. Given the significant F test for the Messorg effect, some form of post hoc test should be executed to determine where the differences occurred. Applications of various post hoc tests (e.g., Scheffe, Tukey, Newman-Keuls) are illustrated in this book. The test employed here is the somewhat controversial Duncan Multiple Range Test (Duncan, 1955) with Kramer's (1956) adjustment for unequal $n$'s. While Glass and Stanley (1970, p. 383) note that Duncan's test is widely used in behavioral and educational research, they also point out that statisticians disagree over its validity and they suggest a moratorium on the use of Duncan's procedure.

The procedures for conducting Duncan's test are much like those used for Newman-Keuls. However, the critical values for significance are derived from tables developed by Duncan. For values of k (number of factor levels) larger than 2, the critical value in Duncan is smaller than that for Newman-Keuls (Winer, 1971, pp. 196-197). Thus, the Duncan procedure is more liberal than Newman-Keuls. Duncan's test is applied to the Messorg effect in the steps which follow.

Step 1.

Rank order the Messorg means from smallest to largest, including the $n$'s.

Example:

| | 1 | 2 | 3 | 4 |
|---|---|---|---|---|
| | 7% | 50% | 75% | 100% |
| X | 15.00 | 15.25 | 32.50 | 35.63 |
| N | 8 | 8 | 8 | 8 |

Step 2.

Find $s = \sqrt{MSerror/n}$. In this case, the pooled term (SSproctor + SSerror/dfproctor + dferror) is substituted for MSerror.

Example:

$$S = \sqrt{102.91/8} = 3.59$$

Step 3.

Find the k-1 Studentized Range Values by entering Duncan's (1955) .05 Table at n(2) for P(2) through P(k). Here, N(2) is the degrees of freedom for error (again, those in the pooled term) and k is the number of factor levels.

Example:

| P | | 2 | 3 | 4 |
|---|---|---|---|---|
| N(2) = 28 | | 2.90 | 3.04 | 3.13 |

Step 4.

Find the Significant Range Factor (R'p) via: R'p=P(k)*S.

Example:

R'2 = 2.90 * 3.59 = 10.41

R'3 = 3.04 * 3.59 = 10.91

R'4 = 3.13 * 3.59 = 11.24

Step 5.

Compute $(\bar{x}(i) - \bar{x}(i))$. Perform these computations in the following order $\bar{x}$(largest) − $\bar{x}$(smallest); $\bar{x}$(largest) − $\bar{x}$(2nd smallest) ... $\bar{x}$(2nd smallest) − $\bar{x}$(smallest). After each computation, check the result against the appropriate value for R'p. The correct value is R'p where p = the number of ordered steps between the means in the comparison. If $R'_p$ is exceeded, the comparison is significant. Otherwise, the comparison is not significant and any comparisons contained within the comparison are not significant.

Example:

(35.63 - 15.00) = 20.63 > 11.24

(35.63 - 15.25) = 20.38 > 10.91

(35.63 - 32.50) =  3.13 < 10.41

(32.50 - 15.00) = 17.50 > 10.91

(32.50 - 15.25) = 17.25 > 10.41

(15.25 - 15.00) =   .25 < 10.41

## Step 6.

All means underlined by the same line are not significantly different. Any other comparisons are significant.

Example:

```
__1_____2_____3_____4____
   7%    50%    75%   100%

  15.00 15.25    32.50 35.63
```

## Step 7.

If the problem has unequal n's, Step 2 becomes $S = \underline{\hspace{1cm}} MS_{error}$ and Step 5 adds the term: $\sqrt{2(n(1)n(1'))/(n(1)+n(i'))}$, using $(\bar{x}(i)-\bar{x}(i'))\sqrt{2(n(i)n(i'))/(n(i)+n(i'))}$.

In this example problem, the 100% and 75% levels of Messorg do not differ significantly. Nor do the 50% and 7% levels. However, both the 100% and 75% levels differ significantly from the 50% and 7% levels.

## Multivariate Analysis of Variance

The following presentations involve multivariate analyses of the example problem. Here, the researcher is interested not only in the effects of message organization upon accuracy in free recall, but also in the effects of message organization upon the degree to which subjects organize their free recall output. A derivation of the category clustering index used to determine the degree of structure in the message is applied to the subject's free recall output for an index of organization and included as a dependent variable (labeled CLUSTER in the program runs). Now, the researcher is dealing with two dependent variables that represent dimensions of learning in a multivariate model.

## Multivariate Analysis: Planned Comparisons

This section contains a multivariate extension of the univariate planned comparisons discussed earlier in the chapter. It is recommended that readers who are unfamiliar with multivariate analysis compare these multivariate applications with the preceding univariate models. The reader should also keep in mind the comments made in Chapter 2 with respect to the importance of a common conceptual basis for dependent variables included in a multivariate model. In this example problem, the two dependent variables represent dimensions in the free recall of message information; the researcher is interested in testing the effects of different levels of the independent variables on the two dependent variables conjunctively.

### Problem

A. Are accuracy and clustering in the free recall of message information dependent upon the level of message organization?

B. Are accuracy and clustering in the free recall of message information dependent upon the proctor orienting the subjects and monitoring the treatments?

### Research Hypotheses

As in the univariate planned comparisons example, these research hypotheses involve planned comparisons for the Messorg factor on the basis of prior theory and research. The Proctor effect will be examined with an overall test.

Research Hypothesis (1A): A message structure with a category clustering index of 100% will be superior to a message structure with a category clustering index of 75% in effects upon accuracy and clustering in the free recall of message information.

Research Hypothesis (2A): A message structure with a category clustering index of 100% will be superior to a message structure with a category clustering index of 50% in effects upon accuracy and clustering in the free recall of message information.

Research Hypothesis (3A): A message structure with a category clustering index of 100% will be superior to a message structure with a category clustering index of 7% in effects upon accuracy and clustering in the free recall of messsage information.

Research Hypothesis (4E): There will be no differences between proctors within levels of message organization in effects upon accuracy and clustering in the free recall of message information.

## Statistical Hypotheses

The symbolic form of the statistical hypotheses matches the research hypotheses. The symbol u(pi) represents the population mean for the dependent variable p(1,2) in Messorg i(1,2,3,4). The symbol $\underline{u}$ represents the vector of means containing both dependent variables in Messorg i. u(pij) represents the mean for variable p in Messorg i under Proctor j(1,2). u(i,j) represents the vector of means containing both dependent variables under Messorg i, Proctor j.

$$
\text{Null Hypothesis (1) } H(01): \begin{bmatrix} u(11) \\ u(21) \end{bmatrix} = \begin{bmatrix} u(12) \\ u(22) \end{bmatrix}
$$

$$
\text{i.e., } H(01): \quad \underline{u}(1) = \underline{u}(2)
$$

$$
\text{Alternate Hypothesis (1) } H(A1): \begin{bmatrix} u(11) \\ u(21) \end{bmatrix} \neq \begin{bmatrix} u(12) \\ u(22) \end{bmatrix}
$$

$$
\text{i.e., } H(A1): \quad \underline{u}(1) \neq \underline{u}(2)
$$

$$
\text{Null Hypothesis (2) } H(02): \begin{bmatrix} u(11) \\ u(21) \end{bmatrix} = \begin{bmatrix} u(13) \\ u(23) \end{bmatrix}
$$

$$
\text{i.e., } H(02): \quad \underline{u}(1) = \underline{u}(3)
$$

$$
\text{Alternate Hypothesis (2) } H(A2): \begin{bmatrix} u(11) \\ u(21) \end{bmatrix} \neq \begin{bmatrix} u(13) \\ u(23) \end{bmatrix}
$$

$$
\text{i.e., } H(A2): \quad \underline{u}(1) \neq \underline{u}(3)
$$

Null
Hypothesis (3) H(03): $\begin{bmatrix} u(11) \\ u(21) \end{bmatrix} = \begin{bmatrix} u(14) \\ u(24) \end{bmatrix}$

    i.e., H(03): $\underline{u}(1) = \underline{u}(4)$


Alternate
Hypothesis (3) H(A3): $\begin{bmatrix} u(11) \\ u(21) \end{bmatrix} \neq \begin{bmatrix} u(14) \\ u(24) \end{bmatrix}$

    i.e., H(A3): $\underline{u}(1) \neq \underline{u}(4)$


Null
Hypothesis (4) H(04): $\begin{bmatrix} u(1i1) \\ u(2i1) \end{bmatrix} = \begin{bmatrix} u(1i2) \\ u(2i2) \end{bmatrix}$ for each i

    i.e., H(04): $\underline{u}(i1) = \underline{u}(i2)$


Alternate
Hypothesis (4) H(A4): $\begin{bmatrix} u(1i1) \\ u(2i1) \end{bmatrix} \neq \begin{bmatrix} u(1i2) \\ u(2i2) \end{bmatrix}$ for 1 or more i's

    i.e., H(A4): $\underline{u}(i1) \neq \underline{u}(i2)$


As in the univariate planned comparison section, the three planned comparisons here are not orthogonal. Thus, the researcher might consider splitting the overall alpha level for tests of each comparison (e.g., .05/3 = .0167). The preliminary test and pooling procedure used in the univariate sections is continued in this section. All hypotheses will be tested at the .05 level of significance.

### Data

The design has the same factors used in the univariate example (Messorg with four levels and Proctor with two levels nested in each level of Messorg). The dependent variables are accuracy and clustering in free recall of message information. The data for the analysis are included in Table 6.7.


No pooling. Table 6.8 summarizes the planned comparison multivariate analysis of variance when Proctor and the error (within) sums of squares are not pooled.

Error and Proctor pooled. Table 6.9 summarizes the planned comparison multivariate analysis of variance when Proctor and the error (within) sums of squares are pooled.

522

## Table 6.7
### Data[1] for a Two-Factor Multivariate Nested Design

| Messorg: | 1 | | | | 2 | | | | 3 | | | | 4 | | | |
|---|---|---|---|---|---|---|---|---|---|---|---|---|---|---|---|---|
| Proctor: | 1 | | 2 | | 3 | | 4 | | 5 | | 6 | | 7 | | 8 | |
| Variable: | A[2] | C | A | C | A | C | A | C | A | C | A | C | A | C | A | C |
| | 19 | 39 | 44 | 41 | 38 | 33 | 35 | 21 | 18 | 9 | 11 | 20 | 3 | 25 | 14 | 16 |
| | 41 | 41 | 39 | 40 | 19 | 22 | 31 | 36 | 38 | 32 | 6 | 13 | 10 | 27 | 8 | 6 |
| | 28 | 36 | 38 | 44 | 44 | 13 | 26 | 34 | 24 | 6 | 6 | 10 | 14 | 2 | 7 | 15 |
| | 40 | 45 | 36 | 46 | 40 | 21 | 27 | 30 | 17 | 4 | 2 | 0 | 25 | 21 | 39 | 9 |

[1]Data modified from Timm (1975, p. 429). See Table 6.1.
[2]A = Accuracy, C = Clustering

Multivariate results. The results for the planned comparison analysis depend on whether one pools or not. In Table 6.8 where no pooling has taken place, we find support for all of the research hypotheses except number one. Thus, when both dependent variables are considered, the 100% structure condition is superior to the 50% and 7% conditions, but does not differ from the 75% condition. Also, there are no differences between proctors with Messorq levels. However, in Table 6.9 where we have pooled the Proctor and error sums of squares, we again find support for research hypotheses 2 through 4, but also support research hypothesis number one. Therefore, when we pool, we find that the 100% condition differs from all conditions including the 75% condition.

Univariate results. After a multivariate test is found to be significant, the researcher may examine the univariate tests on each of the dependent variables associated with the multivariate test. All of the univariate tests associated with the two models discussed here are included in Tables 6.8 and 6.9. Those univariate hypotheses associated with significant multivariate hypotheses are hypotheses two and three in Table 6.8, with no pooling, and hypotheses one, two, and three in Table 6.9, with pooling. When there is no pooling we find that there are univariate differences on both dependent variables between the 100% and 50%, and the 100% and 7% conditions of message organization. (Note that one may not interpret the significant univariate result for clustering in the 100% vs. 75% condition because no multivariate significance was found for this condition.) When pooling is used, we find that the univariate tests under null hypotheses two and three are all significant. However, only the univariate test for clustering is significant under null hypothesis one.

## Multivariate Analysis: Overall and Post Hoc Tests

As in the univariate section on overall and post hoc tests, the researcher in this case has no basis in previous theory or research which would suggest planned comparisons. Thus, the researcher might conduct an overall multivariate test for significance. Given a significant overall multivariate test for an effect, Stevens (1972, 1973) has suggested several procedures which one might apply in further analysis. One approach (Bock, 1975; Finn, 1974) is to examine univariate tests on each dependent variable, then apply post hoc tests wherever significant univariate tests occur. Another approach would involve the following three stages:

Step (1): conduct MANOVA. If none of the MANOVA tests are significant, discontinue testing. If any tests are

Table 6.8

Multivariate Planned Comparisons, No Pooling

| Source of Variation | Sums of Squares and Products | | Multivariate | | | Univariate | | |
|---|---|---|---|---|---|---|---|---|
| | Accuracy | Cluster | Wilks' Lambda | Df | F(Probability) | Df | F (Probablity) Accuracy | Cluster |
| Planned Comparisons | | | | | | | | |
| 100% v. 75% | 39.06 | 190.63 | .21 | 2, 3 | 5.71(-.095) | 1 | .185(-.689) | 14.67*(-.019) |
| | 190.63 | 930.25 | | | | | | |
| 100% v. 50% | 1660.56 | 2424.63 | .06 | 2, 3 | 25.33*(-.013) | 1 | 7.85*(-.049) | 55.83*(-.002) |
| | 2424.63 | 3540.25 | | | | | | |
| 100% v. 7% | 1701.56 | 2175.94 | .07 | 2, 3 | 20.76*(-.017) | 1 | 8.05*(-.047) | 43.88*(-.003) |
| | 2175.94 | 2782.56 | | | | | | |
| Proctor (error term for planned comparisons) | 845.63 | -37.75 | .60 | 8,46 | 1.64(-.133) | 4 | 2.49(-.070) | .97(-.445) |
| | -37.75 | 253.63 | | | | | | |
| Error (within) | 2035.75 | 261.75 | | | | 24 | | |
| | 261.75 | 1576.25 | | | | | | |

*Significant at p<.05.

525

Table 6.9

Multivariate Planned Comparisons, Error and Proctor Pooled

| Source of Variation | Sums of Squares and Products | | Multivariate | | | Univariate | | |
|---|---|---|---|---|---|---|---|---|
| | Accuracy | Cluster | Wilks' Lambda | Df | F(Probability) | Df | F(Probability) Accuracy | Cluster |
| Planned Comparisons | | | | | | | | |
| 100% v. 75% | 39.06 190.63 | 190.63 930.25 | .66 | 2,27 | 6.89*(.004) | 1 | .38(.543) | 14.23*(.001) |
| 100% v. 50% | 1660.56 2424.63 | 2424.63 3540.25 | .30 | 2,27 | 31.42*(.000) | 1 | 16.14*(.000) | 54.17*(.000) |
| 100% v. 7?% | 1701.56 2175.94 | 2175.94 2782.56 | .34 | 2,27 | 26.25*(.000) | 1 | 16.54*(.000) | 42.58*(.000) |
| Error (Pooled) | 2981.38 224.00 | 224.00 1829.88 | | | | 28 | | |

*Significant at p<.05.

526

significant, go to Step (2).

Step (2): Conduct all possible multivariate (Hotelling's) $T^2$'s between groups for each factor where a significant MANOVA test was obtained. If no $T^2$'s are significant, discontinue testing. If any $T^2$'s are significant, go to Step (3).

Step (3): Where significant $T^2$'s are found, execute univariate post hoc tests.

## Problem

A.  Are accuracy and clustering in the free recall of message information dependent upon the level of message organization?

B.  Are accuracy and clustering in the free recall of message information dependent upon the proctor orienting the subjects and monitoring the treatments?

## Research Hypotheses

The research hypotheses are formulated to reflect the researcher's belief that differences will appear among the levels of the Messorg factor. However, in this case, there is no rationale for specific predictions in light of prior research and theory.

Research Hypothesis (1A): The four levels of message organization (100%, 75%, 50% and 7%) will have differing effects upon accuracy and clustering in the free recall of message information.

Research Hypothesis (2B): There will be no differences between proctors within levels of message organization in effects upon accuracy and clustering in the free recall of message information.

## Statistical Hypotheses

As in earlier sections, the statistical hypotheses are in symbolic form. See the multivariate planned comparisons section for an explanation of the u subscripts. H(A1) actually reflects research hypothesis one, while H(02) reflects research hypothesis two.

Null
Hypothesis (1) H(01): $\begin{bmatrix} u(11) \\ u(21) \end{bmatrix} = \begin{bmatrix} u(12) \\ u(22) \end{bmatrix} = \begin{bmatrix} u(13) \\ u(23) \end{bmatrix} = \begin{bmatrix} u(14) \\ u(24) \end{bmatrix}$

Alternate
Hypothesis (1) H(A1): $\begin{bmatrix} u(1i) \\ u(2i) \end{bmatrix} \neq \begin{bmatrix} u(1i') \\ u(2i') \end{bmatrix}$ $(i \neq i'; i, i' = 1, 2, 3, 4)$

Null
Hypothesis (2) H(02): $\begin{bmatrix} u(1i1) \\ u(2i1) \end{bmatrix} = \begin{bmatrix} u(1i2) \\ u(2i2) \end{bmatrix}$ for each i

Alternate
Hypothesis (2) H(A2): $\begin{bmatrix} u(1i1) \\ u(2i1) \end{bmatrix} \neq \begin{bmatrix} u(1i2) \\ u(2i2) \end{bmatrix}$ for 1 cr more i's

Null hypothesis (1) is tested at the .05 level of significance. Again, the preliminary test and pooling procedure (Kirk, 1968) discussed in previous sections are used in this section, and null hypothesis (2) will be tested at the .05 level of significance.

### Data

This analysis is applied to the same data (Table 6.7) used in the multivariate planned comparisons example.

## Multivariate Analysis of Variance

No pooling. Table 6.10 summarizes the overall multivariate analysis of variance when Proctor and the error (within) sums of squares are not pooled.

Error and Proctor pooled. Table 6.11 summarizes the overall multivariate analysis of variance when Proctor and the error (within) sums of squares are pooled.

Multivariate results. The results for the overall analysis do not depend on whether one pools, because in both Tables 6.10 and 6.11 we find support for the first research hypothesis. That is, both tables indicate that there is a sifnificant effect for message organization. In Table 6.10 we also find support for the second research hypothesis, i.e., no effect for proctors.

<u>Univariate results</u>. After a multivariate test is found to be significant, the researcher may examine the univariate tests on each of the dependent variables associated with the multivariate test. All of the univariate tests associated with the two models discussed here are included in Tables 6.10 and 6.11. In these tables we may focus on the univariate tests for Messorg because the multivariate test for this source of variation is significant. In Table 6.10, with no pooling, we find that there is a univariate effect for message organization only on the variable clustering. In Table 6.11, with pooling, we find that there are effects for both dependent variables. In further analysis, the researcher might consider Hotelling's $T^2$ and/or apply some <u>post hoc</u> test in a manner such as the Duncan test illustrated in the univariate section.

## Instruction Input/Output

One instruction I/O is included with this chapter. The program (run number 4) uses SAS's NESTED procedure. NESTED assumes that all factors in the design are random factors (see Appendix D). This run is classified as special because this random effects analysis provides no statistical tests. The output from NESTED simply indicates the percentage of total variance accounted for by each factor in the design.

Table 6.10

Overall Multivariate Analysis, No Pooling

| Source of Variation | Sums of Squares and Products | | Multivariate | | | Univariate | | |
|---|---|---|---|---|---|---|---|---|
| | Accuracy | Cluster | Wilks' Lambda | Df | F(Probability) | Df | F(Probablity) Accuracy | Cluster |
| Messorg | [2908.34<br>[3283.53 | 3283.53]<br>4317.34] | .03 | 6, 6 | 4.58*(.043) | 3 | 4.59(.088) | 22.70*(.006) |
| Proctor (error term for Messorg) | [845.63<br>[-37.75 | -37.75]<br>253.63] | .60 | 8,46 | 1.67(.133) | 4 | 2.49(.070) | .97(.445) |
| Error | [2035.75<br>[261.75 | 261.75]<br>1576.25] | | | | 24 | | |

*Significant at p<.05.

Table 6.11

Overall Multivariate Analysis, Error and Proctor Pooled

| Source of Variation | Sums of Squares and Products | | Multivariate | | | Univariate | |
| --- | --- | --- | --- | --- | --- | --- | --- |
| | Accuracy | Cluster | Wilks' Lambda | Df | F(Probability) | Df | F(Probablity)<br>Accuracy | Cluster |
| Messorg | [2908.34<br>[3283.53 | 3283.53]<br>4317.34] | .22 | 6,54 | 10.01*(.000) | 3 | 9.42*(.000) | 22.02*(.000) |
| Error | [2881.38<br>[ 224.00 | 224.00]<br>1829.88] | | | | 28 | | |

*significant at p<.05.

531

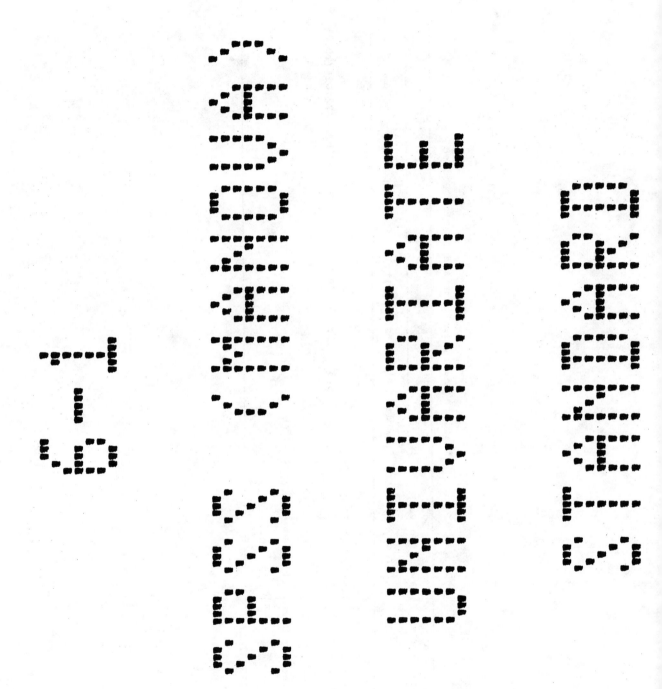

Note: The SPSS input annotations provided here are of value for most problems of this type. Consult the SPSS manual for more general information.

① These are column identifiers and are not part of the program content.

Note: Further annotations for this input and output can be found in the program I/O for SPSS(MANOVA) in Chapter 2. Planned comparisons may be found in program numbered 2-1, and an overall analysis may be found in the program numbered 2-5.

② Four different analyses are shown here to save space. Depending on the assumptions and questions asked, one would usually run only one or two of these analyses at one time.

③ In the first two analyses shown here there is one dependent variable, ACCURACY, and two independent variables, MESSORG, with four levels, and PROCTOR, with two levels nested within each level of MESSORG -- yielding eight proctors.

④ In the DESIGN statement the words MESSORG VS 1 indicate that MESSORG is to be tested using the source of variation designated as 1.

⑤ In this line the word WITHIN indicates that PROCTOR is nested within MESSORG; the '= 1' indicates that PROCTOR is to be used as the error term for the test on MESSORG; and the VS WITHIN indicates that PROCTOR is to be tested using the WITHIN source of variation as the error term.

⑥ In the second analysis the error is specified through the error subcommand as being the term designated as 1.

⑦ Here the nested factor PROCTOR is used as the error term for all sources of variation (here single degree of freedom contrasts) in the DESIGN statement.

```
①
   RUN NAME    CHAPTER 6: NESTED ANOVA
   TASK NAME   IS THE NESTED FACTOR (PROCTOR) SIGNIFICANT?
   DATA LIST   FIXED(1)/1 MESSORG 1 PROCTOR 3 ACCURACY 6-7
   N OF CASES  32
②③ MANOVA     ACCURACY BY MESSORG(1,4) PROCTOR(1,2) /
               PRINT=CELLINFO(MEANS)
               HOMOGENITY(BARTLETT,COCHRAN)
               OMEANS(TABLES(MESSORG))
               POBS/
               PLOT = CELLPLOTS,NORMAL,BOXPLOTS,STEMLEAF,POBS/
               METHOD = SSTYPE(UNIQUE)/
④              DESIGN MESSORG VS 1
⑤              PROCTOR WITHIN MESSORG = 1 VS WITHIN/

   READ INPUT DATA
   1   1   19
   1   1   41
   1   1   28
   1   1   40
   1   2   44
   1   2   38
   1   2   39
   1   2   36
   2   1   38
   2   1   19
   2   1   44
   2   1   40
   2   2   35
   2   2   31
   2   2   26
   2   2   27
   3   1   18
   3   1   38
   3   1   24
   3   1   17
   3   2   11
   3   2   6
   3   2   2
   3   2   2
   4   1   3
   4   1   10
   4   1   14
   4   1   25
   4   2   14
   4   2   8
   4   2   7
   4   2   39

   TASK NAME   PLANNED COMPARISONS ON MAIN FACTOR (MESSORG), NESTED FACTOR IN
②③ MANOVA     ACCURACY BY MESSORG(1,4) PROCTOR(1,2) /
               METHOD = SSTYPE(UNIQUE)/
               PARTITION(MESSORG)/
               CONTRAST(MESSORG) = SPECIAL(1 1 1 1 -1 0 0 -1 0 1 0 -1 0 0 1)/
⑥              ERROR = 1/
               DESIGN = MESSORG(1) MESSORG(2) MESSORG(3)
⑦              PROCTOR WITHIN MESSORG = 1/

   TASK NAME   OVERALL TEST ON MAIN FACTOR, NESTED FACTOR POOLED WITH ERROR
②⑧ MANOVA     ACCURACY BY MESSORG(1,4) PROCTOR(1,2) /
```

```
PRINT = CELLINFO(MEANS)         POBS/
ERROR = W+R/
DESIGN MESSORG/
PLANNED COMPARISONS ON MAIN FACTOR, NESTED POOLED WITH ERROR
ACCURACY BY MESSORG(1,4) PROCTOR(1,2)/
METHOD = SSTYPE(UNIQUE)/
PARTITION(MESSORG)/
CONTRAST(MESSORG) = SPECIAL(1 1 1 -1 1 0 0 -1 0 1 0 -1 0 0 1)/
ERROR = W+R/
DESIGN = MESSORG(1) MESSORG(2) MESSORG(3)/
```

② ⑨ TASK NAME
      MANOVA

① 0000000000111111111122222222223333333333444444444455555555556666666666777777778
   1234567890123456789012345678901234567890123456789012345678901234567890

⑧ In the third analysis the factor PROCTOR has been pooled with the error term. This is done by:

   specifying both MESSORG and PROCTOR in the MANOVA statement,

   designating the error as W (within) + R (residual—here PROCTOR), and

   only specifying MESSORG in the DESIGN statement.

⑨ In the fourth analysis the nested factor PROCTOR has again been pooled with the error term, and this pooled error (W + R) is used to test the contrasts on MESSORG.

534

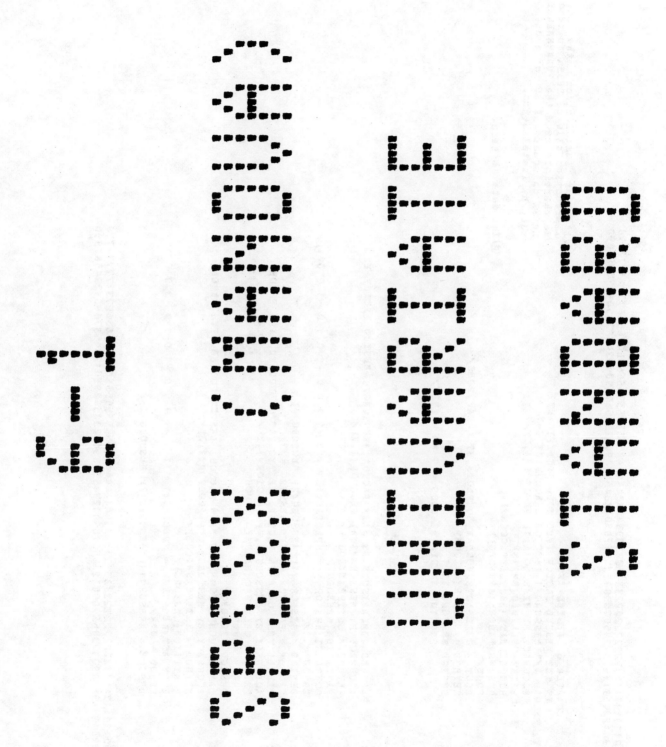

535

```
000000000011111111112222222222333333333344444444445555555555666666666677777777778
12345678901234567890123456789012345678901234567890123456789012345678901234567890
```

① UNNUMBERED
TITLE       CHAPTER 6: NESTED ANOVA
SUBTITLE    IS THE NESTED FACTOR (PROCTOR) SIGNIFICANT?
DATA LIST   RECORD=1/1 MESSORG 1 PROCTOR 3 ACCURACY 6-7
MANOVA      ACCURACY BY MESSORG(1,4) PROCTOR(1,2)/
            PRINT=CELLINFO(MEANS)
            HOMOGENEITY(BARTLETT,COCHRAN)
            OMEANS(TABLES(MESSORG))
            POBS/
            PLOT = CELLPLOTS,NORMAL,BOXPLOTS,STEMLEAF,POBS/
            METHOD = SSTYPE(UNIQUE)/
            DESIGN MESSORG VS 1
            PROCTOR WITHIN MESSORG = 1 VS WITHIN/

BEGIN DATA
②

END DATA
SUBTITLE    PLANNED COMPARISONS ON MAIN FACTOR (MESSORG), NESTED FACTOR IN
MANOVA      ACCURACY BY MESSORG(1,4) PROCTOR(1,2)/
            METHOD = SSTYPE(UNIQUE)/
            PARTITION(MESSORG)/
            CONTRAST(MESSORG) = SPECIAL(1 1 1 1 -1 1 0 0 -1 0 1 0 -1 0 0 1)/
            ERROR = 1/
            DESIGN = MESSORG(1) MESSORG(2) MESSORG(3)
            PROCTOR WITHIN MESSORG = 1/

SUBTITLE    OVERALL TEST ON MAIN FACTOR, NESTED FACTOR POOLED WITH ERROR
MANOVA      ACCURACY BY MESSORG(1,4) PROCTOR(1,2)/
            PRINT = CELLINFO(MEANS)    POBS/
            ERROR = W+R/
            DESIGN MESSORG/

SUBTITLE    PLANNED COMPARISONS ON MAIN FACTOR, NESTED POOLED WITH ERROR
MANOVA      ACCURACY BY MESSORG(1,4) PROCTOR(1,2)/
            METHOD = SSTYPE(UNIQUE)/
            PARTITION(MESSORG)/
            CONTRAST(MESSORG) = SPECIAL(1 1 1 1 -1 1 0 0 -1 0 1 0 -1 0 0 1)/
            ERROR = W+R/
            DESIGN = MESSORG(1) MESSORG(2) MESSORG(3)/
```

① At our installation the default (NUMBERED) instruction allowed SPSSX to read only 72 columns. We therefore used the UNNUMBERED command to allow SPSSX to read all 80 columns. The default may vary by installation.

② The data go here.

```
000000000011111111112222222222333333333344444444445555555555666666666677777777778
12345678901234567890123456789012345678901234567890123456789012345678901234567890
```

536
```

* * * * * * * * * * * * * * * A N A L Y S I S  O F  V A R I A N C E * * * * * * * * * * * * * * * * * * * * * * * *

CELL MEANS AND STANDARD DEVIATIONS

VARIABLE .. ACCURACY

| FACTOR | CODE | MEAN | STD. DEV. | N | 95 PERCENT CONF. INTERVAL |
|---|---|---|---|---|---|
| MESSORG | 1 | | | | |
| PROCTOR | 1 | 32.00000 | 10.48809 | 4 | 15.31135    48.68865 |
| PROCTOR | 2 | 39.25000 | 3.40343 | 4 | 33.83446    44.66554 |
| MESSORG | 2 | | | | |
| PROCTOR | 1 | 35.25000 | 11.11680 | 4 | 17.56094    52.93906 |
| PROCTOR | 2 | 29.75000 | 4.11299 | 4 | 23.20541    36.29459 |
| MESSORG | 3 | | | | |
| PROCTOR | 1 | 24.25000 | 9.67385 | 4 | 8.85697    39.64303 |
| PROCCTOR | 2 | 6.25000 | 3.68556 | 4 | -.38554    12.11446 |
| MESSORG | 4 | | | | |
| PROCTOR | 1 | 13.00000 | 9.20145 | 4 | -1.64135    27.64135 |
| PROCCTOR | 2 | 17.00000 | 14.98888 | 4 | -6.85031    40.85031 |
| FOR ENTIRE SAMPLE | | 24.59375 | 13.66620 | 32 | 19.66656    29.52094 |

- - - - - - - - - - - - - - - - - - - - - - - - - - - - - - - - - - - - - - - - - - - - - - - - - - - - - - - -

UNIVARIATE HOMOGENEITY OF VARIANCE TESTS

VARIABLE .. ACCURACY

COCHRANS C(3,8) =                   .33108, P = .242 (APPROX.)
BARTLETT-BOX F(7,576) =            1.42799, P = .191

- - - - - - - - - - - - - - - - - - - - - - - - - - - - - - - - - - - - - - - - - - - - - - - - - - - - - - - -

32 CASES ACCEPTED.
 0 CASES REJECTED BECAUSE OF OUT-OF-RANGE FACTOR VALUES.
 0 CASES REJECTED BECAUSE OF MISSING DATA.
 8 NON-EMPTY CELLS.

- - - - - - - - - - - - - - - - - - - - - - - - - - - - - - - - - - - - - - - - - - - - - - - - - - - - - - - -

CHAPTER 6: NESTED ANOVA
IS THE NESTED FACTOR (PROCTOR) SIGNIFICANT?

02/02/83          PAGE   8

* * * * * * * * * * * * * * * * A N A L Y S I S   O F   V A R I A N C E * * * * * * * * * * * * * * * * * * * * * *

COMBINED OBSERVED MEANS FOR MESSORG

VARIABLE -- ACCURACY

MESSORG

| | | |
|---|---|---|
| 1 | WGT. | 35.62500 |
| | UNWGT. | 35.62500 |
| 2 | WGT. | 32.50000 |
| | UNWGT. | 32.50000 |
| 3 | WGT. | 15.25000 |
| | UNWGT. | 15.25000 |
| 4 | WGT. | 15.00000 |
| | UNWGT. | 15.00000 |

CORRESPONDENCE BETWEEN EFFECTS AND COLUMNS OF BETWEEN-SUBJECTS DESIGN

| STARTING COLUMN | ENDING COLUMN | EFFECT NAME |
|---|---|---|
| 1 | 1 | CONSTANT |
| 2 | 4 | MESSORG |
| 5 | 8 | PROCTOR WITHIN MESSORG (ERROR 1) |

CHAPTER 6: NESTED ANOVA
IS THE NESTED FACTOR (PROCTOR) SIGNIFICANT?

02/02/83    PAGE    9

* * * * * * * * * * * * * * * * * * A N A L Y S I S   O F   V A R I A N C E * * * * * * * * * * * * * * * * * * * *

TESTS OF SIGNIFICANCE FOR ACCURACY USING UNIQUE SUMS OF SQUARES

| SOURCE OF VARIATION ① | SUM OF SQUARES | DF | MEAN SQUARE | F | SIG. OF F |
|---|---|---|---|---|---|
| WITHIN CELLS | 2035.75000 | 24 | 84.82292 | | |
| CONSTANT | 19355.28125 | 1 | 19355.28125 | 228.18458 | 0.0 |
| PROCTOR WITHIN MESSORG (ERROR 1) | 845.62500 | 4 | 211.40625 | 2.49232 | .070 ② |
| | | | | | |
| ERROR 1 | 845.62500 | 4 | 211.40625 | | |
| MESSORG | 2908.34375 | 3 | 969.44792 | 4.58571 | .088 |

ESTIMATES FOR ACCURACY

CONSTANT

| PARAMETER | COEFF. | STD. ERR. | T-VALUE | SIG. OF T | LOWER .95 CL | UPPER .95 CL |
|---|---|---|---|---|---|---|
| 1 | 24.5937500000 | 1.62810 | 15.10578 | 0.0 | 21.23351 | 27.95399 |

PROCTOR WITHIN MESSORG (ERROR 1)

| PARAMETER | COEFF. | STD. ERR. | T-VALUE | SIG. OF T | LOWER .95 CL | UPPER .95 CL |
|---|---|---|---|---|---|---|
| 5 | -3.6250000000 | 3.25620 | -1.11326 | .277 | -10.34547 | 3.09547 |
| 6 | 2.7500000000 | 3.25620 | .84454 | .407 | -3.97047 | 9.47047 |
| 7 | 9.0000000000 | 3.25620 | 2.76395 | .011 | 2.27953 | 15.72047 |
| 8 | -2.0000000000 | 3.25620 | -.61421 | .545 | -8.72047 | 4.72047 |

MESSORG

| PARAMETER | COEFF. | STD. ERR. | T-VALUE | SIG. OF T | LOWER .95 CL | UPPER .95 CL |
|---|---|---|---|---|---|---|
| 2 | 11.0312500000 | 4.45189 | 2.47788 | .068 | -1.32898 | 23.39148 |
| 3 | 7.9062500000 | 4.45189 | 1.77593 | .150 | -4.45398 | 20.26648 |
| 4 | -9.3437500000 | 4.45189 | -2.09883 | .104 | -21.70398 | 3.01648 |

① This is the overall analysis of variance which is displayed in Table 6.5.

② At the .05 level of significance we find that there are no differences among the proctors or among the levels of message organization.

* * * * * * * * * * * * * * * * * * * A N A L Y S I S   O F   V A R I A N C E * * * * * * * * * * * * * * * * * * *

③ TESTS OF SIGNIFICANCE FOR ACCURACY USING UNIQUE SUMS OF SQUARES

| SOURCE OF VARIATION | SUM OF SQUARES | DF | MEAN SQUARE | F | SIG. OF F |
|---|---|---|---|---|---|
| ERROR 1 | 845.62500 | 4 | 211.40625 | | |
| CONSTANT | 19355.28125 | 1 | 19355.28125 | 91.55492 | .001 |
| ④ MESSORG (1) | 39.06250 | 1 | 39.06250 | .18477 | .689 ⑤ |
| MESSORG (2) | 1660.56250 | 1 | 1660.56250 | 7.85484 | .049 |
| MESSORG (3) | 1701.56250 | 1 | 1701.56250 | 8.04878 | .047 ⑥ |

ESTIMATES FOR ACCURACY

CONSTANT

| PARAMETER | COEFF. | STD. ERR. | T-VALUE | SIG. OF T | LOWER .95 CL | UPPER .95 CL |
|---|---|---|---|---|---|---|
| 1 | 24.5937500000 | 2.57030 | 9.56843 | .001 | 17.45757 | 31.72993 |

MESSORG (1)

| PARAMETER | COEFF. | STD. ERR. | T-VALUE | SIG. OF T | LOWER .95 CL | UPPER .95 CL |
|---|---|---|---|---|---|---|
| 2 | -3.1250000000 | 7.26991 | -.42985 | .689 | -23.30917 | 17.05917 |

MESSORG (2)

| PARAMETER | COEFF. | STD. ERR. | T-VALUE | SIG. OF T | LOWER .95 CL | UPPER .95 CL |
|---|---|---|---|---|---|---|
| 3 | -20.3750000000 | 7.26991 | -2.80265 | .049 | -40.55917 | -.19083 |

MESSORG (3)

| PARAMETER | COEFF. | STD. ERR. | T-VALUE | SIG. OF T | LOWER .95 CL | UPPER .95 CL |
|---|---|---|---|---|---|---|
| 4 | -20.6250000000 | 7.26991 | -2.83704 | .047 | -40.80917 | -.44083 |

③ This is the planned comparisons analysis of variance which is displayed in Table 6.3.

④ The test of MESSORG (1) indicates that there is no significant difference between the 75% and 100% levels of message organization.

⑤ At the .05 level of significance, there is a significant difference between the 50% and 100% levels of message organization.

⑥ At the .05 level of significance, there is a significant difference between the 7% and 100% levels of message organization.

540

\* \* \* \* \* \* \* \* \* \* \* \* \* \* \* \* \* \* \* \* A N A L Y S I S   O F   V A R I A N C E \* \* \* \* \* \* \* \* \* \* \* \* \* \* \* \* \* \* \* \* \* \* \*

TESTS OF SIGNIFICANCE FOR ACCURACY USING SEQUENTIAL SUMS OF SQUARES

| SOURCE OF VARIATION ⑦ | SUM OF SQUARES | DF | MEAN SQUARE | F | SIG. OF F |
|---|---|---|---|---|---|
| WITHIN+RESIDUAL | 2881.37500 | 28 | 102.90625 | | |
| CONSTANT | 19355.28125 | 1 | 19355.28125 | 188.08655 | 0.0 |
| ① MESSORG | 2908.34375 | 3 | 969.44792 | 9.42069 | .000 |

ESTIMATES FOR ACCURACY

CONSTANT

| PARAMETER | COEFF. | STD. ERR. | T-VALUE | SIG. OF T | LOWER .95 CL | UPPER .95 CL |
|---|---|---|---|---|---|---|
| 1 | 24.59375000000 | 1.79327 | 13.71446 | 0.0 | 20.92040 | 28.26710 |

MESSORG

| PARAMETER | COEFF. | STD. ERR. | T-VALUE | SIG. OF T | LOWER .95 CL | UPPER .95 CL |
|---|---|---|---|---|---|---|
| 2 | 11.03125000000 | 3.10604 | 3.55155 | .001 | 4.66882 | 17.39368 |
| 3 | 7.90625000000 | 3.10604 | 2.54545 | .017 | 1.54382 | 14.26868 |
| 4 | -9.34375000000 | 3.10604 | -3.00826 | .006 | -15.70618 | -2.98132 |

541

⑦ This is the overall analysis of variance which is displayed in Table 6.6.

⑧ Here if we assume that there are no differences among the proctors within each level of message organization, then using the pooled error term we find that there are significant differences among the levels of message organization.

* * * * * * * * * * * * * * * * * A N A L Y S I S   O F   V A R I A N C E * * * * * * * * * * * * * * * * * * * * *

TESTS OF SIGNIFICANCE FOR ACCURACY USING UNIQUE SUMS OF SQUARES

| SOURCE OF VARIATION (9) | SUM OF SQUARES | DF | MEAN SQUARE | F | SIG. OF F |
|---|---|---|---|---|---|
| WITHIN+RESIDUAL | 2881.37500 | 28 | 102.90625 | | |
| CONSTANT | 19355.28125 | 1 | 19355.28125 | 188.08655 | 0.0 |
| MESSORG (1) | 39.06250 | 1 | 39.06250 | .37959 | .543 (10) |
| MESSORG (2) | 1660.56250 | 1 | 1660.56250 | 16.13665 | .000 (11) |
| MESSORG (3) | 1701.56250 | 1 | 1701.56250 | 16.53507 | .000 (12) |

ESTIMATES FOR ACCURACY

CONSTANT

| PARAMETER | COEFF. | STD. ERR. | T-VALUE | SIG. OF T | LOWER .95 CL | UPPER .95 CL |
|---|---|---|---|---|---|---|
| 1 | 24.5937500000 | 1.79327 | 13.71446 | 0.0 | 20.92040 | 28.26710 |

MESSORG (1)

| PARAMETER | COEFF. | STD. ERR. | T-VALUE | SIG. OF T | LOWER .95 CL | UPPER .95 CL |
|---|---|---|---|---|---|---|
| 2 | -3.1250000000 | 5.07214 | -.61611 | .543 | -13.51480 | 7.26480 |

MESSORG (2)

| PARAMETER | COEFF. | STD. ERR. | T-VALUE | SIG. OF T | LOWER .95 CL | UPPER .95 CL |
|---|---|---|---|---|---|---|
| 3 | -20.3750000000 | 5.07214 | -4.01705 | .000 | -30.76480 | -9.98520 |

MESSORG (3)

| PARAMETER | COEFF. | STD. ERR. | T-VALUE | SIG. OF T | LOWER .95 CL | UPPER .95 CL |
|---|---|---|---|---|---|---|
| 4 | -20.6250000000 | 5.07214 | -4.06633 | .000 | -31.01480 | -10.23520 |

(9) This is the planned comparison analysis of variance which is displayed in Table 6.4.

(10) At the .05 level of significance, there is no significant difference between the 75% and 100% levels of message organization.

(11) At the .05 level of significance, there is a significant difference between the 50% and 100% levels of message organization.

(12) At the .05 level of significance, there is a significant difference between the 7% and 100% levels of message organization.

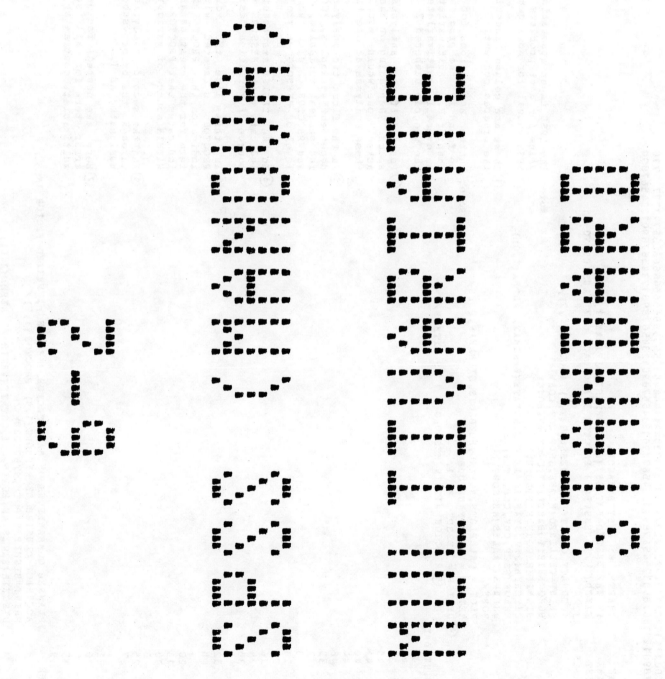

(1)

```
RUN NAME        CHAPTER 6: NESTED MANOVA
TASK NAME       IS THE NESTED FACTOR (PROCTOR) SIGNIFICANT?
DATA LIST       FIXED(1)/1 MESSORG 1 PROCTOR 3 ACCURACY 6-7 CLUSTER 10-11
N OF CASES      32
MANOVA          ACCURACY CLUSTER BY MESSORG(1,4) PROCTOR(1,2)/
                PRINT=CELLINFO(MEANS,SSCP,COV,COR)
                HOMOGENIETY(BARTLETT,COCHRAN,BOXM)
                SIGNIF(HYPOTH,STEPDOWN)
                DISCRIM(RAW,STAN,ESTIM,COR,ROTATE(VARIMAX) ALPHA(1.0) )
                ERROR(SSCP,COV,COR,STDV)/
                OMEANS(TABLES(MESSORG))
                POBS/
                PLOT = CELLPLOTS,NORMAL,BOXPLOTS,STEMLEAF,POBS/
                METHOD = SSTYPE(UNIQUE)/
 (4)            DESIGN = MESSORG VS 1.
     (5)        PROCTOR WITHIN MESSORG = 1 VS WITHIN/

READ INPUT DATA
1 1 19 39
1 1 41 41
1 1 28 36
1 1 40 45
1 2 44 41
1 2 39 40
1 2 38 44
1 2 36 46
2 1 38 33
2 1 19 22
2 1 44 13
2 1 40 21
2 2 35 21
2 2 31 36
2 2 26 34
2 2 27 30
3 1 18 9
3 1 38 32
3 1 24 4
3 1 17 20
3 2 11 20
3 2 6 13
3 2 6 10
3 2 3 0
4 1 2 25
4 1 10 27
4 1 14 2
4 1 25 21
4 2 14 16
4 2 8 6
4 2 7 15
4 2 39 9

TASK NAME       PLANNED COMPARISONS ON MAIN FACTOR (MESSORG), NESTED FACTOR IN
MANOVA          ACCURACY CLUSTER BY MESSORG(1,4) PROCTOR(1,2)/
                PRINT=SIGNIF(HYPOTH,STEPDOWN)
                DISCRIM(RAW,STAN,ESTIM,COR,ROTATE(VARIMAX) ALPHA(1.0) )
                ERROR(SSCP,COV,COR,STDV)/
                METHOD = SSTYPE(UNIQUE)/
```

(2)(3)

(2)(3)

Note: The SPSS input annotations provided here are of value for most problems of this type. Consult the SPSS manual for more general information.

(1) These are column identifiers and are not part of the program content.

Note: Further annotations for this input and output can be found in the program I/O for SPSS (MANOVA) in Chapter 2. Multivariate planned comparisons and an overall multivariate analysis may be found in the program numbered 2-10.

(2) Four different analyses are shown here to save space. Depending on the assumptions and questions asked, one would usually run only one or two of these analyses at one time.

(3) In the first two analyses shown here there are two dependent variables, ACCURACY and CLUSTER, and two independent variables, MESSORG, with four levels, and PROCTOR, with two levels nested within each level of MESSORG -- yielding eight proctors.

(4) In the DESIGN statement the words MESSORG VS 1 indicate that MESSORG is to be tested using the source of variation designated as 1.

(5) In this line the word WITHIN indicates that PROCTOR is nested within MESSORG; the '= 1' indicates that PROCTOR is to be used as the error term for the test on MESSORG; and the VS WITHIN indicates that PROCTOR is to be tested using the WITHIN source of variation as the error term.

(6) In the second analysis the error is specified through the error subcommand as being the term designated as 1.

(7) Here the nested factor PROCTOR is used as the error term for all sources of variation (here multivariate contrasts) in the DESIGN statement.

```
      CONTRAST(MESSORG) = SPECIAL(1 1 1 -1 1 0 0 -1 0 1 0 -1 0 0 1)/
   ⑥ ERROR = 1/
      DESIGN= MESSORG(1) MESSORG(2) MESSORG(3)
           ⑦ PROCTOR WITHIN MESSORG = 1/
      OVERALL TEST ON MAIN FACTOR, NESTED FACTOR POOLED WITH ERROR
      ACCURACY CLUSTER BY MESSORG(1,4) PROCTOR(1,2)/
      PRINT=SIGNIF(HYPOTH,STEPDOWN)
      DISCRIM(RAW,STAN,ESTIM,COR,ROTATE(VARIMAX) ALPHA(1.0))
      ERROR(SSCP,COV,COR,STDV)
      POBS/
      METHOD = SSTYPE(UNIQUE)/
      ERROR = W+R/
      DESIGN = MESSORG/
      PLANNED COMPARISONS ON MAIN FACTOR, NESTED POOLED WITH ERROR
      ACCURACY CLUSTER BY MESSORG(1,4) PROCTOR(1,2)/
      PRINT=SIGNIF(HYPOTH,STEPDOWN)
      DISCRIM(RAW,STAN,ESTIM,COR,ROTATE(VARIMAX) ALPHA(1.0))/
      METHOD = SSTYPE(UNIQUE)/
      PARTITION(MESSORG)/
      CONTRAST(MESSORG) = SPECIAL(1 1 1 -1 1 0 0 -1 0 1 0 -1 0 0 1)/
      ERROR = W+R/
      DESIGN = MESSORG(1) MESSORG(2) MESSORG(3)/

      0000000001111111111222222222233333333334444444444555555555566666666667777777778
      1234567890123456789012345678901234567890123456789012345678901234567890
```

② ⑧ TASK NAME
     MANOVA

② ⑨ TASK NAME
     MANOVA

⑧ In the third analysis the factor PROCTOR has been
   pooled with the error term. This is done by:

   specifying both MESSORG and PROCTOR in the
   MANOVA statement,

   designating the error as W (within) + R
   (residual--here PROCTOR, and

   only specifying MESSORG in the DESIGN
   statement.

⑨ In the fourth analysis the nested factor PROCTOR
   has again been pooled with the error term, and
   this pooled error (W + R) is used to test the
   contrasts on MESSORG.

545

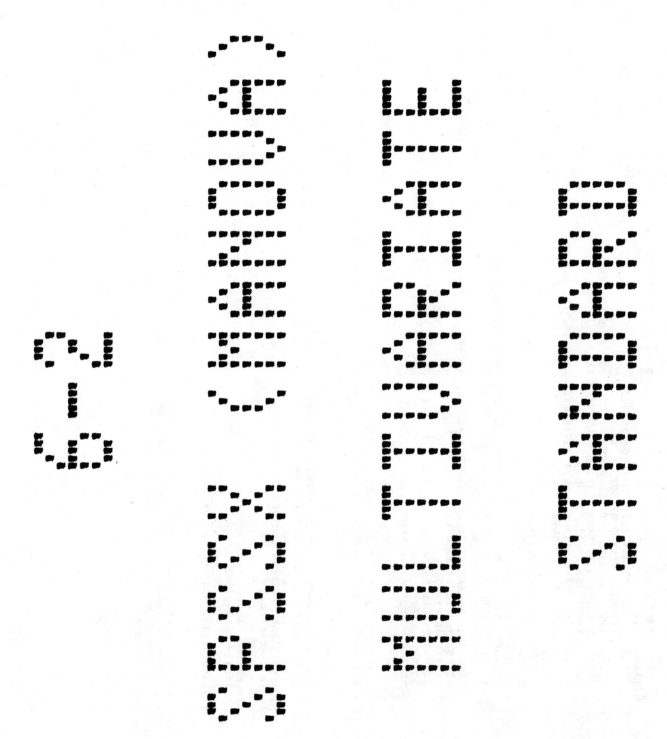

```
00000000011111111112222222222333333333344444444445555555555666666666677777777778
12345678901234567890123456789012345678901234567890123456789012345678901234567890
```

(1) UNNUMBERED
TITLE        CHAPTER 6: NESTED MANOVA
SUBTITLE     IS THE NESTED FACTOR (PROCTOR) SIGNIFICANT?
DATA LIST    RECORD=1/1 MESSCRG 1 PROCTOR 3 ACCURACY 6-7 CLUSTER 10-11
MANOVA       ACCURACY CLUSTER BY MESSORG(1,4) PROCTOR(1,2)/
             PRINT=CELLINFO(MEANS,SSCP,COV,COR)
             HOMOGENEITY(BARTLETT,COCHRAN,BOXM)
             SIGNIF(HYPOTH,STEPDOWN)
             DISCRIM(RAW,STAN,ESTIM,COR,ROTATE(VARIMAX) ALPHA(1.0))
             ERROR(SSCP,COV,COR,STDV)
             OMEANS(TABLES(MESSORG))
             POBS/
             PLOT = CELLPLOTS,NORMAL,BOXPLOTS,STEMLEAF,POBS/
             METHOD = SSTYPE(UNIQUE)/
             DESIGN = MESSORG VS 1.
             PROCTOR WITHIN MESSORG = 1 VS WITHIN/

(2) BEGIN DATA
END DATA
SUBTITLE     PLANNED COMPARISONS ON MAIN FACTOR (MESSORG), NESTED FACTOR IN
MANOVA       ACCURACY CLUSTER BY MESSORG(1,4) PROCTOR(1,2)/
             PRINT=SIGNIF(HYPOTH,STEPDOWN)
             DISCRIM(RAW,STAN,ESTIM,COR,ROTATE(VARIMAX) ALPHA(1.0))
             ERROR(SSCP,COV,COR,STDV)/
             METHOD = SSTYPE(UNIQUE)/
             PARTITION(MESSORG)/
             CONTRAST(MESSORG) = SPECIAL(1 1 1 -1 1 0 0  -1 0 1 0  -1 0 0  1)/
             ERROR = 1/
             DESIGN =  MESSORG(1)  MESSORG(2)  MESSORG(3)
             PROCTOR WITHIN MESSORG = 1/

SUBTITLE     OVERALL TEST ON MAIN FACTOR, NESTED FACTOR POOLED WITH ERROR
MANOVA       ACCURACY CLUSTER BY MESSORG(1,4) PROCTOR(1,2)/
             PRINT=SIGNIF(HYPOTH,STEPDOWN)
             DISCRIM(RAW,STAN,ESTIM,COR,ROTATE(VARIMAX) ALPHA(1.0))
             ERROR(SSCP,COV,COR,STDV)
             POBS/
             METHOD = SSTYPE(UNIQUE)/
             ERROR = W+R/
             DESIGN = MESSORG/
SUBTITLE     PLANNED COMPARISONS ON MAIN FACTOR, NESTED POOLED WITH ERROR
MANOVA       ACCURACY CLUSTER BY MESSORG(1,4) PROCTOR(1,2)/
             PRINT=SIGNIF(HYPOTH,STEPDOWN)
             DISCRIM(RAW,STAN,ESTIM,COR,ROTATE(VARIMAX) ALPHA(1.0))/
             METHOD = SSTYPE(UNIQUE)/
             PARTITION(MESSORG)/
             CONTRAST(MESSORG) = SPECIAL(1 1 1 -1 1 0 0  -1 0 1 0  -1 0 0  1)/
             ERROR = W+R/
             DESIGN = MESSORG(1)  MESSORG(2)  MESSORG(3)/

```
00000000011111111112222222222333333333344444444445555555555666666666677777777778
12345678901234567890123456789012345678901234567890123456789012345678901234567890
```

(1) At our installation the default (NUMBERED) instruction allowed SPSSX to read only 72 columns. We therefore used the UNNUMBERED command to allow SPSSX to read all 80 columns. The default may vary by installation.

(2) The data go here.

* * * * * * * * * * * * * * * A N A L Y S I S   O F   V A R I A N C E * * * * * * * * * * * * * * * * * *

CELL MEANS AND STANDARD DEVIATIONS

VARIABLE -- ACCURACY

| FACTOR | CODE | MEAN | STD. DEV. | N | 95 PERCENT CONF. INTERVAL |
|---|---|---|---|---|---|
| MESSORG | 1 | | | | |
| PROCTOR | 1 | 32.00000 | 10.48809 | 4 | 15.31135   48.68865 |
| PROCTOR | 2 | 39.25000 | 3.40343 | 4 | 33.83446   44.66554 |
| MESSORG | 2 | | | | |
| PROCTOR | 1 | 35.25000 | 11.11680 | 4 | 17.56094   52.93906 |
| PROCTOR | 2 | 29.75000 | 4.11299 | 4 | 23.20541   36.29459 |
| MESSORG | 3 | | | | |
| PROCTOR | 1 | 24.25000 | 9.67385 | 4 | 8.85697   39.64303 |
| PROCTOR | 2 | 6.25000 | 3.68556 | 4 | .38554   12.11446 |
| MESSORG | 4 | | | | |
| PROCTOR | 1 | 13.00000 | 9.20145 | 4 | -1.64135   27.64135 |
| PROCTOR | 2 | 17.00000 | 14.98888 | 4 | -6.85031   40.85031 |
| FOR ENTIRE SAMPLE | | 24.59375 | 13.66620 | 32 | 19.66656   29.52094 |

VARIABLE -- CLUSTER

| FACTOR | CODE | MEAN | STD. DEV. | N | 95 PERCENT CONF. INTERVAL |
|---|---|---|---|---|---|
| MESSORG | 1 | | | | |
| PROCTOR | 1 | 40.25000 | 3.77492 | 4 | 34.24335   46.25665 |
| PROCTOR | 2 | 42.75000 | 2.75379 | 4 | 38.36818   47.13182 |
| MESSORG | 2 | | | | |
| PROCTOR | 1 | 22.25000 | 8.22091 | 4 | 9.16889   35.33111 |
| PROCTOR | 2 | 30.25000 | 6.65207 | 4 | 19.66523   40.83477 |
| MESSORG | 3 | | | | |
| PROCTOR | 1 | 12.75000 | 12.99679 | 4 | -7.93050   33.43050 |
| PROCTOR | 2 | 10.75000 | 8.30161 | 4 | -2.45952   23.95952 |

CHAPTER 6: NESTED MANOVA
IS THE NESTED FACTOR (PROCTOR) SIGNIFICANT?

**** ** ** ** ** ** ** ** ** ** ** ** A N A L Y S I S   O F   V A R I A N C E ** ** ** ** ** ** ** ** ** ** ** ** ** ** ** ** ** **

02/02/83      PAGE    3

CELL MEANS AND STANDARD DEVIATIONS   (CONT.)

VARIABLE -- CLUSTER

| FACTOR | CODE | MEAN | STD. DEV. | N | 95 PERCENT CONF. INTERVAL | |
|---|---|---|---|---|---|---|
| MESSORG | 4 | | | | | |
| PROCTOR | 1 | 18.75000 | 11.44188 | 4 | -.54368 | 36.95632 |
| PROCTOR | 2 | 11.50000 | 4.79583 | 4 | 3.86887 | 19.13113 |
| FOR ENTIRE SAMPLE | | 23.65625 | 14.08181 | 32 | 18.57922 | 28.73328 |

UNIVARIATE HOMOGENEITY OF VARIANCE TESTS

VARIABLE -- ACCURACY

COCHRANS C(3,8) = .33108, P = .242 (APPROX.)
BARTLETT-BOX F(7,576) = 1.42799, P = .191

VARIABLE -- CLUSTER

COCHRANS C(3,8) = .32149, P = .278 (APPROX.)
BARTLETT-BOX F(7,576) = 1.30795, P = .244

CELL NUMBER -- 1

SUM OF SQUARES AND CROSS-PRODUCTS MATRIX

|  | ACCURACY | CLUSTER |
|---|---|---|
| ACCURACY | 330.00000 | |
| CLUSTER | 78.00000 | 42.75000 |

CHAPTER 6: NESTED MANOVA
IS THE NESTED FACTOR (PROCTOR) SIGNIFICANT?

02/02/83      PAGE   20

* * * * * * * * * * * * * * * * * * * * A N A L Y S I S   O F   V A R I A N C E * * * * * * * * * * * * * * * * * * * * * * * *

COMBINED OBSERVED MEANS FOR MESSORG

VARIABLE .. ACCURACY

MESSORG

| | | |
|---|---|---|
| 1 | WGT. | 35.62500 |
| | UNWGT. | 35.62500 |
| 2 | WGT. | 32.50000 |
| | UNWGT. | 32.50000 |
| 3 | WGT. | 15.25000 |
| | UNWGT. | 15.25000 |
| 4 | WGT. | 15.00000 |
| | UNWGT. | 15.00000 |

VARIABLE .. CLUSTER

MESSORG

| | | |
|---|---|---|
| 1 | WGT. | 41.50000 |
| | UNWGT. | 41.50000 |
| 2 | WGT. | 26.25000 |
| | UNWGT. | 26.25000 |
| 3 | WGT. | 11.75000 |
| | UNWGT. | 11.75000 |
| 4 | WGT. | 15.12500 |
| | UNWGT. | 15.12500 |

CHAPTER 6: NESTED MANOVA
IS THE NESTED FACTOR (PROCTOR) SIGNIFICANT?

* * * * * * * * * A N A L Y S I S   O F   V A R I A N C E * * * * * * * * * *

(1) Much of the information in this section is part of the overall multivariate analysis of variance displayed in Table 6.10.

(2) The error sums of squares and cross products matrix is needed for the multivariate Tables 6.8 and 6.10.

(1) WITHIN CELLS SUM-OF-SQUARES AND CROSS-PRODUCTS

|            | ACCURACY    | CLUSTER     |
|------------|-------------|-------------|
| (2) ACCURACY   | 2035.75000  |             |
| CLUSTER    | 261.75000   | 1576.25000  |

CHAPTER 6: NESTED MANOVA
IS THE NESTED FACTOR (PROCTOR) SIGNIFICANT?          02/02/83     PAGE   23

* * * * * * * * * A N A L Y S I S   O F   V A R I A N C E * * * * * * * * * *

(3) The hypothesis sums of squares and cross products matrix is needed for multivariate Table 6.10. It is used as the error sums of squares and cross products matrix in Table 6.8.

(4) At the .05 level of significance we find that there are no multivariate differences among the proctors.

EFFECT -- PROCTOR WITHIN MESSORG (ERROR 1)

ADJUSTED HYPOTHESIS SUM-OF-SQUARES AND CROSS-PRODUCTS

|            | ACCURACY    | CLUSTER     |
|------------|-------------|-------------|
| (3) ACCURACY   | 845.62500   |             |
| CLUSTER    | -37.75000   | 253.62500   |

MULTIVARIATE TESTS OF SIGNIFICANCE (S = 2, M = 1/2, N = 10 1/2)

| TEST NAME  | VALUE   | APPROX. F | HYPOTH. DF | ERROR DF | SIG. OF F (4) |
|------------|---------|-----------|------------|----------|---------------|
| PILLAIS    | .43947  | 1.68970   | 8.00       | 48.00    | .125          |
| HOTELLINGS | .59516  | 1.63668   | 8.00       | 44.00    | .142          |
| WILKS      | .60132  | 1.66505   | 8.00       | 46.00    | .133          |
| RCYS       | .30627  |           |            |          |               |

EIGENVALUES AND CANONICAL CORRELATIONS

| ROOT NO. | EIGENVALUE | PCT.     | CUM. PCT. | CANON. COR. |
|----------|------------|----------|-----------|-------------|
| 1        | .44149     | 74.18079 | 74.18079  | .55342      |
| 2        | .15366     | 25.81921 | 100.00000 | .36496      |

DIMENSION REDUCTION ANALYSIS

| ROOTS   | WILKS LAMBDA | F       | HYPOTH. DF | ERROR DF | SIG. OF F |
|---------|--------------|---------|------------|----------|-----------|
| 1 TO 2  | .60132       | 1.66505 | 8.00       | 46.00    | .133      |
| 2 TO 2  | .86680       | 1.17306 | 3.00       | 47.50    | .330      |

CHAPTER 6: NESTED MANOVA
IS THE NESTED FACTOR (PROCTOR) SIGNIFICANT?

* * * * * * * * * * * * * * * * A N A L Y S I S   O F   V A R I A N C E * * * * * * * * * * * * * * * * * * * * * * * * *

EFFECT .. MESSORG

(5) At the .05 level of significance we find that
    there are one or more multivariate significant
    differences among the levels of message
    organization.

ADJUSTED HYPOTHESIS SUM-OF-SQUARES AND CROSS-PRODUCTS

|  | ACCURACY | CLUSTER |
|---|---|---|
| ACCURACY | 2908.34375 | |
| CLUSTER | 3283.53125 | 4317.34375 |

MULTIVARIATE TESTS OF SIGNIFICANCE (S = 2, M = 0, N = 1/2)

| TEST NAME | VALUE | APPROX. F | HYPOTH. DF | ERROR DF | SIG. OF F |
|---|---|---|---|---|---|
| PILLAIS | 1.23576 | 2.15596 | 6.00 | 8.00 | .155 |
| HOTELLINGS | 21.76233 | 7.25411 | 6.00 | 4.00 | (5) .038 |
| WILKS | .03216 | 4.57608 | 6.00 | 6.00 | .043 |
| BOYS | .95530 | | | | |

EIGENVALUES AND CANONICAL CORRELATIONS

| ROOT NO. | EIGENVALUE | PCT. | CUM. PCT. | CANON. COR. |
|---|---|---|---|---|
| 1 | 21.37256 | 98.20899 | 98.20899 | .97740 |
| 2 | .38977 | 1.79101 | 100.00000 | .52958 |

DIMENSION REDUCTION ANALYSIS

| ROOTS | WILKS LAMBDA | F | HYPOTH. DF | ERROR DF | SIG. OF F |
|---|---|---|---|---|---|
| 1 TO 2 | .03216 | 4.57608 | 6.00 | 6.00 | .043 |
| 2 TO 2 | .71955 | .62609 | 2.00 | 7.00 | .562 |

552

CHAPTER 6: NESTED MANOVA
IS THE NESTED FACTOR (PROCTOR) SIGNIFICANT?

02/02/83          PAGE   32

* * * * * * * * * * * * * * * * * * * * * * A N A L Y S I S   O F   V A R I A N C E * * * * * * * * * * * * * * * * * * * * * * * * * *

EFFECT .. MESSORG        (CONT.)

UNIVARIATE F-TESTS WITH (3,4) D. F.

| VARIABLE | HYPOTH. SS | ERROR SS | HYPOTH. MS | ERROR MS | F | SIG. OF F |
|---|---|---|---|---|---|---|
| ACCURACY | 2908.34375 | 845.62500 | 969.44792 | 211.40625 | 4.58571 | .088 |
| CLUSTER | 4317.34375 | 253.62500 | 1439.11458 | 63.40625 | 22.69673 | ⑥ .006 |

ROY-BARGMAN STEPDOWN F - TESTS

| VARIABLE | HYPOTH. MS | ERROR MS | STEP-DOWN F | HYPOTH. DF | ERROR DF | SIG. OF F |
|---|---|---|---|---|---|---|
| ACCURACY | 969.44792 | 211.40625 | 4.58571 | 3 | 4 | .088 |
| CLUSTER | 504.21338 | 83.97993 | 6.00397 | 3 | 3 | .088 |

⑥ The univariate tests indicate that there is a strong difference among the levels of message organization of the variable we call CLUSTER, the degree to which subjects organize their free recall output.

RAW DISCRIMINANT FUNCTION COEFFICIENTS

FUNCTION NO.

| VARIABLE | 1 | 2 |
|---|---|---|
| ACCURACY | .03142 | -.06144 |
| CLUSTER | .11649 | -.04804 |

STANDARDIZED DISCRIMINANT FUNCTION COEFFICIENTS

FUNCTION NO.

| VARIABLE | 1 | 2 |
|---|---|---|
| ACCURACY | .45684 | -.89330 |
| CLUSTER | .92757 | -.38250 |

553

02/02/83    PAGE  46

* * * * * * * * * * * * * * * * * * * A N A L Y S I S   O F   V A R I A N C E * * * * * * * * * * * * * * * * * * * * * * * *

① 

EFFECT .. MESSORG(3)

ADJUSTED HYPOTHESIS SUM-OF-SQUARES AND CROSS-PRODUCTS

⑦ Note:  The information in this section is part of the second analysis.

⑧ The hypothesis sums of squares and cross products matrix is needed for multivariate Table 6.8.

|          | ⑧ ACCURACY | CLUSTER    |
|----------|------------|------------|
| ACCURACY | 1701.56250 |            |
| CLUSTER  | 2175.93750 | 2782.56250 |

MULTIVARIATE TESTS OF SIGNIFICANCE (S = 1, M = 0, N = 1/2)

| TEST NAME  | VALUE    | APPROX. F | HYPOTH. DF | ERROR DF | SIG. OF F |
|------------|----------|-----------|------------|----------|-----------|
| PILLAIS    | .93262   | 20.76198  | 2.00       | 3.00     | .017  ⑨   |
| HOTELLINGS | 13.84132 | 20.76198  | 2.00       | 3.00     | .017      |
| WILKS      | .06738   | 20.76198  | 2.00       | 3.00     | .017      |
| ROYS       | .93262   |           |            |          |           |

⑨ The test of MESSORG(3) indicates that, at the .05 level of significance, there is a significant difference between the 7% and 100% levels of message organization.

EIGENVALUES AND CANONICAL CORRELATIONS

| RODT NO. | EIGENVALUE | PCT.      | CUM. PCT. | CANON. COR. |
|----------|------------|-----------|-----------|-------------|
| 1        | 13.84132   | 100.00000 | 100.00000 | .96572      |

DIMENSION REDUCTION ANALYSIS

| ROOTS  | WILKS LAMBDA | F        | HYPOTH. DF | ERROR DF | SIG. OF F |
|--------|--------------|----------|------------|----------|-----------|
| 1 TO 1 | .06738       | 20.76198 | 2.00       | 3.00     | .017      |

* * * * * * * * * * * * * * * * * * * * * * *A N A L Y S I S   O F   V A R I A N C E* * * * * * * * * * * * * * * * * * * * * * *

(10) The univariate tests indicate that there are
     differences, at the .05 level of significance,
     between the 7% and 100% levels of message
     organization on both dependent variables.

EFFECT -- MESSORG(3)    (CONT.)

UNIVARIATE F-TESTS WITH (1,4) D. F.

| VARIABLE | HYPOTH. SS | ERROR SS | HYPOTH. MS | ERROR MS | F | SIG. OF F |
|---|---|---|---|---|---|---|
| ACCURACY | 1701.56250 | 845.62500 | 1701.56250 | 211.40625 | 8.04878 | .047 |
| CLUSTER | 2782.56250 | 253.62500 | 2782.56250 | 63.40625 | 43.88467 | (10) .003 |

ROY-EARGMAN STEPDOWN F - TESTS

| VARIABLE | HYPOTH. MS | ERROR MS | STEP-DOWN F | HYPOTH. DF | ERROR DF | SIG. OF F |
|---|---|---|---|---|---|---|
| ACCURACY | 1701.56250 | 211.40625 | 8.04878 | 1 | 4 | .047 |
| CLUSTER | 989.38739 | 83.97993 | 11.78124 | 1 | 3 | .041 |

RAW DISCRIMINANT FUNCTION COEFFICIENTS

FUNCTION NO.

| VARIABLE | 1 |
|---|---|
| ACCURACY | .03142 |
| CLUSTER | .11648 |

STANDARDIZED DISCRIMINANT FUNCTION COEFFICIENTS

FUNCTION NO.

| VARIABLE | 1 |
|---|---|
| ACCURACY | .45689 |
| CLUSTER | .92755 |

* * * * * * * * * * * * * * * * * * * * * * A N A L Y S I S   O F   V A R I A N C E * * * * * * * * * * * * * * * * * * * * * *

EFFECT .. MESSORG(2)

ADJUSTED HYPOTHESIS SUM-OF-SQUARES AND CROSS-PRODUCTS

|  | ACCURACY | CLUSTER |
|---|---|---|
| ACCURACY | 1660.56250 | |
| CLUSTER | 2424.62500 | 3540.25000 |

MULTIVARIATE TESTS OF SIGNIFICANCE (S = 1, M = 0, N = 1/2)

| TEST NAME | VALUE | APPROX. F | HYPOTH. DF | ERROR DF | SIG. OF F |
|---|---|---|---|---|---|
| PILLAIS | .94410 | 25.33209 | 2.00 | 3.00 | .013 ⑪ |
| HOTELLINGS | 16.88806 | 25.33209 | 2.00 | 3.00 | .013 |
| WILKS | .05590 | 25.33209 | 2.00 | 3.00 | .013 |
| ROYS | .94410 | | | | |

⑪ The test of MESSORG(2) indicates that, at the .05 level of significance, there is a significant difference between the 50% and 100% levels of message organization.

EIGENVALUES AND CANONICAL CORRELATIONS

| ROOT NO. | EIGENVALUE | PCT. | CUM. PCT. | CANON. COR. |
|---|---|---|---|---|
| 1 | 16.88806 | 100.00000 | 100.00000 | .97165 |

DIMENSION REDUCTION ANALYSIS

| ROOTS | WILKS LAMBDA | F | HYPOTH. DF | ERROR DF | SIG. OF F |
|---|---|---|---|---|---|
| 1 TO 1 | .05590 | 25.33209 | 2.00 | 3.00 | .013 |

* * * * * * * * * * * * * * * * * * * * * * * A N A L Y S I S   O F   V A R I A N C E * * * * * * * * * * * * * * * * * * * * * * *

EFFECT .. MESSORG(2)     (CONT.)

⑫ The univariate tests indicate that there are
   differences, at the .05 level of significance,
   between the 50% and 100% levels of message
   organization on both dependent variables.

UNIVARIATE F-TESTS WITH (1,4) D. F.

| VARIABLE | HYPOTH. SS | ERROR SS | HYPOTH. MS | ERROR MS | F | SIG. OF F |
|---|---|---|---|---|---|---|
| ACCURACY | 1660.56250 | 845.62500 | 1660.56250 | 211.40625 | 7.85484 | .049 |
| CLUSTER | 3540.25000 | 253.62500 | 3540.25000 | 63.40625 | 55.83440 | ⑫ .002 |

ROY-BARGMAN STEPDOWN F - TESTS

| VARIABLE | HYPOTH. MS | ERROR MS | STEP-DOWN F | HYPOTH. DF | ERROR DF | SIG. OF F |
|---|---|---|---|---|---|---|
| ACCURACY | 1660.56250 | 211.40625 | 7.85484 | 1 | 4 | .049 |
| CLUSTER | 1268.69259 | 83.97993 | 15.10709 | 1 | 3 | .030 |

RAW DISCRIMINANT FUNCTION COEFFICIENTS

FUNCTION NO.

| VARIABLE | 1 |
|---|---|
| ACCURACY | .02874 |
| CLUSTER | .11845 |

STANDARDIZED DISCRIMINANT FUNCTION COEFFICIENTS

FUNCTION NO.

| VARIABLE | 1 |
|---|---|
| ACCURACY | .41788 |
| CLUSTER | .94320 |

* * * * * * * * * * * * * * * * * * * A N A L Y S I S   O F   V A R I A N C E * * * * * * * * * * * * * * * * * * * * * * *

EFFECT .. MESSORG(1)

ADJUSTED HYPOTHESIS SUM-OF-SQUARES AND CROSS-PRODUCTS

|          | ACCURACY   | CLUSTER   |
|----------|------------|-----------|
| ACCURACY | 39.06250   |           |
| CLUSTER  | 190.62500  | 930.25000 |

MULTIVARIATE TESTS OF SIGNIFICANCE (S = 1, M = 0, N = 1/2)

| TEST NAME  | VALUE   | APPROX. F | HYPOTH. DF | ERROR DF | SIG. OF F |
|------------|---------|-----------|------------|----------|-----------|
| PILLAIS    | .79194  | 5.70961   | 2.00       | 3.00     | .095   (13)|
| HOTELLINGS | 3.80641 | 5.70961   | 2.00       | 3.00     | .095      |
| WILKS      | .20806  | 5.70961   | 2.00       | 3.00     | .095      |
| ROYS       | .79194  |           |            |          |           |

(13) The test of MESSORG(1) indicates that, at the .05 level of significance, there is no significant difference between the 75% and 100% levels of message organization.

EIGENVALUES AND CANONICAL CORRELATIONS

| ROOT NO. | EIGENVALUE | PCT.      | CUM. PCT. | CANON. COR. |
|----------|------------|-----------|-----------|-------------|
| 1        | 3.80641    | 100.00000 | 100.00000 | .88991      |

DIMENSION REDUCTION ANALYSIS

| ROOTS  | WILKS LAMBDA | F       | HYPOTH. DF | ERROR DF | SIG. OF F |
|--------|--------------|---------|------------|----------|-----------|
| 1 TO 1 | .20806       | 5.70961 | 2.00       | 3.00     | .095      |

CHAPTER 6: NESTED MANOVA
OVERALL TEST ON MAIN FACTOR, NESTED FACTOR POOLED WITH ERROR

* * * * * * * * * * * * * * * * * A N A L Y S I S   O F   V A R I A N C E * * * * * * * * * * * * * * * * *

Note: The information in this section is part of the third analysis.

Note: Much of the information displayed here is part of the overall multivariate analysis of variance displayed in Table 6.9.

WITHIN+RESIDUAL SUM-OF-SQUARES AND CROSS-PRODUCTS

|  | ACCURACY | CLUSTER |
|---|---|---|
| (14) ACCURACY | 2881.37500 | |
| CLUSTER | 224.00000 | 1829.87500 |

---

CHAPTER 6: NESTED MANOVA
OVERALL TEST ON MAIN FACTOR, NESTED FACTOR POOLED WITH ERROR

* * * * * * * * * * * * * * * * * A N A L Y S I S   O F   V A R I A N C E * * * * * * * * * * * * * * * * *

(14) The pooled error sums of squares and cross products matrix is needed for the multivariate tables, 6.9 and 6.11.

EFFECT .. MESSORG

ADJUSTED HYPOTHESIS SUM-OF-SQUARES AND CROSS-PRODUCTS

(15) The hypothesis sums of squares and cross products matrix is needed for multivariate Table 6.11.

|  | ACCURACY | CLUSTER |
|---|---|---|
| (15) ACCURACY | 2908.34375 | |
| CLUSTER | 3283.53125 | 4317.34375 |

---

MULTIVARIATE TESTS OF SIGNIFICANCE (S = 2, M = 0, N = 12 1/2)

| TEST NAME | VALUE | APPROX. F | HYPOTH. DF | ERROR DF | SIG. OF F |
|---|---|---|---|---|---|
| PILLAIS | .85196 | 6.92620 | 6.00 | 56.00 | .000 |
| HOTELLINGS | 3.11941 | 13.51746 | 6.00 | 52.00 | 0.0 |
| WILKS | .22425 | 10.00524 | 6.00 | 54.00 | .000 |
| ROYS | .75040 | | | | |

(16)

(16) Here if we assume that there are no differences among the proctors within each level of message organization, then using the pooled error term we find that there are significant differences among the levels of message organization.

---

EIGENVALUES AND CANONICAL CORRELATIONS

| ROOT NO. | EIGENVALUE | PCT. | CUM. PCT. | CANON. COR. |
|---|---|---|---|---|
| 1 | 3.00638 | 96.37632 | 96.37632 | .86626 |
| 2 | .11304 | 3.62368 | 100.00000 | .31868 |

---

DIMENSION REDUCTION ANALYSIS

| ROOTS | WILKS LAMBDA | F | HYPOTH. DF | ERROR DF | SIG. OF F |
|---|---|---|---|---|---|
| 1 TO 2 | .22425 | 10.00524 | 6.00 | 54.00 | .000 |
| 2 TO 2 | .89844 | 1.51267 | 2.00 | 55.00 | .229 |

* * * * * * * * * * * * * * * * A N A L Y S I S   O F   V A R I A N C E * * * * * * * * * * * * * * * *

EFFECT .. MESSORG     (CONT.)

UNIVARIATE F-TESTS WITH (3,28) D. F.

| VARIABLE | HYPOTH. SS | ERROR SS | HYPOTH. MS | ERROR MS | F | SIG. OF F |
|---|---|---|---|---|---|---|
| ACCURACY | 2908.34375 | 2881.37500 | 969.44792 | 102.90625 | 9.42069 | .000 |
| CLUSTER | 4317.34375 | 1829.87500 | 1439.11458 | 65.35268 | 22.02074 | .000 (17) |

ROY-BARGMAN STEPDOWN F - TESTS

| VARIABLE | HYPOTH. MS | ERROR MS | STEP-DOWN F | HYPOTH. DF | ERROR DF | SIG. OF F |
|---|---|---|---|---|---|---|
| ACCURACY | 969.44792 | 102.90625 | 9.42069 | 3 | 28 | .000 |
| CLUSTER | 736.60758 | 67.12819 | 10.97315 | 3 | 27 | .000 |

RAW DISCRIMINANT FUNCTION COEFFICIENTS

FUNCTION NO.

| VARIABLE | 1 | 2 |
|---|---|---|
| ACCURACY | -.04684 | -.08728 |
| CLUSTER | -.10326 | -.06918 |

STANDARDIZED DISCRIMINANT FUNCTION COEFFICIENTS

FUNCTION NO.

| VARIABLE | 1 | 2 |
|---|---|---|
| ACCURACY | -.47515 | -.88535 |
| CLUSTER | -.83477 | -.55925 |

(17) The univariate tests indicate that both dependent variables considered separately would differentiate among the levels of message organization.

* * * * * * * * * * * * * * * * * * * *A N A L Y S I S   O F   V A R I A N C E* * * * * * * * * * * * * * * * * * * *

⑩ EFFECT .. MESSORG(3)

⑩ The information in this section is part of the fourth analysis.

ADJUSTED HYPOTHESIS SUM-OF-SQUARES AND CROSS-PRODUCTS

⑲ The hypothesis sums of squares and cross products matrix is needed for multivariate Table 6.9.

|  | ⑲ ACCURACY | CLUSTER |
|---|---|---|
| ACCURACY | 1701.56250 | |
| CLUSTER | 2175.93750 | 2782.56250 |

MULTIVARIATE TESTS OF SIGNIFICANCE (S = 1, M = 0, N = 12 1/2)

| TEST NAME | VALUE | APPROX. F | HYPOTH. DF | ERROR DF | SIG. OF F |
|---|---|---|---|---|---|
| PILLAIS | .66042 | 26.25467 | 2.00 | 27.00 | .000 |
| HOTELLINGS | 1.94479 | 26.25467 | 2.00 | 27.00 | .000 ⑳ |
| WILKS | .33958 | 26.25467 | 2.00 | 27.00 | .000 |
| ROYS | .66042 | | | | |

⑳ The test of MESSORG(3) indicates that, at the .05 level of significance, there is a significant difference between the 7% and 100% levels of message organization.

EIGENVALUES AND CANONICAL CORRELATIONS

| ROOT NO. | EIGENVALUE | PCT. | CUM. PCT. | CANON. COR. |
|---|---|---|---|---|
| 1 | 1.94479 | 100.00000 | 100.00000 | .81266 |

DIMENSION REDUCTION ANALYSIS

| ROOTS | WILKS LAMBDA | F | HYPOTH. DF | ERROR DF | SIG. OF F |
|---|---|---|---|---|---|
| 1 TO 1 | .33958 | 26.25467 | 2.00 | 27.00 | .000 |

* * * * * * * * * * * * * * * * * * * * * * * A N A L Y S I S   O F   V A R I A N C E * * * * * * * * * * * * * * * * * * * * * * *

(21) The univariate tests indicate that there are differences, at the .05 level of significance, between the 7% and 100% levels of message organization on both dependent variables.

EFFECT .. MESSORG(3)     (CONT.)

UNIVARIATE F-TESTS WITH (1,28) D. F.

| VARIABLE | HYPOTH. SS | ERROR SS | HYPOTH. MS | ERROR MS | F | SIG. OF F |
|---|---|---|---|---|---|---|
| ACCURACY | 1701.56250 | 2881.37500 | 1701.56250 | 102.90625 | 16.53507 | .000 |
| CLUSTER | 2782.56250 | 1829.87500 | 2782.56250 | 65.35268 | 42.57764 | .000 (21) |

ROY-BARGMAN STEPDOWN F - TESTS

| VARIABLE | HYPOTH. MS | ERROR MS | STEP-DOWN F | HYPOTH. DF | ERROR DF | SIG. OF F |
|---|---|---|---|---|---|---|
| ACCURACY | 1701.56250 | 102.90625 | 16.53507 | 1 | 28 | .000 |
| CLUSTER | 1543.20605 | 67.12819 | 22.98894 | 1 | 27 | .000 |

RAW DISCRIMINANT FUNCTION COEFFICIENTS

FUNCTION NO.

| VARIABLE | 1 |
|---|---|
| ACCURACY | .04626 |
| CLUSTER | .10372 |

STANDARDIZED DISCRIMINANT FUNCTION COEFFICIENTS

FUNCTION NO.

| VARIABLE | 1 |
|---|---|
| ACCURACY | .46925 |
| CLUSTER | .83847 |

* * * * * * * * * * * * * * * * * * A N A L Y S I S  O F  V A R I A N C E * * * * * * * * * * * * * * * * * * * * * * *

EFFECT .. MESSORG(2)

ADJUSTED HYPOTHESIS SUM-OF-SQUARES AND CROSS-PRODUCTS

(22) ACCURACY        CLUSTER

ACCURACY    1660.56250
CLUSTER     2424.62500    3540.25000

(22) The hypothesis sums of squares and cross products matrix is needed for multivariate Table 6.9.

(23) The test of MESSORG(2) indicates that, at the .05 level of significance, there is a significant difference between the 50% and 100% levels of message organization.

- - - - - - - - - - - - - - - - - - - - - - - - - - - - - - - - - - - - - - - - - - -

MULTIVARIATE TESTS OF SIGNIFICANCE (S = 1, M = 0, N = 12 1/2)

| TEST NAME | VALUE | APPROX. F | HYPOTH. DF | ERROR DF | SIG. OF F |
|-----------|-------|-----------|------------|----------|-----------|
| PILLAIS | .69944 | 31.41631 | 2.00 | 27.00 | .000 |
| HOTELLINGS | 2.32713 | 31.41631 | 2.00 | 27.00 | .000 (23) |
| WILKS | .30056 | 31.41631 | 2.00 | 27.00 | .000 |
| ROYS | .69944 | | | | |

- - - - - - - - - - - - - - - - - - - - - - - - - - - - - - - - - - - - - - - - - - -

EIGENVALUES AND CANONICAL CORRELATIONS

| ROOT NO. | EIGENVALUE | PCT. | CUM. PCT. | CANON. COR. |
|----------|-----------|------|-----------|-------------|
| 1 | 2.32713 | 100.00000 | 100.00000 | .83633 |

- - - - - - - - - - - - - - - - - - - - - - - - - - - - - - - - - - - - - - - - - - -

DIMENSION REDUCTION ANALYSIS

| ROOTS | WILKS LAMBDA | F | HYPOTH. DF | ERROR DF | SIG. OF F |
|-------|--------------|---|------------|----------|-----------|
| 1 TO 1 | .30056 | 31.41631 | 2.00 | 27.00 | .000 |

- - - - - - - - - - - - - - - - - - - - - - - - - - - - - - - - - - - - - - - - - - -

* * * * * * * * * * * * * * * * * * * * * A N A L Y S I S   O F   V A R I A N C E * * * * * * * * * * * * * * * * * * * * *

(24) The univariate tests indicate that there are differences, at the .05 level of significance, between the 50% and 100% levels of message organization on both dependent variables.

EFFECT -- MESSORG(2)    (CONT.)

UNIVARIATE F-TESTS WITH (1,28) D. F.

| VARIABLE | HYPOTH. SS | ERROR SS | HYPOTH. MS | ERROR MS | F | SIG. OF F |
|---|---|---|---|---|---|---|
| ACCURACY | 1660.56250 | 2881.37500 | 1660.56250 | 102.90625 | 16.13665 | .000 (24) |
| CLUSTER | 3540.25000 | 1829.87500 | 3540.25000 | 65.35268 | 54.17146 | .000 |

ROY-BARGMAN STEPDOWN F - TESTS

| VARIABLE | HYPOTH. MS | ERROR MS | STEP-DOWN F | HYPOTH. DF | ERROR DF | SIG. OF F |
|---|---|---|---|---|---|---|
| ACCURACY | 1660.56250 | 102.90625 | 16.13665 | 1 | 28 | .000 |
| CLUSTER | 2013.12165 | 67.12819 | 29.98921 | 1 | 27 | .000 |

RAW DISCRIMINANT FUNCTION COEFFICIENTS

    FUNCTION NO.

| VARIABLE | 1 |
|---|---|
| ACCURACY | -.04068 |
| CLUSTER | .10781 |

STANDARDIZED DISCRIMINANT FUNCTION COEFFICIENTS

    FUNCTION NO.

| VARIABLE | 1 |
|---|---|
| ACCURACY | -.41262 |
| CLUSTER | .87154 |

CHAPTER 6: NESTED MANOVA
PLANNED COMPARISONS ON MAIN FACTOR, NESTED POOLED WITH ERROR

* * * * * * * * * * * * * * * * * * A N A L Y S I S   O F   V A R I A N C E * * * * * * * * * * * * * * * * * * * * * *     02/02/83     PAGE   85

EFFECT .. MESSORG(1)

ADJUSTED HYPOTHESIS SUM-OF-SQUARES AND CROSS-PRODUCTS

(25) The hypothesis sums of squares and cross products matrix is needed for multivariate Table 6.9.

|  | ACCURACY | CLUSTER |
|---|---|---|
| ACCURACY | (25) 39.06250 | |
| CLUSTER | 190.62500 | 930.25000 |

- - - - - - - - - - -

MULTIVARIATE TESTS OF SIGNIFICANCE (S = 1, M = 0, N = 12 1/2)

| TEST NAME | VALUE | APPROX. F | HYPOTH. DF | ERROR DF | SIG. OF F |
|---|---|---|---|---|---|
| PILLAIS | .33801 | 6.89292 | 2.00 | 27.00 | .004 |
| HOTELLINGS | .51059 | 6.89292 | 2.00 | 27.00 | .004 (26) |
| WILKS | .66199 | 6.89292 | 2.00 | 27.00 | .004 |
| RCYS | .33801 | | | | |

(26) The test of MESSORG(1) indicates that, at the .05 level of significance, there is a significant difference between the 75% and 100% levels of message organization.

- - - - - - - - - - -

EIGENVALUES AND CANONICAL CORRELATIONS

| ROOT NO. | EIGENVALUE | PCT. | CUM. PCT. | CANON. COR. |
|---|---|---|---|---|
| 1 | .51059 | 100.00000 | 100.00000 | .58138 |

- - - - - - - - - - -

DIMENSION REDUCTION ANALYSIS

| ROOTS | WILKS LAMBDA | F | HYPOTH. DF | ERROR DF | SIG. OF F |
|---|---|---|---|---|---|
| 1 TO 1 | .66199 | 6.89292 | 2.00 | 27.00 | .004 |

- - - - - - - - - - -

565

\* \* \* \* \* \* \* \* \* \* \* \* \* \* \* \* \* \* \* \* \* \* \* \* \* A N A L Y S I S   O F   V A R I A N C E \* \* \* \* \* \* \* \* \* \* \* \* \* \* \* \* \* \* \* \* \* \* \* \*

EFFECT -- MESSORG(1)    (CONT.)

UNIVARIATE F-TESTS WITH (1,28) D. F.

| VARIABLE | HYPOTH. SS | ERROR SS | HYPOTH. MS | ERROR MS | F | SIG. OF F |
|---|---|---|---|---|---|---|
| ACCURACY | 39.06250 | 2881.37500 | 39.06250 | 102.90625 | .37959 | .543 |
| CLUSTER | 930.25000 | 1829.87500 | 930.25000 | 65.35268 | 14.23431 | .001 (27) |

ROY-BARGMAN STEPDOWN F - TESTS

| VARIABLE | HYPOTH. MS | ERROR MS | STEP-DOWN F | HYPOTH. DF | ERROR DF | SIG. OF F |
|---|---|---|---|---|---|---|
| ACCURACY | 39.06250 | 102.90625 | .37959 | 1 | 28 | .543 |
| CLUSTER | 888.79811 | 67.12819 | 13.24031 | 1 | 27 | .001 |

RAW DISCRIMINANT FUNCTION COEFFICIENTS

FUNCTION NO.

| VARIABLE | 1 |
|---|---|
| ACCURACY | .00653 |
| CLUSTER | .12263 |

STANDARDIZED DISCRIMINANT FUNCTION COEFFICIENTS

FUNCTION NO.

| VARIABLE | 1 |
|---|---|
| ACCURACY | .06624 |
| CLUSTER | .99136 |

(27) The univariate tests indicate that there is a strong difference between the 50% and 100% levels of message organization on the variable we call CLUSTER, the degree to which subjects organize their free recall output.

CHAPTER 7

REPEATED MEASURES DESIGNS
by Charles E. Rich

## Introduction:  Modes of Analysis[1]

A design in which the same subjects are observed under all k levels of one or more treatments is termed repeated measures (see Winer,1971, Chapters 4 and 6).  In this design the repeated measures or treatments are frequently called 'trials' or 'occasions.'  There are two main reasons for using a repeated measures design: 1)  data naturally exists in this form, i.e. we frequently take more than one measurement over time with the same or equivalent instrument on the same subject;  and 2) it allows us to use the subject as his own control, reducing that portion of error variation which is due to subject heterogeneity.  The same repeated measures data may be analyzed using either a univariate or multivariate approach.  The choice of method is dependent on the nature of the data, the research questions, and/or the statistical assumptions involved. Here, given single and multiple groups, we briefly discuss each method or mode of analysis;  for a more detailed discussion see Bock (1975, Chapter 7).

## Univariate Mode

Given a single group of subjects, the univariate analysis may be easily understood as a two-way, subjects by occasions, mixed model design (see Appendix D).  In this two-way design the subjects are considered a random factor and the occasions are considered a fixed factor.  Here there is only one observation per cell, and so the subjects by occasions interaction must serve as the error term.  If two or more groups of subjects are present in the design, then the data are treated as that for a split-plot design with subjects (random) nested within groups (fixed) and both groups and subjects crossed with the occasions (fixed).  Here the group effect is tested using the variation among subjects as the error.  The groups by occasions interaction and the occasions are tested using the subjects within groups by occasions interaction as the error.

The statistical assumptions upon which these univariate analyses depend are that: 1) the observations of each subject were sampled from a multivariate normal distribution; 2)  the observations may be described with a linear model; 3)  the subjects are independent of one another; and, 4)  the matrix of variances and covariances among the repeated measures satisfies a statistical property known as 'circularity' or 'sphericity.' Let it suffice to say that this statistical property describes a certain ideal pattern of relationships between the repeated measures, which should exist for valid univariate tests to be used. The sphericity assumption is said to hold when epsilon equals 1, where,

$$epsilon = \frac{[tr\ (C'SC)]^2}{(k-1)\ tr(C'SC)^2}$$

Here tr stands for the trace of the variance-covariance matrix; $\underline{k}$ is the number of repeated measures; C is a $(\underline{k}-1)$-orthonormal contrast matrix; and, S is the variance-covariance matrix of the multivariate normal distribution from which the repeated measures were selected (Rogan, Keselman, and Mendoza, 1979). When there are two or more groups, S is the pooled estimate (across groups) of the population variance-covariance matrix.

When the circularity assumption is not met, Collier, Baker, Mandeville, and Hayes (1967), Davidson (1972), and Imhof(1962) indicate that the actual level of significance of the F test on the repeated measures factor will exceed the nominal level. In other words, you are more likely to obtain larger F values purely by chance, and hence more likely to wrongly reject the null hypothesis. It is therefore necessary to get a better estimate of the actual probability of our obtained F in order to make decisions concerning the null hypothesis. The latter authors recommend that epsilon, estimated from the data, be multiplied times the degrees of freedom of the F test for the occasions factor. These adjusted degrees of freedom are then used to locate the tabled criterion F statistic.

Huynh and Feldt (1976) have suggested that epsilon be estimated using:

$$\widetilde{e} = \frac{(N \cdot df1 \cdot e) - 2}{df1\ (N - g - df1 \cdot e)}$$

where, e is epsilon, g is the number of groups, df1 is the degrees of freedom for the repeated measures source of variation, and N is the total number of subjects. Huynh and Feldt reviewed a number of publications in education and psychology and found that epsilon rarely fell below .75. Therefore, they modified epsilon to yield $\widetilde{e}$ which they suggested for use when epsilon is greater than or equal to .75. Note that in the BMDP4V programs for this chapter GGI epsilon is the above estimated epsilon (after Greenhouse and Geisser (1959); Imhof (1962)) and H-F epsilon is $\widetilde{e}$ (after Huynh and Feldt).

## Multivariate Mode

Given a single group of subjects with $k$ repeated measures, the multivariate mode may best be thought of as an analysis on a set of $k-1$ measures. In essence one takes the original set of repeated measures and transforms them to a new set having one less measure. In the new set, each measure is really a univariate contrast between one or more of the original measures. In this chapter these contrasts will frequently be referred to as 'contrast variables,' to reflect the fact that they are contrasts or comparisons between several original measures. The null hypothesis is that the mean vector of the transformed measures is equal to the null vector (i.e. a vector of all zeros). When two or more groups of subjects are present in the design, the design is treated as a one-way multivariate analysis with $k-1$ measures or contrast variables in each group.

A more complex analysis occurs when one takes more than one measure on each occasion. For example, in one data set analyzed in this chapter we consider measures of elation and depression taken over five days. Bock (1975, p. 448) refers to this type of data as being 'doubly multivariate' because we have repeated measurements on more than one variable. The data for this design may be analyzed in a doubly multivariate format or treated in what we call a 'univariate-multivariate' format. The doubly multivariate format is an extension of the multivariate approach where one transforms the $k$ measures on each of the $p$ qualitatively distinct variables into $k-1$ contrast variables of interest. In the example described above, $k$ is 5, since the measures were taken over 5 days, and $p$ is 2, since we had 2 qualitatively distinct variables, elation and depression. We then transformed each of the two sets of 5 measures into two sets of 4 measures where each measure was an orthogonal contrast on the original measures, yielding 8 measures for the doubly multivariate analysis. In the univariate-multivariate analysis, one uses the univariate design described above (e.g. groups by occasions by subjects within groups), but in each cell there are measures on two or more variables (e.g. here, depression and elation). That is, the univariate-multivariate analysis of these data consists of the analysis of a multivariate split-plot design with two dependent variables, elation and depression.

The first three statistical assumptions for the multivariate mode of analysis are the same as for the univariate mode. However, the multivariate mode does not require the sphericity assumption. Instead, with two or more groups, it requires homogeniety of the variance-covariance matrices from each group.

# Analysis Selection: Univariate Versus Multivariate

Planned Contrasts. If you are in a position to state planned contrasts among your repeated measures, then either the univariate or multivariate mode may be used because both yield the same statistical tests. Hence you could elect to use a multivariate approach and not have to worry about the sphericity assumption. Furthermore, you may examine planned contrasts without first checking the overall tests of significance. In using planned contrasts, however, you do have to decide between using a pooled error term or a partitioned (i.e. individual) error term. Based on a discussion of this topic by Boik (1981) and Rouanet and Lepine (1970), we recommend that the individual errors be routinely used, because they yield better control of Type I error and independent statistical tests. The pooled error may be used under the combined conditions of homogeneity of the partitioned errors, and if the power for the partitioned errors is poor.

Overall Analysis and Unplanned Contrasts. Since both the univariate and multivariate modes of analysis yield the same statistical tests with planned contrasts, the remaining discussion focuses on the choice when an overall analysis is desired. However, for the same reasons given for planned comparisons, and based on results from Maxwell (1980), we recommend the use of partitioned errors over pooled errors for the post hoc (unplanned) tests which would follow an overall analysis.

Single Group. In a design with repeated measures over one group of subjects, the univariate approach is generally more powerful (even using estimated epsilon or e) compared to the multivariate approach. However, Davidson (1972), based on the work of Imhof (1962), indicates that "when small but reliable effects are present with effects highly variable but averaging to zero over subjects" (p. 452), the multivariate test is far more powerful than the univariate test. Therefore, given an exploratory study, we recommend that both tests be routinely used, because they may differ in the effects which they discern. Furthermore, if you use the univariate test, we recommend that the estimated epsilon be routinely used to modify the degrees of freedom when its population value is believed to be below .75, and that $\tilde{e}$ be used when the population value of epsilon is believed to be greater than or equal to .75. If you have no idea what the population value of epsilon is, then use the estimated sample value.

One problem with the preceding advice occurs when you are faced with data that is best analyzed in the multivariate mode, while the total number of subjects is less than the number of repeated measures. In this case, the univariate test is relatively powerless and the multivariate test cannot be done because the variance-covariance matrix is singular. Marks (1968) suggests some alternatives to this problem, but it remains a difficult situation.

Two or More Groups. Huynh and Feldt (1980) indicate that if the sphericity assumption is violated, and if there are two or more groups, then the univariate test of the interaction between groups and occasions is prone to have an actual level of significance which is vastly distorted. Their Monte Carlo data indicates that this distortion is less if the group sample sizes are equal, but their results encourage the use of the multivariate test even with equal n's. The multivariate test, however, can also have problems when there are two or more groups. Mendoza, Toothaker, and Nicewander (1974) indicate that if the multivariate normality assumption of the multivariate test is violated, then the actual level of significance of the multivariate test is inflated. Therefore, with two or more groups, we recommend the cautious use of the multivariate test.

## Introduction: Carry-Over Effects

In a repeated measures design the responses for any subject across the occasions are usually correlated simply because they are all elicited from that same subject. Part of this correlation between occasions may be due to what are called 'carry-over' effects. These effects entail both advantages and disadvantages, depending on the purposes for which the design is used. In studies of learning and transfer of skills to different situations, these carry-over effects are the prime focus. For example, the influence of a treatment such as practice time, is expected to be found on succeeding trials, where the cumulative effect of prior practice might be seen. The repeated measures design permits the researcher to observe the build-up of practice economically in that he can use the same subjects in all the levels of practice time.

However, when a repeated measures design is used to test the independent effects of several treatment conditions, then differential carry-over effects must be minimized or balanced among the treatments. There are several ways to minimize carry-over effects (see Keppel, 1973, pp. 395-400), but one primary method is to counterbalance the treatments, so that all treatments encounter about the same influence from previous treatments. In other words, the carry-over effects are not eliminated, but they are balanced so that a given level will not be affected by more carry-over than any other level of the treatment. Carry-over effects are thus held constant for all treatment levels. One way to do this is by determining the n orders in which the treatments may be administered and then having n samples of subjects, each sample experiencing treatments in a different order. This is effectively accomplished through what are called latin square designs in which each treatment level succeeds each other level an equal number of times. The latin square design provides a means of counter-balancing the treatment levels. Another method of counter-balancing is to randomly assign treatment level orders to subjects.

Both the latin square and the random assignment of treatment level orders assume that each order of levels has the same carry-over effect. If this is not true, then an interaction exists between treatment level order and the dependent variable. This may be detected on a post hoc basis by plotting the data and looking for intersecting lines. If an interaction exists, then a repeated measures design would be inappropriate and a separate group of subjects should be used for each treatment level. In this chapter no such interaction exists in the data used for illustrations.

## Six Variations on the Repeated Measures Design

The remaining portion of this chapter is organized around six variations of the repeated measures design. More variations are possible by other modifications of what Bock (1975, p. 448) terms the design on the sample and the design on the occasions. Here the design on the occasions will be the same for all setups (i.e. at least one measure taken on each of five days). The design on the sample, however, will change in that some setups use only one group of subjects and others use two independent groups. It is hoped that from these six basic setups the reader may be able to generalize to more complex designs should the need arise.

The six basic setups are determined by combinations of two parameters: the number of groups, and the number of dependent variables that are analyzed simultaneously. The change in groups has been explained already. There will be four ways in which the dependent variables are utilized, creating four different modes of analysis: (1) one dependent variable measured on two or more occasions (univariate mode), (2) contrasts between these same measures analyzed simultaneously (multivariate mode), (3) contrasts between two or more different types of dependent variables analyzed simultaneously (doubly multivariate mode), and (4) the same variables analyzed in a split-plot design (univariate-multivariate mode). Each of the six basic setups is further divided into two sections: planned mean contrasts and unplanned mean contrasts. Although there will be some redundancy in this format, the goal is that the reader will have all the information for a particular setup in very specific locations in the text.

In this chapter each of the six basic setups is illustrated in a portion of the text and then in a section of computer output. In the text portion, each setup is discussed with respect to how the researcher may have organized the analysis of an example study. Following a format suggested by Kerlinger (1973, pp. 16-21), each setup in the text portion is described in terms of a statement of the research problem, statement(s) of one or more research hypotheses and their corresponding statistical hypotheses, a description of the data, and an example of a source table which could be used to report the results of the analysis in a formal report. For simplicity the annotated computer output for all setups is kept together in a separate section at the end of the chapter, and cross-referenced with the text portions by page numbers. Finally, all the univariate setups are presented in one section of text, and then the multivariate, doubly multivariate, and univariate-multivariate setups are presented in two other sections for the convenience of the reader.

Table 7.1 contains a list of the programs run for this chapter and indicates their mode and whether they are 'standard' or 'instruction' runs. As in the other chapters, standard runs illustrate output of general interest while instruction runs illustrate special points of interest. In this table we also number the programs, indicate the page on which a given program's input/output (I/O) is initiated, and present some I/O features that might be of interest.

## Rationale of the Example Study

In this chapter, the repeated measures design will be illustrated in terms of a fictitious study from the social sciences. The data were taken from a study described by Timm (1975, p. 244). Although the Timm data were confined to an equal $\underline{n}$ setup, the data from one subject was eliminated for this chapter, so as to produce the unequal situation which is the more common situation in the field.

The rationale for the example study is as follows. The researcher is interested in the way the emotions of elation and depression fluctuate in intensity over time. Assume that previous research and theory have suggested that emotions fluctuate in response to internal biochemical changes, and hypothesize that a person's overall orientation to other people is important in determining how one's emotions fluctuate in response to interpersonal events. The researcher chooses to define a person's social

Table 7.1
Features of the Programs Run on the
Repeated Measures Data For Chapter 7

| Program | Program Number | Mode[1] | Type[2] | Page | I/O Features |
|---------|---------------|---------|---------|------|--------------|
| | | | | Volume 1: | BMDP |
| BMDP2V | 7-1 | U | S | 443 | Planned (orthogonal polynomial) and overall analyses, one group, Greenhouse-Geisser and Huynh-Feldt sphericity estimates |
| BMDP2V | 7-2 | U | S | 448 | Planned (orthogonal polynomial) and overall analysis, two groups, Greenhouse-Geisser and Huynh-Feldt sphericity estimates |
| BMDP4V | 7-3 | U&M | S | 453 | Planned (orthogonal polynomial) and overall analyses, one group, use of ORTHOGONALIZE paragraph, Greenhouse-Geisser Imhof (GGI) and Huynh-Feldt (H-F) sphericity estimates |
| BMDP4V | 7-4 | U&M | S | 461 | Planned (orthogonal polynomial) and overall analyses, two groups, use of VALUE paragraph to input orthogonal polynomials |
| BMDP4V | 7-5 | DM U-M | S | 471 | Planned (orthogonal polynomial) and overall analyses, doubly multivariate and univariate-multivariate analyses, two groups, Greenhouse-Geisser Imhof (GGI) and Huynh-Feldt (H-F) sphericity estimates |

Table 7.1 (cont.)

| Program | Program Number | Mode[1] | Type[2] | Page | I/O Features |
|---------|---------|---------|---------|------|--------------|
| | | | | | |
| | | Volume 2: | | SAS | |
| | | | | | |
| SAS(GLM) | 7-1 | U | S | 457 | Planned (orthogonal polynomial) and overall analyses, one group, contrasts entered as transformations, data rearranged using program statements, use of pooled error in contrasts |
| SAS(GLM) | 7-2 | U | S | 463 | Planned (orthogonal polynomial) and overall analyses, two groups, use of pooled error in contrasts |
| SAS(REG) | 7-3 | M | S | 469 | Planned (orthogonal polynomial) and overall analyses, one group, use of partitioned error in contrasts |
| SAS(REG) | 7-4 | M | S | 480 | Planned (orthogonal polynomial) and overall analyses, two groups, use of partitioned error in contrasts |
| SAS(GLM) | 7-5 | U-M | S | 494 | Univariate-multivariate overall analysis, two groups |
| SAS(REG) | 7-6 | DM | S | 507 | Planned (orthogonal polynomial) and overall analysis, doubly multivariate, two groups |

Table 7.1 (cont.)

| Program | Program Number | Mode[1] | Type[2] | Page | I/O Features |
|---------|----------------|---------|---------|------|--------------|
| | | Volume 3: | SPSS and SPSSX | | |
| SPSS-SPSSX 7-1 (MANOVA) | | U | S-I | 615 | Overall analysis followed by planned (orthogonal polynomial) analyses first using pooled error; second using partitioned error, one group |
| SPSS-SPSSX 7-2 (RELIABILITY) | | U&M | S | 625 | Overall test, one group, reliability estimate |
| SPSS-SPSSX 7-3 (MANOVA) | | U&M | S | 630 | Planned (orthogonal polynomial) and overall analyses, use of AVERF to obtain univariate results, test of sphericity, one group |
| SPSS-SPSSX 7-4 (MANOVA) | | U&M | S | 642 | Planned (orthogonal polynomial) and overall analyses, two groups |
| SPSS-SPSSX 7-5 (MANOVA) | | U-M | S | 661 | Univariate-multivariate overall analysis, two groups |
| SPSS-SPSSX 7-6 (MANOVA) | | DM | S | 673 | Planned (orthogonal polynomial) and overall analyses, doubly multivariate, two groups |

[1]U=univariate; M=multivariate; U-M=univariate-multivariate; DM=doubly multivariate

[2]S=standard; S-I=standard with instruction features

orientation in terms of whether he is the more shy and retiring introvert or the more outgoing and assertive extravert. He administers an introversion-extraversion test to a sample of subjects and randomly chooses ten introverts and ten extraverts on the basis of the test results. Past research has indicated that the occurrences of introverts and extraverts were approximately equal in the general population. One extravert was unable to complete the study, however, leaving the study with ten introverts and nine extraverts.

To measure fluctuation in elation and depression over time, the researcher administered a Mood Adjective Checklist to each subject at the same time of day on five consecutive days, yielding five repeated measures of elation and five repeated measures of depression for each subject. Thus, a pair of elation and depression scores were measured on each of the five days. Since the researcher is investigating the effect of time on the fluctuation of emotional intensity, time will be considered a factor (a 'within-subjects' factor), referred to generally as the occasions or trials factor and coded in the programs as DAYS.

The DAYS factor has five levels, corresponding to the five occasions when elation and depression were measured on each subject. The groups of introverts and extraverts constitute two levels of the social orientation factor (a 'between-subjects' factor), referred to as SOCIOR. As described earlier, in repeated measures designs the subjects function as an additional factor whether or not they are referred to directly as such. The elation data and design are presented in Table 7.2.

The researcher conducted a planned analysis where he had one main hypothesis which was based on previous research. This hypothesis was that, for both introverts and extraverts, elation and depression would each fluctuate in a quartic fashion over the five days. The term quartic is illustrated in the section below on trend analysis.

## Trend Analysis

In Figure 7.1 below, a quartic trend (or 'profile') is illustrated by plotting the elation means scores for the introverts and extraverts over the five days. This was the type of fluctuation which was predicted by the researcher on the basis of previous research. Other types of trends, not predicted in this case, are the linear (straight line), quadratic (one bend), and cubic (two bends) trends. Of course, many other degrees of trend are possible, but it is rare in the social sciences to encounter a trend beyond the quadratic.

Table 7.2
Raw Elation Data[1] Used in the
Social Orientation Study for the
Univariate and Multivariate Analyses

| Group | Day1 | Day2 | Day3 | Day4 | Day5 |
|---|---|---|---|---|---|
| | 20 | 21 | 42 | 32 | 32 |
| | 67 | 29 | 56 | 39 | 41 |
| | 37 | 25 | 28 | 31 | 34 |
| | 42 | 38 | 36 | 19 | 35 |
| Introverts | 57 | 32 | 21 | 30 | 29 |
| | 39 | 38 | 54 | 31 | 28 |
| | 43 | 20 | 46 | 42 | 31 |
| | 35 | 34 | 43 | 35 | 42 |
| | 41 | 23 | 51 | 27 | 30 |
| | 39 | 24 | 35 | 26 | 32 |
| | 47 | 25 | 36 | 21 | 27 |
| | 53 | 32 | 48 | 46 | 54 |
| | 38 | 33 | 42 | 48 | 49 |
| | 60 | 41 | 67 | 53 | 50 |
| Extraverts | 37 | 35 | 45 | 34 | 46 |
| | 59 | 37 | 52 | 36 | 52 |
| | 67 | 33 | 61 | 31 | 50 |
| | 43 | 27 | 36 | 33 | 32 |
| | 64 | 53 | 62 | 40 | 43 |

[1]Adapted from Timm (1975, p. 244). The last
subject from the group of Extraverts was
omitted to create an unequal n's example.

578

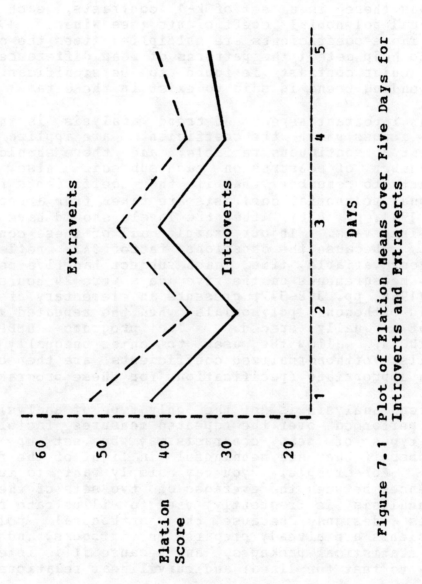

Figure 7.1   Plot of Elation Means over Five Days for
Introverts and Extraverts

579

In a trend analysis where there are <u>k</u> occasions or factor levels, there are <u>k</u>-1 possible trends to be tested. Trends are detected by testing for certain contrasts or patterns of differences between the occasion means. Over <u>k</u> occasions there is a set of <u>k</u>-1 contrasts, each with <u>k</u> orthogonal polynomial coefficients (see Winer, 1971, p. 878). These coefficients are multiplied times the occasion means to help detect the patterns of mean differences. If a particular contrast is found to be significant, the corresponding trend is said to exist in the data.

An important aspect of trend analysis is that the factor across which the coefficients are applied should represent a continuous variable, and there should be an equal number of measures on each subject. Also, it is important to remember that if the coefficients for the orthogonal polynomial contrasts are taken from a book (e.g. Winer, 1971, p. 878), then the levels should have equally spaced intervals. In our example all of these conditions are met, because the occasions factor DAYS reflects the continuous variable, time, each subject had five measures, and the measurements on the five days were 24 hours apart. Myers (1966, pp. 348-372) presents an elementary discussion of using orthogonal polynomials when the repeated measures are not equally spaced. The programs BMDP4V and SPSS(MANOVA) allow the user to enter unequally spaced intervals; orthonormalized coefficients are then obtained through appropriate specifications for these programs.

Trend analysis is not the only type of analysis which may be performed over the repeated measures factor. Any other types of mean contrasts may be set up by the researcher if they are meaningful in light of the research goals. For example, you may simply want to test for differences between the averages of two sets of the means. Trend analysis is frequently used to illustrate repeated measures designs because the orthogonal polynomial coefficients are already prepared in textbooks, and in most of the statistical packages, and because it is interesting to many to test for linear and curvilinear relationships.

### Univariate Mode of Analysis

### Univariate Analysis: Single Group Case, Planned Contrasts

This case is referred to as the single-group case, since there is no factor within which the subjects are nested. The design is simply subjects by occasions.

The Occasions Question. This is the only basic question which may be addressed in the single-group case and is simply asking whether there are differences between the levels of the occasions factor. The particular pattern of differences may describe a trend or some other contrast of interest.

Problem. Does mood change significantly from day to day?

Research hypothesis. The research hypothesis was formulated on the basis of theory and previous research before the data were collected.

Research Hypothesis (1): Mood will change significantly from day to day in a quartic fashion.

Statistical Hypotheses. The statistical hypotheses are written symbolically to match the research hypothesis and take the general form $t = c(1)u(1) + c(2)u(2) + c(3)u(3) + ... + c(k)u(k)$, where t stands for a contrast for a particular trend (t = linear, quadratic, cubic, or quartic), $c(k)$ stands for a given orthogonal polynomial coefficient for a given mean (u), and $k$ is the number of means for the occasions factor (DAYS). H(0) and H(A) below represent the null and alternate hypotheses, respectively, for the research hypothesis that there will be a quartic trend.

H(0):   1 u(1) - 4 u(2) + 6 u(3) - 4 u(4) + 1 u(5) = 0

H(A):   1 u(1) - 4 u(2) + 6 u(3) - 4 u(4) + 1 u(5) ≠ 0

The null hypothesis will be tested at the .05 level of significance.

Data. For this section, only the data for Introverts in Table 7.2 are considered. The design consists of five repeated measures on each subject. A measure of the dependent variable, elation, was taken by administering a mood adjective check list to each subject on each of the five days.

One-Way Repeated Measures ANOVA Table. Table 7.3 is the univariate planned comparison one-way ANOVA table which would appear in a research report on this study. The contents of this table could be drawn from BMDP2V (7-1), BMDP4V(7-3), SAS(GLM) (7-1), SAS(REG) (7-3), SPSS(MANOVA) (7-1), and SPSS(MANOVA) (7-3).

The results in Table 7.3 indicate that the data from this study support rejecting the null hypothesis and accepting the alternate hypothesis. The data suggests that the quartic trend is significant ($p < .003$), thus supporting the research hypothesis. The researcher might interpret this to mean that there was a significant daily change in

Table 7.3
Single Group Repeated Measures, Univariate
Analysis of Variance with Trend Analysis
for Social Orientation Study

| Source of Variation | Degrees of Freedom | Sum of Squares | Mean Square | F Statistic | Prob > F |
|---|---|---|---|---|---|
| Linear Trend | 1 | 207.36 | 207.36 | 2.70(2.96)[1] | .135(.094)[1] |
| Error(Linear) | 9 | 690.64 | 76.74 | | |
| Quadratic Trend | 1 | 55.31 | 55.31 | .68(.79)[1] | .430(.380)[1] |
| Error(Quadratic) | 9 | 730.69 | 81.19 | | |
| Cubic Trend | 1 | 201.64 | 201.64 | 3.23(2.88)[1] | .106(.099)[1] |
| Error(Cubic) | 9 | 561.36 | 62.37 | | |
| Quartic Trend | 1 | 1012.81 | 1012.81 | 16.84*(14.45)*[1] | .003(.001)[1] |
| Error(Quartic) | 9 | 541.39 | 60.15 | | |
| [2]Days(Overall) | 4 | 1477.12 | 369.28 | 5.27* | .002 |
| Error(Overall) | 36 | 2524.08 | 70.11 | | |

[1]These F's and probabilities in parentheses are obtained by using the pooled residual error MS (70.11), instead of using MS error terms corresponding to particular trends.

[2]The Greenhouse-Geisser adjusted overall probability was (.007) and the Huynh-Feldt probability was (.002) based on epsilon = .7054 and $\tilde{e}$ = 1.00, respectively.

*Significant at $p < .05$.

elation in the population of interest, assuming the sample
was representative of the population of introverts.

## Univariate Analysis: Single Group Case. Overall Test and Post Hoc Contrasts

If on the basis of theory and/or past research a
researcher has no planned questions that are appropriate to
ask about the levels of the occasions factor, then he might
conduct an overall test of significance. If the overall
test of the occasions levels is significant, then he could
test for specific trends using a post hoc test. In this
case the problem statement would remain the same, but the
hypotheses would be written differently than in the example
with planned contrasts.

Problem. Does mood change significantly from day to
day? (This is the Occasions Question and is the only basic
question that is addressed in the single-group case.)

Research hypothesis. In this case the researcher
believes that differences will appear among his group
means, but past research was not conclusive enough to
predict whether the differences could be described in terms
of a particular trend or trends.

Research hypothesis: (1): One or more trends will
exist over days on the measures of elation.

Statistical hypothesis:

$H(0): u(1) = u(2) = u(3) = u(4) = u(5)$

$H(A): u(i) \neq u(j)$  $(i \neq j; i,j = 1,2,3,4,5)$

The alternate hypothesis indicates that one or more of
the occasion means are different from others.

The null hypothesis will be tested at the .05 level of
significance.

Data. For this section, only the data for Introverts
in Table 7.2 are considered. The design consists of five
repeated measures on each subject. A measure of the
dependent variable, elation, was taken by administering a
mood adjective check list to each subject on each of the
five days.

One-Way Repeated Measures ANOVA Table. Table 7.4 is
the ANOVA source table that would appear in a research
report on this study. The contents of this table would be
derived from BMDP2V (7-1), BMDP4V (7-3), SAS(GLM) (7-1),
SAS(REG) (7-3), SPSS(MANOVA) (7-1) and SPSS(RELIABILITY)

Table 7.4
Single Group Repeated Measures
Overall Univariate Analysis of Variance
for the Social Orientation Study

| Source of Variation | Degrees of Freedom | Sum of Squares | Mean Square | F Statistic | Prob > F |
|---|---|---|---|---|---|
| [1]Days (Overall) | 4 | 1477.12 | 369.28 | 5.27* | .002 |
| Error | 36 | 2524.08 | 70.11 | | |

[1]The Greenhouse-Geisser adjusted overall probability was (.007) and the Hunyh-Feldt probability was (.002) based on epsilon=.7054 and $\tilde{e}$=1.00, respectively.
*Significant at p<.05.

(7-2). Note that only the BMDP programs provide an estimate of epsilon (with the corresponding F and probability) which we recommend for use here. The results in Table 7.4 indicate that the data from this study support the alternate hypothesis. Therefore, the overall research hypothesis is supported, and individual trends may be tested on a _post hoc_ basis. The reader is reminded that the univariate tests automatically performed by computer programs are done as if the contrasts were planned. However, when they are actually unplanned, the contrasts should be tested with a more conservative test, such as that by Scheffe.

_Scheffe's_ _Post_ _Hoc_ _Test._ Because there are significant (p<.002) overall differences among the occasion level means, the Scheffe _post_ _hoc_ test will be used to determine which trend best describes the fluctuation among the means. The reader is reminded that this _post_ _hoc_ test is done only when a significant overall _F_ is first obtained.

The following material is presented in order to demonstrate how the Scheffe test works. This presentation is based on Kirk (1968, p.25, 90-91). The Scheffe method can be used to test all possible contrasts among means and is sensitive to complex contrasts such as those used in testing for individual trends.

_Step_ _1._ The following formulas for Scheffe's test are based on those given in Kirk (1968, p. 91), but modified to include the partitioned error (PE(i), where i=1,2...k-1) recommended by Boik (1981) and Maxwell (1980).

$$F = \frac{[C(j)X(j) + C(j')X(j') + \ldots + C(j'')X(j'')]^2}{PE(i)\left[\dfrac{C(j)^2}{n(j)} + \dfrac{C(j')^2}{n(j')} + \ldots + \dfrac{C(j'')^2}{n(j'')}\right]}$$

$$F' = (k-1)\, F(alpha,\ v(1),\ v(2))$$

where F is the F value obtained for a given trend, and F' is the value which F must exceed for the given trend to be significant, k is the number of levels of the occasions factor (here, DAYS), F(alpha, v(1), v(2)) is the value obtained from any standard F table at the level of significance, alpha, and with v(1) degrees of freedom (df) for the numerator (df for the given trend comparison) and v(2) df for PE(i); C(j) is the orthogonal polynomial coefficient corresponding to the mean, X(j), of the jth level of the occasions factor; and subsequent levels are denoted by superscripts (e.g., j'' which stands for the

last level); n(j) stands for the number of subjects
measured in each level (here equal n's are assumed).

Example:

k = 5, alpha = .05
v(1) = 1, v(2) = 9
F(.05; 1,9) = 5.12
F' = 20.84
PE(1) (error) = 76.74

Step 2. The orthogonal polynomial coefficients
corresponding to each type of trend may be found in
orthogonal polynomial tables in standard texts (e.g., Kirk,
1968, p. 538; Winer, 1971, p. 878).

Example: The orthogonal polynomial coefficients for
the linear trend comparisons where k=5 are:

-2 -1 0 1 2 , or

C(1) = -2, C(2) = -1, C(3) = 0,
C(4) = 1, C(5) = 2.

Step 3. To find the numerator of the Scheffe formula,
(a) Multiply each occasions level mean, X(j), by its
respective orthogonal polynomial coefficient, C(j),
(b) find the sum of these products, and
(c) square this sum.

Example: (a) (-2) (42.00) + (-1) (28.39) + (0)
            (41.20 ) + (1) (31.20) + 2(33.40)
        (b) -14.40
        (c) 207.36

Step 4. To find the denominator of the Scheffe
formula,
(a) find the PE(i) in the computer output,
(b) square the orthogonal polynomial coefficient,
C(j), for each level of the occasions factor and divide
this square by the corresponding n(j), and sum the
dividends, and
(c) multiply the sums of these dividends by the PE(i)
error

Example:

(a) 76.74
(b) $(-2)^2/10 + (-1)^2/10 + (0)^2/10 + (1)^2/10 +$
    $(2)^2/10 = .40 + .10 + 0.0 + .10 + .40 = 1.00$
(c) 76.74 (1.0) = 76.74

Step 5. Divide the numerator of the Scheffe formula

by its denominator.

Example:

$F(\text{linear}) = 207.36/76.74 = 2.70$

Step 6. Compare this obtained F to F'. In this case F is less than F', and we conclude that the sums of squares for the given trend, here the linear trend, is not significant.

Example:

$F(\text{linear}) = 2.70$
$F' = 20.84$; therefore,
$F(\text{linear})$ is not significant at Scheffe alpha = .05

Step 7. The above six steps are carried out for testing each trend of interest, using the appropriate orthogonal polynomial coefficients and PE(i) error for each trend tested. In all of the following tests F' = 20.84.

Example:

$F(\text{quadratic}) = 77.44/(81.19 \times 1.40) = .68$; therefore,
$F(\text{quadratic})$ is not significant at Scheffe alpha = .05

$F(\text{cubic}) = 201.64/(62.37 \times 1.00) = 3.23$
$F(\text{cubic}) =$ is not significant at Scheffe alpha = .05

$F(\text{quartic}) = 7089.64/(60.15 \times 7.0) = 16.84$
$F(\text{quartic}) =$ is not significant at Scheffe alpha = .05

## Univariate Analysis, Multi-group Case, Planned Contrasts

This is called the multi-group case, since subjects are nested within a grouping factor, SOCIOR. The simplest multi-group case involves two levels of such a grouping factor as is illustrated here. The data are treated as that for a split-plot design with subjects (considered random) nested within groups (considered fixed). Both groups and subjects are crossed with the occasions (considered fixed). Here the groups effect is tested, using the variation among subjects as the error. The groups by occasions interaction and the occasions are tested using the subjects within groups by occasions interaction (here, Subjects within SOCIOR by DAYS) as the error. For planned contrasts this interaction error term is partitioned into its linear, quadratic, cubic, and quartic parts in order to test each of the trends (linear through quartic) and each of their corresponding interactions with the groups factor (SOCIOR).

On the basis of theory and/or previous research the researcher may state planned (a priori) mean contrasts for any of the main and interaction effects. The number of possible mean contrasts, of course, depends on the number of levels in the factors. With five levels of the occasions factor, for example, there are four possible trends to test. Unlike the situation involving unplanned contrasts, planned contrasts may be tested without a prior overall test. Below, each of the three possible overall questions in the multi-group case is discussed and tested, and the same is done for a planned mean contrast on the occasions effect.

The Interaction Question. Of the three possible overall questions, the question which must be asked first is whether there is a groups by occasions interaction. In the absence of such an interaction, the profiles of the means of the groups would essentially be parallel, as in Figure 7.1. If there is no interaction, the effects of the grouping and occasions factors may be interpreted independently of each other. Of course, it is possible, though unusual, to predict an interaction and to have one or more planned contrasts of interest within the interaction (e.g. see Chapters 3 and 4). In this chapter, however, we will be interested only in main effects and in a relevant planned mean contrast. The question of a groups by occasions interaction will be referred to as the Interaction Question and may be phrased simply: may the profiles be considered to be parallel?

The Occasions Question. This question has already been described under the univariate, single-group case. In the multi-group case, the question still remains that of whether there are differences between the levels of the occasions factor, but in the multi-group case the question applies to more than one group of subjects. In Figure 7.1, both introverts and extraverts appear to fluctuate in mood over the five-day period.

The Groups Question. Given no interaction, this question asks whether the profiles are also congruent. That is, are the means of the levels of SOCIOR equal? This is a test of the groups effect. In Figure 7.1 it appears that the profiles of introverts and extraverts may be different.

The rest of this section illustrates how the design and results of this analysis might be presented in a formal research report. To conserve space, each of the possible questions for the multi-group case are presented below under the general headings of 'Problems', 'Research Hypotheses', and so on. The subscripts in parentheses (1,2, and 3) refer to the Interaction, Occasions, and

Groups Questions, respectively. For the occasions effect a specific planned mean contrast is stated.

Problems:

(1) Is one's elation dependent on both social orientation and the day on which the mood is measured?
(2) Does elation change significantly from day to day in a quartic fashion?
(3) Does the day-to-day elation of introverts fluctuate differently from the day-to-day elation of extraverts?

Research Hypotheses: The research hypotheses were formulated on the basis of theory and previous research before the data were collected.

(1) There will be no interaction between social orientation and the day on which elation is measured.
(2) Elation will change significantly from day to day in a quartic fashion.
(3) The fluctuation from day to day in extraverts will occur at a significantly higher level of elation from that occurring in introverts.

Statistical Hypotheses. The statistical hypotheses are written in symbolic form to match the research hypotheses. Here we take the same approach as was developed in Chapter 3 for the 3 x 2 design, i.e. by specifying an observation as:

$$y(ijk) = u + a(i) + b(j) + c(k(i)) + ab(ij) + bc(jk(i)) + e(ijk).$$

Where y is the score of an observation in cell ijk; u is the population grand mean of all observations; a represents the treatment effect for group i of the fixed factor A; b represents the occasions effect for treatment j of the fixed factor B; c represents the effect of random subject k within group i; ab represents the first order interaction between group i of factor A and treatment j of factor B; bc represents the first order interaction between treatment j of factor B and subject k of factor C; and, e(ijk) is that part of y that is not accounted for by the other sources of variation in the design. Then, for this problem, we have the following null and alternate statistical hypotheses, represented by the H(0h) and H(Ah) notations, respectively, where h refers to a given research hypothesis:

H(01): bc(jk(i)) = 0 for all jk(i)

H(A1): bc(jk(i)) $\neq$ 0 for some jk(i)

$$H(02): \quad u(.1) - 4u(.2) + 6u(.3) - 4u(.4) + u(.5) = 0$$

$$H(A2): \quad u(.1) - 4u(.2) + 6u(.3) - 4u(.4) + u(.5) \neq 0$$

$$H(03): \quad a(i) = 0 \text{ for all } i$$

$$H(A3): \quad a(i) \neq 0 \text{ for some } i$$

Here we use the notation $u(.i)$, $i = 1$ to 5, to indicate the mean for all subjects across both groups for occasions level i. Note that because of the complex nature of this problem, we have mixed the mean notation, that in previous chapters we reserved for planned hypotheses, with the effect notation, which we have previously used only with overall hypotheses. These hypotheses will be tested at the .05 level of significance.

Data. The data are those presented for the Introverts and Extraverts in Table 7.2.

Two-Way Repeated Measures ANCVA Source Table. Table 7.5 is the ANOVA source table that would appear in a research report on this study. The contents of this table were derived from BMDP2V (7-2), BMDP4V (7-3), SAS(GLM) (7-2), SAS(REG) (7-4), and SPSS(MANOVA) (7-4).

The results in Table 7.5 suggest that: (1) the SOCIOR x DAYS interaction is not significant (p<.863), that (2) the planned mean contrast for a quartic trend is significant (p<.000), and that (3) the SOCIOR effect is significant (p<.009). These results might be interpreted to suggest that in both introverts and extraverts the mood of elation fluctuates significantly in intensity almost daily over a five-day period, and that the profiles of introverts and extraverts do differ significantly from each other in terms of the quartic trend.

## Univariate Analysis, Multi-group Case, Overall Analysis

The overall analysis presented here differs from the earlier planned analysis only in terms of the research and statistical hypotheses for the Occasions Question, because here the researcher was unable to specify the type of trend expected in the data. Therefore, the data are again treated as that for a split-plot design, and the three basic questions remain the same. As was the case for the planned contrast example, in what follows the subscripts in parentheses, i.e., (1), (2), and (3), refer to the basic questions.

Table 7.5

Two-Group Repeated Measures, Univariate
Analysis of Variance with Trend Analysis
for the Social Orientation Study

| Source of Variation | Degrees of Freedom | Sum of Squares | Mean Square | F Statistic | Prob > F |
|---|---|---|---|---|---|
| Socior | 1 | 1799.07 | 1799.07 | 8.63 | .009 |
| Error(Socior) | 17 | 3543.83 | 208.46 | | |
| Linear Trend | 1 | 319.12 | 319.12 | 3.76(5.28)*[1] | .069(-.025)[1] |
| Linear * Socior | 1 | 3.83 | 3.83 | .05(.06)[1] | .834(-.802)[1] |
| Error | 17 | 1442.06 | 84.83 | | |
| Quadratic Trend | 1 | 293.78 | 293.78 | 5.09*(4.86)*[1] | .038(-.031)[1] |
| Quad.* Socior | 1 | 47.65 | 47.65 | .83(.79)[1] | .376(-.378)[1] |
| Error | 17 | 981.54 | 57.74 | | |
| Cubic Trend | 1 | 350.45 | 350.45 | 8.10*(5.80)*[1] | .011(-.019)[1] |
| Cubic * Socior | 1 | .68 | .68 | .02(.01)[1] | .902(-.916)[1] |
| Error | 17 | 735.16 | 43.24 | | |
| Quartic Trend | 1 | 2388.31 | 2388.31 | 42.62*(39.5)*[1] | .000(-.001)[1] |
| Quartic * Socior | 1 | 25.64 | 25.64 | .46(.42)[1] | .508(-.517)[1] |
| Error | 17 | 952.74 | 56.04 | | |
| Days(Overall)[2] | 4 | 3351.66 | 837.91 | 13.86 | .000 |
| Days * Socior(Ovall.)[2][4] | 4 | 77.80 | 19.45 | .32 | .863 |
| Error (Residual) Socior*Days* Subj(Socior) | 68 | 4111.50 | 60.46 | | |

[1]These F's and probabilities in parentheses are obtained by using the pooled residual error MS (60.46), instead of using the MS error terms corresponding to particular trends.
[2]Here the Greenhouse-Geisser (G-G) epsilon is .8097 and the Huynh-Feldt (H-F) ē is 1.00. The G-G and H-F Days (Overall) probability is .000, and the G-G and H-F Days * Socior (Overall) probabilities are .824 and .863, respectively.
*Significant at p<.05.

<u>Problems.</u>

(1)   Is  one's  elation  dependent  on  both  social
orientation and the day on which the mood is measured?
(2)   Does elation change significantly from day to day
in a linear or non-linear fashion?
(3)   Does   the   day-to-day   elation   of   introverts
fluctuate  differently  from  the  day-to-day  elation  of
extraverts?

<u>Research  Hypotheses.</u>   The  research hypotheses  were
formulated on  the basis  of theory  and previous  research
before the data were collected.

(1)   There  will  be  no  interaction  between  social
orientation and the day on which elation is measured.
(2)   Elation will change significantly from day to day.
(3)   The   day-to-day   fluctuation   in   elation   of
introverts  will  differ  significantly  from  that  of
extraverts.

<u>Statistical  Hypotheses.</u>    The  statistical  hypotheses
for  each  question are  written symbolically  to match  the
research hypotheses.   Here the symbols were taken from the
linear equation for  an observation in a  split-plot design
that was  specified for  the  statistical hypotheses  in the
preceding planned contrasts section.   For each question a
null  hypothesis and  an alternate  hypothesis are  stated,
represented by  the $H(0h)$ and  $H(Ah)$ notations, respectively,
where h refers to a given research hypothesis.

$H(01)$:    $bc(jk(i)) = 0$ for all $jk(i)$
$H(A1)$:    $bc(jk(i)) \neq 0$ for some $jk(i)$

$H(02)$:    $b(j) = 0$ for all $j$
$H(A2)$:    $b(j) \neq 0$ for some $j$

$H(03)$:    $a(i) = 0$ for all $i$
$H(A3)$:    $a(i) \neq 0$ for some $i$

Each  null   hypothesis will  be  tested at   the  .05  level of
significance.

<u>Data.</u>   The  data are  those presented for Introverts  and
Extraverts in Table 7.2.

<u>Two  Group  Repeated  Measures  ANOVA  Source  Table.</u>   Table
7.6 contains the results of  this overall analysis.   These
results  indicate that  there  are significant  differences
between the occasions levels of  DAYS ($p<.000$)  and between
the levels of SOCIOR ($p<.009$).   Here we arrive at the same
conclusion for the occasions factor using the uncorrected F
statistic or  the  F statistic  found using  the Greenhouse-

## Table 7.6
### Two-Group Repeated Measures
### Overall Univariate Analysis of Variance
### for the Social Orientation Study

| Source of Variation | Degrees of Freedom | Sum of Squares | Mean Square | F Statistic | Prob > F |
|---|---|---|---|---|---|
| Socior | 1 | 1799.07 | 1799.07 | 8.63* | .009 |
| Error(Socior) | 17 | 3543.83 | 208.46 | | |
| ¹Days | 4 | 3351.66 | 837.91 | 13.86* | .000 |
| ¹Days*Socior | 4 | 77.80 | 19.45 | .32 | .863 |
| Error (Socior*Days* Subj(Sccior)) | 68 | 4111.50 | 60.46 | | |

¹Here the Greenhouse-Geisser (G-G) epsilon is .8097 and the Huynh-Feldt (H-F) ẽ is 1.00. The G-G and H-F Days (Overall) probabilities are .000, and the G-G and H-F Days*Socior probabilities are .824 and .863, respectively.

*Significant at $p < .05$.

Geisser or Huynh-Feldt degrees of freedom correction coefficient. These results are available from BMDP2V (7-2), BMDP4V (7-4), SAS(GLM) (7-2), SAS(REG) (7-4), and SPSS(MANOVA) (7-4). Only the BMDP programs provide the Greenhouse-Geisser and Huynh-Feldt information.

A Note of Caution: Since many of the computer programs produce the mean contrasts automatically as if the contrasts were planned, finding a particular trend significant in the output should serve only to select contrasts which may then be subjected to a more conservative post hoc test. In the present example, the quadratic, cubic, and quartic trends were found to be significant in the tests performed automatically by the computer programs. However, of those three trends only the quartic trend was found to be significant when subjected to the Scheffe test.

## Multivariate Mode of Analysis

A design is multivariate if there is more than one dependent variable observed per cell. If the univariate repeated measures example design is reconceptualized as multivariate, the occasions factor as such disappears, leaving cell structure to be determined only by the grouping factor. If there is only one group of subjects, there is one cell; two groups of subjects, two cells. Instead of one dependent variable being measured on five occasions for each subject, each subject has five dependent variables. A contrast matrix is then used to reduce the number of dependent variables to one less than the original number, i.e., four in our example. The overall multivariate test is an indication of whether or not it is reasonable to assume that this vector of contrasts was sampled from a multivariate normal distribution with a null mean vector. If this is an unreasonable assumption, i.e., if the overall multivariate null hypothesis is rejected, then individual univariate tests on the contrasts are considered.

If one is interested in planned contrasts, the overall multivariate test is skipped and one considers the univariate tests directly. These univariate tests are exactly the same tests that one would receive from the univariate planned contrasts considered earlier. Therefore, since the univariate and multivariate modes of analysis yield the same planned results, we will not repeat these results here, but refer you to the planned univariate sections. In the next sections we discuss the overall multivariate test for one and multiple groups.

The 'basic questions' which may be addressed in the overall single- and multi-group cases remain the same as they were in the univariate mode, and they will be called the same to illustrate continuity from the univariate to multivariate modes. The difference is that the answer to these questions will be found in different _overall_ effects (see Timm, 1975, pp. 223-250). For example, the Occasions Question is answered by examining the multivariate test of the grand mean (or 'constant') vector instead of the occasions effect, and (in the multi-group case) the Interaction Question is answered by examining the multivariate test of the groups effect in terms of the contrast variable vectors. The Groups Question may also be answered by examining the groups effect, but is done using a subject's total score over occasions as the dependent variable. Specific trends and other mean contrasts are set up by transforming the dependent variables into the contrast variables in question. For example, in the multivariate mode, the five dependent variables are transformed into four variables corresponding to the four possible trends.

## Multivariate Analysis: Single Group Case, Overall Analysis

For this case the data from Group 1 (see Table 7.2) alone is considered. The grouping factor, SOCIOR, has only one level; hence, the design has one cell. An observation consists of the set of five repeated measures on a given subject. In this case there are ten observations. The five occasions are treated as five dependent variables.

In this multivariate, single-group case only the Occasions Question may be addressed by performing an overall multivariate test, and then, by performing a separate univariate test on each contrast variable, which were created by applying orthogonal polynomial transformations to the original five measures of elation. The four resulting dependent variables then correspond to the linear, quadratic, cubic, and quartic trends, respectively.

The rest of this section illustrates how the design and results of this analysis might be presented in a formal research report.

_Problem._ Does mood change significantly from day to day? The Occasions Question is the only appropriate question for the single-group case.

_Research Hypothesis._ In this situation, the researcher believes that one or more trends may exist in the data, but either past research was inconclusive or theory was too poorly formulated to make specific predictions.

Research Hypothesis (1): One or more trends will be found in the measures of elation taken over consecutive days.

Statistical Hypothesis. The statistical hypothesis is stated symbolically so as to match the research hypothesis. Here we use the general form of the multivariate null hypothesis for the full rank procedure (see Timm, 1975, pp. 223-250).

$$H(0): [u(1)\ u(2)\ u(3)\ u(4)\ u(5)] \begin{bmatrix} -2 & 2 & -1 & 1 \\ -1 & -1 & 2 & -4 \\ 0 & -2 & 0 & 6 \\ 1 & -1 & -2 & -4 \\ 2 & 2 & 1 & 1 \end{bmatrix} = [0\ 0\ 0\ 0]$$

$$H(A): [u(1)\ u(2)\ u(3)\ u(4)\ u(5)] \begin{bmatrix} -2 & 2 & -1 & 1 \\ -1 & -1 & 2 & -4 \\ 0 & -2 & 0 & 6 \\ 1 & -1 & -2 & -4 \\ 2 & 2 & 1 & 1 \end{bmatrix} \neq [0\ 0\ 0\ 0]$$

In these hypotheses the first vector contains the means, u(i)'s (i=1 to 5), of elation on each of the five days. The 5x4 matrix contains the orthogonal polynomials in each column, e.g., (-2 -1 0 1 2) is the linear trend. Note that the choice of this matrix is dependent on the univariate questions that you would like to ask following the multivariate test. However, the overall multivariate test is invariant to the choice of contrasts so long as each contrast is not a linear combination of one or more of the other contrasts (e.g. see BMDP4V (7-3)).

The hypothesis will be tested at the .05 level of significance.

Data. The data are those presented for the introverts in Table 7.2.

Single Group Repeated Measures MANOVA Source Table. Table 7.7 is the single group MANOVA table for the overall multivariate test of the trends in the elation data. Here we find a significant multivariate test (p<.043), and the univariate tests indicate that there is a significant quartic trend in the data. Note that although you do not have to worry about the sphericity assumption of the univariate test, the multivariate test is not (in this case) as powerful as the overall univariate test shown in Table 7.4.

Table 7.7
Single Group Multivariate Repeated
Measures Analysis of Variance with
Trend Analysis for the Socior Orientation Study

| Source of Variation | Multivariate | | | Univariate | | | | |
| | Wilks' Lambda | Df | F(Probability) | Df | F(Probability) | | | |
| | | | | | Linear | Quadratic | Cubic | Quartic |
|---|---|---|---|---|---|---|---|---|
| Days | .24 | 4, 6 | 4.87*(.043) | 1,9 | 2.70(.135) | .68(.430) | 3.23(.106) | 16.84*(.003) |

1The SSCP matrices for this table would be put into an appendix, due to the size of the matrices. Because the packages use different algorithms for this analysis, they all yield different SSCP matrices, i.e, see BMDP4V (7-3), SAS (REG) (7-3), and SPSS (MANOVA) (7-3). All of these matrices will yield the same overall multivariate tests, but only the diagonal elements from SPSS (MANOVA) may be used to compute the univariate tests shown here.
*Significant at p<.05.

# Multivariate Analysis: Multi-group Case, Overall Analysis

This multi-group case is so called, because there is more than one group of subjects. Here, both the introverts and the extraverts are included in the analysis. These groups constitute two levels of the grouping factor, SOCIOR. In this multivariate mode of the example study, cell structure is determined only by the grouping factor, since the occasions factor is reconceptualized as five dependent variables instead of five factor levels. These five dependent variables are then transformed (by applying orthogonal polynomials) into four contrast variables corresponding to the four trends of interest.

The three basic questions that may be addressed in the multivariate, multi-group case are the same as those in the univariate, multi-group case, despite the lack of an explicit occasions factor and groups by occasions interaction. Contrasts between variable means are examined instead of contrasts between cell means, but the questions remain the same. To underscore this continuity between the univariate and multivariate modes, the same names are used for the basic questions.

The rest of this section illustrates how the design and results of this analysis might be presented in a formal research report. To conserve space, each of the possible questions for the multi-group case is presented under the general headings of 'Problems', 'Research Hypothesis', and so on. The subscripts in parentheses (1, 2, and 3) refer to the Interaction, Occasions, and Groups Questions, respectively, which were discussed earlier.

## Problems.

(1) Is one's elation dependent on both social orientation and the day on which elation is measured?
(2) Does elation change significantly from day to day in a linear or non-linear fashion?
(3) Does the day-to-day elation of introverts fluctuate differently from the day-to-day elation of extraverts?

Research Hypotheses. The research hypotheses were formulated on the basis of theory and previous research before the data were collected.
(1) There will be no interaction between social orientation and the day on which elation is measured.
(2) One or more trends will be found in the measures of elation taken over consecutive days.
(3) The fluctuation from day to day in extraverts will occur at a significantly different level of elation from that occurring in introverts.

Statistical Hypotheses.    The statistical  hypotheses
for each  question are  written symbolically  to match  the
research hypotheses.    For each  question a null hypothesis
(H(Oh), where h is the  number of the question referenced)
and an alternate hypothesis (H(Ah))   are stated.    Here we
use matrix  notation to  describe the  general form  of the
multivariate null  and alternative hypotheses for  the full
rank procedure (see Timm, 1975, p. 449).

$$H(01): \begin{bmatrix} 1 & -1 \end{bmatrix} \begin{bmatrix} u(11) & u(12) & u(13) & u(14) & u(15) \\ u(21) & u(22) & u(23) & u(24) & u(25) \end{bmatrix} \begin{bmatrix} -2 & 2 & -1 & 1 \\ -1 & -1 & 2 & -4 \\ 0 & -2 & 0 & 6 \\ 1 & -1 & -2 & -4 \\ 2 & 2 & 1 & 1 \end{bmatrix} = \begin{bmatrix} 0 & 0 & 0 & 0 \end{bmatrix}$$

$$H(A1): \begin{bmatrix} 1 & -1 \end{bmatrix} \begin{bmatrix} u(11) & u(12) & u(13) & u(14) & u(15) \\ u(21) & u(22) & u(23) & u(24) & u(25) \end{bmatrix} \begin{bmatrix} -2 & 2 & -1 & 1 \\ -1 & -1 & 2 & -4 \\ 0 & -2 & 0 & 6 \\ 1 & -1 & -2 & -4 \\ 2 & 2 & 1 & 1 \end{bmatrix} \neq \begin{bmatrix} 0 & 0 & 0 & 0 \end{bmatrix}$$

$$H(02): \begin{bmatrix} 1 & 1 \end{bmatrix} \begin{bmatrix} u(11) & u(12) & u(13) & u(14) & u(15) \\ u(21) & u(22) & u(23) & u(24) & u(25) \end{bmatrix} \begin{bmatrix} -2 & 2 & -1 & 1 \\ -1 & -1 & 2 & -4 \\ 0 & -2 & 0 & 6 \\ 1 & -1 & -2 & -4 \\ 2 & 2 & 1 & 1 \end{bmatrix} = \begin{bmatrix} 0 & 0 & 0 & 0 \end{bmatrix}$$

$$H(A2): \begin{bmatrix} 1 & 1 \end{bmatrix} \begin{bmatrix} u(11) & u(12) & u(13) & u(14) & u(15) \\ u(21) & u(22) & u(23) & u(24) & u(25) \end{bmatrix} \begin{bmatrix} -2 & 2 & -1 & 1 \\ -1 & -1 & 2 & -4 \\ 0 & -2 & 0 & 6 \\ 1 & -1 & -2 & -4 \\ 2 & 2 & 1 & 1 \end{bmatrix} \neq \begin{bmatrix} 0 & 0 & 0 & 0 \end{bmatrix}$$

$$H(03): \begin{bmatrix} 1 & -1 \end{bmatrix} \begin{bmatrix} u(11) & u(12) & u(13) & u(14) & u(15) \\ u(21) & u(22) & u(23) & u(24) & u(25) \end{bmatrix} \begin{bmatrix} 1 \\ 1 \\ 1 \\ 1 \\ 1 \end{bmatrix} = 0$$

$$H(A3): \begin{bmatrix} 1 & -1 \end{bmatrix} \begin{bmatrix} u(11) & u(12) & u(13) & u(14) & u(15) \\ u(21) & u(22) & u(23) & u(24) & u(25) \end{bmatrix} \begin{bmatrix} 1 \\ 1 \\ 1 \\ 1 \\ 1 \end{bmatrix} \neq 0$$

These hypotheses are of the form ABC' = D. Here the matrix B contains the means, u(ij) (i = 1,2; j = 1 to 5), of elation for each group, i, on each of the five, j, days. In the first two hypotheses the choice of A is dependent on the overall questions asked, and the choice of C' is dependent on the univariate test questions of concern following the overall multivariate test. In general, however, the overall multivariate test is invariant to the choice of full rank contrasts in the rows of A and the columns of C'. The test of the third hypothesis is the same as that found for groups in the univariate analysis.

Each null hypothesis will be tested at the .05 level of significance.

Data. The data are those presented for the Introverts and Extraverts in Table 7.2.

Two Group Repeated Measures MANOVA Source Table. Table 7.8 is the two group MANOVA table for the overall tests of no interaction, occasions, and groups effects. In this table we see that there is no significant multivariate interaction (p<.667), but that there are significant differences between the measures of elation on different days (p<.000), and between the groups (p<.0092). Here the univariate tests for the repeated measures indicate that there is a strong quartic trend in the data (p<.000), and that one might also include the quadratic (p<.038) and cubic (p<.011) terms in the linear model to describe each observation. The group means indicate that the introverts have lower scores on elation than do the extraverts, 35.24 and 43.96 respectively. The information in Table 7.8 can be obtained from BMDP4V (7-4), SAS(REG) (7-3), and SPSS(MANOVA) (7-4).

## Multiple Measurements On Each Occasion

In the following sections we consider a design with two groups and two measures on each occasion. The data for this design are shown in Table 7.9. Here we have a group of introverts and a group of extraverts measured on elation and depression on each occasion. Therefore, we have simply expanded the data set shown in Table 7.2 to include another variable, depression, measured on each day. As was discussed in the introduction, these data may be analyzed using either of two approaches, univariate-multivariate or doubly multivariate. In the univariate-multivariate approach the data is considered to be that for a multivariate split-plot design, and in the doubly multivariate approach the data is transformed to that for a two group multivariate analysis. However, both of these approaches yield the same results for planned contrasts.

Table 7.8
Two-Group Multivariate Repeated Measures
Analysis of Variance with Trend Analysis
for the Social Orientation Study

| Source of Variation[1] | Multivariate | | | Univariate | | | | |
|---|---|---|---|---|---|---|---|---|
| | Wilks' Lambda | Df | F(Probability) | Df | F(Probability) | | | |
| | | | | | Linear | Quadratic | Cubic | Quartic |
| Days | .22 | 4,14 | 12.16*(.000) | 1,17 | 3.76(.069) | 5.09*(.038) | 8.10*(.011) | 42.62*(.000) |
| Days by Socior | .85 | 4,14 | .60(.667) | 1,17 | .05(.834) | .83(.376) | .02(.902) | .46(.508) |
| Elation | | | | | | | | |
| Socior[2] | | 1,17 | 8.63*(.009) | | | | | |

[1]The SSCP matrices for this table would be put into an appendix, due to the size of the matrices. Because the packages use different algorithms for this analysis, they all yield different sums of squares and products matrices, i.e., see BMDP4v (7-4), SAS(REG) (7-4), and SPSS(MANOVA) (7-4). All of these matrices will yield the same overall multivariate tests, but only the diagonal elements from SPSS(MANOVA) may be used to compute the univariate tests shown here.

[2]The results for this source of variation are the same as that found for the univariate approach, see Table 7.5.

*Significant at $p < .05$.

In what follows we first present a discussion of planned comparisons, and then consider the overall analyses for each approach.

## Univariate-Multivariate and Doubly Multivariate, Planned Comparisons

In preparation for this analysis the researcher had conducted extensive work in the study of elation and depression on introverts and extraverts. The results of these earlier studies indicated that no interaction existed between repeated measures of the variables taken on successive days, and that extraverts generally scored higher on elation and lower on depression than did introverts. The focus of this study was on time. Based on her past research the researcher felt that a quartic trend over time would exist for both measures. This led to the following problem, research hypothesis, and statistical hypotheses.

Problem. Do both elation and depression follow a quartic trend when measured over time for introverts and extraverts considered together?

Research Hypothesis. Elation and depression follow a quartic trend when measured over time for introverts and extraverts considered together.

Statistical Hypotheses. The planned comparison hypotheses are written symbolically to match the research hypothesis.

$$H(0): \underline{u}(.1) - 4\underline{u}(.2) + 6\underline{u}(.3) - 4\underline{u}(.4) + \underline{u}(.5) = 0$$

$$H(A): \underline{u}(.1) - 4\underline{u}(.2) + 6\underline{u}(.3) - 4\underline{u}(.4) + \underline{u}(.5) \neq 0$$

Here $\underline{u}(.i)$ is the mean vector for day i (i = 1 to 5) containing the means, $u(.pi)$ (p = 1, 2), of each dependent variable for day i. We use the dot notation to indicate that the means are based on the data across both groups for a given day. This null hypothesis will be tested at the .05 level of significance.

Data. The data are shown in Table 7.9.

Two-Group, Two Repeated Measures, MANCVA Source Table. Table 7.10 contains the results of the planned multivariate trend analysis. This table is entitled 'Multiple Measures' to imply either the univariate-multivariate or doubly multivariate design, each of which produce the same results for planned contrasts. Here we find a strong indication that there is a significant quartic trend in the multivariate data (p<.000), and our univariate tests

Table 7.9
Raw Data¹ Used in the
Social Orientation Study for the
Doubly Multivariate Analyses

| Group | Day1 | | Day2 | | Day3 | | Day4 | | Day5 | |
|---|---|---|---|---|---|---|---|---|---|---|
| | Elat.² | Dep.² | Elat. | Dep. | Elat. | Dep. | Elat. | Dep. | Elat. | Dep. |
| Introverts | 20 | 30 | 21 | 35 | 42 | 20 | 32 | 27 | 32 | 22 |
| | 67 | 43 | 29 | 50 | 56 | 35 | 39 | 37 | 41 | 26 |
| | 37 | 15 | 25 | 29 | 28 | 16 | 31 | 35 | 34 | 25 |
| | 42 | 31 | 38 | 46 | 36 | 27 | 19 | 32 | 35 | 28 |
| | 57 | 40 | 32 | 59 | 21 | 28 | 30 | 37 | 29 | 23 |
| | 39 | 22 | 38 | 37 | 54 | 33 | 31 | 29 | 28 | 35 |
| | 43 | 24 | 20 | 29 | 46 | 28 | 42 | 26 | 31 | 30 |
| | 35 | 32 | 34 | 56 | 43 | 44 | 35 | 52 | 42 | 47 |
| | 41 | 19 | 23 | 36 | 51 | 15 | 27 | 25 | 30 | 18 |
| | 39 | 25 | 24 | 26 | 35 | 30 | 26 | 21 | 32 | 23 |
| Extraverts | 47 | 35 | 25 | 46 | 36 | 35 | 21 | 42 | 27 | 12 |
| | 53 | 42 | 32 | 52 | 48 | 40 | 46 | 47 | 54 | 35 |
| | 38 | 37 | 33 | 39 | 42 | 38 | 48 | 45 | 49 | 26 |
| | 60 | 49 | 41 | 57 | 67 | 42 | 53 | 45 | 50 | 48 |
| | 37 | 36 | 35 | 37 | 45 | 37 | 34 | 36 | 46 | 26 |
| | 59 | 51 | 37 | 58 | 52 | 50 | 36 | 48 | 52 | 50 |
| | 67 | 42 | 33 | 68 | 61 | 45 | 31 | 32 | 50 | 55 |
| | 43 | 25 | 27 | 43 | 36 | 27 | 33 | 39 | 32 | 37 |
| | 64 | 34 | 53 | 61 | 62 | 36 | 40 | 54 | 43 | 47 |

¹The "elation" measures were adapted from Timm (1975, p. 244), omitting one case of the Timm data to create an unequal n's example here. The depression data were created for this example.
²Elat.=Elation measures, Dep.=Depression measures.

indicate that this trend is found in both dependent variables (p<.000). We also find that the quadratic and cubic multivariate trends are statistically significant and could be included in a statistical model describing the observations. Since the quadratic and cubic trends were not predicted, the corresponding results in Table 7.10 should be used only to suggest which trends should have post hoc tests applied (e.g. Scheffe). If we then find that the quadratic and cubic trends are still significant, we could suggest that their existence in the data was not purely by chance. Future research might then replicate these results and establish that the quadratic, cubic, and quartic trends could all be included in a theoretical research model. The occasion means for elation and depression in each SOCIOB group appear to follow the same quartic pattern, and Figure 7.1 could reasonably be used to describe either variable. The results shown in Table 7.10 can be derived from BMDP4V (7-5), SAS(REG) (7-6), and SPSS(MANOVA) (7-6).

## Univariate-Multivariate Overall Analysis

When you are unable to formulate planned comparisons like those described in the previous section, because of limited previous research or theory, an overall analysis is generally desired. In the overall analysis presented here the data are treated as that for a multivariate split-plot design. The overall questions of interest are the same as those described in 'Univariate Analysis, Multi-group Case, Planned Contrasts,' i.e., concerning Interactions, Occasions, and Groups. One difference here, however, is that we have repeated measures of two different dependent variables, so that these questions are posed for both measures considered simultaneously. In this section, as in previous sections, we use the subscripts in parentheses (1,2, and 3) to refer to the Interaction, Occasions, and Groups questions, respectively.

### Problems.

(1) Is either elation and/or depression dependent on both social orientation and the day on which these emotions are measured?

(2) Is there a significant change in elation and/or depression from day to day?

(3) Does the day-to-day elation and/or depression of introverts fluctuate differently from the day-to-day elation and/or depression of extraverts?

Research Hypotheses. In this case the researcher is unsure of what might happen in the analysis because the

Table 7.10
Two Group, Multiple Measures, Multivariate
Analysis of Variance with Trend Analysis
for the Social Orientation Study

| Source Variation | Sums of Squares and Products | | Multivariate | | | Univariate | | |
|---|---|---|---|---|---|---|---|---|
| | Elation | Depression | Wilks' Lambda | Df | F(Probability) | Df | F(Probability) Elation | Depression |
| Linear | [ 319.17 | 251.36] | .76 | 2,16 | 2.59(.106) | 1 | 3.76(.069) | 3.03(.100) |
| | [ 251.36 | 197.99] | | | | | | |
| Linear Error | [ 1442.06 | 298.18] | | | | 17 | | |
| | [ 298.18 | 1105.82] | | | | | | |
| Quadratic | [ 293.78 | -353.38] | .43 | 2,16 | 10.82*(.001) | 1 | 5.09*(.038) | 20.28*(.000) |
| | [ -353.38 | 425.07] | | | | | | |
| Quadratic Error | [ 981.54 | -81.81] | | | | 17 | | |
| | [ -81.81 | 356.30] | | | | | | |
| Cubic | [ 350.45 | -393.68] | .48 | 2,16 | 8.55*(.003) | 1 | 8.10*(.011) | 8.24*(.011) |
| | [ -393.68 | 442.25] | | | | | | |
| Cubic Error | [ 735.16 | 82.20] | | | | 17 | | |
| | [ 82.20 | 912.62] | | | | | | |
| Quartic | [ 2388.31 | -1727.24] | .15 | 2,16 | 46.60*(.000) | 1 | 42.62*(.000) | 28.56*(.000) |
| | [ -1727.24 | 1249.16] | | | | | | |
| Quartic Error | [ 952.74 | 239.26] | | | | 17 | | |
| | [ 239.26 | 743.42] | | | | | | |

*Significant at p<.05

small amount of past research done in this area was contradictory. Therefore, the research hypotheses were expressed in the following noncommittal manner.

(1) There may or may not be an interaction between social orientation and the day on which elation and depression, considered together, are measured.

(2) Elation and/or depression may or may not change significantly from day-to-day.

(3) The level of day-to-day fluctuation in elation and/or depression may or may not differ significantly between the two social orientation groups.

Statistical Hypotheses. The statistical hypotheses are written in symbolic form to match the research hypotheses. Here we extend the notation developed in the univariate discussion of this split-plot design by specifying an observation as:

$$y(ijk) = \underline{u} + \underline{a}(i) + \underline{b}(j) + \underline{c}(k(i)) + \underline{ab}(ij) + \underline{bc}(jk(i)) + \underline{e}(ijk).$$

Here $\underline{y}$ is the vector of scores for a subject in cell ijk; $\underline{u}$ is the vector of population grand means over all observations; $\underline{a}$ represents the vector of treatment effects for group i of the fixed factor A; $\underline{b}$ represents the vector of repeated measures effects for treatment j of the fixed factor B; $\underline{c}$ represents the vector of effects of random subject k within group i; $\underline{ab}$ represents the vector of first order interactions between group i of factor A and treatment j of factor B; $\underline{bc}$ represents the vector of first order interactions between treatment j of factor B and subject k of factor C; and, $\underline{e}(ijk)$ is that part of $\underline{y}$ that is not accounted for by the other sources of variation in the design. Then, for this problem, we have the following null and alternate hypotheses:

H(01): $\underline{bc}(jk(i)) = 0$ for all jk(i)
H(A1): $\underline{bc}(jk(i)) \neq 0$ for some jk(i)

H(02): $\underline{b}(j) = 0$ for all j
H(A2): $\underline{b}(j) \neq 0$ for some j

H(03): $\underline{a}(i) = 0$ for all i
H(A3): $\underline{a}(i) \neq 0$ for some i

Each null hypothesis will be tested at the .05 level of significance.

Data. The data are shown in Table 7.9.

<u>Univariate-Multivariate MANOVA Source Table.</u>  The
results in Table 7.11 indicate that no DAYS by SOCIOR
interaction was found (p<.991).  A significant multivariate
effect for DAYS on elation and depression was found
(p<.000),  and this effect was also found on the univariate
tests of  both dependent  variables.  A  significant
multivariate effect was also found between the SOCIOR
groups with the extraverts scoring higher on both dependent
variables than the introverts.  The results in Table 7.11
can be derived from BMDP4V (7-5),  SAS(GLM)  (7-5),  and
SPSS(MANOVA)  (7-5).  Further <u>post</u> <u>hoc</u> tests for trends
might be  done using  the Roy-Bose  simultaneous confidence
intervals discussed in Chapter 3.

## Doubly Multivariate Overall Analysis

In this section we consider  the same data,  problems,
and research hypotheses as were  considered in the previous
section  on  univariate-multivariate  analysis.  The
difference here is that in this  analysis the data is first
transformed from ten measures,  five  on each variable,  to
eight measures,  four on each variable.  The analysis is
then  performed  as  that  for  a  two  group multivariate
analysis with  eight measures  on  each subject.  The
difference in the results of this analysis and those of the
preceding one is that the researcher has the opportunity to
specify potential <u>post</u> <u>hoc</u> tests  for trends  of interest,
should a multivariate test be significant.  These <u>post</u> <u>hoc</u>
tests are entered for exploratory  purposes as contrasts in
the transformation of the original data, and they appear as
univariate tests  following the overall  multivariate tests
on occasions and occasions by groups.  These tests are, of
course, <u>post</u> <u>hoc</u> only in a procedural sense;  statistically
they are tested  as any planned contrast might be.  It is
convenient, however,  to be able to specify these contrasts
beforehand,  since we can then  obtain the relevant sums of
squares for the contrasts and error terms.  The partitioned
or  unpartitioned error  terms would  then be  used in  the
actual <u>post</u> <u>hoc</u> tests.

Since the problems and research hypotheses are exactly
the same as those shown in the previous section we will not
repeat them here.  Instead we  will focus on the potential
<u>post</u> <u>hoc</u>  tests that  may be  considered in  this analysis.
The nature  of these  tests may  be seen  in the  following
statistical  hypotheses  for  the  doubly  multivariate
analysis.  As in  the previous sections the  subscripts in
parentheses (1,  2,  and 3)  refer  to the  Interaction,
Occasions, and Groups questions, respectively.

<u>Statistical Hypotheses.</u>  The statistical  hypotheses
for each  question are  written symbolically  to match  the
research hypotheses.  Here we use  the general form of the

## Table 7.11
## Univariate-Multivariate Analysis of
## Variance for the Social Orientation Study

| Source of Variation | Sums of Squares and Products | | Multivariate | | | Univariate | | |
|---|---|---|---|---|---|---|---|---|
| | Elation | Depression | Wilks' Lambda | Df | F(Probability) | Df | F(Probability) Elation | Depression |
| Socior | ⌈ 1799.07 | 2219.26⌉ | .61 | 2,16 | 5.22*(.018) | 1 | 8.63*(.009) | 10.24*(.005) |
| | ⌊ 2219.26 | 2737.57⌋ | | | | | | |
| Error (Socior) | ⌈ 3543.83 | 2875.10⌉ | | | | 17 | | |
| | ⌊ 2875.10 | 4545.56⌋ | | | | | | |
| Days | ⌈ 3351.66 | -2222.95⌉ | .33 | 8,134 | 12.30*(.000) | 4 | 13.86*(.000) | 12.60*(.000) |
| | ⌊ -2222.95 | 2314.46⌋ | | | ¹[3.24][3.16] | | ¹[13.86*(.000)] | [12.60*(.000)] |
| Days by Socior | ⌈ 77.80 | -17.24⌉ | .98 | 8,134 | .20(.991) | 4 | .32(.863) | .04(.996) |
| | ⌊ -17.24 | 7.85⌋ | | | ¹[3.24][3.16] | | ¹[.32(.824)] | [.04(.990)] |
| Error (Socior by Days by Subjects within Socior) | ⌈ 4111.50 | 537.83⌉ | | | | 68 | | |
| | ⌊ 537.83 | 3122.17⌋ | | | | | ¹[55.06][53.75] | |

¹Within the brackets on this line are the Greenhouse-Geisser (G-G) results based on epsilons of .81 and .79 for elation and depression, respectively. First the adjusted degrees of freedom are shown for each variable, followed by the corresponding G-G F values and probabilities.
*Significant at p<.05.

multivariate null and alternative hypotheses for the full
rank procedure (see Timm, 1975, p. 449). Because of the
size of these hypotheses they are presented in Figure 7.2.

The hypotheses in Figure 7.2 are of the form ABC' = D.
Here the matrix B contains the means, u(ij) (i= 1,2; j = 1
to 10), of elation and depression for each group, i, on
each of the five days. The first five means in B are those
on elation, and the second five are those on depression.
These ten measures are indicated with the subscript j.
Each null hypothesis will be tested at the .05 level of
significance. In the first two hypotheses the choice of A
is dependent on the overall questions asked, and the choice
of C' is dependent on the post hoc univariate contrasts of
concern following the overall multivariate test. In
general, however, the overall multivariate test is
invariant to the choice of full rank contrasts in the rows
of A and the columns of C'. In the first two hypotheses we
selected the columns of C' so as to yield post hoc
univariate tests of linear, quadratic, cubic, and quartic
trends on each qualitatively different dependent variable.
The test of the third hypothesis is the same as that found
for SOCIOR in the univariate-multivariate analysis.

Data. The data are shown in Table 7.9.

Doubly Multivariate MANOVA Source Table. The
multivariate results in Table 7.12 yield the same
conclusions found with the univariate-multivariate approach
in Table 7.11, i.e., no DAYS by SOCIOR interaction
(p<.939), and significant effects for DAYS (p<.000) and
SOCIOR (p<.018). (Interestingly, for these data, the
doubly multivariate analysis yields slightly more powerful
multivariate tests on the repeated measures and interaction
sources of variation than does the univariate-multivariate
analysis.) The univariate post hoc tests provided in the
doubly multivariate analysis yield a 'finer grained'
analysis than do the overall univariate tests found in the
univariate-multivariate analysis. The post hoc univariate
tests following the significant multivariate test over days
suggest that there is a strong quartic trend in both
measures of elation and depression over time. The
significant univariate results with respect to the
quadratic and cubic trends indicate that these terms might
be included in a model to describe these data, as has been
discussed earlier. The data for Table 7.12 can be derived
from BMDP4V (7-5), SAS(REG) (7-6), and SPSS(MANOVA) (7-6).
Future research might include a step-wise analysis (see
Appendix C) with the quartic trend ordered first, followed
by the quadratic, cubic, and linear trends.

H(01): $\begin{bmatrix} 1 & -1 \end{bmatrix}$ $\begin{bmatrix} u(11) & u(12) & \cdots & u(1\ 10) \\ u(21) & u(22) & \cdots & u(2\ 10) \end{bmatrix}$ $\begin{bmatrix} -2 & 2 & -1 & 1 & 0 & 0 & 0 & 0 \\ -1 & -1 & 2 & -4 & 0 & 0 & 0 & 0 \\ 0 & -2 & 0 & 6 & 0 & 0 & 0 & 0 \\ 1 & -1 & -2 & -4 & 0 & 0 & 0 & 0 \\ 2 & 2 & 1 & 1 & 0 & 0 & 0 & 0 \\ 0 & 0 & 0 & 0 & -2 & 2 & -1 & 1 \\ 0 & 0 & 0 & 0 & -1 & -1 & 2 & -4 \\ 0 & 0 & 0 & 0 & 0 & -2 & 0 & 6 \\ 0 & 0 & 0 & 0 & 1 & -1 & -2 & -4 \\ 0 & 0 & 0 & 0 & 2 & 2 & 1 & 1 \end{bmatrix}$ $= \begin{bmatrix} 0 & 0 & 0 & 0 & 0 & 0 & 0 & 0 \end{bmatrix}$

H(A1): $\begin{bmatrix} 1 & -1 \end{bmatrix}$ $\begin{bmatrix} u(11) & u(12) & \cdots & u(1\ 10) \\ u(21) & u(22) & \cdots & u(2\ 10) \end{bmatrix}$ $\begin{bmatrix} -2 & 2 & -1 & 1 & 0 & 0 & 0 & 0 \\ -1 & -1 & 2 & -4 & 0 & 0 & 0 & 0 \\ 0 & -2 & 0 & 6 & 0 & 0 & 0 & 0 \\ 1 & -1 & -2 & -4 & 0 & 0 & 0 & 0 \\ 2 & 2 & 1 & 1 & 0 & 0 & 0 & 0 \\ 0 & 0 & 0 & 0 & -2 & 2 & -1 & 1 \\ 0 & 0 & 0 & 0 & -1 & -1 & 2 & -4 \\ 0 & 0 & 0 & 0 & 0 & -2 & 0 & 6 \\ 0 & 0 & 0 & 0 & 1 & -1 & -2 & -4 \\ 0 & 0 & 0 & 0 & 2 & 2 & 1 & 1 \end{bmatrix}$ $\neq \begin{bmatrix} 0 & 0 & 0 & 0 & 0 & 0 & 0 & 0 \end{bmatrix}$

H(02): $\begin{bmatrix} 1 & 1 \end{bmatrix}$ $\begin{bmatrix} u(11) & u(12) & \cdots & u(1\ 10) \\ u(21) & u(22) & \cdots & u(2\ 10) \end{bmatrix}$ $\begin{bmatrix} -2 & 2 & -1 & 1 & 0 & 0 & 0 & 0 \\ -1 & -1 & 2 & -4 & 0 & 0 & 0 & 0 \\ 0 & -2 & 0 & 6 & 0 & 0 & 0 & 0 \\ 1 & -1 & -2 & -4 & 0 & 0 & 0 & 0 \\ 2 & 2 & 1 & 1 & 0 & 0 & 0 & 0 \\ 0 & 0 & 0 & 0 & -2 & 2 & -1 & 1 \\ 0 & 0 & 0 & 0 & -1 & -1 & 2 & -4 \\ 0 & 0 & 0 & 0 & 0 & -2 & 0 & 6 \\ 0 & 0 & 0 & 0 & 1 & -1 & -2 & -4 \\ 0 & 0 & 0 & 0 & 2 & 2 & 1 & 1 \end{bmatrix}$ $= \begin{bmatrix} 0 & 0 & 0 & 0 & 0 & 0 & 0 & 0 \end{bmatrix}$

H(A2): $\begin{bmatrix} 1 & 1 \end{bmatrix}$ $\begin{bmatrix} u(11) & u(12) & \cdots & u(1\ 10) \\ u(21) & u(22) & \cdots & u(2\ 10) \end{bmatrix}$ $\begin{bmatrix} -2 & 2 & -1 & 1 & 0 & 0 & 0 & 0 \\ -1 & -1 & 2 & -4 & 0 & 0 & 0 & 0 \\ 0 & -2 & 0 & 6 & 0 & 0 & 0 & 0 \\ 1 & -1 & -2 & -4 & 0 & 0 & 0 & 0 \\ 2 & 2 & 1 & 1 & 0 & 0 & 0 & 0 \\ 0 & 0 & 0 & 0 & -2 & 2 & -1 & 1 \\ 0 & 0 & 0 & 0 & -1 & -1 & 2 & -4 \\ 0 & 0 & 0 & 0 & 0 & -2 & 0 & 6 \\ 0 & 0 & 0 & 0 & 1 & -1 & -2 & -4 \\ 0 & 0 & 0 & 0 & 2 & 2 & 1 & 1 \end{bmatrix}$ $\neq \begin{bmatrix} 0 & 0 & 0 & 0 & 0 & 0 & 0 & 0 \end{bmatrix}$

Figure 7.2   Statistical Hypotheses for Doubly Multivariate Analysis

$$H(03): \begin{bmatrix} 1 & -1 \end{bmatrix} \begin{bmatrix} u(11) & u(12) & \cdots & u(1\ 10) \\ u(21) & u(22) & \cdots & u(2\ 10) \end{bmatrix} \begin{bmatrix} 1 & 0 \\ 1 & 0 \\ 1 & 0 \\ 1 & 0 \\ 1 & 0 \\ 0 & 1 \\ 0 & 1 \\ 0 & 1 \\ 0 & 1 \\ 0 & 1 \end{bmatrix} = \begin{bmatrix} 0 & 0 \end{bmatrix}$$

$$H(A3): \begin{bmatrix} 1 & -1 \end{bmatrix} \begin{bmatrix} u(11) & u(12) & \cdots & u(1\ 10) \\ u(21) & u(22) & \cdots & u(2\ 10) \end{bmatrix} \begin{bmatrix} 1 & 0 \\ 1 & 0 \\ 1 & 0 \\ 1 & 0 \\ 1 & 0 \\ 0 & 1 \\ 0 & 1 \\ 0 & 1 \\ 0 & 1 \\ 0 & 1 \end{bmatrix} \neq \begin{bmatrix} 0 & 0 \end{bmatrix}$$

Figure 7.2 (cont.)

Table 7.12
Doubly Multivariate Analysis of Variance
for the Social Orientation Study

| Source of Variation[1] | Multivariate | | | Variable | Univariate F(Probability) | | | |
|---|---|---|---|---|---|---|---|---|
| | Wilks' Lambda | Df | F(Probability) | | Linear | Quadratic | Cubic | Quartic |
| Days | .08 | 8,10 | 14.06*(.000) | Elation | 3.76(.069) | 5.09*(.038) | 8.10*(.011) | 42.62*(.000) |
| | | | | Depression | 3.03(.100) | 20.28*(.000) | 8.24*(.011) | 28.56*(.000) |
| Days by Socior | .79 | 8,10 | .32(.939) | Elation | .05(.834) | .83(.376) | .02(.902) | .46(.508) |
| | | | | Depression | .04(.838) | .19(.667) | .02(.894) | .00(.984) |
| | | | | | Elation | | Depression | |
| Socior[2] | .61 | 2,16 | 5.22*(.018) | | 8.63*(.009) | | 10.24(.005) | |

[1] The SSCP matrices for this table would be put into an appendix due to their size. Because the packages use different algorithms for this mode, they all yield different sums of squares and products matrices for Days and Days by Socior, i.e., see BMDP4v (7-5), SAS(REG) (7-6) and SPSS (MANOVA) (7-6). All of these matrices will yield the same overall multivariate tests, but only the diagonal elements from SPSS(MANOVA) may be used to compute the univariate tests shown here.

[2] The results for this source of variation are the same as that found for the univariate-multivariate approach.

*Significant at p<.05.

## Summary

In this chapter we have presented an introduction to repeated measures designs, and, through examples, we have illustrated the two different modes of analyzing these designs. The examples considered here consisted of the single group design, and the two group design with five repeated measures. The univariate analyses were those for mixed models and consisted of a two-way analysis and split-plot analysis for the single and two group examples, respectively. The multivariate analyses were also performed on the same single and two group data, in this mode; however, the nature of the dependent variables allowed for more detailed post hoc univariate tests. These univariate and multivariate analyses were juxtaposed in their presentation in order to demonstrate the differences and similarities of these modes of analysis.

## Other Designs

Repeated measures factors may be found in combination with any of the designs that we have discussed in the earlier chapters, and with many designs which space prohibits us from discussing. Here we mention some of these designs and helpful references.

Carlson (1981), Carlson and Timm (1980), Ceurvorst and Stock (1978), Davidson (1980), and Delaney and Maxwell (1981) discuss the problems in using covariates on the repeated measures. Davidson (1980) also discusses problems in using the multivariate mode of analysis with certain counterbalanced designs. Winer (1971, pp. 539-603) presents many examples (e.g. three factor designs with one and two repeated measures factors) of complex repeated measures designs.

## Notes

[1]This section was written by Robert S. Barcikowski and edited by Chuck Rich.

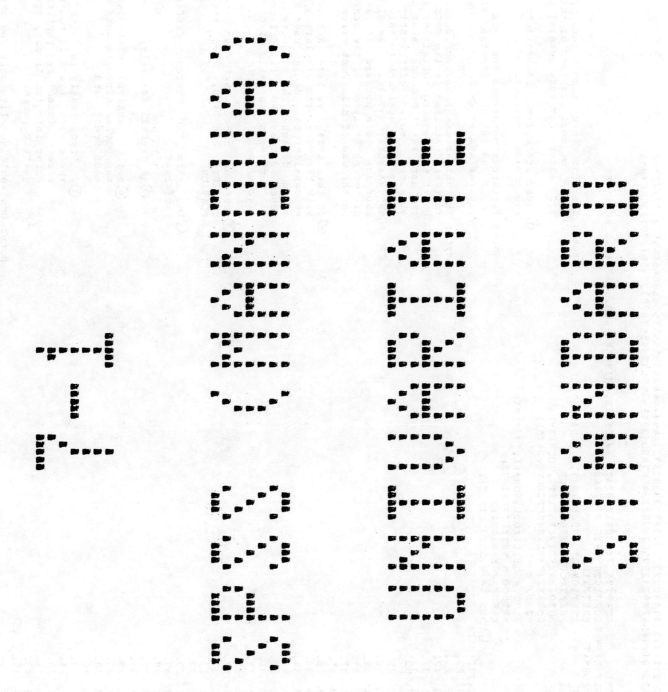

```
②③ RUN NAME        CHAPTER 7:  UNIVARIATE ANALYSIS, SINGLE GROUP REPEATED MEASURES
③ VARIABLE LIST   SUBJECTS DAYS ELATION
④ INPUT FORMAT    FREEFIELD
④⑤ MANOVA         ELATION BY SUBJECTS(1,10) DAYS(1,5)/
                   PRINT=CELLINFO(MEANS)
                   HOMOGENEITY(BARTLETT,COCHRAN)
                   OMEANS(TABLES(SUBJECTS,DAYS))
                   PCBS/
                   PLOT = CELLPLOTS,NORMAL,STEMLEAF/
                   METHOD = SSTYPE(UNIQUE)/
                   ERROR = RESIDUAL/
           ⑧⑤  DESIGN = SUBJECTS DAYS/
       READ INPUT DATA
           1   1  20.
           1   2  42.
           1   3  42.
           1   4  32.
           1   5  32.
           2   1  67.
           2   2  29.
           2   3  56.
           2   4  39.
           2   5  41.
           3   1  37.
           3   2  25.
           3   3  28.
           3   4  31.
           3   5  34.
           4   1  42.
           4   2  38.
           4   3  36.
           4   4  19.
           4   5  35.
           5   1  57.
           5   2  32.
           5   3  21.
           5   4  30.
           5   5  29.
           6   1  39.
           6   2  38.
           6   3  54.
           6   4  31.
           6   5  28.
           7   1  43.
           7   2  20.
           7   3  46.
           7   4  42.
           7   5  31.
           8   1  35.
           8   2  34.
           8   3  43.
           8   4  35.
           8   5  42.
           9   1  41.
           9   2  23.
           9   3  51.
```

Note: The SPSS input annotations provided here are of value for most problems of this type. Consult the SPSS manual for more general information.

① These are column identifiers and are not part of the program content.

Note: Further annotations for this input and output can be found in the program I/O for SPSS(MANOVA), program number 2-10.

Note: The univariate approach described in this I/O is further described in the SPSS manual (1981, p.48) under the heading "Obtaining a Univariate Analysis the Hard Way," because most of the output can be obtained more efficiently through MANOVA's multivariate approach to this problem, e.g., see SPSS(MANOVA) (7-3). We display the univariate approach here because it allows us to present different analyses of the same data, and to focus on the use of different error terms.

② In this design we have a single group of subjects with five measures of elation on each subject. If we consider the design used here to be a two-way mixed design with subjects a random factor and repeated measures a fixed factor, then the sources of variation in this I/O may be easier to understand.

③ Here we named the two independent variables SUBJECTS and DAYS, and the dependent variable ELATION.

④ In this I/O three different analyses are performed:

⑤ an overall analysis,

⑥ a trend analysis with planned contrasts where the pooled error is used as the error to test each trend, and

⑦ a trend analysis with planned contrasts, where each trend is tested using individual errors found by partitioning the overall error into its linear, quadratic, cubic, and quartic parts.

Note: One would usually only run one of these analyses for any given problem, we present them together for illustrative purposes.

```
 9   4   27.
 9   5   30.
10   1   39.
10   2   24.
10   3   35.
10   4   26.
10   5   32.
END INPUT DATA
```

④⑥⑦ MANOVA    ELATION BY SUBJECTS(1,10)  DAYS(1,5) /
            PARTITION(DAYS) /
            CONTRAST(DAYS) = POLYNOMIAL/
⑥⑧ METHOD = SSTYPE(UNIQUE)/
⑨ DESIGN = SUBJECTS  DAYS(1)  DAYS(2)  DAYS(3)  DAYS(4)/
⑦ DESIGN = DAYS(1) VS 1 DAYS(1) BY SUBJECTS = 1
           DAYS(2) VS 2 DAYS(2) BY SUBJECTS = 2
           DAYS(3) VS 3 DAYS(3) BY SUBJECTS = 3
           DAYS(4) VS 4 DAYS(4) BY SUBJECTS = 4/

```
①00000000011111111112222222222333333333344444444445555555555666666666677777777778
   12345678901234567890123456789012345678901234567890123456789012345678901234567890
```

⑧ This error specification is optional here because the program will automatically take the error to be the residual when there is only one subject per cell. Indeed it does just this in the first DESIGN statement in the second call of MANOVA.

⑨ In this DESIGN statement individual errors are selected by partitioning the overall error. For example, the linear trend, DAYS(1) is tested using the linear part of the error, here denoted by 1. The 1 represents the interaction of the linear part of DAYS with SUBJECTS.

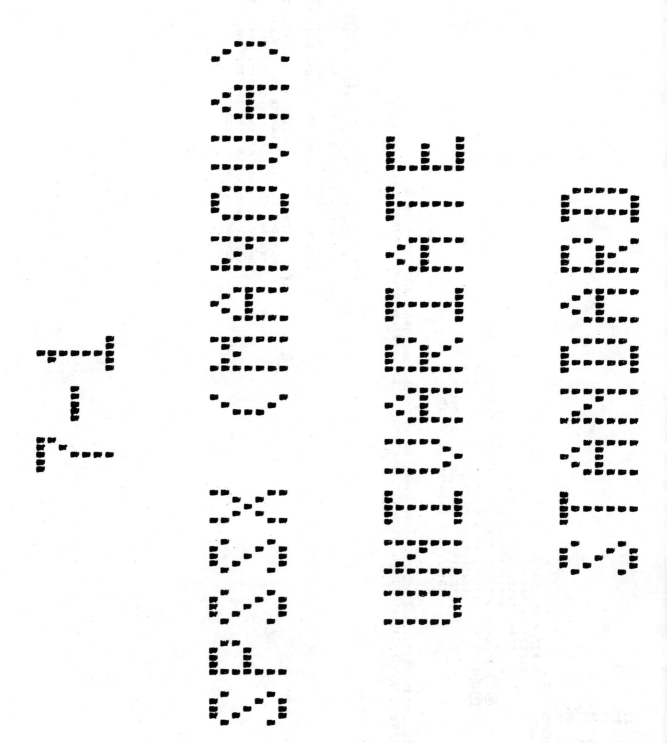

```
0000000000111111111122222222223333333333444444444455555555556666666666777777777778
1234567890123456789012345678901234567890123456789012345678901234567890123456789 0
```

① UNNUMBERED
TITLE   CHAPTER 7:   UNIVARIATE ANALYSIS, SINGLE GROUP REPEATED MEASURES
② DATA LIST LIST/ SUBJECTS DAYS ELATION
MANOVA      ELATION BY SUBJECTS(1,10) DAYS(1,5)/
            PRINT=CELLINFO(MEANS)
            HOMOGENEITY(BARTLETT,COCHRAN)
            OMEANS(TABLES(SUBJECTS,DAYS))
            POBS/
            PLOT = CELLPLOTS,NORMAL,STEMLEAF/
            METHOD = SSTYPE(UNIQUE)/
            ERROR = RESIDUAL/
            DESIGN = SUBJECTS DAYS/
BEGIN DATA
③
END DATA
MANOVA      ELATION BY SUBJECTS(1,10) DAYS(1,5)/
            PARTITION(DAYS)/
            CONTRAST(DAYS) = POLYNOMIAL/
            METHOD = SSTYPE(UNIQUE)/
            DESIGN = SUBJECTS DAYS(1) DAYS(2) DAYS(3) DAYS(4)/
            DESIGN = DAYS(1) VS 1 DAYS(1) BY SUBJECTS = 1
                     DAYS(2) VS 2 DAYS(2) BY SUBJECTS = 2
                     DAYS(3) VS 3 DAYS(3) BY SUBJECTS = 3
                     DAYS(4) VS 4 DAYS(4) BY SUBJECTS = 4/

```
0000000000111111111122222222223333333333444444444455555555556666666666777777777778
1234567890123456789012345678901234567890123456789012345678901234567890123456789 0
```

① At our installation the default (NUMBERED) instruction allowed SPSSX to read only 72 columns. We therefore used the UNNUMBERED command to allow SPSSX to read all 80 columns. The default may vary by installation.

② If a title is more than 60 characters, only the first 60 characters are printed.

③ The data go here.

619

* * * * * * * * * * * * * * * A N A L Y S I S   O F   V A R I A N C E * * * * * * * * * * * * * * * * * * * * * * * *

COMBINED OBSERVED MEANS FOR SUBJECTS

VARIABLE -- ELATION

SUBJECTS

| 1 | WGT. | 29.40000 |
| | UNWGT. | 29.40000 |
| 2 | WGT. | 46.40000 |
| | UNWGT. | 46.40000 |
| 3 | WGT. | 31.00000 |
| | UNWGT. | 31.00000 |
| 4 | WGT. | 34.00000 |
| | UNWGT. | 34.00000 |
| 5 | WGT. | 33.80000 |
| | UNWGT. | 33.80000 |
| 6 | WGT. | 38.00000 |
| | UNWGT. | 38.00000 |
| 7 | WGT. | 36.40000 |
| | UNWGT. | 36.40000 |
| 8 | WGT. | 37.80000 |
| | UNWGT. | 37.80000 |
| 9 | WGT. | 34.40000 |
| | UNWGT. | 34.40000 |
| 10 | WGT. | 31.20000 |
| | UNWGT. | 31.20000 |

COMBINED OBSERVED MEANS FOR DAYS

VARIABLE -- ELATION

DAYS

| 1 | WGT. | 42.00000 |

* * * * * * * * * * * * * * * A N A L Y S I S   O F   V A R I A N C E * * * * * * * * * * * * * * * * * * * * * *

COMBINED OBSERVED MEANS FOR DAYS        (CONT.)

VARIABLE -- ELATION    (CONT.)

|   | | UNWGT. | 42.00000 |
|---|---|---|---|
| 2 | WGT.   | 28.40000 |
|   | UNWGT. | 28.40000 |
| 3 | WGT.   | 41.20000 |
|   | UNWGT. | 41.20000 |
| 4 | WGT.   | 31.20000 |
|   | UNWGT. | 31.20000 |
| 5 | WGT.   | 33.40000 |
|   | UNWGT. | 33.40000 |

CORRESPONDENCE BETWEEN EFFECTS AND COLUMNS OF BETWEEN-SUBJECTS DESIGN

| STARTING COLUMN | ENDING COLUMN | EFFECT NAME |
|---|---|---|
| 1  | 1  | CONSTANT |
| 2  | 10 | SUBJECTS |
| 11 | 14 | DAYS |

621

\* \* \* \* \* \* \* \* \* \* \* \* \* \* \* \* \* A N A L Y S I S   O F   V A R I A N C E \* \* \* \* \* \* \* \* \* \* \* \* \* \* \* \* \* \* \* \*

TESTS OF SIGNIFICANCE FOR ELATION USING UNIQUE SUMS OF SQUARES

SOURCE OF VARIATION (1)

| | SUM OF SQUARES | DF | MEAN SQUARE | F | SIG. OF F |
|---|---|---|---|---|---|
| RESIDUAL | 2524.08000 | 36 | 70.11333 | | |
| CONSTANT | 62092.88000 | 1 | 62092.88000 | 885.60730 | 0.0 |
| SUBJECTS | 1063.92000 | 9 | 118.21333 | 1.68603 | .129 |
| DAYS | 1477.12000 | 4 | 369.28000 | 5.26690 | (2) .002 |

ESTIMATES FOR ELATION

CONSTANT

| PARAMETER | COEFF. | STD. ERR. | T-VALUE | SIG. OF T | LOWER .95 CL | UPPER .95 CL |
|---|---|---|---|---|---|---|
| 1 | 35.2400000000 | 1.18417 | 29.75915 | 0.0 | 32.83838 | 37.64162 |

SUBJECTS

| PARAMETER | COEFF. | STD. ERR. | T-VALUE | SIG. OF T | LOWER .95 CL | UPPER .95 CL |
|---|---|---|---|---|---|---|
| 2 | -5.8400000000 | 3.55252 | -1.64390 | .109 | -13.04485 | 1.36485 |
| 3 | 11.1600000000 | 3.55252 | 3.14143 | .003 | 3.95515 | 18.36485 |
| 4 | -4.2400000000 | 3.55252 | -1.19352 | .240 | -11.44485 | 2.96485 |
| 5 | -1.2400000000 | 3.55252 | -.34905 | .729 | -8.44485 | 5.96485 |
| 6 | -1.4400000000 | 3.55252 | -.40535 | .688 | -8.64485 | 5.76485 |
| 7 | 2.7600000000 | 3.55252 | .77691 | .442 | -4.44485 | 9.96485 |
| 8 | 1.1600000000 | 3.55252 | .32653 | .746 | -6.04485 | 8.36485 |
| 9 | 2.5600000000 | 3.55252 | .72062 | .476 | -4.64485 | 9.76485 |
| 10 | -.8400000000 | 3.55252 | -.23645 | .814 | -8.04485 | 6.36485 |

DAYS

| PARAMETER | COEFF. | STD. ERR. | T-VALUE | SIG. OF T | LOWER .95 CL | UPPER .95 CL |
|---|---|---|---|---|---|---|
| 11 | 6.7600000000 | 2.36835 | 2.85431 | .007 | 1.95677 | 11.56323 |
| 12 | -6.8400000000 | 2.36835 | -2.88809 | .007 | -11.64323 | -2.03677 |
| 13 | 5.9600000000 | 2.36835 | 2.51652 | .016 | 1.15677 | 10.76323 |
| 14 | -4.0400000000 | 2.36835 | -1.70583 | .097 | -8.84323 | -.76323 |

(1) The information in the ANOVA source table shown here may be used to construct an overall ANOVA table, see Table 7.4.

(2) Here we find a significant difference between the measures of elation taken on different days (p<.002).

* * * * * * * * * * * * * * * A N A L Y S I S   O F   V A R I A N C E * * * * * * * * * * * * * * * *

TESTS OF SIGNIFICANCE FOR ELATION USING UNIQUE SUMS OF SQUARES (3)

SOURCE OF VARIATION (4)

| | SUM OF SQUARES | DF | MEAN SQUARE | F | SIG. OF F |
|---|---|---|---|---|---|
| RESIDUAL | 2524.08000 | 36 | 70.11333 | | |
| CONSTANT | 62092.88000 | 1 | 62092.88000 | 885.60730 | 0.0 |
| SUBJECTS | 1063.92000 | 9 | 118.21333 | 1.68603 | .129 |
| DAYS(1) | 207.36000 | 1 | 207.36000 | 2.95750 | .094 |
| DAYS(2) | 55.31429 | 1 | 55.31429 | .78893 | .380 |
| DAYS(3) | 201.64000 | 1 | 201.64000 | 2.87592 | .099 |
| DAYS(4) | 1012.80571 | 1 | 1012.80571 | 14.44527 | .001 (5) |

ESTIMATES FOR ELATION

CONSTANT

| PARAMETER | COEFF. | STD. ERR. | T-VALUE | SIG. OF T | LOWER .95 CL | UPPER .95 CL |
|---|---|---|---|---|---|---|
| 1 | 35.24000000000 | 1.18417 | 29.75915 | 0.0 | 32.83838 | 37.64162 |

SUBJECTS

| PARAMETER | COEFF. | STD. ERR. | T-VALUE | SIG. OF T | LOWER .95 CL | UPPER .95 CL |
|---|---|---|---|---|---|---|
| 2 | -5.84000000000 | 3.55252 | -1.64390 | .109 | -13.04485 | 1.36485 |
| 3 | 11.16000000000 | 3.55252 | 3.14143 | .003 | 3.95515 | 18.36485 |
| 4 | -4.24000000000 | 3.55252 | -1.19352 | .240 | -11.44485 | 2.96485 |
| 5 | -1.24000000000 | 3.55252 | -.34905 | .729 | -8.44485 | 5.96485 |
| 6 | -1.44000000000 | 3.55252 | -.40535 | .688 | -8.64485 | 5.76485 |
| 7 | 2.76000000000 | 3.55252 | .77691 | .442 | -4.44485 | 9.96485 |
| 8 | 1.16000000000 | 3.55252 | .32653 | .746 | -6.04485 | 8.36485 |
| 9 | 2.56000000000 | 3.55252 | .72062 | .476 | -4.64485 | 9.76485 |
| 10 | -.84000000000 | 3.55252 | -.23645 | .814 | -8.04485 | 6.36485 |

DAYS(1)

| PARAMETER | COEFF. | STD. ERR. | T-VALUE | SIG. OF T | LOWER .95 CL | UPPER .95 CL |
|---|---|---|---|---|---|---|
| 11 | -4.55367988306 | 2.64789 | -1.71974 | .094 | -9.92385 | .81649 |

(3) The information in this ANOVA source table may be used to construct a planned ANOVA table, see Table 7.3.

(4) This overall error term is used to test each trend. Although it yields a more powerful test than the use of individual errors, it requires that the circularity assumption be met, and provides statistical tests that are not independent of one another.

(5) Here we find a significant quartic trend over DAYS (p<.001).

\* \* \* \* \* \* \* \* \* \* \* \* \* \* \* \* \* \* \* A N A L Y S I S  O F  V A R I A N C E \* \* \* \* \* \* \* \* \* \* \* \* \* \* \* \* \* \* \*

TESTS OF SIGNIFICANCE FOR ELATION USING UNIQUE SUMS OF SQUARES

| SOURCE OF VARIATION ⑥ | SUM OF SQUARES | DF | MEAN SQUARE | F | SIG. OF F |
|---|---|---|---|---|---|
| ⑦ RESIDUAL | 1063.92000 | 9 | 118.21333 | | |
| CONSTANT | 62092.88000 | 1 | 62092.88000 | 525.26122 | 0.0 |
| ⑦ ERROR 1 | 690.64000 | 9 | 76.73778 | | |
| DAYS(1) | 207.36000 | 1 | 207.36000 | 2.70219 | .135 |
| ⑦ ERROR 2 | 730.68571 | 9 | 81.18730 | | |
| DAYS(2) | 55.31429 | 1 | 55.31429 | .68132 | .430 |
| ⑦ ERROR 3 | 561.36000 | 9 | 62.37333 | | |
| DAYS(3) | 201.64000 | 1 | 201.64000 | 3.23279 | .106 |
| ⑦ ERROR 4 | 541.39429 | 9 | 60.15492 | | |
| DAYS(4) | 1012.80571 | 1 | 1012.80571 | 16.83662 | ⑧ .003 |

⑥ The information in the ANOVA source table shown here may be used to construct a planned ANOVA table, see Table 7.3.

ESTIMATES FOR ELATION

CONSTANT

| PARAMETER | COEFF. | STD. ERR. | T-VALUE | SIG. OF T | LOWER .95 CL | UPPER .95 CL |
|---|---|---|---|---|---|---|
| 1 | 35.24000000000 | 1.53762 | 22.91858 | 0.0 | 31.76167 | 38.71833 |

DAYS(1)

| PARAMETER | COEFF. | STD. ERR. | T-VALUE | SIG. OF T | LOWER .95 CL | UPPER .95 CL |
|---|---|---|---|---|---|---|
| 2 | -4.5536798306 | 2.77016 | -1.64383 | .135 | -10.82021 | 1.71285 |

DAYS(2)

| PARAMETER | COEFF. | STD. ERR. | T-VALUE | SIG. OF T | LOWER .95 CL | UPPER .95 CL |
|---|---|---|---|---|---|---|
| 12 | 2.3518989288 | 2.84934 | .82542 | .430 | -4.09375 | 8.79755 |

DAYS(3)

| PARAMETER | COEFF. | STD. ERR. | T-VALUE | SIG. OF T | LOWER .95 CL | UPPER .95 CL |
|---|---|---|---|---|---|---|
| 22 | -4.4904342774 | 2.49747 | -1.79800 | .106 | -10.14009 | 1.15922 |

⑦ In this analysis the error terms are found by partitioning the error (RESIDUAL) into its linear, quadratic, cubic and quartic parts. Use of these individual error terms is preferred by many statisticians (Gatio and Wiley, 1966, pp. 83-84; Rouanet and Lepine, 1970).

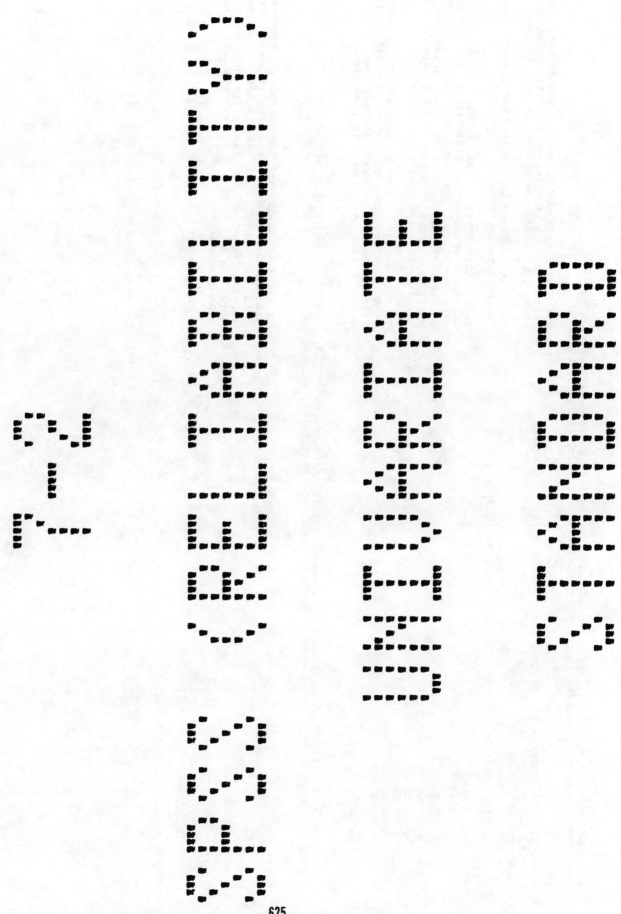

Note: The SPSS input annotations provided here are of value for most problems of this type. Consult the SPSS manual for more general information.

```
RUN NAME       CHAPTER 7: MANOVA, SINGLE GROUP REPEATED MEASURES
VARIABLE LIST  DAY1 DAY2 DAY3 DAY4 DAY5
INPUT FORMAT   FIXED(2X,5F3.0)
N OF CASES     10
RELIABILITY    VARIABLES = DAY1 TO DAY5/ SCALE(ELATION) = DAY1 TO DAY5
STATISTICS     1,10,12
READ INPUT DATA
20 21 42 32 32
67 29 56 39 41
37 25 28 31 34
42 38 36 19 35
57 32 21 30 29
39 38 54 31 28
43 20 46 42 31
35 34 43 35 42
41 23 51 27 30
39 24 35 26 32
```

① These are column identifiers and are not part of the program content.

Note: SPSS(RELIABILITY) was primarily written to calculate measures of reliability for multiple-item additive scales. However, subprogram RELIABILITY also provides both univariate and multivariate statistics for a single group repeated measures analysis.

② In this design we have a single group of subjects with five measures of elation on each subject. Here we decided to name the measures of elation taken on each day as DAY1 through DAY5.

③ On the STATISTICS card the number 1 requests that the mean and standard deviation for each level of DAYS be printed; the 10 requests a univariate repeated measures analysis; and the 12 requests Hotelling's T² for the multivariate repeated measures analysis.

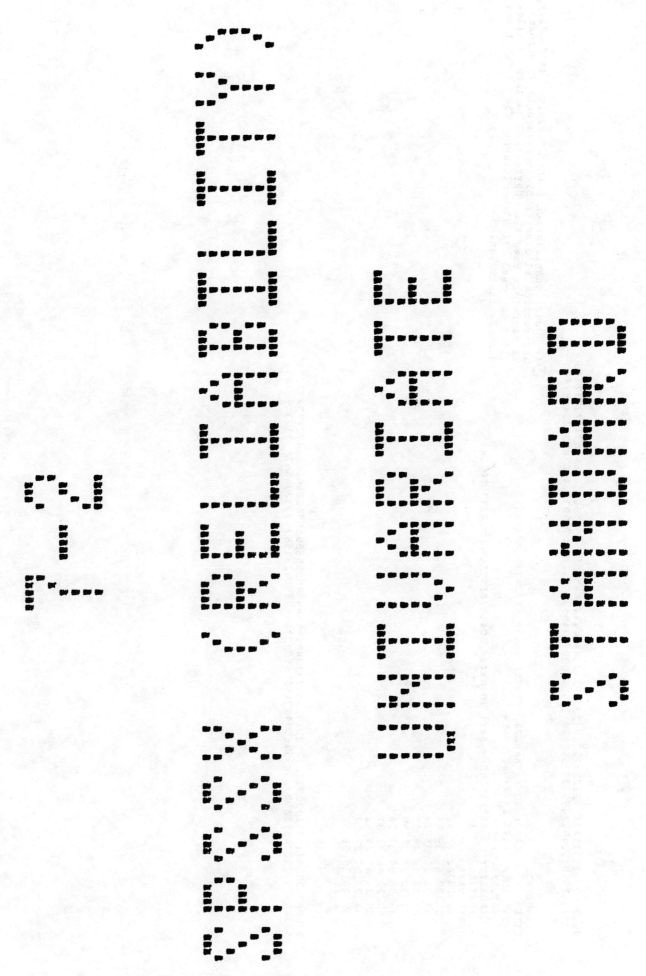

```
00000000011111111112222222222333333333344444444445555555555666666666677777777778
12345678901234567890123456789012345678901234567890123456789012345678901234567890
```

① UNNUMBERED
TITLE        CHAPTER 7:  MANOVA, SINGLE GROUP REPEATED MEASURES
DATA LIST/ DAY1 DAY2 DAY3 DAY4 DAY5
      (2X,5F3.0)
RELIABILITY      VARIABLES = DAY1 TO DAY5/ SCALE(ELATION) = DAY1 TO DAY5
STATISTICS      1,10,12
BEGIN DATA
20 21 42 32 32
67 29 56 39 41
37 25 28 31 34
42 38 36 19 35
57 32 21 30 29
39 38 54 31 28
43 20 46 42 31
35 34 43 35 42
41 23 51 27 30
39 24 35 26 32
END DATA

```
00000000011111111112222222222333333333344444444445555555555666666666677777777778
12345678901234567890123456789012345678901234567890123456789012345678901234567890
```

① At our installation the default (NUMBERED) instruction allowed SPSSX to read only 72 columns. We therefore used the UNNUMBERED command to allow SPSSX to read all 80 columns. The default may vary by installation.

FILE   NCNAME   (CREATION DATE = 02/02/83)

* * * * * * * * R E L I A B I L I T Y   A N A L Y S I S   F O R   S C A L E   ( E L A T I O N ) * * * * * * * * *

|    |      | MEANS | STD DEV | CASES |
|----|------|-------|---------|-------|
| 1. | DAY1 |       |         |       |
| 2. | DAY2 |       |         |       |
| 3. | DAY3 |       |         |       |
| 4. | DAY4 |       |         |       |
| 5. | DAY5 |       |         |       |

|    |      | MEANS    | STD DEV  | CASES |
|----|------|----------|----------|-------|
| 1. | DAY1 | 42.00000 | 12.59630 | 10.0  |
| 2. | DAY2 | 28.40000 | 6.78561  | 10.0  |
| 3. | DAY3 | 41.20000 | 11.32156 | 10.0  |
| 4. | DAY4 | 31.20000 | 6.56252  | 10.0  |
| 5. | DAY5 | 33.40000 | 4.76562  | 10.0  |

\# OF CASES =   10.0

(1)        ANALYSIS OF VARIANCE  (2)

| SOURCE OF VARIATION | SS         | DF | MEAN SQUARE | F       | PROBABILITY      |
|---------------------|------------|----|-------------|---------|------------------|
| BETWEEN PEOPLE      | 1063.92000 | 9  | 118.21333   |         |                  |
| WITHIN PEOPLE       | 4001.20000 | 40 | 100.03000   |         |                  |
| BETWEEN MEASURES    | 1477.12000 | 4  | 369.28000   | 5.26690 | (3) 0.00191      |
| RESIDUAL            | 2524.08000 | 36 | 70.11333    |         |                  |
| TOTAL               | 5065.12000 | 49 | 103.36980   |         |                  |

GRAND MEAN =   35.24000

(4) HOTELLINGS T-SQUARED = (5) 29.20114        F =   4.86686  (6)
DEGREES OF FREEDOM ** NUMERATOR = 4    DENOMINATOR= 6    PROBABILITY = 0.04306

RELIABILITY COEFFICIENTS         5 ITEMS
ALPHA = 0.40689       STANDARDIZED ITEM ALPHA =   0.44391

(1) If we consider the univariate design used here to be a two-way mixed design with subjects a random factor and repeated measures a fixed factor, then the univariate sources of variation in this I/O may be easier to understand.

(2) The information in the ANOVA source table shown here may be used to construct an overall ANOVA table, see Table 7.4.

(3) Here we find a significant difference between the measures of elation taken on different days ($p < .00191$).

(4) In the multivariate mode we have a single group of subjects with four dependent variables on each subject. These dependent variables result from automatic transformations done on the original five measures of elation.

(5) Hotelling's $T^2$ is the overall multivariate test of the null hypothesis that the vector of mean differences is equal to the null vector. At the .05 level of significance, we reject the latter null hypothesis, and conclude that there are differences between the measures of elation taken on different days. (Note that in this example the univariate test is more powerful.)

(6) This output does not provide all of the information shown in Table 7.7, however the F statistic and its probability are the same as those shown in Table 7.7.

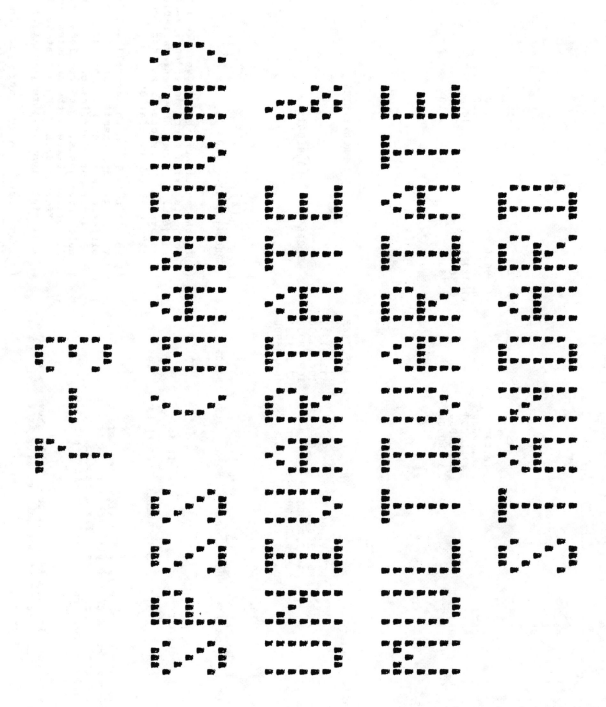

Note: The SPSS input annotations provided here are of value for most problems of this type. Consult the SPSS manual for more general information.

Note: Further annotations for this input and output can be found in the program I/O for SPSS(MANOVA), program numbered 2-10.

② In this design we have a single group of subjects with five measures of elation on each subject. Here we decided to name the measures of elation taken on each day as DAY1 through DAY5.

③ In this I/O two different approaches to the same analyses are performed:

④ one using the standard approach described in the SPSS manual (1981, pp. 50-51), and

⑤ one using transformation matrices.

⑥ Both of these approaches yield both univariate and multivariate analyses of these data. However, one would usually only run one of these analyses for any given problem, we present them together for illustrative purposes.

⑦ The WSFACTOR (within subjects factor) subcommand indicates that there is one occasions factor named DAYS and that this factor has 5 levels (5 repeated measures).

⑧ Here we request orthogonal polynomial contrasts on the occasions factor DAYS.

⑨ The WSDESIGN (within subjects design) subcommand specifies the design on the within subjects factor, just as the DESIGN subcommand would specify the design on a between subjects factor.

⑩ In the SIGNIF subcommand the specification AVERF requests that the univariate repeated measures statistics be compiled from the multivariate matrices. This results in an overall univariate test of DAYS.

⑪ The ANALYSIS subcommand with the specification REPEATED indicates that a repeated measures analysis is requested.

⑫ The RENAME subcommand is recommended as a means of identifying the repeated measures effects after transformation by the orthogonal polynomials. Here the first variable, MEAN, represents the grand mean across the repeated measures; the second variable, LINEAR, represents the linear trend, etc.

```
① 0000000001111111111222222222233333333334444444444555555555566666666667777777778
  1234567890123456789012345678901234567890123456789012345678901234567890123456789 0

② RUN NAME       CHAPTER 7: MANOVA, SINGLE GROUP REPEATED MEASURES
  VARIABLE LIST  DAY1 DAY2 DAY3 DAY4 DAY5
  INPUT FORMAT   FIXED(2X,5F3.0)
③ ④ ⑥ N OF CASES   10
  MANOVA         DAY1 TO DAY5/
           ⑦    WSFACTOR = DAYS (5)/
           ⑧    CONTRAST(DAYS) = POLYNOMIAL/
           ⑨    WSDESIGN = DAYS/
                PRINT=CELLINFO(MEANS,SSCP,COV,COR)
                  HOMOGENEITY(BARTLETT,COCHRAN,BOXM)
           ⑩     SIGNIF(HYPOTH,STEPDOWN AVERF)
                  DISCRIM(RAW,STAN,ESTIM,COR,ROTATE(VARIMAX),ALPHA(1.0))
                  ERROR(SSCP,COV,COR,STDV)
                  POBS/
                PLOT = CELLPLOTS,BOXPLOTS,STEMLEAF,ZCORR,POBS/
           ⑪    ANALYSIS(REPEATED)/
           ⑫    RENAME = MEAN LINEAR QUADRATIC CUBIC QUARTIC

  READ INPUT DATA
     20 21 42 32 32
     67 29 56 39 41
     37 25 28 31 34
     42 38 36 19 35
     57 32 21 30 29
     39 38 54 31 28
     43 20 46 42 31
     35 34 43 35 42
     41 23 51 27 30
     39 24 35 26 32
③ ⑤ ⑥ ⑬ MANOVA    DAY1 TO DAY5/
           ⑭    TRANSFORM = POLYNCMIAL/
           ⑮    RENAMF = MEAN LINEAR QUADRATIC CUBIC QUARTIC/
           ⑯    ANALYSIS = LINEAR TO QUARTIC/
```

```
① 0000000001111111111222222222233333333334444444444555555555566666666667777777778
  1234567890123456789012345678901234567890123456789012345678901234567890123456789 0
```

⑬ In the second call to MANOVA we illustrate how the multivariate repeated measures analysis can be performed using the TRANSFORM subcommand.

⑭ The data matrix is first transformed by post multiplying it by the transpose of the orthogonal polynomial matrix (this orthogonal polynomial matrix is displayed in the output). This creates contrast variables corresponding to the grand mean and each trend.

⑮ The resultant variables are then renamed using the RENAME subcommand.

⑯ A traditional single-group multivariate analysis is then performed on the contrast variables of interest. Note that we are not interested in whether or not the grand mean is equal to zero, and so the variable MEAN is not included in the analysis.

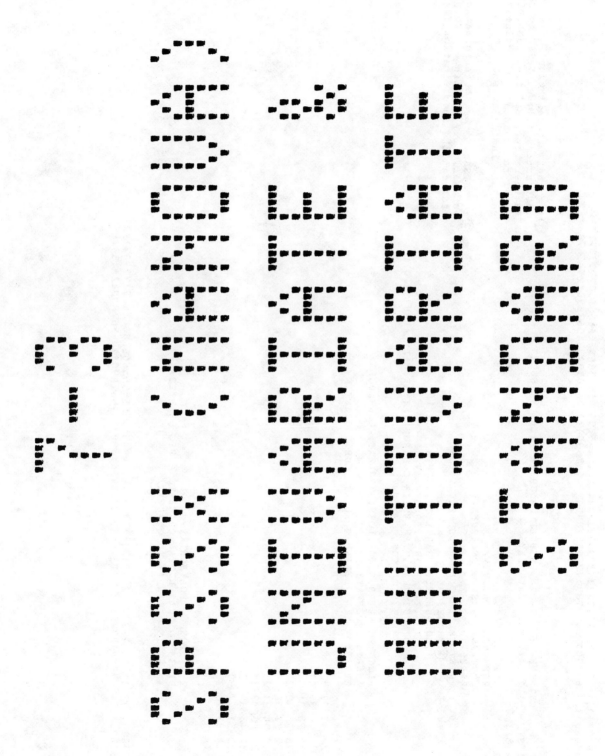

```
00000000001111111111222222222233333333334444444444555555555566666666667777777778
12345678901234567890123456789012345678901234567890123456789012345678901234567890
① UNNUMBERED
  TITLE     CHAPTER 7:  MANOVA, SINGLE GROUP REPEATED MEASURES
  DATA LIST/ DAY1 DAY2 DAY3 DAY4 DAY5
            (2X,5F3.0)
  MANOVA    DAY1 TO DAY5/
            WSFACTOR = DAYS(5)/
            CONTRAST(DAYS) = POLYNOMIAL/
            WSDESIGN = DAYS/
            PRINT=CELLINFO(MEANS,SSCP,COV,COR)
②           TRANSFORM
            HOMOGENEITY(BARTLETT,COCHRAN,BOXM)
            SIGNIF(HYPOTH,STEPDOWN AVERF)
            DISCRIM(RAW,STAN,ESTIM,COR,ROTATE(VARIMAX),ALPHA(1.0))
            ERROR(SSCP,COV,COR,STDV)
            POBS/
            PLOT = CELLPLOTS,BOXPLOTS,STEMLEAF,ZCORR,POBS/
            ANALYSIS(REPEATED)/
            RENAME = MEAN LINEAR QUADRATC CUBIC QUARTIC/

BEGIN DATA
  20 21 42 32 32
  67 29 56 39 41
  37 25 28 31 34
  42 38 36 19 35
  57 32 21 30 29
  39 38 54 31 28
  43 20 46 42 31
  35 34 43 35 42
  41 23 51 27 30
  39 24 35 26 32
END DATA
  MANOVA    DAY1 TO DAY5/
            TRANSFORM = POLYNCMIAL/
            RENAME = MEAN LINEAR QUADRATIC CUBIC QUARTIC/
            ANALYSIS = LINEAR TO QUARTIC/

00000000001111111111222222222233333333334444444444555555555566666666667777777778
12345678901234567890123456789012345678901234567890123456789012345678901234567890
```

* * * * * * * * * * * * * * * * * * * * A N A L Y S I S   O F   V A R I A N C E * * * * * * * * * * * * * * * * * * * * *

CELL MEANS AND STANDARD DEVIATIONS

VARIABLE -- DAY1

|  | MEAN | STD. DEV. | N | 95 PERCENT CONF. INTERVAL |
|---|---|---|---|---|
| FOR ENTIRE SAMPLE | 42.00000 | 12.59630 | 10 | 32.98916   51.01084 |

VARIABLE -- DAY2

|  | MEAN | STD. DEV. | N | 95 PERCENT CONF. INTERVAL |
|---|---|---|---|---|
| FOR ENTIRE SAMPLE | 28.40000 | 6.78561 | 10 | 23.54587   33.25413 |

VARIABLE -- DAY3

|  | MEAN | STD. DEV. | N | 95 PERCENT CONF. INTERVAL |
|---|---|---|---|---|
| FOR ENTIRE SAMPLE | 41.20000 | 11.32156 | 10 | 33.10105   49.29895 |

VARIABLE -- DAY4

|  | MEAN | STD. DEV. | N | 95 PERCENT CONF. INTERVAL |
|---|---|---|---|---|
| FOR ENTIRE SAMPLE | 31.20000 | 6.56252 | 10 | 26.50546   35.89454 |

VARIABLE -- DAY5

|  | MEAN | STD. DEV. | N | 95 PERCENT CONF. INTERVAL |
|---|---|---|---|---|
| FOR ENTIRE SAMPLE | 33.40000 | 4.76562 | 10 | 29.99088   36.80912 |

CHAPTER 7: MANOVA, SINGLE GROUP REPEATED MEASURES

* * * * * * * * * * * * * * * * * * * * A N A L Y S I S   O F   V A R I A N C E * * * * * * * * * * * * * * * * * * * * * * *

02/02/83          PAGE   10

ORTHONORMALIZED TRANSFORMATION MATRIX (TRANSPOSED)

|   | 1 | 2 | 3 | 4 | 5 |
|---|---|---|---|---|---|
| 1 | .44721 | -.63246 | .53452 | -.31623 | -.11952 |
| 2 | .44721 | -.31623 | -.26726 | .63246 | -.47809 |
| 3 | .44721 | 0.-0 | -.53452 | 0.-0 | -.71714 |
| 4 | .44721 | -.31623 | -.26726 | -.63246 | -.47809 |
| 5 | .44721 | .63246 | .53452 | .31623 | -.11952 |

(1) This matrix of orthogonal polynomial coefficients is post multiplied times the data matrix to form the variables for the repeated measures analyses.

CORRESPONDENCE BETWEEN EFFECTS AND COLUMNS OF BETWEEN-SUBJECTS DESIGN

| STARTING COLUMN | ENDING COLUMN | EFFECT NAME |
|---|---|---|
| 1 | 1 | CONSTANT |

ORDER OF VARIABLES FOR ANALYSIS

| VARIATES | COVARIATES | NOT USED |
|---|---|---|
| MEAN |  | LINEAR |
|  |  | QUADRATC |
|  |  | CUBIC |
|  |  | QUARTIC |

1 DEPENDENT VARIABLE
0 COVARIATES
4 VARIABLES NOT USED

\* \* \* \* \* \* \* \* \* \* \* \* \* \* \* \* \* \* \*A N A L Y S I S   O F   V A R I A N C E \* \* \* \* \* \* \* \* \* \* \* \* \* \* \* \* \* \* \*

ORDER OF VARIABLES FOR ANALYSIS (CCNT.)

VARIATES     COVARIATES     NOT USED

4 DEPENDENT VARIABLES
0 COVARIATES
1 VARIABLE NOT USED

WITHIN CELLS CORRELATIONS WITH STD. DEVS. ON DIAGONAL

|  | LINEAR | QUADRATC | CUBIC | QUARTIC |
|---|---|---|---|---|
| LINEAR | 8.76001 | | | |
| QUADRATC | -.59591 | 9.01040 | | |
| CUBIC | -.07712 | -.16276 | 7.89768 | |
| QUARTIC | -.07738 | -.51960 | -.24322 | 7.75596 |

② The Bartlett and F(max) tests are used together to determine if the sphericity index is equal to 1. See Bock (1975, pp. 459-460) for a discussion of these tests, and Timm (1975, pp. 253-260) for a discussion of a single test that is frequently used in the literature for the same purpose. Rogan, Keselman and Mendoza (1979, p. 281) indicate that these tests are 'sensitive to departures from multivariate normality and from their respective null hypotheses,' and are therefore not worth doing. However, one must decide on the value of these tests given one's particular situation.

DETERMINANT =       -.33319
② BARTLETT TEST OF SPHERICITY =   7.51006 WITH 6 D. F. ④
 SIGNIFICANCE =      -.276    ③

② F(MAX) CRITERION =    1.34964 WITH (4,9) D. F.

③ Here we find that the sphericity index does not differ significantly from 1, and so one may perform the univariate analysis.

WITHIN CELLS VARIANCES AND CCVARIANCES

|  | LINEAR | QUADRATC | CUBIC | QUARTIC |
|---|---|---|---|---|
| LINEAR | 76.73778 | | | |
| QUADRATC | -47.03565 | 81.18730 | | |
| CUBIC | 5.33556 | -11.58237 | 62.37333 | |
| QUARTIC | 5.25707 | -36.31161 | -14.89852 | 60.15492 |

④ Note that Bartlett's sphericity test is of no value in this program unless the transformation matrix is orthonormalized. This matrix is orthonormalized here because we are using an orthogonal polynomial transformation matrix, but care must be used when considering other transformation matrices.

* * * * * * * * * * * * * * * * * * A N A L Y S I S   O F   V A R I A N C E * * * * * * * * * * * * * * * * * * * * * * * * * * *

WITHIN CELLS SUM-OF-SQUARES AND CROSS-PRODUCTS

|  | LINEAR | QUADRATC | CUBIC | QUARTIC |
|---|---|---|---|---|
| LINEAR | (5) 690.64000 | | | |
| QUADRATC | -423.32086 | 730.68571 | | |
| CUBIC | 48.02000 | -104.24133 | 561.36000 | |
| QUARTIC | 47.31359 | -326.80453 | -134.08668 | 541.39429 |

(5) This matrix would be placed in the overall multivariate analysis of variance table, see Table 7.7.

* * * * * * * * * * * * * * * * * * A N A L Y S I S   O F   V A R I A N C E * * * * * * * * * * * * * * * * * *

EFFECT .. DAYS
ADJUSTED HYPOTHESIS SUM-OF-SQUARES AND CROSS-PRODUCTS

⑥ This matrix would be placed in the overall multivariate analysis of variance table, see Table 7.7.

|          | LINEAR ⑥   | QUADRATC   | CUBIC      | QUARTIC     |
|----------|-----------|-----------|-----------|------------|
| LINEAR   | 207.36000 |           |           |            |
| QUADRATC | -107.09795 | 55.31429 |           |            |
| CUBIC    | -204.48000 | -105.61048 | 201.64000 |          |
| QUARTIC  | -458.27436 | 236.69099 | -451.90944 | 1012.80571 |

MULTIVARIATE TESTS OF SIGNIFICANCE (S = 1, M = 1, N = 2)

⑦ Here we find a significant multivariate difference between the measures of elation taken on different days (p<.043).

| TEST NAME  | VALUE   | APPROX. F | HYPOTH. DF | ERROR DF | SIG. OF F |
|------------|---------|-----------|------------|----------|-----------|
| PILLAIS    | .76440  | 4.86686   | 4.00       | 6.00     | .043 ⑦    |
| HOTELLINGS | 3.24457 | 4.86686   | 4.00       | 6.00     | .043      |
| WILKS      | .23560  | 4.86686   | 4.00       | 6.00     | .043      |
| ROYS       | .76440  |           |            |          |           |

EIGENVALUES AND CANONICAL CORRELATIONS

| ROOT NO. | EIGENVALUE | PCT.      | CUM. PCT. | CANON. CCR. |
|----------|------------|-----------|-----------|-------------|
| 1        | 3.24457    | 100.00000 | 100.00000 | .87430      |

DIMENSION REDUCTION ANALYSIS

| ROOTS  | WILKS LAMBDA | F       | HYPOTH. DF | ERROR DF | SIG. OF F |
|--------|--------------|---------|------------|----------|-----------|
| 1 TO 1 | .23560       | 4.86686 | 4.00       | 6.00     | .043      |

EFFECT .. DAYS   (8)   (CONT.)

(8) The information in this ANOVA source table may be used to construct a planned ANOVA table, see Table 7.3.

UNIVARIATE F-TESTS WITH (1,9) D. F.

| VARIABLE | HYPOTH. SS | ERROR SS | HYPOTH. MS | ERROR MS | F | SIG. OF F |
|---|---|---|---|---|---|---|
| LINEAR | 207.36000 | 690.64000 | 207.36000 | 76.73778 | 2.70219 | .135 |
| QUADRATC | 55.31429 | 730.68571 | 55.31429 | 81.18730 | .68132 | .430 |
| CUBIC | 201.64000 | 561.36000 | 201.64000 | 62.37333 | 3.23279 | .106 |
| QUARTIC | 1012.80571 | 541.39429 | 1012.80571 | 60.15492 | 16.83662 | (10) .003 |

Note: In SPSSX the Avereged F-Test has been moved so that it follows the Correlations Between Dependent and Canonical Variables (not shown here).

(9) ERROR MS column: 76.73778, 81.18730, 62.37333, 60.15492

AVERAGED F-TEST WITH (4,36) D. F.

| | HYPOTH. SS | ERROR SS | HYPOTH. MS | ERROR MS | F | SIG. OF F |
|---|---|---|---|---|---|---|
| (11) (AVER.) | 1477.12000 | 2524.08000 | 369.28000 | 70.11333 | 5.26690 | .002 |

ROY-BARGMAN STEPDOWN F - TESTS

| VARIABLE | HYPOTH. MS | ERROR MS | STEP-DOWN F | HYPOTH. DF | ERROR DF | SIG. OF F |
|---|---|---|---|---|---|---|
| LINEAR | 207.36000 | 76.73778 | 2.70219 | 1 | 9 | .135 |
| QUADRATC | 1.48377 | 58.90193 | .02519 | 1 | 8 | .878 |
| CUBIC | 138.06018 | 78.02072 | 1.76953 | 1 | 7 | .225 |
| QUARTIC | 459.31541 | 47.91846 | 9.58535 | 1 | 6 | .021 |

RAW DISCRIMINANT FUNCTION COEFFICIENTS

| | FUNCTION NO. | 1 |
|---|---|---|

| VARIABLE | 1 |
|---|---|
| LINEAR | .01322 |
| QUADRATC | .09741 |
| CUBIC | .01273 |
| QUARTIC | .15870 |

(9) In this analysis the error terms are found by partitioning the overall error into its linear, quadratic, cubic and quartic parts. Use of these individual error terms is preferred by many statisticians (Gatio and Wiley, 1966, pp. 83-84: Rouanet and Lepine, 1970).

(10) Here we find a significant quartic trend over DAYS (p<.003).

(11) This is the overall univariate test of significant differences on the occasions factor, DAYS. The sums of squares for this test are found by summing the diagonal elements of the error and hypotheses sums of squares and cross products matrices. Here we have a significant difference between the measures of elation taken on each day (p<.002).

\* \* \* \* \* \* \* \* \* \* \* \* \* \* \* \* \* \*A N A L Y S I S   O F   V A R I A N C E\* \* \* \* \* \* \* \* \* \* \* \* \* \* \* \* \* \*

EFFECT .. CONSTANT    (12)

MULTIVARIATE TESTS OF SIGNIFICANCE (S = 1, M = 1, N = 2)

| TEST NAME | VALUE | APPROX. F | HYPOTH. DF | ERROR DF | SIG. OF F |
|---|---|---|---|---|---|
| PILLAIS | .76440 | 4.86686 | 4.00 | 6.00 | .043 |
| HOTELLINGS | 3.24457 | 4.86686 | 4.00 | 6.00 | .043 |
| WILKS | .23560 | 4.86686 | 4.00 | 6.00 | .043 |
| ROYS | .76440 | | | | |

- - - - - - - - - - - - - - - -

EIGENVALUES AND CANONICAL CORRELATIONS

| ROOT NO. | EIGENVALUE | PCT. | CUM. PCT. | CANON. COR. |
|---|---|---|---|---|
| 1 | 3.24457 | 100.00000 | 100.00000 | .87430 |

- - - - - - - - - - - - - - - -

DIMENSION REDUCTION ANALYSIS

| ROOTS | WILKS LAMBDA | F | HYPOTH. DF | ERROR DF | SIG. OF F |
|---|---|---|---|---|---|
| 1 TO 1 | .23560 | 4.86686 | 4.00 | 6.00 | .043 |

- - - - - - - - - - - - - - - -

UNIVARIATE F-TESTS WITH (1,9) D. F.

| VARIABLE | HYPOTH. SS | ERROR SS | HYPOTH. MS | ERROR MS | F | SIG. OF F |
|---|---|---|---|---|---|---|
| LINEAR | 207.36000 | 690.64000 | 207.36000 | 76.73778 | 2.70219 | .135 |
| QUADRATC | 55.31429 | 730.68571 | 55.31429 | 81.18730 | .68132 | .430 |
| CUBIC | 201.64000 | 561.36000 | 201.64000 | 62.37333 | 3.23279 | .106 |
| QUARTIC | 1012.80571 | 541.39429 | 1012.80571 | 60.15492 | 16.83662 | .003 |

- - - - - - - - - - - - - - - -

(12) This output is from the second call to MANOVA where we created orthogonal polynomial contrasts using the TRANSFORM subcommand. It yields the same multivariate and univariate tests as before, but under the effect for the CONSTANT (grand mean).

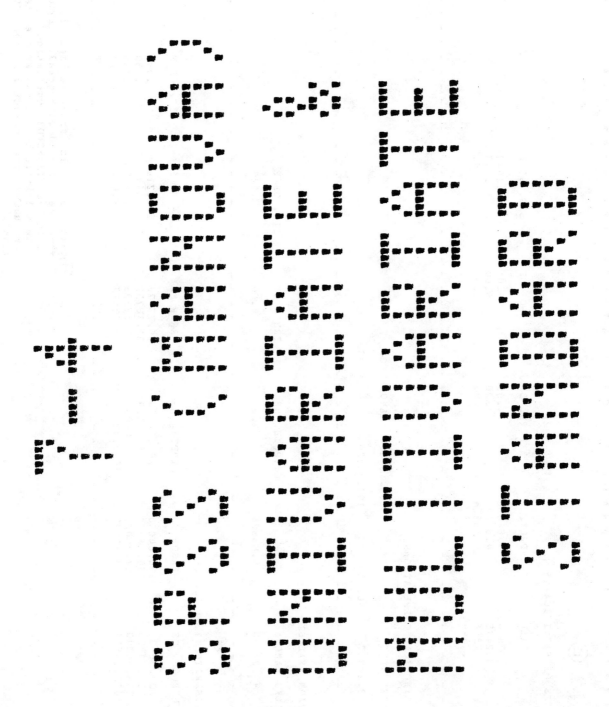

```
RUN NAME       CHAPTER 7:  MANOVA, ONE FACTOR (2 GROUPS) REPEATED MEASURES
VARIABLE LIST  SOCIOR DAY1 DAY2 DAY3 DAY4 DAY5
INPUT FORMAT   FIXED(F2.0,5F3.0)
N OF CASES     19
② MANOVA
               DAY1 TO DAY5 BY SOCIOR(1,2)/
③ ④           WSFACTOR = DAYS(5)/
               CONTRAST(DAYS) = POLYNOMIAL/
⑤             WSDESIGN = DAYS/
               PRINT=CELLINFO(MEANS,SSCP,COV,COR)
               HOMOGENEITY(BARTLETT,COCHRAN,BOXM)
⑥             SIGNIF(HYPOTH,STEPDOWN AVERF)
               OMEANS (TABLES(CONSTANT SOCIOR))
               DISCRIM(RAW,STAN,ESTIM,COR,ROTATE(VARIMAX),ALPHA(1.0))
               ERROR(SSCP,COV,COR,STDV)
               POBS/
               PLOT = CELLPLOTS,BOXPLOTS,STEMLEAF,ZCORR,POBS/
               METHOD = SSTYPE(UNIQUE)/
⑦             ANALYSIS(REPEATED)/
⑧             RENAME = MEAN LINEAR QUADRATIC CUBIC QUARTIC/
               DESIGN = SOCIOR/

READ INPUT DATA
1 20 21 42 32 32
1 67 29 56 39 41
1 37 25 28 31 34
1 42 38 36 19 35
1 57 32 21 30 29
1 39 38 54 31 28
1 43 20 46 42 31
1 35 34 43 35 42
1 41 23 51 27 30
1 39 24 35 26 32
2 47 25 36 21 27
2 53 32 48 46 54
2 38 33 42 48 49
2 60 41 67 53 50
2 37 35 45 34 46
2 59 37 52 36 52
2 67 33 61 31 50
2 43 27 36 33 32
2 64 53 62 40 43
```

**Note:** The SPSS input annotations provided here are of value for most problems of this type. Consult the SPSS manual for more general information.

① These are column identifiers and are not part of the program content.

**Note:** Further annotations for this input and output can be found in the program I/O for SPSS(MANOVA), program numbered 2-10.

② In this design we have two groups of subjects with five measures of elation on each subject. Here we decided to identify the factor levels with the variable name SOCIOR and the measures of elation taken on each day as DAY1 through DAY5.

③ The WSFACTOR (within subjects factor) subcommand indicates that there is one occasions (within subjects) factor named DAYS and that this factor has 5 levels (5 repeated measures).

④ Here we request orthogonal polynomial contrasts on the repeated measures factor DAYS.

⑤ The WSDESIGN (within subjects design) subcommand specifies the design on the within subjects factor, just as the DESIGN subcommand specifies the design on the between subjects factor.

⑥ In the SIGNIF subcommand the specification AVERF requests that the univariate repeated measures statistics be compiled from the multivariate matrices. This results in an overall univariate test of DAYS.

⑦ The ANALYSIS subcommand with the specification REPEATED indicates that a repeated measures analysis is requested.

⑧ The RENAME subcommand is recommended as a means of identifying the repeated measures effects after transformation by the orthogonal polynomials. Here the first variable, MEAN, represents the grand mean across the repeated measures; the second variable, LINEAR, represents the linear trend, etc.

① 00000000011111111112222222222333333333344444444445555555555666666666677777777778
1234567890123456789012345678901234567890123456789012345678901234567890123456789 0

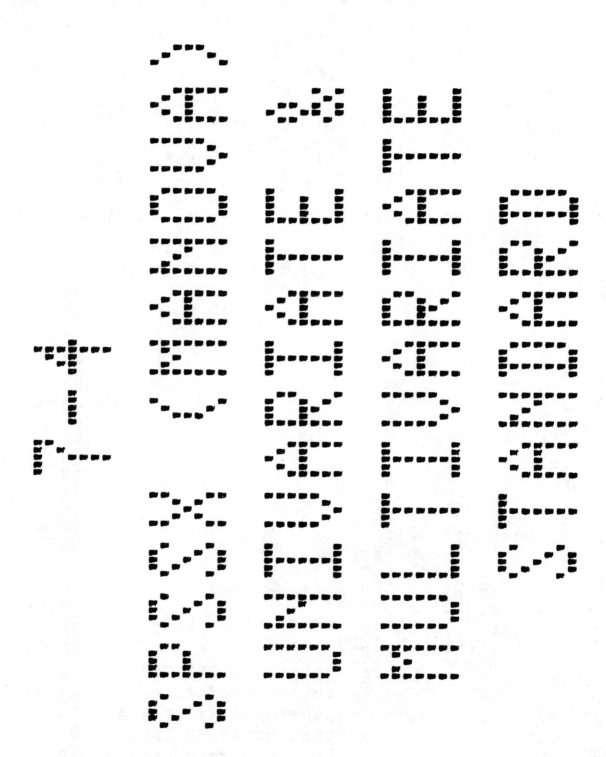

① At our installation the default (NUMBERED) instruction allowed SPSSX to read only 72 columns. We therefore used the UNNUMBERED command to allow SPSSX to read all 80 columns. The default may vary by installation.

② In SPSSX the transformation matrix is not automatically printed. To print this matrix we included the specification TRANSFORM.

```
0000000001111111111222222222233333333334444444444555555555566666666667777777778
1234567890123456789012345678901234567890123456789012345678901234567890123456789

① UNNUMBERED
  TITLE    CHAPTER 7:  MANOVA, ONE FACTOR (2 GROUPS) REPEATED MEASURES
  DATA LIST/ SOCIOR DAY1 DAY2 DAY3 DAY4 DAY5
     (F2.0,5F3.0)
  MANOVA   DAY1 TO DAY5 BY SOCIOR(1,2)/
           WSFACTOR = DAYS(5)/
           CONTRAST(DAYS) = POLYNOMIAL/
           WSDESIGN = DAYS/
           PRINT=CELLINFO(MEANS,SSCP,COV,COR)
② TRANSFORM
           HOMOGENEITY(BARTLETT,COCHRAN,BOXM)
           SIGNIF(HYPOTH,STEPDOWN AVERF)
           OMEANS (TABLES(CONSTANT SOCIOR))
           DISCRIM(RAW,STAN,ESTIM,COR,ROTATE(VARIMAX),ALPHA(1.0))
           ERROR (SSCP,COV,COR,STDV)
           POBS/
           PLOT = CELLPLOTS,BOXPLOTS,STEMLEAF,ZCORR,POBS/
           METHOD = SSTYPE(UNIQUE)/
           ANALYSIS(REPEATED)/
           RENAME = MEAN LINEAR QUADRATC CUBIC QUARTIC/
           DESIGN = SOCIOR/

BEGIN DATA
1 20 21 42 32 32
1 67 29 56 39 41
1 37 25 28 31 34
1 42 38 36 19 35
1 57 32 21 30 29
1 39 38 54 31 28
1 43 20 46 42 31
1 35 34 43 35 42
1 41 23 51 27 30
1 39 24 35 26 32
2 47 25 36 21 27
2 53 32 48 46 54
2 38 33 42 48 49
2 60 41 67 53 50
2 37 35 45 34 46
2 59 37 52 36 52
2 67 33 61 31 50
2 43 27 36 33 32
2 64 53 62 40 43
END DATA

0000000001111111111222222222233333333334444444444555555555566666666667777777778
1234567890123456789012345678901234567890123456789012345678901234567890123456789
```

645

* * * * * * * * * * * * * * * * * * A N A L Y S I S   O F   V A R I A N C E * * * * * * * * * * * * * * * * * * * *

CELL MEANS AND STANDARD DEVIATIONS

VARIABLE -- DAY1

| FACTOR | CODE | MEAN | STD. DEV. | N | 95 PERCENT CONF. INTERVAL | |
|---|---|---|---|---|---|---|
| SOCIOR | 1 | 42.00000 | 12.59630 | 10 | 32.98916 | 51.01084 |
| SOCIOR | 2 | 52.00000 | 11.23610 | 9 | 43.36318 | 60.63682 |
| FOR ENTIRE SAMPLE | | 46.73684 | 12.71850 | 19 | 40.60672 | 52.86696 |

VARIABLE -- DAY2

| FACTOR | CODE | MEAN | STD. DEV. | N | 95 PERCENT CONF. INTERVAL | |
|---|---|---|---|---|---|---|
| SOCIOR | 1 | 28.40000 | 6.78561 | 10 | 23.54587 | 33.25413 |
| SOCIOR | 2 | 35.11111 | 8.25295 | 9 | 28.76734 | 41.45488 |
| FOR ENTIRE SAMPLE | | 31.57895 | 8.07132 | 19 | 27.68870 | 35.46920 |

VARIABLE -- DAY3

| FACTOR | CODE | MEAN | STD. DEV. | N | 95 PERCENT CONF. INTERVAL | |
|---|---|---|---|---|---|---|
| SOCIOR | 1 | 41.20000 | 11.32156 | 10 | 33.10105 | 49.29895 |
| SOCIOR | 2 | 49.88889 | 11.41758 | 9 | 41.11257 | 58.66521 |
| FOR ENTIRE SAMPLE | | 45.31579 | 11.91196 | 19 | 39.57441 | 51.05717 |

VARIABLE -- DAY4

| FACTOR | CODE | MEAN | STD. DEV. | N | 95 PERCENT CONF. INTERVAL | |
|---|---|---|---|---|---|---|
| SOCIOR | 1 | 31.20000 | 6.56252 | 10 | 26.50546 | 35.89454 |
| SOCIOR | 2 | 38.00000 | 9.84886 | 9 | 30.42951 | 45.57049 |
| FOR ENTIRE SAMPLE | | 34.42105 | 8.76429 | 19 | 30.19680 | 38.64531 |

CHAPTER 7: MANOVA, ONE FACTOR (2 GROUPS) REPEATED MEASURES

02/02/83   PAGE   3

* * * * * * * * * * * * * * * * * * * * * A N A L Y S I S   O F   V A R I A N C E * * * * * * * * * * * * * * * * * * * * * * *

CELL MEANS AND STANDARD DEVIATIONS   (CONT.)

VARIABLE -- DAY5

| FACTOR | CODE | MEAN | STD. DEV. | N | 95 PERCENT CONF. INTERVAL | |
|---|---|---|---|---|---|---|
| SOCIOR | 1 | 33.40000 | 4.76562 | 10 | 29.99088 | 36.80912 |
| SOCIOR | 2 | 44.77778 | 9.31099 | 9 | 37.62073 | 51.93483 |
| FOR ENTIRE SAMPLE | | 38.78947 | 9.16260 | 19 | 34.37324 | 43.20570 |

UNIVARIATE HOMOGENEITY OF VARIANCE TESTS

VARIABLE -- DAY1

COCHRANS C(9,2) =   .55689, P =   .370 (APPROX.)
BARTLETT-BOX F(1,859) =   .10365, P =   .748

VARIABLE -- DAY2

COCHRANS C(9,2) =   .59665, P =   .285 (APPROX.)
BARTLETT-BOX F(1,859) =   .30671, P =   .580

VARIABLE -- DAY3

COCHRANS C(9,2) =   .50422, P =   .490 (APPROX.)
BARTLETT-BOX F(1,859) =   .00057, P =   .981

VARIABLE -- DAY4

COCHRANS C(9,2) =   .69253, P =   .121 (APPROX.)
BARTLETT-BOX F(1,859) =  1.30420, P =   .254

VARIABLE -- DAY5

COCHRANS C(9,2) =   .79241, P =   .029 (APPROX.)
BARTLETT-BOX F(1,859) =  3.44012, P =   .064

\* \* \* \* \* \* \* \* \* \* \* \* \* \* \* \* \* \* \* A N A L Y S I S   O F   V A R I A N C E \* \* \* \* \* \* \* \* \* \* \* \* \* \* \* \* \* \* \* \* \* \* \* \* \* \* \*

COMBINED OBSERVED GRAND MEANS

VARIABLE -- DAY1

|   | MEAN |   |
|---|------|---|
|   | WGT. | 46.73684 |
|   | UNWGT. | 47.00000 |

---

VARIABLE -- DAY2

|   | MEAN |   |
|---|------|---|
|   | WGT. | 31.57895 |
|   | UNWGT. | 31.75556 |

---

VARIABLE -- DAY3

|   | MEAN |   |
|---|------|---|
|   | WGT. | 45.31579 |
|   | UNWGT. | 45.54444 |

---

VARIABLE -- DAY4

|   | MEAN |   |
|---|------|---|
|   | WGT. | 34.42105 |
|   | UNWGT. | 34.60000 |

---

CHAPTER 7: MANOVA, ONE FACTOR (2 GROUPS) REPEATED MEASURES

* * * * * * * * * * * * * * * * * * *A N A L Y S I S  O F  V A R I A N C E* * * * * * * * * * * * * * * * * * * * * * * * * * * *    02/02/83    PAGE    24

VARIABLE -- DAY5

MEAN

WGT.-     38.78947
UNWGT.-   39.08889

- - - - - - - - - - - - - - - - - - - - - - - - - - - - - - - - - - - - - - - - - -

COMBINED OBSERVED MEANS FOR SCCIOR

VARIABLE -- DAY1

SCCIOR

1        WGT.-     42.00000
         UNWGT.-   42.00000

2        WGT.-     52.00000
         UNWGT.-   52.00000

- - - - - - - - - - - - - - - - - - - - - - - - - - - - - - - - - - - - - - - - - -

VARIABLE -- DAY2

SCCIOR

1        WGT.-     28.40000
         UNWGT.-   28.40000

2        WGT.-     35.11111
         UNWGT.-   35.11111

- - - - - - - - - - - - - - - - - - - - - - - - - - - - - - - - - - - - - - - - - -

VARIABLE -- DAY3

SOCIOR

649

CHAPTER 7: MANOVA, ONE FACTOR (2 GROUPS) REPEATED MEASURES

* * * * * * * * * * * * * * * * * * * A N A L Y S I S   O F   V A R I A N C E * * * * * * * * * * * * * * * * * * * * * * * * *

02/02/83          PAGE   25

VARIABLE .. DAY3      (CONT.)

```
              1        WGT.     41.20000
                       UNWGT.   41.20000

              2        WGT.     49.88889
                       UNWGT.   49.88889
```

- - - - - - - - - - - - - - - - - - - - - - - - - - - - - - - - - - - - - - - - - - -

VARIABLE .. DAY4

SOCIOR

```
              1        WGT.     31.20000
                       UNWGT.   31.20000

              2        WGT.     38.00000
                       UNWGT.   38.00000
```

- - - - - - - - - - - - - - - - - - - - - - - - - - - - - - - - - - - - - - - - - - -

VARIABLE .. DAY5

SOCIOR

```
              1        WGT.     33.40000
                       UNWGT.   33.40000

              2        WGT.     44.77778
                       UNWGT.   44.77778
```

- - - - - - - - - - - - - - - - - - - - - - - - - - - - - - - - - - - - - - - - - - -

CORRESPONDENCE BETWEEN EFFECTS AND COLUMNS OF WITHIN-SUBJECTS DESIGN

```
STARTING  ENDING
COLUMN    COLUMN    EFFECT NAME

   1        1       CONSTANT
   2        5       DAYS
```

- - - - - - - - - - - - - - - - - - - - - - - - - - - - - - - - - - - - - - - - - - -

*  *  *  *  *  *  *  *  *  *  *  *  *  *  *  *  * A N A L Y S I S   O F   V A R I A N C E *  *  *  *  *  *  *  *  *  *  *  *  *  *  *  *  *  *  *

TESTS OF SIGNIFICANCE FOR MEAN USING UNIQUE SUMS OF SQUARES

| SOURCE OF VARIATION | SUM OF SQUARES | DF | MEAN SQUARE | F | SIG. OF F |
|---|---|---|---|---|---|
| (1) WITHIN CELLS (2) | 3543.83111 | 17 | 208.46065 | | 0.0 (4) |
| CONSTANT | 148545.85310 | 1 | 148545.85310 | 712.58461 | |
| SOCIOR | 1799.07415 | 1 | 1799.07415 | (3) 8.63028 | .009 |

STANDARD DEVIATIONS FOR DEPENDENT VARIABLE MEAN

| ERROR TERM | STD. DEV. |
|---|---|
| WITHIN CELLS | 14.43817 |

ESTIMATES FOR MEAN

CONSTANT

| PARAMETER | COEFF. | STD. ERR. | T-VALUE | SIG. OF T | LOWER .95 CL | UPPER .95 CL |
|---|---|---|---|---|---|---|
| 1 | 88.5433228690 | 3.31694 | 26.69428 | 0.0 | 81.54519 | 95.54145 |

SOCIOR

| PARAMETER | COEFF. | STD. ERR. | T-VALUE | SIG. OF T | LOWER .95 CL | UPPER .95 CL |
|---|---|---|---|---|---|---|
| 2 | -9.7442873419 | 3.31694 | -2.93773 | .009 | -16.74242 | -2.74616 |

Note: The matrix of orthogonal polynomial coefficients, which is post multiplied times the data matrix to form the variables for the repeated measures analyses, is exactly the same as that shown in the previous SPSS(MANOVA) output (7-3), and is not shown here.

Note: In the univariate analysis if we consider the design used here to be a split-plot design with subjects a random factor, and occasions and groups as fixed factors, then the sources of variation in this output may be easier to understand.

(1) The information for the test on SOCIOR would be placed in the overall univariate (Table 7.6), or multivariate (Table 7.8) analysis of variance table.

(2) Here the error term (WITHIN CELLS) is the subjects within SOCIOR source of variation in the univariate design. It is used to test the SOCIOR source of variation. Here we do find a significant difference between the SOCIOR groups (p<.009).

(3) Because there are only two groups in the multivariate design, the univariate and multivariate tests of the SOCIOR effect are the same.

(4) The WITHIN CELLS error term is also used to test the null hypotheses that the grand mean is equal to zero. This test is of little interest here, since the grand mean is usually not equal to zero.

* * * * * * * * * * * * * * * * * * * * * * * * A N A L Y S I S   O F   V A R I A N C E * * * * * * * * * * * * * * * * * * * * * *

ORDER OF VARIABLES FOR ANALYSIS (CCNT.)

```
     VARIATES      COVARIATES      NOT USED

     4 DEPENDENT VARIABLES
     0 COVARIATES
     1 VARIABLE NOT USED
```

---

WITHIN CELLS CORRELATIONS WITH STD. DEVS. ON DIAGONAL

|          | LINEAR   | QUADRATC | CUBIC    | QUARTIC |
|----------|----------|----------|----------|---------|
| LINEAR   | 9.21017  |          |          |         |
| QUADRATC | -.39422  | 7.59854  |          |         |
| CUBIC    | -.03728  | -.13485  | 6.57607  |         |
| QUARTIC  | -.23749  | -.19947  | -.14622  | 7.48621 |

---

DETERMINANT =                     .65506
⑤ BARTLETT TEST OF SPHERICITY =   6.27500 WITH 6 D. F.
   SIGNIFICANCE =                 ⑥ .393

---

⑤ F(MAX) CRITERION =   1.96156 WITH (4,17) D. F.

---

WITHIN CELLS VARIANCES AND CCVARIANCES

|          | LINEAR    | QUADRATC  | CUBIC     | QUARTIC  |
|----------|-----------|-----------|-----------|----------|
| LINEAR   | 84.82719  |           |           |          |
| QUADRATC | -27.58915 | 57.73782  |           |          |
| CUBIC    | -2.25765  | -6.73837  | 43.24471  |          |
| QUARTIC  | -16.37446 | -11.34682 | -7.19822  | 56.04336 |

---

⑤ The Bartlett and F(max) tests are used together to
determine if the sphericity index is equal to 1.
See Bock (1975, pp. 459-460) for a discussion of
these tests, and Timm (1975, pp. 253-260) for a
discussion of a single test that is frequently
used in the literature for the same purpose.
Bogan, Keselman and Mendoza (1979, p. 281)
indicate that these tests are 'sensitive to
departures from multivariate normality and from
their repective null hypotheses,' and are
therefore not worth doing. However, one must

⑥ Here we find that the sphericity index does not
differ significantly from 1, and so, on the basis
of this test, we may perform the univariate
analysis.

Note: Bartlett's sphericity test is of no value in this
program unless the transformation matrix is
orthonormalized. This matrix is orthonormalized
here because we are using an orthogonal polynomial
transformation matrix, but care must be used when
considering other transformation matices.

652

************************A N A L Y S I S   O F   V A R I A N C E************************************

WITHIN CELLS SUM-OF-SQUARES AND CROSS-PRODUCTS

①            LINEAR        QUADRATC        CUBIC        QUARTIC

LINEAR     1442.06222
QUADRATC   -469.01554     981.54286
CUBIC       -38.38000    -114.55221     735.16000
QUARTIC    -278.36579    -192.89600    -122.36978     952.73714

① This matrix would be  placed  in  the  overall
  multivariate analysis of variance table, see Table
  7.8.

* * * * * * * * * * * * * * * * * * * * * A N A L Y S I S   O F   V A R I A N C E * * * * * * * * * * * * * * * * * * * * * *

EFFECT -- SOCIOR AND DAYS

(8) This matrix would be placed in the overall multivariate analysis of variance table, see Table 7.8.

ADJUSTED HYPOTHESIS SUM-OF-SQUARES AND CROSS-PRODUCTS

|  | ⑧ LINEAR | QUADRATC | CUBIC | QUARTIC |
|---|---|---|---|---|
| LINEAR | 3.83251 |  |  |  |
| QUADRATC | 13.51298 | 47.64511 |  |  |
| CUBIC | 1.61684 | 5.70079 | .68211 |  |
| QUARTIC | 9.91354 | 34.95395 | 4.18228 | 25.64331 |

⑨ MULTIVARIATE TESTS OF SIGNIFICANCE (S = 1, M = 1, N = 6)

| TEST NAME | VALUE | APPROX. F | HYPOTH. DF | ERROR DF | SIG. OF F |
|---|---|---|---|---|---|
| PILLAIS | .14700 | .60317 | 4.00 | 14.00 | .667 |
| HOTELLINGS | .17233 | .60317 | 4.00 | 14.00 | .667 ⑩ |
| WILKS | .85300 | .60317 | 4.00 | 14.00 | .667 |
| RCYS | .14700 |  |  |  |  |

EIGENVALUES AND CANONICAL CORRELATIONS

| ROOT NO. | EIGENVALUE | PCT. | CUM. PCT. | CANON. CCR. |
|---|---|---|---|---|
| 1 | .17233 | 100.00000 | 100.00000 | .38341 |

DIMENSION REDUCTION ANALYSIS

| ROOTS | WILKS LAMBDA | F | HYPOTH. DF | ERROR DF | SIG. OF F |
|---|---|---|---|---|---|
| 1 TO 1 | .85300 | .60317 | 4.00 | 14.00 | .667 |

⑨ The first test considered in this analysis should be the DAYS by SOCIOR interaction, because if this is significant we must consider each SOCIOR group separately. Here none of the significance tests (univariate or multivariate) indicate a significant interaction, so we may move on to consider the main effects.

⑩ This is the multivariate test of the days by

654

* * * * * * * * * * * * * * * * A N A L Y S I S   O F   V A R I A N C E * * * * * * * * * * * * * * * * *

EFFECT .. SOCIOR AND DAYS     (CONT.)

UNIVARIATE F-TESTS WITH (1,17) D. F.

| VARIABLE | HYPOTH. SS | ERROR SS | HYPOTH. MS | ERROR MS | F | SIG. OF F |
|---|---|---|---|---|---|---|
| LINEAR | 3.83251 | 1442.06222 | 3.83251 | 84.82719 | .04518 | .834 |
| QUADRATC | 47.64511 | 981.54286 | 47.64511 | 57.73782 | .82520 | .376 |
| CUBIC | .68211 | 735.16000 | .68211 | 43.24471 | .01577 | .902 |
| QUARTIC | 25.64331 | 952.73714 | 25.64331 | 56.04336 | .45756 | .508 |

Note: In SPSSX the Avereged F-Test has been moved so that it follows the Correlations Between Dependent and Canonical Variables (not shown here).

AVERAGED F-TEST WITH (4,68) D. F.

| | HYPOTH. SS | ERROR SS | HYPOTH. MS | ERROR MS | F | SIG. OF F |
|---|---|---|---|---|---|---|
| (11) (AVER.) | 77.80304 | 4111.50222 | 19.45076 | 60.46327 | .32170 | .863 |

ROY-BARGMAN STEPDOWN F - TESTS

| VARIABLE | HYPOTH. MS | ERROR MS | STEP-DOWN F | HYPOTH. DF | ERROR DF | SIG. OF F |
|---|---|---|---|---|---|---|
| LINEAR | 3.83251 | 84.82719 | .04518 | 1 | 17 | .834 |
| QUADRATC | 56.68976 | 51.81253 | 1.09413 | 1 | 16 | .311 |
| CUBIC | 3.85945 | 47.64479 | .08100 | 1 | 15 | .780 |
| QUARTIC | 67.27766 | 54.29423 | 1.23913 | 1 | 14 | .284 |

RAW DISCRIMINANT FUNCTION COEFFICIENTS

FUNCTION NO.

| VARIABLE | 1 |
|---|---|
| LINEAR | -.08092 |
| QUADRATC | .13681 |
| CUBIC | -.05521 |
| QUARTIC | .11123 |

Note: In a repeated measures design the planned single degree of freedom contrasts (here, for trends) yield the same results from both the univariate and multivariate analyses, see table 7.5).

(11) This is the overall univariate test of significant differences on the DAYS by SOCIOR interaction. The sums of squares for this test are found by summing the diagonal elements of the error and hypotheses sums of squares and cross products matrices. Here we have no significant difference ($p<.863$). This result is shown in Table 7.6.

* * * * * * * * * * * * * * * * * * * * * A N A L Y S I S   O F   V A R I A N C E * * * * * * * * * * * * * * * * * * * * * * * *

EFFECT .. DAYS

⑫ This matrix would be placed in the overall multivariate analysis of variance table, see Table 7.8.

ADJUSTED HYPOTHESIS SUM-OF-SQUARES AND CROSS-PRODUCTS

⑬ In the overall multivariate test we find that there is a significant difference in elation as measured on different days (see Table 7.8).

|        | ⑫ LINEAR | QUADRATC | CUBIC | QUARTIC |
|--------|----------|----------|-------|---------|
| LINEAR | 319.11673 | | | |
| QUADRATC | -306.18664 | 293.78045 | | |
| CUBIC | 334.41684 | -320.86682 | 350.45053 | |
| QUARTIC | -873.01146 | 837.63846 | -914.86818 | 2388.30797 |

MULTIVARIATE TESTS OF SIGNIFICANCE (S = 1, M = 1, N = 6)

| TEST NAME | VALUE | APPROX. F | HYPOTH. DF | ERROR DF | SIG. OF F |
|-----------|-------|-----------|------------|----------|-----------|
| PILLAIS | .77650 | 12.16016 | 4.00 | 14.00 | .000 |
| HOTELLINGS | 3.47433 | 12.16016 | 4.00 | 14.00 | .000 ⑬ |
| WILKS | .22350 | 12.16016 | 4.00 | 14.00 | .000 |
| ROYS | .77650 | | | | |

EIGENVALUES AND CANONICAL CORRELATIONS

| ROOT NO. | EIGENVALUE | PCT. | CUM. PCT. | CANON. CCR. |
|----------|------------|------|-----------|-------------|
| 1 | 3.47433 | 100.00000 | 100.00000 | .88119 |

DIMENSION REDUCTION ANALYSIS

| ROOTS | WILKS LAMBDA | F | HYPOTH. DF | ERROR DF | SIG. OF F |
|-------|--------------|---|------------|----------|-----------|
| 1 TO 1 | .22350 | 12.16016 | 4.00 | 14.00 | .000 |

\* \* \* \* \* \* \* \* \* \* \* \* \* \* \* \* \* \* A N A L Y S I S   O F   V A R I A N C E \* \* \* \* \* \* \* \* \* \* \* \* \* \* \* \* \* \*

EFFECT .. DAYS        (CONT.)

UNIVARIATE F-TESTS WITH (1,17) D. F.

(14)

| VARIABLE | HYPOTH. SS | ERROR SS | HYPOTH. MS | ERROR MS | F | SIG. OF F |
|---|---|---|---|---|---|---|
| LINEAR | 319.11673 | 1442.06222 | 319.11673 | 84.82719 | 3.76196 | .069 |
| QUADRATC | 293.78045 | 981.54286 | 293.78045 | 57.73782 | 5.08818 | .038 |
| CUBIC | 350.45053 | 735.16000 | 350.45053 | 43.24471 | 8.10389 | .011 |
| QUARTIC | 2388.30797 | 952.73714 | 2388.30797 | 56.04336 | 42.61536 | .000 |

(15) near ERROR MS column     (16) near SIG. OF F

Note: In SPSSX the Avereged F-Test has been moved so
that it follows the Correlations Between Dependent
and Canonical Variables (not shown here).

AVERAGED F-TEST WITH (4,68) D. F.

(17)

| VARIABLE | HYPOTH. SS | ERROR SS | HYPOTH. MS | ERROR MS | F | SIG. OF F |
|---|---|---|---|---|---|---|
| (AVER.) | 3351.65567 | 4111.50222 | 837.91392 | 60.46327 | 13.85823 | .000 |

ROY-BARGMAN STEPDOWN F - TESTS

| VARIABLE | HYPOTH. MS | ERROR MS | STEP-DOWN F | HYPOTH. DF | ERROR DF | SIG. OF F |
|---|---|---|---|---|---|---|
| LINEAR | 319.11673 | 84.82719 | 3.76196 | 1 | 17 | .069 |
| QUADRATC | 105.10910 | 51.81253 | 2.02864 | 1 | 16 | .174 |
| CUBIC | 221.51573 | 47.64479 | 4.64932 | 1 | 15 | .048 |
| QUARTIC | 1126.52989 | 54.29423 | 20.74861 | 1 | 14 | .000 |

RAW DISCRIMINANT FUNCTION COEFFICIENTS

FUNCTION NO.

| VARIABLE | 1 |
|---|---|
| LINEAR | .02063 |
| QUADRATC | -.07166 |
| CUBIC | -.02226 |
| QUARTIC | .13114 |

(14) In a repeated measures design the planned single degree of freedom contrasts (here, for trends) yield the same results from both the univariate and multivariate analyses (see Table 7.5).

(15) In the trend analysis the error terms are found by partitioning the error (the interaction) into its linear, quadratic, cubic, and quartic parts. Use of these individual error terms is preferred by most statisticians (Boik, 1978; Gatio and Wiley, 1966, pp. 83-84; Rouanet and Lepine, 1970); however, in SAS(GLM) (7-2) the unpartitioned error term is used to test each trend. These results are shown in Table 7.5.

(16) Here, given the .05 level of significance for each test, we find a significant quartic trend, as predicted, but we also find that the quadratic (p<.038) and cubic (p<.011) trends are also statistically significant. However, since these later trends were not predicted, they should be further tested with a more conservative post hoc test, such as that by Scheffe. Then if they are still significant, they might be included in a discussion of the theoretical research model.

(17) This is the overall univariate test of significant differences on the occasions factor. The sums of squares for this test are found by summing the diagonal elements of the error and hypotheses sums of squares and cross products matrices. Here we have a significant difference between the measures of elation taken on each day (p<.000).

657

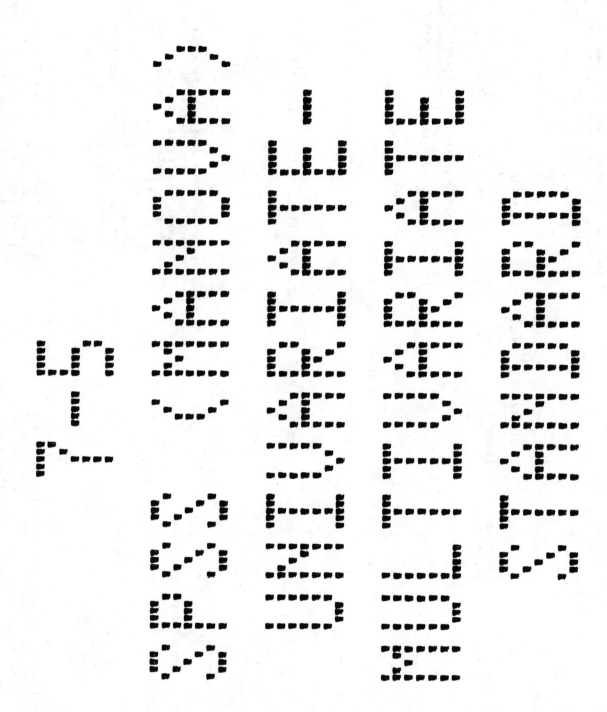

```
RUN NAME      CHAPTER 7:  MANOVA, ONE FACTOR (TWO GROUPS) REPEATED MEASURES
VARIABLE LIST SOCIOR SUBJECTS DAYS ELATION DEPRESS
INPUT FORMAT  FREEFIELD
② MANOVA       ELATION DEPRESS BY SOCIOR(1,2) SUBJECTS(1,10) DAYS(1,5) /
              PRINT=CELLINFO(MEANS,SSCP,COV,COR)
                    HOMOGENEITY(BARTLETT,COCHRAN,BOXM)
                    SIGNIF(HYPOTH,STEPDOWN)
                    OMEANS(TABLES(SOCIOR,DAYS,SOCIOR BY DAYS))
                    DISCRIM(RAW,STAN,ESTIM,COR,ROTATE(VARIMAX),ALPHA(1.0))
                    ERROR(SSCP,COV,COR,STDV)
                    POBS/
              PLOT = CELLPLOTS,STEMLEAF,ZCORR,POBS/
              METHOD = SSTYPE(UNIQUE)/
③ ERROR = RESIDUAL/
④ DESIGN = SOCIOR VS 1, SUBJECTS WITHIN SOCIOR = 1,
                    DAYS, SOCIOR BY DAYS/

READ INPUT DATA
1 1 20 30
1 2 21 35
1 3 42 20
1 4 32 27
1 5 32 22
2 1 67 43
2 2 29 50
2 3 56 35
2 4 39 37
2 5 41 26
3 1 37 15
3 2 25 29
3 3 28 16
3 4 31 35
3 5 34 25
4 1 42 31
4 2 38 46
4 3 36 27
4 4 19 32
4 5 35 28
5 1 57 40
5 2 32 59
5 3 21 28
5 4 30 37
5 5 29 23
6 1 39 22
6 2 38 37
6 3 54 33
6 4 31 29
6 5 28 35
7 1 43 24
7 2 20 29
7 3 46 28
7 4 42 26
7 5 31 30
8 1 35 32
8 2 34 56
8 3 43 44
8 4 35 52
```
(data rows prefixed with column-1 value "1" in the leftmost position)

**Note:** The SPSS input annotations provided here are of value for most problems of this type. Consult the SPSS manual for more general information.

① These are column identifiers and are not part of the program content.

**Note:** Further annotations for this input and output can be found in the program I/O for SPSS(MANOVA), program numbered 2-10.

② In this design we have two groups of subjects with five measures of elation and depression on each subject. In this I/O we analyze these data with what we have referred to in the text as the univariate-multivariate approach. This approach may be easier to understand if you consider the design used here to be a multivariate (two dependent variables) split-plot design with SUBJECTS a random factor, and DAYS and SOCIOR as fixed factors.

③ Here the RESIDUAL is the SUBJECTS within SOCIOR by DAYS interaction. This specification is optional here because the program will automatically take the error to be the residual when there is only one subject per cell.

④ In the DESIGN subcommand the error used to test the SOCIOR source of variation is 1, the SUBJECTS WITHIN SOCIOR source of variation. However, because we used the SSTYPE(UNIQUE) specification, the test for SOCIOR is not correct here, and we must repeat this design in a second call to MANOVA. This input is included here to illustrate how the design setup might look correct on the surface when, in reality, the wrong error term would be used. The other terms in the model (DAYS and SOCIOR by DAYS) will be tested correctly using the residual as the error term. The residual is used for these terms by default, since no special error term was specified in the DESIGN specification.

```
1  8  5  42  47
1  9  1  41  19
1  9  2  23  36
1  9  3  51  15
1  9  4  27  25
1  9  5  30  18
1 10  1  39  25
1 10  2  24  26
1 10  3  35  30
1 10  4  26  21
1 10  5  32  23
2  1  1  47  35
2  1  2  25  46
2  1  3  36  35
2  1  4  21  42
2  1  5  27  12
2  2  1  53  42
2  2  2  32  52
2  2  3  48  40
2  2  4  46  47
2  2  5  54  35
2  3  1  38  37
2  3  2  33  39
2  3  3  42  38
2  3  4  48  45
2  3  5  49  26
2  4  1  60  49
2  4  2  41  57
2  4  3  67  42
2  4  4  53  45
2  4  5  50  48
2  5  1  37  36
2  5  2  35  37
2  5  3  45  37
2  5  4  34  36
2  5  5  46  26
2  6  1  59  51
2  6  2  37  58
2  6  3  52  50
2  6  4  36  48
2  6  5  52  50
2  7  1  67  42
2  7  2  33  68
2  7  3  61  45
2  7  4  31  32
2  7  5  50  55
2  8  1  43  25
2  8  2  27  43
2  8  3  36  27
2  8  4  33  39
2  8  5  32  37
2  9  1  64  34
2  9  2  53  61
2  9  3  62  36
2  9  4  40  54
2  9  5  43  47
END INPUT DATA
⑤ MANOVA  ELATION DEPRESS BY SOCIOR(1,2) SUBJECTS(1,10) DAYS(1,5) /
   DESIGN = SOCIOR VS 1, SUBJECTS WITHIN SOCIOR = 1,
   DAYS, SOCIOR BY DAYS/
```

⑤ In the second call to MANOVA we eliminate the METHOD = SSTYPE(UNIQUE) subcommand so that through the DESIGN subcommand we are able to arrive at the correct test on the social orientation groups, SOCIOR.

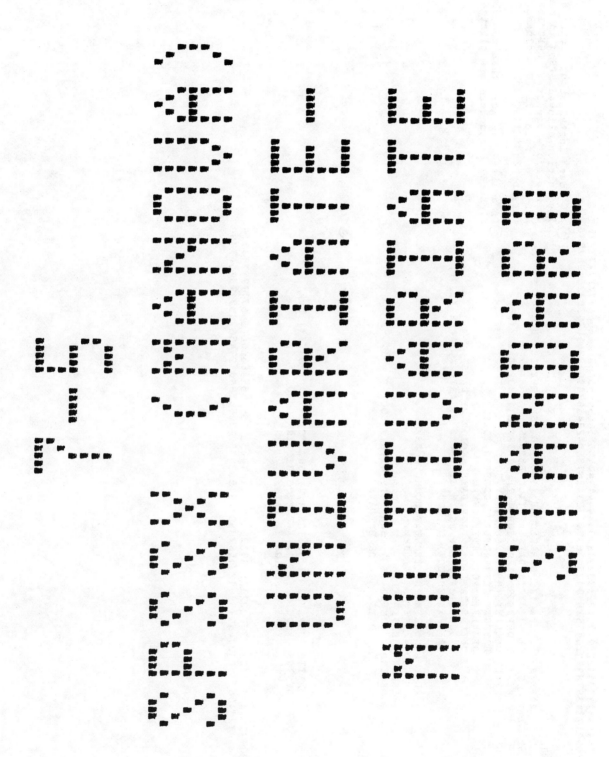

```
00000000011111111112222222222333333333344444444445555555555666666666677777777778
12345678901234567890123456789012345678901234567890123456789012345678901234567890
```

① UNNUMBERED
② TITLE      CHAPTER 7:   MANOVA, ONE FACTOR (TWO GROUPS)  REPEATED MEASURES
DATA LIST LIST/  SOCIOR SUBJECTS DAYS ELATION DEPRESS
MANOVA      ELATION DEPRESS BY SOCIOR(1,2) SUBJECTS(1,10) DAYS(1,5)/
            PRINT=CELLINFO(MEANS,SSCP,COV,COR)
               HOMOGENEITY(BARTLETT,COCHRAN,BOXM)
               SIGNIF(HYPOTH,STEPDOWN)
               OMEANS(TABLES(SOCIOR,DAYS,SOCIOR BY DAYS))
               DISCRIM(RAW,STAN,ESTIM,COR,ROTATE(VARIMAX),ALPHA(1.0))
               ERROR(SSCP,COV,COR,STDV)
               POBS/
            PLOT = CELLPLOTS,STEMLEAF,ZCORR,POBS/
            METHOD = SSTYPE(UNIQUE)/
            ERROR = RESIDUAL/
            DESIGN = SOCIOR VS 1, SUBJECTS WITHIN SOCIOR = 1,
                     DAYS, SOCIOR BY DAYS/

③ BEGIN DATA

③ The data go here.

END DATA
MANOVA      ELATION DEPRESS BY SOCIOR(1,2) SUBJECTS(1,10) DAYS(1,5)/
            DESIGN = SOCIOR VS 1, SUBJECTS WITHIN SOCIOR = 1,
                     DAYS, SOCIOR BY DAYS/

```
00000000011111111112222222222333333333344444444445555555555666666666677777777778
12345678901234567890123456789012345678901234567890123456789012345678901234567890
```

① At our installation the default  (NUMBERED)
instruction allowed SPSSX to read only 72 columns.
We therefore used the UNNUMBERED command to allow
SPSSX to read all 80 columns.  The default may
vary by installation.

② If a title is more than 60 characters,  only the
first 60 characters are printed.

* * * * * * * * * * * * * * * * * * A N A L Y S I S   O F   V A R I A N C E * * * * * * * * * * * * * * * * * *

CORRESPONDENCE BETWEEN EFFECTS AND COLUMNS OF BETWEEN-SUBJECTS DESIGN

```
STARTING   ENDING
COLUMN     COLUMN   EFFECT NAME

   3         20     SUBJECTS WITHIN SOCIOR (ERROR 1)
  21         24     DAYS
  25         28     SOCIOR BY DAYS
```

REDUNDANCIES IN DESIGN MATRIX

```
COLUMN     EFFECT

  20       SUBJECTS WITHIN SOCIOR (ERROR 1)
```

```
* * * * * * * * * * * * * * * * * * * * * * * * * *
*                                                 *
*  W A R N I N G   *  UNIQUE SUMS-OF-SQUARES ARE OBTAINED ASSUMING   *
*                  *  THE REDUNDANT EFFECTS ARE ACTUALLY NULL.       *
*                  *  DIFFERENT RECORDERINGS OF THE MODEL OR DATA     *
*                  *  MAY RESULT IN DIFFERENT UNIQUE SUMS-OF-SQUARES. *
*                  *                                                 *
* * * * * * * * * * * * * * * * * * * * * * * * * *
```

RESIDUAL  CORRELATIONS WITH STD. DEVS. ON DIAGONAL

```
           ELATION      DEPRESS

ELATION    7.77581
DEPRESS     .15011      6.77601
```

```
DETERMINANT =                      .97747
BARTLETT TEST OF SPHERICITY =     1.51564 WITH 1 D. F.
SIGNIFICANCE =                     .218
```

F(MAX) CRITERION =          1.31687 WITH (2,68) D. F.

①Because we are treating this design as a multivariate split-plot design, this test of sphericity is not appropriate.

CHAPTER 7: MANOVA, ONE FACTOR (TWO GROUPS) REPEATED MEASURES                    02/02/83          PAGE  18

* * * * * * * * * * * * * * * * * A N A L Y S I S   O F   V A R I A N C E * * * * * * * * * * * * * * * * * * * * * * *

RESIDUAL VARIANCES AND COVARIANCES

                ELATION          DEPRESS

ELATION        60.46327
DEPRESS         7.90928         45.91425

- - - - - - - - - - - - - - - - - - - - - - -

RESIDUAL SUM-OF-SQUARES AND CROSS-PRODUCTS

                ELATION          DEPRESS

ELATION      4111.50222
DEPRESS       537.83111       3122.16889

- - - - - - - - - - - - - - - - - - - - - - -

②This matrix would be placed in an overall
univariate-multivariate analysis of variance
table, see Table 7.11.

(2)

* * * * * * * * * * * * * * * * A N A L Y S I S   O F   V A R I A N C E * * * * * * * * * * * * * * * * * * * * * * * * *

COMBINED OBSERVED MEANS FOR SCCIOR
VARIABLE -- ELATION

SOCIOR

1       WGT.      35.24000
        UNWGT.    35.24000

2       WGT.      43.95556
        UNWGT.    43.95556

VARIABLE -- DEPRESS

SOCIOR

1       WGT.      31.16000
        UNWGT.    31.16000

2       WGT.      41.91111
        UNWGT.    41.91111

COMBINED OBSERVED MEANS FOR DAYS
VARIABLE -- ELATION

DAYS

1       WGT.      46.73684
        UNWGT.    46.73684

2       WGT.      31.57895
        UNWGT.    31.57895

3       WGT.      45.31579
        UNWGT.    45.31579

4       WGT.      34.42105

665

CHAPTER 7:  MANOVA, ONE FACTOR (TWO GROUPS) REPEATED MEASURES

* * * * * * * * * * A N A L Y S I S   O F   V A R I A N C E * * * * * * * * * * * * * * * * * * * * * * *     (CONT.)

02/02/83      PAGE  15

COMBINED OBSERVED MEANS FOR DAYS      (CONT.)

VARIABLE -- ELATION (CONT.)

|       |         | UNWGT. | 34.42105 |
|-------|---------|--------|----------|
| 5     | WGT.    |        | 38.78947 |
|       | UNWGT.  |        | 38.78947 |

VARIABLE -- DEPRESS

DAYS

| 1 | WGT.   | 33.26316 |
|---|--------|----------|
|   | UNWGT. | 33.26316 |
| 2 | WGT.   | 45.47368 |
|   | UNWGT. | 45.47368 |
| 3 | WGT.   | 32.94737 |
|   | UNWGT. | 32.94737 |
| 4 | WGT.   | 37.31579 |
|   | UNWGT. | 37.31579 |
| 5 | WGT.   | 32.26316 |
|   | UNWGT. | 32.26316 |

COMBINED OBSERVED MEANS FOR SOCIOR BY DAYS

VARIABLE -- ELATION

|      | SOCIOR  | 1        | 2        |
|------|---------|----------|----------|
| DAYS |         |          |          |
| 1    | WGT.    | 42.00000 | 52.00000 |
|      | UNWGT.  | 42.00000 | 52.00000 |
| 2    | WGT.    | 28.40000 | 35.11111 |
|      | UNWGT.  | 28.40000 | 35.11111 |

666

COMBINED OBSERVED MEANS FOR SCCIOR BY DAYS     (CONT.)

VARIABLE -- ELATION     (CONT.)

| 3 | WGT.   | 41.20000 | 49.88889 |
|   | UNWGT. | 41.20000 | 49.88889 |
| 4 | WGT.   | 31.20000 | 38.00000 |
|   | UNWGT. | 31.2C000 | 38.00000 |
| 5 | WGT.   | 33.40000 | 44.77778 |
|   | UNWGT. | 33.40000 | 44.77778 |

VARIABLE -- DEPRESS

|      |        | SOCIOR |          |
|------|--------|--------|----------|
| DAYS |        | 1      | 2        |
| 1 | WGT.   | 28.10000 | 39.00000 |
|   | UNWGT. | 28.10000 | 39.00000 |
| 2 | WGT.   | 40.30000 | 51.22222 |
|   | UNWGT. | 40.30000 | 51.22222 |
| 3 | WGT.   | 27.6000C | 36.88889 |
|   | UNWGT. | 27.60000 | 36.88889 |
| 4 | WGT.   | 32.10000 | 43.11111 |
|   | UNWGT. | 32.10000 | 43.11111 |
| 5 | WGT.   | 27.70000 | 37.33333 |
|   | UNWGT. | 27.70000 | 37.33333 |

CORRESPONDENCE BETWEEN EFFECTS AND COLUMNS OF BETWEEN-SUBJECTS DESIGN

| STARTING COLUMN | ENDING COLUMN | EFFECT NAME |
|-----------------|---------------|-------------|
| 1 | 1 | CCNSTANT |
| 2 | 2 | SOCIOR |

667

\* \* \* \* \* \* \* \* \* \* \* \* \* \* \* \* \* \* \* \* \* \* \* A N A L Y S I S   O F   V A R I A N C E \* \* \* \* \* \* \* \* \* \* \* \* \* \* \* \* \* \* \* \* \* \* \*

EFFECT -- SOCIOR BY DAYS

ADJUSTED HYPOTHESIS SUM-OF-SQUARES AND CROSS-PRODUCTS

③ This matrix would be placed in an overall univariate-multivariate analysis of variance table, see Table 7.11.

|  | ELATION | DEPRESS |
|---|---|---|
| ELATION | 77.80304 | |
| DEPRESS | -17.24164 | 7.85216 |

④

MULTIVARIATE TESTS OF SIGNIFICANCE (S = 2, M = 1/2, N = 32 1/2)

| TEST NAME | VALUE | APPROX. F | HYPOTH. DF | ERROR DF | SIG. OF F |
|---|---|---|---|---|---|
| PILLAIS | .02292 | .19711 | 8.00 | 136.00 | .991 |
| HOTELLINGS | .02341 | .19314 | 8.00 | 132.00 | .991 ⑤ |
| WILKS | .97710 | .19514 | 8.00 | 134.00 | .991 |
| ROYS | .02180 | | | | |

EIGENVALUES AND CANONICAL CORRELATIONS

| ROOT NO. | EIGENVALUE | PCT. | CUM. PCT. | CANON. CCR. |
|---|---|---|---|---|
| 1 | .02229 | 95.20949 | 95.20949 | .14766 |
| 2 | .00112 | 4.79051 | 100.00000 | .03347 |

DIMENSION REDUCTION ANALYSIS

| ROOTS | WILKS LAMBDA | F | HYPOTH. DF | ERROR DF | SIG. OF F |
|---|---|---|---|---|---|
| 1 TO 2 | .97710 | .19514 | 8.00 | 134.00 | .991 |
| 2 TO 2 | .99888 | .02532 | 3.00 | 135.50 | .995 |

④ The first test considered should be the DAYS by SOCIOR interaction, because if this is significant we must consider each SOCIOR group separately. Here none of the significance tests (univariate or multivariate) indicate a significant interaction, so we may move on to consider the main effects.

⑤ This is the multivariate test of the DAYS by SOCIOR interaction (see Table 7.11).

\* \* \* \* \* \* \* \* \* \* \* \* \* \* \* \* \* \* \* \* \* \* \* A N A L Y S I S   O F   V A R I A N C E \* \* \* \* \* \* \* \* \* \* \* \* \* \* \* \* \* \* \* \* \* \*

EFFECT .. SOCIOR BY DAYS          (CONT.)

UNIVARIATE F-TESTS WITH (4,68) D. F.

| VARIABLE | HYPOTH. SS | ERROR SS | HYPOTH. MS | ERROR MS | F | SIG. OF F |
|---|---|---|---|---|---|---|
| ELATION | 77.80304 | 4111.50222 | 19.45076 | 60.46327 | .32170 | .863 |
| DEPRESS | 7.85216 | 3122.16889 | 1.96304 | 45.91425 | .04275 | .996 |

ROY-BARGMAN STEPDOWN F - TESTS

| VARIABLE | HYPOTH. MS | ERROR MS | STEP-DOWN F | HYPOTH. DF | ERROR DF | SIG. OF F |
|---|---|---|---|---|---|---|
| ELATION | 19.45076 | 60.46327 | .32170 | 4 | 68 | .863 |
| DEPRESS | 3.37871 | 45.54947 | .07418 | 4 | 67 | .990 |

(6) These univariate test results are those that would be found if you did two repeated measures analyses, one on each dependent variable.

RAW DISCRIMINANT FUNCTION COEFFICIENTS

| VARIABLE | FUNCTION NO. 1 | FUNCTION NO. 2 |
|---|---|---|
| ELATION | .12572 | .03337 |
| DEPRESS | .05952 | .13689 |

STANDARDIZED DISCRIMINANT FUNCTION COEFFICIENTS

| VARIABLE | FUNCTION NO. 1 | FUNCTION NO. 2 |
|---|---|---|
| ELATION | .97760 | .25952 |
| DEPRESS | .40333 | .92757 |

669

* * * * * * * * * * * * * * * * * * * * * * * A N A L Y S I S   O F   V A R I A N C E * * * * * * * * * * * * * * * * * * * * * * *

EFFECT -- SOCIOR BY DAYS      (CONT.)

EFFECT -- DAYS

(7) This matrix would be placed in the overall multivariate analysis of variance table, see Table 7.11.

(8) In the overall multivariate test we find that there are significant multivariate differences in elation and depression when measured across the five days (see Table 7.11).

ADJUSTED HYPOTHESIS SUM-OF-SQUARES AND CROSS-PRODUCTS

|            | ELATION      | DEPRESS    |
|------------|--------------|------------|
| ELATION    | (7) 3351.65567   |            |
| DEPRESS    | -2222.94690  | 2314.46269 |

MULTIVARIATE TESTS OF SIGNIFICANCE (S = 2, M = 1/2, N = 32 1/2)

| TEST NAME  | VALUE    | APPROX. F | HYPOTH. DF | ERROR DF | SIG. OF F |
|------------|----------|-----------|------------|----------|-----------|
| PILLAIS    | .74210   | 10.02921  | 8.00       | 136.00   | 0.0       |
| HOTELLINGS | 1.78294  | 14.70924  | 8.00       | 132.00   | 0.0   (8) |
| WILKS      | .33252   | 12.29736  | 8.00       | 134.00   | 0.0       |
| RCYS       | .62216   |           |            |          |           |

EIGENVALUES AND CANONICAL CORRELATIONS

| ROOT NO. | EIGENVALUE | PCT.     | CUM. PCT. | CANON. CCR. |
|----------|------------|----------|-----------|-------------|
| 1        | 1.64666    | 92.35633 | 92.35633  | .78877      |
| 2        | .13628     | 7.64367  | 100.00000 | .34632      |

DIMENSION REDUCTION ANALYSIS

| ROOTS    | WILKS LAMBDA | F        | HYPOTH. DF | ERROR DF | SIG. OF F |
|----------|--------------|----------|------------|----------|-----------|
| 1 TO 2   | .33252       | 12.29736 | 8.00       | 134.00   | 0.0       |
| 2 TC 2   | .88006       | 2.97943  | 3.00       | 135.50   | .034      |

* * * * * * * * * * * * * * * * * * * A N A L Y S I S   O F   V A R I A N C E * * * * * * * * * * * * * * * * * * * * * * * * * *

EFFECT .. DAYS   (CONT.)

UNIVARIATE F-TESTS WITH (4,68) D. F.

| VARIABLE | HYPOTH. SS | ERROR SS | HYPOTH. MS | ERROR MS | F | SIG. OF F |
|---|---|---|---|---|---|---|
| ELATION | 3351.65567 | 4111.50222 | 837.91392 | 60.46327 | 13.85823 | .000 ⑨ |
| DEPRESS | 2314.46269 | 3122.16889 | 578.61567 | 45.91425 | 12.60209 | .000 |

ROY-BARGMAN STEPDOWN F - TESTS

| VARIABLE | HYPOTH. MS | ERROR MS | STEP-DOWN F | HYPOTH. DF | ERROR DF | SIG. OF F |
|---|---|---|---|---|---|---|
| ELATION | 837.91392 | 60.46327 | 13.85823 | 4 | 68 | .000 |
| DEPRESS | 501.08317 | 45.54947 | 11.00086 | 4 | 67 | .000 |

⑨ The univariate tests indicate that there are differences in terms of both elation and depression across DAYS.

RAW DISCRIMINANT FUNCTION COEFFICIENTS

FUNCTION NO.

| VARIABLE | 1 | 2 |
|---|---|---|
| ELATION | -.10071 | -.08233 |
| DEPRESS | -.11075 | -.10008 |

STANDARDIZED DISCRIMINANT FUNCTION COEFFICIENTS

FUNCTION NO.

| VARIABLE | 1 | 2 |
|---|---|---|
| ELATION | -.78310 | -.64016 |
| DEPRESS | -.75046 | -.67813 |

671

\* \* \* \* \* \* \* \* \* \* \* \* \* \* \* \* \* \* \* \* A N A L Y S I S   O F   V A R I A N C E \* \* \* \* \* \* \* \* \* \* \* \* \* \* \* \* \* \* \* \* \*

(10)(11) EFFECT .. SOCIOR

MULTIVARIATE TESTS OF SIGNIFICANCE (S = 1, M = 0, N = 7)

| TEST NAME | VALUE | APPROX. F | HYPOTH. DF | ERROR DF | SIG. OF F |
|-----------|-------|-----------|------------|----------|-----------|
| PILLAIS | .39490 | 5.22091 | 2.00 | 16.00 | (12) .018 |
| HOTELLINGS | .65261 | 5.22091 | 2.00 | 16.00 | .018 |
| WILKS | .60510 | 5.22091 | 2.00 | 16.00 | .018 |
| RCYS | .39490 | | | | |

EIGENVALUES AND CANONICAL CORRELATIONS

| ROOT NO. | EIGENVALUE | PCT. | CUM. PCT. | CANON. CCR. |
|----------|------------|------|-----------|-------------|
| 1 | .65261 | 100.00000 | 100.00000 | .62841 |

DIMENSION REDUCTION ANALYSIS

| ROOTS | WILKS LAMBDA | F | HYPOTH. DF | ERROR DF | SIG. OF F |
|-------|--------------|---|------------|----------|-----------|
| 1 TO 1 | .60510 | 5.22091 | 2.00 | 16.00 | .018 |

UNIVARIATE F-TESTS WITH (1,17) D. F.

| VARIABLE | HYPOTH. SS | ERROR SS | HYPOTH. MS | ERROR MS | F | SIG. OF F |
|----------|------------|----------|------------|----------|---|-----------|
| ELATION | 1799.07415 | 3543.83111 | 1799.07415 | 208.46065 | 8.63028 | (13) .009 |
| DEPRESS | 2737.57240 | 4545.56444 | 2737.57240 | 267.38614 | 10.23827 | .005 |

(10) This output is from the second call to MANCVA (we do not show the first test on SOCIOR).

(11) The error and hypothesis sum of squares and cross products matrices for this test on SOCIOR are shown in SPSS(MANOVA) 7-6, pp. 685 and 686.

(12) Here we find that there is a significant multivariate difference between the SOCIOR groups when both elation and depression are considered.

(13) Here we find that significant univariate differences between the SOCIOR groups would be found on both elation and depression.

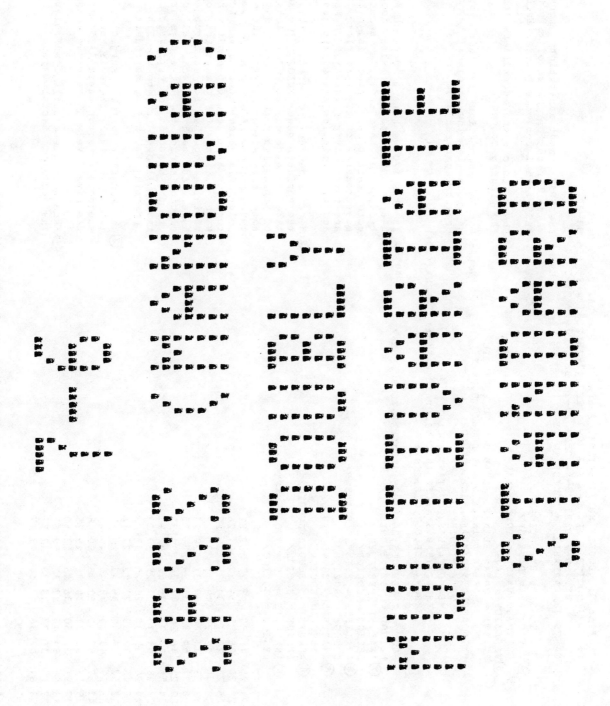

```
RUN NAME     CHAPTER 7: DOUBLY MULTIVARIATE, 2 MEASURES PER DAY FOR 5 DAYS
DATA LIST    FIXED/1 SOCIOR 1 EL1 3-4 EL2 10-11 EL3 17-18 EL4 24-25 EL5 31-32
             DEP1 6-7 DEP2 13-14 DEP3 20-21 DEP4 27-28 DEP5 34-35
LIST CASES   CASES=19/VARIABLES = SOCIOR TO DEP5
N OF CASES   19
MANOVA       EL1 TO DEP5 BY SOCIOR (1,2)/
             WSFACTORS = DAYS(5)/
             CONTRAST(DAYS) = POLYNOMIAL/
             WSDESIGN = DAYS/
             RENAME = EMEAN ELINEAR EQUAD ECUBIC EQUARTIC
                      DMEAN DLINEAR DQUAD DCUBIC DQUARTIC/
             PRINT=CELLINFO(MEANS,SSCP,COV,COR)
                   SIGNIF(HYPOTH)
                   OMEANS(TABLES(CONSTANT SOCIOR))
                   DISCRIM(RAW,STAN,ESTIM,COR,ROTATE(VARIMAX),ALPHA(1.0))
                   ERROR(SSCP,COV,CCR,STDV)
                   POBS/
             PLOT = CELLPLOTS,BOXPLOTS,STEMLEAF,ZCORR,POBS/
             METHOD = SSTYPE(UNIQUE)/
             ANALYSIS(REPEATED)/
             DESIGN = SOCIOR/
             ANALYSIS = ELINEAR DLINEAR/
             DESIGN = SOCIOR/
             ANALYSIS = EQUAD DQUAD/
             DESIGN = SOCIOR/
             ANALYSIS = ECUBIC DCUBIC/
             DESIGN = SOCIOR/
             ANALYSIS = EQUARTIC DQUARTIC/
             DESIGN = SOCIOR/
READ INPUT DATA
1 20 30 21 35 42 20 32 27 32 22
1 67 43 29 50 56 35 39 37 41 26
1 37 15 25 29 28 16 31 35 34 25
1 42 31 38 46 36 27 19 32 35 28
1 57 40 32 59 21 28 30 37 29 23
1 39 22 38 37 54 33 31 29 28 35
1 43 24 20 29 46 28 42 26 31 30
1 35 32 34 56 43 44 35 52 42 47
1 41 19 23 36 51 15 27 25 30 18
1 39 25 24 26 35 30 26 21 32 23
2 47 35 25 46 36 35 21 42 27 12
2 53 42 32 52 48 40 46 47 54 35
2 38 37 33 39 42 38 48 45 49 26
2 60 49 41 57 67 42 53 45 50 48
2 37 36 35 37 45 37 34 36 46 26
2 59 51 37 58 52 50 36 48 52 50
2 67 42 33 68 61 45 31 32 50 55
2 43 25 27 43 36 27 33 39 32 37
2 64 34 53 61 62 36 40 54 43 47
```

Note: The SPSS input annotations provided here are of value for most problems of this type. Consult the SPSS manual for more general information.

① These are column identifiers and are not part of the program content.

Note: Further annotations for this input and output can be found in the program I/O for SPSS(MANOVA), program numbered 2-10.

Note: In this I/O we have a design that Bock (1975, p. 448) refers to as being "doubly multivariate" because we have multiple measurements on two or more variables. That is, here we have five measurements on two variables; the measurements are taken over five days in each of two groups, and the variables are elation and depression.

② Here we decided to identify the factor levels with the variable name SOCIOR, the measures of elation taken on each day as EL1 to EL5, and the measures of depression taken on each day as DEP1 to DEP5. Note that since we used the same data as that found for the BMDP4V run (7-5), we identified the columns in which the data were found. SPSS(MANOVA) requires that the dependent variables be entered with all of the measures on each dependent variable together for each subject. For example, here, for each subject, all of the measures of elation across the five days are followed by all of the measures of depression. Our method of input allowed us to use the keyword TO when referring to the ten dependent variables.

③ The WSFACTOR (within subjects factor) subcommand indicates that there is one occasions (within subjects) factor named DAYS and that this factor has five levels (5 repeated measures).

④ Here we request orthogonal polynomial contrasts on the occasions factor DAYS.

⑤ The WSDESIGN (within subjects design) subcommand specifies the design on the within subjects

⑥ The RENAME subcommand is recommended as a means of identifying the repeated measures effects after transformation by the orthogonal polynomials. Here the first variable, EMEAN, represents the grand mean across the repeated measures taken on elation; the second variable, ELINEAR, represents the linear trend on the measures of elation; etc.; DMEAN, represents the grand mean across the repeated measures taken on depression; the seventh variable, DLINEAR, represents the linear trend on the measures of depression, etc.

⑦ The ANALYSIS subcommand with the specification REPEATED indicates that a repeated measures analysis is requested. This subcommand is used here to obtain the overall doubly multivariate repeated measures analysis.

⑧ The ANALYSIS subcommand is also used here to obtain the planned contrast doubly multivariate analyses by specifying the transformed dependent variables for each trend. For example, the test for linear trend is found by specifying ELINEAR and DLINEAR in the first planned contrast ANALYSIS subcommand. Each of the subsequent ANALYSIS subcommands then requests tests of the quadratic, cubic, and quartic planned contrasts in the doubly multivariate analyses.

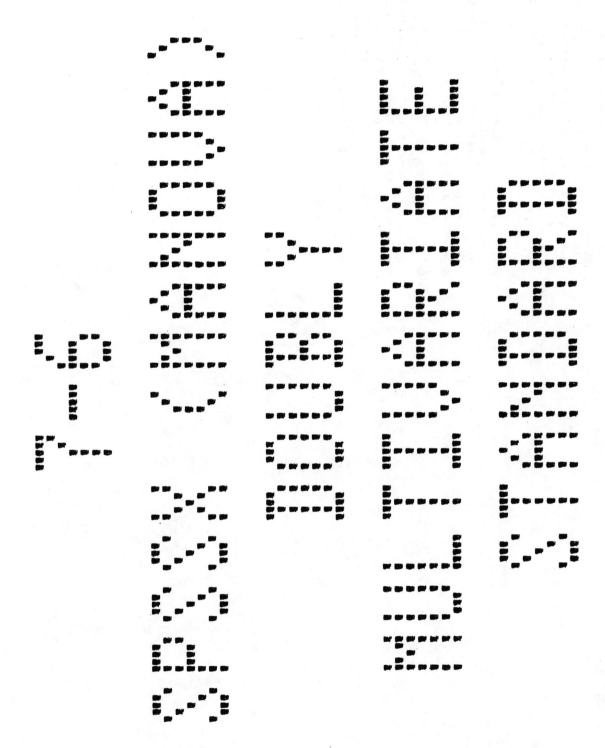

① UNNUMBERED
② TITLE    CHAPTER 7:  DOUBLY MULTIVARIATE, 2 MEASURES PER DAY FOR 5 DAYS
   DATA LIST /1 SOCIOR 1 EL1 3-4 EL2 10-11 EL3 17-18 EL4 24-25 EL5 31-32
             DEP1 6-7 DEP2 13-14 DEP3 20-21 DEP4 27-28 DEP5 34-35

MANOVA
   EL1 TO DEP5 BY SOCIOR(1,2)/
   WSFACTORS = DAYS(5)/
③ MEASURE = ELATION DEPRESS/
   CONTRAST(DAYS) = POLYNOMIAL/
   WSDESIGN = DAYS/
   RENAME = EMEAN ELINEAR EQUAD ECUBIC EQUARTIC
            DMEAN DLINEAR DQUAD DCUBIC DQUARTIC/
   PRINT=CELLINFO(MEANS,SSCP,COV,COR)
④      TRANSFORM
⑤      SIGNIF(HYPOTH AVERF)
       DISCRIM(RAW,STAN,ESTIM,COR,ROTATE(VARIMAX),ALPHA(1.0))
       OMEANS(TABLES(CONSTANT SOCIOR))
       ERROR(SSCP,COV,COR,STDV)
       POBS/
   PLOT = CELLPLOTS,BCXPLOTS,STEMLEAF,ZCORR,POBS/
   METHOD = SSTYPE(UNIQUE)/
   ANALYSIS(REPEATED)/
   DESIGN = SOCIOR/
   ANALYSIS = ELINEAR DLINEAR/
   DESIGN = SOCIOR/
   ANALYSIS = EQUAD DQUAD/
   DESIGN = SOCIOR/
   ANALYSIS = ECUBIC DCUBIC/
   DESIGN = SOCIOR/
   ANALYSIS = EQUARTIC DQUARTIC/
   DESIGN = SOCIOR/

BEGIN DATA
1 20 30 21 35 42 20 32 27 32 22
1 67 43 29 50 56 35 39 37 41 26
1 37 15 25 29 28 16 31 35 34 25
1 42 31 38 46 36 27 19 32 35 28
1 57 40 32 59 21 28 30 37 29 23
1 39 22 38 37 54 33 31 29 28 35
1 43 24 20 29 46 28 42 26 31 30
1 35 32 34 56 43 45 35 52 42 47
1 41 19 23 36 51 15 27 25 30 18
1 39 25 24 26 35 30 26 21 32 23
2 47 35 25 46 36 35 21 42 27 12
2 53 42 52 48 40 46 47 54 35
2 38 37 33 39 42 38 48 45 49 26
2 60 49 41 57 67 42 53 45 50 48
2 37 36 35 37 45 37 34 36 46 26
2 59 51 37 58 52 50 36 48 52 50
2 67 42 33 68 61 45 31 32 50 55
2 43 25 27 43 36 27 33 39 32 37
2 64 34 53 61 62 36 40 54 43 47
END DATA
LIST    VARIABLES = SOCIOR TO DEP5

① At our installation the default (NUMBERED) instruction allowed SPSSX to read only 72 columns. We therefore used the UNNUMBERED command to allow SPSSX to read all 80 columns. The default may vary by installation.

② If a title is more than 60 characters, only the first 60 characters are printed.

③ The MEASURE command names the variables in the univariate-multivariate output.

④ In SPSSX the transformation matrix is not automatically printed. To print this matrix we included the specification TRANSFORM.

⑤ Here the specification AVERF yields univariate-multivariate output. (This is referred to as univariate output in the SPSSX manual.)

```
0000000000111111111122222222223333333333444444444455555555556666666666777777777778
1234567890123456789012345678901234567890123456789012345678901234567890123456789890
```

677

FILE  NCNAME   (CREATION DATE = 02/02/83)

* * * * * * * * * * * * * * * * * * * * * A N A L Y S I S   O F   V A R I A N C E * * * * * * * * * * * * * * * * * * * *

CELL MEANS AND STANDARD DEVIATIONS

VARIABLE -- EL1

| FACTOR | CODE | MEAN | STD. DEV. | N | 95 PERCENT CONF. INTERVAL | |
|---|---|---|---|---|---|---|
| SOCIOR | 1 | 42.00000 | 12.59630 | 10 | 32.98916 | 51.01084 |
| SOCIOR | 2 | 52.00000 | 11.23610 | 9 | 43.36318 | 60.63682 |
| FOR ENTIRE SAMPLE | | 46.73684 | 12.71850 | 19 | 40.60672 | 52.86696 |

VARIABLE -- EL2

| FACTOR | CODE | MEAN | STD. DEV. | N | 95 PERCENT CONF. INTERVAL | |
|---|---|---|---|---|---|---|
| SOCIOR | 1 | 28.40000 | 6.78561 | 10 | 23.54587 | 33.25413 |
| SOCIOR | 2 | 35.11111 | 8.25295 | 9 | 28.76734 | 41.45488 |
| FOR ENTIRE SAMPLE | | 31.57895 | 8.07132 | 19 | 27.68870 | 35.46920 |

VARIABLE -- EL3

| FACTOR | CODE | MEAN | STD. DEV. | N | 95 PERCENT. CONF. INTERVAL | |
|---|---|---|---|---|---|---|
| SOCIOR | 1 | 41.20000 | 11.32156 | 10 | 33.10105 | 49.29895 |
| SOCIOR | 2 | 49.88889 | 11.41758 | 9 | 41.11257 | 58.66521 |
| FOR ENTIRE SAMPLE | | 45.31579 | 11.91196 | 19 | 39.57441 | 51.05717 |

VARIABLE -- EL4

| FACTOR | CODE | MEAN | STD. DEV. | N | 95 PERCENT CONF. INTERVAL | |
|---|---|---|---|---|---|---|
| SOCIOR | 1 | 31.20000 | 6.56252 | 10 | 26.50546 | 35.89454 |
| SOCIOR | 2 | 38.00000 | 9.84886 | 9 | 30.42951 | 45.57049 |
| FOR ENTIRE SAMPLE | | 34.42105 | 8.76429 | 19 | 30.19680 | 38.64531 |

* * * * * * * * * * * * * * * * * *A N A L Y S I S   O F   V A R I A N C E* * * * * * * * * * * * * * * * * *

CELL MEANS AND STANDARD DEVIATIONS  (CCNT.)

VARIABLE -- EL5

| FACTOR | CODE | MEAN | STD. DEV. | N | 95 PERCENT CONF. INTERVAL | |
|---|---|---|---|---|---|---|
| SOCIOR | 1 | 33.40000 | 4.76562 | 10 | 29.99088 | 36.80912 |
| SOCIOR | 2 | 44.77778 | 9.31099 | 9 | 37.62073 | 51.93483 |
| FOR ENTIRE SAMPLE | | 38.78947 | 9.16260 | 19 | 34.37324 | 43.20570 |

VARIABLE -- DEP1

| FACTOR | CODE | MEAN | STD. DEV. | N | 95 PERCENT CONF. INTERVAL | |
|---|---|---|---|---|---|---|
| SOCIOR | 1 | 28.10000 | 8.87506 | 10 | 21.75117 | 34.44883 |
| SOCIOR | 2 | 39.00000 | 8.00000 | 9 | 32.85066 | 45.14934 |
| FOR ENTIRE SAMPLE | | 33.26316 | 9.95458 | 19 | 28.46521 | 38.06111 |

VARIABLE -- DEP2

| FACTOR | CODE | MEAN | STD. DEV. | N | 95 PERCENT CONF. INTERVAL | |
|---|---|---|---|---|---|---|
| SOCIOR | 1 | 40.30000 | 11.73835 | 10 | 31.90289 | 48.69711 |
| SOCIOR | 2 | 51.22222 | 10.62753 | 9 | 43.05319 | 59.39126 |
| FOR ENTIRE SAMPLE | | 45.47368 | 12.26725 | 19 | 39.56106 | 51.38631 |

VARIABLE -- DEP3

| FACTOR | CODE | MEAN | STD. DEV. | N | 95 PERCENT CONF. INTERVAL | |
|---|---|---|---|---|---|---|
| SOCIOR | 1 | 27.60000 | 8.88444 | 10 | 21.24446 | 33.95554 |
| SOCIOR | 2 | 38.88889 | 6.52772 | 9 | 33.87125 | 43.90653 |
| FOR ENTIRE SAMPLE | | 32.94737 | 9.58861 | 19 | 28.32580 | 37.56893 |

* * * * * * * * * * * * * * * * * * * * * A N A L Y S I S   O F   V A R I A N C E * * * * * * * * * * * * * * * * * * * * * *

CELL MEANS AND STANDARD DEVIATIONS   (CONT.)

VARIABLE -- DEP4

| FACTOR | CODE | MEAN | STD. DEV. | N | 95 PERCENT CONF. INTERVAL | |
|---|---|---|---|---|---|---|
| SOCIOR | 1 | 32.10000 | 8.81224 | 10 | 25.79611 | 38.40389 |
| SOCIOR | 2 | 43.11111 | 6.67915 | 9 | 37.97706 | 48.24516 |
| FOR ENTIRE SAMPLE | | 37.31579 | 9.51638 | 19 | 32.72904 | 41.90254 |

VARIABLE -- DEP5

| FACTOR | CODE | MEAN | STD. DEV. | N | 95 PERCENT CONF. INTERVAL | |
|---|---|---|---|---|---|---|
| SOCIOR | 1 | 27.70000 | 8.24688 | 10 | 21.80054 | 33.59946 |
| SOCIOR | 2 | 37.33333 | 14.07125 | 9 | 26.51723 | 48.14944 |
| FOR ENTIRE SAMPLE | | 32.26316 | 12.10070 | 19 | 26.43081 | 38.09551 |

CELL NUMBER .. 1

SUM OF SQUARES AND CROSS-PRODUCTS MATRIX

|  | EL1 | EL2 | EL3 | EL4 | EL5 | DEP1 |
|---|---|---|---|---|---|---|
| EL1 | 1428.00000 | | | | | |
| EL2 | 191.00000 | 414.40000 | | | | |
| EL3 | 78.00000 | -7.80000 | 1153.60000 | | | |
| EL4 | 165.00000 | -147.80000 | 253.60000 | 387.60000 | | |
| EL5 | 113.00000 | 53.40000 | 94.20000 | 73.20000 | 204.40000 | |
| DEP1 | 580.00000 | 170.60000 | -21.20000 | 96.80000 | 166.60000 | 708.90000 |
| DEP2 | 632.00000 | 442.80000 | -140.60000 | 12.40000 | 215.80000 | 732.70000 |
| DEP3 | 291.00000 | 293.60000 | -213.80000 | 166.80000 | 207.60000 | 387.40000 |
| DEP4 | 198.00000 | 267.60000 | -102.20000 | 126.20000 | 266.60000 | 303.90000 |
| DEP5 | -105.00000 | 268.20000 | 172.60000 | 146.60000 | 175.20000 | 68.30000 |

* * * * * * * * * * * * * * * * * * * * * * * A N A L Y S I S   O F   V A R I A N C E * * * * * * * * * * * * * * * * * * * * * * * *

COMBINED OBSERVED GRAND MEANS

VARIABLE -- EL1

          MEAN          WGT.    46.73684
                        UNWGT.  47.00000

VARIABLE -- EL2

          MEAN          WGT.    31.57895
                        UNWGT.  31.75556

VARIABLE -- EL3

          MEAN          WGT.    45.31579
                        UNWGT.  45.54444

VARIABLE -- EL4

          MEAN          WGT.    34.42105
                        UNWGT.  34.60000

* * * * * * * * * * * * * * * * * * * A N A L Y S I S   O F   V A R I A N C E * * * * * * * * * * * * * * * * * * * * * * * *

VARIABLE -- EL5

    MEAN

        WGT.    38.78947
        UNWGT.  39.08889

------------------------------------------------------------

VARIABLE -- DEP1

    MEAN

        WGT.    33.26316
        UNWGT.  33.55000

------------------------------------------------------------

VARIABLE -- DEP2

    MEAN

        WGT.    45.47368
        UNWGT.  45.76111

------------------------------------------------------------

VARIABLE -- DEP3

    MEAN

        WGT.    32.94737
        UNWGT.  33.24444

------------------------------------------------------------

* * * * * * * * * * * * * * * * * * * * * * * * A N A L Y S I S   O F   V A R I A N C E * * * * * * * * * * * * * * * * * * * * * * * * *
*

VARIABLE -- DEP4

VARIABLE -- DEP4     (CONT.)

      MEAN                 WGT.        37.31579
                           UNWGT.      37.60556

- - - - - - - - - - - - - - - - - - - - - - - - - - - - - - - - - - - - - - - - - - - - - - - - - - - - - - - - - - - - - - - - - - - -

VARIABLE -- DEP5

      MEAN                 WGT.        32.26316
                           UNWGT.      32.51667

- - - - - - - - - - - - - - - - - - - - - - - - - - - - - - - - - - - - - - - - - - - - - - - - - - - - - - - - - - - - - - - - - - - -

COMBINED OBSERVED MEANS FOR SCCIOR

VARIABLE -- EL1

      SCCIOR

         1               WGT.         42.00000
                         UNWGT.       42.00000

         2               WGT.         52.00000
                         UNWGT.       52.00000

- - - - - - - - - - - - - - - - - - - - - - - - - - - - - - - - - - - - - - - - - - - - - - - - - - - - - - - - - - - - - - - - - - - -

VARIABLE -- EL2

      SOCIOR

         1               WGT.         28.40000

* * * * * * * * * * * * * * * * * * * * * * * A N A L Y S I S   O F   V A R I A N C E * * * * * * * * * * * * * * * * * * * * * * * * * * * *

VARIABLE -- EL2       UNWGT.   (CONT.)
                               28.40000

               2       WGT.    35.11111
                       UNWGT.  35.11111

- - - - - - - - - - - - - - - - - - - - - - - - - - - - - - - - - - - - - - - - - - - - - - - - - - - - - - - - - - - - - - - - - - - - - - -

VARIABLE -- EL3

       SOCIOR

               1       WGT.    41.20000
                       UNWGT.  41.20000

               2       WGT.    49.88889
                       UNWGT.  49.88889

- - - - - - - - - - - - - - - - - - - - - - - - - - - - - - - - - - - - - - - - - - - - - - - - - - - - - - - - - - - - - - - - - - - - - - -

VARIABLE -- EL4

       SOCIOR

               1       WGT.    31.20000
                       UNWGT.  31.20000

               2       WGT.    38.00000
                       UNWGT.  38.00000

- - - - - - - - - - - - - - - - - - - - - - - - - - - - - - - - - - - - - - - - - - - - - - - - - - - - - - - - - - - - - - - - - - - - - - -

VARIABLE -- EL5

       SOCIOR

               1       WGT.    33.40000
                       UNWGT.  33.40000

               2       WGT.    44.77778

* * * * * * * * * * * * * * * * * * A N A L Y S I S   O F   V A R I A N C E * * * * * * * * * * * * * * * * * * * * * * * *

VARIABLE -- EL5       UNWGT.  (CONT.)
                      UNWGT.  44.77778

---

VARIABLE -- DEP1

     SOCIOR

        1        WGT.    28.10000
                 UNWGT.  28.10000

        2        WGT.    39.00000
                 UNWGT.  39.00000

---

VARIABLE -- DEP2

     SOCIOR

        1        WGT.    40.30000
                 UNWGT.  40.30000

        2        WGT.    51.22222
                 UNWGT.  51.22222

---

VARIABLE -- DEP3

     SCCIOR

        1        WGT.    27.60000
                 UNWGT.  27.60000

        2        WGT.    38.88889
                 UNWGT.  38.88889

---

* * * * * * * * * * * * * * * * * * * * * * * A N A L Y S I S   O F   V A R I A N C E * * * * * * * * * * * * * * * * * * * * * *

VARIABLE -- DEP4

   SOCIOR

      1        WGT.     32.10000
             UNWGT.   32.10000

      2        WGT.     43.11111
             UNWGT.   43.11111

VARIABLE -- DEP5

   SOCIOR

      1        WGT.     27.70000
             UNWGT.   27.70000

      2        WGT.     37.33333
             UNWGT.   37.33333

CORRESPONDENCE BETWEEN EFFECTS AND COLUMNS OF WITHIN-SUBJECTS DESIGN

| STARTING COLUMN | ENDING COLUMN | EFFECT NAME |
|---|---|---|
| 1 | 1 | CONSTANT |
| 2 | 5 | DAYS |

* * * * * * * * * * * * * * * * * * A N A L Y S I S   O F   V A R I A N C E * * * * * * * * * * * * * * * * * * * * * *

ORTHONORMALIZED TRANSFORMATION MATRIX (TRANSPOSED)  ①

|   | 1 | 2 | 3 | 4 | 5 | 6 |
|---|---|---|---|---|---|---|
| 1 | .44721 | -.63246 | .53452 | -.31623 | -.11952 | 0.0 |
| 2 | .44721 | -.31623 | -.26726 | .63246 | -.47809 | 0.0 |
| 3 | .44721 | 0.0 | -.53452 | 0.0 | -.71714 | 0.0 |
| 4 | .44721 | .31623 | -.26726 | -.63246 | -.47809 | 0.0 |
| 5 | .44721 | .63246 | .53452 | .31623 | -.11952 | 0.0 |
| 6 | 0.0 | 0.0 | 0.0 | 0.0 | 0.0 | -.44721 |
| 7 | 0.0 | 0.0 | 0.0 | 0.0 | 0.0 | -.44721 |
| 8 | 0.0 | 0.0 | 0.0 | 0.0 | 0.0 | -.44721 |
| 9 | 0.0 | 0.0 | 0.0 | 0.0 | 0.0 | -.44721 |
| 10 | 0.0 | 0.0 | 0.0 | 0.0 | 0.0 | -.44721 |

|   | 7 | 8 | 9 | 10 |
|---|---|---|---|---|
| 1 | 0.0 | 0.0 | 0.0 | 0.0 |
| 2 | 0.0 | 0.0 | 0.0 | 0.0 |
| 3 | 0.0 | 0.0 | 0.0 | 0.0 |
| 4 | 0.0 | 0.0 | 0.0 | 0.0 |
| 5 | 0.0 | 0.0 | 0.0 | 0.0 |
| 6 | -.63246 | -.53452 | -.31623 | -.11952 |
| 7 | -.31623 | -.26726 | .63246 | -.47809 |
| 8 | 0.0 | -.53452 | 0.0 | -.71714 |
| 9 | .31623 | -.26726 | -.63246 | -.47809 |
| 10 | .63246 | .53452 | .31623 | -.11952 |

① This is the matrix of orthogonal polynomial coefficients, which is post multiplied times the data matrix to form the contrast variables for the grand mean and trends in the repeated measures analyses.

CORRESPONDENCE BETWEEN EFFECTS AND COLUMNS OF BETWEEN-SUBJECTS DESIGN

| STARTING COLUMN | ENDING COLUMN | EFFECT NAME |
|---|---|---|
| 1 | 1 | CONSTANT |
| 2 | 2 | SOCIOR |

ORDER OF VARIABLES FOR ANALYSIS

| VARIATES | COVARIATES | NOT USED |
|---|---|---|
| EMEAN |  | ELINEAR |
| DMEAN |  | EQUAD |

\* \* \* \* \* \* \* \* \* \* \* \* \* \* \* \* \* \* \* \* A N A L Y S I S   O F   V A R I A N C E \* \* \* \* \* \* \* \* \* \* \* \* \* \* \* \* \* \* \* \* \* \* \*

WITHIN CELLS SUM-OF-SQUARES AND CROSS-PRODUCTS

   ②     EMEAN      DMEAN

| | EMEAN | DMEAN |
|---|---|---|
| EMEAN | 3543.83111 | |
| DMEAN | 2875.10222 | 4545.56444 |

② This matrix would be placed in the overall doubly multivariate analysis of variance table, see Table 7.12.

* * * * * * * * * * * * * * * * A N A L Y S I S   O F   V A R I A N C E * * * * * * * * * * * * * * * * * * * *

EFFECT .. SOCIOR

ADJUSTED HYPOTHESIS SUM-OF-SQUARES AND CROSS-PRODUCTS

(3)  EMEAN      DMEAN

| | EMEAN | DMEAN |
|---|---|---|
| EMEAN | 1799.07415 | |
| DMEAN | 2219.25567 | 2737.57240 |

MULTIVARIATE TESTS OF SIGNIFICANCE (S = 1, M = 0, N = 7)

| TEST NAME | VALUE | APPROX. F | HYPOTH. DF | ERROR DF | SIG. OF F |
|---|---|---|---|---|---|
| PILLAIS | .39490 | 5.22091 | 2.00 | 16.00 | .018 |
| HOTELLINGS | .65261 | 5.22091 | 2.00 | 16.00 | .018  (4) |
| WILKS | .60510 | 5.22091 | 2.00 | 16.00 | .018 |
| ROYS | .39490 | | | | |

EIGENVALUES AND CANONICAL CORRELATIONS

| ROOT NO. | EIGENVALUE | PCT. | CUM. PCT. | CANON. COR. |
|---|---|---|---|---|
| 1 | .65261 | 100.00000 | 100.00000 | .62841 |

DIMENSION REDUCTION ANALYSIS

| ROOTS | WILKS LAMBDA | F | HYPOTH. DF | ERROR DF | SIG. OF F |
|---|---|---|---|---|---|
| 1 TO 1 | .60510 | 5.22091 | 2.00 | 16.00 | .018 |

(3) This matrix would be placed in the overall doubly multivariate analysis of variance table, see Table 7.12.

(4) This is the overall multivariate test of significant differences on the SOCIOR factor. Here we find that there is a significant multivariate difference between the SOCIOR groups when both elation and depression are considered.

* * * * * * * * * * * * * * * * * * * * A N A L Y S I S   O F   V A R I A N C E * * * * * * * * * * * * * * * * * * * * * * * * * *

EFFECT .. SOCIOR          (CONT.)

UNIVARIATE F-TESTS WITH (1,17) D. F.

| VARIABLE | HYPOTH. SS | ERROR SS | HYPOTH. MS | ERROR MS | F | SIG. OF F |
|----------|-----------|----------|-----------|----------|---|-----------|
| EMEAN | 1799.07415 | 3543.83111 | 1799.07415 | 208.46065 | 8.63028 | .009 ⑤ |
| DMEAN | 2737.57240 | 4545.56444 | 2737.57240 | 267.38614 | 10.23827 | .005 |

⑤ The univariate tests indicate  that both dependent
variables  considered  alone  would  differentiate
between the SOCIOR groups.

RAW DISCRIMINANT FUNCTION COEFFICIENTS

     FUNCTION NO.

VARIABLE          1

EMEAN          .02758
DMEAN          .04131

STANDARDIZED DISCRIMINANT FUNCTICN COEFFICIENTS

     FUNCTION NO.

VARIABLE          1

EMEAN          .39814
DMEAN          .67544

ESTIMATES OF EFFECTS FOR CANCNICAL VARIABLES

     CANONICAL VARIABLE

PARAMETER          1

     2          -.76521

690

\* \* \* \* \* \* \* \* \* \* \* \* \* \* \* \* \* \* \* \* \* \*A N A L Y S I S   O F   V A R I A N C E\* \* \* \* \* \* \* \* \* \* \* \* \* \* \* \* \* \* \* \* \* \* \*

WITHIN CELLS VARIANCES AND COVARIANCES

| | ELINEAR | EQUAD | ECUBIC | EQUARTIC | DLINEAR | DQUAD | DCUBIC | DQUARTIC |
|---|---|---|---|---|---|---|---|---|
| ELINEAR | 84.82719 | | | | | | | |
| EQUAD | -27.58915 | 57.73782 | | | | | | |
| ECUBIC | -2.25765 | -6.73837 | 43.24471 | | | | | |
| EQUARTIC | -16.37446 | -11.34682 | -7.19822 | 56.04336 | | | | |
| DLINEAR | 17.53987 | -27.76746 | 9.60000 | -1.92391 | 65.28366 | | | |
| DQUAD | 5.43771 | -4.81232 | -6.02545 | 12.85770 | 7.88590 | 20.95892 | | |
| DCUBIC | -31.04837 | 6.99324 | 4.83529 | 28.13538 | 11.08954 | 17.09808 | 53.68366 | |
| DQUARTIC | 21.24131 | -9.68537 | -3.66937 | 14.07429 | 2.94442 | 9.85436 | -1.85128 | 43.73076 |

WITHIN CELLS SUM-OF-SQUARES AND CROSS-PRODUCTS

⑥

| | ELINEAR | EQUAD | ECUBIC | EQUARTIC | DLINEAR | DQUAD | DCUBIC | DQUARTIC |
|---|---|---|---|---|---|---|---|---|
| ELINEAR | 1442.06222 | | | | | | | |
| EQUAD | -469.01554 | 981.54286 | | | | | | |
| ECUBIC | -38.38000 | -114.55221 | 735.16000 | | | | | |
| EQUARTIC | -278.36579 | -192.89600 | -122.36978 | 952.73714 | | | | |
| DLINEAR | 298.17778 | -472.04682 | 163.20000 | -32.70653 | 1109.82222 | | | |
| DQUAD | 92.44109 | -81.80952 | -102.43270 | 218.58097 | 134.06025 | 356.30159 | | |
| DCUBIC | -527.82222 | 118.88503 | 82.20000 | 478.30144 | 188.52222 | 290.66733 | 912.62222 | |
| DQUARTIC | 361.10222 | -164.65127 | -62.37926 | 239.26286 | 50.05510 | 167.52408 | -31.47184 | 743.42286 |

⑥ This matrix would be placed in the overall doubly multivariate analysis of variance table (see Table 7.12) or in an appendix.

CHAPTER 7: DOUBLY MULTIVARIATE, 2 MEASURES PER DAY FOR 5 DAYS          02/02/83      PAGE  68

* * * * * * * * * * * * * * * * * * * * * A N A L Y S I S   O F   V A R I A N C E * * * * * * * * * * * * * * * * * * * * * *

EFFECT -- SOCIOR AND DAYS

ADJUSTED HYPOTHESIS SUM-OF-SQUARES AND CROSS-PRODUCTS

(7)         ELINEAR        EQUAD        ECUBIC       EQUARTIC       DLINEAR        DQUAD

ELINEAR      3.83251
EQUAD       13.51298     47.64511
ECUBIC       1.61684      5.70079       .68211
EQUARTIC     9.91354     34.95395      4.18228     25.64331
DLINEAR     -3.29357    -11.61272     -1.38947     -8.51945      2.83041
DQUAD       -3.92231    -13.82957     -1.65472    -10.14581      3.37073      4.01420
DCUBIC      -1.94620     -6.86206      -.82105     -5.03422      1.67251      1.99180
DQUARTIC     -.27160      -.95764       .11458       .70256      -.23341      -.27797

             DCUBIC      DQUARTIC

DCUBIC       -.98830
DQUARTIC     -.13792      -.01925

(8)

MULTIVARIATE TESTS OF SIGNIFICANCE (S = 1, M = 3, N = 4)

TEST NAME      VALUE     APPROX. F    HYPOTH. DF    ERROR DF     SIG. OF F

PILLAIS       .20509       .32251        8.00        10.00         .939
HOTELLINGS    .25801       .32251        8.00        10.00         .939 (9)
WILKS         .79491       .32251        8.00        10.00         .939
ROYS          .20509

EIGENVALUES AND CANONICAL CORRELATIONS

RCOT NO.    EIGENVALUE      PCT.      CUM. PCT.    CANON. CCR.

   1         .25801     100.00000    100.00000      .45287

(7) This matrix would be placed in the overall doubly multivariate analysis of variance table (see Table 7.12) or in an appendix.

(8) The first test considered should be the DAYS by SOCIOR interaction, because if this is significant we must consider each SOCIOR group separately. Here none of the significance tests (univariate or multivariate) indicate a significant interaction, so we may move on to consider the main effects.

(9) This is the multivariate test of the DAYS by SOCIOR interaction (see Table 7.12).

692

* * * * * * * * * * * * * * * * * * * * A N A L Y S I S  O F  V A R I A N C E * * * * * * * * * * * * * * * * * * * * * * * * *
*

EFFECT .. SOCIOR AND DAYS        (CONT.)

DIMENSION REDUCTION ANALYSIS

| ROOTS   | WILKS LAMBDA | F      | HYPOTH. DF | ERROR DF | SIG. OF F |
|---------|--------------|--------|------------|----------|-----------|
| 1 TO 1  | .79491       | .32251 | 8.00       | 10.00    | .939      |

UNIVARIATE F-TESTS WITH (1,17) D. F.  ⑩

| VARIABLE | HYPOTH. SS | ERROR SS   | HYPOTH. MS | ERROR MS | F       | SIG. OF F |
|----------|------------|------------|------------|----------|---------|-----------|
| ELINEAR  | 3.83251    | 1442.06222 | 3.83251    | 84.82719 | .04518  | .834      |
| EQUAD    | 47.64511   | 981.54286  | 47.64511   | 57.73782 | .82520  | .376      |
| ECUBIC   | .68211     | 735.16000  | .68211     | 43.24471 | .01577  | .902      |
| EQUARTIC | 25.64331   | 952.73714  | 25.64331   | 56.04336 | .45756  | .508      |
| DLINEAR  | 2.83041    | 1109.82222 | 2.83041    | 65.28366 | .04336  | .838      |
| DQUAD    | 4.01420    | 356.30159  | 4.01420    | 20.95892 | .19153  | .667      |
| DCUBIC   | .98830     | 912.62222  | .98830     | 53.68366 | .01841  | .894      |
| DQUARTIC | .01925     | 743.42286  | .01925     | 43.73076 | .00044  | .984      |

RAW DISCRIMINANT FUNCTION COEFFICIENTS

FUNCTION NO.

| VARIABLE | 1       |
|----------|---------|
| ELINEAR  | -.06888 |
| EQUAD    | -.14802 |
| ECUBIC   | -.04757 |
| EQUARTIC | -.15908 |
| DLINEAR  | -.05033 |
| DQUAD    | -.05683 |
| DCUBIC   | -.06962 |
| DQUARTIC | -.03990 |

⑩ These are the univariate trend tests on the DAYS by SOCIOR interaction. These tests would only be considered if a significant multivariate test of the interaction were found.

\* \* \* \* \* \* \* \* \* \* \* \* \* \* \* \* \* \* \* \* \* \* \* A N A L Y S I S   O F   V A R I A N C E \* \* \* \* \* \* \* \* \* \* \* \* \* \* \* \* \* \* \* \* \* \*

EFFECT .. DAYS

ADJUSTED HYPOTHESIS SUM-OF-SQUARES AND CROSS-PRODUCTS

(11)

|          | ELINEAR    | EQUAD      | ECUBIC     | EQUARTIC    | DLINEAR    | DQUAD      |
|----------|------------|------------|------------|-------------|------------|------------|
| ELINEAR  | 319.11673  |            |            |             |            |            |
| EQUAD    | -306.18664 | 293.78045  |            |             |            |            |
| ECUBIC   | 334.41684  | -320.86682 | 350.45053  |             |            |            |
| EQUARTIC | -873.01146 | 837.63846  | -914.63818 | 2388.30797  |            |            |
| DLINEAR  | 251.35906  | -241.17440 | 263.41053  | -687.64602  | 197.98830  |            |
| DQUAD    | 368.30142  | -353.37845 | 385.95971  | -1007.56663 | 290.10043  | 425.06683  |
| DCUBIC   | -375.67251 | 360.45088  | -393.68421 | -1027.73182 | -295.90643 | -433.57402 |
| DQUARTIC | 631.36883  | -605.78679 | 661.63994  | -1727.24331 | 497.31107  | 728.68019  |

|          | DCUBIC     | DQUARTIC   |
|----------|------------|------------|
| DCUBIC   | 442.25146  |            |
| DQUARTIC | -743.26382 | 1249.15609 |

MULTIVARIATE TESTS OF SIGNIFICANCE (S = 1, M = 3, N = 4)

(12)

| TEST NAME  | VALUE    | APPROX. F | HYPOTH. DF | ERROR DF | SIG. OF F |
|------------|----------|-----------|------------|----------|-----------|
| PILLAIS    | .91834   | 14.05806  | 8.00       | 10.00    | .000      |
| HOTELLINGS | 11.24645 | 14.05806  | 8.00       | 10.00    | .000      |
| WILKS      | .08166   | 14.05806  | 8.00       | 10.00    | .000      |
| ROYS       | .91834   |           |            |          |           |

EIGENVALUES AND CANONICAL CORRELATIONS

| ROOT NO. | EIGENVALUE | PCT.      | CUM. PCT. | CANON. COR. |
|----------|------------|-----------|-----------|-------------|
| 1        | 11.24645   | 100.00000 | 100.00000 | .95830      |

(11) This matrix would be placed in the overall doubly multivariate analysis of variance table (see Table 7.12) or in an appendix.

(12) In the overall multivariate test we find that there is a significant difference across DAYS when both elation and depression are considered together.

\* \* \* \* \* \* \* \* \* \* \* \* \* \* \* \* \* A N A L Y S I S   O F   V A R I A N C E \* \* \* \* \* \* \* \* \* \* \* \* \* \* \* \* \* \* \* \* \* \* \*

EFFECT .. DAYS          (CONT.)

DIMENSION REDUCTION ANALYSIS

| ROOTS | WILKS LAMBDA | F | HYPOTH. DF | ERROR DF | SIG. OF F |
|---|---|---|---|---|---|
| 1 TO 1 | .08166 | 14.05806 | 8.00 | 10.00 | .000 |

UNIVARIATE F-TESTS WITH (1,17) D. F.  [13]

| VARIABLE | HYPOTH. SS | ERROR SS | HYPOTH. MS | ERROR MS | F | SIG. OF F |
|---|---|---|---|---|---|---|
| ELINEAR | 319.11673 | 1442.06222 | 319.11673 | 84.82719 | 3.76196 | .069 |
| EQUAD | 293.78045 | 981.54286 | 293.78045 | 57.73782 | 5.08818 | .038 |
| ECUBIC | 350.45053 | 735.16000 | 350.45053 | 43.24471 | 8.10389 | .011 |
| EQUARTIC | 2388.30797 | 952.73714 | 2388.30797 | 56.04336 | 42.61536 | .000 [14] |
| DLINEAR | 197.98830 | 1109.82222 | 197.98830 | 65.28366 | 3.03274 | .100 |
| DQUAD | 425.06683 | 356.30159 | 425.06683 | 20.95892 | 20.28095 | .000 |
| DCUBIC | 442.25146 | 912.62222 | 442.25146 | 53.68366 | 8.23810 | .011 |
| DQUARTIC | 1249.15609 | 743.42286 | 1249.15609 | 43.73076 | 28.56470 | .000 [14] |

RAW DISCRIMINANT FUNCTION COEFFICIENTS

FUNCTION NO.          1

| VARIABLE | |
|---|---|
| ELINEAR | -.07245 |
| EQUAD | -.04435 |
| ECUBIC | -.03976 |
| EQUARTIC | -.12250 |
| DLINEAR | -.00888 |
| DQUAD | .17373 |
| DCUBIC | -.05438 |
| DQUARTIC | .08573 |

[13] In the univariate trend analysis the error terms are found by partitioning the error into its linear, quadratic, cubic, and quartic parts. Use of these individual error terms is preferred by most statisticians (Boik, 1981; Gatio and Wiley, 1966, pp. 83-84; Rouanet and Lepine.

[14] Here, given the .05 level of significance for each test, we find a significant quartic trend, as predicted, but we also find that, for both dependent variables, the quadratic ad cubic terms are statistically significant. However, since these latter trends were not predicted, they should be further tested with a more conservative post hoc test, such as that by Scheffe. Then if they are still significant, they might be included in a discussion of the theoretical research model.

Note: In SPSSX the univariate-multivariate output was printed here.

695

* * * * * * * * * * * * * * * * * * * * A N A L Y S I S   O F   V A R I A N C E * * * * * * * * * * * * * * * * * * * * * * * * * * * *

WITHIN CELLS SUM-OF-SQUARES AND CROSS-PRODUCTS

⑮                ELINEAR          DLINEAR

ELINEAR       1442.06222
DLINEAR        298.17778       1109.82222

⑮ This error matrix would be placed in the planned contrast doubly multivariate analysis of variance table, see Table 7.10.

* * * * * * * * * * * * * * * * * * * A N A L Y S I S   O F   V A R I A N C E * * * * * * * * * * * * * * * * * * * * * * * *

(16) EFFECT -- SOCIOR

ADJUSTED HYPOTHESIS SUM-OF-SQUARES AND CROSS-PRODUCTS

(17)          ELINEAR      DLINEAR

ELINEAR      3.83251
DLINEAR     -3.29357      2.83041

MULTIVARIATE TESTS OF SIGNIFICANCE (S = 1, M = 0, N = 7)

| TEST NAME | VALUE | APPROX. F | HYPOTH. DF | ERROR DF | SIG. OF F |
|---|---|---|---|---|---|
| PILLAIS | .00677 | .05451 | 2.00 | 16.00 | .947 |
| HOTELLINGS | .00681 | .05451 | 2.00 | 16.00 | .947 (18) |
| WILKS | .99323 | .05451 | 2.00 | 16.00 | .947 |
| ROYS | .00677 | | | | |

EIGENVALUES AND CANONICAL CORRELATIONS

| ROOT NO. | EIGENVALUE | PCT. | CUM. PCT. | CANON. CCR. |
|---|---|---|---|---|
| 1 | .00681 | 100.00000 | 100.00000 | .08227 |

DIMENSION REDUCTION ANALYSIS

| ROOTS | WILKS LAMBDA | F | HYPOTH. DF | ERROR DF | SIG. OF F |
|---|---|---|---|---|---|
| 1 TO 1 | .99323 | .05451 | 2.00 | 16.00 | .947 |

(16) In order to obtain the planned contrast analysis we conducted individual multivariate analyses on each pair of transformed variables. When we do this, the resulting tests are not labeled properly by MANOVA. For example, the tests under the label EFFECT -- SOCIOR are really our tests of trend effect within the DAYS by SOCIOR interaction, depending on the contrast variables selected. Here the contrast variables are ELINEAR and DLINEAR, so these tests are for the linear by SOCIOR interaction.

(17) This hypothesis matrix would be placed in the planned contrast doubly multivariate analysis of variance table, see Table 7.10.

(18) Here the multivariate test indicates that there is no linear by SOCIOR interaction.

* * * * * * * * * * * * * * * * * * * A N A L Y S I S   O F   V A R I A N C E * * * * * * * * * * * * * * * * * * * * * *

(19) EFFECT -- CONSTANT

ADJUSTED HYPOTHESIS SUM-OF-SQUARES AND CROSS-PRODUCTS

|  | ELINEAR | DLINEAR |
|---|---|---|
| ELINEAR | (20) 319.11673 | |
| DLINEAR | 251.35906 | 197.98830 |

MULTIVARIATE TESTS OF SIGNIFICANCE (S = 1, M = 0, N = 7)

| TEST NAME | VALUE | APPROX. F | HYPOTH. DF | ERROR DF | SIG. OF F |
|---|---|---|---|---|---|
| PILLAIS | .24473 | 2.59222 | 2.00 | 16.00 | .106 |
| HOTELLINGS | .32403 | 2.59222 | 2.00 | 16.00 | .106 |
| WILKS | .75527 | 2.59222 | 2.00 | 16.00 | .106 |
| ROYS | .24473 | | | | |

EIGENVALUES AND CANONICAL CORRELATIONS

| ROOT NO. | EIGENVALUE | PCT. | CUM. PCT. | CANON. CCR. |
|---|---|---|---|---|
| 1 | .32403 | 100.00000 | 100.00000 | .49470 |

DIMENSION REDUCTION ANALYSIS

| ROOTS | WILKS LAMBDA | F | HYPOTH. DF | ERROR DF | SIG. OF F |
|---|---|---|---|---|---|
| 1 TO 1 | .75527 | 2.59222 | 2.00 | 16.00 | .106 |

(19) The tests under the label EFFECT -- CONSTANT are the multivariate planned contrast tests of trend over DAYS, depending on the contrast variables. Here the contrast variables are ELINEAR and DLINEAR, and so this is the multivariate test of linear trend in elation and depression over DAYS. Here no significant trend is found.

(20) This hypothesis matrix would be placed in the planned contrast doubly multivariate analysis of variance table, see Table 7.10.

CHAPTER 7: DOUBLY MULTIVARIATE, 2 MEASURES PER DAY FOR 5 DAYS          02/02/83          PAGE  128

* * * * * * * * * * * * * * * * * * A N A L Y S I S   O F   V A R I A N C E * * * * * * * * * * * * * * * * * * * * * * * *

WITHIN CELLS SUM-OF-SQUARES AND CRCSS-PRODUCTS

          EQUAD        DQUAD

   (21)
EQUAD   981.54286
DQUAD   -81.80952    356.30159

(21) This error matrix would be placed in  the planned
     contrast doubly multivariate  analysis of variance
     table, see Table 7.10.

699

* * * * * * * * * * * * * * * * * * * * * * * A N A L Y S I S   O F   V A R I A N C E * * * * * * * * * * * * * * * * * * * * * * * *

EFFECT -- SOCIOR

ADJUSTED HYPOTHESIS SUM-OF-SQUARES AND CROSS-PRODUCTS

                EQUAD           DQUAD
(22)
EQUAD     47.64511
DQUAD    -13.82957       4.01420

MULTIVARIATE TESTS OF SIGNIFICANCE (S = 1, M = 0, N = 7)

| TEST NAME | VALUE | APPROX. F | HYPOTH. DF | ERROR DF | SIG. OF F |
|-----------|-------|-----------|------------|----------|-----------|
| PILLAIS    | .05157 | .43502 | 2.00 | 16.00 | .655 |
| HOTELLINGS | .05438 | .43502 | 2.00 | 16.00 | .655 (23) |
| WILKS      | .94843 | .43502 | 2.00 | 16.00 | .655 |
| ROYS       | .05157 |         |      |       |      |

EIGENVALUES AND CANONICAL CORRELATIONS

| ROOT NO. | EIGENVALUE | PCT. | CUM. PCT. | CANON. COR. |
|----------|------------|------|-----------|-------------|
| 1 | .05438 | 100.00000 | 100.00000 | .22710 |

DIMENSION REDUCTION ANALYSIS

| ROOTS | WILKS LAMBDA | F | HYPOTH. DF | ERROR DF | SIG. OF F |
|-------|--------------|---|------------|----------|-----------|
| 1 TO 1 | .94843 | .43502 | 2.00 | 16.00 | .655 |

(22) This hypothesis matrix would be placed in the planned contrast doubly multivariate analysis of variance table, see Table 7.10.

(23) Here the multivariate test indicates that there is no quartic by SOCIOR interaction.

700

* * * * * * * * * * * * * * * * * * * * * * A N A L Y S I S   O F   V A R I A N C E * * * * * * * * * * * * * * * * * * * *

EFFECT .. CONSTANT

ADJUSTED HYPOTHESIS SUM-OF-SQUARES AND CROSS-PRODUCTS

(24)                  EQUAD           DQUAD

EQUAD       293.78045
DQUAD      -353.37845    425.06683

- - - - - - - - - - - - - - - - - - - - - - - - - - - - - - - - - - - - - - - - - - - - - - - - - - - - - - - -

MULTIVARIATE TESTS OF SIGNIFICANCE (S = 1, M = 0, N = 7)

| TEST NAME | VALUE | APPROX. F | HYPOTH. DF | ERROR DF | SIG. OF F |
|---|---|---|---|---|---|
| PILLAIS | .57499 | 10.82291 | 2.00 | 16.00 | .001 |
| HOTELLINGS | 1.35286 | 10.82291 | 2.00 | 16.00 | .001 (25) |
| WILKS | .42501 | 10.82291 | 2.00 | 16.00 | .001 |
| RCYS | .57499 | | | | |

- - - - - - - - - - - - - - - - - - - - - - - - - - - - - - - - - - - - - - - - - - - - - - - - - - - - - - - -

EIGENVALUES AND CANONICAL CORRELATIONS

| ROOT NO. | EIGENVALUE | PCT. | CUM. PCT. | CANON. COR. |
|---|---|---|---|---|
| 1 | 1.35286 | 100.00000 | 100.00000 | .75828 |

- - - - - - - - - - - - - - - - - - - - - - - - - - - - - - - - - - - - - - - - - - - - - - - - - - - - - - - -

DIMENSION REDUCTION ANALYSIS

| ROOTS | WILKS LAMBDA | F | HYPOTH. DF | ERROR DF | SIG. OF F |
|---|---|---|---|---|---|
| 1 TO 1 | .42501 | 10.82291 | 2.00 | 16.00 | .001 |

- - - - - - - - - - - - - - - - - - - - - - - - - - - - - - - - - - - - - - - - - - - - - - - - - - - - - - - -

(24) This hypothesis matrix would be placed in the planned contrast doubly multivariate analysis of variance table, see Table 7.10.

(25) Here the multivariate test indicates that there is a significant quadratic trend over DAYS, see Table 7.10.

\* \* \* \* \* \* \* \* \* \* \* \* \* \* \* \* A N A L Y S I S   O F   V A R I A N C E \* \* \* \* \* \* \* \* \* \* \* \* \* \* \* \* \* \*

EFFECT .. CONSTANT    (CONT.)

UNIVARIATE F-TESTS WITH (1,17) D. F.

| VARIABLE | HYPOTH. SS | ERROR SS | HYPOTH. MS | ERROR MS | F | SIG. OF F |
|---|---|---|---|---|---|---|
| EQUAD | 293.78045 | 981.54286 | 293.78045 | 57.73782 | 5.08818 | -038 (26) |
| DQUAD | 425.06683 | 356.30159 | 425.06683 | 20.95892 | 20.28095 | .000 |

(26) Here the univariate tests indicate that there is a significant quadratic trend over DAYS on both dependent variables. Note that these tests are the same as those found following the overall doubly multivariate test on DAYS, the difference being that these tests were preceded by the more powerful multivariate test on a single trend.

RAW DISCRIMINANT FUNCTION COEFFICIENTS
    FUNCTION NO.

| VARIABLE | 1 |
|---|---|
| EQUAD | -.04568 |
| DQUAD | .19463 |

STANDARDIZED DISCRIMINANT FUNCTION COEFFICIENTS
    FUNCTION NO.

| VARIABLE | 1 |
|---|---|
| EQUAD | -.34709 |
| DQUAD | -.89104 |

ESTIMATES OF EFFECTS FOR CANONICAL VARIABLES
    CANONICAL VARIABLE

| PARAMETER | 1 |
|---|---|
| 1 | -1.10173 |

CHAPTER 7: DOUBLY MULTIVARIATE, 2 MEASURES PER DAY FOR 5 DAYS                    02/02/83        PAGE 145

*******************ANALYSIS OF VARIANCE****************************************

WITHIN CELLS SUM-OF-SQUARES AND CROSS-PRODUCTS

         ECUBIC         DCUBIC

(27) This error matrix would be placed in the planned
     contrast doubly multivariate analysis of variance
     table, see Table 7.10.

(27)  735.16000
ECUBIC
DCUBIC    82.20000    912.62222

-------------------------------------------------------------------------------------------------

703

* * * * * * * * * * * * * * * * * * *A N A L Y S I S   O F   V A R I A N C E* * * * * * * * * * * * * * * * * * * * * *

EFFECT -- SOCIOR

ADJUSTED HYPOTHESIS SUM-OF-SQUARES AND CROSS-PRODUCTS

| | ECUBIC | DCUBIC |
|---|---|---|
| ECUBIC | -.68211 | |
| DCUBIC | -.82105 | -.98830 |

---

MULTIVARIATE TESTS OF SIGNIFICANCE (S = 1, M = 0, N = 7)

| TEST NAME | VALUE | APPROX. F | HYPOTH. DF | ERROR DF | SIG. OF F |
|---|---|---|---|---|---|
| PILLAIS | .00223 | .01788 | 2.00 | 16.00 | .982 |
| HOTELLINGS ㉙ | .00223 | .01788 | 2.00 | 16.00 | .982 |
| WILKS | .99777 | .01788 | 2.00 | 16.00 | .982 |
| ROYS | .00223 | | | | |

---

EIGENVALUES AND CANONICAL CORRELATIONS

| ROOT NO. | EIGENVALUE | PCT. | CUM. PCT. | CANON. COR. |
|---|---|---|---|---|
| 1 | .00223 | 100.00000 | 100.00000 | .04722 |

---

DIMENSION REDUCTION ANALYSIS

| ROOTS | WILKS LAMBDA | F | HYPOTH. DF | ERROR DF | SIG. OF F |
|---|---|---|---|---|---|
| 1 TO 1 | .99777 | .01788 | 2.00 | 16.00 | .982 |

---

㉘ This hypothesis matrix could be placed in the planned contrast doubly multivariate analysis of variance table, see Table 7.10.

㉙ Here the multivariate test indicates that there is no cubic by SOCIOR interaction.

704

* * * * * * * * * * * * * * * * * * * A N A L Y S I S   O F   V A R I A N C E * * * * * * * * * * * * * * * * * * *

EFFECT .. CONSTANT

(30) This hypothesis matrix would be placed in the planned contrast doubly multivariate analysis of variance table, see Table 7.10.

(31) Here the multivariate test indicates that there is a significant cubic trend over DAYS, see Table 7.10.

ADJUSTED HYPOTHESIS SUM-OF-SQUARES AND CROSS-PRODUCTS

|         | ECUBIC      | DCUBIC    |
|---------|-------------|-----------|
| (30)    |             |           |
| ECUBIC  | 350.45053   |           |
| DCUBIC  | -393.68421  | 442.25146 |

MULTIVARIATE TESTS OF SIGNIFICANCE (S = 1, M = 0, N = 7)

| TEST NAME  | VALUE    | APPROX. F | HYPOTH. DF | ERROR DF | SIG. OF F |
|------------|----------|-----------|------------|----------|-----------|
| PILLAIS    | .51656   | 8.54817   | 2.00       | 16.00    | .003      |
| HOTELLINGS | 1.06852  | 8.54817   | 2.00       | 16.00    | .003 (31) |
| WILKS      | .48344   | 8.54817   | 2.00       | 16.00    | .003      |
| ROYS       | .51656   |           |            |          |           |

EIGENVALUES AND CANONICAL CORRELATIONS

| ROOT NO. | EIGENVALUE | PCT.      | CUM. PCT. | CANON. COR. |
|----------|------------|-----------|-----------|-------------|
| 1        | 1.06852    | 100.00000 | 100.00000 | .71872      |

DIMENSION REDUCTION ANALYSIS

| ROOTS    | WILKS LAMBDA | F       | HYPOTH. DF | ERROR DF | SIG. OF F |
|----------|--------------|---------|------------|----------|-----------|
| 1 TO 1   | .48344       | 8.54817 | 2.00       | 16.00    | .003      |

705

* * * * * * * * * * * * * * * * * *A N A L Y S I S   O F   V A R I A N C E* * * * * * * * * * * * * * * * * * * * * * * *

EFFECT .. CONSTANT     (CONT.)

UNIVARIATE F-TESTS WITH (1,17) D. F.

| VARIABLE | HYPOTH. SS | ERROR SS | HYPOTH. MS | ERROR MS | F | SIG. OF F |
|----------|-----------|----------|-----------|----------|---|-----------|
| ECUBIC | 350.45053 | 735.16000 | 350.45053 | 43.24471 | 8.10389 | .011 |
| DCUBIC | 442.25146 | 912.62222 | 442.25146 | 53.68366 | 8.23810 | .011 (32) |

(32) Here the univariate tests indicate that there is a
significant cubic trend over DAYS on both
dependent variables.

RAW DISCRIMINANT FUNCTION COEFFICIENTS

FUNCTION NO.

VARIABLE               1

ECUBIC             -.11298
DCUBIC              .10209

STANDARDIZED DISCRIMINANT FUNCTION COEFFICIENTS

FUNCTION NO.

VARIABLE               1

ECUBIC             -.74299
DCUBIC              .74800

ESTIMATES OF EFFECTS FOR CANONICAL VARIABLES

CANONICAL VARIABLE

PARAMETER              1

1                 .97913

\* \* \* \* \* \* \* \* \* \* \* \* \* \* \* \* \* A N A L Y S I S   O F   V A R I A N C E \* \* \* \* \* \* \* \* \* \* \* \* \* \* \* \* \* \* \* \*

WITHIN CELLS SUM-OF-SQUARES AND CROSS-PRODUCTS

(33)

|          | EQUARTIC   | DQUARTIC   |
|----------|------------|------------|
| EQUARTIC | 952.73714  |            |
| DQUARTIC | 239.26286  | 743.42286  |

(33) This error matrix would be placed in  the planned
contrast doubly multivariate  analysis of variance
table, see Table 7.10.

\* \* \* \* \* \* \* \* \* \* \* \* \* \* \* \* \* \* \* \* A N A L Y S I S   O F   V A R I A N C E \* \* \* \* \* \* \* \* \* \* \* \* \* \* \* \* \* \* \* \* \*

EFFECT .. SOCIOR

ADJUSTED HYPOTHESIS SUM-OF-SQUARES AND CROSS-PRODUCTS

(34)    EQUARTIC          DQUARTIC

| | EQUARTIC | DQUARTIC |
|---|---|---|
| EQUARTIC | 25.64331 | |
| DQUARTIC | .70256 | -.01925 |

MULTIVARIATE TESTS OF SIGNIFICANCE (S = 1, M = 0, N = 7)

| TEST NAME | VALUE | APPROX. F | HYPOTH. DF | ERROR DF | SIG. OF F |
|---|---|---|---|---|---|
| PILLAIS | .02799 | .23035 | 2.00 | 16.00 | .797 |
| HOTELLINGS | .02879 | .23035 | 2.00 | 16.00 | .797 (35) |
| WILKS | .97201 | .23035 | 2.00 | 16.00 | .797 |
| RCYS | .02799 | | | | |

EIGENVALUES AND CANONICAL CORRELATIONS

| ROOT NO. | EIGENVALUE | PCT. | CUM. PCT. | CANON. COR. |
|---|---|---|---|---|
| 1 | .02879 | 100.00000 | 100.00000 | .16730 |

DIMENSION REDUCTION ANALYSIS

| ROOTS | WILKS LAMBDA | F | HYPOTH. DF | ERROR DF | SIG. OF F |
|---|---|---|---|---|---|
| 1 TO 1 | .97201 | .23035 | 2.00 | 16.00 | .797 |

(34) This hypothesis matrix could be placed in the planned contrast doubly multivariate analysis of variance table, see Table 7.10.

(35) Here the multivariate test indicates that there is no quartic by SOCIOR interaction.

708

* * * * * * * * * * * * * * * * * * * * * * A N A L Y S I S   O F   V A R I A N C E * * * * * * * * * * * * * * * * * * * * * *

EFFECT .. CONSTANT

(36) This hypothesis matrix would be placed in the planned contrast doubly multivariate analysis of variance table, see Table 7.10.

(37) Here the multivariate test indicates that there is a significant quartic trend over DAYS, see Table 7.10.

ADJUSTED HYPOTHESIS SUM-OF-SQUARES AND CROSS-PRODUCTS

|            | EQUARTIC      | DQUARTIC    |
|------------|---------------|-------------|
| (36) EQUARTIC | 2388.30797  |             |
| DQUARTIC   | -1727.24331   | 1249.15609  |

MULTIVARIATE TESTS OF SIGNIFICANCE (S = 1, M = 0, N = 7)

| TEST NAME  | VALUE   | APPROX. F | HYPOTH. DF | ERROR DF | SIG. OF F |
|------------|---------|-----------|------------|----------|-----------|
| PILLAIS    | .85348  | 46.59832  | 2.00       | 16.00    | .000      |
| HOTELLINGS | 5.82479 | 46.59832  | 2.00       | 16.00    | .000 (37) |
| WILKS      | .14652  | 46.59832  | 2.00       | 16.00    | .000      |
| ROYS       | .85348  |           |            |          |           |

EIGENVALUES AND CANONICAL CORRELATIONS

| ROOT NO. | EIGENVALUE | PCT.      | CUM. PCT. | CANON. COR. |
|----------|------------|-----------|-----------|-------------|
| 1        | 5.82479    | 100.00000 | 100.00000 | .92384      |

DIMENSION REDUCTION ANALYSIS

| ROOTS  | WILKS LAMBDA | F        | HYPOTH. DF | ERROR DF | SIG. OF F |
|--------|--------------|----------|------------|----------|-----------|
| 1 TO 1 | .14652       | 46.59832 | 2.00       | 16.00    | .000      |

\* \* \* \* \* \* \* \* \* \* \* \* \* \* \* \* \* \* A N A L Y S I S   O F   V A R I A N C E \* \* \* \* \* \* \* \* \* \* \* \* \* \* \* \* \* \* \* \* \* \*

EFFECT .. CONSTANT     (CONT.)

UNIVARIATE F-TESTS WITH (1,17) D. F.

| VARIABLE | HYPOTH. SS | ERROR SS | HYPOTH. MS | ERROR MS | F | SIG. OF F |
|---|---|---|---|---|---|---|
| EQUARTIC | 2388.30797 | 952.73714 | 2388.30797 | 56.04336 | 42.61536 | .000 |
| DQUARTIC | 1249.15609 | 743.42286 | 1249.15609 | 43.73076 | 28.56470 | .000 (38) |

(38) Here the univariate tests indicate that there is a significant quartic trend over DAYS on both dependent variables.

RAW DISCRIMINANT FUNCTION COEFFICIENTS

          FUNCTION NO.

VARIABLE                1

EQUARTIC          -.11753
DQUARTIC          -.11904

STANDARDIZED DISCRIMINANT FUNCTION COEFFICIENTS

          FUNCTION NO.

VARIABLE                1

EQUARTIC          -.87983
DQUARTIC           .78723

ESTIMATES OF EFFECTS FOR CANONICAL VARIABLES

          CANONICAL VARIABLE

PARAMETER               1

     1            -2.28607

# APPENDICES

## Two-Way Nonorthogonal (Unequal $n$ )Analyses
### by Robert S. Barcikowski

### Introduction

In a workshop for social scientists that I have conducted in different parts of the United States for the past several years, I frequently ask participants who are familiar with a particular program package to run the 2 x 2 univariate design shown in Figure 3.1 of Chapter 3. I then ask them to consider their analysis as an overall analysis where each source of variation is tested at the .05 level of significance, and to verbally report their results to the other participants. The participants are usually quite surprised to find that the results reported depend on the statistical package and the particular program within a package that has been run. For example, those who run BMDP programs usually find no significant differences between any of the treatments; those who run SPSS(ANOVA) generally find a significant difference between students who have been taught with different methods; those who run SPSS(MANOVA) usually find that both main effects are significant; while those who run SAS(GLM) find that their output contains significant treatment differences under 'TYPE I SS' and no significant treatment differences under 'TYPE III SS'. These findings, shown in Table A.1, represent the many different ways that one can perform a two-way unequal $n$ analysis of variance. In this Appendix we consider several of these approaches; illustrate them with program I/O; and, tell you why we have selected what is called the 'method of weighted squares of means' approach for use in this text.

### Nonorthogonal Methods of Analysis

The discussion that follows relies on a presentation by Speed, Hocking, and Hackney (1978) for a description of different nonorthogonal methods.

### The Method of Weighted Squares of Means

Through out this text we use the method of weighted squares of means[1]. Why? Because in a fixed-effects analysis of variance this method allows us to test hypotheses concerning the unweighted means that we are interested in. It therefore allows us to effectively plan questions concerning treatment mean differences, and to be aware of the mean differences being tested in an overall analysis. For example, in the 2 X 2 design that we considered earlier this method allows us to test the following hypotheses:

## Table A.1
## Standard[1] Statistical Package Output
## For The Example Experiment

| Source of Variation | Degrees of Freedom | Sum of Squares | Mean Squares | F Values | Probability |
|---|---|---|---|---|---|
| **BMDP7D, BMDP2V, BMDP4V, and SAS(GLM, Type III & IV SS)** | | | | | |
| Factor A (Test Type) | 1 | 9.61 | 9.61 | 4.50 | .0521 |
| Factor B (Method) | 1 | 9.61 | 9.61 | 4.50 | .0521 |
| Interaction[2] | 1 | .13 | .13 | .06 | .8111 |
| Error[2] | 14 | 29.89 | 2.13 | | |
| **SPSS and SPSSX (MANOVA) and SAS (GLM, Type I SS)** | | | | | |
| Factor A (Test Type) | 1 | 23.36 | 23.36 | 10.94 | .0052* |
| Factor B (Method) | 1 | 10.90 | 10.90 | 5.11 | .0404* |
| **SPSS and SPSSX (ANOVA)** | | | | | |
| Factor A (Test Type) | 1 | 9.57 | 9.57 | 4.48 | .0527 |
| Factor B (Method) | 1 | 10.90 | 10.90 | 5.11 | .0404* |

[1]These are the "standard" or "default" results (i.e. no options).
[2]The interaction and error (within) sources of variation remain the same across packages for a two-way ANOVA, and were not included in the other source tables.
*p<.05.

H(01)     u(1.) =  u(2.)

H(02)     u(.1) =  u(.2)

H(03)     u(11) - u(21) =  u(12) -  u(22), and

in general, this method allows us to test the two-way
hypotheses:

H(01)     u(i.) =  u(i'.)

H(02)     u(j.) =  u(j'.)

H(03)     u(ij) - u(i'j) =  u(ij') -  u(i'j')

for all i,i',j,j' where i ≠ i' and j ≠ j' and n(ij) >0.

The method of weighted squares of means has been
advocated for use with fixed effects analysis of variance
designs by many authors, including Carlson and Timm (1974);
Hemmerle (1979); Overall, Lee and Hornick (1981); Overall,
Spiegel and Cohen (1975) and Speed, Hocking, and Hackney
(1978). It is the standard output from all of the BMDP
programs; it is 'TYPE III' and 'TYPE IV' analyses in
SAS(GLM); it is arrived at by selecting option 9 in
SPSS(ANOVA), and by including the specification 'METHOD =
SSTYPE(UNIQUE)' in SPSS (MANOVA). These features and
specifications were indicated and included for most of the
programs run in this book.

## The Method of Fitting Constants

This method is advocated by those who are interested
in building a model to fit data. For example Appelbaum and
Cramer (1974) and Cramer and Applebaum (1980) consider all
of the following models:

A:  Y(ijk) = u + a(i) + b(j) + g(ij) + e(ijk)
B:  Y(ijk) = u + a(i) + b(j) + e(ijk)
C:  Y(ijk) = u + a(i) + e(ijk)
D:  Y(ijk) = u + b(j) + e(ijk)
E:  Y(ijk) = u + e(ijk)

Here Y is the score of subject k in cell (i,j); u is the
population grand mean of all observations; a represents the
treatment effect for treatment i of factor A; b represents
the treatment effect for treatment j of factor B; g
represents the interaction between treatment i of factor A
and treatment j of factor B; and, e(ijk) is that part of Y
which is not accounted for by the other sources of
variation (i.e. u, a, b, g) in the design.

Appelbaum and Cramer suggest that the following steps

are "for the logical flow of decisions and conclusions that are made in such an analysis, but do not dictate the actual order in which the computations need be performed (p. 340)."

1. Test model A for an interaction; if this test is significant then stop; if this test is not significant go to the next step.

2. Test model B with a eliminating b and b eliminating a; if both are significant adopt model B; if a is significant adopt model C; if b is significant adopt model d; if neither is significant go to step 3.

3. Test model C (a ignoring b) and model D (b ignoring a); if both are significant adopt either model C or D but not both because the choice is indeterminent (i.e. more experimentation is necessary). If only a is significant adopt model C; if only b is significant adopt model D; if neither is significant adopt model E.

Many authors (e.g. Overall and Spiegel (1969), and Winer (1971)) suggest that only steps 1 and 2 be conducted, the approach using only these two steps is the standard output (i.e. no options) found with SPSS (ANOVA) and may be found using 'TYPE II' sums of squares in SAS(GLM). All three steps may be found in BMDP4V by assigning SIZES to the BETWEEN sentence in the WEIGHTS paragraph. All three steps indicated by Appelbaum and Cramer can be constructed from all of the packages by manipulating the models; we have done this with the I/O of this Appendix.

Reservations. We have strong reservations about this approach, in full or in part, for the following reasons:
(1) The researcher is allowed to build a model based on the observed data, and is not required to build a model based on logic, past research and/or theory. We feel that anyone can interpret an analysis after it was run, and that therefore it is inappropriate to establish a model based on observed data alone.
(2) Changing the model and reordering the effects, especially without a priori predictions, plays havoc with Type I error.
(3) Overall, Lee, and Hornick (1981) have indicated, through a Monte Carlo study, that in general the Appelbaum and Cramer (1974) comparison of models strategy does not provide superior estimates of the true treatment effects. Indeed, it generally provides poorer estimates than does the method of weighted squares of means.

716

(4) Several authors (e.g. Bock, 1975, p. 295;
    Hocking, Speed, and Coleman, 1980, pp.120-121;
    Overall, Lee, and Hornick, 1981, p.372)
    indicate that there are many situations where
    one might test for main effects in the presence
    of a significant interaction. This is not
    possible after step 1 in the Applebaum and
    Cramer strategy.

## The Method of A Priori Ordering

Speed, Hocking and Hackney (1978) subsume this method
under the heading 'The Methods of Overall and Spiegel',
based on Overall and Spiegel's (1969) presentation of three
different nonorthogonal analysis methods. Overall and
Spiegel called their first method 'complete least squares;'
it is the method of weighted squares of means. Their
second method, labeled the 'experimental design method', we
have already described as the first two steps of Appelbaum
and Cramer. The method of a priori ordering is Overall and
Spiegel's third method. This method is actually a special
case of the method of fitting constants, but we decided to
present it separately because it is standard output from
SPSS (MANOVA); is available as 'TYPE I SS' from SAS (GLM);
and, is strongly advocated by Bock (1975) and Finn (1974).

In the method of a priori ordering one tests models A,
B, C and E in the following manner:
1. Step 1 is the same as that of Applebaum and
   Cramer (although Bock (1975, p. 245) does
   mention the possibility of considering main
   effects following this step).
2. Test model B with b eliminating a; stop if
   a is significant; go to step 3 if b is not
   significant.
3. Test model C (a ignoring b); if a is
   significant adopt model C, if not,
   adopt model E.

Note that if in steps 1 or 2 a significant effect is found,
testing stops. This requires that the researcher using
this approach decide in advance on the order of testing of
the effects. In factorial designs the interaction effects
are generally tested first followed by the main effects.
Bock (1975) makes the following comment with respect to
ordering of the effects to be tested:

Fortunately, there is usually sufficient asymmetry of
interest in the main-class effects to dictate the
order of elimination. Effects that are known a priori
to be significant are always eliminated from doubtful
effects, which require a critical test. Similarly
effects that are well understood and accepted as

717

explanatory variables should generally be eliminated from new and unfamiliar sources of variation. This places on the investigator the burden of demonstrating that the new source explains variation in the dependent variable that is not already accounted for by the established variable. (pp. 288-289)

Both Finn (1974) and Bock admit that often a researcher has difficulty on deciding on the order of testing for some effects. In this case Finn suggests that more than one order of testing be considered, but warns: "The number of alternative orders should be kept to a minimum, to avoid compounding statistical error rates" (p. 326).

We like the method of a priori ordering as described by Bock and Finn because it places a good deal of emphasis in the researcher having given careful consideration to planning the analysis in terms of theory and/or past research. However, in light of the work done by Overall, Lee, and Hornick (1981), and for overall analyses, we believe the method of weighted squares of means as presented in this text is a superior approach.

## Organization of the Programs

We illustrate the method of fitting constants using the Appelbaum and Cramer (1974) strategy with the (2 X 2) data shown in Figure 3.1 of Chapter 3. In the process we also illustrate the method of a priori ordering. The programs run were BMDP4V, SPSS(ANOVA), SPSS(MANOVA), and SAS(GLM). These programs and their features are listed in Table A.2. Although we only illustrate a univariate data analysis, the reader familiar with multivariate analysis may easily generalize to multivariate data.

Table A.2
Programs Run and Their Features Using
the Appelbaum and Cramer Strategies

| Program | Program Code | Page | Features |
|---|---|---|---|
| BMDP4V | A-1 | 721 | Use of 'SIZES' in 'BETWEEN' sentence of the 'WEIGHT' paragraph |
| SAS(GLM) | A-2 | 725 | Use of all four available sums of squares |
| SPSS(ANOVA) | A-3 | 729 | Standard output and option 10 |
| SPSS(MANOVA) | A-4 | 734 | Use of two DESIGN statements in a single call to the subprogram MANOVA |

## Notes

[1]The method of weighted squares of means should not be confused with the method of unweighted means. The latter method is an approximate method because it does not yield exact F tests. The method of unweighted means was suggested by Yates (1934) because of its computational simplicity, but this advantage is lost in today's world of computers. However, several texts describe the method of unweighted means for use with unequal $n$ ANOVA (e.g. Glass and Stanley (1970), Kleinbaum and Kupper (1978), Winer (1971)).

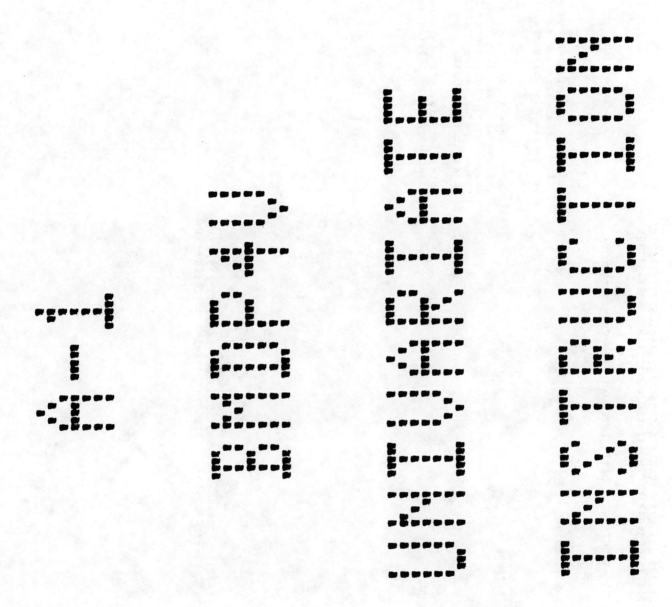

```
0000000000111111111122222222223333333333444444444455555555556666666666777777778
1234567890123456789012345678901234567890123456789012345678901234567890

/PROB  TITLE IS 'TWO-WAY (2 X 2)--BARCIKOWSKI DATA--APPLEBAUM AND CRAMER METHOD'.
/INPUT  VARIABLE = 3.
        FORMAT = '(3F2.0)'.
        CASES = 18.
/VARIABLE NAME = TESTTYPE,METHOD,ATTITUDE.
/GROUP CODES(1) = 1,2.
       NAME(1) = EASY,HARD.
       CODES(2) = 1,2.
       NAME(2) = AUDITOFY,HEURIST.
/BETWEEN FACTORS = TESTTYPE,METHOD.
/WEIGHTS BETWEEN ARE SIZES.
/PRINT MARGINALS = ALL.
/END
 1 1 6
 1 4 4
 1 2 5
 1 2 7
 1 2 8
 1 2 6
 2 1 3
 2 1 3
 2 1 2
 2 1 4
 2 1 6
 2 1 6
 2 2 5
 2 2 2
 2 2 2
 2 2 1
 2 2 6
 2 2 5
 2 2 4
ANALYSIS PROC = FACT./

0000000000111111111122222222223333333333444444444455555555556666666666777777778
1234567890123456789012345678901234567890123456789012345678901234567890
```

NOTE: This I/O illustrates how Appelbaum and Cramer's (1974) strategies are found using BMDP4V. In the process we also illustrate the method of a _priori_ ordering.

NOTE: On input this program contains the same information as that found for this data in program (3-3) of Chapter 3 in Volume I, except the specification SIZES replaced the specification EQUAL.

NOTE: Only the statistical tests are shown here; all other output was deleted to save space.

PAGE   7   BMDP4V TWO-WAY (2 X 2)--EARCIKOWSKI DATA--APPLEBAUM AND CRAMER METHOD

===================================================================

--- ANALYSIS SUMMARY ---

THE FOLLOWING EFFECTS ARE COMPONENTS OF THE SPECIFIED
LINEAR MODEL FOR THE BETWEEN DESIGN.  ESTIMATES AND TESTS
OF HYPOTHESES FOR THESE EFFECTS CONCERN PARAMETERS OF THAT MODEL.

        CVALL: GRAND MEAN
            TM
            T|M
            M|T

THE FOLLOWING EFFECTS INVOLVE WEIGHTED COMBINATIONS OF CELL MEANS.
THEY ARE NOT COMPONENTS OF THE LINEAR MODEL FOR THE BETWEEN DESIGN.

        T: TESTTYPE
        M: METHOD

===================================================================
===================================================================

| EFFECT | VARIATE | STATISTIC | F | DF | P |
| --- | --- | --- | --- | --- | --- |
| OVALL: GRAND MEAN | | | | | |
| | ATTITUDE | SS= 346.722 | | | |
| | | MS= 346.722 | 162.41 | 1, 14 | 0.0000 |
| T: TESTTYPE | | | | | |
| ⑤ | ATTITUDE | SS= 23.3611 | | | |
| | | MS= 23.3611 | 10.94 | 1, 14 | 0.0052 |
| M: METHCD | | | | | |
| ⑥ | ATTITUDE | SS= 24.6934 | | | |
| | | MS= 24.6934 | 11.57 | 1, 14 | 0.0043 |

NOTE: The statistical tests considered first are on the next page.

723

PAGE   8   BMDP4V TWO-WAY (2 X 2)--BARCIKOWSKI DATA--APPLEBAUM AND CRAMER METHOD

TM
① ATTITUDE    SS= 0.126615
             MS= 0.126615      0.06   1,   14   0.8111

T|M
② ATTITUDE    SS= 9.56891
             MS= 9.56891       4.48   1,   14   0.0526

M|T
③ ④ ATTITUDE  SS= 10.9012
             MS= 10.9012       5.11   1,   14   0.0403

ERROR
  ATTITUDE    SS= 29.888889
             MS= 2.1349206

=================================================

NO MORE CONTROL LANGUAGE.

PROGRAM TERMINATED

NUMBER OF INTEGER WORDS OF STORAGE USED IN PRECEDING   PROBLEM   2512
CPU TIME USED       5.719 SECONDS

724

① The first step in the Appelbaum and Cramer strategies and the method of a priori ordering is to test for a significant interaction; here none is found so we proceed to step 2.

② In step 2 of the Appelbaum and Cramer strategies we test a (effects of test type) eliminating b (method of instruction) and this effect is not significant.

③ In step 2 we also test b eliminating a; this is significant. Therefore, for this data, we would adopt model D from this Appendix. That is we have found a significant difference between the methods of instruction. Here, the unweighted cell means indicate that students who were taught using the heuristic method had better attitudes ($\bar{Y}$ = 5.86) than did the students taught using the auditory method ($\bar{Y}$ = 3.46).

④ In the method of a priori ordering the second step is to test b eliminating a, and since this is significant, further testing would not be appropriate. Using this method the researcher could not test a, but could conclude that there is a significant difference between methods of instruction.

NOTE: Since we have adopted model D through the Appelbaum and Cramer strategies and have stopped testing using the method of a priori ordering, the following tests are commented on to show what they are in the testing processes.

⑤ This is the test of model C (a ignoring b). It is the last test in the method of a priori ordering, and is part of step 3 of the Appelbaum and Cramer strategies.

⑥ This is the test of model D (b ignoring a) which is part of step 3 of the Appelbaum and Cramer strategies.

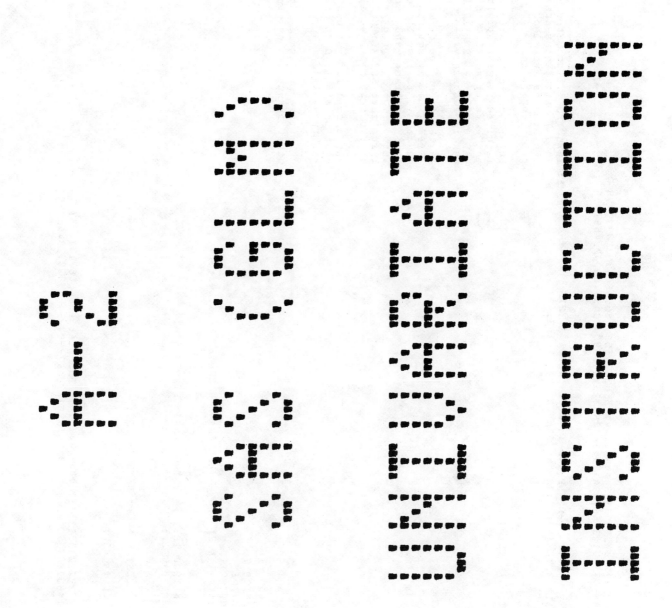

COMMENT   CHAPTER 3:  TWO-WAY (2 X 2) UNEQUAL N UNIVARIATE ANALYSIS
          BARCIKOWSKI DATA WITH APPLEBAUM AND CRAMER STRATEGIES;
DATA TWOWAY:
INPUT TEST METHOD ATTITUDE:
LABEL TEST = TEST TYPE
      METHOD = INSTRUCTIONAL METHOD;
CARDS:
1 1 6
1 1 4
1 2 5
1 2 7
1 2 8
1 2 6
2 1 3
2 1 3
2 1 2
2 1 4
2 1 6
2 1 2
2 1 2
2 1 1
2 2 6
2 2 5
2 2 4

PROC FORMAT;
VALUE FACTA 1 = 1:    EASY
            2 = 2:    DIFFICULT:
VALUE FACTB 1 = 1:    AUDITORY
            2 = 2:    HEURISTIC;

TITLE CHAPTER 3:  TWO-WAY (2 X 2) ANOVA (APPLEBAUM & CRAMER STRATEGIES);
PROC GLM:
CLASS TEST METHOD;
① MODEL ATTITUDE = TEST METHOD TEST  * METHOD /SS1 SS2 SS3 SS4;
FORMAT TEST FACTA. METHOD FACTB.;
PROC GLM;
CLASS TEST METHOD;
② MODEL ATTITUDE = METHOD TEST TEST  * METHOD /SS1;
LSMEANS TEST METHOD;
FORMAT TEST FACTA. METHOD FACTB.;

NOTE: This I/O illustrates how Appelbaum and Cramer's (1974) strategies are found using SAS(GLM). In the process we also illustrate the method of a priori ordering.

NOTE: In order to be able to test all of the models required by the Appelbaum and Cramer strategies you have to run PROC GLM twice. However, to use the method of a priori ordering only the first run is necessary.

① In the first run of GLM you need only request SS1 (TYPE I sum of squares) and SS2 (TYPE II sum of squares) to test the various models required for the Appelbaum and Cramer strategies and the method of a priori ordering. However, to illustrate SS3 (TYPE III SS) and SS4 (TYPE IV SS) at the same time, we also requested them.

② The second run of GLM is required to obtain the test of model D (b ignoring a). Here only SS1, was requested.

NOTE: Only the statistical tests are shown here; all other output was deleted to save space.

CHAPTER 3: TWO-WAY (2 X 2) ANCVA (APPLEBAUM & CRAMER STRATEGIES)

GENERAL LINEAR MODELS PROCEDURE

DEPENDENT VARIABLE: ATTITUDE

| SOURCE | DF | SUM OF SQUARES | MEAN SQUARE | F VALUE | PR > F | R-SQUARE | C.V. |
|---|---|---|---|---|---|---|---|
| MODEL | 3 | 34.38888889 | 11.46296296 | 5.37 | 0.0114 | 0.53004 | 33.2917 |
| ERROR | 14 | 29.88888889 | 2.13492063 | | | STD DEV | ATTITUDE MEAN |
| CORRECTED TOTAL | 17 | 64.27777778 | | | | 1.46113676 | 4.38888885 |

| SOURCE | DF | TYPE I SS | F VALUE | PR > F | TYPE II SS | F VALUE | PR > F |
|---|---|---|---|---|---|---|---|
| ⑤① TEST | 1 | 23.36111111 | 10.94 | 0.0052 | 9.56891171 | 4.48 | 0.0526 |
| ③④ METHOD | 1 | 10.90116279 | 5.11 | 0.0403 | 10.90116279 | 5.11 | 0.0403 |
| ① TEST*METHOD | 1 | 0.12661499 | 0.06 | 0.8111 | 0.12661499 | 0.06 | 0.8111 |

| SOURCE | DF | TYPE III SS | F VALUE | PR > F | TYPE IV SS | F VALUE | PR > F |
|---|---|---|---|---|---|---|---|
| ① TEST | 1 | 9.61498708 | 4.50 | 0.0521 | 9.61498708 | 4.50 | 0.0521 |
| METHOD | 1 | 9.61498708 | 4.50 | 0.0521 | 9.61498708 | 4.50 | 0.0521 |
| ① TEST*METHOD | 1 | 0.12661499 | 0.06 | 0.8111 | 0.12661499 | 0.06 | 0.8111 |

① The first step in the Appelbaum and Cramer strategies and the method of a priori ordering is to test for a significant interaction; here none is found so we proceed to step 2. Note that all 4 types of sums of squares yield the same interaction test.

② In step 2 of the Appelbaum and Cramer strategies we test a (effects of test type) eliminating b (method of instruction) and this effect is not significant.

③ In step 2 we also test b eliminating a; this is significant. Therefore, for this data, we would adopt model D from this Appendix. That is we have found a significant difference between the methods of instruction. Here, the unweighted cell means indicate that students who were taught using the heuristic method had better attitudes ($\overline{X}$ = 5.86) than did the students taught using the auditory method ($\overline{X}$ = 3.46).

④ In the method of a priori ordering the second step is to test b eliminating a, and since this is significant, further testing would not be appropriate. Using this method the researcher could not test a, but could conclude that there is a significant difference between methods of instruction.

NOTE: Since we have adopted model D through the Appelbaum and Cramer strategies and have stopped testing using the method of a priori ordering, the following tests are commented on to show what they are in the testing processes.

⑤ This is the test of model C (a ignoring b). It is the last test in the method of a priori ordering, and is part of step 3 of the Appelbaum and Cramer strategies.

⑥ This is the test of model D (b ignoring a) which is part of step 3 of the Appelbaum and Cramer strategies.

⑦ The TYPE III SS and TYPE IV SS are not part of the testing processes described here, but were output to illustrate that they yield the same results, i.e., the method of weighted squares of means, when all cells have one or more observations.

GENERAL LINEAR MODELS PROCEDURE

DEPENDENT VARIABLE: ATTITUDE

| SOURCE | DF | SUM OF SQUARES | MEAN SQUARE | F VALUE | PR > F | R-SQUARE | C.V. |
|---|---|---|---|---|---|---|---|
| MODEL | 3 | 34.38888889 | 11.46296296 | 5.37 | 0.0114 | 0.535004 | 33.2917 |
| ERROR | 14 | 29.88888889 | 2.13492063 | | | STD DEV | ATTITUDE MEAN |
| CORRECTED TOTAL | 17 | 64.27777778 | | | | 1.46113676 | 4.38888889 |

| SOURCE | DF | TYPE I SS | F VALUE | PR > F |
|---|---|---|---|---|
| METHOD | 1 | 24.69336219 | 11.57 | 0.0043 |
| TEST | 1 | 9.56891171 | 4.48 | 0.0526 |
| TEST*METHOD | 1 | 0.12661499 | 0.06 | 0.8111 |

728

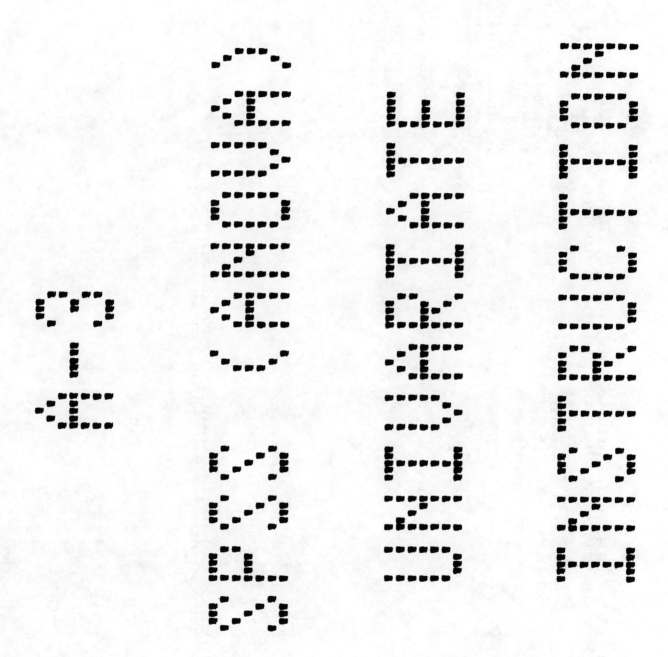

```
0000000000111111111122222222223333333333444444444455555555556666666666777777777 8
1234567890123456789012345678901234567890123456789012345678901234567890123456789 0
```

RUN NAME        CHAPTER 3:  TWO-WAY ANOVA (STANDARD & OPTION 10)
DATA LIST       FIXED(1)/1 TESTTYPE 2 METHOD 4 ATTITUDE 6
① N OF CASES      18
ANOVA           ATTITUDE BY TESTTYPE(1,2),METHOD(1,2)
STATISTICS      ALL
READ INPUT DATA
1 1 6
1 1 4
1 1 5
1 2 7
1 2 8
1 2 6
2 1 3
2 1 3
2 1 2
2 1 4
2 1 6
2 1 5
2 1 2
2 1 2
2 1 1
2 2 6
2 2 5
2 2 4
② ANOVA          ATTITUDE BY TESTTYPE(1,2),METHOD(1,2)
OPTIONS        10
ANOVA          ATTITUDE BY METHOD(1,2),TESTTYPE(1,2)
② OPTIONS        10

```
0000000000111111111122222222223333333333444444444455555555556666666666777777777 8
1234567890123456789012345678901234567890123456789012345678901234567890123456789 0
```

NOTE: This I/O illustrates how Appelbaum and
      Cramer's (1974) strategies are found using
      SPSS(ANOVA). In the process we also
      illustrate the method of a priori ordering.

NOTE: In order to evaluate all of the Applebaum
      and Cramer strategies three runs of ANOVA
      are necessary, however, to use the method of
      a priori ordering only the first two runs
      are necesary.

① The first run of ANCOVA yields this program's
   standard (i.e. no options) output.

② The second and third runs require option 10
   for the third step in the Appelbaum and
   Cramer strategies.

NOTE: Only the statistical tests are shown here:
      all other output was deleted to save space.

730

CHAPTER 3: TWO-WAY ANOVA (STANDARD & OPTION 10)

FILE NONAME (CREATION DATE = 01/06/83)

* * * * * * * * A N A L Y S I S   O F   V A R I A N C E * * * * * * * * * * * * * * *
       ATTITUDE
    BY TESTTYPE
       METHOD
* * * * * * * * * * * * * * * * * * * * * * * * * * * * * * * * * * * * * * * * * * *

| SOURCE OF VARIATION | SUM OF SQUARES | DF | MEAN SQUARE | F | SIGNIF OF F |
|---|---|---|---|---|---|
| MAIN EFFECTS | 34.262 | 2 | 17.131 | 8.024 | 0.005 |
| ② ③ TESTTYPE | 9.569 | 1 | 9.569 | 4.482 | 0.053 |
| ③ METHOD ④ | 10.901 | 1 | 10.901 | 5.106 | 0.040 |
| 2-WAY INTERACTIONS | 0.127 | 1 | 0.127 | 0.059 | 0.811 |
| ① TESTTYPE METHOD | 0.127 | 1 | 0.127 | 0.059 | 0.811 |
| EXPLAINED | 34.389 | 3 | 11.463 | 5.369 | 0.011 |
| RESIDUAL | 29.889 | 14 | 2.135 | | |
| TOTAL | 64.278 | 17 | 3.781 | | |

18 CASES WERE PROCESSED.
0 CASES ( 0.0 PCT) WERE MISSING.

① The first step in the Applebaum and Cramer strategies and the method of a priori ordering is to test for a significant interaction; here none is found so we proceed to step 2.

② In step 2 of the Appelbaum and Cramer strategies we test a (effects of test type) eliminating b (method of instruction) and this effect is not significant.

③ In step 2 we also test b eliminating a; this is significant. Therefore, for this data, we would adopt model D from this Appendix. That is we have found a significant difference between the methods of instruction. Here, the unweighted cell means indicate that students who were taught using the heuristic method had better attitudes ($\bar{X} = 5.86$) than did the students taught using the auditory method ($\bar{X} = 3.46$).

④ In the method of a priori ordering the second step is to test b eliminating a, and since this is significant, further testing would not be appropriate. Using this method the researcher could not test a, but could conclude that there is a significant difference between methods of instruction.

NOTE: Since we have adopted model D through the Appelbaum and Cramer strategies and have stopped testing using the method of a priori ordering, the following tests are commented on to show what they are in the testing processes.

CHAPTER 3:  TWO-WAY ANOVA (STANDARD & OPTION 10)

FILE    NONAME    (CREATION DATE = 01/06/83)

* * * * * * * * * * * A N A L Y S I S   O F   V A R I A N C E * * * * * * * * * * * * * * * * * *
                    ATTITUDE
                 BY TESTTYPE
                    METHOD
* * * * * * * * * * * * * * * * * * * * * * * * * * * * * * * * * * * * * * * * * * * * * * * * *

| SOURCE OF VARIATION | SUM OF SQUARES | DF | MEAN SQUARE | F | SIGNIF OF F |
|---|---|---|---|---|---|
| MAIN EFFECTS | 34.262 | 2 | 17.131 | 8.024 | 0.005 |
| ⑤ TESTTYPE | 23.361 | 1 | 23.361 | 10.942 | 0.005 |
| METHOD | 10.901 | 1 | 10.901 | 5.106 | 0.040 |
| 2-WAY INTERACTIONS | 0.127 | 1 | 0.127 | 0.059 | 0.811 |
| TESTTYPE METHOD | 0.127 | 1 | 0.127 | 0.059 | 0.811 |
| EXPLAINED | 34.389 | 3 | 11.463 | 5.369 | 0.011 |
| RESIDUAL | 29.889 | 14 | 2.135 | | |
| TOTAL | 64.278 | 17 | 3.781 | | |

18 CASES WERE PROCESSED.
 0 CASES ( 0.0 PCT) WERE MISSING.

NOTE: The second run of ANOVA yields   this output
      which allows us to test model C (a ignoring
      b).

⑤ This is the test of model C (a ignoring b).
  It is the last test in the method of a
  priori ordering, and is part of step 3 of
  the Appelbaum and Cramer strategies.

FILE   NONAME   (CREATION DATE = 01/06/83)

* * * * * * * * * * * A N A L Y S I S   O F   V A R I A N C E * * * * * * * * * * * * * * * * * * * *
            ATTITUDE
       BY METHOD
            TESTTYPE
* * * * * * * * * * * * * * * * * * * * * * * * * * * * * * * * * * * * * * * * * * * * * * * * * * *

| SOURCE OF VARIATION | SUM OF SQUARES | DF | MEAN SQUARE | F | SIGNIF OF F |
|---|---|---|---|---|---|
| MAIN EFFECTS | 34.262 | 2 | 17.131 | 8.024 | 0.005 |
| ⑥ METHOD | 24.693 | 1 | 24.693 | 11.566 | 0.004 |
| TESTTYPE | 9.569 | 1 | 9.569 | 4.482 | 0.053 |
| 2-WAY INTERACTIONS | .0.127 | 1 | 0.127 | 0.059 | 0.811 |
| METHOD   TESTTYPE | 0.127 | 1 | 0.127 | 0.059 | 0.811 |
| EXPLAINED | 34.389 | 3 | 11.463 | 5.369 | 0.011 |
| RESIDUAL | 29.889 | 14 | 2.135 | | |
| TOTAL | 64.278 | 17 | 3.781 | | |

18 CASES WERE PROCESSED.
0 CASES ( 0.0 PCT) WERE MISSING.

NOTE:   The third run of ANOVA allows us to test
        model D (b ignoring a).

⑥ This is the test of model D (b ignoring a)
   which is part of step 3 of the Appelbaum and
   Cramer strategies.

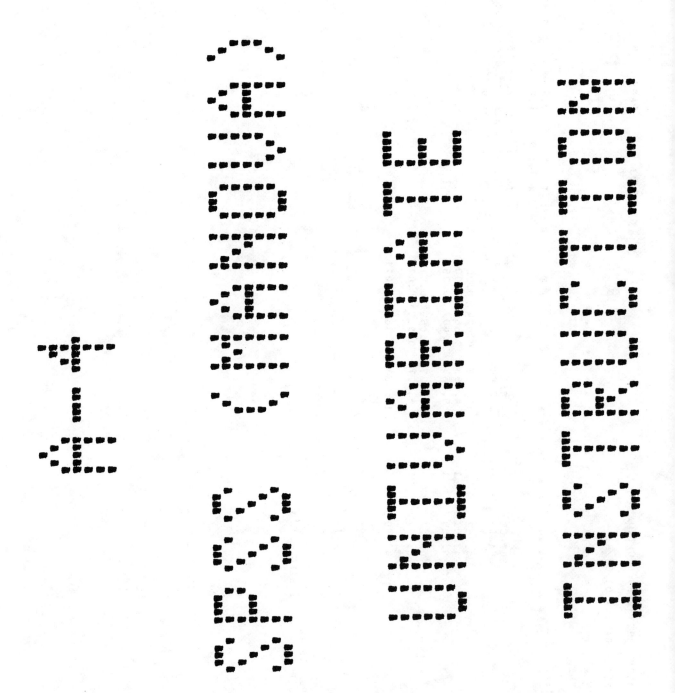

```
RUN NAME      CHAPTER 3:  TWO-WAY UNIVARIATE ANALYSIS
DATA LIST     FIXED(1)/1 TESTTYPE 2 METHOD 4 ATTITUDE 6
N OF CASES    18
MANOVA        ATTITUDE BY TESTTYPE(1,2) METHOD(1,2)/
              PRINT = CELLINFO(MEANS)
                      OMEANS(TABLES(TESTTYPE,METHOD))/
           ① DESIGN = TESTTYPE,METHOD,TESTTYPE BY METHOD/
           ② DESIGN = METHOD,TESTTYPE/

READ INPUT DATA
1 1 6
1 1 4
1 2 5
1 2 7
1 2 8
1 2 6
2 1 3
2 1 3
2 1 2
2 1 6
2 1 5
2 1 2
2 1 2
2 1 1
2 2 6
2 2 5
2 2 4
```

NOTE: This I/O illustrates how Appelbaum and Cramer's (1974) strategies are found using SPSS(MANOVA). In the process we also illustrate the method of a priori ordering.

① The standard output from SPSS(MANOVA) is the method of a priori ordering.

② To arrive at all of the tests necessary for the Appelbaum and Cramer strategies a second run of MANOVA is required with METHOD placed before TESTTYPE; here the interaction need not be specified.

NOTE: Only the statistical tests are shown here; all other output was deleted to save space.

\* \* \* \* \* \* \* \* \* \* \* \* \* \* \* A N A L Y S I S   O F   V A R I A N C E \* \* \* \* \* \* \* \* \* \* \* \* \* \* \* \* \* \* \* \* \* \* \*

TESTS OF SIGNIFICANCE FOR ATTITUDE USING SEQUENTIAL SUMS OF SQUARES

| SOURCE OF VARIATION | SUM OF SQUARES | DF | MEAN SQUARE | F | SIG. OF F |
|---|---|---|---|---|---|
| WITHIN CELLS | 29.88889 | 14 | 2.13492 | | |
| CONSTANT ⑥ | 346.72222 | 1 | 346.72222 | 162.40520 | 0.0 |
| TESTTYPE ⑤ | 23.36111 | 1 | 23.36111 | 10.94238 | .005 |
| METHOD ④ | 10.90116 | 1 | 10.90116 | 5.10612 | .040 |
| TESTTYPE ① BY METHOD | .12661 | 1 | .12661 | .05931 | .811 |

⑦ ESTIMATES FOR ATTITUDE

CONSTANT

| PARAMETER | COEFF. | STD. ERR. | T-VALUE | SIG. OF T | LOWER .95 CL | UPPER .95 CL |
|---|---|---|---|---|---|---|
| 1 | 4.9027777778 | .39922 | 12.28085 | 0.0 | 4.04653 | 5.75902 |

TESTTYPE

| PARAMETER | COEFF. | STD. ERR. | T-VALUE | SIG. OF T | LOWER .95 CL | UPPER .95 CL |
|---|---|---|---|---|---|---|
| 2 | -.8472222222 | .39922 | 2.12219 | .052 | -.00902 | 1.70347 |

METHOD

| PARAMETER | COEFF. | STD. ERR. | T-VALUE | SIG. OF T | LOWER .95 CL | UPPER .95 CL |
|---|---|---|---|---|---|---|
| 3 | -.8472222222 | .39922 | -2.12219 | .052 | -1.70347 | -.00902 |

TESTTYPE BY METHOD

| PARAMETER | COEFF. | STD. ERR. | T-VALUE | SIG. OF T | LOWER .95 CL | UPPER .95 CL |
|---|---|---|---|---|---|---|
| 4 | -.0972222222 | .39922 | -.24353 | .811 | -.75902 | .95347 |

CORRESPONDENCE BETWEEN EFFECTS AND COLUMNS OF BETWEEN-SUBJECTS DESIGN

| STARTING COLUMN | ENDING COLUMN | EFFECT NAME |
|---|---|---|
| 1 | 1 | CONSTANT |

① The first step in the Appelbaum and Cramer strategies and the method of a priori ordering is to test for a significant interaction; here none is found so we proceed to step 2.

② For the first part of step 2 in the Appelbaum and Cramer strategies we must go to the last output,

③ This second output yields the tests of a eliminating b and ignoring a. This step's output is on the next page.

④ In step 2 we also test b eliminating a; this is significant. Therefore, for this data, we would adopt model D from this Appendix. That is we have found a significant difference between the methods of instruction. Here, the unweighted cell means indicate that students who were taught using the heuristic method had better attitudes ($\overline{X}$ = 5.86) than did the students taught using the

\* \* \* \* \* \* \* \* \* \* \* \* \* \* \* \* \* \* \* A N A L Y S I S  O F  V A R I A N C E \* \* \* \* \* \* \* \* \* \* \* \* \* \* \* \* \* \* \* \* \* \* \*

TESTS OF SIGNIFICANCE FOR ATTITUDE USING SEQUENTIAL SUMS OF SQUARES

② SOURCE OF VARIATION

| | SUM OF SQUARES | DF | MEAN SQUARE | F | SIG. OF F |
|---|---|---|---|---|---|
| WITHIN CELLS | 29.88889 | 14 | 2.13492 | | |
| CONSTANT | 346.72222 | 1 | 346.72222 | 162.40520 | 0.0 |
| ⑧ METHOD | 24.69336 | 1 | 24.69336 | 11.56641 | .004 |
| ③ TESTTYPE | 9.56891 | 1 | 9.56891 | 4.48209 | .053 |

⑨ ESTIMATES FOR ATTITUDE

CONSTANT

| PARAMETER | COEFF. | STD. ERR. | T-VALUE | SIG. OF T | LOWER .95 CL | UPPER .95 CL |
|---|---|---|---|---|---|---|
| 1 | 4.8643410853 | .36670 | 13.26528 | 0.0 | 4.07785 | 5.65083 |

METHOD

| PARAMETER | COEFF. | STD. ERR. | T-VALUE | SIG. OF T | LOWER .95 CL | UPPER .95 CL |
|---|---|---|---|---|---|---|
| 2 | -.8720930233 | .38594 | -2.25967 | .040 | -1.69985 | -.04434 |

TESTTYPE

| PARAMETER | COEFF. | STD. ERR. | T-VALUE | SIG. OF T | LOWER .95 CL | UPPER .95 CL |
|---|---|---|---|---|---|---|
| 3 | .8449612403 | .39911 | 2.11710 | .053 | -.01105 | 1.70097 |

⑤ In the method of a priori ordering the second step is to test b eliminating a, and since this is significant, further testing would not be appropriate. Using this method the researcher could not test a, but could conclude that there is a significant difference between methods of instruction.

NOTE: Since we have adopted model D through the Appelbaum and Cramer strategies and have stopped testing using the method of a priori ordering, the following tests are commented on to show what they are in the testing processes.

⑥ This is the test of model C (a ignoring b). It is the last test in the method of a priori ordering, and is part of step 3 of the Appelbaum and Cramer strategies.

⑦ These are the default deviation linear contrasts, which are tested using the method of weighted squares of means.

NOTE: In step 2 of the Appelbaum and Cramer strategies we test a (effects of test type) eliminating b (method of instruction) and this effect is not significant.

⑧ This is the test of model D (b ignoring a) which is part of step 3 of the Appelbaum and Cramer strategies.

⑨ These are the default deviation linear contrasts, tested using the method of weighted squares of means, where the interaction is assumed to be zero. (Here these tests yield the same tests as the standard output from ANOVA and TYPE II SS from SAS(GLM).)

## APPENDIX B

## MULTIVARIATE STATISTICAL TESTS
by Robert S. Barcikowski

### Introduction

This Appendix was written in order to assist you to interpret the multivariate statistical tests which are output by the packages. In Table B.1 we present six standard multivariate tests and what they are called in each of the multivariate programs run in this book. You will notice that all six tests are not reported by each program. However, several programs output more than one test for a multivariate analysis, e.g., SAS(GLM) and SPSS(MANOVA) produce four tests, and BMDP4V yields five. You may wonder: Why more than one test? and What do I do if these tests yield different results? Fortunately, Olson (1976) and Stevens (1979) provide information to help answer these questions, and Timm (1975) provides tables for the major tests along with example problems on which the tests are calculated. However, there is still another problem; it concerns the probabilities reported with these multivariate tests. In order to avoid having to use the tabled values of the multivariate statistics, they are usually converted to the more familiar F or chi-square statistics. And, when more than two mean groups are involved, the probabilities found with these converted statistics are only approximations. These approximations may vary in accuracy and may be determined using different methods, e.g., see the Note in Table B.1. Therefore, Olson (1976) has urged research writers to name both the statistical test they have used and whose approximation was employed. In what follows we further discuss some frequent questions about the six tests.

### Why More Than One Test?

First let us dispose of Hotelling's $T^2$ (denoted here as $Th^2$) and Mahalanobis' $D^2$. These two tests are primarily used when only one or two groups are being investigated. In this situation the F and chi-square conversions yield the same exact probabilities, i.e., the probability you would find using the original multivariate statistic. Since these two multivariate statistics yield the same result, they offer no problem in interpretation. Indeed, when only one or two groups are involved, all of the multivariate tests shown in Table B.1 yield the same result.

The four multivariate tests which may cause you some confusion are Roy's largest root, R, Hotelling's trace, T, Wilks' lambda, W, and Pillai's trace, V. These tests are

Table B.1
Multivariate Statistical Tests and
How They are Identified in the
Programs Considered in This Text

| Multivariate Program | Roy's Largest Root | Hotelling's Trace | Wilks' Lambda | Pillai's Trace | Hotelling's T² | Mahalanobis' D² |
|---|---|---|---|---|---|---|
| EMDP3D | ---- | ---- | ---- | ---- | Hotelling's T Square | ---- |
| BMDP7M | ---- | ---- | U-Statistic or Wilks' Lambda | ---- | ---- | Mahalanobis' D Square |
| BMDP4V | MXROOT | TRACE TZSQ¹ | LRATIO | ---- | TSQ² | ---- |
| SAS(DISCRIM) | ---- | ---- | ---- | ---- | ---- | Generalized Squared Distance |
| SAS(GLM) & SAS(ANOVA) | Roy's Maximum Root Criterion | Hotelling- Lawley Trace | Wilks' Criterion | Pillai's Trace | ---- | ---- |
| SAS(REG) & SAS(CANDISC) | Roy's Greatest Root | Hotelling- Lawley Trace | Wilks' Lambda | Pillai's Trace | ---- | ---- |
| SAS(STEPDISC) | ---- | ---- | Wilks' Lambda | Pillai's Trace | ---- | ---- |
| SPSS & SPSSX (DISCRIMINANT) | ---- | ---- | Wilks' Lambda³ (U-Statistic) | ---- | ---- | ---- |
| SPSS & SPSSX (MANOVA) | Roys | Hotellings | Wilks | Pillais | ---- | ---- |
| SPSS & SPSSX (RELIABILITY) | ---- | ---- | ---- | ---- | Hotelling's T Square | ---- |

NOTE: The F approximation for Roy's Largest Root is based on Harris (1975) in BMDP and Pillai (1965) for SPSS and SAS; for Hotelling's trace BMDP's chi-square approximation is based on Tiku (1971) and SAS and SPSS's F approximation is based on Pillai (1960); Wilk's Lambda F approximation for all programs is based on Rao (1973); Pillai's Trace F approximation is based on Pillai (1960) for SAS and SPSS.

¹TZSQ is found by multiplying the value for TRACE by $(V_e + V_h - t)$, where $V_e$ and $V_h$ are the degrees of freedom associated with the error (E) and hypothesis (H) sums of squares and crossproducts matrices, respectively, and $t$ is the maximum of the rank of $(E + H)$ or $V_h$.
²TSQ is the only multivariate test performed in BMDP4V when the null hypothesis consists of only one or two mean vectors.
³Uses Bartlett's (1947) Chi-square approximation.

output by the programs because they have a desirable statistical property, i.e., they are invariant to changes in the origin, and the units of measurement, of the original data, and because they can each have a different statistical power. Olson (1976, p. 581) indicates that the power of these tests is dependent upon whether differences among population mean vectors occur in one or more multivariate dimensions. That is, if a discriminant analysis were run on a data set would only a single significant discriminant function be found, yielding a concentrated noncentrality structure, or would more than one significant function be found, yielding a diffuse noncentrality structure. Given a concentrated noncentrality structure, the multivariate tests tend to be ranked as R, T, W, V, from most powerful to least powerful. Given a diffuse noncentrality structure, the multivariate tests are generally ranked in reverse order from most powerful to least powerful, i.e., V, W, T, R, with the power differences among the tests being small. In considering the intermediate noncentrality structures found in the work of Schatzoff (1966), Olson concluded that this type of structure "must become heavily concentrated before it ceases to produce test criterion behavior like that in the diffuse structure" (p.582). Since the power of a particular multivariate test is dependent on the structure of a data set's multivariate dimensions, the packaged programs are forced to report more than one test. Let us now consider how we might select a particular test.

## What Do I Do If These Tests Yield Different Results?

Before we can answer the question that provides the heading to this section we must consider V, W, T, and R with respect to robustness to violations of the multivariate model's assumptions. This is exactly what Olson (1976) did after he considered their power with respect to noncentrality structure. In considering the assumption of multivariate normality, he found that kurtosis reduces the power of these tests, and that "R develops a severely inflated Type I error rate in situations in which only one of several groups is subject to kurtosis" (p.582). Olson also found that departure from homogeniety among the variance-covariance matrices had a dramatic effect on the Type I and Type II error rates of these tests. He indicated that: "The R test in particular is prone to an excessively high Type I error rate, and T and W follow close behind, whereas V's increase in Type I errors tends to be much less severe" (p.582). Based on these findings, and his intuition that most multivariate data has a diffuse noncentrality structure, Olson concluded that researchers should generally use Pillai's trace, V, to test multivariate hypotheses. However, based on his Monte Carlo work, he also concluded that if the ratio of the degrees of freedom for error to the degrees of freedom for hypothesis is greater than or equal to ten times the number of variables, then one could use V, W, or T, as well. Finally, Olson determined that Roy's largest root, R, is unacceptable as a routinely used multivariate test statistic because of its susceptability to large Type I errors under violations of assumptions, and its dependence on a concentrated structure.

Stevens (1979) took issue with Olson's conclusions. Basically, Stevens felt that Olson's choice of Pillai's trace for general use was partially based on data with a concentrated noncentrality structure that one would be unlikely to encounter in practice. Stevens stated: "For concentrated noncentrality structures with covariance heterogeneity, it is recommended that any of these three statistics be used since the slight robustness advantages V has is offset by the greater power of T and W in these situations" (p. 355). Stevens agreed, however, with Olson's conclusions concerning V in a diffuse noncentrality structure. Further comments were made by Olson (1979).

Recommendation. Based on the discussions by Olson (1975, 1976, 1979) and Stevens (1979) we believe that the choice of which multivariate statistic to use is dependent on whether one is conducting a confirmatory or an exploratory study. In a confirmatory study one has a good deal of prior information on the data structure and the data's likelihood of violating one or more assumptions. Therefore, given a confirmatory study, we recommend that if the noncentrality structure is:

1. concentrated and the multivariate model's assumptions appear reasonable, use Roy's largest root, R;

2a. concentrated and it is likely that the assumption of normality and/or homogeneity of variance-covariance matrices will be violated, but not seriously, use either Wilks' lambda, W, or Hotelling's trace, T;

2b. concentrated and it is likely that the assumption of homogeneity of variance-covariance matrices will be seriously violated, i.e. where one group's variances are expected to be as large as or larger than 36 times those of another group, use Pillai's trace, V;

3. diffuse and it is likely that the assumption of homogeniety of variance-covariance matrices is tenable, use either Wilks' lambda, W, or Hotelling's trace, T;

4. diffuse and it is likely that the assumption of

742

homogeniety of variance-covariance matrices is not tenable, use Pillai's trace, V.

Given an exploratory study where little is known about the data, we recommend the use of Pillai's trace, V. Note that this is not what we have practiced in the preceding chapters where we always used Wilks' lambda in our tables. We choose W because it was available from more of the programs than any other statistic. Wilks' lambda was not a poor choice, however, in light of Stevens' arguments, and the concentrated nature of all of our data sets. (Interestingly, it appears to have been pure chance that all of our data sets exhibited a concentrated data structure.)

## Calculation of the Test Criteria

In this section we present formulas for the calculation of the multivariate tests discussed in the previous section, and demonstrate the use of these formulas using the multivariate data from the 3 X 2 design in Chapter 3. All of the test criteria that we have discussed may be found as functions of the eigenvalues, $c(i)$, $l(i)$, $r(i)$, of the matrix products $HE^{-1}$, $H(H + E)^{-1}$, $E(H + E)^{-1}$, respectively. Here H and E are the hypothesis and error sums of squares and cross products matrices. In Table B.2 (taken from Olson, (1976)) we display the formulas for R, T, W, and V in terms of the latter eigenvalues. The relationship among these eigenvalues is:

$$c(i) = 1 / (1 - l(i)) = (1 - r(i))/r(i),$$

In general Hotelling's $Th^2$ (TZSQ in BMDP4V) may be found as the following function of Hotelling's trace:

$$Th^2 = (ve + vh - t)T,$$

Here ve and vh are the degrees of freedom associated with the error (E) and hypothesis (H) sums of squares and cross product matrices, respectively, and t is the maximum of the rank of (E + H) and vh. Given only two groups this formula reduces to:

$$Th^2 = (n1 + n2 - 2)T,$$

where n1 and n2 are the number of subjects in groups one and two, respectively. Mahalanobis' $D^2$ may be found as:

$$D^2 = [(n1 + n2)/(n1 * n2)]Th^2$$

Example. To illustrate the various test criteria, we have chosen the 3 X 2 factorial design in Chapter 3. In the SAS(GLM) (3-5) and SPSS(MANOVA) (3-8) output in Chapter

Table B.2

Four Test Criteria for MANOVA[1]

| Descriptive label of criterion | Symbol and range | Criterion in terms of $HE^{-1}$ | Criterion in terms of $H(H+E)^{-1}$ | Criterion in terms of $E(H+E)^{-1}$ |
|---|---|---|---|---|
| Roy's largest root | $0 < R < 1$ | $\dfrac{c(1)}{1+c(1)}$ | $l(1)$ | $1-r(1)$ |
| Hotelling's trace | $0 < T < 1$ | $\sum_1^s c(i)$ | $\sum_1^s \dfrac{l(i)}{1-l(i)}$ | $\sum_1^s \dfrac{1-r(i)}{r(i)}$ |
| Wilks' likelihood ratio | $0 < W < 1$ | $\prod_1^s \dfrac{1}{1+c(i)}$ | $\prod_1^s (1-l(i))$ | $\prod_1^s r(i)$ |
| Pillai's trace | $0 < V < s$ | $\sum_1^s \dfrac{c(i)}{1+c(i)}$ | $\sum_1^s l(i)$ | $\sum_1^s (1-r(i))$ |

Note: $c(i)$, $l(i)$, and $r(i)$ are the eigenvalues of $HE^{-1}$, $H(H+E)^{-1}$ and $E(H+E)^{-1}$, respectively; s is the number of eigenvalues that are greater than zero.

[1]This table was taken from Olson (1976).

3 we find that the eigenvalues of HE-¹ for CONTENT are:

c(1) = 55.28347

c(2) =  0.00283

c(3) =  0.00000

Since there are two eigenvalues greater than zero, the rank of HE-¹ is two.  The rank of (H + E) is found to be 3, and therefore, t in the equation for Th² is 3.  Also, from the information given just before the multivariate test results for CONTENT in SAS(GLM) (3-5) we have that:

ve = 15, and

vh = 2.

Then,

R = 55.28347/(1 + 55.28347) = .9822

T = 55.28347 + 0.00283 = 55.2863

W = 1/(1 + 55.28347) * 1/(1 + .00283) = .0177

V = 55.28347/(1 + 55.28347) + .00283/(1 + .00283) = .9851

TZSQ = Th² = (15 + 2 - 3) 55.2863 = 774.0082.

APPENDIX C

Step-Down Analysis
by Robert S. Barcikowski

Step-down analysis, introduced by Roy and Bargmann (1958), is a multivariate procedure which is an optional part of the output in the program SPSS(MANOVA). The computational procedures for this analysis are outlined in Finn (1974, pp. 157-160 and pp. 322-324) and Stevens (1973). An important part of step-down analysis is that one must have decided in advance on an order for the dependent variables in the analysis. If the dependent variables cannot be placed in some a priori order e.g., according to complexity or time, the step-down analysis option in SPSS(MANOVA) should not be selected. When the dependent variables can be placed in some a priori order then, the step-down analysis allows the researcher to test whether those variables ordered last in the analysis contribute to the explanation of main or interaction effects above and beyond those dependent variables ordered first in the analysis. To interpret the step-down analysis one starts with the F test of the variable ordered last; if the last F test is not significant, one considers the next to the last F test; if it is not significant, one considers the F test next in order, etc. This process continues until a significant F test is found, at which point the analysis stops. Those dependent variables that had a nonsignificant F test are considered to have not contributed to the between group differences beyond that found by the variables placed higher in order. Testing of the importance of the variables ordered above the variable found signficant is not considered appropriate because the effects of the higher ordered variables are confounded with those variables placed below. Reordering of the dependent variables without a good theoretical rationale "plays havoc" with the Type I error rate.

Stevens (1973) presented an excellent example of a problem where one would use step-down analysis. He considered a one-way MANOVA where the levels were teaching methods and the dependent variables were tests of knowledge, comprehension and application. In the step-down analysis the variables were ordered according to complexity based on Bloom's Taxonomy. That is, knowledge was ordered first, comprehension was ordered second and complexity was ordered third. The first test considered would be on the dependent variable ordered third, complexity. Here the researcher would want to know if a part of the difference found between teaching methods could be attributed to the measure of complexity, above and beyond that due to knowledge and comprehension. If the latter test was not significant, the researcher would test to see if the measure of comprehension accounted for significant differences between the groups beyond that accounted for by knowledge. Finally, if this test was found to be nonsignificant, the researcher could test to see if knowledge was primarily responsible for the difference between the teaching methods. On the other hand, if comprehension was found to be significant then knowledge could not be tested since, in the taxonomy, knowledge is necessary before one can have comprehension, i.e., knowledge is confounded with comprehension.

In a step-down analysis the overall level of significance, alpha, is found by considering one minus the product of $(1 - a(i))$'s where $a(i)$ is the level of significance for test i. That is,

$$\text{alpha} = 1 - \prod_{i=1}^{P}(1 - a(i))$$

where $\prod$ stands for the product over p dependent variables. For example, if in the previous example the researcher tested knowledge at $a(1) = .025$; comprehension at $a(2) = .015$ and application at $a(3) = .010$, then:

alpha = 1 - (1 - .025) (1 - .015) (1 - .010)
alpha = .05

Provided a researcher can decide on an a priori order of his dependent variables, one can use step-down analysis in place of the overall multivariate test. Finn (1974, pp. 342-344) provides an example of this. Bock (1975, pp. 411-412 and pp. 497-502) provides applications of step-down analysis to discriminant analysis and repeated measures designs.

# APPENDIX D

## Statistical Tests When The Factors
## Have Fixed, Random and Mixed Levels
## by Robert S. Barcikowski

The levels of a factor in a design can be of two types, called either "fixed" or "random". The levels are called fixed if a researcher is only interested in those specific levels; the levels are called random if they are considered to be a random sample from a population of levels, and a researcher is interested in generalizing to the population of levels. Research designs consisting of one or more factors whose levels are fixed, are called "fixed effects" designs. When a design consists of one or more factors whose levels were selected at random, it is called a "random effects" design. Research designs that consist of one or more factors whose levels are fixed, and one or more factors whose levels were selected at random, are called "mixed effects" designs.

In a mixed effects design the following questions might be asked:

1) Does the time of day that a third grade reading examination is given affect the results on the examination?

2) Will the method of teaching reading affect the results on the examination?

3) Are there interaction effects between time of day and method of teaching reading that will affect the results on the examination?

In order to answer these questions a two factor (two-way) analysis of variance was planned. The first factor was "time of day" and five levels of this factor were selected at random from the population of times of day available during a school day. The second factor was methods of teaching reading and it consisted of three levels. The three methods were considered fixed since they were the only methods of interest (i.e., they were the only reading methods used in the school system involved). The unit of analysis was the classroom score on the dependent variable, reading comprehension. Five classrooms were randomly assigned to each cell in the design.

The topic of fixed, random, and mixed effects designs was put in this Appendix because different denominator mean square (error terms) are used to form the F statistics in higher order designs, depending on the type of levels. All of the programs described in this book, except for BMDP2V,

BMDP4V and BMDP8V, automatically use the mean square error (MSE) in the denominator of the F statistic to test the sources of variation. The denominator of the F statistic in higher order random and mixed effects designs may be selected in the SAS programs ANOVA and GLM, and in SPSS(MANOVA). The selection of a denominator for the F statistic is referred to as the selection of an "error effect" in SAS, and as an "error term" in SPSS(MANOVA). The denominator mean square is referred to as the "error term" in this Appendix.

In order to select an appropriate denominator mean square for an F statistic one must be familiar with the expected mean square associated with each source of variation in the design under consideration. Cornfield and Tukey (1956) presented an algorithm which enables researchers to find these mean squares. The Cornfield-Tukey algorithm is discussed in Winer (1971, pp. 371-378) and Dayton (1970, pp. 215-217). Tables D.1, D.2, and D.3 were constructed to provide appropriate error terms for different fixed, mixed, and random, equal n, designs, to save the user the time and effort involved in using the Cornfield-Tukey algorithm for two and three factor crossed and nested designs.

Table D.1 contains the denominator mean squares for the F statistic for two-way, equal n, fixed, random, and mixed designs. The error term in Table D.1 for a two-way fixed effects design is the mean square error, i.e., the denominator of the F statistic for each main effect and the interaction is MSE. In a two-way random effects design the error term for all main effects is the mean square for interaction, and the error term for the interaction is MSE. In a two-way mixed effects design the error term for the fixed main effect is the interaction mean square; the error term for the random effect and the interaction effect is MSE.

The error terms for the F statistic in a three-way design are listed in Table D.2. In Table D.2 the error term for all F statistics in the fixed effects design is the MSE. For the three-way random effects design the error term for the main effects does not exist, but can be estimated (Winer, 1971, pp. 375-378). The error term for the two-way interactions is the mean square for the three-way interaction; the error term for the three-way interaction is the MSE. The error terms for the mixed effects model depend on which factors have fixed or random levels. For example, in the three-way design where factor A has fixed levels and factors B and C have random levels, there is no error term available to test the effects of factor A, and the B and C main effects are tested using the mean square for the BC interaction as the error term.

Table D.1

Denominator Mean Squares (Error Terms) For F Statistics From
Two-Way, Equal $\underline{n}$ ($\underline{n}>1$), Fixed, Random and Mixed Designs

| Source of Variation | Fixed | Random | Mixed A Fixed, B Random |
|---|---|---|---|
| A | MSE[1] | AB[2] | AB |
| B | MSE | AB | MSE |
| AB | MSE | MSE | MSE |

[1]MSE=mean square error
[2]AB=interaction mean square

The denominator mean squares for the F statistics from
two and three factor nested, equal $\underline{n}$ ($\underline{n}>1$) mixed designs are
presented in Table D.3. If all of the factors are fixed in a
nested design, the MSE is the error term (not in Table D.3).
If the factors all have random levels, then there is no
appropriate error term. In a mixed model each factor has a
unique error term for the F statistic, as is indicated in
Table D.3.

Table D.2
Denominator Mean Squares (Error Terms) For F Statistics
From Three-Way, Equal n (n>1), Fixed, Random and Mixed Designs

| Source of Variation | Fixed | Random | A=Fixed B,C=Random | B=Fixed A,C=Random | C=Fixed A,B=Random | A,B=Fixed C=Random | A,C=Fixed B=Random | B,C=Fixed A=Random |
|---|---|---|---|---|---|---|---|---|
| F(A) | MSE[1] | AB+AC-ABC[2] | ---[3] | AC | AB | AC | AB | MSE |
| F(B) | MSE | AB+BC-ABC | BC | --- | AB | BC | MSE | AB |
| F(C) | MSE | BC+AC-ABC | BC | AC | --- | MSE | BC | AC |
| F(AB) | MSE | ABC | ABC | ABC | MSE | ABC | MSE | MSE |
| F(AC) | MSE | ABC | ABC | MSE | ABC | MSE | ABC | MSE |
| F(BC) | MSE | ABC | MSE | ABC | ABC | MSE | MSE | ABC |
| F(ABC) | MSE | MSE | MSE | MSE | MSE | MSE | MSE | MSE |

Note: The letter products indicate interaction mean squares, e.g., BC is the mean square interaction between factors B and C.
[1]MSE=mean square error
[2]Approximations (see Winer, 1971, pp.375-378)
[3]No error term is available

## Table D.3

Denominator Mean Square (Error Terms) For Statistics From Two and Three Factor Nested, Equal $\underline{n}$ ($\underline{n}>1$), Mixed Designs

| Sources of Variation | Factor Levels | Error Term |
|---|---|---|
| A<br>B(A) | A fixed<br>B random | B(A)<br>MSE[1] |
| A<br>B(A) | A random<br>B fixed | MSE<br>A |
| A<br>B(A)<br>C(AB) | A fixed<br>B random<br>C random | B(A)<br>C(AB)<br>MSE |
| A<br>B<br>C(AB) | A fixed<br>B fixed<br>C random | C(AB)<br>C(AB)<br>MSE |

Note: The letter products indicate interaction and/or nested mean squares, e.g., C(AB) is the mean square for C nested within A and B.
[1]MSE=mean square error

Skewness and Kurtosis Measures in SAS
by Robert S. Barcikowski

Measures of skewness and kurtosis provide a means of checking on the assumptions that the scores in each cell of a design follow a normal distribution. However, to be profitably used the cell $n$ should be reasonably large, i.e., larger than thirty. As Fisher (1958) indicated: "Departures from normal form, unless strangely marked, can only be detected in large samples; conversely, they make little difference to statistical tests on other questions" (p. 52).

The measures of skewness and kurtosis in SAS were taken from R.A. Fisher's Statistical Methods for Research Workers (1958). In the 13th printing of this text these measures are illustrated on page 53 with the pertinent formulas given in Appendix A of Chapter 2 (pp. 70-77). These measures of skewness and kurtosis are not those found in many texts (e.g., Glass & Stanley, 1970; Snedecor & Cochran, 1968), but they are directly related to the latter formulas because they involve the cubed and quartic powers of deviations from the mean. They are found here as follows:

Let

$$S(2) = \sum(X-X)^2, \quad S(3) = \sum(X-X)^3,$$

$$S(4) = \sum(X-X)^4$$

and,

$$k(2) = S(2)/(n-1), \quad k(3) = nS(3)/(n-1)(n-2),$$

$$k(4) = n/(n-1)(n-2)(n-3)$$
$$[(n+1)S(4) - 3(n-1)S(2)2/n],$$

then,

skewness $= g(1) = k(3)/k(2)^{3/2}$

and

kurtosis $= g(2) = k(4)/k(2)^2$

For example, the values of $g(1)$ and $g(2)$ for the Oral presentation in Chapter 2 on the four credibility scores (3,5,4,1) can be found as follows:.

$$S(2) = 8.75 \quad S(3) = -5.625 \quad S(4) = 35.328125$$

$$k(2) = 2.9167 \quad k(3) = -3.75 \quad k(4) = 2.9167$$

skewness $g(1) = k(3)/k(2)^{3/2}$
$$-3.75/(2.9167)^{3/2} = -.7528$$

kurtosis $g(2) = k(4)/k(2)^2 = 2.9167/(2.9167)^2$
$$= .34285$$

When calculated on a normal distribution $g(1) = g(2) = 0$, and their respective sampling variances are:

$$Var(g(1)) = \frac{6N(N-1)^2}{(N-2)(N+1)(N+3)}$$

$$Var(g(2)) = \frac{24N(N-1)}{(N-3)(N-2)(N+3)(N+5)}.$$

The sampling standard deviations of $g(1)$ and $g(2)$ may be used to construct a confidence interval for each of these values.
For the data from the Oral presentation we have that:

standard deviation of $g(1) = 1.0142$;

standard deviation of $g(2) = 2.6186$.

Therefore, the 95% confidence intervals are:

skewness $= -.7528 \pm 1.9878$;

kurtosis $= .3429 \pm 5.1325$.

Since both of these intervals contain the value zero, the evidence is that neither the measure of skewness nor that of kurtosis is significantly different from those found in a normal distribution.

When $g(1)$ (skewness) is negative this is an indication of a negatively skewed (i.e. a long left tail) distribution; if $g(1)$ is positive this is an indication of a positively skewed ( i.e. a long right tail) distribution. When $g(1)$ equals zero the distribution is symmetric and normally distributed. Then $g(2)$ (kurtosis) is negative this is an indication that the distribution is platykurtic (i.e. flatter, with more frequency in the tails); if $g(2)$ is positive the distribution is leptokurtic (i.e. peaked); if $g(2)$ equals 0 the distribution is mesokurtic and normally distributed.

WARNING: These measures of skewness and kurtosis may be strongly affected by a few extreme values, therefore you should always check for this possibility by considering a stem-and-leaf plot or a histogram.

REFERENCES

Amick, D. J., & Walberg, H. J. Introductory multivariate analysis . Berkeley: McCutchan, 1975.

Anscomb, F. J. Examination of residuals. Procedures of the Fourth Berkley Symposium of Mathematical Statistics and Probability , 1961, I , 1-36.

Applebaum, M. I., & Cramer, E. M. Some problems in the nonorthogonal analysis of variance. Psychological Bulletin , 1974, 81 , 335-343.

Atiqullah, M. The robustness of the covariance analysis of a one-way classification. Biometrika , 1964, 51 , 365-373.

Barcikowski, R. S. Statistical power with group mean as the unit of analysis. Journal of Educational Statistics , 1981, 6 , 267-285.

Barcikowski, R. S., & Stevens, J. P. A Monte Carlo study of the stability of canonical correlations, canonical weights, and canonical variate-variable correlations. The Journal of Multivariate Behavioral Research , 1975, 10 , 353-364.

Barnett, V. Probability plotting methods and order statistics. Applied Statistics , 1975, 1 , 95-108.

Barnett, V., & Lewis, T. Outliers in statistical data . New York: Wiley, 1978.

Bartlett, M. S. Properties of sufficiency and statistical tests. Proceedings of the Royal Society , 1937, A160 , 268-282.

Bartlett, M. S. Multivariate analysis. Journal of the Royal Statistical Supplement, Series B , 1947, 9 , 176-197.

Bettinghaus, E. P. Persuasive Communication (3rd ed.). New York: Holt, Rinehart and Winston, 1980.

Betz, M. A., & Gabriel, K. R. Type IV errors and analysis of simple effects. Journal of Educational Statistics , 1978, 3 , 121-143.

Bock, R. D. Multivariate statistical methods in behavioral research . New York: McGraw-Hill, 1975.

Boik, R. J. A priori tests in repeated measures designs: Effects of nonsphericity. Psychometrika , 1981, 46 , 241-255.

Borgen, F. H., & Seling, M. J. Uses of discriminant analysis following MANOVA: Multivariate statistics for multivariate purposes. Journal of Applied Psychology , 1978, 63 , 689-697.

Box, G. E. P. A general distribution theory for a class of likelihood criteria. Biometrika , 1949, 36 ,317-346.

Brown, M. B., & Forsythe, A. B. Robust tests for the equality of variances. Journal of the American Statistical Association , 1974, 69 , 364-367. (a)

Brown, M. B., & Forsythe, A. B. The small sample behavior of some statistics which test the equality of several means. Technometrics , 1974, 16 , 129-132. (b)

Carlson, J. E. Multivariate models in analysis of repeated measures designs with a covariate. Paper presented at the Canadian Conference on Applied Statistics, Montreal, April, 1981.

Carlson, J. E., & Timm, N. H. Analysis on nonorthogonal fixed-effects designs. Psychological Bulletin , 1974, 81 , 563-570.

Carlson J. E., & Timm, N. H. Some extensions of the full rank multivariate linear model. Paper presented an the annual meeting of the American Educational Research Association, Boston, April, 1980.

Carmer, S. G., & Swanson, M. R. An evaluation of ten pairwise multiple comparison procedures by Monte Carlo methods. Journal of the American Statistical Association , 1973, 68 , 66-74.

Ceurvorst, R. W., & Stock, W. A. Comments on the analysis of covariance with repeated measures designs. The Journal of Multivariate Behavioral Research , 1978, 13 , 509-513.

Cochran, W. G. Analysis of covariance: Its nature and uses. Biometrics , 1957, 13 , 261-281.

Cohen, J. Statistical power analysis for the behavioral sciences (2nd ed.). New York: Academic Press, 1977.

Cohen, J., & Cohen, P. *Applied multiple regression/correlation analysis for the behavioral sciences* . New York: Wiley, 1975.

Collier, R. O., Jr., Baker, F. B., Mandeville, G. K., & Hayes, T. F. Estimates of test size for several test procedures on conventional variance ratios in the repeated measures design. *Psychometrika* , 1967, *32* , 339-353.

Cook, G. C., & Juergenson, E. M. *Approved practices in poultry production* . Danville, Ill.: The Interstate, 1955.

Cook, T. D., & Campbell D. T. *Quasi-experimentation: Design & analysis issues for field settings* . Chicago: Rand McNally, 1979.

Cooley, W. W., & Lohnes, P. R. *Multivariate data analysis* . New York: Wiley, 1971.

Cornfield, J., & Tukey, J. W. Average values of mean squares in factorials. *The Annals of Mathematical Statistics* , 1956, *27* , 907-949.

Cox, D. R. The use of a concomitant variable in selecting an experimental design. *Biometrika* , 1957, *44* , 150-158.

Cramer, E. M., & Appelbaum, M. I. Nonorthogonal analysis of variance--once again. *Psychological Bulletin* , 1980, *87* , 51-57.

Cramer, E. M., & Nicewander, W. A. Some symmetric, invariant measures of multivariate association. *Psychometrika* , 1979, *44* , 43-54.

Croft, R., Stimpson, D. V., Ross, W. L., Bray, R. M., & Breglio, V. J. Comparison of attitude changes elicited by live and video-tape classroom presentations. *A V Communication Review* , 1969, *17* , 315-321.

Daniel, C., & Wood, F. S. *Fitting equations to data* . New York: Wiley, 1971.

Davidson, M. L. Univariate versus multivariate tests in repeated-measures experiments. *Psychological Bulletin* , 1972, *77* , 446-452.

Davidson, M. L. *The multivariate approach to repeated measures* (Report No. 75). Los Angeles: BMDP Statistical Software, 1980.

Dayton, C. M.   The design of educational experiments .
New York:   McGraw-Hill, 1970.

Delaney H. D., & Maxwell, S. E.   On using analysis of
covariance in repeated measures designs.   The Journal of
Multivariate Behavioral Research , 1981, 16 , 105-123.

Dixon, W. J. (Ed.).   BMDP statistical software, 1981
edition . Los Angeles:  University of California Press,
1981.

Dixon, J. W., & Massey, F. J.   Introduction to
statistical analysis (3rd ed.).  New York:  McGraw-Hill,
1969.

Draper, N. R., & Smith, H.   Applied regression analysis
(2nd ed.).  New York:  Wiley, 1981.

Duncan, D. B.   Multiple range and multiple F tests.
Biometrics , 1955, 11 , 1-42.

Elashoff, J. D.   Analysis of covariance:   A delicate
instrument.   American Educational Research Journal ,
1969, 6 , 383-401.

Evans, S. H., & Anastasio, E. J.   Misuse of analysis of
covariance when treatment effect and covariate are
confounded.   Psychological Bulletin , 1968, 69 ,
225-234.

Feldt, L. S.   A comparison of the precision of three
experimental designs employing a concomitant variable.
Psychometrika , 1958, 23 , 335-354.

Ferguson, G. A.   Statistical analysis in psychology and
education (5th ed.).  New York:  McGraw-Hill, 1981.

Finn, J. D.   A general model for multivariate analysis .
New York:   Holt, Rinehart and Winston, 1974.

Fisher, R. A.  Design of experiments (13th ed).   New
York:  Hafner, 1973.

Frase, L. T.  Paragraph organization of written
materials:  the influence of conceptual clustering upon
the level and organization of recall.   Journal of
Educational Psychology , 1969, 60 , 39-401.

Fryer H. C.   Concepts and methods of experimental
statistics . Boston, Mass.:  Allyn and Baycon, 1966.

Games, P. A. Multiple comparisons of means. American Educational Research Journal , 1971, 8 , 531-565.

Games, P. A. Type IV errors revisted. Psychological Bulletin , 1973, 80 ,30-307.

Games, P. A., & Howell, J. F. Pairwise multiple comparison procedures with unequal n's and/or variances: A Monte Carlo study. Journal of Educational Statistics , 1976, 1 , 113-125.

Gatio, J., & Wiley, D. E. Univariate analysis procedures in the measurement of change. In C. W. Harris (Ed.), Problems in measuring change . Madison, Wis.: The University of Wisconsin Press, 1967.

Glass, G. V, Peckham, P. D., & Saunders, J. R. Consequences of failure to meet assumptions underlying the fixed effects analysis of variance and covariance. Review of Educational Research , 1972, 42 , 237-284.

Glass, G. V, & Stanley, J. C. Statistical methods in education and psychology . Englewood Cliffs, N. J.: Prentice-Hall, 1970.

Green, B. F. The two kinds of linear discriminant functions and their relationship. Journal of Education Statistics . 1979, 4 , 247-163.

Greenhouse, S. W., & Geisser, S. On methods in analysis of profile data. Psychometrika , 1959, 24 , 95-112.

Gregory, R. W. (Ed.) Poultry problems in production, marketing, and management . Chicago: J. B. Lippincott, 1938.

Harris, R. J. A primer of multivariate statistics . New York: Academic Press, 1975.

Hays, W. L. Statistics: For the social sciences (2nd ed.). New York: Holt, Rinehart and Winston, 1973.

Heck, D. L. Charts of some upper percentage points of the distribution of the largest characteristic root. The Annals of Mathematical Statistics , 1960, 31 , 625-642.

Hemmerle, W. J. Balanced hypotheses and unbalanced data. Journal of the American Statistical Association , 1979, 74 , 794-798.

Heuser, G. F. _Feeding poultry_. New York: Wiley, 1955.

Hocking, R. R., Speed, F. M., & Coleman, A. T. Hypotheses to be tested with unbalanced data. _Communications in Statistics: Theory and Methods_, 1980, _A9(2)_, 117-129.

Hoerl, A. E. Fitting curves to data. In J. H. Perry (Ed.), _Chemical Business Handbook_. New York: McGraw-Hill, 1954.

Hopkins, K. D., & Glass, G. V _Basic statistics for the behavioral sciences_. Englewood Cliffs, N. J.: Prentice-Hall, 1978.

Hotelling, H. The generalization of Student's ratio. _The Annals of Mathematical Statistics_, 1931, _2_, 360-378.

Huberty, C. J. Discriminant analysis. _Review of Educational Research_, 1975, _45_, 543-598.

Huitema, B. E. _The analysis of covariance and alternatives_. New York: Wiley, 1980.

Hull, C. H., & Nie, N. H. _SPSS: Update_. New York: McGraw-Hill, 1979.

Hull, C. H., & Nie, N. H. _SPSS: Update 7-9_. New York: McGraw-Hill, 1981.

Hummel, T. J., & Sligo, J. R. Empirical comparison of univariate and multivariate analysis of variance procedures. _Psychological Bulletin_, 1971, _76_, 49-57.

Huynh, H., & Feldt, L. S. Estimation of the Box correction for degrees of freedom from sample data in randomized block and split-plot designs. _Journal of Educational Statistics_, 1976, _1_, 69-82.

Huynh, H., & Feldt, L. S. Performance of traditional F tests in repeated measures designs under covariance hetrogeneity. _Communications in Statistics: Theory and Methods_, 1980, _A9(1)_, 61-74.

Imhof, J. P. Testing the hypothesis of no fixed main-effects in Scheffe's mixed model. _The Annals of Mathematical Statistics_, 1962, _33_, 1085-1095.

Kahneman, D. Control of spurious association and the reliability of the controlled variable. Psychological Bulletin , 1965, 64 , 326-329.

Kennedy, J. J. An introduction to the design and analysis of experiments in education and psychology . Washington D. C.: University Press of America, 1978.

Keppel, G. Design and analysis: A researcher's handbook . Englewook Cliffs, N. J.: Prentice-Hall, 1973.

Kerlinger, F. N. Foundations of behavioral research (2nd ed.). New York: Holt, Rinehart and Winston, 1973.

Kerlinger, F. N., & Pedhazur, E. J. Multiple regression in behavioral research . New York: Holt, Rinehart and Winston, 1973.

Keselman, H. J., & Rogan, J. C. A comparison of the modified-Tukey and Scheffe methods of multiple comparisons for pairwise contrasts. Journal of the American Statistical Association , 1978, 73 , 47-52.

Kirk, R. E. Experimental design: Procedures for the behavioral sciences . Belmont, Ca: Brooks/Cole, 1968.

Kleinbaum, D. G., & Kupper, L. L. Applied regression and other multivariable methods . North Scituate, Mass.: Duxbury Press, 1978.

Knower, F. H. Experimental studies of changes in attitudes: A study of the effect of oral argument on changes of attitude. Journal of Social Psychology , 1935, 6 , 315-347.

Knower, F. H. Experimental studies of changes in attitude (II): A study of the effect of printed argument on changes in attitude. Journal of Abnormal and Social Psychology , 1936, 30 , 522-532.

Kramer, C. Y. Extension of multiple range tests to group means with unequal numbers of replication. Biometrics , 1956, 12 , 307-310.

Lawley, D. N. Tests of significance in canonical analysis. Biometrika , 1959, 46 , 59-66.

Levin, J. R., & Marascuilo, L. A. Type IV errors and Games. Psychological Bulletin , 1973, 80 , 308-309.

Lindeman, R. H. Analysis of variance in complex experimental designs . San Francisco: W. H. Freeman and Company, 1974.

Lindeman, R. H., Merenda, P. F., & Gold, R. Z. Introduction to bivariate and multivariate analysis . Glenview, Illinois: Scott, Foresman and Company, 1980.

Lord, F. M. Large-sample covariance analysis when the control variable is fallible. Journal of the American Statistical Association , 1960, 55 , 307-322.

Lord, F. M., & Novick, M. R. Statistical theories of mental test scores . Reading, Mass.: Addison-Wesley, 1968.

Mahalanobis, P. C. On the generalized distance in statistics. Proceedings of the National Institute of Science (India), 1936, 12 , 49-55.

Marascuilo, L. A., & Levin, J. R. Appropriate post hoc comparisons for interaction and nested hypotheses in analysis of variance designs: The elimination of type IV errors. American Educational Research Journal , 1970, 7 , 397-421.

Marascuilo, L. A., & Levin, J. R. The simultaneous investigation of interaction and nested hypotheses in two-factor analysis of variance designs. American Education Research Journal , 1976, 13 , 61-65.

Marks, E. Some profile methods useful with singular covariance matrices. Psychological Bulletin , 1968, 70 , 179-184.

Maxwell, S. E. Pairwise multiple comparisons in repeated measures designs. Journal of Educational Statistics , 1980, 5 , 269-287.

Mendoza, J. L., Toothaker, L. E., & Nicewander, W. A. A Monte Carlo comparison of the univariate and multivariate methods for the groups by trials repeated measures design. The Journal of Multivariate Behavioral Research , 1974, 9 , 165-178.

Meyer, V. H., & Gute, J. The effects of channel variation on attitude change and source credibility. Paper presented at the Western Speech Communication Association convention, Honolulu, Hawaii, November, 1972.

Miller, R. G. Simultaneous statistical inference . New York: McGraw-Hill, 1966.

Morrison, D. F. Multivariate statistical methods . New York: McGraw Hill, 1967.

Myers, J. L. Fundamentals of experimental design . Boston: Allyn and Bacon, 1966.

Myers, J. L., Pezdek, K., & Coulson, D. Effect of prose organization upon free recall. Journal of Educational Psychology , 1973, 65 , 313-320.

Nie, N. N., Hull, C. H., Jenkins, J. G., Steinbrenner, K., & Brent, D. H. SPSS: Statistical package for the social sciences (2nd ed.). New York: McGraw-Hill, 1975.

Olson, C. L. A Monte Carlo investigation of the robustness of multivariate analysis of variance (Doctoral dissertation, University of Toronto, 1973). Dissertation Abstracts International , 1975, 35 , 6106B. (Microfilm, National Library of Canada, Ottawa)

Olson, C. L. On choosing a test statistic in multivariate analysis. Psychological Bulletin , 1976, 83 , 579-586.

Olson, C. L. Practical considerations in choosing a MANOVA test statistic: A rejoinder to Stevens. Psychological Bulletin , 1979, 86 , 1350-1352.

Overall, J. E., & Klett, C. J. Applied multivariate analysis . New York: McGraw-Hill, 1972.

Overall, J. E., Lee, D. M., & Hornick, C. W. Comparison of two strategies for analysis of variance in nonorthogonal designs. Psychological Bulletin , 1981, 90 , 367-375.

Overall J. E., & Spiegel, D. K. Concerning least squares analysis of experimental data. Psychological Bulletin , 1969, 72 , 311-322.

Overall, J. E., Spiegel, D. K., & Cohen, J. Equivalence of orthogonal and nonorthogonal analysis of variance. Psychological Bulletin , 1975, 82 , 182-186.

Overall, J. E., & Woodward, J. A. Common misconceptions concerning the analysis of covariance. The Journal of Multivariate Behavioral Research , 1977, 12 , 171-185.

Parnell, E. D. Profitable poultry production . New York: Wiley, 1957.

Patel, H. I., & Bonus, L. Analysis of repeated measures experiments: One-and two-way classifications. In '80 SUGI: Proceedings of the sixth annual SAS user's group international conference . Cary, NC: SAS Institute, 1980.

Pearson, E S., & Hartley, H. O. Biometrika Tables for Statisticians: Volume I (3rd ed.). Cambridge, Great Britain: Cambridge University Press, 1966.

Peckham, P. D. An investigation of the effects of non-homogeneity of regression slopes upon the F-test of analysis of covariance (Report No. 16). Boulder Colorado: University of Colorado, 1968.

Perlmutter, J., & Royer, J. M. Organization of prose materials: Stimulus, storage and retrieval. Canadian Journal of Psychology , 1973, 27 , 200-209.

Pillai, K. C. S. Statistical tables for tests of multivariate hypotheses . Manila: Statistical Center, University of the Philippines, 1960.

Pillai, K. C. S. On the distribution of the largest characteristic root of a matrix in multivariate analysis. Biometrika , 1965, 52 , 405-414.

Press, S. J. Applied multivariate analysis . New York: Holt, Rinehart and Winston, 1972.

Rao, C. R. Linear statistical inference and its applications (2nd ed.). New York: Wiley, 1973.

Rogan, J. C., Keselman, H. J., & Mendoza, J. L. Analysis of repeated measurements. British Journal of Mathematical and Statistical Psychology , 1979, 32 , 269-286.

Rouanet, H., & Lepine, D. Comparison between treatments in a repeated-measurement design: ANOVA and multivariate methods. British Journal of Mathematical and Statistical Psychology , 1970, 23 , 17-163.

Roy, S. N., & Bargmann, R. E. Tests of multiple independence and the associated confidence bounds. The Annals of Mathematical Statistics , 1958, 29 , 491-503.

Roy, S. N., & Bose, R. C. Simultaneous confidence interval estimation. The Annals of Mathematical Statistics , 1953, 24 , 513-536.

SAS Institute Inc.   SAS user's guide: Basics, 1982 edition . Cary, NC: Sas Instuite Inc., 1982. (a)

SAS Institute Inc.   SAS user's guide: Statistics, 1982 edition . Cary, NC: Sas Instuite Inc., 1982. (b)

Schatzoff, M.  Sensitivity comparisons among tests of the general linear hypothesis.  Journal of the American Statistical Association , 1966,  61 , 415-435.

Scheffe, H.   The analysis of variance . New York: Wiley, 1953.

Schultz, C. G., & DiVesta, F. J.  Effects of passage organization and note-taking on the selection of clustering stratgies and on recall of textual materials. Journal of Educational Psychology , 1972,  63 , 244-252.

Shapiro, S. S., & Wilk, M. B.  An analysis of variance test for normality (complete samples). Biometrika , 1965,  52 , 591-611.

Snedecor, G. W., & Cochran, W. G.   Statistical methods (6th ed.).  Ames, Iowa:  Iowa University Press, 1967.

Speed, S. M., Hocking, R. R., & Hackney, O. P.  Methods of analysis of linear models with unbalanced data. Journal of the American Statistical Association , 1978, 73  105-111.

SPSS Inc.  SPSSX: User's guide . New York: McGraw-Hill, 1983.

Stevens, J. P.  Four methods of analyzing between variation for the k group MANOVA problem.  The Journal of Multivariate Behavioral Research , 1972,  7 , 499-522.

Stevens, J. P.  Step-down analysis and simultaneous confidence intervals in manova.  The Journal of Multivariate Behavioral Research ,  1973,  8 , 391-402.

Stevens, J. P.  Comment on Olson:  Choosing a test statistic in multivariate analysis of variance. Psychological Bulletin , 1979,  86 , 355-360.

Stevens, J. P., & Barcikowski, R. S.   Applied multivariate statistics for the social sciences . Book in preparation, 1984.

Tatsuoka, M. M.   Multivariate analysis . New York: Wiley, 1971.

Tatsuoka, M. M. Classification procedures: Profile similarity . Champaign, Illinois: Institute for Personality and Ability Testing, 1974.

Tiku, M. L. A note on the distribution of Hotelling's generalized $T^2$. Biometrika , 1971, 58 , 237-241.

Timm, N. H. Multivariate analysis with applications in education and psychology . Monterey, Ca: Brooks/Cole, 1975.

Titus, H. W. The scientific feeding of chickens (2nd ed.). Danville, Ill: The Interstate, 1949.

Tukey, J. W. Exploratory data analysis . Reading, Mass.: Addison-Wesley, 1977.

Ware, J. E., & Williams, R. G. The Dr. Fox effect: A study of lecturer effectiveness and ratings of instruction. Journal of Medical Education , 1975, 50 , 149-156.

Welch, B. L. On the comparison of several mean values: An alternative approach. Biometrika , 1951, 38 , 330-336.

Whitman, R. F., & Timmis, J. H. The influence of verbal organizational structure and verbal organizing skills on selected measures of learning. Human Communication Research , 1975, 1 , 293-301.

Wiley, D. Review of Exploratory Data Analysis by J. W. Tukey. Applied Psychological Measurement , 1978, 2 , 151-155.

Williams, R. G., & Ware, J. E. An extended visit with Dr. Fox: Validity of student satisfaction with instruction ratings after repeated exposures to a lecturer. American Educational Research Journal , 1977, 14 , 449-457.

Winer, B. J. Statistical principles in experimental design (2nd ed.). New York: McGraw-Hill, 1971.

Yates, F. The analysis of multiple classifications with unequal numbers in the different classes. Journal of the American Statistical Association , 1934, 29 , 52-66.

## COMPLETE PROGRAM LISTINGS AVAILABLE

The program output in Chapters 3 through 7 was limited primarily to statistical tests. A tape containing a complete set of program input and output is available. For the cost of this I/O please specify the statistical package(s), i.e., BMDP, SAS, SPSS or SPSSX, and write:

Ms. E. Waters
19 Canterbury Drive
Athens, Ohio  45701

## WORKSHOP ON COMPUTER SOFTWARE

## AND MULTIVARIATE ANALYSES

Dr. Robert Barcikowski and Dr. James Stevens offer a 3-day workshop on computer software and multivariate analyses. This book compliments the workshop wherein the following topics are discussed:

Criteria for the Selection of a Statistical Package
Multiple Regression
Principal Components Analysis
Cross-Validation
Multiple and Multivariate Regression Analyses
Canonical Correlation and Partial Canonical
  Correlation Analyses
Redundancy Analysis
Why Use Multivariate Analysis of Variance (MANOVA)?
One-Way MANOVA
Multivariate "Planned" and Post Hoc Comparison Techniques
  (Is an overall test desirable? If so, what can be done
  after overall significance?)
Violations of Assumptions: How to Detect Them and
  What To Do If You Have Them
Two-Way MANOVA
Discriminant Analysis
Repeated Measures Analysis: Univariate and Multivariate
  Approaches
Multivariate Analysis of Covariance

For further information about the availability of this software and multivariate analyses workshop write or call:

Workshops Office
Memorial Auditorium
Ohio University
Athens, Ohio  45701

(614) 594-6851